The Origins of the Irish Constitution, 1928–1941

The Origins of the Irish Constitution, 1928–1941

GERARD HOGAN

Documents Editor
EOIN KINSELLA

The Origins of the Irish Constitution, 1928–1941

First published 2012

by Royal Irish Academy
19 Dawson St
Dublin 2

www.ria.ie

The author and publisher are grateful to the following for permission to reproduce the documents, photographs and illustrations in this book: National Archives of Ireland; National Library of Ireland; UCD Archives, School of History and Archives; UCD-OFM Partnership; Áras an Uachtaráin; Attorney General's Office; Incorporated Law Reporting Council of Ireland; *Irish Times*; *Irish Independent*; Irish Press plc; Irish Jesuit Archives; Royal Irish Academy.

ISBN 978-1-904890-75-1

British Library Cataloguing in Publication Data. A CIP catalogue record for this book is available from the British Library.

Design by Fidelma Slattery
Typeset by Carole Lynch
Copyedited by Linda Longmore
Index compiled by Julitta Clancy
Printed in Northern Ireland by Nicholson and Bass

10 9 8 7 6 5 4 3 2 1

CONTENTS

EDITORIAL ADVISORY BOARD

ABBREVIATIONS

The following is a list of the most commonly used abbreviations in the volume, particularly those used in document headers to denote archival sources.

DFA
Department of Foreign Affairs Collection, NAI, Dublin

DT S
Department of the Taoiseach, S series files, NAI, Dublin

Farrell (ed.), *De Valera's Constitution*
Brian Farrell (ed.), *De Valera's Constitution and Ours: the Thomas Davis Lecture Series* (Dublin, 1988)

ILTSJ
Irish Law Times and Solicitors' Journal

IR
Irish Law Reports

ILRM
Irish Law Reports Monthly

JA
Jesuit Archives of Ireland, Dublin

Kelly, *Irish Constitution*
J.M. Kelly, *The Irish Constitution* (4th edn, Dublin, 2003)

Kohn, *Constitution of the I.F.S.*
Leo Kohn, *The Constitution of the Irish Free State* (London, 1932)

LQR
Law Quarterly Review

NAI
National Archives of Ireland

O'Sullivan, *I.F.S. and its Senate*
Dónal O'Sullivan, *The Irish Free State and its Senate: a Study in Contemporary Politics* (London, 1940)

PRES
Office of the Secretary to the President Collection, NAI, Dublin

TD
Teachta Dála (Member of Dáil Éireann)

UCDA
University College Dublin, Archives Department

PREFACE

Following the success of the *Documents on Irish Foreign Policy* series, it seemed only natural that a similar volume should be produced dealing with the key documents which led to the drafting of the Constitution of Ireland. A chance remark by Professor Mary E. Daly MRIA to the then President of the Royal Irish Academy, Professor James Slevin MRIA, set the Origins of the Irish Constitution project in train. The present volume is thus the fruit of a project of the Academy in conjunction with the Office of the Attorney General and the National Archives of Ireland.

The project was endorsed by the then Attorney General, the late Rory Brady SC, and was also welcomed by the Director of the National Archives of Ireland, Dr David Craig, whose permission was necessary for access to the material in his care. The then Director General of the Office of the Attorney General, Ms Finola Flanagan, and Ms Catriona Crowe, Senior Archivist at the National Archives, accordingly kindly agreed to become members of the Editorial Advisory Board. The Royal Irish Academy became a partner in the project when the Council approved the outline proposal in 2007. A preliminary meeting of the Editorial Advisory Board chaired by the former Chief Justice, Ronan Keane, was held at the Academy on 14 February 2008. At that meeting it was agreed to approve the appointment of Eoin Kinsella as the research assistant, and Dr Gerard Hogan SC was appointed as Project Director.

The aim of the project was to publish a comprehensive selection of key documents relating to the development and drafting of the Constitution. The documents are collected from a variety of archival holdings and other sources and cover the period from 1928 to the enactment of the Second Amendment of the Constitution Act, 1941. The principal archival holdings are the National Archives themselves, along with the Archives Department of UCD where the de Valera papers are held. In addition, an extensive commentary accompanies each chapter, which seeks to guide the reader through the complex legal, political and philosophical problems that arose during the drafting process. The reader should, however, note that not only was there a proliferation of drafts (some fragmentary, others very advanced) in the period September 1936 to March 1937, but between March and June

1937 there were no less than eight full draft Constitutions printed, with the ninth printing being the draft as approved by Dáil Éireann and submitted to the people. Due to restrictions of space, it has not been possible to print them here. However, at various points in this volume readers are directed to the website www.irishconstitution.ie in order to access further documentary material. This is especially true for the period January–June 1937. Readers will also find a guide to many important Dáil debates relating to constitutional questions, from the late 1920s up to and including the debate on the Second Amendment of the Constitution Bill 1941. The website has been designed to mirror the structure of the volume, with fourteen separate sections corresponding to the chapters of this volume. Considerable editorial judgment has been necessary in terms of the selection of material for inclusion in this printed volume, and it is important to stress that a host of drafts attended virtually every constitutional provision. Some of the suggested changes were purely verbal, but others were of considerable significance.

The evolution of Irish constitutional law during this period was and is a topic of profound legal and political importance, given the centrality of the Constitution to much contemporary legal and political discourse. Yet, until the pioneering work of Professor Dermot Keogh MRIA was published some twenty years ago, almost nothing was known about the drafting of the Constitution. This volume thus aims to assist the reader better to understand the nature of the constitutional revolution begun by Eamon de Valera in the 1930s, culminating with the enactment of the Constitution itself.

The project would not have been possible without the assistance provided by several archives in Dublin. The Editorial Board wishes to thank Mr Seamus Helferty and the staff of the University College Dublin Archives; Noelle Dowling of the Dublin Diocesan Archives; Fr Fergus O'Donoghue and Damien Burke of the Irish Jesuit Archives, and Catriona Crowe and the staff of the National Archives of Ireland. All documents from the papers of Eamon de Valera and George Gavan Duffy held in University College Dublin Archives published in this volume are reproduced by kind permission of the UCD-OFM Partnership. Material from the papers of Alfred O'Rahilly and Hugh Kennedy are reproduced by kind permission of UCD Archives. Dr Dónal Coffey kindly drew the Board's attention to an important file from October 1936 dealing with a proposal for a Constitutional Court (see document no. 86).

The project's research assistant, Eoin Kinsella, would like to thank Catriona Crowe for her assistance and guidance during the course of the research. Special mention must be made of Dr Michael Kennedy and Dr Kate O'Malley of the *Documents on Irish Foreign Policy* project, who provided a warm working environment and invaluable advice over a period of two years.

Thanks are also due to Geraldine Kennedy MRIA, former Editor of the *Irish Times*, Gerard O'Regan, Editor, the *Irish Independent* and Eamon de Valera, Chairman, Irish Press plc for permission to reproduce extracts from their respective newspapers in the commentary, and the Editorial Board is likewise grateful to the Incorporated Law Reporting Council of Ireland for permission to reproduce extracts from *The Irish Reports*.

The original version of this work as submitted to the Board was deemed to be simply too large for publication. The Board is enormously indebted to Professor Ronan Fanning MRIA who took on the thankless task of adapting the work and by judicious editing reduced the volume to a manageable size so that it was ready for publication.

A special word of thanks is also due to Ruth Hegarty, Managing Editor of the Royal Irish Academy. Ms Hegarty oversaw the publication of this large work, and the attractive layout, style and design provides its own tribute to her consummate pro-fessionalism.

The Board would finally wish to pay a special tribute to the outstanding work of its research assistant, Eoin Kinsella. Mr Kinsella assembled the material almost from scratch and attended to a host of detailed queries. This volume could not possibly have been produced without his assistance, and the Board is deeply indebted to him for his efficiency and dedication to the project.

Biographical Notes

This list is intended as a guide to the principal figures involved in the development of the 1937 Constitution. Minor figures, such as those mentioned briefly in documents or in the accompanying commentary, have been identified where possible in footnotes. Most of the names listed can be consulted in further depth in the Royal Irish Academy's *Dictionary of Irish Biography.*

Bartley, Patrick, SJ (1879–1941): Born in Grange, Co. Limerick; educated at Sacred Heart College, Crescent, Limerick; entered the Society of Jesus (1894); graduated MA from the Royal University of Ireland; further education at University of Beirut, the French Scholasticate, Jersey, and Milltown Park, Dublin; ordained in 1912; Professor of Scholastic Philosophy, Church History, Sacred Scripture and Hebrew at Milltown Park; member of the Jesuit Constitution Committee (1936).

Bennett, Louie (1870–1956): Born in Dublin; novelist, suffragist and trade unionist; co-founder of Irish Women's Suffrage Federation (1911); founder, Irish Women's Reform League; member of the national executive of the Irish Trade Union Congress (1927–32, 1944–50); President of the ITUC (1932, 1947).

Bewley, Charles (1888–1969). Diplomat and barrister. Born to a wealthy Dublin Quaker family and educated at Park House and Winchester School. A graduate of New College, Oxford (1910), he was called to the Bar in 1914. Repudiating his Anglo-Irish inheritance, he took the Treaty side during the Civil War. Appointed resident minister to the Vatican (1929) and Berlin (1933). Dismissed at the outset of the Second World War by de Valera for his pro-Nazi views, he died in Rome in 1969.

Byrne, Edward Joseph (1872–1940): Born in Dublin; educated at Belvedere College, Dublin, Holy Cross College, Clonliffe, and graduated from the Royal University of Ireland; Vice-Rector of the Irish College in Rome (1901–4); Roman Catholic Archbishop of Dublin (1921–40).

Cahill, Edward, SJ (1868–1941): Born in Callow, Ballingrane, Co. Limerick; educated at Mungret College, Limerick, and St Patrick's College, Maynooth; joined the Society of Jesus (1890); pamphleteer, author of *Freemasonry and the Anti-Christian Movement* (1929) and *The Framework of a Christian State: An Introduction to Social Science* (1932); co-founder of An Ríoghacht (1926); member of the Jesuit Constitution Committee (1936).

Canavan, Joseph, SJ (1886–1950): Born in Khandalla, India; educated at St Mary's High School, Bombay (Mumbai), Clongowes Wood College (1901–4);

entered the Society of Jesus (1904); further educated at the Gregorian University, Rome (1922–4); Professor of Philosophy at Milltown Park, Dublin, and St Stanislaus College, Tullamore (1924–33); Professor of Theology, Milltown Park (1934–50); member of the Jesuit Constitution Committee (1936).

Codling, Arthur Dean (1876–1950): Born in Lytham, Lancashire, England; educated in Lancashire, North Wales and the University of London; Irish civil servant (1900–44); Principal Officer, Department of Finance (1923–8); Assistant Secretary, Department of Finance (1928–44).

Connolly, Joseph (1885–1961): Born in Belfast; educated at St Malachy's College, Belfast; appointed Irish consul general to the United States of America in 1921, resigned in 1922; Fianna Faíl member of the Irish Free State Senate (1928–36); Minister for Posts and Telegraphs (1932–3); Minister for Lands and Fisheries (1933–6); Member of the Second House Commission (1936); Controller of Censorship (1939–41); Chairman of the Office of Public Works (1936–50).

Cosgrave, William Thomas (1880–1965) TD Sinn Féin, Cumann na nGaedheal and Fine Gael: Born in Dublin; educated at Christian Brothers' School, Marino; elected MP while in prison in 1917 Kilkenny by-election; elected TD for Carlow-Kilkenny in 1918; Minister for Local Government, Dáil Éireann (April 1919–September 1922); Minister for Local Government, Provisional Government (January–August 1922); Chairman of the Provisional Government (August–December 1922); President of the Executive Council of the Irish Free State (1922–32); Acting Minister for Finance (September 1922–September 1923); Acting Minister for External Affairs (July–October 1927); Leader of Cumann na nGaedheal and later Fine Gael (1922–44).

Costello, John Aloysius (1891–1976) TD Cumann na nGaedheal and Fine Gael: Born in Dublin; educated at Christian Brothers' School, North Richmond St; graduated BA from University College Dublin in 1911, LLB 1913; Senior Counsel (1925); Bencher of King's Inns (1926); Attorney General (1926–32); TD (1933–69); Taoiseach (1948–51 and 1954–7); returned to legal practice at the Bar (1951–4; 1957–75).

Coyne, Edward Joseph, SJ (1896–1958): Born in Dublin; educated at Clongowes Wood College and St Stanislaus College, Tullamore, Franz Ferdinand University, Innsbruck (1926–8) and University College Dublin; teacher, Belvedere College; Professor of Ethics, St Stanislaus College (1933–8); appointed Professor of Moral Theology, Milltown Park, Dublin (1938); member of the Jesuit Constitution Committee (1936).

Derrig, Thomas (1897–1956) TD Sinn Féin and Fianna Fáil: Born in Westport, Co. Mayo; educated at Christian Brothers' School, Westport, and University College Galway (1915–19); elected as Sinn Féin TD for Mayo North and West (May 1921); opposed the Anglo-Irish treaty; founder member of Fianna Fáil; TD (June 1927–56); Minister for Education (March 1932–September 1939 and June 1940–February 1948); Minister for Lands (September 1939–July 1943 and June 1951–June 1954); Minister for Posts and Telegraphs (8–27 September 1939).

Dillon, James Mathew (1902–86) TD Independent, National Centre Party and Fine Gael: Born in Dublin; son of John Dillon, last leader of the Irish Parliamentary Party; educated at Mt St Benedict, Gorey, Co. Wexford, and University College Dublin (1919–21); elected as independent TD for Donegal (1932) and Monaghan (1937–69); joint leader, National Centre Party (1932–3); joined Fine Gael (1933); resigned from Fine Gael (February 1942); Minister for Agriculture (1948–51, 1954–7); rejoined Fine Gael 1952; Leader of Fine Gael (1959–65); TD (1932–69).

Dixon, Kevin (1902–59): Born in Dalkey, Co. Dublin; educated at Belvedere College, Dublin, University College Dublin and the King's Inns; graduated B.Sc. from UCD (1923); called to the Bar (1926); Senior Counsel (1940); Bencher of King's Inns (1942); Attorney General (1942–6); Justice of the High Court (1946–59).

de Valera, Eamon (1882–1975) TD Sinn Féin and Fianna Fáil: Born in New York, brought to Ireland in 1885 by an uncle; educated at Bruree National School, Co. Limerick, Christian Brothers School, Charleville, Co. Cork, Blackrock College, Co. Dublin, graduating from the Royal University of Ireland, Dublin, and Trinity College Dublin; teacher of mathematics at Rockwell College, Co. Tipperary and Blackrock College, Co. Dublin; elected MP for East Clare (July 1917); elected President of Sinn Féin (October 1917); imprisoned in England (1918–19); returned unopposed for East Clare and elected for East Mayo in the 1918 general election, also elected for North Down (1921–7) and South Down (1933–8) to the Parliament of Northern Ireland; President of Dáil Éireann (1 April 1919–9 January 1922); opposed the Treaty; announced re-organisation of Sinn Féin (January 1923); arrested by Irish Free State troops and imprisoned (August 1923–July 1924; TD for Clare (1923–59); resigned Presidency of Sinn Féin (March 1926); founder of Fianna Fáil (May 1926); became leader of the opposition in Dáil Éireann (August 1927); President of the Executive Council and Minister for External Affairs (1932–7); President of the Council of the League of Nations and acting President of the Assembly of the League of Nations (1932–3); Taoiseach and Minister for External Affairs (1937–48); Minister for Education (September 1939–June 1940); Minister for Local Government (August 1941); Taoiseach (1951–4 and 1957–9); President of Ireland (1959–73).

Douglas, James Green (1887–1954): Born in Dublin; educated at the Friend's School, Lisburn; member of the drafting committee of the Irish Free State Constitution (1922); member of the Irish Free State Senate (1922–36); Member of Seanad Éireann (1938–43, 1944–54).

Duffy, George Gavan (1882–1951) TD Sinn Féin: Born in Cheshire, England;

educated at Stonyhurst College, Lancashire; solicitor for Roger Casement (1916), called to the Irish Bar (1917); elected MP for Sinn Féin (1918); Irish Representative of Dáil Éireann in Paris (1919–September 1920); roving envoy in Europe (September 1920–Spring 1921); representative in Rome (1921); Member of the Irish Treaty delegation (October–December 1921); supported the Treaty; Dáil Éireann Minister for Foreign Affairs (10 January–25 July 1922); called to the Inner Bar (1929); Justice of the High Court (1936–46); President of the High Court (1946–50)

Edward VIII (1894–1972): British Monarch (1936) (abdicated); married Wallis Simpson (1937); created Duke of Windsor; Governor of the Bahamas (1940–5).

Esmonde, Sir Osmond Thomas Grattan (1896–1936) TD Cumann na nGaedheal: Born in Ballynastragh, Co. Wexford; educated at Mt St Benedict School, Gorey, Co. Wexford; attended both Balliol College, Oxford and University College Dublin, but graduated from neither; Assistant Secretary, Department of External Affairs (1923); TD for Wexford for Cumann na nGaedheal (1923–7) (joined the National Group in 1924); rejoined Cumann na nGaedheal in early 1927 and again served as TD (September 1927–36).

Fahy, Francis Patrick ('Frank') (1879–1953) TD Sinn Féin and Fianna Fáil: Born in Loughrea, Co. Galway; educated at Mungret College, Limerick, and University College Galway; founder member of the Irish Volunteers; elected MP for Galway South (1918); TD (1919–53); Ceann Comhairle (1932–51).

Fay, William Patrick Ignatius (1909–69): Born in Dublin; educated at Clongowes Wood College, King's Inns and University College Dublin; called to the Irish Bar in 1931; Assistant, Attorney General's Office (1937–41); First Secretary, Department of External Affairs (1941–6); Secretary to the Irish High Commission, London (1946–7); Chargé d'affaires en titre, Brussels (1947–50); Minister Plenipotentiary to Sweden (1950–1); Legal Adviser, Department of External Affairs (1951–4); Ambassador to France (1954–60); Ambassador to Canada (1960–4); Ambassador to Washington (1964–9).

FitzGerald, Desmond (1889–1947) TD Sinn Féin and Cumann na nGaedheal: Born in London; educated at West Ham Grammar School; Dáil Éireann substitute Director of Propaganda (17 June 1919–11 February 1921 and 15 July 1921–8 September 1922) (subsequently styled Secretary for Publicity, August 1921, then Minister for Publicity, January 1922); Minister for External Affairs (1922–7); Minister for Defence (1927–32); member of Seanad Éireann (1938–47).

Fitzgibbon, Gerald (1866–1942) Independent TD: Educated at Bassets College and Clifton College. Called to the Bar (1891) and the Inner Bar (1908); Bencher of King's Inns (1912); MP for Dublin University (1912–21); TD for Dublin University (1921–3); Justice of the Supreme Court (1924–38).

Geoghegan, James (1886–1951) TD Cumann na nGaedheal and Fianna Fáil: Born in Walshestown, Co. Westmeath; educated at Christian Brothers' School, Mullingar; called to the Irish Bar (1915) and to the English Bar (1923); Senior

Counsel (1925); Minister for Justice (1932–3); Attorney General (2 November–22 December 1936); Justice of the Supreme Court (1936–50); served as TD for Fianna Fáil (1930–6).

Gregg, John Allen Fitzgerald (1873–1961): Born in North Cerney, Gloucestershire, England; educated at Christ's College, Cambridge (1891–4); Archbishop King Professor of Divinity, Trinity College Dublin (1911–15); Church of Ireland Bishop of Ossory (1915–20); Church of Ireland Archbishop of Dublin (1920–9); Church of Ireland Archbishop of Armagh and Primate of all Ireland (1939–59).

Hanna, Henry (1871–1946): Born in Belfast; educated at Belfast Academy; graduated from Queen's University, Belfast, and London University; called to the Bar (1896); King's Counsel (1911); elected Bencher of King's Inns (1915); Justice of the High Court (1925–42).

Haugh, Kevin (1901–69): Born in Dublin; educated at Belvedere College, Blackrock College and University College Dublin; called to the Irish Bar (1925); Senior Counsel (1938); Attorney-General (January 1940); Justice of the High Court (1942–61); Justice of the Supreme Court (1961–9).

Hayden, Mary Teresa (1862–1942): Born in Dublin; educated at Mt Anville convent, Dublin, the Ursuline convent, Thurles, Co. Tipperary; graduated BA (1885) and MA (1887) from the Royal University of Ireland; founder member of the Irish Association for Women Graduates (1902); Professor of modern Irish history, University College Dublin (1909–38); co-founder, Irish Catholic Women's Suffrage Society (1915); President, National University Women Graduates' Association, 1937.

Hearne, John Joseph (1893–1969): Born in Waterford; educated at Waterpark College, Waterford and University College Dublin; called to the Irish Bar (1919); Assistant Parliamentary Draftsman (1923–9); Legal Adviser, Department of External Affairs (1929–39); called to Inner Bar (1939); High Commissioner to Canada (1939–49); Ambassador to the United States of America (1950–60).

Hogan, Gabriel Patrick Sarsfield (1901–89): Educated at the Catholic University School, Dublin, and University College Dublin (BA, 1921; LLM, 1923); called to the Irish Bar (1923); Private Secretary to the Secretary, Department of Finance (1923–5); Private Secretary to the Minister, Department of Finance (1925–7); Parliamentary and Estimates Clerk, Department of Finance (1927–38); Assistant Secretary, Department of the Taoiseach (1938–9); Principal Officer, Department of Finance (1940–8); Assistant Secretary, Department of Finance (1948–61).

Hyde, Douglas (1860–1949): Born in Castlerea, Co. Roscommon; educated at Trinity College Dublin (LLB, 1887 and LLD, 1888); President of the National Literary Society (1892); President of the Gaelic League (1893–1915); Professor of Irish, University College Dublin (1909–32); member of the Irish Free State Senate (1925); First President of Ireland (1938–45).

Keane, Sir John (1873–1956): Educated at Clifton College, Bristol, and the Royal Military Academy, Woolwich; member of the Irish Free State Senate (1922–34); Member of Seanad Éireann (1938–48).

Keith, Arthur Berriedale (1879–1944): Born in Edinburgh; educated at the Royal High School, Edinburgh (1887–94), Edinburgh University and Balliol College, Oxford; Regius Professor of Sanskrit and Comparative Philology, Edinburgh University (1914–44); Author of *Responsible government in the Dominions* (1909, 1912, 1928), *Constitutional history of the first British Empire* (1930) and *The Dominions as Sovereign States* (1938).

Kennedy, Hugh Boyle (1879–1936) TD Cumann na nGaedheal: Born in Dublin; graduated with a BA and LLB from the Royal University of Ireland; called to the Bar (1902); King's Counsel, (1920); Legal adviser to the Department of Local Government in the first Dáil; member of the drafting committee of the Irish Free State Constitution (1922); Law Officer to the Provisional Government (1922); TD (1923–4). Attorney General (1923–4); Chairman, Second House Commission (1936); Chief Justice (1924–36).

Lemass, Seán (1899–1971) TD Fianna Fáil: Educated at O'Connell Schools, Dublin; elected to Dáil Éireann (1924) but abstained; founder member of Fianna Fáil (1926); Minister for Industry and Commerce (1932–9, 1941–8, 1951–4 and 1957–9); Minister for Supplies (1939–45); Tánaiste (1945–8, 1951–4 and 1957–9); Managing Director, *Irish Press* (1948–51); Taoiseach (1959–66).

Leydon, John (1895–1979): Born in Co. Roscommon; educated at St Mel's College, Longford; entered seminary at St Patrick's College, Maynooth (1913–14); entered British civil service in 1915; transferred to Ireland, Department of Finance (1923–32); Secretary, Department of Industry and Commerce (1932–9); Secretary, Department of Supplies (1939–45); Secretary, Department of Industry and Commerce (1945–55); President, Institute of Public Administration (1957–9).

Little, Patrick John (1884–1963) TD Fianna Fáil: Born in Dundrum, Co. Dublin; educated at Clongowes Wood College and University College Dublin; elected Sinn Féin MP for Dublin Rathmines (1918); Diplomatic representative for Dáil Éireann (1921); Founder member of Fianna Fáil; TD (June 1927–54); Parliamentary secretary to de Valera (1933–9); Minister for Posts and Telegraphs (1939–48); Director, Arts Council (1951–6).

Lynch, Patrick Gregory (1866–1947): Born in Co. Clare; graduated from the Royal University of Ireland; called to the Irish Bar (1888) and the Inner Bar (1906); Senior crown prosecutor for Kerry (1908); Member of the Irish Free State Senate (Fianna Fáil, 1934–6); Attorney General (22 December 1936–1 March 1940).

Macardle, Dorothy Margaret (1889–1958): Born in Dundalk, Co. Louth; founder member of Fianna Fáil; author of *The Irish Republic* (1937).

Macaulay, William J. Babbington (1892–1964): Born in Dublin; Secretary to the Irish legation in Washington (1925–9); Counsellor to the Irish legation in Washington (1929–30); Consul General in New York (1930–4); Irish Minister to the Vatican (1934–41).

MacBride, Seán (1904–88) TD Clann na Poblachta: Born in Paris; called to the Irish Bar (1937); Senior Counsel (1943); co-founder of Clann na Poblachta (1946); TD (1947–57); Minister for External Affairs (1948–51); Nobel peace prize laureate (1974).

MacDermot, Frank (1886–1975) TD Independent Centre Party and Fine Gael: Educated at Queen's College, Oxford (BA, 1909); called to the English Bar (1911); founder member of National Centre Party (1932) (merged in 1933 with Cumann na nGaedheal and the Army Comrades Association to form Fine Gael); TD (1933–7); left Cumann na nGaedheal 1935; member of Seanad Éireann (1938–43).

MacEntee, Seán (1889–1984), TD Sinn Féin and Fianna Fáil: Educated at St Malachy's College, Belfast, and Belfast Municipal College of Technology; TD (1919–22 and 1927–69); founder member of Fianna Fáil (1926); Joint-Treasurer of Fianna Fáil (1926–32); Minister for Finance (1932–9 and 1951–4); Minister for Industry and Commerce (1939–41); Minister for Local Government and Public Health (1941–8); Member of the Council of State from 1948; Minister for Social Welfare (1957–61); Minister for Health (1957–65); Tánaiste (1959–65).

MacErlean, John Campbell, SJ (1870–1950): Born in Belfast; entered Jesuit novitiate at Tullabeg, King's County (County Offaly) (1888); graduated BA from the Royal University of Ireland (1892); member of the Jesuit Constitution Committee (1936).

MacMahon, Peadar (1893–1975): Born near Ballybay, Co. Monaghan; joined the Irish army (1922); Major-General (1923); Chief of Staff (1924–7); Secretary, Department of Defence (1927–58).

MacRory, Joseph (1861–1945): Born in Ballygawley, Co. Tyrone; Professor of Moral Theology and Sacred Scripture, Oscott College, Birmingham (1887–9); Professor of Sacred Scripture and Hebrew, Maynooth College (1889–1905); Professor of Hermeneutics and New Testament Exegesis, Maynooth College (1905–12); Roman Catholic Bishop of Down and Connor (1915–28); Roman Catholic Archbishop of Armagh (1928–45); appointed Cardinal (1929).

McDunphy, Michael (1890–1971): Born in Dublin; educated at Christian Brothers' School, North Richmond St; entered Civil Service in 1911 and dismissed in 1918 for refusing to take the oath of allegiance; Assistant Secretary to the Provisional Government (January–December 1922); Assistant Secretary to the Executive Council (1922–37); Secretary to the President of Ireland (1937–54); Director of Irish Life Assurance Company and Irish Estates Ltd. (1954–64); Director of the Bureau of Military History (1947–57).

McElligott, James J. (1893–1974): Born in Tralee, Co. Kerry; educated at Christian Brothers' School, Tralee, and at University College Dublin; Secretary, Department of Finance (1927–53).

McGilligan, Patrick (1889–1979) TD Cumann na nGaedheal and Fine Gael: Educated at Clongowes Wood College and University College Dublin; called to the Bar (1921); Private Secretary, Minister of Home Affairs (1922); Secretary to the High Commissioner's Office, London (1923); TD (1923–65); Minister for Industry and Commerce (1924–32); Minister for External Affairs (1927–32); called to the Inner Bar (1946); Minister for Finance (1948–51); Attorney General (1954–7); Chair of Constitutional, International Law and Criminal Law and Procedure at University College Dublin.

McQuaid, John Charles (1895–1973): Born in Cootehill, Co. Cavan; member of the Holy Ghost Fathers; President of Blackrock College (1931–9); Archbishop of Dublin (1940–72).

Maguire, Conor (1889–1971) TD Fianna Fáil: Born in Claremorris, Co. Mayo, educated at Clongowes Wood College and University College, Dublin; judge in the Republican Courts (1920–2); called to the Bar (1922); Senior Counsel (1932); TD (1932–6); Attorney General (1932–6); High Court Judge (1936), President of the High Court (1936–46); Chief Justice (1946–61); Judge of the European Court of Human Rights, (1965–71).

Matheson, Arthur (1878–1946): Born in Dublin; educated at Trinity College, Dublin and King's Inns; called to the Bar (1903); First Parliamentary Draftsman of the Irish Free State.

Moynihan, Maurice (1902–99): Educated at Christian Brothers' School, Tralee, and at University College Cork; entered the Department of Finance (1925); Secretary to the Government (1937–48 and 1951–60); Secretary, Department of the Taoiseach (1937–60); Governor of the Central Bank of Ireland (1961–9); brother of Seán Moynihan.

Moynihan, John (Seán) (1891–1964): Educated at Christian Brothers' School, Tralee; Secretary to Eamon de Valera (1929); Assistant Editor, *Irish Press* (September 1931–March 1932); Secretary to the Government (1932–7); Assistant Secretary, Department of Finance (1937–52); brother of Maurice Moynihan.

Mulcahy, Richard (1886–1971) TD Sinn Féin, Cumann na nGaedheal and Fine Gael: Born in Waterford City; educated at the Christian Brothers' Schools of Mt Sion and Thurles; IRA Chief of Staff (1918); Minister for National Defence (1919); Assistant Minister for National Defence (1920–1); Minister for Defence (1922–4); Commander in Chief of the Irish Army (1922–4); Minister for Local Government and Public Health (1927–32); TD (1919–37, 1938–43, 1944–61); Member of Seanad Éireann (1938, 1943–4); Minister for Education (1948–51; 1954–7).

Murnaghan, James Augustine (1881–1973): Born in St Louis, Missouri; educated at University College Dublin, graduated MA and LLB from the Royal

University of Ireland; called to the Irish Bar (1903); Professor of Jurisprudence, Roman Law and International Law, UCD (1910–24); member of the drafting committee of the Irish Free State Constitution (1922); Justice of the High Court (1924–5), Justice of the Supreme Court (1925–53).

Murphy, Seán (1896–1964): Educated at Clongowes Wood College and University College Dublin; solicitor; Secretary, Irish Mission to Paris (1920); Representative of the Irish Free State in Paris (1923); Administrative Officer, Department of External Affairs (1925–7); Assistant Secretary, Department of External Affairs (1927–38); Minister to France (1938–50); Ambassador to Canada (1950–5); Secretary, Department of External Affairs (1955–7).

Ó Broin, León (1902–90): Born in Dublin; educated at Synge St Christian Brothers' School; clerk, Dáil Éireann Department of Agriculture (1921–2); called to the Irish Bar (1924); involved in the launch of An Gúm while working in the Department of Education (1925–7); Parliamentary Clerk, Department of Finance (1927–31); Private Secretary to the Minister for Finance (1931–2); Assistant Principal Officer (1932–9) and Principal Officer (1939–45), Department of Finance; Assistant Secretary (1945–8) and Secretary (1948–67), Department of Posts and Telegraphs.

Ó Cinnéide, Pádraig (1899–1981): Educated at Belvedere College, Dublin, and University College Dublin; Higher Executive Officer, Department of Justice (1922–7); Assistant Principal Officer, Department of Finance (1927–32); Chief Clerk of the Land Commission (1932–7); Assistant Secretary to the Cabinet (1937–47); Assistant Secretary, Department of Health (1947); Secretary, Department of Health (1947–59); Chairman of the Hospitals' Commission (1963).

O'Connell, Kathleen (1888–1956): Born in Caherdaniel, Co. Kerry; emigrated to America (1904); returned to Ireland with de Valera (1920); Personal Secretary to de Valera (1919–54); Personal Secretary to the Taoiseach (1944–8, 1951–4).

O'Connell, Thomas Joseph (1882–1969) TD Labour Party: Born in Spotfield, Bekan, Co. Mayo; qualified as a teacher from St Patrick's College, Drumcondra; General Secretary of the Irish National Teachers' Organisation (1916–48); TD, leader of the Labour Party (1927–32); founder of Educational Building Society (1935); member of Seanad Éireann (1938–44, 1948–51, 1954–7).

O'Donoghue, (Patrick) Philip (1896–1987): Born in Macroom, Co. Cork; called to the Irish Bar (1919); Legal Assistant to the Attorney General (1929–59); called to the Inner Bar (1939); Irish member of the European Commission on Human Rights (1965); Judge, European Court of Human Rights (1971–80).

Ó Foghludha, Risteard (1871–1957): Born in Knockmonlea, Co. Cork; educated at the Christian Brothers' School, Youghal; clerk at the first meeting of Dáil Éireann, 21 January 1919; founder of Craobh an Chéitinnigh (1901); contributor to the *Freeman's Journal* and *An Claidheamh Soluis*; editor of several collections of Munster Irish poetry; director of Coimisiún na Logainmneacha (Commission for Placenames).

O'Hegarty, Diarmuid (1892–1958): Born in Lowertown, Skibbereen, Co. Cork; educated at Christian Brothers' School, St Patrick's Place, Cork; joined the Civil Service (1910); dismissed from the Civil Service for refusing to take the oath of allegiance (1918); Clerk of the first Dáil and Secretary to the Dáil cabinet (1919–21); Secretary to the Irish delegation during the Anglo-Irish treaty negotiations (1921); Secretary to the Executive Council and Principal Private Secretary to W.T. Cosgrave (1922–32); appointed as Commissioner of Public Works (1932); Chairman of Public Works (1949–57).

O'Higgins, Kevin (1892–1927) TD Sinn Féin and Cumann na nGaedheal: Born in Stradbally, Queen's County (Co. Laois); educated at the Christian Brothers' School, Maryborough (Portlaoise), Clongowes Wood and Knockbeg College, Co. Carlow; Deputy Minister for Local Government (1920–1); supported the Treaty; Minister for Home Affairs (1922–4); Vice President of the Executive Council (1922–7); Minister for Justice (1924–7); assassinated on 10 July 1927.

O'Kelly, Seán Thomas (1883–1966) TD Sinn Féin and Fianna Fáil: Educated at O'Connell Schools, Dublin; Ceann Comhairle of Dáil Éireann (1919); Irish representative to the Paris Peace Conference (1919) and representative in Paris (1919–22); Sinn Féin Envoy to Italy (1920); Sinn Féin Envoy to the United States of America (1924–6); founder member of Fianna Fáil (1926); Minister for Local Government and Public Health (1932–9); Tánaiste (1937–45); Minister for Finance (1939–45); President of Ireland (1945–59).

O'Neill, Joseph (1878–1953): Born in Tuam, Co. Galway; Secretary, Department of Education (1923–44); Author of *Wind from the North* (1934), *Land under England* (1935), *Day of wrath* (1936), *Philip* (1940), *Chosen by the Queen* (1947).

O'Rahilly, Alfred (1884–1969): Born in Listowel, Co. Kerry; educated at St Michael's College, Listowel, Blackrock College and University College Dublin; trained as a member of the Society of Jesus (1901–14), but not then ordained; assistant lecturer in mathematics and mathematical physics, University College Cork (1914–17); Professor of mathematical physics, UCC (1917–43); Registrar, UCC (1920–43); President, UCC (1943–54) ordained as a priest in 1955 and resided at Blackrock College.

O'Sullivan, John Marcus (1881–1948) TD Cumann na nGaedheal and Fine Gael: Born in Killarney, Co. Kerry; educated at St Brendan's College, Killarney, and Clongowes Wood College; graduated from University College Dublin BA (1902) and MA (1903); received a doctorate from the University of Heidelberg; appointed to the chair of modern history at UCD in 1910; TD (1923–43); parliamentary secretary to the Minister for Finance (1924–6); Minister for Education (1926–32); delegate to the League of Nations (1924, 1928, 1929 and 1930).

Robinson, Paschal (1870–1948): Born in Dublin, christened Charles Edward Neville Robinson; associate editor of the *North American Review* (1892–4);

educated at Holy Cross College, Worcester, Massachusetts (1894–6), St Bonaventure College, Alleghany, New York (1896–9, where he adopted the name Paschal) and St Anthony's International Franciscan College, Rome; founder of the *Laurel* (1899); ordained in 1901; Professor of Medieval History, Catholic University of America, Washington, D.C. (1913–25); Papal Nuncio to the Irish Free State (1929–37) and Ireland (1937–48).

Roche, Stephen Anselm (1890–1949): Born in Caherciveen, Co. Kerry; educated at Blackrock College; entered Civil Service (1909); graduated from Trinity College Dublin in 1914, BA and LLB; Assistant Secretary, Department of Justice (1926); Acting Secretary (1930–4) and Secretary (1934–49), Department of Justice.

Ruttledge, Patrick Joseph (1892–1952) TD Sinn Féin and Fianna Fáil: Born in Ballina, Co. Mayo; educated at St Muredach's College, Ballina, St Enda's School, Dublin and Trinity College Dublin; solicitor; TD (1921–54); Acting 'President of the Republic' (1923–4); Minister for Lands and Fisheries (1932–3); Minister for Justice (1933–9); Minister for Local Government and Public Health (1939–41).

Ryan, James (1891–1970) TD Sinn Féin and Fianna Fáil: Born in Tomcoole, Co. Wexford; educated at St Peter's College, Ring, Co. Waterford and University College Dublin; medical doctor; founder member of Fianna Fail (1926); Minister for Agriculture (1932–47); Minister for Health and Social Welfare (1947–8 and 1951–4); Minister for Finance (1957–65); Member of Seanad Éireann (1965–9).

Rynne, Michael Andrew Lysaght (1899–1981): Born in Knockacarn, Ennistymon, Co. Clare; called to the Irish Bar (1925); Assistant Legal Adviser, Department of External Affairs (1932–6); Legal Adviser, Department of External Affairs (1936–50); Assistant Secretary, Department of External Affairs (1950–5); Ambassador to Spain (1955–61).

Sullivan, Timothy (1874–1949): Born in Dublin, educated at Belvedere College, Dublin; called to the Bar (1895); King's Counsel (1918); Bencher of King's Inns (1921); President of the High Court (1924–36); Chief Justice (1936–46).

Tierney, Michael (1894–1975) TD Cumann na nGaedheal: Born in Esker, Co. Galway; educated at St Joseph's College, Ballinasloe and University College Dublin; appointed Professor of Greek, University College Dublin (1922); TD (1923–32); member of Seanad Éireann (1938–44); President, University College Dublin (1947–64).

Traynor, Oscar (1886–1963) TD Sinn Féin and Fianna Fáil: Born in Upper Abbey St, Dublin; Minister for Posts and Telegraphs (1936–9); Minister for Defence (1939–48, 1951–4); Minister for Justice (1957–61).

Walsh, Louis Joseph (1880–1942): Born in Maghera, Derry; educated at St Columb's College, Derry and University College Dublin; playwright and author; Justice of the District Court (1922–42).

Walshe, Joseph Patrick (1886–1956): Born in Killenaule, Co. Tipperary; educated at Mungret College, Limerick; graduated from University College Dublin BA (1916) and MA (1917); former Jesuit seminarian and teacher at Clongowes Wood College; solicitor; served on the Irish delegation in Paris (November 1920–January 1922); Secretary to Dáil Ministry of Foreign Affairs (1922); Acting Secretary, Department of External Affairs (1922–7); Secretary, Department of External Affairs (1927–46); Ambassador to the Holy See (1946–54).

List of Documents Reproduced

1928

No.	Type of Document	Subject	Date	Page
1	Memorandum, O'Hegarty to Cosgrave	Deletion of Article 48	17 Feb.	30
2	Memorandum, O'Hegarty to Costello	Deletion of Articles 47 and 48	1 June	31
3	Memorandum, McDunphy to Costello	Amendment of Article 50	13 Nov.	32

1934

No.	Type of Document	Subject	Date	Page
4	Memorandum by McDunphy	Establishment of 1934 Constitution Committee	24 May	48
5	Minutes	1st meeting of 1934 Constitution Committee	28 May	48
6	Minutes	2nd meeting of 1934 Constitution Committee	29 May	49
7	Memorandum by McDunphy	Objectives of 1934 Constitution Committee	31 May	54
8	Minutes	3rd meeting of 1934 Constitution Committee	1 June	55
9	Letter, Roche to McElligott	Fundamental financial articles of the 1922 Constitution	2 June	58
10	Draft Report	1st draft of 1934 Constitution Committee's Report	9 June	59
11	Memorandum, McDunphy to 1934 Constitution Committee members	Fundamental Articles of the 1922 Constitution	12 June	60
12	Memorandum, Roche to 1934 Constitution Committee members	Article 2A of the 1922 Constitution	14 June	61
13	Letter, McDunphy to O'Neill	Article 10 of the 1922 Constitution	15 June	64

1935

1936

No.	Type of Document	Subject	Date	Page
50	Letter, de Valera to Cahill	Suggestions for a new Constitution	19 Sept.	239
51	Letter, Cahill to de Valera	Suggestions for a new Constitution	21 Sept.	239
52	Minutes	1st meeting of the Jesuit Constitution Committee	24 Sept.	240
53	Letter, Bartley to Kiernan	Instructions for Cahill	11 Oct.	241
54	Letter, Bartley to Kiernan	Instructions for Cahill	15 Oct.	242
55	Letter, Kiernan to Cahill	Instructions for Cahill	16 Oct.	242
56	Minutes	5th meeting of the Jesuit Constitution Committee	18 Oct.	243
57	Letter, Cahill to de Valera	Enclosing 'Suggestion for a Catholic Constitution'	21 Oct.	244
58	Draft Preamble and Articles	Jesuit Constitution Committee's 'Suggestions for a Catholic Constitution'	18 Oct.	246
59	Letter, Cahill to de Valera	Enclosing Cahill's 'Supplementary Suggestions'	13 Nov.	251
60	Draft Articles	Cahill's 'Supplementary Suggestions'	13 Nov.	252
61	Memorandum, Executive Council to Edward VIII	Introduction of a new Constitution	8 June	259
62	Memorandum, Hearne to S. Moynihan	Explanatory memo for a draft Foreign Relations Bill	6 Sept.	260
63	Draft Bill by Hearne	Draft Foreign Relations Bill	6 Sept.	261
64	Cabinet Minutes	Abdication of Edward VIII	10 Dec.	262
65	Memorandum by McDunphy	Drafting of Constitution (Amndt 27) Bill	10 Dec.	263
66	Note by Geoghegan	Necessity for External Relations Act	11 Dec.	264
67	Briefing notes, McDunphy to de Valera	Constitution (Amndt 27) Bill and Executive Authority (External Relations) Bill	11 Dec.	264
68	Memorandum by McDunphy	Office of the Governor General	16 Dec.	267
69	Memorandum by McDunphy	Office of the Governor General	22 Dec.	269
70	Memorandum by Hearne	'Plan of Fundamental Constitutional Law'	20 Aug.	280
71	Draft Constitution	Draft Constitution used at Cabinet discussions	20–22 Oct.	286
72	Memorandum	'Summary of Main Provisions of the Constitution [No. 2]'	5 Nov.	298

1937

No.	Type of Document	Subject	Date	Page
184	Letter, Cahill to de Valera	Observations on the draft Constitution as published	13 May	555
185	Letter, Dowling to Hurson	Observations on religious Article	13 May	556
186	Memorandum by Hearne	Meeting with deputations from women's organisations	14 May	558
187	Memorandum, Roche to M. Moynihan	Observations on Article 9	15 May	559
188	Letter, J. Walshe to de Valera	Position of women under the Constitution	15 May	560
189	Letter, O'Mullane to de Valera	Position of women under the Constitution	18 May	561
190	Letter, Bennett to de Valera	Position of women under the Constitution	18 May	562
191	Memorandum by Department of Education	Qualification for the electoral register	19 May	562
192	Letter, Whelehan to McDunphy	Sale of the draft Constitution	19 May	563
193	Letter, Ditchburn to de Valera	Position of women under the Constitution	20 May	565
194	Letter, Macardle to de Valera	Position of women under the Constitution	21 May	566
195	Memorandum, M. Moynihan to Codling	Appointment of Committee on Spelling of Irish in the draft Constitution	21 May	567
196	Memorandum, Douglas to McDunphy	Observations on the draft Constitution as published	21 May	568
197	Letter, Hassard and Conan to de Valera	Position of women under the Constitution	22 May	570
198	Letter, Scott to Little	Christian Scientists and the religious Article	22 May	570
199	Letter, Cahill to de Valera	Observations on the draft Constitution as published	23 May	571
200	Letter, Hayden and M. Hogan to the Executive Council	Position of women under the Constitution	23 May	574
201	Letter, Bennett to de Valera	Position of women under the Constitution	24 May	576
202	Letter, W. O'Hegarty to M. Moynihan	Position of women under the Constitution	24 May	577
203	Letter, de Valera to Cahill	Letter of thanks	24 May	579
204	Memorandum, O'Donoghue to M. Moynihan	Article 40	25 May	579

No.	Type of Document	Subject	Date	Page
225	Memorandum by McDunphy	Date of coming into operation of the Constitution	10 July	601
226	Memorandum, Matheson to M. Moynihan	Legislation for the coming into operation of the Constitution	15 July	602
227	Memorandum, M. Moynihan to Matheson	Legislation for the coming into operation of the Constitution	17 July	604
228	Letter, Browne to McDunphy	Number of votes cast in the general election and the Constitution plebiscite	11 Aug.	604
229	Memorandum, Matheson to M. Moynihan	Operation of the Council of State	28 Aug.	605
230	Memorandum, Matheson to M. Moynihan	Constitution (Consequential Provisions) Bill	28 Aug.	606
231	Memorandum, McDunphy to M. Moynihan	Powers of the President of Ireland	6 Sept.	607
232	Memorandum, McDunphy to M. Moynihan	Operation of the Council of State	15 Sept.	608
233	Memorandum by McDunphy	Powers of the President of Ireland	30 Sept.	609
234	Memorandum, McDunphy to all Ministers	Date of coming into operation of the Constitution	11 Oct.	609
235	Memorandum, McDunphy to M. Moynihan	Enrolment of the Constitution in the Supreme Court	19 Oct.	610
236	Memorandum by McDunphy	Appointment of McDunphy as Secretary to the President of Ireland	5 Nov.	611
237	Memorandum by McDunphy	Legislation for the coming into operation of the Constitution	14 Dec.	612
238	Letter, McDunphy to all Ministers and Lynch	Action to be taken on the date of the coming into operation of the Constitution	16 Dec.	613
239	Memorandum, Irwin to M. Moynihan	Action to be taken on the date of the coming into operation of the Constitution	[?] Dec.	613
240	Memorandum by McDunphy	Constitution Day	20 Dec.	614
241	Letter, Ó Cinnéide to Wilson	Religious service in St Patrick's Cathedral	21 Dec.	615
242	Memorandum by Ó Cinnéide	Religious services	22 Dec.	615
243	Letter, M. Moynihan to Baker	Religious services	23 Dec.	616
244	Memorandum, Ó Cinnéide to McDunphy	Presidential Commission	28 Dec.	617

1938

1939

1940

No.	Type of Document	Subject	Date	Page
281	Transcript of verbal statement	de Valera's statement at the 1st meeting of the Council of State	8 Jan.	735
282	Minutes	1st meeting of the Council of State	8 Jan.	735
283	Supreme Court reference	Reference by Hyde of the Offences Against the State (Amendment) Bill to the Supreme Court	8 Jan.	737
284	Memorandum by McDunphy	Refusal of Cosgrave to attend meeting of the Council of State	10 Jan.	737
285	Memorandum by McDunphy	Council of State procedure	10 Jan.	738
286	Memorandum by McDunphy	Council of State procedure	10 Jan.	738
287	Memorandum by M. Moynihan	Amendment of Article 26	10 Jan.	740
288	Memorandum, M. Moynihan to McDunphy	Amendment of Article 26	11 Jan.	741
289	Memorandum, M. Moynihan to Ó Cinnéide	Procedure for considering proposed constitutional amendments	11 Jan.	742
290	Memorandum, McDunphy to M. Moynihan	Amendment of Article 26	18 Jan.	742
291	Memorandum, McDunphy to M. Moynihan	Amendment of Article 26	19 Jan.	743
292	Memorandum, Ó Cinnéide to M. Moynihan	Procedure for considering proposed constitutional amendments	22 Jan.	745
293	Memorandum, Codling to all government departments	Inviting suggestions for constitutional amendments	29 Jan.	746
294	Memorandum by S. Moynihan	Potential for conflict between English and Irish texts	7 Feb.	746
295	Supreme Court judgment	Offences Against the State (Amendment) Bill	8 Feb.	747
296	Letter, Hyde to de Valera	Signature of the Offences Against the State (Amendment) Bill	9 Feb.	756
297	Telegram, Department External Affairs to Hearne	Inviting suggestions for constitutional amendments	4 Sept.	756
298	Telegram, Hearne to Department External Affairs	Suggestions for amendment of Constitution	16 Sept.	757
299	Report	Report of the constitutional amendments committee	[Sept.]	757
300	Memorandum, Roche to M. Moynihan	Judicial system under the Constitution	13 Sept.	788

TABLE OF CONSTITUTIONAL ARTICLES, INTERNATIONAL TREATIES, ETC

CONSTITUTION OF THE IRISH FREE STATE

CONSTITUTION OF IRELAND

INTERNATONAL TREATIES AND CONVENTIONS

CONSTITUTIONS OF OTHER JURISDICTIONS

TABLE OF STATUTES

TABLE OF CASES

INTRODUCTION

The Constitution of the Irish Free State[1] entered into force on December 6, 1922 after six turbulent years that saw rebellion against British rule, the success of the Sinn Féin party at the 1918 general election, the War of Independence, the partition of the island of Ireland and, ultimately, the Anglo-Irish Treaty of December 1921. The 1921 Treaty had provided for the establishment of the Irish Free State, with Dominion status within the emerging British Commonwealth. While the new state was to be internally sovereign within its borders, its external sovereignty was, at least theoretically, compromised by the uncertainties associated with Dominion status. Yet, within a space of fifteen years, that Constitution was itself replaced following years of political and constitutional turmoil and debate, a process which accelerated following the accession of de Valera to power in March 1932. A new state thus emerged whose external sovereignty was now put beyond question.

The Treaty had contained provisions which were decidedly unpalatable so far as nationalist opinion was concerned: the British side had insisted on a number of essentially symbolic constraints on Irish sovereignty which, with hindsight, can fairly be described as a faint endeavour on their part to camouflage the extent to which a new independent State was being created. At the time, however, the British side certainly considered these to be real constraints which squarely confined the Irish Free State within the existing parameters of the prevailing Imperial/Commonwealth constitutional theory. There seems to have been no realisation on the part of the British side that the Irish Free State would successfully challenge and push back these boundaries over the next fifteen years.[2] These provisions were also incorporated into the Constitution and were declared by section 2 of the Constitution of the Irish Free State (Saorstát Éireann) Act, 1922 to be beyond the amending power of the Oireachtas:

[1] For the drafting of the Irish Free State Constitution, see J.M. Curran, *The Birth of the Irish Free State, 1921–1923* (Alabama, 1980), 200–18; D.H. Akenson and J.F. Fallin, 'The Irish Civil War and the Drafting of the Irish Free State Constitution', *Éire-Ireland* 5, (1970), (no. 1), 10–26; (no. 2) 42–93; (no. 4), 28–70; Brian Farrell, 'The Drafting of the Irish Free State Constitution' in *Irish Jurist*, 5 (1970), 115–40, 343–56 and *Irish Jurist*, 6 (1971), 111–35, 345–59.

[2] Indeed, 'only in the summer of 1936 did the implications of the constitutional developments of the past two decades really dawn upon the British Government' (Deirdre McMahon, *Republicans and Imperialists* (Yale, 1982)), 186.

> The said Constitution shall be construed with reference to the Articles of Agreement for a Treaty between Great Britain and Ireland set forth in the Second Schedule hereto annexed (hereinafter referred to as 'the Scheduled Treaty') which are hereby given the force of law, and if the provisions of the said Constitution or of any amendment thereof or of any law made thereunder is in any respect repugnant to any of the provisions of the Scheduled Treaty, it shall, to the extent only of such repugnancy, be absolutely void and inoperative and the Parliament and the Executive Council of the Irish Free State (Saorstát Éireann) shall respectively pass such further legislation and do all such other things as may be necessary to implement the Scheduled Treaty.

Thus, the Treaty provided for the position of Governor-General who was to be the King's representative.[3] While the Governor-General retained the power to 'reserve' Bills passed by the Oireachtas (i.e., not to sign them into law), this reserve power was purely theoretical and was never exercised.[4] Although the Governor-General's position was entirely ceremonial, his position as the representative of the Crown meant that the very existence of the office remained a constant irritant. In much the same vein, Article 4 of the Treaty provided that members of the Oireachtas were required to swear an oath of allegiance to the Constitution and fidelity to the British Crown. Article 2 of the Treaty also envisaged that there would be a right of appeal to the Privy Council.[5]

The Constitution of the Irish Free State was, in many respects, a unique experiment:

> Ostensibly it created an Irish constitutional monarchy, but by force of will the Provisional Government ensured that key republican values were written into constitutional law for the first time, including popular sovereignty, parliamentary control of the war power, and entrenched civil rights.[6]

[3] Article 3 of the Treaty.

[4] Although in 1922 the British Government 'clearly believed that Instructions to reserve could and, if necessary, should be sent to the Governor-General of the Irish Free State': see Brendan Sexton, *Ireland and the Crown, 1922–1936: The Governor Generalship of the Irish Free State* (Dublin, 1989), 85.

[5] It did this through a somewhat oblique mechanism in that Article 2 provided that 'the law, practice and constitutional usage governing the relationship of the Crown or the representative of the Crown and of the Imperial Parliament to the Dominion of Canada shall govern their relationship to the Irish Free State'. Since a right of appeal to the Privy Council was unarguably part of the constitutional practice and usage in Canada, this also imported the necessity for a similar right of appeal in the Irish Free State as well, a point which the Privy Council itself was to confirm in *Performing Right Society v. Bray Urban District Council*, [1930] IR 509.

[6] A.J. Ward, *The Irish Constitutional Tradition: Responsible Government and Modern Ireland, 1782–1922* (Dublin, 1994), 187.

Articles 65 and 66 of the 1922 Constitution, which vested the High Court (and, on appeal, the Supreme Court) with express powers of judicial review of legislation, represented a radical break with the previous British constitutional tradition, where the doctrine of the supremacy of parliament was fundamental.[7] Indeed, these provisions may be thought to represent the coping stone of the entire constitutional experiment – at least, so far as the 'republican' element of that Constitution was concerned.[8]

Thus, the Constitution of the Irish Free State introduced the conspicuous novelties of judicial review of legislation and the protection of traditional civil rights such as personal liberty, free speech, the inviolability of the dwelling and religious freedoms.[9] In theory, this ought to have meant that legislation enacted by the Oireachtas which unfairly encroached upon these rights would have been unconstitutional and invalid. However, at the time that Constitution was introduced, the legal system was in a state of crisis. The Civil War was raging and a form of martial law prevailed. The reaction of the courts to the *habeas corpus* applications brought during the Civil War demonstrated that the judges were either unwilling or unable to provide effective protection of the fundamental rights of the population.[10] There probably could not have been a more inauspicious time in which to introduce the novelties of a written Constitution with protections for fundamental rights along with the power of judicial review of legislation. At all events, the courts were (with few exceptions) unwilling to subject the exercise of far-reaching and draconian executive and legislative powers to any searching scrutiny during the entire period of the Irish Free State's existence.

In the event, the 1922 Constitution did not prove—in this respect, at least—to be a success. In the period between 1922 and 1937, there were only two occasions when judicial review was actually exercised[11] and a combination of circumstances conspired to ensure that the provision of this power never played the significant role that the drafters

[7] Judicial review conferred on the courts the power to invalidate a statute on the ground that it contravened a provision of the Constitution. This was completely unknown in the British system.

[8] *I.e.*, in contrast to those features which were either inspired by previous British constitutional practice (e.g., the rules as to parliamentary privilege in Articles 18 and 19) or which established the institutions of the State in a manner which roughly paralleled the Westminster model (e.g., the Executive Council based on the principle of collective responsibility contained in Article 51).

[9] Article 16 of the Treaty contained guarantees for religious freedom.

[10] See, *e.g., R.* (*Childers*) *v. Adjutant General, Provisional Forces*, [1923] 1 IR 5, and *R.* (*Johnstone*) *v. O'Sullivan*, [1923] 1 IR 13. See Gerard Hogan, 'Hugh Kennedy, the Childers *Habeas Corpus* Application and the Return to the Four Courts' in Caroline Costello (ed.), *The Four Courts: 200 years* (Dublin, 1996), 177–219; Ronan Keane, '"The Will of the General": Martial Law in Ireland, 1535–1924' in *Irish Jurist*, 25–27 (1990–2), 151.

[11] *R.* (*O'Brien*) *v. Governor of the North Dublin Military Barracks*, [1924] 1 IR 32; *ITGWU v. TGWU*, [1936] IR 471.

of the Constitution had evidently intended. There were essentially two reasons for this. First, the legal culture was largely unreceptive and inhospitable. Unfamiliarity with the concept of judicial review led the judiciary to give the personal rights guarantees of the new Constitution of the Irish Free State a highly restricted ambit. As J.M. Kelly perceptively observed:

> The judges [of this period] were used to the idea of the sovereignty of parliament, and notions of fundamental law were foreign to their training and tradition. The effect of these clauses in the 1922 Constitution was thus minimal.[12]

Secondly, the manner in which the language of Article 50 of the Constitution was judicially interpreted effectively set at naught the possibility of the evolution of any significant constitutional jurisprudence. This, in turn, served to create the impression that these guarantees counted for little and that the power of judicial review of legislation would seldom (if ever) be exercised. This process reached its apotheosis with the decision of the Supreme Court in *The State* (*Ryan*) *v. Lennon.*[13] In that case a majority of the Court held that, subject to the provisions of the Scheduled Treaty, there were no limits to the power of the Oireachtas to amend the 1922 Constitution, thereby negating (should the legislature so see fit) the fundamental rights guarantees.

Article 50 of the 1922 Constitution

One of the innovatory features of the 1922 Constitution was that it provided that future amendments would have to be subjected to a referendum. Article 50 of the 1922 Constitution as enacted provided that:

> Amendments of this Constitution within the terms of the Scheduled Treaty may be made by the Oireachtas, but no such amendment, passed by both Houses of the Oireachtas, *after the expiration of a period of eight years from the date of the coming into operation of this Constitution*, shall become law, unless the same shall, after it has been passed or deemed to have been passed by the said two Houses of the Oireachtas, have been submitted to a Referendum of the people, and unless a majority of voters on the register, or two-thirds of the vote

[12] J.M. Kelly, *Fundamental Rights in the Irish Law and Constitution* (Dublin, 1967), 16–17.
[13] See Chapter III of this volume for a discussion of this case.

> recorded, shall have been cast in favour of such amendment. *Any such amendment may be made within the said period of eight years by way of ordinary legislation and as such shall be subject to the provisions of Article 47 hereof.*

The italicised words were added at the last minute during the course of the Dáil Debates. However, had the drafters' original intentions in this regard been fulfilled, the path of constitutional development in the 1920s and 1930s would surely have taken a different route. In particular, the radical constitutional changes of the 1930s (such as the abolition of the oath and the office of Governor General and the end of the appeal to the Privy Council) might not have been possible had each amendment been subject to the referendum process which would have required a majority of voters on the register or two-thirds of the voters who actually voted.[14] However, as just mentioned, a last-minute alteration to the text of Article 50 allowed for amendments by ordinary legislation during an initial eight-year period from the date the Constitution came into force, i.e., until 6 December 1930. As Chief Justice Kennedy (himself a member of that Constitution's drafting committee) was later to explain:

> It was originally intended, as appears by the draft, that amendment of the Constitution should not be possible without the consideration due to so important a matter affecting the fundamental law and framework of the State, and the draft provided that the process of amendment should be such as to require full and general consideration [sc. by means of referendum]. At the last moment, however, it was agreed that a provision be added to Article 50, allowing amendment by way of ordinary legislation during a limited period so that drafting or verbal amendments, not altogether unlikely to appear necessary in a much debated text, might be made without the more elaborate process proper for the purpose of more important amendments. This clause was, however, afterwards used for effecting alterations of a radical and far-reaching character, some of them far

[14] It will be noted that this was a far more restrictive requirement than that required of amendments to the present Constitution, as Article 47.1 merely requires a majority of the votes actually cast at that referendum. Indeed, the 1937 Constitution would not have been passed had it been required to satisfy the conditions stipulated by Article 50 of the 1922 Constitution. As O'Sullivan observed:

> Under Article 62 of the [1937 Constitution] only a bare majority of those actually voting was required, and so the new Constitution had been enacted by the people. But if the conditions laid down in Article 50 had been incorporated in Article 62 it would have been decisively rejected (*I.F.S. and its Senate*, 502).

But it might be said that the original version of Article 50 was unrealistic in its rigidity and set an unfairly high (and, indeed, arbitrary) threshold requirement in respect of the majority required in respect of a referendum, especially when that Constitution had itself never been adopted by referendum.

> removed in principle from the ideas and ideals before the minds of the first authors of the instrument.[15]

As we shall presently see, the eight-year clause—originally intended simply to cover minor and technical amendments—ultimately proved to be the means whereby the entire 1922 Constitution was undone.[16]

The last minute amendment to which Kennedy referred took place during what amounted to a Committee Stage debate on the draft Constitution by the Third Dáil, sitting as a Constituent Assembly. During the debate on Article 50,[17] Kevin O'Higgins (Minister for Home Affairs) moved an amendment, which would have allowed amendments by means of ordinary legislation for a five-year period:

> It is realised that in all the circumstances of the time, this Constitution is going through with what would, if the circumstances were otherwise, be considered undue haste. It is realised that only when the Constitution is actually at work will the latent defects that may be contained in it show themselves, and it would be awkward to have to effect changes in the Constitution—changes about which there might be unanimity in the Dáil and in the Senate—if it were necessary to go to a referendum and get the majority of the voters on the register to record their votes in favour of such amendment. That would be a cumbrous process, and very often it might be out of all proportion to the importance of the amendment we might wish to make. If the Article were to stand as it is in the text of this Draft Constitution we would have, for the slightest amendment, to go to the country and go through all the elaborate machinery of a

[15] Foreword to Kohn, *Constitution of the I.F.S.*, xiii. Cf. his comments in dissent on this point in *The State (Ryan) v. Lennon*, [1935] IR 170, and the observations of Justice Murnaghan (who was also a member of the 1922 drafting committee) by way of rejoinder:

> I am ready to conjecture that when Article 50 was framed it was not considered probable that any such use of the power would be made as has been made, but the terms in which Article 50 is framed does authorise the amendment made and there is not in the Article any express limitation which excludes Article 50 itself from the power of amendment (244).

[16] As Justice Fitzgibbon later remarked in *The State (Ryan) v. Lennon*:

> The framers of our Constitution may have intended 'to bind man down from mischief by the chains of the Constitution' but if they did, they defeated their object by handing him the key of the padlock in Article 50 (see document no. 33).

In more recent times, a former Chief Justice, writing extra-judicially, has expressed the same view regarding the effect of Article 50:

> The repressive measures which became necessary [during and immediately after the Civil War] against those whose actions threatened the State and the maintenance of law and order, required a duration or continuance which was, at first, not apparent. This in turn exposed an internal weakness in the [1922] Constitution – a weakness which subsequently, and perhaps inevitably, led to its collapse (Thomas O'Higgins, 'The Constitution and the Courts' in Patrick Lynch and James Meenan (eds), *Essays in memory of Alexis FitzGerald* (Dublin, 1987), 125–6).

[17] Originally Article 49.

> referendum. Now we are providing, by this Government amendment, that for five years there can be changes by ordinary legislation in the Constitution, and after that time the Referendum will be necessary to secure a change. The only provision is that while we are stating that amendments may be made by ordinary legislation, the provisions of Article 46 will apply, which provisions enable a certain proportion of the Senate to call for a Referendum and in that case a Referendum would have to be held.[18]

This amendment was warmly welcomed by prominent opposition deputies, including Thomas Johnson[19] and George Gavan Duffy.[20] Johnson, however, pressed for a longer period because he thought it obvious 'that constitutional matters will not be in the minds of the people if [pressing] legislative demands are being attended to in the Parliament'.[21] The Minister agreed to this suggestion and, accordingly, the five-year period was subsequently extended at Report Stage to eight years.[22] The suggestion that the Constitution might be amended by ordinary legislation for a short transitional period probably made a good deal of sense at the time. After all, a written Constitution with judicial review was a complete novelty and given the inauspicious circumstances in which it had come to be drafted and debated, it was reasonable that the Oireachtas should retain the power to make amendments without the necessity for a referendum. Moreover, it was clear from the tenor of the Minister's speech ('latent defects', 'slightest amendment') that it was intended that this transitional power would be used to remedy what amounted to drafting errors or to make a number of technical changes.

No one foresaw at the time the amendment was accepted by the Dáil that this power could be used to undermine the Constitution in three significant ways. First, there was the possibility (which was ultimately accepted by the courts) that during this transitional period the Constitution could be implicitly amended by ordinary legislation which

[18] 1 *Dáil Debates*, Col. 1237 (5 October 1922).

[19] Thomas Johnson (1872–1963) was a TD from 1922–7 and leader of the Labour Party. During this period—prior to the entry of Fianna Fáil to the Dáil in August 1927—Johnson was leader of the opposition. See J.A. Gaughan, *Thomas Johnson, 1872–1963: First Leader of the Labour Party in Dáil Éireann* (Dublin, 1980); Arthur Mitchell, 'Thomas Johnson, 1872–1963, a Pioneer Labour Leader' in *Studies*, 58 (1969), 396–404.

[20] Gavan Duffy said:

> I wish to congratulate the Minister very heartily on the amendment which he has proposed which, I think, is an excellent one, and goes a long way to meet certain objections (1 *Dáil Debates*, Col. 1238 (5 October 1922)).

But he was subsequently quickly alive to the implications of the defective drafting of Article 50: see 4 *Dáil Debates*, Cols 418–9 (10 July 1923).

[21] 1 *Dáil Debates*, Col. 1238 (5 October 1922).

[22] 1 *Dáil Debates*, Cols 1748–9 (19 October 1922).

was in conflict with it. Secondly, there was nothing to prevent conditional or even temporary amendments of the Constitution which were made contingent on other events (such as a Government order bringing an amendment into force for a temporary period), so that, especially in the latter years of its life, it was not always easy to determine what the current text of the Constitution actually was. Finally, there was the prospect that the eight-year period might itself be extended by the Oireachtas, so that the Constitution would be rendered entirely vulnerable to legislative abrogation. This is what ultimately happened and it led to the complete undermining of the Constitution.

Article 2A

Faced with the growing threat of political conflict from both the IRA and other groups,[23] by early autumn of 1931 the then Cumann na nGaedheal Government decided that stern new legislative measures were necessary in advance of the general election which was but a few months away. Despite the grand promise of Article 73 that no extraordinary courts would be created, the unfortunate reality of political life almost a decade later was that the jury system had more or less broken down.[24] Accordingly, on 14 October 1931, the President of the Executive

[23] For the nature of these threats, see Eunan O'Halpin, *Defending Ireland: The Irish State and its Enemies* (Oxford, 1999), 77–80; O'Sullivan, *I.F.S. and its Senate*, 256–65. The threats were certainly perceived as very real ones by the Government and so, for example, the then Minister for Justice (James Fitzgerald-Kenney) wrote in September 1931 to Chief Justice Kennedy directing him not to arrange for a formal opening of the re-constructed Four Courts lest an attempt be made to blow up the building. The Minister explained that:

> The political situation in the country is far worse than the public knows. The forces making for anarchy are stronger than men dream of. I have endeavoured to wake the country up; but I have been very careful to understate rather than overstate my case. We are taking all possible precautions to see that the Four Courts are not blown up or otherwise destroyed some night. I believe that they will prove adequate. But I would prefer that such an attempt would not be made entailing as it would a potentiality of a huge destruction of public property. A formal opening would be a direct incentive to the making of an attempt to wreck the building and if there be a formal opening an attempt of this nature will inevitably be made.
>
> We are confident that we are strong enough to defeat lawlessness in this State. But we are going to have a terrible winter. No advantage can be derived from shaking a red rag in the face of a raging bull. These are considerations that I dare say are quite new to you but I am sure that you will appreciate them. (UCDA, P4/1058)

See Hogan, 'Hugh Kennedy, the Childers Habeas Corpus Application and the Return to the Four Courts' in Costello (ed.), *The Four Courts*, 177, 214.

[24] O'Halpin observed that one effect of Article 2A was that the 'virtual immunity conferred on those engaged in acts of defiance against the State by the failure of the jury system was now gone' (*Defending Ireland*, 79). O'Sullivan catalogued a long list of outrages associated with jury intimidation by the IRA and its associates and then concluded that by 1931 'trial by jury had broken down' (*I.F.S. and its Senate*, 255–61). On the other hand, J.M. Regan concludes that the outrages in question 'were not exceptional in the broader context of the post-civil war Free State' and that the:

> hysteria and speed with which the [Article 2A] Bill was introduced and processed through the Dáil protected it from protracted criticism from the opposition benches, which would have exposed further the exaggerated picture of a disturbed country Cosgrave and his Government painted: *The Irish Counter-Revolution 1921–1936* (Dublin, 1999), 289–90.

Council introduced the Constitution (Amendment No. 17) Bill 1931 into the Dáil. This Bill was subsequently signed into law 'in the teeth of bitter and indignant criticism from Mr de Valera and his supporters'.[25] This Amendment effected the most radical amendments of the Constitution to date, since it introduced a new Article 2A. This, in reality, was little more than a variation of a radical Public Safety Act which was incorporated into the Constitution. Section 2 of the new Article 2A provided that:

> Article 3 and every subsequent Article of this Constitution shall be read and construed subject to the provisions of this Article and, in the case of inconsistency between this Article and the said Article 3 or any subsequent Article, this Article shall prevail.

This device was open to the objection that the provisions of the Constitution were effectively contingent on the making of executive orders bringing these amendments or quasi-amendments into force. This was illustrated in the case of Article 2A, since, as we shall see, it was brought into force, later suspended and subsequently brought into force once again. At all events, there was no doubt as to the radical and draconian character of Article 2A: it provided for a standing military court[26] (from which there was to be no appeal) which was empowered to impose any penalty (including the death penalty) in respect of any offence, even if such a penalty was greater than that provided by the ordinary law. In *The State* (*O'Duffy*) *v. Bennett*[27] (an application brought by General Eoin O'Duffy[28] to restrain his trial before the Special Powers Tribunal, decided a few months before *Ryan's* case), Justice Hanna did not mince his words about the nature of Article 2A:

> In considering the creation of this new Tribunal under Article 2A, this Court must recognise that there are times when the Legislature may legitimately clip the wings of the individual freedom and liberty of thought and action and when the civil population must, for the general good, submit to strict discipline by having their national charter set aside even though no one can see the ultimate benefits or

[25] Kelly, *Fundamental Rights*, 272.

[26] W.T. Cosgrave informed the Dáil in the course of the debate on Article 2A that the two judges of the Supreme Court had intimated to him that they would resign if they were required to preside over a non-jury court: 40 *Dáil Debates*, Col. 45 (14 October 1931).

[27] [1935] IR 70.

[28] Eoin O'Duffy (1892–1944) TD: revolutionary leader, General and former Garda Commissioner; leader of the quasi-fascist Blueshirt movement. See Fearghal McGarry, *Eoin O'Duffy: A Self Made Hero* (Oxford University Press, 2005).

> evil to which it may ultimately lead. The Constitution contemplated martial law (Article 6) as known to the common law as exercised in most countries, but martial law depends on a state of war or armed rebellion as a matter of fact so as to be capable of being tested by the Courts of the land. But this Act goes beyond the original Constitution inasmuch as no Court can question whether as a matter of fact it is necessary or expedient that this power should be put into force. That decision lies in the hands of the Executive Council of any Government that may be in power, and if improperly used it might possibly become, as was said of the Star Chamber, a potent and odious auxiliary of a tyrannous administration.[29]

Having then described the amendment as creating 'a kind of intermittent martial law under the harmless name of a constitutional amendment', Hanna continued:

> As to trials by the Tribunal of offences which are within their jurisdiction, there is no provision that they are to be conducted according to law. This would be impossible with a lay tribunal. There is no legal member provided for the Court nor have they any legal advice or Judge Advocate allocated to them by the Article. Their decision, involving as it may, life, liberty or property, is that of three (possibly two) laymen without any knowledge of criminal or other law, and no knowledge or experience of the laws of evidence according to the common law. Are they any more than three jurymen, doing their best to decide fairly between the prosecution, which is always in the hands of able and educated counsel, and on the other hand, the accused, who are frequently uneducated and undefended peasants? There is no provision for giving the accused legal assistance. Now, any Judge of experience and knowledge recognises the difficulty of holding the balance in such cases. These provisions blot out of the Constitution, with reference to the offences in the Article, the rights as to legal trial preserved by Article 70 of the Constitution, which enacts that no one shall be tried save in due course of law and that extraordinary courts shall not be established and the jurisdiction of the military Tribunals shall not be extended or exercised over the civil population save in time of war, and also the provisions of Article 72 that no person shall be tried on any criminal charge without a jury. Those who have no legal experience, or little

[29] [1935] IR 70 86.

> experience, think that criminal law, and the law of evidence as to criminal offences, is simple and clear, whereas, in fact it is most technical and difficult. The decisions of the Court of Criminal Appeal on such subjects as accomplices, corroboration, evidence of previous statements or character; the admissibility of statements made to the police; the doctrine of reasonable doubt; *mens rea* and other technical matters, shows how easily this small and inexperienced lay Tribunal could go astray and pass a conviction and sentence that would not stand the slightest legal consideration...Undoubtedly, this Tribunal has great powers, especially in respect to sentence within its jurisdiction – powers beyond those of any constitutional Court in this State. For example, there is no limit upon its sentence, either as to length of imprisonment, or as to any of the cases in which it could give sentence of death, and it could, in any case, if it thought it expedient or necessary, deport or flog convicted persons or order the forfeiture or destruction of their property.[30]

The incoming Fianna Fáil Government had suspended the operation of Article 2A on accession to power in March 1932. The political mood of the country was, however, increasingly bitter and, in some respects, unstable. The Army Comrades Association had been formed in the wake of the 1932 General Election. It was originally an unobtrusive organisation designed to promote the welfare of ex-Army officers, but, under new leadership and re-organisation in late 1932 and 1933, its objectives changed. During the snap 1933 General Election it sought to protect the pro-Treaty supporters from attack by IRA supporters[31] and to organise by wearing the distinctive blueshirt. It underwent another re-organisation in June 1933, when the mercurial General O'Duffy, the former Garda Commissioner, took over the organisation and re-named it the National Guard.[32] When O'Duffy planned a major march towards the gardens of Leinster House in August 1933, the Government decided to re-activate Article 2A and promptly banned the march.[33] While the Blueshirt threat finally fizzled out in the subsequent two to three years, the Fianna Fáil Government was also finally forced to take action against the IRA. By late 1933, members of the IRA were appearing before the

[30] [1935] IR 97–8.
[31] Maurice Manning, *The Blueshirts* (Dublin, 1970), 48–53.
[32] Maurice Manning, *The Blueshirts*, 73–6. Following the amalgamation of Cumann na nGaedheal and the Centre Party in September 1933, it was announced that the National Guard was to be re-formed as an organisation within the Fine Gael Party and that its name would be changed to the Young Ireland Association: Maurice Manning, *The Blueshirts*, 94.
[33] Maurice Manning, *The Blueshirts*, 85–8; O'Halpin, *Defending Ireland*, 117.

Military Tribunal[34] and it suffered the ultimate indignity of being suppressed under Article 2A in June 1936.[35] The fact that Article 2A had been opposed by Fianna Fáil in opposition but (following a period of suspension) employed by them on their return to power gave rise to the following bitterly sarcastic comments of Justice Fitzgibbon in *The State* (*Ryan*) *v. Lennon* when he described Article 2A as:

> an enactment which appears to have received the almost unanimous support of the Oireachtas for we have been told that those of our legislators by whom it was opposed most vehemently as unconstitutional and oppressive, when it was first introduced, have since completely changed their opinions, and now accord it their unqualified approval. It is true that even a unanimous vote of the Legislature does not decide the validity of a law, but it is some evidence that none of those whose duty it is to make the laws see anything in it which they regard as exceptionally iniquitous, or as derogating from the standard of civilisation which they deem adequate for Saorstát Éireann.[36]

The validity of Constitution (Amendment No. 16) Act, 1929 (extending the time for amendment to sixteen years) and Constitution (Amendment No. 17) Act, 1931 (introducing Article 2A and the military tribunals) were ultimately challenged in the great case of *The State* (*Ryan*) *v. Lennon.*[37] Far reaching though these challenges were, it is important to stress that this case did *not* raise the question as to whether the Oireachtas had the power to amend *the Treaty.*

In *Ryan* four prisoners challenged the legality of their detention and sought orders of prohibition restraining the Constitution (Special Powers) Tribunal from proceeding to try them in respect of a variety of offences, including attempting to shoot with intent to murder and unlawful possession of firearms, which applications were first dismissed by a unanimous Divisional High Court[38] and, subsequently, by a majority of the Supreme Court.[39]

In the Supreme Court, Justice Gerald Fitzgibbon first rejected the argument that the power to amend the Constitution should be confined

[34] According to statistics supplied by de Valera in the Dáil, 513 persons were convicted by the Military Tribunal during the period from 1 September 1933 to 5 February 1935, of which 357 were Blueshirts and 138 were members of the IRA: 54 *Dáil Debates*, Col. 1759 (13 February 1935).

[35] O'Halpin, *Defending Ireland*, 124–6.

[36] [1935] IR 170, 235.

[37] See Chapter III of this volume.

[38] Timothy Sullivan, President of the Court, Justices James Creed Meredith and John O'Byrne.

[39] Justices Gerald Fitzgibbon and James Augustine Murnaghan, with Chief Justice Hugh Kennedy dissenting.

to circumstances where the amendment effected an 'improvement' of the Constitution. If this construction were correct, then the validity of an amendment would depend upon the decision of the High Court that it effected such an improvement, so that:

> the Judges and not the Oireachtas would be made the authority to decide upon the advisability of any particular amendment of the Constitution, and this would involve a direct contravention of the principles [of the separation of powers].[40]

The judge then turned to consider the wider question of whether the power to amend the Constitution included the power to amend Article 50 itself. While he observed that 'however undesirable it may appear to some' that the Oireachtas should have the power to extend the period during which the Constitution might be amended by ordinary legislation, nevertheless 'if this be the true construction of Article 50, the Court is bound to give effect to that construction'.[41]

The judge continued by noting that whereas both the Constituent Act and Article 50 contained restrictions on the power of amendment—they both precluded amendments which were in conflict with the terms of the Treaty—the *expressio unius*[42] principle came into play, suggesting that no further restrictions on the power to amend were thereby intended:

> It is conceded that there is no express prohibition against amendment of Article 50 to be found in the Constitution. It is not unusual to find that Constitutions or Constituent Acts impose such restrictions upon the legislative bodies set up by them, and the omission of any such restriction in regard to amendments of Article 50 is at least a negative argument that Dáil Éireann as a Constituent Assembly did not intend to impose any such restriction upon the Oireachtas. This negative argument is supported by the fact that both the Constituent Act and Article 50 itself do contain an express restriction upon the powers of the Oireachtas to amend the Constitution, and it is a legitimate inference that, when certain restrictions were expressly imposed, it was not intended that other undefined restrictions should be imposed by implication.

[40] See document no. 33.
[41] See document no. 33.
[42] The mention of one thing is to the (implied) exclusion of the other. This is a standard principle of statutory and constitutional interpretation.

Fitzgibbon then emphasised the fact that it was Dáil Éireann sitting as a Constituent Assembly which had created the Oireachtas and had limited its powers in particular ways:

> Therefore the supreme legislative authority, speaking as the mouthpiece of the people, expressly denied to the Oireachtas the power of enacting *any* legislation, by way of amendment of the Constitution or otherwise, which might be 'in any respect repugnant to any of the provisions of the Scheduled Treaty', and it reiterated this prohibition in Article 50, which empowered the Oireachtas to make '*amendments of this Constitution within the terms of the Scheduled Treaty*'.
>
> It is further observed that this power to make amendments is limited to '*amendments of this Constitution*', and that the Constituent Assembly did not confer upon the Oireachtas any power to amend the Constituent Act itself.
>
> These express limitations, imposed by the mouthpiece of the people upon the legislative powers of the Oireachtas which it set up, support the view that the Oireachtas was intended to have full power of legislation and amendment outside the prohibited area, and, as there was no prohibition against amendment of Article 50, I am of opinion that Amendment No. 10 in 1928, and Amendment No. 16 in 1929, were within the powers conferred upon the Oireachtas by the Constituent Act.

Fitzgibbon concluded by noting that the Constitutions of other jurisdictions often contained express restrictions upon the power of the Legislature to amend the amendment power itself[43] so that it followed that:

> Our Constituent Assembly could in like manner have excepted Article 50 from the amending powers conferred upon the Oireachtas, but it did not do so, and in my opinion the Court has no jurisdiction to read either into the Constituent Act or into Article 50 a proviso excepting it, and it alone, from those powers.

Justice James Augustine Murnaghan spoke in similar terms and concluded that:

[43] He instanced section 152 of the South Africa Act, 1909 which provided that 'no repeal or alteration of the provisions contained in this section…shall, be valid' unless the Bill embodying such an amendment to the amending power itself shall have been passed in a particular way or by a specified majority. Article V of the US Constitution also contained certain restrictions on the power of amendment of certain clauses of Article I prior to 1808.

> the terms in which Article 50 is framed does authorise the amendment made and there is not in the Article any express limitation which excludes Article 50 itself from the power of amendment. I cannot, therefore, find any ground upon which the suggested limitation can be properly based. It must also be remembered that in this country the Referendum was an untried political experiment and it cannot be assumed that the Referendum should be incapable of alteration or removal. I feel bound by the words of Article 50, which allows amendment of the Constitution as a whole, of which Article 50 is declared to be a part.[44]

While this line of argument was 'simple in its logic and devastating in its implications'[45] and while the sympathy of most modern commentators is with the dissenting judgment of Chief Justice Kennedy, it is nonetheless difficult dogmatically to assert that the majority were wrong on this point.

The dismantling of the 1922 Constitution

Ryan's case gave the imprimatur to a development which was already gathering speed, namely, the wholescale dismantling of the 1922 Constitution by ordinary legislation. After that decision, the only remaining check on the amendment power was that the Oireachtas could not legislate in contravention of the Treaty, but even this restriction had been purportedly removed by the Constitution (Removal of Oath) Act, 1933.[46]

Had the decision in *Ryan* been otherwise, every amendment after December 1930 would have had to be by way of referendum. One can only conjecture how the electorate would have responded to referenda on such topics as Article 2A and the abolition of the oath,[47] the appeal to the Privy Council,[48] the Senate,[49] the Governor General and all references to the Crown in the Constitution.[50] In this respect, it must be recalled that

[44] See document no. 34.
[45] Rory O'Connell, 'Guardians of the Constitution: Unconstitutional Constitutional Norms' in *Journal of Civil Liberties*, vol. 4, no. 48 (1999), 58.
[46] Section 2 of the 1933 Act had repealed section 2 of the Constitution of the Irish Free State Act, 1922 (which precluded the Oireachtas from legislating in a manner inconsistent with the Treaty) and section 3 had deleted the words 'within the terms of the Scheduled Treaty' from Article 50 of the Constitution.
[47] Constitution (Removal of Oath) Act,1933.
[48] Constitution (Amendment No. 22) Act, 1933.
[49] Constitution (Amendment No. 24) Act, 1936. For the background to the abolition of the Seanad, see O'Sullivan, *I.F.S. and its Senate*, 464–9. O'Sullivan argued (468) that the real reason for the abolition of the Senate was that 'Mr de Valera knew it would reject his quasi-republican Constitution for which he had no mandate from the people'.
[50] Constitution (Amendment) (No. 27) Act, 1936. For the background to this legislation, see Brendan Sexton, *Ireland and the Crown 1922–1936: The Governor-Generalship of the Irish Free State* (Dublin, 1992), 163–70.

Article 50 of the 1922 Constitution required for a valid amendment of the Constitution either *a majority of the voters on the register or two-thirds of the votes recorded.*[51] These conditions were far more stringent than currently apply in the case of referenda on constitutional amendments under the Constitution, where Article 47.1 simply requires a majority of the voters who actually voted.

At all events, the drafters of the 1937 Constitution clearly learnt from this experience. While the 1937 Constitution allowed for amendments by way of ordinary legislation during a transitional period, the drafters were careful to include safeguards not found in the 1922 Constitution. First, the transitional period was much shorter—three years from the date the first President entered office[52]—and even then the President was entitled to require, following consultation with the Council of State, that the amendment be submitted to referendum if he were of the opinion that the proposal was 'of such a character and importance that the will of the people thereon ought to be ascertained by Referendum before its enactment into law'.

Secondly, the combined effect of Articles 46.3 and Article 46.4 was to rule out all forms of implicit amendments and to prevent a repetition of cases such as *Cooney* and *McBride:*

> 46.3. Every such Bill shall be expressed to be 'An Act to amend the Constitution'.
> 46.4 A Bill containing a proposal or proposals for the amendment of the Constitution shall not contain any other proposal.

Had Article 50 of the 1922 Constitution contained a provision similar to that contained in Article 46.3, the Court of Appeal could not have reasoned as it did in *Cooney*. Likewise, had Article 50 contained the safeguard found in Article 46.4, the Public Safety Act, 1927 could not have purported to amend the Constitution indirectly by means of legislation containing other substantive proposals which were not in themselves directly intended to effect amendments to the Constitution. In short, Article 46.3 precludes the enactment of the type of drag-net amendment clause contained in s.3 of the 1927 Act.

Thirdly, the entire tenor of the Constitution is to exclude contingent or temporary amendments. If the Constitution is amended, that

[51] In the case of a majority of the voters on the register, this makes the percentage required to carry the Bill contingent on the actual turn-out. Thus, for example, in a 70 per cent turnout, the majority for the Bill would need to approach 72 per cent in order to constitute a majority of the voters on the register.
[52] Article 51.1. The first President (Dr Douglas Hyde) entered office on 25 June 1938 and so the transitory period expired on 25 June 1941.

amendment is permanent unless and until it is subsequently repealed or varied in another referendum.

Finally, Article 51.1 contained the crucial type of safeguard which Article 50 lacked and which, as we have seen, ultimately led to the demise of the 1922 Constitution. It provided that:

> Notwithstanding anything contained in Article 46 hereof, any of the provisions of this Constitution, except the provisions of the said Article 46 and this Article may, subject as hereafter provided, be amended by the Constitution, whether by way of variation, addition or repeal, within a period of three years after the date on which the first President shall have entered upon his office.[53]

Thus, Article 51.1 prevented any further extensions of time beyond the original three-year period since, unlike Article 50 of the 1922 Constitution, it precluded the amendment of the amendment provisions themselves by means of ordinary legislation. After 25 June 1941, the Constitution became a rigid one and could only be amended by means of a referendum. If there was any single provision which contributed to the success of the present Constitution, it was this. The relative rigidity of the Constitution thus gave it stability and permanence, enabling it to take root within the political and legal system – an opportunity which was denied to the Constitution of the Irish Free State. Although there were two relatively minor amendments enacted during the transitional period,[54] some thirty-five years would elapse before the next amendment—(and the first to be enacted by means of a referendum) Third Amendment of the Constitution Act, 1972 (permitting membership of the European Economic Community)—was enacted.

[53] The drafters had at all stages been conscious of this point. In the very first complete draft of the new Constitution (submitted by John Hearne on 22 October 1935), the (draft) Article 50 had provided:

> The Oireachtas may amend any Articles of this Constitution with the exception of the Articles relating to fundamental rights...and this Article by way of ordinary legislation expressed to be an amendment of the Constitution.
>
> The Articles relating to fundamental rights...and this Article shall not be amended by the Oireachtas unless and until the Bill containing the proposed amendment or amendments of any such Article, after it has been passed by Dáil Éireann and before being presented to the President for his assent, shall have been submitted to a Referendum and either the votes of a majority of the voters on the register or two thirds of the votes recorded shall have been cast in favour of such amendment or amendments.

[54] The First Amendment of the Constitution Act, 1939 (enacted in September 1939) extended the meaning of 'time of war' for the purposes of the emergency provisions of Article 28.3.3; the Second Amendment of the Constitution Act, 1941 effected a series of miscellaneous amendments, including the provision for the 'one judgment rule', the immutability of decisions given pursuant to the Article 26 reference procedure and a series of changes to *habeas corpus* procedure. See Chapters XIII and XIV of this volume respectively.

The Statute of Westminster

Externally, the single most important change during this period was the enactment by the British Parliament of the Statute of Westminster, 1931. This legislation gave effect to the recommendations of the Imperial Conferences of 1926 and 1930 and paved the way for the individual Dominions to achieve full external sovereignty.[55] Section 2 (2) provided that:

> No law and no provision of any law made after the commencement of this Act by the Parliament of a Dominion shall be void or inoperative on the ground that it is repugnant to the law of England, or to the provisions of any existing or future Act of the Parliament of the United Kingdom, or to any order, rule or regulation made under any such Act, and the powers of the Parliament of a Dominion shall include the power to repeal or amend any such Act, order, rule or regulation in so far as the same is part of the law of the Dominion.

Section 3 declared that each Dominion had the full power to legislate with extra-territorial effect and section 4 provided that, henceforth, no Act of the Parliament of the United Kingdom should extend to a Dominion, unless it was expressly declared in that Act that the Dominion had 'requested, and consented to, the enactment thereof'.

So far as the Irish Free State was concerned, the significance here was that the Statute of Westminster now permitted the Oireachtas to dismantle entirely the 1921 Treaty. So far as the British were concerned, the Irish Free State had been the creation of the Westminster Parliament. As the Judicial Committee of the Privy Council was later to hold in *Moore v. Attorney General of the Irish Free State*,[56] both the Treaty and the Constitution derived their validity from the statute law of the United Kingdom, the former from the Irish Free State (Agreement) Act, 1922 and the latter from the Constitution of Irish Free State (Saorstát Éireann) Act, 1922.[57] This legislation had given effect to the Treaty and had debarred the Oireachtas from amending the Treaty. It followed from this line of reasoning that the restrictions which had been imposed on the Oireachtas by the Treaty had been the creation of an Act of Westminster. If that were so, then in the wake of the passage of the Statute of

[55] Dominions were defined by section 1 of the statute as meaning Canada, Australia, New Zealand, South Africa, the Irish Free State and Newfoundland.

[56] See Chapter III. For a full account of this remarkable litigation, see Mohr, 'Law without Loyalty' 37 *Irish Jurist* (2005), 187. It is interesting to note the memoranda from Conor Maguire and John Hearne, who both anticipated this very result and line of reasoning: see document nos 30, 31.

[57] 12 and 13 Geo. 5, c.4 and 13 Geo. 5., c.1, respectively.

Westminster, the Oireachtas was thus free to amend the Treaty, since it had been a statute of the Westminster parliament which had imposed the restrictions in the first place.

This was the very point which the Privy Council had made in *Moore* in June 1935 in upholding the validity of the Constitution (Amendment No. 22) Act, 1933. This Act had not only removed the right of appeal from the Supreme Court to the Privy Council, but it also amounted to a breach of the Treaty. In *Ryan* the Supreme Court had clearly implied that amendments to the Treaty would be void, since it had been Dáil Éireann sitting as a *constituent assembly* which, in enacting the Constitution of 1922, had entrenched the Treaty and put it beyond the reach of the amending power of the Oireachtas. On this basis, therefore, many of the fundamental changes effected by de Valera following his entry into Government in March 1932—such as the removal of the oath, the appeal to the Privy Council and the ultimate abolition of the office of Governor General—would have been unlawful.[58] The Privy Council had, of course, disagreed with this conclusion, since they proceeded from the different premise, namely, that these legislative restrictions derived from United Kingdom statutes, which, courtesy of the Statute of Westminster, the Oireachtas was now free to amend.

This divergence of judicial views certainly placed de Valera in an unpalatable predicament:

> Mr de Valera was thus in a kind of legal limbo. He must of necessity have accepted the Supreme Court's view [in *Ryan*] on the Constitution's root of title; anything else would have been a denial of his previous career. On the other hand, the Judicial Committee [of the Privy Council's] conclusion [in *Moore*] was eminently acceptable – but unfortunately it was based on an inadmissible premise.[59]

These uncertainties must have provided a further impetus for the drafting of an entirely new Constitution. Indeed, Article 34.5 of the Constitution now requires every judge to make a declaration to 'uphold the Constitution and the laws', so that any judge who declined or neglected to swear this would be 'deemed to have vacated his office' and Article 58 (a transitory provision) applied this requirement to all the judges who were then in office on the date the new Constitution came into force. This requirement effectively precluded the judiciary from

[58] It seems curious that no litigant came forward to challenge these changes at that time and had the courts then been confronted with this issue they would undoubtedly have been placed in a difficult situation.
[59] J.P. Casey, *Constitutional Law in Ireland* (3rd edn, Dublin, 2000), 20–1.

questioning the manner in which the Constitution came into being and de Valera 'thus astutely disarmed in advance anyone who was prepared to argue before an Irish court that the new Constitution was invalid'.[60]

It is against this general background that the documentary material commences in 1928. A word of explanation regarding the nature of the material and its sequencing is now, perhaps, in order. While the material broadly speaks for itself, a commentary has been provided at the start of each chapter for the assistance of the reader. The material has been presented for the most part in chronological order, although this has not always proved possible. While the focus is generally on the archival material which has hitherto, to some extent at least, remained hidden from public view, extracts from public sources such as Oireachtas debates, Acts of the Oireachtas, court judgments and contemporary newspaper accounts are also included, since much of this material also makes for essential reading. The volume does not purport to deal with constitutional law doctrine, although some reference is made to subsequent case law.

Some editorial judgment has been necessary. In that regard, while some key drafts of the Constitution have been reproduced, the reader should bear in mind that as the drafting process reached its zenith in the hectic months of April, May and June 1937, the drafting team worked quickly and left an incomplete documentary record. Many changes must have been agreed orally and informally. While the significance of certain changes were obvious and well documented, in other cases the reasons for the change can now only be conjectured. Nevertheless, this volume seeks to assist the reader to understand and appreciate the thought processes and concerns of the drafting team and their political master, de Valera, to the extent to which they can now be reproduced. The volume ends with the enactment of the Second Amendment of the Constitution Act, 1941.

Chapter I thus deals with the undermining of the 1922 Constitution, beginning with the removal of the Initiative and the Referendum in 1928–9. The principal change here was, of course, the Constitution (Amendment No. 16) Act, 1929 which extended the time period during which the 1922 Constitution could be amended from eight years to sixteen years. Major constitutional changes were effected by the

[60] Kelly, *Fundamental Rights*, 7.

new Fianna Fáil Government following their successes in the 1932 and 1933 general elections. The Constitution (Removal of Oath) Act, 1933 not only removed the oath, but also purported to enable the Oireachtas to make constitutional amendments which varied or amended the 1921 Treaty.

Chapter II deals with the role of the Constitution Committee of 1934. This Committee was given the task of reviewing the existing Constitution on an article by article basis. Its report proved to be of considerable importance so far as the drafting of the Constitution is concerned, as three of the four members—Michael McDunphy, Philip O'Donoghue and (especially) John Hearne—were later to play a pivotal role in its drafting.

Chapter III deals with the decisions of the Supreme Court in *Ryan* in December 1934 and that of the Privy Council in *Moore* in June 1935 and other material directly related to these decisions. There is here a slight break in the chronological sequence to ensure that all relevant material is conveniently located in one place.

Chapter IV deals with the early drafts of the new Constitution, starting with the 'squared paper draft' (probably dating from May 1935) which contains de Valera's notes regarding the initial set of instructions to John Hearne for the drafting of the new Constitution. It is clear that Hearne's early drafts and his associated commentary were hugely influential in the subsequent structure and layout of the Constitution. For reasons which are not entirely clear, the drafting process fell into abeyance from the autumn of 1935 for another twelve months.

Chapter V deals with the abolition of the Seanad in 1936 and the subsequent appointment of the Second House of the Oireachtas Commission. The Seanad's opposition to Fianna Fáil's programme of constitutional reform had sealed its fate and it was finally abolished in May 1936. The Second House of the Oireachtas Commission was established in June 1936 with a broad range of membership and with Chief Justice Kennedy (who as Attorney General from 1922 to 1924 had been a noted opponent of de Valera) as Chairman. The Committee reported with impressive speed at the end of September 1936 and its recommendations proved hugely influential.

Chapter VI deals with the role of Father Edward Cahill SJ and the Jesuit Constitution Commission in Autumn 1936. The Jesuit submission was an impressive document, which also drew heavily from the then contemporary constitutions of other European Catholic countries such as Poland, Austria and Portugal, as well as directly from Papal encyclicals.

There are strong echoes of this draft in the Constitution, although by the end of the entire drafting process Father Cahill—whose own views were regarded as somewhat idiosyncratic by other members of his community—seems to have felt somewhat marginalized. The contribution of Fr John Charles McQuaid is dealt with here.

Chapter VII deals with the External Relations Act 1936 and the abolition of the office of Governor General. The abdication of Edward VIII in December 1936 provided de Valera with the opportunity to remove all references to the Crown in the Constitution. John Hearne's draft Foreign Relations Bill of September 1936 also proved to be hugely influential.

Chapter VIII deals with the drafting of the new Constitution in the period from September 1936 until March 1937. The drafting process appears to have begun again in the autumn of 1936 and the first full draft of the Constitution was discussed at a Government meeting which took place over three days in October 1936. Following the abdication crisis, early 1937 saw the preparation of further drafts and other work done, largely it seems by John Hearne, with assistance from the parliamentary draftsman, Arthur Matheson. The first submissions from Fr John Charles McQuaid also seem to date from this period.

Chapter IX deals with invited observations on and criticisms of the Draft Constitution. The material here, along with that contained in chapter X, deals with one of the most crucial phases of the entire drafting process, namely, the period from 16 March 1937 to 2 May 1937. The first published draft (save for the Preamble and the provisions dealing with religion) to be widely circulated was sent to Ministers, Government Departments, the Revenue Commissioners, the Ceann Comhairle and a number of members of the judiciary on 16 March 1937. The Government Departments responded promptly, often with specialist comments particular to their own area of expertise. Some other contributions were especially influential, not least those of Michael McDunphy and Justice George Gavan Duffy. Two contributions, however, stand out, namely those of Stephen Roche, Secretary of the Department of Justice and J.J. McElligott, Secretary of the Department of Finance. Both submitted trenchant critiques of the draft and both expressed considerable hostility to the very idea of judicial review. On this the drafting committee was generally unyielding, save that it was agreed to avoid the potential impact of what are sometimes known as socio-economic rights through the creation of a new Article 45, the provisions of which would not be justiciable (i.e., enforceable) in the courts. The copious nature of the memoranda and the different drafts which were generated during this period bear testimony to the fact that this was one of the most intense phases of the drafting process.

Chapter X outlines the revision of the Constitution in April 1937. Following the initial responses to the 16 March draft, de Valera formally appointed Maurice Moynihan, Michael McDunphy, Philip O'Donoghue and John Hearne as members of the drafting committee. A printed draft of the revised document was available by 1 April. The scene was then set for a busy month in which the drafting committee was occupied with a host of submissions and further drafting points. In addition, the material dating from this period shows de Valera wrestling with the most sensitive issue of religion and the exchanges with the various Churches. In the end, de Valera elected not to yield to clerical demands. Readers should note that commentary on the documentary material in Chapter X is found in the introductory remarks to Chapter IX.

Chapter XI deals with the reaction in the media and the debate in the Dáil following the publication of the Constitution on 1 May 1937. Much of the debate focused on the role of the President and the position of women in the Constitution. There were significant amendments made during the course of the Dáil debates, with de Valera responding on certain aspects of women's rights. Another important change which was made at this juncture was to restore the High Court's power of judicial review, with a right of appeal to the Supreme Court. The original draft had envisaged that the Supreme Court would have a full, original jurisdiction in all constitutional matters.

Chapter XII details the preparations for the coming into force of the Constitution following the plebiscite of 1 July 1937, held in conjunction with the general election. Much of the material here deals with the legislation which was to be enacted as a necessary consequence of the coming into operation of the Constitution. There was also an anxiety that a copy of the Constitution should be quickly enrolled with the Office of the Supreme Court, as it was anticipated that the validity of the new Constitution would soon be challenged in the courts.

Chapter XIII deals with the First Amendment of the Constitution Act, 1939, which was enacted by means of ordinary legislation during the transitional period contemplated by Article 51. The First Amendment (enacted on 2 September 1939) effected an amendment to Article 28.3.3°, extending the definition of 'time of war', so as to cater for the circumstances of a European war in which Ireland was neutral. Preparations for this had been in train since the Munich crisis the previous autumn.

Chapter XIV deals with the Supreme Court and the Constitution and the Second Amendment of the Constitution Act, 1941. The decision of Justice Gavan Duffy in *The State* (*Burke*) *v. Lennon* on 1 December 1939 presented the Government with an early reminder of the potential impact which the Constitution might have. Here the High Court held that the internment provisions of the Offences against the State Act, 1939 were unconstitutional and ordered the release of the detainee who had sought *habeas corpus.* When the Supreme Court held that it had no jurisdiction to hear an appeal in *habeas corpus* matters, the Government felt that it had no alternative but to release the remaining prisoners. A serious crisis then ensued with the recall of the Oireachtas in the opening days of 1940, the first meeting of the Council of State and the reference of a new Offences against the State Bill to the Supreme Court by President Hyde. The Court duly upheld the Bill, albeit apparently by a majority.

As early as December 1938, the Department of Finance had been planning one omnibus amendment Bill which would take effect before the transitional period expired in June 1941, i.e., some three years after the entry into office of the first President. The events surrounding the *Burke* case formed the background to some of the amendments, but most of the changes were largely technical or even purely verbal in nature.

Chapter I

The Irish Free State Constitution Undermined, 1928–34

One of the innovatory features of the 1922 Constitution was that it provided that future amendments to the Constitution would have to be subjected to a referendum. This was no mere technical question, since the mode of constitutional amendment (referendum or ordinary legislation) was (and is) critical to the ease with which significant constitutional change can be brought about.

Article 50 of the 1922 Constitution as enacted provided that:

> Amendments of this Constitution within the terms of the Scheduled Treaty may be made by the Oireachtas, but no such amendment, passed by both Houses of the Oireachtas, [after the expiration of a period of eight years from the date of the coming into operation of this Constitution,] shall become law, unless the same shall, after it has been passed or deemed to have been passed by the said two Houses of the Oireachtas, have been submitted to a Referendum of the people, and unless a majority of voters on the register, or two-thirds of the vote recorded, shall have been cast in favour of such amendment. [Any such amendment may be made within the said period of eight years by way of ordinary legislation and as such shall be subject to the provisions of Article 47 hereof.]

The vital words in brackets were added at the last minute during the course of the Dáil debates. [1]

[1] 1 *Dáil Debates*, Cols 1748–9 (19 October 1922).

The Constitution (Amendment No. 10) Act, 1928

In June 1928 the Oireachtas considered the Constitution (Amendment No. 10) Bill 1928. The object of this Bill was to remove the referendum and initiative provisions of Articles 47 and 48 of the Constitution and also to effect some minor changes in Article 50 itself. But before considering the implications of these changes, it is necessary to say something first about the 'referendum' and the 'initiative' devices. These provisions appear to have been inspired by the post First World War Constitutions in continental Europe and were designed to foster 'an active association of the people with law-making' and to provide a 'valuable safeguard' for minorities.[2]

Prior to the enactment of the Constitution (No. 10) Act, a referendum might be held in any of three possible circumstances. First, Article 47 permitted a referendum to be held in respect of a Bill other than a Money Bill or a Bill declared to be necessary for the immediate preservation of public peace, health or safety if demanded by either three-fifths of Seanad Éireann or by a petition signed by not less than one-twentieth of the voters on the electoral roll. Second, Article 50 required a referendum to be held in respect of a Bill to amend the Constitution once the eight-year period had expired. Finally, Article 50 permitted—but, of course, did not require—a referendum in respect of a Bill to amend the Constitution which took place within the original eight years.

The Initiative was a continental device which the 1922 Constitution Committee had evidently borrowed from the Swiss Constitution[3] as Article 48 provided that in relevant part:

> The Oireachtas may provide for the Initiation by the people of proposals for laws or constitutional amendments. Should the Oireachtas fail to make such provision within two years, it shall on the petition of not less than seventy-five thousand voters on the register, of whom not more than fifteen thousand shall be voters in any one constituency, either make such provisions or submit the question to the people for decision in accordance with the ordinary regulations governing the Referendum.

[2] For first quotation, see Kohn, *Constitution of the I.F.S.*, 238. For second quotation see O'Sullivan, *I.F.S. and its Senate*, 229.

[3] Kohn commented that the Initiative proposals 'went further than those of almost any of its Continental models in enabling an extra-parliamentary system of legislation to be set up', *Constitution of the I.F.S.*, 242. Kohn was also not enamoured of the Initiative, and he considered that it was 'subversive of the authority of Parliament, destroyed the coherence of representative government, and substituted crude voting under the influence of demagogic agitation for the deliberative methods of an elected Assembly', 244. O'Sullivan likewise observed that 'no tears need have been shed over the disappearance of the Initiative', which was a 'constitutional device quite unsuited to Ireland in its present stage of political development', *I.F.S. and its Senate*, 229.

As it happens, the Oireachtas never regulated the procedure governing the presentation of a petition for an initiative. However, on 3 May 1928, the opposition party Fianna Fáil sought leave of the Dáil to present a petition for an Initiative to amend the Constitution in order to abolish the Oath.[4] Following a protracted debate,[5] the Dáil adjourned a consideration of the petition, but further discussion of this was forestalled by the decision of the Oireachtas to enact the Constitution (Amendment No. 10) Act, 1928.[6] The effect of this measure was to delete Articles 47 and 48 and to effect (what seemed) a minor amendment to Article 50. In short, the Initiative was abolished and the referendum was retained only in respect of Bills to amend the Constitution. However, the change made to Article 50 meant that the referendum was no longer optional during the transitional period: henceforth, during the transitional period a Bill to amend the Constitution took effect once it was passed by both Houses and duly signed into law. This latter change seemed a minor one as, at the time of the enactment of the 1928 Act, the eight-year transitional period had only eighteen months to run. Nevertheless, as Donal O'Sullivan observed:

> The whole situation was transformed, however, by the action of the same Government in the following year (1929), when a Bill was passed extending the eight years' period to sixteen years.[7]

In the Dáil Debate on the Constitution (Amendment No. 10) Bill, the Government made it clear that it considered that Article 50 was too restrictive. As President W.T. Cosgrave explained:

> I unquestionably give the guarantee that it is our intention within a two-year period to extend or amend at any rate that Article of the Constitution, which will not make it necessary for a majority Referendum to take place in order to effect an amendment of the Constitution.[8]

[4] 23 *Dáil Debates*, Cols 806–7 (3 May 1928).
[5] 23 *Dáil Debates*, Cols 1498–1531 (16 May 1928); 1898–1926 (23 May 1928); 2519–47 (1 June 1928).
[6] Over the fervent protests of the opposition, the Dáil passed the appropriate resolution under Article 47 that the immediate passage of the Bill was necessary for the 'preservation of the public peace, health or safety': see 24 *Dáil Debates*, Cols 1758–1851 (28 June 1928). The Government thereby avoided the possibility of a referendum being demanded under Article 47 itself by either a resolution of three-fifths of the Senate or by a petition signed by one-twentieth of the voters. The resolution that the immediate passage of the Bill was necessary for public peace and order was simply a colourable device to circumvent the possibility of a referendum under Article 47 and it would have been interesting to see how the courts would have reacted to a challenge to the validity of the Constitution (Amendment No. 10) Act, 1928, had the opposition sought to challenge the measure on this ground.
[7] O'Sullivan, *I.F S. and its Senate*, 230.
[8] 24 Dáil Debates, Col. 896 (20 June 1928).

It seems a fair inference that the very rigidity of Article 50 (with its weighted majority requirements) was the principal reason why both the Government and Opposition were anxious not to allow the original deadline of December 1930 to expire.[9]

Constitution (Amendment No. 16) Act, 1929

The Government duly honoured its commitment and on 13 March 1929 the Dáil debated the second stage of the Constitution (Amendment No. 16) Bill 1928.[10] The object of this Bill was to extend the eight-year transitional period for a further eight years from December 1930 until December 1938. While the debate in the Dáil was perfunctory, the Bill subsequently passed all stages in the Seanad without debate. It seems extraordinary that a Bill with such radical implications should pass through the Oireachtas virtually without any discussion.[11]

Fianna Fáil and the dismantling of the 1921 Treaty

The full import of the Constitution (Amendment No. 16) Act became apparent on the accession to government of Fianna Fáil. The Sixth Dáil was dissolved on 29 January 1932 and the new Dáil assembled on 9 March. The election results enabled Fianna Fáil to govern with the support of the Labour Party.[12] Fianna Fáil's election programme was more or less to effect a gradual dismantling of the 1921 Treaty settlement. The first legislative item introduced in the new Dáil was the Constitution (Removal of Oath) Bill 1932. This Bill purported to delete the requirement of Article 17 of the 1922 Constitution that all members of the Oireachtas swear 'to be faithful to HM King George V, his heirs and successors at law, in virtue of the common citizenship of Ireland with Great Britain and her adherence to and membership of the group of nations forming the British Commonwealth of Nations'.

[9] Cf. the comments of Patrick McGilligan in the Seanad on the Amendment No. 10 Bill: 'People here should not consider that they are in the position of the Americans with regard to their Constitution. We have not a Constitution in its final form, and they should not imagine that the mould of the Constitution is the final shape of the Constitution... We intend to allow a longer period in which amendments to the Constitution can be made by ordinary legislation. People have not had full time to consider the final form of the Constitution, and to experience what are the good points in the Constitution and what are the evil points', 10 *Seanad Debates*, Col. 839 (4 July 1928).

[10] For a guide to relevant Dáil debates, see www.irishconstitution.ie.

[11] For passage through the Seanad, see 12 *Seanad Debates*, Col. 46 (Second Stage, 10 April 1929); Col. 225 (Committee, 24 April 1929); Col. 456 (Report, 2 May 1929) and Col. 531 (Passage, 9 May 1929). Introducing the Bill on 10 April, Cosgrave explained in a single sentence that it was a Bill to extend the eight-year period for a further eight years. Not one word was uttered by a Senator during the entirety of the Bill's passage through the Seanad.

[12] The Seventh Dáil consisted of 153 members, with the following composition: Fianna Fáil 72, Cumann na nGaedheal 57, Independents 11, Labour 7, Farmers 4, Independent Labour 2.

Of course, the Oireachtas was then free to amend the Constitution by ordinary legislation without the need for a referendum.[13] In the case of the oath requirement in Article 17, there was, however, a further complication. Article 4 of the 1921 Treaty had provided for the oath and this requirement had been reflected in Article 17 of the Constitution. It was thus necessary also to amend Section 2 of the Irish Free State Constitution Act, 1922:[14] this section had given the Treaty the force of law and had provided that any amendment of the Constitution which was repugnant to the Treaty would be inoperative. It was also necessary to amend Article 50 (which dealt with the power of amendment) by deleting the words 'within the terms of the Scheduled Treaty'. The deletion of Section 2 of the 1922 Act and the amendment of Article 50 were designed to remove the power of the High Court and the Supreme Court to declare the Bill (when enacted) to be unconstitutional and invalid.

Following protracted debate the Bill passed the Dáil,[15] but while it technically passed the Seanad,[16] it had been made subject to a number of amendments which were unacceptable to the Dáil.[17] The Seanad subsequently insisted upon the amendments and so if the suspensory period were to run its ordinary course, the Bill would have become law (as passed by the Dáil) on 18 November 1933, some 180 days after the Dáil had received the Bill from the Seanad, unless a general election intervened.

The Dáil was, however, dissolved in early 1933, with the general election held on 24 January. Fianna Fáil gained five seats and it now had a Dáil majority. The fact that a general election had taken place also assumed significance so far as the Removal of the Oath Bill was concerned, since the suspensory period during which the Seanad could delay the coming into force of the legislation was reduced from eighteen months to sixty days.[18] The Bill was then sent to the Seanad on 1 March. The Seanad declined to pass the Bill, but the Dáil insisted on its enactment.[19] The Constitution (Removal of Oath) Act, 1933 was then signed on 3 May 1933 and immediately came into law.

[13] See Introduction to this volume.

[14] The Irish Free State Constitution Act, 1922 had been enacted by Dáil Éireann sitting as a constituent assembly, i.e., a body elected for the principal purpose of drafting and enacting a Constitution.

[15] 41 *Dáil Debates*, Cols 171–6 (20 April 1932), Cols 567–668 (27 April 1932), Cols 707–842 (28 April 1932), Cols 921–1116 (29 April 1932), Cols 1127–1207 (3 May 1932), Cols 1384–1408 (4 May 1932) Cols 2012–2142 (19 May 1932).

[16] 15 *Seanad Debates*, Cols 673–756 (25 May 1932), Cols 757–840 (1 June 1932), Cols 841–956 (2 June 1932), Cols 957–1016 (8 June 1932), Cols 1082–4 (15 June 1932), Cols 1090–1101 (28 June 1932).

[17] 43 *Dáil Debates*, Cols 616–717 (12 July 1932). One of these was that the Bill would not come into force until there had been a fresh agreement between the Government and the British Government providing that Article 4 of the 1921 Treaty shall cease to have effect: see O'Sullivan, *I.F.S. and its Senate*, 312.

[18] Under Article 38A of the 1922 Constitution.

[19] 47 *Dáil Debates*, Cols 438–9 (3 May 1933).

To modern eyes, the most remarkable feature of the entire affair was the absence of any challenge to the validity of this constitutional amendment, especially as one year later, in December 1934, the Supreme Court confirmed in its decision in *The State (Ryan) v. Lennon* that there was no power to delete Section 2 of the Constitution Act.[20] This issue, however, is bound up with the impact of the Statute of Westminster 1931, the abolition of the right of appeal to the Privy Council by the Constitution (Amendment No. 22) Act, 1933 and the Privy Council's decision in *Moore v. Attorney General for the Irish Free State*, and is thus best considered in a separate chapter.[21]

The process of constitutional amendment continued throughout this period. Two further (largely formal) powers of the Governor General were removed. The Constitution (Amendment No. 20) Act, 1933 transferred from the Governor General to the Executive Council the power of recommending the appropriation of money. The Constitution (Amendment No. 21) Act, 1933 abolished the Governor General's power to withhold the King's assent to Bills to reserve them for the signification of the King's pleasure. The next step involved an entire reconsideration of the 1922 Constitution itself.[22]

No. 1: NAI, DT S4469/10

Memorandum from Diarmuid O'Hegarty to William T. Cosgrave

Department of the President
17 February 1928

President,
The matter of [Constitution (Amendment No. 6)] Bill was considered by the Cabinet on the 10th instant. No decision was taken. It is entirely a question of policy as to whether the Bill should be allowed to drop.

It would clearly be in the public interest, at any rate in the present circumstances, to have Article 48 deleted from the Constitution. Even in the most ideal conditions, legislation by initiative is hard to foresee.

[20] It is quite remarkable that all three members of the Court regarded Section 2 of Constitution Act, 1922 as still effective and valid, even though the Constitution (Removal of Oath) Act, 1933 had purported to repeal that provision. Thus, Justice Fitzgibbon said of Section 2: 'It is further to be observed that this power to make amendments is limited to '*amendments of this Constitution*' and that the Constituent Assembly did not confer upon the Oireachtas any power to amend the Constituent Act itself'. (see document no. 33).

[21] See Chapter III of this volume.

[22] See Chapter II of this volume.

Its second reading was opposed by the Farmers' Party and by Messrs. Byrne, Coburn and Captain Redmond as well as other independent members who are not now members of the House.[23] The Labour Party, who was also antagonistic, had left the Chamber before the debate and division took place.

It would appear from the Press that Fianna Fáil are collecting signatures to a petition which it is hoped will force the Dáil to make provision for an initiative. I believe the petition is so drawn that it will be imperative. But it is worth considering whether the most suitable time to reintroduce this measure would not be when this petition is handed in and when the financial and administrative difficulties are clearly before Deputies.

If and when the petition is handed in some action will be called for, and it may be that the reintroduction of this measure, which at the moment might be regarded as provocative or inconvenient, might then prove the timely course.[24]

No. 2: NAI, DT S4469/10

Memorandum from Diarmuid O'Hegarty to John A. Costello

Department of the President
1 June 1928

A chara,

I have to inform you that the Executive Council at their meeting on Tuesday the 29th ultimo decided that legislation should be prepared deleting Articles 47 and 48 from the Constitution.

It is intended that the requisite Bills should be introduced early next week and I have to request, therefore, that instructions may be issued to the Parliamentary Draftsman accordingly.

The intended effect of the measure is to secure that the provision for the initiative and all reference thereto should be deleted from the

[23] Alfred Byrne (1882–1956) (Independent); James Coburn (1882–1953) (National League, later joined Fine Gael); Captain William Archer Redmond (1886–1932) (National League, later joined Cumann na nGaedheal).

[24] At a meeting of the Cabinet on 27 March 1928, a subcommittee was established to consider the question of amendments to the Constitution generally, and particularly Amendment No. 6. According to a note by Michael McDunphy, dated 14 June 1928: 'The Committee appointed by the Executive Council on 27 March 1928 never effectively operated and produced no report. The appointment of a Joint Committee of the Dáil and Seanad on 2 March to consider and report on the changes, if any, necessary in the Constitution and powers of, and methods of election to Seanad Éireann, rendered the existence of the Sub-Committee of the Cabinet to a great extent unnecessary, NAI, DT S2483. At the Cabinet meeting of 29 May, it was decided to delete Articles 47 and 48 from the Constitution *in toto* (see document no. 2). This decision was taken in the light of the report of the Joint Committee on the Constitution of Seanad Éireann, delivered on 16 May 1928.

Constitution (*vide* Articles 14 and 48) and that provision for a Referendum save in so far as it relates to Article 50 of the Constitution should also be deleted.

No. 3: NAI, AGO 2002/14/700

Memorandum from Michael McDunphy to John A. Costello

Department of the President
13 November 1928

I have to inform you that the Executive Council decided at their meeting today to introduce a Bill providing for the extension by a further eight years of the period prescribed in Article 50 of the Constitution within which amendments may be made by the Oireachtas by way of legislation.

I have to request that instructions may be given to the Parliamentary Draftsman accordingly. The Bill is to be placed in Priority One.

CHAPTER II

THE CONSTITUTION COMMITTEE, 1934

Much of the groundwork in respect of the new Constitution was done in the first instance by the 1934 Constitution Committee, appointed on 24 May.[1] While it may be surmised that de Valera had toyed for some time with the idea that a new Constitution was necessary to replace the Constitution of the Irish Free State, the initial impetus for the establishment of the Committee resulted from an opposition amendment which had been put down in respect of the Constitution (Amendment No. 24) Bill, 1934. This Bill proposed to abolish the existing Seanad, but the amendment sought to ensure in the wake of such abolition that certain provisions of the Constitution could no longer be amended by ordinary legislation unless a general election had intervened in the meantime.[2]

The Constitution Committee was then established, and its terms of reference were to review the existing 1922 Constitution.[3] The Committee consisted of four senior civil servants, all of whom were legally qualified: Stephen Roche, Secretary, Department of Justice; Michael McDunphy, Assistant Secretary, Department of the President of the Executive

[1] See Gerard Hogan, 'The Constitution Review Committee of 1934', in Fionán Ó Muircheartaigh (ed.), *Ireland in the Coming Times: Essays to Celebrate T.K. Whitaker's 80 Years* (Dublin, 1997), 342–69.

[2] For a guide to relevant Dáil debates, see www.irishconstitution.ie. The amendment, which was in the name of W.T. Cosgrave, J.A. Costello and Patrick McGilligan, sought to amend Article 50 of the 1922 Constitution by providing that no ordinary law amending the Constitution passed by the Oireachtas in respect of: 'Articles 6, 7, 8, 9, 18, 19, 24, 28, 43, 46, 49, 50, 61, 62, 63, 64, 65, 66, 68, 69, 70 shall become law until after a General Election shall have been held and a Resolution approving of such amendment shall have been passed by Dáil Éireann on the recommendation of the Executive Council first elected after such General Election'. For the background to this, see O'Sullivan, *I.F.S. and its Senate*, 363–5. The author comments that the opposition was concerned that de Valera's real object 'was to establish himself as a dictator behind the facade of single-chamber parliamentary government', 364.

[3] See document no. 4.

Council; John Hearne, Legal Adviser, Department of External Affairs and Philip O'Donoghue, Assistant to the Attorney General. The composition of the Committee was in itself significant, as the latter three members were subsequently to play a pivotal role in the drafting of the new Constitution.[4]

The Roche memorandum

By 14 June, Stephen Roche, the Secretary of the Department of Justice, had prepared a memorandum for circulation to the other members of the Committee.[5] While the memorandum chiefly dealt with the topic of Article 2A, Roche first took the opportunity to express his views on the issue of constitutional change:

> I believe that in a unitary State with full adult suffrage the idea of a written Constitution, not capable of alteration by a majority of the elected representatives of the people is unsound in theory and dangerous in practice. It is unsound in theory *because no Parliament (whether it calls itself a Dáil or a Constituent Assembly or any other name) and no generation* has any right to bind future Parliaments or future generations... That is the theoretical side. The practical side is that majorities will have their way, anyhow, and if they can't have it 'constitutionally', or only after great delay, then they will (and quite rightly) have it 'unconstitutionally'.

The italicised words were underlined by McDunphy, who commented in the margins: 'Not rigidly—but a Constituent Assembly should have some authority of an exceptional kind'. While Roche did not expressly address the question of amendment by means of a referendum, it seems a fair inference from the tenor of his remarks that he was generally against it.

Roche then continued in a manner which suggests that he was strongly opposed to the idea of judicial review of legislation:

> I believe that what this country wants at present and probably will continue to want for many years is a strong Executive, not liable, so long as it has the support of the people, to be delayed, hampered and humiliated at every

[4] The drafting committee for the Constitution itself consisted of McDunphy, Hearne and O'Donoghue, together with de Valera's private secretary Maurice Moynihan who took Roche's place on that Committee: see Ronan Fanning, 'Mr de Valera Drafts a Constitution', in Brian Farrell (ed.), *De Valera's Constitution and Ours* (Dublin, 1988), 39.

[5] See document no. 12.

> step by long arguments in the Courts, or by propaganda of a threatening and seditious type. A Government should not allow itself to be insulted.
>
> Further, I believe that the doctrines of 'judicial independence' and 'the separation of the functions' are being overdone and that the Courts have been given or have assumed a position in our civic life to which they are not entitled. There was a time in England when the Judges' job was to save the people from an irresponsible Executive: it may be necessary, in turn, for a responsible Executive to save the people from irresponsible Judges.

McDunphy placed a question mark in the margin beside the reference to 'irresponsible Judges' and then commented 'a "strong" Executive could conceivably be a real danger instead of a blessing. Something more than "strength" is essential.'

Roche continued by making comments on a number of specific Articles of the Constitution. These remarks are of exceptional interest to any constitutional historian, since they contain the genesis of a number of innovatory provisions of the present Constitution:

> With particular reference to Article 2A, I agree that, *in form*, that Article is grotesque as an Article of the Constitution. It must go.[6] On the other hand, so long as we keep to the idea of a 'normal' written Constitution, with all sorts of snags and pit-falls for the Executive, we must have something, somewhere, on the lines of Article 2A. What I have done in my draft is to split the task into two parts, viz.:
>
> (a) The declaration of an 'emergency period' and
> (b) The measures which may be taken by the Executive once an 'emergency period' has been declared.
>
> I have put part (a) in the Constitution and left part (b) to be dealt with by ordinary legislation with the proviso that such legislation shall not be subject to the ordinary constitutional limitations. I see no other way of making adequate provision without overloading the actual Constitution with details.

Roche then went on to sketch out a scheme whereby the bringing into force of such legislation would be contingent on the consent of the judiciary voting in secret ballot. He added that he had taken this

[6] McDunphy noted in the margins of his copy: 'I agree'.

approach mainly because he gathered from de Valera 'that he was anxious, for obvious and weighty reasons, to get some form of judicial, or, at least, non-political sanction for such a declaration'. We see here for the first time the outlines of what subsequently emerged as Article 28.3.3° of the present Constitution, whereby during the occurrence of a State of Emergency, the Oireachtas is freed from the ordinary constitutional constraints. It is significant, however, that Article 28.3.3° follows the main features of Roche's model.[7] As we shall see presently, following further discussion, the Committee ultimately agreed to a further related proposal, namely, that in addition to the emergency powers provisions, provision should be made for the establishment of special courts where the ordinary courts proved to be inadequate for this purpose.[8] On this vital question the first draft of the Committee's report as prepared by McDunphy stated as follows:

> The Committee are in favour of requiring that there must be a popular vote in a referendum in favour of any change in any of these fundamental Articles before such change can become law, except where a dissolution has occurred subsequent to the submission of the proposal in the form of a Bill to the Dáil.
>
> In such case it should be competent for the Executive Council appointed by the new Dáil to secure by ordinary legislation the enactment of the proposed amendment in the form in which it was submitted to or, in the case of any alteration, agreed to, by the Dáil prior to the General Election.[9]

These comments are significant because, in the event, the Committee never reported on Part II of its terms of reference (i.e. on the question of the manner of constitutional amendment). McDunphy noted in hand on the cover of the Committee's file: 'No action was taken on Part II of the Committee's terms of reference. The matter gradually became one of Government Policy and was dealt with on that basis.'[10]

Whatever reservations Roche may have had about the referendum process, it seems nonetheless fair to infer from this (admittedly draft) passage that the other members of the Committee were in favour of this

[7] Save that the emergency is declared only following the passage of resolutions by both Houses of the Oireachtas. See further F.F. Davis, *The History and Development of the Special Criminal Court, 1922–2005* (Dublin, 2006), 56–70.

[8] Roche then proceeded to make a number of comments about other specific Articles including 64 and 65.

[9] See document no. 10.

[10] See document no. 26.

method of amendment. Since these three members of the Committee were later to form the nucleus of the group who either drafted or, as the case may be, revised the 1937 Constitution, it is scarcely surprising that the referendum option was the one chosen. With the exception of the transitory three-year period,[11] Article 46 provided that the Constitution could henceforth only be amended by way of referendum. While this rigidity has certain disadvantages, this choice was ultimately to prove to be an enlightened one which ensured durability and continuity, guarded against ephemeral change and reinforced popular sovereignty. Indeed, if there was one single change which ensured the success of the present Constitution, it was this.

The eighth meeting of the committee also considered Roche's proposals in relation to Article 2A and the matter was ultimately referred to him to revise in the light of the discussion. Roche's revised draft—prepared overnight—was then discussed at the ninth meeting on 29 June where it appears to have suffered heavy revisions.[12] However, the revised draft had contained a most important new suggestion:

> 5. In addition and apart from 'emergency' periods and 'emergency' legislation, the proposed Article (or else an addendum to one of the 'judicial power' Articles) should authorise the enactment of special legislation, to provide as a part of new permanent judicial machinery for the trial by special courts of persons accused of crime, as regards whose trial the ordinary Judge or Justice certifies at any stage of the proceedings, that it is desirable in the interests of justice that the trial be removed to a special court.
>
> As regards this last suggestion we desire to point out, as against the obvious objections to Special Courts, that the ordinary Courts have been unable, in the past, to deal effectively with certain forms of crime, and that it is perhaps too optimistic to hope for any permanent improvement in that respect. The choice appears to lie therefore between the alternatives of
>
> (a) allowing such forms of crime to go unpunished,

[11] Article 51 had provided that any provision of the 1937 Constitution (other than Article 46 and Article 51) might be amended by means of ordinary legislation for a period of three years from the date on which the first President took office. The First Amendment of the Constitution Act, 1939 and the Second Amendment of the Constitution Act, 1941 were enacted by means of ordinary legislation during this transitional period, which expired on 25 June 1941. However, even during this transitional period the President had a discretion to require that any such proposal be submitted to a referendum before it was enacted into law.

[12] See document nos 20–2. The revised draft contained in the NAI is very heavily annotated and lines have been drawn through several paragraphs.

> (b) declaring a 'state of emergency' for the mere purpose of setting up a special court every time such crimes occur,
>
> (c) making permanent provision for a Special Court on the lines indicated in para. (5) above.
>
> As between these alternatives we recommend the last mentioned, mainly because we feel that its adoption will provide a remedy for outbreaks of disorder which would otherwise necessitate the formal declaration of a 'state of emergency' with inevitable damage to the national credit.[13]

Here we see for the first time the clear outline of what ultimately was to become Article 38.3 of the Constitution,[14] which permits of the establishment by law of special courts quite independently of any declaration of emergency under Article 28.3.3°.

The Committee's Report

The Report consisted of an Introduction and eight Appendices.[15] The Introduction recited the terms of reference and indicated the subsequent layout of the Report. Appendix A contained the text of the Articles regarded as fundamental by the Committee and 'to the extent and with such modifications as are recommended in this Report, [which should] be rendered immune from easy alteration'. In those cases where amendments to such constitutional provisions were proposed, the Committee indicated that 'we have confined ourselves to indicating the nature of the changes suggested and our reasons therefore. We have assumed that it is not our function to submit drafts of articles as so revised.'

The following Articles were, however, regarded as fundamental by the Committee:

> Article 6: The liberty of the person (including *habeas corpus*).
> Article 7: Inviolability of the Dwellings of Citizens.
> Article 8: Freedom of Conscience.

[13] A line has, however, been drawn in the manuscript through these paragraphs and they do not feature in the final report.

[14] Article 38.3.1 provides that: 'Special courts may be established by law for the trial of offences in cases where it may be determined in accordance with law that the ordinary courts are inadequate to secure the effective administration of justice, and the preservation of public peace and order'.

[15] See document no. 27. The contents of Appendices B and C are dealt with below. Appendix D contained extracts from foreign constitutions dealing with freedom of assembly; Appendix E contained extracts from foreign constitutions dealing with the annual assembly of parliament; Appendix F contained extracts from foreign constitutions dealing with the declaration of war; Appendix G contained an excerpt of a letter from the Secretary of the Department of Education dealing with free primary education (see also document no. 23) and Appendix H contained the text of Article 36 of the Constitution.

Article 9: Right of Free Expression of Opinion and Peaceable Assembly.[16]
Article 18: Immunity of Members of the Oireachtas.
Article 19: Privilege of Official Reports etc. of the Oireachtas.[17]
Article 24:
  (a) Summoning and Dissolving the Oireachtas in the name of the King.
  (b) Holding of at least one session of the Oireachtas each year.[18]
Article 28:
  (a) Date of assembly of Dáil Éireann after a general election.
  (b) Duration of Parliament.
Article 41: Presentation of Bills for the King's Assent.[19]
Article 43: Non-declaration of Acts to be infringements of the law which were not so at the date of their commission.

[16] The Committee recommended that Article 9 be amended so as to make it clear that '...laws may be passed, and police action taken, to prevent or control open-air meetings which might interfere with normal traffic or which otherwise become a nuisance or danger to the general public. We understand that legislation on these lines has been delayed by reason of doubts as to whether such legislation could be validly enacted in view of the present wording of the Article'.

The Committee included in Appendix D copies of the relevant Articles dealing with freedom of assembly that were contained in the constitutions of Belgium (1921), Czechoslovakia (1920), Denmark (1915), Estonia (1920), Germany (Weimar Constitution, 1919), Yugoslavia (1921) and Spain (1931).

The Committee's recommendation was acted on, as Article 40.6.1.ii of the Constitution now provides by way of qualification of the right of the citizens to assemble peaceably and without arms that: 'Provision may be made by law to prevent or control meetings which are determined in accordance with law to be calculated to cause a breach of the peace or to be a danger or nuisance to the general public and to prevent or control meetings in the vicinity of either House of the Oireachtas'.

[17] The minutes of the third meeting record that the Committee observed that Article 19 might be modified so as to secure that 'objectionable pronouncements in Parliament may not be utilised outside for the purpose of inciting to violence or other breaches of the law'. These comments—which, significantly, did not feature in the final Report nor were they acted upon in respect of the corresponding provisions (Article 15.12)—were probably made in the light of the deteriorating security situation at the time, with clashes between the IRA and the Blueshirts, O'Sullivan, *I.F.S. and its Senate*, 342–4, 359–62.

[18] The Committee recommended that there be at least one session of the Oireachtas each year (now contained in Article 15.7) and that the Dáil should fix the date of its re-assembly following a general election, which should be regarded as fundamental. The Committee examined the constitutions of Czechoslovakia (1920), Denmark (1915), Germany (Weimar Constitution, 1919), Yugoslavia (1921), Estonia (1920), Mexico (1917) and Poland (1921) (which were set out in Appendix E to the main Report) by way of comparative analysis of these questions and concluded: 'In other Constitutions (see Appendix E) the desired result is secured by providing: (i) that Parliament shall meet on a specified date in each year, if not previously convoked, and/or (ii) that if a certain proportion of the total number of its members so requires, Parliament must be convened within a prescribed time. We recommend that an effective provision on the lines of (i) be substituted for the first sentence of Article 24. We also suggest for favourable consideration the insertion of an additional provision on the lines of (ii)'. Article 15.7 incorporates a modified version of (i), but no action was taken in respect of (ii).

[19] The Committee observed that the principle that 'an Executive should have no power to delay the last formal stage of enactment of Bills which have been duly passed by Parliament through all legislative stages is fundamental'. As 'the trend of policy' was that it was not desirable 'to make permanent the present machinery of assent', the Committee thought it better, if possible, to separate these two features of this Article into separate articles, so 'that relating to machinery of assent or promulgation [could be] left open to amendment by ordinary legislation'. Article 25.1 of the Constitution now provides that, save for the special case of a Bill to amend the Constitution, a Bill passed by both Houses of the Oireachtas shall be presented by the Taoiseach to the President for signature.

Article 46: The raising and maintenance of an armed force.[20]
Article 49: Participation in War.[21]
Article 50: Amendments of the Constitution.[22]
Article 61:
- (a) Central Fund etc;
- (b) Appropriation of Public Money only in accordance with law;[23]

Articles 62 and 63: Comptroller and Auditor General—Tenure of Office;
Articles 64, 65, 66, 68, 69: The Judiciary;[24]
Article 70:
- (a) Provision for legal trials of civilians;
- (b) Trial of Military Offenders by Military Tribunals;
- (c) The extension of the authority of military tribunals to civilians in time of war and armed rebellion.[25]

Some specific comments of the Committee in relation to particular topics merit further consideration.

The Courts

The Committee's comments in relation to the courts were particularly interesting. It first concluded that Article 64—which provided, *inter alia*, that the judicial power 'shall be exercised and justice administered

[20] The Committee commented that '(a) the reference to the Treaty and (b) the limitation to the territory of the Irish Free State should be eliminated'. The Committee added that the suggested amendment 'in regard to (b) is a corollary to recent constitutional developments whereby the right of Saorstát Éireann to raise and maintain armed forces outside its own territory has been recognised'.

[21] Article 49 provided that: 'Save in the case of actual invasion, the Irish Free State (Saorstát Éireann) shall not be committed to active participation in any war without the assent of the Oireachtas'.

The Committee commented that 'The restriction imposed by the word "active" in reference to participation of the Saorstát in war should be removed. This word was not in the draft of the Treaty before being submitted to the British Government in 1922. It was inserted at the instance of the latter Government in conformity with the theory that once the King has declared war, even though in making such declaration he acts on the advice of British Ministers only, the declaration automatically involves the Dominions also in the state of war created'. In view of these comments it is not surprising therefore that the reference to 'active participation' has been omitted in the present Constitution. Article 28.3.1° now provides that 'War shall not be declared and the State shall not participate in any war save with the assent of Dáil Éireann'.

[22] The Committee originally commented that: 'The subject matter of this Article, which has a direct bearing on Part II of our terms of reference, will be dealt with in a separate report'. As already noted, the Committee ultimately never reported on Part II of its terms of reference.

[23] At its third meeting the Committee noted that the Department of Finance was to be consulted 'as to whether this Article is fundamental'. Roche wrote to J.J. McElligott on 2 June 1934 requesting the urgent views of the Department as to whether Article 61 'or any other Article should be so regarded' (see document no. 9). The Department of Finance does not appear to have responded formally to this request, but in the final Report the Committee observed that it understood 'from informal conversations that the Department of Finance regard this Article as fundamental'.

[24] The Committee's comments are dealt with below.

[25] The Committee noted that if its proposals in relation to the revision of Article 2A were to be adopted, it might necessitate a revision of the text of Article 70, but 'this question would naturally receive attention in connection with the drafting of the new provisions'.

in the public courts established by the Oireachtas by judges appointed in manner hereinafter provided'—was to be regarded as fundamental, subject to the following proviso:

> We suggest, however, that it should be carefully re-drafted so as to meet the present position in which judicial or quasi-judicial functions are necessarily performed by persons who are not judges within the strict terms of the Constitution, e.g., Revenue Commissioners, Land Commissioners, Court Registrars, etc.[26]

Indeed, following a discussion of this very point at the Committee's third meeting, Roche had put forward a sketch of a possible addendum to Article 64:

> Provided, [for the removal of doubts and for the more expeditious and economical administration of justice and transaction of public business], that nothing in this Article shall be deemed to render invalid any enactment, or any rule, order, or arrangement made under the authority of any enactment, whereby powers or duties (not being powers or duties of a judicial nature in connection with criminal trials) have been conferred or shall hereafter be conferred, on an officer of any Court in relation to the business of the Court or any Board, Commission, or Tribunal (by whatever name known) or any member thereof.[27]

This draft proved to be very influential, since it clearly anticipates the present Article 37 which permits the Oireachtas to vest non-judicial personages with limited judicial powers in matters 'other than criminal matters'. Indeed, during the Dáil Debates on the 1937 Constitution, de Valera had expressly acknowledged that such concerns had given rise to Article 37:

> There were questions about the Land Commission, as to whether their functions were of a judicial character or not...So as not to get tied in the knot that judicial powers or functions could only be exercised by the ordinary courts

[26] See document no. 27, Appendix A. The Committee had already noted at its third meeting that the provisions of Article 64 might need to be re-examined as far as its effect 'on the exercise of quasi-judicial functions such as those exercised by the Land Commission, the Master of the High Court, etc., should be further considered'. It may be noted that, a few years earlier, the constitutionality of the Land Commission's activities had survived challenge only following very elaborate judgments from the Supreme Court which attempted to essay a definition of what constituted a judicial power: see *Lynham v. Butler* (*No. 2*), [1933] IR 74.

[27] See document no. 12. The section in square parenthesis was annotated by McDunphy: 'Omit this.'

> established here, you have to have a provision of this type.[28]

The Committee also agreed that the express power of judicial review of legislation vested in the High Court by Article 65 was fundamental. No agreement could, however, be reached on two very interesting suggestions which had been discussed by the Committee. The first was whether:

> the power of deciding the validity of laws, having regard to the provisions of the Constitution, should be vested
> (a) in the Supreme Court alone, or
> (b) in a special 'Constitution' Court appointed or designated for that purpose, e.g., a combination of the Supreme and High Courts, or
> (c) in the High Court with a right of appeal to the Supreme Court as at present.

Had the suggestion that a special Constitutional Court might be established become public at that time, it would almost certainly have been regarded with deep suspicion by the judicial and legal establishments of the day. Hostility from the bar and bench had already killed off far more modest proposals for reform of court costume and dress in the 1920s[29] and radical, *avant garde* proposals of this kind would doubtless have met a similar fate. However, irrespective of the merits of such a proposal in the context of a small, common law jurisdiction such as Ireland, the fact that it was seriously considered by the Committee (and, clearly, supported by some of its members) demonstrates that the members of the Committee must have had a very sophisticated understanding of the dynamics of constitutional law. It provides yet further evidence of the ability and remarkable open-mindedness of what one leading historian has described as the 'meritocratic administrative elite' who were later to serve on the Constitution's drafting committee.[30]

However, the suggestion that a Constitutional Court might be established clearly impacted on de Valera who admitted in the Dáil Debates on the Constitution that he was wary of giving the powers of judicial review to the ordinary courts:

[28] 67 *Dáil Debates*, Cols 1511–12 (2 June 1937). See also to similar effect the memorandum of 7 April 1937 submitted by the Revenue Commissioners on the first draft of the Constitution: Document no. 126.

[29] See Ronan Keane, 'The Voice of the Gael: Chief Justice Kennedy and the Emergence of the new Irish Court System, 1921–1936', in *Irish Jurist*, 31 (1996), 205–25; Tom Garvin, *1922: The Birth of Irish Democracy* (Dublin, 1996), 171–3; O'Sullivan, *I.F.S. and its Senate*, 533–4.

[30] Dermot Keogh, 'Church, State and Society', in Farrell (ed.), *De Valera's Constitution*, 108. Keogh also observes that de Valera, Hearne and Moynihan '...were all people of wide culture. They were wholly free of the stridency associated with certain vociferous elements in the Irish Catholic Church in the 1930s. All three had broad intellectual horizons. None were the victims of then fashionable ideological phobias', 107.

> This matter of the Constitution is going to be interpreted, ultimately, by the Courts. I know that in other countries courts are set up, roughly, as constitutional courts, which take a broader view—I do not wish to be hurtful—or not so narrow a view, as the ordinary Courts which, strictly interpreting the ordinary law from day-to-day, have to take. If I could get from anybody any suggestion of some court to deal with such matters other than the Supreme Court, I would be willing to consider it. I confess that I have not been able to get anything better than the Supreme Court to fulfil this function.[31]

The second suggestion was that the Constitution should contain a time limit within which the constitutionality of legislation might be challenged. This proposal had first been put forward by Roche in his memorandum. He had suggested that Article 65 (which vested the High Court and Supreme Court with express powers of judicial review of legislation) should be amended by the addition of the following proviso:

> But no question as to such validity shall be considered unless it is brought before the High Court for determination within three months after the enactment of such law.

He added:

> The idea is that we should get *certainty* as to what is the law and not be discussing in 1934 whether a law which has been in operation since 1925 is valid or not.[32]

The Committee was ultimately to be divided on the question of a fixed time limit, but, like the constitutional court proposal, 'thought it well…to place on record' that these suggestions had been put forward. McDunphy was, however, clearly against the proposal, since he had commented on the margins of the Roche memorandum 'I am afraid of this'.

Roche's proposal did not find its way into the corresponding provision—Article 34.3.2°—of the Constitution and, indeed, by any standards, it would have to be rejected as unsound. Experience has shown that the constitutionality of most legislation cannot be tested on an *a priori*, abstract basis, but has to be judged by reference to the special

[31] 67 *Dail Debates*, Cols 53–4 (11 May 1937). Indeed, the draft Constitution had originally proposed that the Supreme Court alone should have original jurisdiction in constitutional matters. However, in response to opposition suggestions, de Valera agreed to an amendment at committee stage whereby the power was transferred to the High Court with a right of appeal to the Supreme Court, 67 *Dail Debates*, Cols 1492–5 (2 June 1937). The idea of a Constitutional Court was evidently put forward by Hearne: see documents no. 43 and 86.

[32] See document no. 12.

circumstances of a particular litigant. The circumstances in which such a litigant may require to challenge the constitutionality of legislation affecting him adversely may not arise for many years or even decades after it has been enacted. Moreover, legislation which was valid at the date it was enacted may become unconstitutional by reason of changing circumstances, such as inflation, population movements and mortality tables. In addition, where a court upholds the validity of legislation in a case which depends on an appraisal of the prevailing scientific or other relevant expert evidence as to the effect of such legislation, it would seem unjust if this question could not be re-opened if new evidence were later to materialise.[33] At the same time, a procedure which provided for a swift and certain determination of the constitutionality of a particular law—which was the gist of Roche's proposals—might prove to be of great value. And thus it may be that this proposal contained the germ of an idea which ultimately led to the present Article 26 of the Constitution (which had no counterpart in the 1922 Constitution) whereby the constitutionality of a Bill may be determined before it ever comes into law following a reference by the President to the Supreme Court.

Appendix B and the plan for a Special Criminal Court

Appendix B contained the Committee's recommendations in relation to Article 2A which closely followed Roche's proposals for the establishment of special criminal courts (Scheme A) and declarations of emergency (Scheme B). The Committee clearly envisaged that the Special Criminal Court would be the first step in curbing civil disorder and that the declaration of a state of emergency would be necessary in the final resort:

> 1. What may be regarded as the first serious phase in the development of a grave state of disorder throughout the country is the failure of the ordinary Courts, either through intimidation of jurors and/or witnesses, or lack of civic spirit on the part of either or both, to secure the conviction of offenders, particularly in the case of offences of a semi-political nature.
> 2. The resultant immunity of offenders from punishment leads inevitably to the spread of offences of this character,

[33] This point was made by the Supreme Court in *Ryan v. Attorney General,* [1965] IR 294, in dismissing a challenge to the constitutionality of the Health (Fluoridation of Water Supplies) Act, 1960. In this case the available evidence strongly suggested that the fluoridation of water did not have the deleterious consequences apprehended by the plaintiff, but Chief Justice O Dálaigh was careful to stress that 'if in the future the scientific evidence available should be such as to warrant a different conclusion on the facts, the question of the validity of the Act could be reopened'.

resulting sometimes in a serious situation with which the ordinary processes of law are unable to cope.

3. We are of opinion that the development of a situation of this nature could in most cases be arrested by the application of suitable measures in the early stages, and we think that, to this end, the Constitution should contain a permanent provision to supplement the operation of the ordinary Courts.[34]

In its introduction to the Report the Committee had anticipated its recommendations in relation to Scheme B, the declaration of emergency provisions:

> We are of opinion that Article 2A in its present form is not a proper one for retention in the Constitution. We suggest that it should be replaced by a simple Article which would enable the Oireachtas, by ordinary legislation, to empower an Executive to take any measures necessary to deal effectively with a state of public emergency not amounting to armed rebellion or a state of war, including, when necessary, the temporary suspension of many Articles of the Constitution which under normal conditions are rightly regarded as fundamental.

As we have noted, these recommendations clearly formed the basis for Article 38.3.1° and Article 28.3.3° of the present Constitution.

Recommendations regarding language, education and jury trial

The Committee dealt with three heterogeneous provisions dealing respectively with language (Article 4), education (Article 10) and the right to jury trial (Article 72) in Appendix C. In the case of Article 4 (which, unlike the present Article 8, provided that while Irish was the 'national language', English was 'equally recognised as an official language') the Committee observed that:

> While…this Article is not fundamental in the sense that it safeguards democratic rights, we recognise that from the National point of view it is important because of the status which it gives to the Irish language.
>
> We realise, however, that in the course of time it may be found desirable to modify the recognition which it accords

[34] See document no. 27, Appendix B.

> to English as an equally official language throughout the State, and for that reason we are of opinion that the Article should be left open to change by ordinary legislation.

In relation to the guarantee contained in Article 10 that all citizens 'have the right to free elementary education', the Committee recommended against including this in the fundamental list having first obtained the views of Joseph O'Neill, then Secretary of the Department of Education[35] who adverted to possible difficulties to which this provision might give rise:

> (1) Whether a small number of children, say, two, three, or four, living on an island, or at a long distance from a National School, could successfully claim the right to be transported daily to a National School; or to have a School established for their own use;
> (2) Whether the Article could be construed to put an obligation on the State not only to pay the teachers but also to build, equip and maintain schools, and provide free books and requisites for the schoolchildren.[36]

While Article 42.4 still protects the right to free primary education, O'Neill's letter—and the Committee's evident support for his views—produced an important change. Article 42.4 provides that the State's duty is now only to 'provide *for* free primary education (as opposed to 'provide free primary education')—a change which has significantly diluted the extent of the State's obligations in this area.[37]

Somewhat surprisingly, the Committee also recommended against the inclusion of Article 72—guaranteeing the right to jury trial—in the list of fundamental articles. It noted that in England and America the jury system had been subjected 'in recent years to very considerable

[35] O'Neill's letter of 2 July 1934 (document no. 23) to the Committee was set out in Appendix G. McDunphy had written on 15 June 1934 (document no. 13) requesting O'Neill's views. As will be seen in Chapter IX, similar concerns were expressed in March and April 1937 by a number of government departments—including Finance, Lands and Education—about the corresponding provisions of Article 42.4 lest this provision be subsequently interpreted so as to impose additional financial burdens on the State.

[36] See document no. 23.

[37] This very point was made by the Supreme Court in both *Crowley v. Ireland,* [1980] IR 102, and *O'Keeffe v. Hickey,* [2009] 2 IR 302. The importance of this distinction was stressed by Justice Hardiman in the latter case:

> At Article 42.4 it is seen that the State is to '*provide for*' free primary education and in that connection to 'endeavour to supplement and give reasonable aid to private and corporate educational initiative'. It is, however, obliged 'to provide' other educational facilities when the public good requires it. The distinction between 'providing for' and 'providing' lies at the heart of the distinction between a largely State funded but entirely clerically administered system of education on the one hand and a State system of education on the other hand.

criticism' and that 'in our State it cannot even claim to be a spontaneous national growth'. The Committee continued:

> With an Executive dependent on, and responsible to, a parliament elected on a full adult suffrage, and with Judges whose independence is guaranteed by the Constitution, which also forbids the setting up of 'extraordinary Courts' the right to trial by jury has lost its original importance.

The Committee concluded that if they had included the Article in the list of fundamental articles, they would have recommended amendments designed to make it clear:

> (a) that the Article does not bind us to the present English system of requiring a jury of twelve and an unanimous verdict, and
>
> (b) that when the Oireachtas has designated any particular offence as a 'minor' offence, fit to be tried summarily, it shall not be open to a defendant to raise the point that the offence is so serious that it cannot reasonably be called a 'minor' offence and that the law declaring it to be triable summarily is therefore *ultra vires* Article 72 and invalid.

While these recommendations were ultimately not acted on—and, if anything, the new Constitution has strengthened and reinforced the right to jury trial, the provisions of Article 38.3.1° and the Special Criminal Court notwithstanding—these recommendations again demonstrate the far-sighted character of the Committee's Report.

Nevertheless, the entire tenor of the 1934 Report was essentially two-fold. It first emphasised the necessity to protect fundamental rights via a written Constitution and a system of judicial review. It secondly stressed the desirability of maintaining continuity where possible with the existing 1922 Constitution. The Report clearly took the view that the better features of that Constitution should be retained, while at the same time paving the way for innovatory improvements. As will shortly be seen, the entire structure of the new Constitution was subsequently substantially built upon these recommendations. In sum, the Committee's recommendations paved the way for the successful transition from the Constitution of 1922 to the present Constitution. Although the 1922 Constitution was by that stage close to total collapse, the Committee by its recommendations managed to salvage the best features of that document while coming up with new innovations. The Committee's Report may fairly be regarded as a critical step in the entire process leading to the drafting of the Constitution.

No. 4: NAI, DT S2979

Memorandum by Michael McDunphy

Department of the President
24 May 1934

The President by verbal direction today appointed a committee consisting of the following: Mr Roche, LL.B, Secretary, Department of Justice; Mr McDunphy, B.L., Assistant Secretary, Department of the President; Mr John Hearne, B.L., Legal Adviser, Department of External Affairs and Mr Philip O'Donoghue, B.L., Attorney General's Office, to examine the Constitution with a view to ascertaining what Articles should be regarded as fundamental, on the ground that they safeguard democratic rights, and to make recommendations as to steps which should be taken to secure that such Articles should not be capable of being altered by the ordinary process of legislation.

No. 5: NAI, DT S2979

Minutes of first meeting of the Constitution Committee

Government Buildings
28 May 1934

Held in Mr Roche's room, Government Buildings, 10.30am–11.30am. In attendance:

Mr Stephen Roche, LLB., Secretary, Department of Justice,
Mr Michael McDunphy, Assistant Secretary, Department of the President,
Mr John Hearne, B.L., Legal Adviser, Department of External Affairs.

Absent:

Mr Philip O'Donoghue, B.L., Assistant to the Attorney General (ill).

1. The procedure to be adopted was discussed and it was decided that before the next meeting each member of the Committee should examine the Constitution in the light of the Committee's terms of reference.
2. The next meeting was arranged for Tuesday, the 29 May, 1934 at 5.30pm.[38]

No. 6: NAI, DT S2979

Minutes of the second meeting of the Constitution Committee

Government Buildings, Dublin
29 May, 1934

Held in Mr Roche's room, Government Buildings, 5.30pm–7.30pm.
In attendance:

Mr Stephen Roche, LLB., Secretary, Department of Justice,
Mr Michael McDunphy, B.L., Assistant Secretary, Department of the President,
Mr John Hearne, B.L., Legal Adviser, Department of External Affairs.

Absent:

Mr Philip O'Donoghue, B.L., Assistant to the Attorney General (ill).

1. The Constitution was examined Article by Article.
2. It was agreed that the report of the Committee should take the form of an entirely new Constitution.
3. It was not proposed to present a finished draft, that being considered a matter for the Parliamentary Draftsman.
4. It was first intended to limit the new Constitution to matters relating to fundamental rights but it was found that the insertion of others, e.g. those relating to Parliament, etc., was essential if a complete Constitution were to result.

[38] Appended to file DT S2979, which contains all of the proceedings of the 1934 Constitution Committee, is a memo drawn up by Eoin MacNeill during the drafting of the 1922 Constitution. The 1934 Committee appear to have used the following quotation as a guiding principle: 'The test of any provision in a constitution is not whether it is good but whether it is necessary, whether bad government would be a probable result of its omission. A constitution should avoid defining anything that is not necessary to be defined. Its provisions should be cut down to a necessary minimum'; original found at 'Document 61', NAI, DT S1769/3.

5. It was provisionally agreed that the new Constitution should contain the equivalent of the following Articles of the present Constitution with such modifications as further examination would suggest:

   1, 2, 2A, 4, 5, 6, 7, 8, 9, 10, 11, 12, 14, 15, 18, 19, 24, 26, 28, 41, 42, 43, 46, 49, 50, 51, 53, 54, 61, 62, 63, 64, 65, 66, 67, 68, 69, 70, 71, 72, 73.

6. The importance of these varies considerably, but it was felt that it would be difficult to omit any of them.
7. The annexed Schedule [below] sets out briefly the Committee's reasons for the proposed inclusion or exclusion of the various Articles of the present Constitution, with other relevant notes.
8. It was observed that in an amendment moved by Deputies Cosgrave, Costello and McGilligan on the 17 May on the report stage of the Constitution (Amendment no. 24) Bill, 1934, that the following Articles had been selected for special treatment to prevent them being changed by ordinary legislation:

   6, 7, 8, 9, 18, 19, 24, 28, 43, 46, 49, 50, 61, 62, 63, 64, 65, 66, 68, 69, 70.

All of these Articles are included in those named in paragraph five above.

Schedule

Article 1: Title and status of the State
To be retained. The title alone should be provided for. The reference to the British Commonwealth should be omitted.

Article 2: Derivation of powers and authority from the people
To be retained. This Article has little practical value but it was felt that popular sentiment would be in favour of its retention.

Article 2A: Constitution (Special Powers) Tribunal
It was felt that this Article in its present form was not proper to be retained in the Constitution, but that nevertheless power should be provided for the taking of special powers by the Executive to deal with disorder not amounting to actual rebellion or state of war. This matter is to be further considered.

Article 3: Nationality
To be omitted. The subject matter is already covered by proposals for legislation which it is hoped shortly to introduce in the Dáil.

Article 4: Language
To be retained.

Article 5: Titles of Honour
To be retained.[39]

Article 6: Liberty of the person
To be retained.

Article 7: Inviolability of dwellings
To be retained.

Article 8: Freedom of conscience
To be retained.

Article 9: Right of free expression of opinion and peaceable assembly
To be retained.

Article 10: Right to free elementary education
It was not clear that this Article had any practical value.[40]

Article 11: Ownership of lands, waters, etc
To be retained subject to careful revision.

Article 12: Composition of the Legislature
The King being a constituent part of the legislature it was felt that further instructions as to the form which this Article should take should be sought from the President.

Article 13: Place of assembly of the Oireachtas
To be omitted.

Article 14: Right to vote
To be retained.

Article 15: Eligibility for membership of Dáil Éireann
To be retained.

Article 16: Concurrent membership of both houses
Already repealed by Constitution (Amendment no. 24) Bill.

Article 17: The Oath
Already repealed by Constitution (Removal of Oath) Act, 1933.

Article 18: Privilege of members of the Oireachtas
To be retained.

Article 19: Privilege of Official Reports, etc., of the Oireachtas
To be retained.

[39] Annotated by McDunphy: 'Subject to amendment'. All annotations to this document, unless otherwise specified, were made by McDunphy.
[40] Annotated: 'But popular sentiment would probably resent its repeal'.

Article 20: Rules, etc., of Dáil Éireann
To be omitted.

Article 21: Election of Chairman and Deputy Chairman of Dáil Éireann
To be omitted.

Article 22: Mode of determining decisions of the Oireachtas
To be omitted.

Article 23: Payment of members of the Oireachtas
To be omitted.

Article 24: Holding of at least one session a year of the Oireachtas
To be retained with necessary amendment by way of improvement.

Article 25: Provision for private sittings of the Oireachtas
To be omitted

Article 26: Composition of and constituencies for election to Dáil Éireann
To be retained.

Article 27: University representation in Parliament
Repealed by Constitution (Amendment no. 23) Bill.

Article 28:
(a) Date of assembly of Dáil Éireann after General Election
(b) Duration of Parliament
To be retained.

Article 29: Filling of casual vacancies in Dáil Éireann
To be omitted.

Articles 30, 31, 31A, 32, 32A, 32B, 32C, 33, 34, 35: Matters relating to Seanad Éireann
Repealed by Constitution (Amendment no. 24) Bill.

Article 36: Presentation of annual estimates
To be omitted.

Article 37: Money Messages
To be omitted.

Article 38, 38A, 39, 40: Seanad Éireann
Repealed by Constitution (Amendment no. 25) Bill.

Article 41: Presentation of Bills for the King's assent
To be included in such modified form as might later be decided.

Article 42: Enrolment of signed copies of Acts
To be retained.

Article 43: Non-declaration of Acts to be infringements of the law which were not so at the date of their commission
To be retained.

Article 44: Power to create subordinate legislatures
To be omitted.

Article 45: Power to establish functional or educational councils
To be omitted.

Article 46: The raising and maintaining of an armed force
To be retained with the omission of
(a) the reference to the Treaty
(b) the limitation to the territory of the Irish Free State

Article 47: The Referendum
Repealed by Constitution (Amendment no. 10) Act.

Article 48: The Initiative
Repealed by Constitution (Amendment no. 10) Act.

Article 49: Participation in war
To be retained subject to redrafting, if necessary.

Article 50: Amendments to the Constitution
To be entirely redrafted.

Article 51: Executive authority
Further instructions from the President would require to be obtained regarding this Article which in its present form declares the Executive Authority to be vested in the King.

Article 52: Constitution of the Executive Council
To be omitted.[41]

Article 53: Formation of the Executive Council and right to advise dissolution
To be retained.

Article 54:
(a) Collective responsibility of the Executive Council
(b) Presentation of estimates
To be retained as regards (a). Would require further examination as regards (b).

Article 55, 56: Extern Ministers
To be omitted.

Article 57: Provision of Seanad Éireann
Repealed by Constitution (Amendment no. 24) Bill.

Article 58: Resignation of his seat by a deputy on appointment as minister
To be omitted.

[41] Annotated: 'Why omit?'.

Article 59: Payment of Ministers
To be omitted.

Article 60: Appointment, salary, etc, of the Governor General
These provisions are sufficiently covered by the Treaty.

Article 61: Central fund, etc
To be retained.

Article 62: Appointment and powers of Comptroller General and Auditor General
To be retained.

Article 63: Comptroller and Auditor General—tenure of office
To be retained.

Articles 64, 65, 66, 67, 68, 69: Judiciary
To be retained.

Article 70: Provision for legal trials and military tribunals
To be retained.

Article 71: Trial of members of the armed forces
To be retained.

Article 72: Trial by jury on criminal charges
To be retained.

Article 73: Continuance in force of pre-Treaty British statutes
To be retained.

Articles 74, 75, 76, 77, 78, 79, 80, 81: Transitory Provisions
To be omitted.

Article 82: The First Seanad Éireann
Repealed by Constitution (Amendment no. 24) Bill.

Article 83: Enactment of the 1922 Constitution
To be omitted.

No. 7: NAI, DT S2979

Memorandum by Michael McDunphy

Department of the President
31 May 1934

Subsequent to the meeting of 29 May it became clear as a result of pronouncements by the President and of conversations which individual members of the Committee had with him, that what he really wanted was not a new Constitution but

(a) A selection within the framework of the present Constitution of those Articles which should be regarded as fundamental and
(b) A recommendation as to how these should be rendered immune from alteration by ordinary legislation.

The President himself had already created a precedent which should serve as a guide in regard to (b).

In Constitution (Amendment no. 24) Bill, 1934, which provides for the abolition of the Seanad as a constituent house of the Oireachtas, he has provided in respect of Article 63 (the tenure of Office of the Comptroller and Auditor General) and Article 68 (the tenure of Office of Judges) as follows:

> Notwithstanding anything contained in any other Article of this Constitution, a Bill for legislation to amend this Article in relation to the passing of the said resolution shall not be introduced in Dáil Éireann unless or until the amendment proposed by such Bill has been approved by a resolution of Dáil Éireann for the passing of which not less than four-sevenths (exclusive of the Chairman or presiding member) of the full membership of Dáil Éireann shall have voted.

No. 8: NAI, DT S2979

Minutes of third meeting of the Constitution Committee

Government Buildings, Dublin
1 June 1934

In attendance:
Mr Stephen Roche, LLB.., Secretary, Department of Justice,
Mr Michael McDunphy, B.L., Assistant Secretary, Department of the President.

Absent:
Mr John Hearne, B.L., Legal Adviser, Department of External Affairs,
Mr Philip O'Donoghue, B.L., Assistant to the Attorney General (ill).

1. It was agreed, Mr Hearne's concurrence being secured by telephone, that it was now clear that what the President wanted was not a new Constitution, but
   - (a) a selection within the framework of the present Constitution of those Articles which should be regarded as fundamental and
   - (b) a recommendation as to how these should be rendered immune from alteration by ordinary legislation.
2. The work of the previous meeting was reviewed from this point of view.
3. It was decided that the following Articles should be regarded as fundamental and, subject to the modifications indicated, be rendered immune from change by ordinary legislation:

Article 6—The liberty of the person (including *habeas corpus*).
Article 7—Inviolability of the dwellings of citizens.
Article 8—Freedom of conscience.
Article 9—Right of free expression of opinion and peaceable assembly.
Article 18—Immunity of members of the Oireachtas.
Article 19—Privilege of Official Reports, etc, of the Oireachtas.
(Subject to modification so as to secure that objectionable pronouncements in Parliament may not be utilised outside for the purpose of inciting to violence or other breaches of the law.)
Article 24 –
(a) Summoning and Dissolving the Oireachtas in the name of the King.
(b) Holding of at least one Session of the Oireachtas each year.
Portion (b) is clearly fundamental. It should be differentiated from (a). Two separate Articles might meet the situation.
Article 28 –
(a) Date of assembly of Dáil Éireann after a General Election.
(b) Duration of Parliament.
Article 41—Presentation of Bills for the King's Assent.

It was agreed that the provision that Bills should be presented for the Royal Assent as soon as may be after they have been passed by both houses of the Oireachtas or under the new arrangement created by Constitution (Amendment no. 24) Bill, 1924 [*sic* 1934], by Dáil Éireann was regarded as fundamental but that the actual machinery of presentation was one which should be left flexible. The position might be met by dividing the Article into two parts.

Article 43—Non-declaration of Acts to be infringements of the law which were not so at the date of their commission.

Article 46—The raising and maintenance of an armed force.

The reference to the Treaty and the limitation to the territory of the Irish Free State might be omitted.

Article 49—Participation in war.

The restriction imposed by the word 'active' in reference to participation of the Saorstát in war should be further examined. This word was not in the draft of the Treaty before being submitted to the British Government in 1922. It is understood that it was inserted at the request of the British Government in conformity with the theory that once the King has declared war even though the actual declaration concerned Great Britain, it automatically involved the Dominions in the state of war created.

Article 50—Amendments to the Constitution.

The terms of this Article would require careful consideration in the light of the proposals to be submitted by the Committee.

Article 61— (a) Central fund, etc.
(b) Appropriation of public money only in accordance with law.

The Department of Finance to be consulted as to whether this Article is fundamental.

Articles 62 and 63—Comptroller and Auditor General: tenure of office.

Articles 64, 65, 66, 68, 69—The Judiciary.

The effect of these Articles on the exercise of quasi-judicial functions such as those exercised in practice by the Land Commission, the Master of the High Court, etc,. should be further considered.

Article 70— (a) Provision for legal trials of civilians.
(b) Trial of military offenders by military tribunals.
(c) The extension of the authority of military tribunals to civilians in time of war or armed rebellion (see Article 6).

With regard to Article 2A it was agreed that this Article in its present form was not a proper one for retention in the Constitution, but that nevertheless, it was essential that power should be provided to enable the Executive to deal with conditions of disorder not amounting to actual rebellion or state of war and that these powers should include the temporary suspension of the Constitution except those [articles] relating to:

(a) The Constitution and Assembly of Parliament
(b) *Habeas Corpus*
(c) The independence of the Judiciary, and other matters of a like nature.

It was arranged:

(a) That Mr McDunphy should prepare a skeleton report for consideration of the next meeting;
(b) That a confidential letter should be addressed to the Department of Finance asking for their views as to what Articles should be regarded as fundamental from the point of view of that Department.[42]

In addition to the Articles mentioned above there were two other Articles which, though not fundamental in the same sense, might have the pressure of public opinion behind them from the sentimental point of view, viz:

Article 4—Language.
Article 10—Right to free elementary education.

No. 9: NAI, DT S2979

Stephen Roche to J.J. McElligott

Department of Finance
2 June 1934

Dear McElligott,
An informal Committee has been set up by the President to consider and make recommendations as to what Articles of the Constitution should be immune from amendment by the ordinary process of legislation, on the ground that they are fundamental from the point of view of safeguarding rights of individuals, of Parliament, or of the Executive.

[42] See document no. 9.

Articles previously coming within this category are those relating to the liberty of the person, inviolability of dwellings, freedom of conscience, the independence of the judiciary, etc.

It has been suggested that certain Articles dealing with Finance, such as Article 61, might possibly be regarded as coming within this category, and I would be glad to have from you, at the earliest possible moment, a brief reasoned statement as to whether this or any other Article should be so regarded.

We would like to complete the work early next week, if possible, and for that reason I would be glad if you would treat the matter as urgent.

No. 10: NAI, DT S2979

First Draft of Committee Report[43]

Michael McDunphy, Department of the President
9 June 1934

[The text of this initial draft was largely similar—though not as comprehensive—to that finally submitted to Eamon de Valera on 3 July, for which see document no. 27 below. It is included here for the following relevant extract]:

With regard to section (b) [i.e. part 2] of our terms of reference, you will recollect that on the fifth stage in the Dáil of Constitution (Amendment No. 24) Bill, 1934, which provides for the abolition of Seanad Éireann as a constituent house of the Oireachtas, you stated as follows:

> We can guarantee these Articles against constant change either by way of requiring a vote of this House so large as to ensure that, if it is obtained, there must be a strong popular demand for the change or else provide that a change, to be effective must be approved of by the people through the means of a Referendum.

The Committee are in favour of requiring that there must be a popular vote in a referendum in favour of any change in any of these fundamental Articles before such change can become law, except where a dissolution has occurred subsequent to the submission of the proposal in the form of a Bill to the Dáil.

In such case it should be competent for the Executive Council appointed by the new Dáil to secure by ordinary legislation the enactment

[43] A copy of the report and covering letter was given to each member of the Constitution Committee on 9 June. It does not appear to have been supplied to de Valera at this point.

of the proposed amendment in the form in which it was submitted to or, in the case of any alteration, agreed to, by the Dáil prior to the General Election.

No. 11: NAI, DT S2979

Memorandum from Michael McDunphy to all Constitution Committee members

Department of the President
12 June 1934

You will perhaps recollect that on seventeenth ultimo the following motion in the name of Deputies William T. Cosgrave, John A. Costello and Patrick McGilligan was moved to Constitution (Amendment no. 24) Bill, 1934, which provides for the abolition of Seanad Éireann as a constituent house of the Oireachtas:

> 'In page 3, Schedule, Part II, at the end of the portion of the column relating to Article 50 to add the words 'The insertion after the words "but no such amendment passed by the Oireachtas in respect of Articles 6, 7, 8, 9, 18, 19, 24, 28, 43, 46, 49, 50, 61, 62, 63, 64, 65, 66, 68, 69, 70 shall become law until after a General Election shall have been held and a Resolution approving of such amendment shall have been passed by Dáil Éireann on the recommendation of the Executive Council first elected after such General Election."'[44]

A good deal of the debate on this proposal, which was rejected by the Government, has a bearing on the work of our Committee and the following references to appropriate portions of the debate may be found useful. They appear in Dáil Debates of seventeenth May, 1934, Vol. 55, no. 3 and relate to the Report Stage of the Bill.

Speaker	Columns
Mr John Costello	1167–72
Professor J. O'Sullivan	1180–1
Professor J. O'Sullivan	1183–4
President	1192–4
Attorney General	1201
President	1218–20
President	1249–50

[44] 51 *Dáil Debates*, Cols 1168–72, 1178–83 (17 May 1934).

The following portion of the debate on the fifth stage of the Bill may also be of interest. It will be found in Dáil Debates of 25 May, 1934, Vol. 52, no. 4.

Speaker	Columns
President	1876–8

The following statements by the President on the second stage of the Bill in the Seanad are also relevant. They are both contained in Vol. 18, no. 16 of 30 May—1 June, 1934.

Date	Columns
30 May 1934	1217
1 June 1934	1514–15.[45]

No. 12: NAI, DT S2979

Memorandum by Stephen Roche
Note, with special reference to Article 2A

Department of Justice
14 June 1934

I attach separate notes on points which have occurred to me after reading Mr McDunphy's excellent preliminary draft, and in particular, I attach a rough draft of an Article to replace Article 2A.[46]

I take the opportunity to put down, as shortly as I can, my own views on the question generally, not that I intend in the least to insist on them unduly but because I think it as well to put them on record.

I believe that in a unitary State with full adult suffrage, the idea of a written Constitution, not capable of alteration by a majority of the elected representatives of the people, is unsound in theory and dangerous in practice. It is unsound in theory *because no Parliament (whether it calls itself a Dáil or a Constituent Assembly or any other name) and no generation* has any right to bind future Parliaments or future generations.[47] The men and women of 1964 will be in a better position than we are in 1934 of saying what ought to be regarded, in 1964, as fundamental principles of Government and it is an impertinence on our part to try to fetter them

[45] Annotated by McDunphy: 'Other refs are Dáil 26 April 1934, cols 2479–82'.

[46] Not transcribed. A revised version of this draft is found at document no. 21.

[47] Italicised section underlined by McDunphy. Annotated: 'Not rigidly but a Constituent Assembly should have some authority of an exceptional kind. 15 June 1934'. All annotations to this document, unless otherwise specified, were made by McDunphy.

in advance. That is the theoretical side. The practical side is that majorities will have their way, anyhow, and if they can't have it 'constitutionally', or only after great delay, then they will (and quite rightly) have it 'unconstitutionally'.

I believe that what this country wants at present and probably will continue to want for many years is a strong Executive, not liable, so long as it has the support of the people, to be delayed, hampered and humiliated at every step by long arguments in the Courts, or by propaganda of a threatening and seditious type. A Government should not allow itself to be insulted.[48]

Further, I believe that the doctrine of 'judicial independence' and 'the separation of the functions' are being overdone and that the Courts have been given or have assumed a position in our civic life to which they are not entitled. There was a time in England when the Judges' job was to save the people from an irresponsible Executive: it may be necessary, in turn, for a responsible Executive to save the people *from irresponsible Judges*.[49]

With particular reference to Article 2A, I agree that, *in form*, that Article is grotesque as an Article of the Constitution. It must go.[50] On the other hand, so long as we keep to the idea of a 'normal' written Constitution, with all sorts of snags and pit-falls for the Executive, we must have something, somewhere, on the lines of Article 2A. What I have done in my draft is to split the task into two parts, viz:

(a) The Declaration of an 'emergency period' and
(b) The measures which may be taken by the Executive once an 'emergency period' has been declared.

I have put part (a) in the Constitution and left part (b) to be dealt with by ordinary legislation with the proviso that such ordinary legislation shall not be subject to the ordinary Constitutional limitations.[51] I see no other way of making adequate provision without overloading the actual Constitution with details.

I have made the declaration of an 'emergency period' contingent on the consent of those Judges and Justices[52] who travel the country and deal with crime locally. I have done this mainly because I gathered from

[48] Paragraph annotated: 'A "strong" Executive could conceivably be a real danger instead of a blessing. Something more than "strength" is essential'.
[49] Italicised section underlined by McDunphy. Annotated with a question mark.
[50] Annotated: 'I agree'.
[51] Annotated with a 'yes' tick.
[52] Annotated here as follows: 'Including, I presume, the Supreme Court. Otherwise the decision would rest with the lower courts to the exclusion of, or with a doubt existing as to the right of appeal to, the Supreme Court'.

the President that he was anxious, for obvious and weighty reasons, to get some form of judicial, or at least non-political sanction for such a declaration. Those Judges and Justices have a strong incentive to shift the burden of dealing with organised crime from their own shoulders; they see at close quarters the inadequacy of ordinary police and court methods in semi-revolutionary periods; they even run definite personal risks, and they are in the main sensible decent men, so that I have some hope that in any real emergency they will not be obstructive. I have, as will be seen, taken pains to avoid giving any ground for the charge that the Executive will be in a position to mark down for victimisation any individual Judge or Justice who opposes the Government's wishes.[53]

I need hardly add, I hope, that I see, myself, many objections to this proposal and that it is put forward largely in the hope of inducing someone else to propose something better.

(Notes on selected articles)

Article 4: I am not inclined to make this Article semi-irrevocable, at the present moment. I am by no means opposed to the sentiment of this Article, but I do not regard its form as satisfactory and I do not at the moment know how it could be made satisfactory. On the sentimental side, I suppose the majority of our people would say that as between 'the Faith' and 'the Language' the former is the more important, but we don't say anything about it in the Constitution.[54]

Article 9: This Article is too wide and too vague. What is 'public morality'? What does 'regulating' mean? I suggest: '*Subject to law*, the right, etc is guaranteed. Such laws shall, etc.'

Article 10: I would not put this Article in the select class.

Proposed addendum to Article 64: 'Provided, [for the removal of doubts and for the more expeditious and economical administration of justice and transaction of public business,][55] that nothing in this Article shall be deemed to render invalid any enactment, or any rule, order or arrangement made under the authority of any enactment, whereby powers or duties (not being powers or duties of a judicial nature in connection with criminal trials) have been conferred or shall hereafter be conferred, on any officer of any Court in relation to the business of the Court or on any Board, commission or Tribunal (by whatever name known) or any member thereof.'[56]

[53] Paragraph annotated: '*Prima Facie* this seems sound. 16 June 1934'.
[54] Annotated: 'We cannot make any religious distinction between Catholics and persons professing other religions'.
[55] Section in square parentheses annotated: 'Omit this'.
[56] This is probably the original model for the present Article 37.1.

Proposed addendum to Article 65: 'but no question as to such validity shall be considered unless it is brought before the High Court for determination within three months after the enactment of such law'.[57]

The idea is that we should get *certainty* as to what is law and not be discussing in 1934 whether a law which has been in operation since 1925 is valid or not.

Article 68: In first sentence say 'shall be appointed by the Executive Council'.

At the end of the sentence 'such remuneration may not be diminished during their continuance in office' add the words 'save by way of legislation and the remuneration of a Judge shall not in any event be reduced to less than three-quarters of the amount of remuneration which he received when first appointed, and no reduction shall be made in the case of any particular Judge or Judges unless the remuneration of all other Judges (if any) in receipt of the same remuneration is reduced to the same amount at the same time.'[58]

Article 69: I don't like the first sentence. If the word 'and' were omitted it would be better. What is the justification for the word 'and'? I object to it because it creates a dangerous vagueness.

Article 70: Omit the words in the first sentence *after* the words 'due course of law' (What does the expression 'extraordinary courts' mean, anyhow? If a person cannot be tried except 'in due course of law' how can he be tried by an 'extraordinary court' unless that expression includes a court set up by law, and if it does include that kind of court how are we to distinguish the courts which are extraordinary from those which are not? This provision seems to be a relic of the time when the King or Executive could set up a court without parliamentary authority).

No. 13: NAI, DT S2979

Michael McDunphy to Joseph O'Neill

Department of the President
15 June 1934

Confidential

Dear O'Neill.

As mentioned in our phone conversation today, a Committee set up by the President is at present working on the Constitution with a view to

[57] Annotated: 'I am afraid of this'.

[58] Annotated: 'The principle seems sound enough'.

selecting for special treatment those Articles which should be regarded as fundamental and rendered incapable of change by ordinary legislation.

Amongst those which have come up for consideration is Article 10 which provides that:

> 'All citizens of the Irish Free State (Saorstát Éireann) have the right to free elementary education.'

Before coming to any decision regarding this Article, we would like to have your views as to whether:

(a) This Article is really fundamental.
(b) Whether, in practice, it is rigidly adhered to.
(c) What difficulties have arisen in its application.
(d) Whether it should be rendered permanent in its present form.

If you could let me have four copies of a memorandum on the subject, it would be a distinct convenience.[59]

No. 14: NAI, DT S2979

Minutes of the 4th meeting of the Constitution Committee

Government Buildings, Dublin
18 June 1934

Held in Mr Roche's room, Government Buildings, 10.30am–1.30pm. [All committee members in attendance]

1. It was agreed that the draft circulated by Mr McDunphy on the 9th instant should serve as a basis for discussion subject to the inclusion of Articles 71 and 72.
2. The following Articles were discussed in detail: 4, 6, 7, 8, 9, 10, 18, 19, 24, 28, 41, 43, 46, 49, 50, 61, 62, 63, 64.
3. It was decided to hold the next meeting at 5pm on Tuesday, 19th instant.

[59] For reply see document no. 23.

No. 15: NAI, DT S2979

Minutes of the fifth meeting of the Constitution Committee

Government Buildings, Dublin
19 June 1934

Held in Mr Roche's room, Government Buildings, 5–7pm
[All committee members in attendance]

1. The following articles were covered in detail:
   65, 66, 68, 69, 70.
2. The next meeting was fixed for Wednesday, the 20th instant at 5pm.

No. 16: NAI, DT S2979

Minutes of sixth meeting of the Constitution Committee

Government Buildings, Dublin
20 June 1934

Held in Mr Roche's room in Government Buildings, 3.30–5pm
[All committee members in attendance]

Consideration of the Constitution was continued. It was agreed that Mr McDunphy should prepare a draft of the Committee's report for consideration at the next meeting, the date of which would be arranged later.

No. 17: NAI, DT S2979

Memorandum from Michael McDunphy to all Constitution Committee members

Department of the President
25 June 1934

I enclose herewith a rough draft of our suggested report.[60] Needless to say, it does not purport to be a finished product, but it contains, I believe,

[60] Not transcribed. This copy of the letter is annotated by McDunphy: 'Copy not attached. In essence it was the same as the report as presented'.

sufficient material, seasoned in parts with controversial views of my own, to serve as a basis for discussion at our next meeting.

With regard to the substitute for Article 2A, I have provided for the insertion in the draft report of the scheme exactly in the form as proposed by Mr Roche.

I think that we are in general agreement with the main idea, but we have not yet discussed details.

No. 18: NAI, DT S2979

Rosita Austin[61] to Michael McDunphy

Department of External Affairs
26 June 1934

Dear Mr McDunphy,
I enclose copy of Spanish Constitution—in Spanish. The French copy is out. We have no English or French copies of the German Constitution but I may be able to get you a summary of it, if that is any use.

No. 19: NAI, DT S2979

Minutes of seventh meeting of the Constitution Committee

Government Buildings, Dublin
27 June 1934

Held in Mr Roche's room, Government Buildings, 3.30–4.45pm
[All committee members in attendance]

1. A draft report prepared by Mr McDunphy, as arranged at the previous meeting, was considered.
2. The draft consisted of the report with seven appendices—A to G inclusive.
3. Subject to examination as to details it was agreed to adopt the draft as the basis of the Committee's report.
4. The draft was then examined in detail, and subject to minor amendments and to redrafting of the observations under

[61] Rosita Austin (1883–1974), translator and librarian of the Department of External Affairs. For more on Austin, see Michael Kennedy, '"It is a disadvantage to be represented by a woman": the experiences of women in the Irish diplomatic service', in *Irish Studies in International Affairs*, 13 (2002), 215–35.

Article 9 (Appendix A, 4) and Article 72 (Appendix C, 3) the following portions were approved:

I. The text of the report proper.
II. Appendix A (Pages 1 to 10 inclusive, Articles 6, 7, 8, 9, 18, 19 and 24)
III. Appendix C
IV. Appendix D
V. Appendix E
VI Appendix G

No. 20: NAI, DT S2979

Minutes of 8th meeting of the Constitution Committee

Government Buildings, Dublin
28 June 1934

Held in Mr Roche's room, Government Buildings, 3.30–5.45pm
[All committee members in attendance]

1. Consideration of Mr McDunphy's draft was continued and completed, various textual amendments being agreed on.
2. The suggested scheme to replace Article 2A was discussed, and referred to Mr Roche to revise in the light of the discussion.
3. It was decided that the revised scheme should be discussed at the next meeting of the Committee on Friday, the 29th instant.

No. 21: NAI, DT S2979

Memorandum from Stephen A. Roche to Michael McDunphy

Department of Justice
29 June 1934

Mr McDunphy,
I attach herewith a copy of the proposals as regards the Article to replace Article 2A of the Constitution, as revised by me following our conference yesterday evening.

I direct special attention to paragraph five thereof which I added last night.[62] I attach considerable importance to it and I hope that it will be possible to agree to something on these lines.

I suggest a meeting at 4pm today, Friday, with a view to settling the draft.[63]

Notes of a scheme for an Article to replace Article 2A of the Constitution[64]
[28 June 1934]

1. It should be set out in the proposed Article that such provision, including, if thought proper, the suspension of any article of the Constitution, [which] may be made by way of ordinary legislation (and such provision should be capable of being repealed, amended, or added to by way of ordinary legislation), as may be necessary to meet the requirements of any period during which the ordinary laws are not adequate to preserve public order. All such legislation should, by way of title or preamble, indicate expressly that its object is to carry out the purpose of the proposed Article.
2. The Article should provide that if and whenever the Executive Council is of opinion that it is desirable so to do they shall request the President, or the senior available Judge, of the High Court (hereinafter called the summoning officer) to summon all the Judges or Justices exercising criminal jurisdiction (but not judges of the Supreme or High Court nor any person acting only as a temporary Judge or Justice) to meet at a stated place and time (not being sooner than three days or later than seven days after the issue of such summons), for the purpose of advising the Executive Council as to whether the state of the country is such as that the ordinary laws are not adequate to preserve public order.

   The said Judges shall meet accordingly under the Chairmanship of the summoning officer, and shall, after such discussion as they shall think fit, decide, by way of majority vote, on a secret ballot, on the question referred to them by the Executive Council, and the summoning officer shall report to

[62] In the draft attached to this file, McDunphy has drawn a line through paragraph five in its entirety. However, the paragraph appears almost verbatim in Appendix B of the Constitution Committee's final report (see document no. 27).
[63] Annotated by McDunphy: 'Meeting: Roche and Self, 4pm, 29/6, 4–4.45. O'D[onoghue] absent, Hearne [?]' [sic]. For minutes of the meeting, see document no. 22.
[64] This part of the document is heavily annotated by McDunphy. This transcription sets out the text as it appears it was intended to read following all of the emendations. At the head of the document is the note 'Revise of scheme of 14 June 1934' (see document no. 12).

the Executive Council in writing (attested to by the signatures of all present at the meeting) as to the result of the vote, without specifying the names or numbers of persons voting for or against.

To provide against wilful abstention from the meeting of Judges and Justices, severe penalties, amounting even to automatic removal from office, should be provided in the case of any Judge or Justice who is absent unless the summoning officer shall certify that such absence was unavoidable.

3. If and whenever the Executive Council receives such report in the affirmative, they may by Order declare that the provisions of all such legislation as is mentioned in paragraph 1 above shall come into operation on a day which shall be appointed in such Order and the said provisions shall come into operation on such day.

   The Order, and a statement as to the prior receipt of the report referred to in the preceding paragraph, shall be published in *Iris Oifigiúil* not later than the day preceding the appointed day, and shall be laid before the Dáil as soon as may be after.

4. The legislation mentioned in paragraph 1 above shall cease to be in operation (without prejudice to anything done under it) either
   (a) On a date named in an Order of the Executive Council, published in *Iris Oifigiúil*, or
   (b) On a date named in a resolution of the Dáil, or
   (c) If not sooner terminated as at (a) or (b) six months after the commencing date, but it may be renewed at any time for a further six months and so on from time to time by the same procedure (meeting of Judges, etc.).

5. In addition and apart from 'emergency' periods, and 'emergency' legislation, the proposed Article (or else an addendum to one of the 'judicial power' Articles) should authorise the enactment of special legislation, to provide as a part of new permanent judicial machinery for the trial by special courts of persons accused of crime, as regards whose trial the ordinary Judge or Justice certifies at any stage of the proceedings, that it is desirable in the interests of Justice that the trial be removed to a special court.

   As regards this last suggestion we desire to point out, as against the obvious objections to Special Courts, that the ordinary Courts have been unable, in the past, to deal effectively with certain forms of crime, and that it is perhaps too optimistic to hope for any permanent improvement in that respect. The choice appears to lie therefore between the alternatives of

(a) Allowing such forms of crime to go unpunished,
(b) Declaring a 'state of emergency' for the mere purpose of setting up a special court every time such crimes occur,
(c) Making permanent provision for a Special Court on the lines indicated in para. 5 above.

As between these alternatives we recommend the last mentioned, mainly because we feel that its adoption will provide a remedy for outbreaks of disorder which would otherwise necessitate the formal declaration of a 'state of emergency' with inevitable damage to the national credit.

No. 22: NAI, DT S2979

Minutes of ninth meeting of the Constitution Committee

Government Buildings, Dublin
29 June 1934

Held in Mr Roche's room, Government Buildings, 4.00–4.45pm

In attendance:
Mr S. Roche, LLB., Secretary, Department of Justice,
Mr McDunphy, B.L., Assistant Secretary, Department of the President.

Absent:
Mr P. O'Donoghue, B.L., Assistant to the Attorney General
Mr J. Hearne, B.L., Legal Adviser to the Department of External Affairs

1. Mr Roche's revised draft of the scheme to deal with a public emergency was examined. The principle was agreed on but it was decided to set it out in a different form.[65]
2. It was arranged that Mr McDunphy should do this and prepare for final consideration the text of the whole of the Committee's report on Part 1 of their terms of reference.

[65] Annotated by McDunphy: 'Mr Hearne and Mr O'Donoghue who were absent had already intimated their concurrence verbally'.

No. 23: NAI, DT S2979

Joseph O'Neill to Michael McDunphy

Department of Education
2 July 1934

Dear McDunphy,
In reply to your semi-official letter (S.2979) of 15th ultimo on the subject of Article 10 of the Constitution, I would like to mention at the outset that the principal query (a) of your letter appears to us to raise an important issue of constitutional policy and to be rather outside the province of departmental consideration or opinion.

There is a further difficulty in dealing with your enquiries inasmuch as Article 10 has never been formally invoked, and we have not so far obtained a legal interpretation of it, or of the obligations which it imposes.

The present position is that elementary education is free except in a few of the Model Schools, and in these Schools the practice of charging fees is being gradually terminated and in a few years it will have disappeared.

Apart however from the obligation that elementary education should be free, there are other claims which might possibly be made under the Article in question. These include:

(i) Whether a small number of children, say two, three or four, living on an island, or at a long distance from a National School, could successfully claim the right to be transported daily to a National School; or to have a School established for their use;
(ii) Whether the Article could be construed to put an obligation on the State not only to pay the teachers but also to build, equip and maintain schools, and provide free books and requisites for the schoolchildren.

In my opinion the present position is that the principle underlying the Article is fundamental and should be preserved if possible, but in the absence of a clear definition of the States [*sic*] obligation under the Article it would be undesirable to put it in such a position as to make it more difficult to deal by legislation with any problem that might arise thereunder.

No. 24: NAI, DT S2979

Michael McDunphy to all Constitution Committee members

Department of the President
2 July 1934

I send you herewith, for your perusal, draft of the final text of the Committee's report on part 1 of our terms of reference.

Subject to agreement on the text it is hoped to sign the report tomorrow.

No. 25: NAI, DT S2979

Minutes of tenth meeting of the Constitution Committee

Government Buildings, Dublin
3 July 1934

Held in Mr Roche's room, Government Buildings, 12.30–12.45pm
[All committee members in attendance]

The text of the Committee's report on part 1 of their terms of reference, which was circulated by Mr McDunphy the previous day, was approved and the report signed by all four members of the Committee as a unanimous report.

No. 26: NAI, DT S2979

Memorandum by Michael McDunphy

Department of the President
3 July 1934

Report on part 1 of the Committees' terms of reference signed today by all members of the Committee and given to President by Mr Roche.

No action was taken on part 2 of the Committee's terms of reference. The matter gradually became one of Government Policy and was dealt with on that basis.[66]

[66] This sentence appears to have been added some time after the memorandum was originally drafted.

No. 27: UCDA, P150/2365

Report of the Constitution Committee[67]

3 July 1934

President,

1. In accordance with your verbal direction of the 24 May, we have examined the Constitution from the point of view of:
   (i) ascertaining which of its Articles should be regarded as fundamental in the sense that they safeguard democratic rights, and;
   (ii) submitting a recommendation as to how these Articles might be specially protected from change.
2. We have now completed our task as regards part 1 of our terms of reference and accordingly submit this our report thereon.
3. After careful examination we have come to the conclusion that the following twenty-two Articles, or portions thereof, should be regarded as fundamental, and should, to the extent and with such modifications as are recommended in this report, be rendered immune from easy alteration, viz:

   6, 7, 8, 9, 18, 19, 24, 28, 41, 43, 46, 49, 50, 61, 62, 63, 64, 65, 66, 68, 69, 70.
4. In dealing with these Articles we have taken their text in the form which will obtain when the following Bills, which are either held up by the Seanad, or are in the course of passage through the Oireachtas, have become law, viz:

   Constitution (Amendment no. 24) Bill, 1934: Abolition of Seanad Éireann as a constituent House of the Oireachtas (rejected by Seanad Éireann on 1 June, 1934), and;

   Constitution (Amendment no. 23) Bill, 1934: Abolition of the University representation in the Oireachtas (at present with Dáil Éireann).
5. For convenient reference we have set out in Appendix A the text of each of the Articles in question as so modified, together with a note as to our views in respect of each.
6. In those cases where we have proposed amendments, we have confined ourselves to indicating the nature of the changes suggested and our reasons therefore. We have assumed that it

[67] A copy of the report is also filed at NAI, DT S2979.

is not our function to submit drafts of articles as so revised.

7. We have given special consideration to Article 2A, and in doing so we have borne in mind the statement made by you in the Dáil on Committee Stage of the Constitution (Amendment No. 24) Bill on 26 April last, column 2480, viz: 'that it is necessary to ensure, in cases of real urgency and real public emergency, that an Executive would not be prevented from taking the action that might be considered necessary to safeguard public interests'.
8. We are of opinion that Article 2A in its present form is not a proper one for retention in the Constitution. We suggest that it should be replaced by a simple Article which would enable the Oireachtas, by ordinary legislation, to empower an Executive to take any measures necessary to deal effectively with a state of public emergency not amounting to armed rebellion or state of war, including, when necessary, the temporary suspension of many Articles of the Constitution which under normal conditions are rightly regarded as fundamental.
9. We realise the great importance of providing safeguards to prevent such drastic powers being resorted to except in the abnormal circumstances for which they are designed, and at the same time to secure that an Executive which has real occasion to use them will not be in danger of finding its efforts to cope with a serious situation hampered or defeated by appeals to the Courts based on normal constitutional rights.
10. A suggested scheme which might meet the position is briefly outlined in Appendix B.
11. In addition to the Articles referred to in paragraphs 3 and 7 above we have given special consideration to the following:

    Article 4 – THE NATIONAL AND OFFICIAL LANGUAGE
    Article 10 – EDUCATION
    Article 72 – TRIAL BY JURY

    We have not, however, included these among the fundamental Articles, and we set out in Appendix C annexed, our reasons for their omission.
12. As bearing on the suggestion made by you in the course of the Debate in the Dáil on 17 May, 1934, (Column 1193) on Report Stage of Constitution (Amendment No. 24) Bill that agreement might be obtained between both sides of the House as to what Articles are fundamental, it will be observed that the

Articles selected by us, after independent examination, as falling within that category, including all of those proposed for special treatment by Deputies William T. Cosgrave (former Attorney General) and Patrick McGilligan (former Minister for Industry and Commerce and Minister for External Affairs), viz:

6, 7, 8, 9, 18, 24, 28, 43, 46, 49, 50, 61, 62, 63, 64, 65, 66, 68, 69, 70,

the only difference between our respective selections being that we have included Article 41 which compels the Executive Council to present, without delay, for the last formal stage of enactment, bills which have been duly passed by Parliament through all other legislative stages.

(Signed) S.A. Roche
M. McDunphy
John J. Hearne
P.P. O'Donoghue

3 July, 1934

Appendix A

Articles 6, 7, 8, 9, 18, 19, 24, 28, 41, 43, 46, 49, 50. 51, 62, 63, 64, 65, 66, 68, 69, 70: For explanation see paragraphs 3, 4, 5 and 6 of the report.

Article 6

The liberty of the person is inviolable, and no person shall be deprived of his liberty except in accordance with law. Upon complaint made by or on behalf of any person that he is being unlawfully detained, the High Court and any and every judge thereof shall forthwith enquire into the same and may make an order requiring the person in whose custody such person shall be detained to produce the body of the person so detained before such Court or judge without delay and to certify in writing as to the cause of the detention and such Court or judge shall thereupon order the release of such person unless satisfied that he is being detained in accordance with the law:

Provided, however, that nothing in this Article contained shall be invoked to prohibit control or interfere with any act of the military forces of the Irish Free State (Saorstát Éireann) during the existence of a state of war or armed rebellion.

Observations of the Committee:
In our opinion this Article should be regarded as fundamental. We do not suggest that any alteration should be made in the text.

Article 7
The dwelling of each citizen is inviolable and shall not be forcibly entered except in accordance with law.

Observations of the Committee:
In our opinion this Article should be regarded as fundamental. We do not suggest that any alteration should be made in the text.

Article 8
Freedom of conscience and the free profession and practice of religion are, subject to the public order and morality, guaranteed to every citizen, and no law may be made either directly or indirectly to endow any religion, or prohibit or restrict the free exercise thereof or give any preference, or impose any disability on account of religious belief or religious status, or affect prejudicially the right of any child to attend a school receiving public money without attending the religious instruction at the school or make any discrimination as respects State aid between schools under the management of different religious denominations, or divert from any religious denomination or any educational institution any of its property except for the purpose of roads, railways, lighting, water or drainage works, or other works of public utility, and on payment of compensation.

Observations of the Committee:
In our opinion this Article should be regarded as fundamental. We do not suggest that any alteration should be made in the text.

Article 9
The right of free expression of opinion as well as the right to assemble peaceably and without arms, and to form associations or unions is guaranteed for purposes not opposed to public morality. Laws regulating the manner in which the right of forming associations and the right of free assembly may be exercised shall contain no political, religious or class distinction.

Observations of the Committee:
Subject to the observations which follow, we are of opinion that this Article should be regarded as fundamental.
We recommend that it be amended so as to make it clear that laws may be passed, and police action taken, to prevent or control open-air

meetings which might interfere with normal traffic or which otherwise become a nuisance or danger to the general public.

We understand that legislation on these lines has been delayed by reason of doubts as to whether such legislation could be validly enacted in view of the present wording of the Article.

Copies of Articles in other Constitutions which bear on this matter are annexed (See Appendix D).

Article 18
Every member of the Oireachtas shall, except in case of treason, felony or breach of the peace, be privileged from arrest in going to and returning from, and while within the precincts of Dáil Éireann, be amenable to any action or proceeding in any Court other than Dáil Éireann itself.

Observations of the Committee:
In our opinion this Article should be regarded as fundamental. We do not suggest that any alteration should be made in the text.

Article 19
All official reports and publications of the Oireachtas or of Dáil Éireann shall be privileged and utterances made in Dáil Éireann wherever published shall be privileged.

Observations of the Committee:
In our opinion this Article should be regarded as fundamental. We do not suggest that any alteration should be made in the text.

Article 24
The Oireachtas shall hold at least one session each year. The Oireachtas shall be summoned and dissolved by the Representative of the Crown in the name of the King and subject as aforesaid Dáil Éireann shall fix the date of re-assembly of the Oireachtas.

Observations of the Committee:
This Article provides for three distinct matters, viz:

(a) The holding of at least one session of the Oireachtas each year.
(b) The summoning and dissolving of the Oireachtas by the representative of the Crown in the name of the King.
(c) The right of Dáil Éireann subject to (b) to fill the date of re-assembly.

In our opinion, the principles embodied in portions (a) and (c) are fundamental.

Subject to the observations which follow, we recommend that they should be separated from (b) and made the subject of a distinct Article or Articles.

With regard to (a), the obvious intention of this provision, which is contained in the first sentence of the Article, is to ensure that democratic control through Parliament will not be defeated by unduly prolonged non-assembly of that body, but as no specific machinery is prescribed and no individual or institution is charged with the responsibility of putting it into effect, the provision might in practice prove to be of little real value.

We realise that the necessity for invoking it is not likely to arise, as long as the present practice continues of requiring the Oireachtas to assemble annually for the purpose of granting the Executive the necessary monies for the carrying on of the administration of the State.

It is not inconceivable, however, that a situation might arise in which the Oireachtas might be induced to forego this practice and to empower an Executive to obtain the necessary moneys without having to resort annually to Parliament.

The apparently strict requirements of Article 36, a copy of which is annexed (see Appendix 4), might in such circumstances prove to be no safeguard.

In other Constitutions (see Appendix E) the desired result is secured by providing:

(i) That Parliament shall meet on a specified date in each year, if not previously convoked, and/or
(ii) That if a certain proportion of the total number of its members so requires, Parliament must be convened within a prescribed time.

We recommend that an effective provision on the lines of (i) be substituted for the first sentence of Article 24.

We suggest also for favourable consideration the insertion of an additional provision on the lines of (ii).

Article 28
At a General Election for Dáil Éireann the polls shall be held on the same day throughout the country, and that day shall be a day not later than thirty days after the date of dissolution. Dáil Éireann shall meet within one month of such day, and shall unless earlier dissolved continue for six years or such shorter period as may be fixed by legislation from the date of its first meeting, and not longer. Dáil Éireann may not at any time be dissolved except on the advice of the Executive Council.

Observations of the Committee:
The provisions of this Article deal with five distinct matters:

(a) The holding of the polls for a general election on the same day throughout the country.
(b) The period after a dissolution within which a general election must be held.
(c) The date of assembly of Dáil Éireann after a general election.
(d) The maximum duration of Dáil Éireann.
(e) A provision that Dáil Éireann may not be dissolved except on the advice of the Executive Council.

We are of opinion that the principles underlying (b) (c) (d) and (e) are fundamental.

The trend of policy, however, indicates that it is not desirable to make permanent the present form of the portion dealing with heading (c) which is based on the procedure laid down in the present form of Article 24 whereby the Oireachtas is summoned and dissolved by the Representative of the Crown in the name of the King.

We suggest that this aspect of the Article should be separated from the other aspects and left open for the present to amendment by ordinary legislation.

With regard to (a) we do not consider this provision to be fundamental.

Article 41
So soon as any Bill shall have been passed by Dáil Éireann, the Executive Council shall present the same to the Representative of the Crown for the signification by him, in the King's name, of the King's assent.

Observations of the Committee:
In our opinion the principle that an Executive should have no power to delay the last formal stage of enactment of Bills which have been duly passed by Parliament through all other legislative stages is fundamental.

The trend of policy, however, indicates that it is not desirable to make permanent the present machinery of assent.

If the two aspects of the Article, viz. the principle which we have referred to, and the machinery which has to be utilised in its application, can be separated, we suggest that they be made the subject of two distinct Articles, that relating to the machinery of assent or promulgation being left open to amendment by ordinary legislation.

Article 43
The Oireachtas shall have no power to declare acts to be infringements of the law which were not so at the date of their commission.

Observations of the Committee:
In our opinion this Article should be regarded as fundamental. We do not suggest that any alteration should be made in the text.

Article 46
The Oireachtas has the exclusive right to regulate the raising and maintaining of such armed forces as are mentioned in the Scheduled Treaty in the territory of the Irish Free State (Saorstát Éireann) and every such force shall be subject to the control of the Oireachtas.

Observations of the Committee:
We are of opinion that the principle underlying this Article is fundamental.

We suggest, however, that:

(a) The reference to the Treaty, and
(b) The limitation to the territory of the Irish Free State should be eliminated.

The suggested amendment in regard to (b) is a corollary to recent constitutional developments whereby the right of Saorstát Éireann to raise and maintain armed forces outside its own territory has been recognised.

Article 49
Save in the case of actual invasion, the Irish Free State (Saorstát Éireann) shall not be committed to active participation in any war without the assent of the Oireachtas.

Observations of the Committee:
We are of opinion that the principle underlying this Article is fundamental.

We suggest, however, that the Article should be re-drafted in the light of the following considerations:

(i) The restriction imposed by the word 'active' in reference to participation of the Saorstát in war should be removed.

This word was not in the draft of the Treaty submitted by the Provisional Government to the British Government in 1922. It was inserted at the instance of the latter Government in conformity with the theory that once the King has declared war, even though in making such declaration he acts on the advice of British Ministers only, the declaration automatically involves the Dominions also in the state of war created.

This theory is contrary to the principle now accepted that the King in respect of matters affecting the Saorstát can act only on the advice of the Executive Council of the Saorstát, and a provision based on this theory should not, therefore, be permitted to remain in the Constitution.

(ii) It is clear that an Executive should have power to take immediate steps to deal with an invasion, but we are of opinion that it should not be possible for an Executive to take advantage of such an occasion to commit the State, without the specific approval of the Oireachtas, to participation in a war which might conceivably involve the country to an extent far beyond that necessary to deal with the invasion.

We think that the principle that the country shall not be committed to participation in any war without the prior assent of the Oireachtas should be absolute, but that subject thereto, powers should be conferred on the Executive to take such measures as are necessary to deal with an invasion.

Copies of Articles from other Constitutions bearing on this matter are attached (See Appendix F).

Article 50
Amendments of this Constitution may be made by the Oireachtas, but no such amendment, passed by Dáil Éireann after the expiration of a period of sixteen years from the date of the coming into operation of this Constitution, shall become law, unless the same shall, after it has been passed by Dáil Éireann, have been submitted to a Referendum of the people, and unless a majority of the voters on the register shall have recorded their votes on such Referendum, and either the votes of a majority of the voters on the register, or two-thirds of the votes recorded, shall have been cast in favour of such amendment. Any such amendment may be made within the said period of sixteen years by way of ordinary legislation.

Observations of the Committee:
The subject matter of this Article, which has a direct bearing on Part II of our terms of reference, will be dealt with in a separate report.

Article 61
All revenue of the Irish Free State (Saorstát Éireann) from whatever source arising, shall, subject to such exception as may be provided by law, form one fund, and shall be appropriated for the purposes of the Irish Free State (Saorstát Éireann) in the manner and subject to the charges and liabilities imposed by law.

Observations of the Committee:
We understand from informal conversations that the Department of Finance regard this Article as fundamental. A formal expression of their views on the financial provisions of the Constitution generally has been promised.

Article 62
Dáil Éireann shall appoint a Comptroller and Auditor-General to act on behalf of the Irish Free State (Saorstát Éireann). He shall control all disbursements and shall audit all accounts of moneys administered by or under the authority of the Oireachtas and shall report to Dáil Éireann at stated periods to be determined by law.

Observations of the Committee:
We are of opinion that this Article should be regarded as fundamental. We do not suggest that any alteration should be made in the text.

Article 63
The Comptroller and Auditor-General shall not be removed except for stated misbehaviour or incapacity on a resolution of Dáil Éireann for the passing of which not less than four-sevenths (exclusive of the Chairman or presiding member) of the full membership of Dáil Éireann shall have voted. Subject to this provision the terms and conditions of his tenure of office shall be fixed by law. He shall not be a member of the Oireachtas nor shall he hold any other office or position of emolument.

Notwithstanding anything contained in any other Article of this Constitution, a bill for legislation to amend this Article in relation to the passing of the said resolution shall not be introduced in Dáil Éireann unless or until the amendment proposed by such Bill has been approved by a resolution of Dáil Éireann for the passing of which not less than four-sevenths (exclusive of the Chairman or presiding member) of the full membership of Dáil Éireann shall have voted.

Observations of the Committee:
In our opinion this Article should be regarded as fundamental. The provision contained in the second paragraph however, will naturally arise

for consideration in connection with Part II of our terms of reference.

Article 64
The judicial power of the Irish Free State (Saorstát Éireann) shall be exercised and justice administered in the public courts established by the Oireachtas, by judges appointed in manner hereinafter provided. These Courts shall comprise Courts of First Instance and a Court of Final Appeal to be called the Supreme Court. The Courts of First Instance shall include a High Court, invested with full original jurisdiction in and power to determine all matters and questions whether of law or fact, civil or criminal, and also Courts of local and limited jurisdiction with a right to appeal as determined by law.

Observations of the Committee:
We are of opinion that this Article should be regarded as fundamental. We suggest, however, that it should be carefully re-drafted so as to meet the present position in which judicial or quasi-judicial functions are necessarily performed by persons who are not judges within the strict terms of the Constitution, e.g. Revenue Commissioners, Land Commissioners, Court Registrars, etc.

Article 65
The judicial power of the High Court shall extend to the question of the validity of any law having regard to the provisions of the Constitution. In all cases in which such matters shall come into question, the High Court alone shall exercise original jurisdiction.

Observations of the Committee:
The principle that some court should have power to decide on the validity of laws having regard to the provisions of the Constitution is in our opinion fundamental.
In the course of our consideration of this Article, the following points were discussed, viz:

I. Whether the power of deciding the validity of laws, having regard to the provisions of the Constitution, should be vested
   (a) In the Supreme Court alone, or
   (b) In a special 'Constitution' Court appointed or designated for that purpose, e.g. a combination of the Supreme and High Courts, or
   (c) in the High Court with a right of appeal to the Supreme Court as at present.

II. Whether a time limit, commencing from the date of enactment in each case should be fixed within which the question of validity of any law could be submitted to or decided on by the Courts.

We have been unable to reach unanimity on either of these questions and, therefore, make no recommendation regarding them. We think it well, however, to place on record that they have arisen.

Article 66
The Supreme Court of the Irish Free State (Saorstát Éireann) shall, with such exceptions (not including cases which involve questions as to validity of any law) and subject to such regulations as may be prescribed by law, have appellate jurisdiction from all decisions of the High Court. The decision of the Supreme Court shall in all cases be final and conclusive, and shall not be reviewed or capable of being reviewed by any other Court, Tribunal or Authority whatsoever and no appeal shall lie from a decision of the Supreme Court or of any other Court in Saorstát Éireann to his Majesty in Council, and it shall not be lawful for any person to petition His Majesty for leave to bring any such appeal.

Observations of the Committee:
We are of opinion that this Article should be regarded as fundamental, subject, however, to the observations which follow.

The reference to Appeals to His Majesty in Council should, if possible, be now repealed.

The purpose for which this portion of the Article was inserted has been effected, and we understand that its repeal if enacted in appropriate terms would not result in the restoration of the position which its enactment brought to an end.

If this amendment is not regarded as feasible, at present, the Article should be left open to change by ordinary legislation.

Article 68
The judges of the Supreme Court and of the High Court and of all other Courts established in pursuance of this Constitution shall be appointed by the representative of the Crown on the advice of the Executive Council. The Judges of the Supreme Court and of the High Court shall not be removed except for stated misbehaviour or incapacity, and then only by a resolution of Dáil Éireann for the passing of which not less than four-sevenths (exclusive of the Chairman or presiding member) of the full membership of Dáil Éireann shall have voted. The age of retirement, the remuneration and the pension of such judges on

retirement and the declarations to be taken by them on appointment be diminished during their continuance in office. The terms of appointment of the judges of such other courts as may be created shall be prescribed by law.

Notwithstanding anything contained in any other Article of this Constitution, a bill for legislation to amend this Article in relation to the passing of the said resolution shall not be introduced in Dáil Éireann unless or until the amendment proposed by such Bill has been approved by a resolution of Dáil Éireann for the passing of which not less than four-sevenths (exclusive of the Chairman or presiding member) of the full membership of Dáil Éireann shall have voted.

Observations of the Committee:
We are of opinion that this Article should in the main be regarded as fundamental.

It deals with two separate matters, viz:

(a) The method of appointment of Judges, and
(b) Their tenure of office and other relevant matters.

The trend of policy makes it clear that it is not desirable to make permanent the present machinery of appointment, and for that reason the Article might be divided into two separate Articles dealing respectively with (a) and (b).

We suggest that the provisions relating to (b) should be amended so as to make it clear that the age of retirement of all Judges, whether of the Supreme, High, Circuit or District Courts, their remuneration, their pension on retirement and the declarations to be made by them on appointment, shall be prescribed by law. The present wording is ambiguous.

Having regard to the possibility of wide variations in the purchasing power of money over long periods, and the undesirability of the Oireachtas being debarred from adjusting, within reasonable limits, the salaries of any class of State functionary, we further suggest that powers be taken in the Article to regulate the salaries of Judges by law, safeguards being provided to prevent the possibility of individuals or particular classes of Judges being victimised or subjected to undue influence by this means.

The provision contained in the second paragraph of the Article will naturally arise for consideration in connection with part II of our terms of reference.

Article 69
All judges shall be independent in the exercise of their functions, and subject only to the Constitution and the law. A judge shall not be eligible to sit in the Oireachtas, and shall not hold any other office or position of emolument.

Observations of the Committee:
We are of opinion that this Article should be regarded as fundamental. We do not suggest that any alteration should be made in the text.

Article 70
No one shall be tried save in due course of law and extraordinary courts shall not be established, save only such Military Tribunals as may be authorised by law for dealing with military offenders against military law. The jurisdiction of Military Tribunals shall not be extended to or exercised over the civil population save in time of war or armed rebellion, and for acts committed in time of war or armed rebellion, and in accordance with the regulations to be prescribed by law. Such jurisdiction shall not be exercised in any area in which all civil courts are open or capable of being held, and no person shall be removed from one area to another, for the purpose of creating such jurisdiction.

Observations of the Committee:
We are of opinion that this Article should be regarded as fundamental. Subject to the appended note we do not suggest that any alteration should be made in the text.

Note: The suggestions submitted by us under the heading 'Emergency Provisions'—see paragraphs 7, 8, 9 and 10 of the Report in conjunction with Appendix B—might, if adopted, necessitate a revision of the text of Article 70, but this question would naturally receive attention in connection with the drafting of the new provisions.

Appendix B

Emergency Provisions: For explanation see paragraphs 7, 8, 9 and 10 of the Report.

Suggestions of the Committee:

1. What may be regarded as the first serious phase in the development of a grave state of disorder throughout the country is the failure of the ordinary Courts, either through intimidation of jurors and/or witnesses, or lack of civic spirit on the part of either or both, to secure the conviction of offenders, particularly in the case of offences of a semi-political nature.
2. The resultant immunity of offenders from punishment leads inevitably to the spread of offences of this character, resulting sometimes in a serious situation with which the ordinary processes of law are unable to cope.
3. We are of opinion that the development of a situation of this nature could in most cases be arrested by the application of suitable measures in the early stages, and we think that, to this end, the Constitution should contain a permanent provision to supplement the operation of the ordinary Courts.
4. Our suggestion, which for convenient reference we call Scheme A is as follows:
   Scheme A
   (a) Power should be provided in the Constitution for the enactment of legislation to provide, as part of the permanent judicial machinery of the State, for the trial by special Courts of persons accused of crime, in respect of whom the appropriate ordinary Judge or Justice certifies, at any stage of the proceedings, either on his own initiative, or on the application of the Attorney General, that it is desirable, in the interests of justice, that the trial should be removed to a special court set up under this scheme.
   (b) The exact constitution and powers of these special courts would remain to be settled by legislation, but what we have in contemplation is something in the nature of the Constitution (Special Powers) Tribunal, with such changes as experience has shown to be desirable.
5. In addition to the Scheme A outlined above, which may be regarded as a preventive measure, aimed at stopping, where

possible, the development of a state of public emergency, we consider it essential that the State should be in a position to deal effectively with such an emergency in the event of its occurring, and for that purpose, we suggest Scheme B which is outlined hereunder:

Scheme B

(a) In substitution for the present Article 2A, a new Article should be inserted in the Constitution which would authorise the Oireachtas to provide by ordinary legislation such powers as the Oireachtas might consider necessary, (including power to suspend temporarily any Article of the Constitution), to meet the requirements of any period during which the ordinary laws are not adequate for the preservation of public order, such legislation to come into effect at the times and in the manner set out hereunder.

(b) The Article should provide that nothing in the Constitution or in any Act should be capable of being invoked or cited as invalidating anything in the Article or in any legislation enacted or any other action taken under it.

(c) All such legislation should, by way of title or preamble state expressly that its object is to carry out the provisions of the said Article.

(d) The Article should provide that, if and whenever the Executive Council is of opinion that it is desirable so to do, they may request the President, or the senior available Judge, of the High Court (hereinafter called the summoning officer) to summon all Judges or Justices of the Supreme or High Court nor any person acting only as a temporary Judge or Justice, to meet at a stated place and time, (not being sooner than three days or later than seven days after the issue of such summons) for the purposes of advising the Executive Council as to whether the state of the country is such that the ordinary laws are not adequate for the preservation of public order.

(e) The said Judges shall meet accordingly under the Chairmanship of the summoning officer, and shall, after such discussion as they shall think fit, decide, by way of majority vote, on a secret ballot, on the question referred to them by the Executive Council, and the summoning officer shall report to the Executive Council in writing (attested by the signatures of all present at the meeting) as to the result of the vote, without specifying the names or numbers of persons voting for or against.

(f) To provide against wilful abstention from the meeting of judges and justices, severe penalties, amounting if necessary to automatic removal from office, should be provided. In case of unavoidable absence, a certificate from the summoning officer setting out the reasons for such absence would be essential.

(g) If and whenever the Executive Council receives from the summoning officer a report in the affirmative, they may by Order declare that the provisions of all such legislation as is mentioned in paragraph (a) above shall come into operation on a day which shall be appointed in such Order and the said provisions shall come into operation on such day.

(h) The Order of the Executive Council should, inter alia

- (1) Cite that the report referred to in the preceding paragraph has been duly received.
- (2) Be so worded and operate as to summon the Dáil forthwith if not already in session.
- (3) Be published in *Iris Oifigiúil* not later than the day preceding the appointed day.
- (4) Be laid before the Dáil forthwith, and unless and until a resolution annulling such Order is passed by the Dáil within the next subsequent twenty-one days on which the Dáil has sat after such Order is laid before it, such Order shall have full force and effect, but no such resolution shall operate to prejudice the validity of anything previously done under such Order.

(i) The effect of the Order and the operation of all legislation brought into effect under it shall cease, without prejudice to anything done under it:

- (a) Six months after the appointed day, or
- (b) On an earlier date named in an ad hoc Order, by the Executive Council, or
- (c) On an earlier date named in an express resolution passed by Dáil Éireann for that purpose.

(j) If the Executive Council consider it is desirable that the period of six months should be extended, they may at any time, either during the operation of the Order, or after its termination, take steps as provided in paragraph (d) *et. seq.* above with a view to the making of a new Order to bring the scheme into operation for a further period.

6. With regard to the meeting of Judges and Justices provided for in paragraph (d) of Scheme B above, our proposal to exclude the High Court and Supreme Court Judges is deliberate, on the grounds:
   (a) That their jurisdiction is in practice almost exclusively civil, that they function in Dublin only, and that they are accordingly not in the same position as District Justices and Circuit Court Judges to assess the general condition of the country from the point of view of maintenance of law and order;
   (b) That these Judges may have to decide Constitutional questions arising out of the operation of the Article.

Appendix C

Articles 4, 10 and 72: For explanation see paragraph 11 of the Report.

Article 4
The National language of the Irish Free State (Saorstát Éireann) is the Irish language, but the English language shall be equally recognised as an official language. Nothing in this Article shall prevent special provisions being made by the Parliament of the Irish Free State (otherwise called and herein generally referred to as the 'Oireachtas') for districts or areas in which only one language is in general use.

Observations of the Committee:
While in our opinion this Article is not fundamental in the sense that it safeguards democratic rights, we recognise that from the National point of view it is important because of the status which it gives to the Irish language.

We realise, however, that in course of time it may be found desirable to modify the recognition which it accords to English as an equally official language throughout the State, and for that reason we are of opinion that the Article should be left open to change by ordinary legislation.

Article 10
All citizens of the Irish Free State (Saorstát Éireann) have the right to free elementary education.

Observations of the Committee:
The views of the Department of Education on this Article were sought and were duly furnished in a letter from the Secretary dated 2 July, 1934.

A relevant extract is quoted in Appendix G (4) annexed.

Having regard to these views we recommend that Article 10 be not included in the category of fundamental Articles.

Article 72
No person shall be tried on any criminal charge without a jury save in the case of charges in respect of minor offences triable by law before a Court of Summary Jurisdiction and in the case of charges for offences against military law triable by Court Martial or other Military Tribunal.

Observations of the Committee:
We have decided not to recommend this Article for inclusion in the category of fundamental Articles.

The relations between the Executive, the judiciary, and the ordinary citizen, are very different in a modern democratic State, such as ours, from those which prevailed in England at the time when the establishment of the right to trial by jury was regarded as a matter of the first importance.

Both in England and in America the jury system has been subjected in recent years to considerable criticism and in our State it cannot even claim to be a spontaneous national growth.

With an Executive dependent on, and responsible to, a Parliament elected on full adult suffrage, and with Judges whose independence is guaranteed by the Constitution, which also forbids the setting up of 'extraordinary Courts', the right to trial by jury has lost its original importance.

This change in conditions is reflected in the modern tendency to give more and more criminal jurisdiction to magistrates, sitting without a jury.

We are inclined to think that the question of how far this tendency should be allowed to develop in this State is one which might safely be left to the discretion of the Oireachtas, and we observe, in this connection that the Article in question was not included by the leaders of the Opposition in the list of fundamental articles referred to in paragraph 12 of our report.

It may be useful to observe that if we had decided to include the Article in our list we would have recommended amendments designed to make it clear:

(a) That the Article does not bind us to the present English system of requiring a jury of twelve and an unanimous verdict, and
(b) That when the Oireachtas has designated any particular offence as a 'minor' offence, fit to be tried summarily, it shall not be open to a defendant to raise the point that the offence is so serious that it cannot reasonably be called a 'minor' offence and that the law declaring it to be triable summarily is therefore *ultra vires* Article 72 and invalid.

Appendix D

Right of Assembly: For explanation see the Committee's observations under Article 9 in Appendix A to the Report.

Copies of provisions in the Constitution of:

1. Belgium	Article 19
2. Czechoslovakia	Article 113
3. Denmark	Article 86
4. Estonia	Article 18
5. Germany (Constitution of 1919)	Article 123
6. Jugo Slavia	Article 14
7. Spain	Article 38

1. Constitution of Belgium (15 October 1921) Article 19
   Belgians have the right, without previous authorisation, to assemble peaceably and without arms, conforming themselves to the laws which regulate the exercise of this right. This provision does not apply to assemblies in the open air, which remain entirely under police laws.
2. Constitution of Czechoslovakia (29 February 1920)
   Article 113
   1. The freedom of the Press and the right to meet peaceably and without arms and to form associations shall be guaranteed. It is therefore in principle forbidden to subject the Press to any preliminary censorship. The exercise of the

rights of meeting and forming associations shall be regulated by law.

2. An association may not be dissolved unless it acts in violation of the criminal law or contrary to public peace and order.
3. Restrictions may be imposed by law, particularly as regards meetings in public places, the formation of associations for purposes of profit, and the participation of foreigners in political associations. The law may likewise determine what restrictions may be placed on the application of the principles of the preceding sections in case of war or of outbreak of internal troubles seriously threatening the republican form of the State, the Constitution of public peace and order.

3. Constitution of Denmark (10 September 1920)
   Article 86
   Citizens have the right of meeting unarmed. Police may be present at public meetings. Meetings in the open air may be forbidden when they become a danger to the public peace.
4. Constitution of Estonia (15 June 1920)
   Article 18
   All persons are free to assemble peaceably and unarmed.
   All citizens have the right to form associations.
   The right to strike is assured.
   These rights may be limited only by law and solely in the interests of public safety.
5. Constitution of Germany (11 August 1919)[68*]
   Article 123
   All Germans have the right without notification or special permission to assemble peaceably and unarmed.
   Open-air meetings may be made notifiable by a law of the Reich, and in case of direct danger to public security may be forbidden.
6. Constitution of Jugo Slavia (28 June 1921)
   Article 14
   Citizens shall have the right to form associations, to assemble meetings, and to take collective action. Detailed provisions as to these matters shall be prescribed by law. Citizens may not attend meetings armed. Meetings in the open air must be

[68] Annotated by McDunphy: 'Suspended 1932 by Hitler Constitution'.

notified to the competent authority at least twenty-four hours in advance. Citizens shall have the right of forming associations for purposes not contrary to law.

7. Constitution of Spain (1931)
   Article 38
   The right to assemble peaceably and without arms is recognised. The right of assembly in the open air and of public demonstrations shall be regulated by a special law.

Appendix E

Annual Assembly of Parliament: For explanation see the Committee's observations under Article 24 in Appendix A to the Report.

Copies of Articles from the Constitutions of:

1. Czechoslovakia	Article 28
2. Denmark	Article 40
3. Estonia	Article 41
4. Germany (Constitution of 1919)	Article 24
5. Jugo Slavia	Article 75
6. Mexico	Article 65
7. Poland	Article 25

1. Constitution of Czechoslovakia (29 February 1920)
   Article 28
   1. The President of the Republic shall summon both Chambers for two ordinary sessions each year—the Spring and the Autumn session, the former to begin in March, the latter in October.
   2. Furthermore, he may summon the National Assembly for extraordinary sessions whenever he may deem it necessary. If an absolute majority of the members of either Chamber makes application to the President of the Council of Ministers, stating the subject to be discussed, the President of the Republic shall summon the Assembly within a fortnight from the date of such application; should he fail to do so, the Chairman of both Chambers shall convoke the Assembly within the following fortnight.
   3. If not less than four months have elapsed since the last ordinary session, the President of the Republic shall, upon

demand being made by not less than two-fifths of the members of either Chamber, summon the National Assembly to meet within a fortnight from the date of the demand. Should he fail to do so, the Chairman of both Chambers shall convoke the Assembly within the following fortnight.

2. Constitution of Denmark (5 June 1915)
   Article 40
   The Rigsdag meets in ordinary session on the first Tuesday of October if the King has not previously convoked it.
3. Constitution of Estonia (15 June 1930)
   Article 41
   The ordinary sessions of the State Assembly commence each year on the first Monday in October.
4. Constitution of Germany (11 August 1919)
   Article 24
   The Reichstag assembles annually on the first Wednesday in November at the seat of the Government of the Reich. The President of the Reichstag must summon it earlier if requested by the President of the Reich or by at least one-third of the members. The Reichstag determines the conclusion of the session and the day of re-assembly.
5. Constitution of Jugo Slavia (28 June 1921)
   Article 75
   The National Assembly shall meet in the capital, Beograd (Belgrade), in regular session on 20th October in each year, unless earlier summoned in extraordinary session by decree by the King. The regular session may not terminate until the State Budget has been voted. In time of war, the National Assembly shall sit continuously save as it may itself otherwise decide.
6. Constitution of Mexico (31 January 1917)
   Article 65
   The Congress shall meet on the first day of September of each year in regular session for the consideration of the following matters:
   I. To audit the accounts of the previous year, which shall be submitted to the House of Representatives not later than ten days after the opening of the session. The audit shall not be confined to determining whether the expenditures do or do not conform with the respective items in the

Budget, but shall comprise an examination of the exactness of, and authorisation for, payment made thereunder, and of any liability arising from such payments.

No other secret item shall be permitted than those which the Budget for that year may consider necessary as such; these amounts shall be paid out by the Secretaries of Executive Departments under written orders of the President.

II. To examine, discuss and approve the Budget for the next fiscal year, and to levy such taxes as may be needed to meet the expenditure.

III. To study, discuss, and vote on all Bills presented and to discuss all other matters incumbent upon the Congress by virtue of this Constitution.

7. Constitution of Poland (17 March 1921)

Article 25

The President of the Republic convenes, opens, adjourns and dissolves the Diet and the Senate.

The Diet must be convened for its first session on the third Tuesday following the date of the elections, and in every year in October at latest in order to pass the Budget, determine the strength and recruitment of the Army, and to deal with current business.

The President of the Republic may, if he thinks necessary, convene an extraordinary session of the Diet at any time, and is bound to do so within two weeks if one-third of the total number of Deputies so require.

Other extraordinary sessions of the Diet are held as provided by the Constitution.

The Diet can be adjourned only with its own prior consent if it is the second adjustment in the same ordinary session or if the adjournment is for a period exceeding thirty days.

The ordinary session of the Diet in the month of October may not be terminated until the Budget has been passed.

Appendix F

Declaration of War: For explanation see the Committee's observations under Article 49 in Appendix A to the Report.

Copy of provisions in the Constitution of:

1. Czechoslovakia	Article 33
	Article 64.1 (3)
2. Denmark	Article 18
3. Estonia	Article 60 (4)
	Article 82
4. France	Article 9
5. Jugo Slavia	Article 51
6. Mexico	Article 89 (VIII)
7. Poland	Article 50
8. Spain	Article 77
9. Sweden	Article 13
10. Switzerland	Article 8
11. U.S.A.	Article 8

1. Czechoslovakia (29 February 1920)

Article 33

The decision as to a declaration of war...shall require a three-fifths majority of all the members in each Chamber.

Article 64.1(3)

The functions of the President shall be as follows:

He shall proclaim the existence of a state of war, declare war with the prior consent of the National Assembly, and shall present Treaties of Peace to the Assembly for its approval.

2. Denmark (5 June 1915)

Article 18

The King cannot without the consent of the Rigsdag declare war, conclude peace, make or dissolve alliances or commercial treaties, cede any of the national territory, nor contract any obligation which varies the existing conditions of public law.

3. Estonia (15 June 1920)

Article 60 (4)

The Government declares war and concludes peace in accordance with the decisions of the State Assembly.[69]

[69] Though Article 82 of the Estonian Constitution is listed on the contents page of Appendix F, it is not included in the appendix itself.

4. France (1875–1919)
   Article 9
   The President of the Republic shall not declare war without the previous consent of the two Chambers.
5. Jugo Slavia (28 June 1921)
   Article 51
   The King shall represent the State in all its relations with foreign States. He shall declare war and conclude peace. If the country has not been attacked or if war has not been declared against the country by another State, the prior consent of the National Assembly is necessary for war to be declared.
   If war is declared on the country, or if the country is attacked, the National Assembly must be immediately summoned.
6. Mexico (31 January 1917)
   Article 89 (VIII)
   The President shall have the following powers and duties:
   To declare war in the name of the United States of Mexico, after the passage of the corresponding resolution by the Congress of the Union.
7. Poland (17 March 1921)
   Article 50
   The President of the Republic cannot declare war or conclude peace without the prior consent of the Diet.
8. Spain (1930)
   Article 77
   The President of the Republic may not declare war except after having been so authorised in each case by a special law.
9. Sweden (6 June 1809)
   Article 13
   If the King wishes to declare war or to conclude peace he shall convene all the members of the Council of State into extraordinary council, shall lay before them the causes and circumstances to be considered, and shall require their opinions concerning the matter; each of them shall separately enter his opinion in the minutes, under the responsibility referred to in Article 107. The King may then make and execute such a decision as he considers in the best interests of the country.

10. Switzerland (29 May 1874)
    Article 8
    The Confederation has the sole right to declare war and conclude peace, and to make alliances and treaties, particularly customs and commercial treaties, with foreign States.
11. United States of America (1787)
    Article 8
    The Congress shall have power:
    ...
    (II) To declare war...

Appendix G

Extract from letter from the Department of Education dated 2 July, 1934 on the right of Free Elementary Education, guaranteed in Article 10 of the Constitution.

For explanation see the Committee's observations under Article 10 in Appendix C[70] to the Report.

[See Document no. 23, from paragraph two onwards.]

Appendix H

Copy of Article 36: For explanation see Committee's observations under Article 24, Appendix A.

Article 36
Dáil Éireann shall as soon as possible after the commencement of each financial year consider the Estimates of receipts and expenditure of the Irish Free State (Saorstát Éireann) for that year, and, save in so far as may be provided by specific enactment in each case, the legislation required to give effect to the Financial Resolutions of each year shall be enacted within that year

[70] Incorrectly referenced in the original as Appendix B.

Dréaċt-Ḃunreaċt

(Draft Constitution)

Mar do haontuíodh ag Dáil Eireann.

As approved by Dáil Eireann.

To Mr. John Hearne, Barrister at Law
Legal adviser to the Department of
External affairs architect in chief
and Draftsman of this Constitution,
as a Souvenir of the successful
issue of his work and in testimony
of the fundamental part he took
in framing this the first Free
Constitution of the Irish People

Éamon de Valéra

Constitution Day. 29.XII.37.

Inset: Eamon de Valera's dedication of a copy of the Draft Constitution to John Hearne. He calls Hearne 'Architect in chief and Draftsman of this Constitution'. Ms. 23,508. Courtesy of the National Library of Ireland.

John J. Hearne, Legal Adviser to the Department of Foreign Affairs (1929–39). Private collection, reproduced with permission.

Right: Arthur Matheson, the first parliamentary draftsman of the Irish Free State. Courtesy of the Attorney General's Office.

Below: Hugh Kennedy, a member of the drafting committee of the Irish Free State Constitution (1922) and Chief Justice (1924-36). UCDA P4/Kennedy.

An early photograph of Gavan Duffy, centre with beard, who was Justice of the High Court when the 1937 Constitution was being drafted. NLI Hog3. Courtesy of the National Library of Ireland.

Portrait of the First Council of State presided over by Douglas Hyde in 1940. By Simon Coleman, RHA. Courtesy of Áras an Uachtaráin. © Coleman Estate.

Eamon de Valera with
Conor Maguire, president
of the High Court,
UCDA P150/2181.

Dr John Charles McQuaid, Papal Nuncio Paschal Robinson & Taoiseach Eamon de Valera in the grounds of Blackrock College. See Chapter VI for an account of the discussions with the churches. UCDA P150/2224.

Fr Edward Cahill, a personal friend of de Valera's, who was the driving force of the Jesuit Constitution Committee. Courtesy of the Jesuit Archives.

The Senate Cask was presented to the first Seanad by Alice Stopford Green and came into the Royal Irish Academy's safekeeping when the Seanad was disbanded in 1936. Courtesy of the Royal Irish Academy Library.

CHAPTER III

THE STATE (RYAN) V. LENNON AND APPEALS TO THE PRIVY COUNCIL, 1934–5

It may fairly be said that the decision of the Supreme Court in *The State (Ryan) v. Lennon*[1] ultimately led to the entire downfall of the Irish Free State Constitution and paved the way for the enactment of the present Constitution. The decision raised a host of novel and difficult issues, including the validity of two separate constitutional amendments, whether any provisions of the Constitution of the Irish Free State had been placed beyond the amending power of the Oireachtas, the role of natural law and the response of the courts to extreme legal measures, and the nature of the sovereignty of the Irish Free State.

To understand the complex constitutional background to this case, it is important to recall that Article 70 of the 1922 Constitution had originally provided in relevant part that: '...extraordinary tribunals shall not be established, save only such Military Tribunals as may be authorised by law for dealing with military offences against military law.' Against the backdrop of the Civil War of 1922–3 and the continued disturbed conditions which prevailed thereafter, this guarantee was not, unfortunately, a very realistic one.[2] Throughout the 1920s the Oireachtas found itself forced to pass a variety of public safety legislation providing either for a power of internment or, alternatively, for trial by standing military tribunal. Despite the fact that such swingeing legislation

[1] See document nos 32–4; [1935] IR 170. For contemporary comment, see Owen Hood Philips, 'Ryan's Case', in *LQR*, 52 (1936), 241; W.I. Jennings, 'The Statute of Westminster and Appeals to the Privy Council', in *LQR*, 52 (1936), 173; Anon., 'The Amendment of the Saorstát Constitution', in *ILTSJ* 69 (1935), 55.

[2] As Justice Dodd put it—speaking of the enactment of the Constitution in 1922—what 'was supposed to herald an era of settled government turned out to be the harbinger of unrest and rebellion': *R. (O'Connell) v. Military Governor of Hare Park,* [1924] 2 IR 104, 115.

generally rested uneasily with the solemn guarantees (ranging from Article 6 (personal liberty) to Article 70 contained in that Constitution, the constitutionality of such legislation was upheld in a series of cases, chiefly on the ground that during the initial eight-year period following the entry into force of the Constitution, any legislation enacted by the Oireachtas which was found in conflict with the Constitution had the effect, *ipso facto*, of amending that Constitution, whether on a permanent[3] or temporary basis.[4] As has been noted already, these developments came about as a result of a last-minute alteration to the text of Article 50 which allowed of amendments by ordinary legislation during an initial eight-year period from the date the Constitution came into force, i.e., until 6 December 1930.[5]

The State (Ryan) v. Lennon

The validity of both the Constitution (Amendment No. 16) Act, 1929 and Constitution (Amendment No. 17) Act, 1931 were the key issues in *The State (Ryan) v. Lennon*. In this case the four applicants had been arrested on 22 April 1934 and were charged with the attempted murder of a rate collector and other serious public order offences.[6] They were detained in custody pending their trial before the Constitutional (Special Powers) Tribunal.

In the High Court it was conceded on behalf of the Attorney General that the Constitution (Amendment No. 17) Act, 1931 was inconsistent with the Constitution as originally enacted.[7] It followed that if this Act was valid, it could only be so as an amendment to the Constitution which was authorised by Article 50. As this question in turn depended on whether Article 50 itself had been validly amended by Constitution (Amendment No. 16) Act, 1929, the Divisional High Court then went to consider whether this amendment was itself valid. Again, the manner in which Justices Sullivan (President of the Court), Meredith and O'Byrne rejected the arguments that the power to amend in Article 50 should be confined in some way or that Article 50 should itself fall outside the amendment power was quite striking.[8]

[3] *R. (Cooney) v. Clinton*, [1935] IR 245 (decided in 1924, but belatedly reported).
[4] *Attorney General v. M'Bride*, [1928] IR 451.
[5] This consisted of an addition of the following words at the end of Article 50: 'Any such amendment may be made within the said period of eight years by way of ordinary legislation'. See Chapter I of this volume.
[6] *Irish Times*, 24 April 1934. See Davis, *History and Development of the Special Criminal Court*, 42–55.
[7] See the comments of Justice Sullivan, [1935] IR 170, 175–6. In the Supreme Court Justice Fitzgibbon made comments to similar effect: 220.
[8] [1935] IR 177–8 (Sullivan, President of the Court); 179 (Justice Meredith); 181 (Justice O'Byrne). Meredith subsequently admitted that even 'inviolable provisions' of the Constitution—such as the position of the judiciary—could be amended in this way, but such was 'the devastating effect of Article 50'.

From this judgment the applicants appealed to the Supreme Court which dismissed the appeals by a majority.[9] These judgments are, however, notable for the range of issues which they traverse. The first key issue facing the Court on appeal was whether the Oireachtas had an unlimited power of amendment of the Constitution during the transitory period of eight years. The Court was divided on this question and it may be convenient to turn first to the reasoning of the majority judges, Fitzgibbon and Murnaghan.

Justice Fitzgibbon first rejected the argument that the power to amend the Constitution should be confined to circumstances where the amendment effected an 'improvement' of the Constitution. He then considered the wider question of whether the power to amend the Constitution included the power to amend Article 50 itself. While he observed that 'however undesirable it may appear to some' that the Oireachtas should have the power to extend the period during which the Constitution might be amended by ordinary legislation, nevertheless 'if this be the true construction of Article 50, this Court is bound to give effect to that construction'.[10] He continued by noting that whereas both the Constituent Act and Article 50 contained restrictions on the power of amendment—they both precluded amendments which were in conflict with the terms of the Treaty—the *expressio unius* principle came into play, suggesting that no further restrictions on the power to amend were thereby intended.

Fitzgibbon then emphasised the fact that it was Dáil Éireann sitting as a Constituent Assembly which had created the Oireachtas and which had limited its powers in particular ways.[11] He concluded by noting that other Constitutions often contained express restrictions upon the power of the legislature to amend the amendment power itself,[12] so that it followed that:

[9] One measure of the importance of the case is that the applicants were represented by no less than seven counsel, while the respondents (led in person by Attorney General Conor Maguire) had six counsel. The legal teams thus included a future Chief Justice (Conor Maguire), a President of the High Court (George Gavan Duffy), four future ordinary Supreme Court judges (Lavery, Martin Maguire, Geoghegan and Haugh); two future High Court judges (Overend and Casey), as well as a former Attorney General (John A. Costello) who would later become Taoiseach in the 1948–51 and 1954–7 Inter-Party Governments.

[10] For all quotations from Fitzgibbon's judgment, see document no. 33. See also [1935] IR 170, 220–37.

[11] Fitzgibbon added that an amendment of Article 50 by the deletion of the words 'within the terms of the Scheduled Treaty' would be 'totally ineffective', as effect was given to those words by the Constituent Act itself, 'which the Oireachtas has no power to amend'.

[12] He instanced section 152 of the South Africa Act, 1909 which provided that no 'repeal or alteration of the provisions contained in this section…shall, be valid' unless the Bill embodying such an amendment to the amending power itself shall have been passed in a particular way or by a specified majority. Article V of the US Constitution also contained certain restrictions on the power of amendment of certain clauses of Article I prior to 1808.

> Our Constituent Assembly could in like manner have exempted Article 50 from the amending powers conferred upon the Oireachtas, but it did not do so, and, in my opinion, the Court has no jurisdiction to read either into the Constituent Act or into Article 50 a proviso excepting it, and it alone, from these powers.[13]

From these judgments, the Chief Justice delivered a remarkable and vigorous dissent. Chief Justice Kennedy's dissent on this point contains echoes of his later natural law argument:

> The Third Dáil Éireann has, therefore, as a Constituent Assembly, of its own supreme authority, proclaimed its acceptance of and declared, in relation to the Constitution which it enacted, certain principles, and in language which shows that beyond doubt that they are stated as governing principles which are fundamental and absolute (except as expressly qualified) and, so, necessarily immutable. Can the power of amendment given to the Oireachtas be lawfully exercised in such a manner as to violate these principles which, as principles, the Oireachtas has no power to change? In my opinion there can be only one answer to that question, namely, that the Constituent Assembly cannot be supposed to have in the same breath declared certain principles to be fundamental and immutable, or conveyed that sense in other words, as by a declaration of inviolability, and at the same time to have conferred upon the Oireachtas power to violate them or to alter them. In my opinion, any amendment of the Constitution, purporting to be made under the power given by the Constituent Assembly, which would be a violation of, or be inconsistent with, any fundamental principle so declared, is necessarily outside the scope of the power and invalid and void.[14]

Colonel Ryan was ultimately convicted by the Tribunal and sentenced to nine months' imprisonment for the attack on the home of the rate collector.[15]

[13] As we have already seen, Justice Murnaghan spoke in similar terms: [1935] IR 170, 224.
[14] [1935] IR 209.
[15] *Irish Press*, 8 February 1935.

Chief Justice Kennedy and natural law principles

Ryan's case is also justly famous for the fact that the Chief Justice Kennedy was willing to invalidate a constitutional amendment by reference to natural law or higher law principles. Kennedy stressed that the Constitution was subject to the certain immutable limitations:

> The Constituent Assembly declared in the forefront of the Constitution Act (an Act which it is not within the power of the Oireachtas to alter, or amend or repeal) that all lawful authority comes from God to the people, and that it is declared by Article 2 of the Constitution that 'all powers of government and all authority, legislative, executive, and judicial, in Ireland are derived from the people of Ireland…' It follows that every act, whether legislative, executive or judicial, in order to be lawful under the Constitution, must be capable of being justified under the authority thereby declared to be derived from God. From this it seems clear that, if any legislation of the Oireachtas (including any purported amendment of the Constitution) were to offend against that acknowledged ultimate Source from which the legislative authority has come through the people to the Oireachtas, as, for instance, if it were repugnant to the Natural Law, such legislation would be necessarily unconstitutional and invalid, and it would be, therefore, absolutely null and void and inoperative. I find it very difficult to reconcile with the Natural Law actions and conduct which would appear to be within the legalising intendment of the provisions of the new Article 2A relating to interrogation. I find it impossible to reconcile as compatible with the Natural Law the vesting, in three military servants of the Executive, power to impose as punishment for any offence within the indefinite, but certainly extensive, ambit of the Appendix, the penalty of death, whenever these three persons are of opinion that it is *expedient.* Finally, the judicial power has been acknowledged and declared (and the acknowledgment and declaration remain) to have come from God through the people to its appointed depositary, the judiciary and the Courts of the State. While they can fulfil that trust, dare any one say that the Natural Law permits

> it, or any part of it, to be transferred to the Executive or their military or other servants?[16]

The two majority judges responded to this issue in slightly different ways. It brought forth in Justice Fitzgibbon a withering, contemptuous response, full of savage and biting irony. He noted first that the appellants had argued that there are:

> certain rights, inherent in every individual, which are so sacred that no legislature has authority to deprive him of them. It is useless to speculate upon the origin of a doctrine which may be founded in the writings of Rousseau, Thomas Paine, William Godwin and other philosophical writers, but we have not to decide between their theories and those of de Lolme and Burke, not to mention Bentham and Locke, upon what Leslie Stephen described as a 'problem which has not yet been solved, nor are even the appropriate methods definitely agreed upon', as we are concerned, not with the principles which might or ought to have been adopted by the framers of our Constitution, but with the powers which have actually been entrusted by it to the Legislature and Executive which it set up.

He then went on to reject the argument that the Constitution, like its American counterpart on which it was to some degree modelled, had attempted to enshrine fundamental principles, since the American experience had been founded upon historical considerations which did not obtain in the case of the Irish Free State:

> I can find no justification for the inference which the counsel for the appellants ask us to draw from the provisions of the American Declaration of Independence and the Constitution founded thereon, or from the fact that some of these provisions have been embodied in other Constitutions, including our own, that the rights thereby secured are universal and inalienable rights of all citizens in all countries or even in the Saorstát which, we have been assured, was, or is, or ought to be Gaelic and Catholic, attributes to either of which few other States can claim a title, while there is no other which can even suggest a claim to both.
>
> There is no ground for surprise, therefore, that this State should, as the Chief Justice has said, 'point new ways' in its 'pioneer Constitution draftsmanship', or that it

[16] [1935] IR 170, 204–5.

> should prefer to secure liberty and justice to its citizens by the simple processes of Amendment No. 17 in preference to the complicated British and American machinery of an independent judiciary, trial by jury and *habeas corpus*.
>
> I cannot presume, either, that rights and privileges which the inhabitants of England have always enjoyed, either by virtue of their common law…or under the provisions of special statutes, are also indigenous to the citizens of this Gaelic and Catholic State, in the sense in which the American colonists claimed them as their birthright by virtue of *their* status as British subjects—a status which I understand to be repudiated by *our* legislators—or that our national conceptions of liberty and justice must necessarily coincide with those of citizens of any other State.

Fitzgibbon continued by harking back to the all-embracing power of amendment in Article 50:

> Unless, therefore, these rights appear plainly from the express provisions of our Constitution to be inalienable, and incapable of being modified or taken away by legislative act, I cannot accede to the argument that the Oireachtas cannot alter, modify or repeal them. The framers of our Constitution may have intended 'to bind man down from mischief by the chains of the Constitution', but if they did, they defeated their object by handing him the key of the padlock in Article 50.[17]

But this remarkable judgment had yet to reach its apotheosis. Fitzgibbon next surveyed the Constitutions as diverse as those of Poland and Mexico, demonstrating the extraordinary lengths to which such provisions protected fundamental liberty and then continued:

> But the fact that the Constitutions of other countries prohibit such invasions of the rights of liberty and property, and such extraordinary innovations in the methods of administering justice in criminal cases as have been introduced into our Constitution by Amendment No. 17, affords no ground for condemning as unconstitutional in

[17] As Hood Phillips remarked, this case confirmed that there are no 'fundamental laws or "natural rights" in the Constitution of the Irish Free State, whatever continental observers who read that document may have thought' ('Ryan's Case', 242–3). The reference to 'continental observers' is to Kohn's *Constitution of the I.F.S.* Kohn had, of course, been heavily influenced by the thinking of Kennedy. The two had become friendly and the Chief Justice had written the foreword to Kohn's masterly work: see Geoffrey Hand, 'A reconsideration of a German study (1927–32) of the Irish Constitution', in Roland Bieber and Dietmar Nickel (eds), *Das Europa der zweiten Generation: Gedächtnisschrift für Christoph Sasse* (2 vols, Baden-Baden, 1981).

this country, or as contrary to any inalienable rights of an Irish citizen, an enactment which appears to have received the almost unanimous support of the Oireachtas, for we have been told that those of our legislators by whom it was opposed most vehemently as unconstitutional and oppressive, when it was first introduced, have since completely changed their opinions, and now accord it their unqualified approval.[18] It is true that even a unanimous vote of the Legislature does not decide the validity of a law, but it is some evidence that none of those whose duty it is to make the laws see anything in it which they regard as exceptionally iniquitous, or as derogating from the standard of civilisation which they deem adequate for Saorstát Éireann. Indeed, it is possible that our Constituent Assembly may have followed too slavishly the constitutional models of other nationalities, and that, just as the constitutional safeguards of Freedom of Speech, Trial by Jury, Security of the Person and Property, with others, were only introduced into the Constitution of the United States by way of amendment a year after the original Constitution had been adopted, so the amendments of our Constitution which have been enacted during recent years, whereby these and similar safeguards have been minimised or abrogated, more truly represent our national ideals. If this be so, we find the Briton's conception of liberty and justice set forth in his Magna Carta and his Bill of Rights; those of the American in his Declaration of Independence and his Constitution; while those of the Gael are enshrined in Amendment No. 17 (which is to prevail, in case of inconsistency, over everything in the Constitution except Articles 1 and 2), and subsequent amendments. However this may be, I can find no justification for a declaration that there was some 'spirit' embodied in our original Constitution which is so sacrosanct and immutable that nothing antagonistic to it may be enacted by the Oireachtas.[19]

[18] This, of course, is an intentionally ironic reference to the fact that while Fianna Fáil in opposition had vehemently opposed Article 2A and suspended it as soon as they came into Government in March 1932, they were forced to re-introduce it in 1933: see O'Sullivan, *I.F.S. and its Senate*, 334–5.

[19] Fitzgibbon quoted two American decisions at State court level to illustrate this point, including the following quotation from *Walker v. Cincinnati* 21 Ohio 41:

> Courts cannot nullify an Act of the State Legislature on the vague ground that they think it opposed to a general latent spirit supposed to pervade or underlie the Constitution where neither the terms nor the implications of the instrument disclose any such restriction.

The judgment of the other majority judge—Murnaghan—was only somewhat more muted. While he acknowledged that the 'extreme rigour' of the provisions of Article 2A passed 'far beyond anything having the semblance of legal procedure' and that the 'judicial mind is staggered at the very complete departure from legal methods in use in these courts',[20] he evinced no sympathy whatever for the natural law arguments of the appellants:

> It is sought to be established that many Articles of the Constitution are so fundamental as to be incapable of alteration and that the true meaning of the word 'amendment' in Article 50 of the Constitution does not authorise any change in these fundamental Articles or doctrines. It has to be admitted that the Constitution itself does not segregate as fundamental specified Articles or doctrines, nor does it in terms make any distinction between the different classes of Articles. At most, certain Articles such as Article 8, by which freedom of conscience is guaranteed, and Article 9, by which the right of public meeting is guaranteed subject to certain safeguards, may be said to secure what may, in the sphere of ethics and politics, be regarded as fundamental rights. These Articles are not, however, those which have been said to have been weakened; and, in reference to other Articles which are alleged to be fundamental, the only criteria which the appellants can suggest is that the Court should undertake the responsibility of deciding in any set of circumstances which Articles should be held to be fundamental. Before the Court should seek to assume such a power it is, in my opinion, necessary that the Court should find a very stable foundation for such an exercise of jurisdiction. If we regard closely the substance of the matter it is plain that, after the eight-year period, proposed amendments of the Constitution were to be submitted to the people for approval, and were to become law only if they had been accepted by the requisite majority of the voters entitled to vote. This direct consultation of the people's will does indicate that all matters, however fundamental, might be the subject of amendment. On the other hand the view contended for by the appellants must go to this extreme

[20] [1935] IR 170, 237–8.

> point, viz., that certain Articles or doctrines of the Constitution are utterly incapable of alteration at any time, even if demanded by an absolute majority of the voters.[21]

Kennedy's dissent on the natural law issue—magnificent though it was—must really be regarded as a personal judicial response to an extreme and draconian constitutional amendment which had been enacted almost by a legislative sleight of hand without the sanction of the electorate in the manner in which the Constitution had originally intended.[22]

Ryan's case and the sovereignty of the Irish Free State

The other major question addressed in *Ryan* concerned the nature of the sovereignty of the Irish Free State. While by any standards the Irish Free State was an independent, sovereign State at the time of its establishment, the Sinn Féin negotiators had been forced, following the 1921 Treaty negotiations, to accept an unusual abridgement of that sovereignty in that the then Oireachtas was precluded from enacting legislation which was in conflict with that Treaty. This was provided for in section 2 of the Constitution of the Irish Free State (Saorstát Éireann) Act, 1922:

> The said Constitution shall be construed with reference to the Articles of Agreement for a Treaty between Great Britain and Ireland set forth in the Second Schedule hereto annexed...which are hereby given the force of law, and if any provision of the said Constitution or of any amendment thereof or of any law made thereunder is in any respect repugnant to any of the provisions of the Scheduled Treaty, it shall, to the extent only of such repugnancy, be absolutely void and inoperative and the Parliament and the Executive Council of the Irish Free State (Saorstát Éireann) shall respectively pass such further legislation and do all such other things as may be necessary to implement the Scheduled Treaty.

[21] [1935] IR 240.

[22] In the preface to Kohn's *Constitution of the I.F.S.*, Kennedy (who had himself been a member of that Constitution's drafting committee) had explained:

> It was originally intended, as appears by the draft, that amendment of the Constitution should not be possible without the consideration due to so important a matter affecting the fundamental law and framework of the State, and the draft provided that the process of amendment should be such as to require full and general consideration [sc. by means of referendum]. At the last moment, however, it was agreed that a provision be added to Article 50, allowing amendment by way of ordinary legislation during a limited period so that drafting or verbal amendments, not altogether unlikely to appear necessary in a much debated text, might be made without the more elaborate process proper for the purpose of more important amendments. This clause was, however, afterwards used for effecting alterations of a radical and far-reaching character, some of them far removed in principle from the ideas and ideals before the minds of the first authors of the instrument.

Article 50 of the Constitution provided that any amendments to the Constitution had to be 'within the terms of the Scheduled Treaty'. Following de Valera's accession to power in March 1932, he immediately set about dismantling those elements of the Constitution (such as the Oath of Allegiance, the appeal to the Privy Council and the Governor-General) to which he was so resolutely opposed. This was done in the first instance by the Constitution (Removal of Oath) Act, 1933. As the provision for the Oath of Allegiance had been incorporated in Article 4 of the Treaty; as well as in Article 17 of the Constitution, it would not have sufficed simply for the Oireachtas to have attempted to delete Article 17.[23] The 1933 Act therefore took the opportunity to delete section 2 of the 1922 Constitution Act; the reference in Article 50 to 'within the terms of the Scheduled Treaty' and purported to deprive the High Court and Supreme Court of their jurisdiction under Articles 65 and 66 to declare a constitutional amendment invalid on the ground that it was inconsistent with the Scheduled Treaty.

The Supreme Court was agreed in *Ryan* that the Oireachtas had no power whatever to amend the terms of the Constituent Act and the Scheduled Treaty, although, of course, there was no suggestion that Article 2A violated the terms of the Scheduled Treaty.[24] But a further extraordinary dimension of the *Ryan* case is that the Supreme Court completely ignored the 1933 Act—which had been in force for over a year[25]—and treated section 2 of the 1922 Act as if it had not been amended. There is simply no other precedent for a court purporting to ignore and treat a constitutional amendment as a complete nullity.

A further complication was provided by the Privy Council's decision some six months later in June 1935 in *Moore v. Attorney General of the Irish Free State.*[26] Here the issue was whether the Constitution (Amendment No. 22) Act, 1933—which had purported to abolish the right of appeal from the Supreme Court to the Privy Council—was valid.

[23] None of the earlier constitutional amendments—however radical—had attempted unilaterally to alter the provisions of the Treaty.

[24] Cf. the comments of Justice Murnaghan:

> The only limitation specified in the text of Article 50 itself is that the amendment of the Constitution must be within the terms of the Scheduled Treaty. This limitation is emphasised by the Constituent Act itself, which provides that if any amendment of the Constitution is in any respect repugnant to any of the provisions of the Scheduled Treaty it shall to the extent only of such repugnancy be absolutely void and inoperative. This conception of the power of amendment as entertained by the framers of the Constitution does not at all accord with the limitation now attempted to be put forward. As a matter of construction I am satisfied that the power of amendment extends to any limits other than those specified in the Article and in the Constituent Act, and it is not argued that the Act of 1931 is in any way inconsistent with the Scheduled Treaty (241).

[25] The 1933 Act became law on 3 May 1933.

[26] See document no. 35. See also Thomas Mohr, 'Law without Loyalty, 187'.

As this right of appeal was held to have been protected by the Treaty,[27] the Judicial Committee was thus confronted directly with the issue of whether the Oireachtas had power to amend the Constitution in a manner inconsistent with the Treaty. The Statute of Westminster 1931 had provided that a Dominion Parliament had power to abrogate an enactment of the Imperial Parliament. Although the Irish Free State had never purported to legislate by reference to the Statute of Westminster, Lord Chancellor Viscount Sankey held that the Constitution (Amendment No. 22) Act was valid. As he pithily put it:

> The simplest way of stating the situation is that the Statute of Westminster gave to the Irish Free State a power under which they could abrogate the Treaty, and that, as a matter of law, they have availed themselves of that power.[28]

In so doing, the Privy Council held that the Irish Free State derived its authority from an Act of the Imperial Parliament and rejected the contrary views expressed in *Ryan.* Of course, in more recent times the Supreme Court has re-affirmed the views expressed in Ryan's case that the Constitution of 1922 derived its authority from an Act of Dáil Éireann and not from an Act of the Imperial Parliament.[29]

If Ryan's case effectively heralded the collapse of the 1922 Constitution since it established that, the terms of the Scheduled Treaty aside, there were no legislative barriers to amendments of that

[27] Article 2 of the Treaty provided that the position of the Irish Free State 'in relation to the Imperial Parliament and Government…shall be that of the Dominion of Canada' and the 'law, practice and constitutional usage governing the relationship of the Crown or the representative of the Crown and of the Imperial Parliament to the Dominion of Canada shall govern their relationship to the Irish Free State'. In *Performing Right Society v. Bray Urban District Council,* [1930] IR 509, the Privy Council held that Article 2 of the Treaty specifically ensured the right to petition the Judicial Committee for leave to appeal, because the right was part of the law, practice and constitutional usage then governing the relationship of the Crown and of the Imperial Parliament to the Dominion of Canada.

[28] See document no. 35. It bears emphasis that—remarkable as it seems to modern eyes—Lord Sankey as Lord Chancellor was a member of the British Government as well as being its most senior judge. He was also a member of the Irish Situation Committee (a Cabinet Committee which dealt with Irish affairs), yet it is a tribute to his judicial impartiality that as a judge he delivered a judgment which released the Irish Free State from the restraints of the Treaty.

A further striking fact is that Lord Sankey was effectively dismissed from his position the day after delivering the judgment in *Moore.* This seems to have been totally bound up with the reconstruction of the National Government in Britain and the replacement of Ramsay MacDonald as Prime Minister by Stanley Baldwin. As Robert Heuston notes:

> Sankey's place in the Cabinet does not seem to have been very strong. The experienced politicians regarded some of Sankey's contributions to debate with a mixture of amusement and contempt…Baldwin and his party had no reason to love Sankey. In addition, Baldwin had a long friendship for and serious political obligations to his ex-Lord Chancellor, Hailsham. So that unless MacDonald made Sankey's continuance [as Lord Chancellor] an indispensable condition of his own membership of the Cabinet, it was plain that Sankey's position was precarious. But in fact MacDonald was anxious to secure a Cabinet post for his son Malcolm so he jettisoned Sankey, *Lives of the Lord Chancellors, 1885–1940* (Oxford, 1964), 527.

[29] *Re Article 26 and Criminal Law (Jurisdiction) Bill 1976,* [1977] IR 129, 146–7, per Chief Justice O'Higgins.

Constitution, that process was completed by *Moore's* case. In the wake of the Privy Council's interpretation of the Statute of Westminster in that case the Oireachtas was now free to dismantle the Treaty as well.

The lessons of *Ryan* were clearly learnt by the drafters of the new Constitution, as in the three-year transitory period during which the Constitution could be amended by ordinary legislation, Article 51 was careful to ensure that the referendum provisions of Article 46 and the three-year period itself were beyond the reach of ordinary legislation. This was a vital step in ensuring the stability and success of the new Constitution, since it ensured that, thereafter, a referendum would be necessary to effect constitutional change. And so thus, the practical lessons of *Ryan* having being learnt and as the endless debates over the Treaty and the 1922 Constitution were effectively ended by the new Constitution, the practical significance of this remarkable decision began to wane.

No. 28: NAI, DFA 3/1

Memorandum from Conor Maguire to Joseph P. Walshe

Office of the Attorney General
11 May 1934

I think it well to inform the President that the document, copy of which I enclose, has been served upon me.[30] You will observe that it is a notice of intention to argue before the Privy Council that the Act (No. 45 of 1933) abolishing the appeal to the Privy Council is *ultra vires* the Parliament of the Irish Free State and consequently void. They also bring to the attention of the Privy Council the refusal of the Supreme Court Registrar to receive the order of the Privy Council which purported to give leave to the Plaintiffs to appeal or to transmit the record of the Proceedings of the Privy Council.

They pray (1) that copies of the relevant documents in their possession may be received by the Registrar of the Privy Council in order to complete the record. (2) That if the Council thinks fit for a special day for a preliminary hearing to decide on the validity of the Act abolishing the appeal to the Privy Council may be fixed.

[30] Not transcribed. The document was a copy of a petition by Robert Lyon Moore and others to the King, applying for leave to deliver to the Registrar of the Privy Council several documents relating to their case and for a preliminary hearing in the Privy Council to establish the validity of Constitution (Amendment No. 22) Act, 1933.

I take it that it is not the desire of the Government to recognise the right of the Privy Council to enquire into the validity of the Act (No. 45 of 1933).

I do not intend, unless specifically instructed, to enter a *caveat* or appear on the proceedings. I think it well however that the President should be aware of the steps which are being taken.

No. 29: NAI, DFA 3/1

Minute by John Hearne

[Department of External Affairs]
15 May 1934

Note: Secretary discussed this matter with me on Monday, 14 May.[31] Agreed that no action be taken.

Secretary discussed the position with the President later same day and on return directed me to inform the Attorney General that President agreed that no action be taken.

Informed Attorney General by telephone today in the sense of the Secretary's direction.

No. 30: NAI, DT S6757

Memorandum from Conor Maguire to Eamon de Valera

Office of the Attorney General
19 September 1934

President,
Re/ Appeal to Privy Council.
Moore and Others v. Attorney General and Others. (Known as the Erne Fisheries Case)

I have now been served with a copy of the order made by the King in Council of the 25th day of July last in this case. I enclose a copy of the order.

The order in its recitals gives the history of the case since leave to appeal was given by the Privy Council on the tenth day of November 1933. It states 'that on the sixteenth November, 1933, the Parliament of the Irish Free State purported to pass an Act (No. 45 of 1933) providing

[31] See document no. 28.

inter alia that no appeal should be from a decision of the Supreme Court to your Majesty in Council'.

It recites that when the order was lodged with the Registrar of the Supreme Court on the first December the Registrar returned the order to the Solicitors with an endorsement as follows: 'Having regard to the recent legislation amending Article 66 of the Constitution I cannot receive or act on this order without a direction of the Supreme Court...'

On 1 March 1934, the order was again served on the registrar with a letter formally requesting the Registrar to act on the order and to transmit the record to the Privy Council.

On 6 March 1934, the Registrar returned the order refusing by reason of Act No. 45 of 1933 to transmit the record.

The Lords of the Committee having heard the appellant's prayer reported to the King (*inter alia*) that *it ought to be referred* to the Lords of the Committee to determine in the first instance the preliminary question as to the validity and effect of Act No. 45 of 1933 in relation to this appeal. The order goes on:

'His Majesty having taken the report into consideration was pleased by and with the advice of the Privy Council to approve thereof and order and it was thereby ordered that the same be punctually observed, obeyed and carried into execution. The Governor General or officer administering the Government of the Irish Free State for the time being are to take notice and *govern themselves accordingly*.'

There is here a definite order by the King in Council made on the advice of the Judicial Committee.

The question as to whether a protest should be made against the action of the Privy Council in undertaking the determination of the question of the validity of an Act of the Oireachtas has already been considered and was postponed on the ground that, while not directly an issue, the question of the validity of the Act was involved in the *Ryan* case then pending before the Supreme Court in the Saorstát, to the extent that if the Court decided that the amendment of the Constitution could not be made by ordinary legislation since the passing of eight years from the enactment of the Constitution the Act abolishing the Appeal to the Privy Council would require to be submitted to a referendum before it became effective as a law. The Supreme Court have indicated a majority view that the Act cannot be challenged on this ground but, as they have left it open to themselves to decide otherwise, the question can still in a sense be considered *sub judice*.

The decision to await the judgment of the Supreme Court before making a protest was partly inspired by the hope that the Government's hand would be strengthened by an affirmative decision as to an alleged ground of invalidity and partly by the feeling that an adverse decision would make the protest for a moment appear futile.

The Privy Council has now acted on the suggestion of the Judicial Committee that the question of the validity of the Act of the Oireachtas abolishing the Appeal be referred to it as a preliminary question. This action means that the Privy Council accepted the view of the Judicial Committee that the Privy Council has the jurisdiction to pronounce on the validity of the Act notwithstanding its formal enactment by the Oireachtas.

It must be borne in mind that consideration of questions arising out of the dominion relationship in the Commonwealth are approached both by the Judges in England and the British Government from the point of view that it is possible to discover from the Acts of the British Parliament the principles which underlie that relationship and in particular the extent and scope of the legislative power granted to the Dominions.

They will regard the relationship between the two countries as statutory and will measure our freedom to legislate away the prerogative by the extent to which liberty so to legislate has been conferred by Statute.

It follows that they will almost certainly reject the view that the Privy Council should not advise the King as to the precise position created by the various British Statutes which have from the British side ratified the arrangements made in the Treaty.

Before the Statute of Westminster the Commonwealth of Australia and the Union of South Africa had both limited the cases in which an appeal can be brought. In both, the provision so limiting the appeal has been effected by Imperial Acts.[32] Canada attempted by a unilateral Act (section 1025 of the Criminal Code) to abolish the appeal to the Privy Council in criminal cases. In *Nadan's* case[33] this section was held to be void by the Privy Council on the ground, firstly, that there was nothing in the North America Act to authorise the Parliament of Canada to abrogate a right long established and expressly confirmed by the Judicial Committee Acts of 1833 and 1844, and, secondly, that the prerogative could only be annulled by Imperial Statute.

It was there pointed out that the modifications of the prerogative in Australia and South Africa were modified in that way.

Further, the Section was held repugnant to the Judicial Committee Acts 1833 and 1844 and therefore void by reason of the Colonial Laws Validity Act, 1865.

[32] Commonwealth of Australia Act, 1900, s.74; Union of South Africa Act, 1909, s.106.
[33] [1926] AC, 482.

This latter ground of challenge is not now open as regards a Saorstát Act since the Statute of Westminster.

Although the view is also held here that the prerogative can be annulled by a Saorstát Act; the Privy Council may hold that it is open to argument whether this view is correct.

It may possibly be argued that the treaty crystallised the Free State in the Canadian position as in 1922.

This view could not in my opinion receive support from any Court.

I can understand the English Government striving for such an interpretation of the position, but I cannot see how *in law* such a contention can be upheld.

The Privy Council will deal or pretend to deal with the question as one of pure law. If it is a question of law it is difficult to discover a precedent for advising the King not to allow the Privy Council to give him advice on a matter which, it will be argued, depends upon the construction to be placed upon the Treaty and the various Acts confirming it and giving it the force of law.

As head of the Executive, the King no doubt is bound to Act in Executive matters as advised by the Executive Council. In asking him to accept an advice that he no longer can invite an opinion from the Privy Council we must adopt the position that we are to be the sole judges as to the precise effect of the Treaty. Is this not laying ourselves open to the answer that in adopting this line we are begging the question?

On the other hand, we can hardly await calmly the situation which will arise if advice is given by the Judicial Committee to the effect that the Act abolishing the appeal is void. The King will, in order to make such decision effective, have to order that the decision be carried out.

The Government here will be faced with the necessity of either obeying the Order or allowing the Appellants to seek its enforcement through the machinery of the Courts.

The Government can hardly allow the decision to be enforced and may have to resort to *ad hoc* legislation to deal with the position, which legislation may again be challenged.

In view of the possible developments it may be thought well to make clear in advance what the attitude of the Government will be if any attempt is made to carry into effect any decision of the Privy Council.

I have given the reasons why I find it difficult to justify the giving of an advice in the sense that this term is understood when it refers to Executive Acts. The place of the King in the Commonwealth system and the relationship between him and the Executive is a matter of law. The Privy Council will regard the question to be determined as an aspect of the law governing Commonwealth relationship, with particular reference to the precise nature of the relationship created by the Irish Treaty and the legislation which followed it.

If we adopt the view that this question is outside the jurisdiction of the Privy Council and is really a question of Treaty interpretation, objection to its being considered by the Privy Council would more appropriately take the form of a diplomatic protest to the British Government than of tendering advice to the King.

The Privy Council action already taken makes it clear that they take the view that the Treaty is inextricably linked up with the status quo which existed at the date of its making. This view they will support by pointing out that each change from the old order agreed to be made by the Treaty was effected by legislation. The fact that the new order differs so fundamentally from the old does not dispose of the view that the change was brought about by law. The Treaty in its basic provision provided that this State is given a position in the commonwealth similar to that of Canada. Canada's position was originally defined by an Act of the British Parliament. Therefore, they will argue the question as to how the Privy Council appeal as a piece of Commonwealth legal machinery came to be embodied in our Constitution and the question as to whether it survives the recent changes in the Constitutional structure of the Commonwealth made by the Statute of Westminster and the Act under discussion is a question of law upon which the King may seek advice from the body which the Canadian Constitution, our Constitution and the Act under consideration recognised as having hitherto had the Constitutional right to advise him on such matters.

It is difficult to advise you that such a reasoning cannot be supported. What I have stated, I hope, makes clear why I regard the question as to the course of action now to be followed as both delicate and difficult.

It should be borne in mind that a decision to make a diplomatic protest against the action of the Privy Council leaves it open later to tender advice to the King if this course commends itself to the Government. If advice to the King is now given and disregarded it would considerably weaken the effect of a diplomatic protest.

The step now to be taken is a vital one as the reasoned basis for adopting it will rule all future controversy.

No. 31: NAI, DT S6757

Memorandum from John Hearne to Eamon de Valera

[Department of External Affairs]
25 September 1934

Minister,
I have read the Attorney General's opinion of the nineteenth instant relating to the proceedings in the above mentioned case now pending in the Judicial Committee of the Privy Council.[34] Basing myself on the views expressed by the Attorney General I submit the following observations.

1) The Order in Council made on the 25 July 1934 directs that the hearing of the substance of the petition be postponed until after the determination of the preliminary question as to the validity of the Constitution (Amendment no. 22) Act, 1933 (No. 45 of 1933). The hearing of the arguments for the determination of the preliminary question is fixed (by that Order) for the 3 December 1934 or some convenient date thereafter. In these circumstances it is submitted that no action should be taken by the Government until the Supreme Court has decided the *Attorney General v. Ryan and Others*. The Government could not appropriately advise the King or take any other action which assumes the validity of the Constitution (Amendment no. 22) Act, 1933 while the validity of that statute is in fact in issue in the Courts of Saorstát Éireann. No doubt the statute is challenged—the *Ryan* case—on one ground only but its validity is to that extent *sub judice*.
2) There is little doubt as to what the decision of the Supreme Court will be. That Court will by implication if not actually by express reference decide that the Constitution (Amendment no. 22) Act, 1933 was a valid amendment of the Constitution. But the Court will make no pronouncement as to the consistency or otherwise of the said statute with the Treaty of 1921.
3) Once the Supreme Court has given its decision the internal constitutional situation will be cleared up and the Government will be in a position to take action with regard to the proceedings now pending in the Privy Council in the case

[34] See document no. 30.

of *Moore and Others v. the Attorney-General and Others.* Their action must be based upon the supreme authority of the Oireachtas to regulate and control the prerogatives of the King. The whole issue is a constitutional issue between the Parliament and Government of Saorstát Éireann and the constitutional monarch. The correct course for the Government to take will be to advise the King in the terms of the Constitution (Amendment No. 22) Act, 1933. The advice should be in the form and sense of the Submission drafted some weeks ago.[35]

4) The Government should firmly decline to be drawn into any discussion with the British Government on the question of the propriety or otherwise of the advice tendered to the King. The British Government argument on Article 2 of the Treaty is trite and threadbare. It would no doubt be urged again (should the Government of Saorstát Éireann enter into any discussion with the British Government on the present issue) notwithstanding the assurances given in the year 1931 that when the Statute of Westminster became law the objections of the British Government—based on Article 2 of the Treaty— to the abolition of the appeal to the Privy Council would be definitely dropped.

5) The King will not refuse to accept the advice of the Government of Saorstát Éireann, if given in the order suggested before 3 December 1934. The advice would be correct on every conceivable ground. It would be correct on the legal ground of the statute of the Oireachtas barring the prerogative appeal in express terms; correct on the constitutional ground of the relations which exist between the King and the Government of Saorstát Éireann in an affair so obviously internal as the organisation of the judicial system; correct on the political ground of a unanimous Dáil and a practically undivided public opinion; correct on the international ground of the judicial sovereignty of the Irish Free State and its responsibility in international law for the acts of its judicial tribunals.

6) Neither the British Government nor his Majesty the King will receive any support from the Governments or peoples of the States of the Commonwealth of Nations in any action which

[35] Document not located.

challenges the right of the Parliaments of those States to abolish the appeal to the Privy Council should the electorate of those States determine to abolish it.

No. 32: [1935] IR pp 219

Extract from the opinion of Chief Justice Hugh Kennedy in *The State (Ryan) v. Lennon*

Supreme Court, Dublin
19 December 1934

I am of opinion that the Constitution (Amendment no. 16) Act, No. 10 of 1929, is invalid and the amendment of the Constitution contained in it inoperative null and void. It follows that, in my opinion, no amendment of the Constitution passed by both Houses of the Oireachtas after 6 December 1930 could become law unless and until it had been submitted for decision to a referendum of the people and had received the approval of the people in the manner prescribed.

It follows that, in my opinion, the Constitution (Amendment No. 17) Act, no. 37 of 1931, has never become law, and that the matters of which the applicants here complain, being acts and proceedings under that invalid statute, are all wholly illegal and indefensible in law.

I have just stated my opinion that the Act no. 37 of 1931, as a whole enactment, has never become law. I have further to add that I am also of opinion that, for the reasons already given, parts of the amendment (the new 'Article 2A') are incapable of being validly enacted under the Constitution, some as repugnant to the source of power and authority acknowledged and declared by the Constituent Assembly, others as repugnant to some of the principles postulated by the Constituent Assembly as fundamental.

Therefore, after most anxious and grave consideration of this very serious and critical case, I have arrived at the clear and deliberate opinion that the judgment of the High Court should be reversed and that the cause shown should be disallowed and the conditional order of *Habeas corpus* and Prohibition made absolute.

No. 33: [1935] IR 220–37

Opinion of Justice Gerald Fitzgibbon in *The State (Ryan) v. Lennon*

Supreme Court, Dublin
19 December 1934

It is impossible to overestimate the importance of the questions which we have to decide on this appeal, involving as they do, on the one hand, the validity of several Acts already passed by the Oireachtas and the powers possessed by that body over future legislation, and on the other, rights and privileges of the citizens of the Saorstát which are stated by our own Constitution to be 'inviolable', or to be 'guaranteed', and which are all alleged by the Appellants to be 'fundamental', 'immutable', and incapable of being taken away by any enactment whatsoever. The detailed analysis which has just been read by the Chief Justice, upon which I cannot hope to improve, makes it unnecessary for me to recapitulate the character and effect of the legislation which we have to consider. It is no part of my duty to express an opinion upon anything connected with the legislation except its validity under the Constitution, and I refrain from any kind of criticism of its merits.

The Appellants contend that 'The Constitution (Amendment No. 17) Act, 1931', No. 37 of the Acts of 1931, which I shall refer to as 'Amendment No. 17', is *ultra vires*, unconstitutional and void, in that it is contrary to Article 72 of the Constitution, which enacts that 'No person shall be tried on any criminal charge without a jury save in the case of charges in respect of minor offences triable by law before a Court of Summary Jurisdiction, and in the cases of charges for offences against military law triable by Court Martial or other Military Tribunal'; to Article 6 of the Constitution which enacts that 'The liberty of the person is inviolable, and no person shall be deprived of his liberty except in accordance with law'; and to Article 64 of the Constitution which enacts that 'The judicial power of the Irish Free State (Saorstát Éireann) shall be exercised and justice administered in the public courts established by the Oireachtas by judges appointed in manner hereinafter provided.'

There is no doubt, and it is indeed admitted by the Attorney General and his colleagues, that Amendment No. 17 expressly contravenes, in these and many other respects, the Constitution as originally enacted by Dáil Éireann, sitting as a Constituent Assembly, but they contend that Amendment No. 17 was a valid amendment of the Constitution by the Oireachtas under the powers conferred on the Oireachtas by Article 50, as amended by the Constitution (Amendment No. 16) Act, 1929, No. 10 of 1929, and the Constitution (Amendment No. 10) Act, 1928, No. 8 of 1928.

To this contention the appellants reply that the Acts by which the Oireachtas purported to amend Article 50 of the Constitution were themselves invalid and *ultra vires* of the Oireachtas, and, consequently, that any amendment of the Constitution which rests upon them must also be invalid. The validity of Amendment No. 17 is also attacked upon a substantive ground of far reaching importance, namely, that it violates certain rights of citizenship which are alleged to be fundamental, and 'inviolable' and 'immutable', apparently by any legislative authority whatsoever.

It is obvious that if the Oireachtas had no power to amend Article 50 of the Constitution at all, or in the particular way in which it was amended by the Amendments No. 10 and No. 16, it will be unnecessary to consider any of the other objections to Amendment No. 17, and I shall therefore endeavour to deal with that objection first.

Article 50 is in these terms: 'Amendments of this Constitution within the terms of the Scheduled Treaty may be made by the Oireachtas, but no such Amendment, passed by both Houses of the Oireachtas, after the expiration of a period of eight years from the date of the coming into operation of this Constitution, shall become law, unless the same shall, after it has been passed or deemed to have been passed by the said two Houses of the Oireachtas, been submitted to a Referendum of the people, and unless a majority of the voters on the register shall have recorded their votes on such Referendum, and either the votes of a majority of the voters on the register, or two thirds of the votes recorded, shall have been cast in favour of such Amendment. Any such Amendment may be made within the said period of eight years by way of ordinary legislation and as such shall be subject to the provisions of Article 47 hereof.' Article 47 made provisions for the suspension, in certain events, of any Bill, for a period of ninety days, and of the submission of any Bill so suspended to the decision of the people by Referendum, if a demand should be made within the ninety days either by a resolution of Seanad Éireann, assented to by three-fifths of its members, or by a petition signed by one-twentieth of the voters on the register of voters. This Article was repealed in 1928 by Amendment No. 10, and as consequential upon that repeal the reference to the provisions of Article 47 in the last clause of Article 50 was deleted.

The first contention of the appellants is that the terms 'Amendments' and 'Amendment' in Article 50 do not connote 'repeal', and they have referred us to dictionary interpretations of 'Amend' and 'Amendment' in the sense of 'to improve', 'to make better', and so on. There are, however, other equally common and authentic interpretations which do include the sense of 'repeal', and 'improvement' that may quite properly be effected by addition, alteration, or omission. 'Amend. V.t. 1. To correct, to rectify by expunging a mistake; as, to amend a law. Amend 2. To change or alter, as a law, bill, motion or constitutional provision by the will of a legislative body, or by competent authority; as to amend the Constitution.'[36] 'Amendment. The act of changing a fundamental law, as of a political constitution, or any change made in it according to a prescribed mode of procedure; as, to alter the law by amendment; an Amendment to the Constitution.'[37]

In legislation, the words 'Amendment' and 'Amend' are constantly employed in the sense of 'repeal', especially when reference is made to the amendment of a lengthy document, such as the Constitution or an Act of Parliament, by a repeal, total as to some provisions of the enactment, by partial when considered in relation to the document as a whole. Taking a volume of the Statutes of the Imperial Parliament[38] and opening it at random, I find, within a few pages, the following instances: Chapter 3. 'An Act to amend the Prosecution of Offences Acts, 1879 and 1884.' Section 3. (1) 'The enactments mentioned in the Schedule to this Act are hereby repealed to the extent specified in the third column of that schedule', and the schedule, of 'Enactments Repealed' repeals the whole of one section and parts of two others of the Act of 1879 and part of one section of the Act of 1884. Chapter 15 of the same year, 'An Act to consolidate and amend the Law relating to the payment of costs in Criminal Cases' repeals by Section 10 (1) portions of twenty sections and the whole of each of thirty-two sections, in thirty-six different Statutes. Chapter 8 of the same year is perhaps the most apt illustration of all. 'An Act to amend section eleven of the Savings Bank Act, 1904.' Section 1 (2). 'Section eleven of the Savings Bank Act, 1904, shall be and is hereby repealed.' These instances might, I expect, be multiplied by hundreds of English legislation; and they may be paralleled from

[36] Noted in margin: 'Ogilvic's Imperial Dict. S.V. amend'.
[37] Noted in margin: 'Standard Dictionary, Funk and Wagnalls. 1894'.
[38] Statutes, 8 Edward VIII.

the comparatively few enactments of our own legislature. The usage of Parliamentary Draughtsmen appears in the promiscuous interchange of the words 'amend' and 'repeal' in the text and marginal headings of different sections, but that of the Legislature itself may be seen in the 'Local Elections Postponement (Amendment) Act, 1924'. 'An Act to Amend the Local Elections Postponement Acts, 1922 and 1923.' Section 1. 'The Local Elections Postponement (Amendment) Act, 1923, (No. 48), shall be and is hereby repealed.'

Article V of the Constitution of the United States enables Congress to propose 'Amendments to this Constitution', (the very expression used, with the substitution of 'of' for 'to' in Article 50 of our own Constitution), and 'Amendments' and 'Amendment' are the only terms employed, yet 'Amendment No. 22' is in these words: 'The Eighteenth Article of Amendment to the Constitution of the United States is hereby repealed. This Article shall be inoperative unless it has been ratified as an Amendment to the Constitution by conventions in the several States as provided in the Constitution within seven years from the date of submission hereof to the States by Congress.'

A further reason, conclusive in my opinion, against the limitation of the meaning of the word 'amendment' to 'improvement' is to be found in Article 65, which extends the judicial power of the High Court to the 'question of the validity of any law, having regard to the provisions of the Constitution'. If the validity of an Amendment of the Constitution were to depend upon the decision of the High Court that it was an 'improvement', the Judges and not the Oireachtas would be made the authority to decide upon the advisability of any particular amendment of the Constitution, and this would involve a direct contravention of the principles by which their respective spheres are assigned to the Legislative, the Executive and the Judicial organisations in the Irish Free State. The Executive decides that the Constitution would be improved by a particular alteration, the Oireachtas, if it approves of the alteration proposed by the Executive, embodies it in the form of an act, and the Judiciary decides whether that act can be and has been validly enacted, and then, and not till then, the Executive enforces it as a law upon the people at large.

For all these reasons I am quite satisfied that the power conferred upon the Oireachtas by Article 50 of the Constitution to make amendments of the Constitution, includes a power to amend by alteration or repeal, and that the Oireachtas alone has the right to decide whether any particular alteration, addition or omission is desirable, and accordingly that neither Amendment No. 10, nor Amendment No. 16, nor Amendment No. 17, is *ultra vires* of the Oireachtas merely because it involves a partial repeal of the Constitution.

The next objection is that even if there be a power to amend or repeal portions of the Constitution, this power does not extend to an amendment or repeal of all or any part of Article 50.

However undesirable it may appear to some that the Oireachtas should have power, by merely passing an Amendment, to extend, as they have done, the period within which amendments to the Constitution may be made by way of ordinary legislation, or to legalise, as they have done, amendments of the Constitution without submitting them to a Referendum of the people, as contemplated by the Constitution itself, nevertheless, if this be the true construction of Article 50, the Court is bound to give effect to that construction.

It is conceded that there is no express prohibition against amendment of Article 50 to be found in the Constitution. It is not unusual to find that Constitutions or Constituent Acts impose such restrictions upon the legislative bodies set up by them, and the omission of any such restriction in regard to amendments of Article 50 is at least a negative argument that Dáil Éireann as a Constituent Assembly did not intend to impose any such restriction upon the Oireachtas. This negative argument is supported by the fact that both the Constituent Act and Article 50 itself do contain an express restriction upon the powers of the Oireachtas to amend the Constitution, and it is a legitimate inference that, when certain restrictions were expressly imposed, it was not intended that other undefined restrictions should be imposed by implication. The Constitution was enacted by Dáil Éireann, sitting as a Constituent Assembly, unfettered by any oath or test, open to all elected representatives of the constituencies in that Irish Free State whose establishment was therein and thereby proclaimed, and it was the only act of legislation of that Constituent Assembly.

By the Constituent Act it was decreed and enacted as follows: '1. The Constitution set forth in the First Schedule hereto annexed shall be the Constitution of the Irish Free State (Saorstát Éireann). 2. The said Constitution (that is the Constitution set forth in the First Schedule hereto annexed) shall be construed with reference to the Articles of Agreement for a Treaty between Great Britain and Ireland set forth in the Second Schedule hereto annexed (hereafter referred to as 'the Scheduled Treaty') which are hereby given the force of law, and if any provision of the said Constitution or of any amendment thereof or of any law made thereunder is in any respect repugnant to any of the provisions of the Scheduled Treaty, it shall, to the extent only of such repugnancy, be absolutely void and inoperative and the Parliament and the Executive Council of the Irish Free State (Saorstát Éireann) shall respectively pass such further legislation and do all such other things as may be necessary to implement the Scheduled Treaty. 3. This Act may be cited for all purposes as the Constitution of the Irish Free State (Saorstát Éireann) Act, 1922.'

Then follows the 'First Schedule above referred to. Constitution of the Irish Free State (Saorstát Éireann)', which contains eighty-three separate numbered 'Articles', of which those numbered 73 and 83 inclusive are preceded by a descriptive heading 'Transitory Provisions', which is, for what it may be worth, the sole indication of any intended distinction between any one Article or group of Articles and any other.

If there ever was an assembly which could claim to represent the inhabitants of Saorstát Éireann, it was that Dáil Éireann, sitting as a Constituent Assembly, which every elected representative of every constituency within the Saorstát was free to attend, unfettered by any test, and in which there was no nominated or unrepresentative element, and I am not disposed to quarrel with the statement of the Attorney General that 'the framers of the Constitution framed that instrument in accordance with doctrines of popular sovereignty, and the instrument must be construed as indicating the powers conferred upon the Oireachtas', or, subject to two modifications, with the propositions stated by Mr Gavan Duffy as the foundation of his argument, that '1. The Constituent Assembly proclaimed the Constitution by virtue of its own supreme legislative authority. 2. It transmitted that authority to its successor the Oireachtas at least for eight years. 3. It gave the Oireachtas complete amending power for eight years, subject to checks which are merely checks voluntarily imposed by the Supreme authority, and removable at its will, and 4. That the Constitution was proclaimed in the name of the people by Dáil Éireann as an act of Supreme Authority, which it alone had the right to do, because it was the mouthpiece of the people, requiring and receiving no Royal assent.'

The points in which it seems to me that Mr Gavan Duffy[39] has overstated the powers conferred by the Constituent Assembly upon the Oireachtas are his assertions (a) that Dáil Éireann '*transmitted* that authority', i.e. '*Supreme* legislative authority' to the Oireachtas, and (b) that 'It gave the Oireachtas *complete* amending power for eight years'. An examination of the Constituent Act and of the Constitution will

[39] Senior Counsel for the State defendants.

demonstrate that these statements exaggerate the powers of the Oireachtas. Assuming that the legislative authority of the Constituent Assembly was Supreme, it expressly decreed and enacted by the Constituent Act that 'The said Constitution' namely, 'The Constitution set forth in the First Schedule' to the Constituent Act, 'shall be construed with reference to the Articles of Agreement for a Treaty between Great Britain and Ireland set forth in the Second Schedule hereto annexed…which are *hereby* given the force of law, and if any provision of the said Constitution *or of any amendment thereof or of any law made thereunder* is in any respect repugnant to any of the provisions of the Scheduled Treaty, *it shall*, to the extent only of such repugnancy, *be absolutely void and inoperative*'.

Therefore the Supreme legislative authority, speaking as the mouthpiece of the people, expressly denied to the Oireachtas the power of enacting *any* legislation, by way of amendment of the Constitution or otherwise, which might be 'in any respect repugnant to any of the provisions of the Scheduled Treaty', and it reiterated this prohibition in Article 50, which empowered the Oireachtas to make '*amendments of this Constitution within the terms of the Scheduled Treaty*'. *It is further to be observed that this power to make amendments is limited to 'amendments of the Constitution', and that the Constituent Assembly did not confer upon the Oireachtas any power to amend the Constituent Act itself.* These express limitations imposed by the mouthpiece of the people upon the legislative powers of the Oireachtas which it set up, support the view that the Oireachtas was intended to have full power of legislation and amendment outside the prohibited area, and, as there was no prohibition against amendment of Article 50, I am of opinion that Amendment No. 10 in 1928, and Amendment No. 16 in 1929, were within the powers conferred upon the Oireachtas by the Constituent Act.

In this connection I may add that in my opinion an amendment of Article 50 by the deletion of the words 'Within the terms of the Scheduled Treaty' would be totally ineffective, as effect is given to these words by the Constituent Act itself, which the Oireachtas has no power to amend.

In my opinion the object of Article 50 was to prescribe the method by which legislative sanction was to be given to those Amendments of the Constitution which the Oireachtas was empowered to make, and the Oireachtas had full power, during eight years, in the absence of any express prohibition, to alter, modify or repeal the method prescribed. The extension of the period of eight years to sixteen was, in the absence of any such express prohibition, an amendment within the powers conferred. I can find no sound justification for the exclusion of Article 50 from the powers of Amendment which appear to me to exist in respect of every other Article of the constitution except those which embody provisions of the Scheduled Treaty, and in respect even of those Articles so far as the Amendments made to them are not repugnant to any provision of the Scheduled Treaty.

It is by no means unusual to find in Constitutions, especially in those of States of recent formation, express restrictions upon the power of the Legislature to amend them imposed in respect of particular articles; and in the case of the Union of South Africa Section 152 of the South Africa Act, 1909 which enacts that 'Parliament may by law repeal or alter any of the provisions of this Act' (a declaration which appears to me indistinguishable in substance from 'Amendments of this Constitution may be made by the Oireachtas within a period of eight years by way of ordinary legislation'), goes on to declare expressly 'that no repeal or alteration of the provisions contained *in this Section*...shall be valid unless the Bill embodying such repeal or alteration' shall have been passed in a particular way and by a specified majority.

Our Constituent Assembly could in like manner have excepted Article 50 from the amending powers conferred upon the Oireachtas, but it did not do so, and in my opinion this court has no jurisdiction to read either into the Constituent Act or into Article 50 a proviso excepting it, and it alone, from those powers.

Mr Overend has endeavored to support his argument on this point by analogies from the law of principal and agent, master and servant, trustee and *cestuique* trust, and principal and attorney. 'Who', said he, 'ever heard of a power of attorney by which the attorney could extend the term of his own authority?' Perhaps there has never been such an instrument, but I do not see any legal objection to the insertion in a power of attorney, given for a specified period, of a proviso authorising the attorney, by deed poll registered or executed in compliance with the law or in any specified manner, to extend the period of his authority, provided that such an extension was made while the power was still in force, and did not offend against any statutory prohibition. The objections that the Oireachtas had no power to amend Article 50, that Amendment No. 17 was made after the period of eight years originally fixed by Article 50 had expired, and that it was not submitted to a Referendum of the people as provided by Article 47, therefore fail.

The next objection is founded upon the provisions of Amendment No. 17 itself.

It has been admitted, as I have already stated, that many of these provisions are directly opposed to the express enactments contained in many Articles of the Constitution, for instance, in Articles 43, 64, 65, 68, 69, 70 and 72, all of which have been abrogated in whole or in part. The most emphatic of these is probably Article 43; 'The Oireachtas shall have no power to declare Acts to be infringements of the law which were not so at the date of their commission', and Article 72; 'No person shall be tried on any criminal charge without a jury save in the case of charges in respect of minor offences triable by law before a Court of Summary Jurisdiction, and in the case of charges for offences against military law triable by Court Martial or other Military Tribunal.'

I can see no ground that either of these Articles could not have been amended by the Oireachtas subject to a Referendum of the people after a period of eight years, and if so, it follows that the same amendment, e.g. the deletion of the word 'no' in Article 43, could be made 'by way of ordinary legislation' within that period, or within sixteen years, after eight had been altered to sixteen.

The same reasoning which applies to the power of the Oireachtas to amend Article 50 applies with at least equal force to amendments of any other Article. Outside the area covered by the provisions of the Scheduled Treaty, no limit was imposed by the Constituent Assembly upon the power of the Oireachtas to amend the Constitution. In many other Constitutions there are Articles, Laws or provisions which are specifically described as 'Fundamental', e.g. Sweden, or 'Constitutional', e.g. Austria, Czechoslovakia and France, in respect of which the Constitution expressly restricts the power of amendment, but in the Constitution of the Saorstát there is no such segregation, and the power of amendment which applies to any Article appears to me to be equally applicable to all others, subject, of course, to the restriction in respect of the Scheduled Treaty. In Article 6 it is declared that 'The liberty of the person is inviolable' but that is not a law of universal application, for the Article proceeds 'and no person shall be deprived of his liberty *except in accordance with law*'. The law may, therefore, make provisions in accordance with which a person may be deprived of his liberty. It is for the legislature to prescribe these provisions, and for the Courts to enforce them, and even if, under Amendment No. 17, a person has been deprived of his liberty by the mere caprice of an Executive Minister (Section 24 (2) and Appendix, clause 7), or the unfounded suspicion, 'incapable of being rebutted or questioned by cross examination, rebutting evidence, or otherwise', 'of any member of the Garda Síochána' (Sections 13 and 29), 'or of the Defence Forces of Saorstát Éireann' (Sec. 13), such a deprivation would be 'in accordance with law', and the prisoner would have no redress.

The particular method of amendment adopted, by enacting that every Article of the Constitution subsequent to Article 3 shall be subject to the provisions of Amendment 17, and that the provisions of that Amendment shall prevail whenever there is any inconsistency between them and any other Article of the Constitution, is unquestionably very inconvenient, and throws almost insuperable obstacles in the way of any citizen or Judge whose duty it is to ascertain the actual law of the Constitution, but an Act of the Legislature is not *ultra vires* or invalid because it is difficult to construe, and amendments of the Constitution which might be made clearly and one at a time are not invalidated because they have been enacted *en masse* in a manner calculated to create the utmost uncertainty and inconvenience. It is our duty to ascertain and declare the law to the best of our ability, and we are not concerned with either the wisdom or the propriety of the Acts of the Legislature. Since the argument I have come across a passage in the opinion of Chief Justice John Marshall, who was for thirty-four years Chief Justice of the Supreme Court of the United States during a period when that Court was engaged in settling questions of fundamental importance which arose upon the interpretation of the recently adopted Constitution, which seems to me to have a bearing upon more than one aspect of the present case.

> 'The proposition is that a power which is in itself capable of being exerted to the total destruction of the grant is inconsistent with the grant; and is therefore, impliedly relinquished by the grantor, though the language of the instrument contains no allusion to the subject. If this be an abstract truth, it may be supposed universal. But it is not universal; and therefore its truth cannot be admitted, in these broad terms, in any case. We must look for the exemption in the language of the instrument, and if we do not find it there, it would be going very far to insert it by construction. The power of legislation, and consequently of taxation, operates on all the persons and property belonging to the body politic. This is an original principle which has its foundation in Society itself. It is granted by all for the benefit of all…This vital power may be abused, but the Constitution of the

> United States was not intended to furnish the correction for every abuse of power which may be committed by the State Governments. The interest, wisdom and justice of the representative body, and its relations with its constituents, furnish the only security, *where there is no express contract*, against unjust and excessive taxation, *as well as against unwise legislation* generally.'

In my opinion the repeals, alterations and modifications of the Constitution by Amendment No. 17 so far as they have been discussed before us upon this appeal, do not exceed the powers of amendment conferred upon the Oireachtas by Article 50, as amended in 1928 and 1929, and as it has not been suggested that they are in any respect repugnant to the Scheduled Treaty, I hold that they are valid Amendments of the Constitution.

There is, however, a broader ground upon which Mr Costello and Mr Overend have endeavoured to found an argument. They assert that there are certain rights, inherent in every individual, which are so sacred that no legislature has authority to deprive him of them. It is useless to speculate upon the origin of a doctrine which may be found in the writings of Rousseau, Thomas Paine, William Godwin and other philosophical writers, but we have not to decide between their theories and those of de Lolme and Burke, not to mention Bentham and Locke, upon what Leslie Stephen describes as 'a problem which has not yet been solved, nor are even the appropriate methods definitely agreed upon', as we are concerned, not with the principles which might or ought to have been adopted by the framers of our Constitution, but with the powers which have actually been entrusted by it to the Legislature and Executive which it set up.

'The Declaration of the Rights of Man and of Citizens' by the National Assembly of France on 5 October 1789, that 'Liberty, property, security and resistance of oppression are the natural and imprescriptible rights of man', cannot be invoked to overrule the provisions of a written Constitution. When a written Constitution declares that 'The liberty of the person is inviolable', but goes on to provide that 'no person shall be deprived of his liberty *except in accordance with law*', then, if a law is passed that a citizen may be imprisoned indefinitely upon a *lettre de cachet* signed by a Minister or, as we have seen, even by a Minister's clerk the citizen *may* be deprived of his 'inviolable' liberty, but, as the deprivation will have been 'in accordance with law', he will not be as devoid of redress as he would have been under the regime of a French or Neapolitan Bourbon.

Nations and constituent Assemblies are not agreed as to the rights and privileges which have been variously described in different Constitutions as 'inalienable', 'inviolable', fundamental', constitutional' or 'guaranteed'. For instance; among the 'repeated injuries and usurpations, all having in direct object the establishment of an absolute Tyranny over these States', which the Signatories of the American Declaration of Independence published as 'Facts submitted to a candid world' in justification of their rebellion, were the following acts of George III:

> He has dissolved Representative Houses for opposing with manly firmness his Invasions on the rights of the people. He has made Judges dependent on his will alone, for the tenure of their offices, and the amount and payment of their salaries. He has created a multitude of new offices, and sent hither swarms of officers to harass our people and eat out their substance. He has affected to render the military independent of and superior to the Civil Power. He has combined with others to subject us to a jurisdiction foreign to our constitution and unacknowledged by our laws, giving his Assent to their acts of pretended legislation. For quartering large bodies of armed troops among us. For protecting them by a mock trial from punishment for any murders which they should commit on the inhabitants of these States. For cutting off our trade with all parts of the world. For depriving us in many cases of the benefits of trial by jury. For taking away our charters, abolishing our most valuable laws and altering fundamentally the forms of our governments. A prince whose character is thus marked by every act which may define a tyrant, is unfit to be the ruler of a free people.

These rights, of which 'the people of these colonies' had been deprived, were claimed by them not as inalienable rights of all mankind, but by virtue of their former status as British colonists, but when the American colonists set to work to frame a Democratic and Republican Constitution for themselves they realised the danger of merely substituting the will of a majority for that of a single individual, probably because many of the framers of the Constitution of the United States had suffered from the tyranny of a political or religious majority. The States of Connecticut, Rhode Island and New Hampshire were founded by refugees driven out from Massachusetts; Delaware by refugees from New York and Pennsylvania by Quakers in search of freedom and they were resolved to impose constitutional restraints upon the power of the majority in the new legislature of the Confederation. In this Constitution, accordingly, they embodied the English, or Anglo-Saxon, principles of trial by jury, an independent judiciary, *habeas corpus* and other safeguards of liberty derived from Magna Carta, the English bill of Rights and the Act of Settlement, and they imposed severe restrictions upon the power of the legislature, and placed almost insuperable obstacles in the path of Amendments to the Constitution. They sought to bind within the limits of the Constitution, as framed by them, not only the Executive but the Legislature itself. 'An elective despotism', said Jefferson, 'was not the government for which we fought...a group of tyrants would be less manageable than one...In question of power, then, let no more be heard of confidence in man, but bind him down from mischief by the chains of the Constitution.' To the same effect is the opinion of the Supreme Court of the United States delivered a century later in a case in which the legislature of a State had attempted to appropriate private property under the guise of the imposition of a tax:

> 'It must be conceded that there are private rights in every free government beyond the control of the State. A government which recognised no such rights, which held the lives, the liberty and the property of its citizens subject at all times to the absolute disposition and unlimited control of even the most democratic depositary of power, is after all but a despotism. It is true it is a despotism of the many, of the majority, if you choose to call it so, but it is none the less a despotism. It may well be doubted if a man is to hold all that he is accustomed to call his own, all in which he has placed his happiness, and the security of which is essential to that happiness, under the unlimited dominion of others, whether it is not wiser that this power should be exercised by one man than by many. The theory of our governments, State and National, is opposed to the deposit of unlimited power *anywhere*.'[40]

But that is only the Anglo-Saxon, or American, conception of Constitutional liberty. Another view was taken by Rousseau, who declared that 'Each of us puts his person and all his power in common under the supreme direction of the General Will', that is, of the majority, and this appears to have been adopted by the French constitution makers. I can find no justification for the inference which the Counsel for the Appellants ask us to draw from the provisions of the American Declaration for Independence and the Constitution founded thereon, or

[40] *Loan Association v. Topeka*, 20 Wall. 655.

from the fact that some of these provisions have been embodied in other constitutions, including our own, that the rights thereby secured are universal and inalienable rights of all citizens in all countries, or even in the Saorstát, which, we have been assured, was or is or ought to be Gaelic and Catholic, attributes to either of which few other States can assert a title, while there is no other which can even suggest a claim to both.

There is no ground for surprise, therefore, that this State should, as the Chief Justice has said, 'point new ways' in its 'pioneer Constitution Draftsmanship', or that it should prefer to secure liberty and justice to its citizens by the simple processes of Amendment No. 17 in preference to the complicated British and American machinery of an independent judiciary, trial by jury, and *habeas corpus.* I cannot presume either, that rights and privileges which the inhabitants of England have always enjoyed, either by virtue of their Common Law (which was only introduced into Ireland bit by bit between the last years of the twelfth century and the beginning of the seventeenth), or under the provisions of special statutes, are also indigenous to the citizens of this Gaelic and Catholic State, in the sense in which the American colonists claimed them as their birthright by virtue of *their* status as British subjects, a status which I understand to be repudiate by *our* legislators, or that our national conceptions of liberty and justice must necessarily coincide with those of the citizens of any other State. Two extracts from fathers of American independence will suffice to show, if there be any doubt, the source from which the principles embodied in their Constitution were derived.

> 'What is the subject of our controversy with the Mother Country? It is this: Whether we shall preserve that security in our lives and properties which the laws of nature, the genius of the British constitution, and our charters afford us; or whether we shall resign them into the hands of the British House of Commons, which is no more privileged to dispose of them than the Great Mogul?'[41]

> 'No constitution of government has appeared in the world so admirably adapted to these great purposes [liberty and knowledge, civil and religious] as that of Great Britain. Every British subject in America is, of common right, entitled to all the essential privileges of Britons.'[42]

Unless, therefore, these rights appear plainly from the express provisions of our Constitution to be inalienable, and incapable of being modified

[41] Works of Alexander Hamilton, vol. 2, 4.
[42] James Otis, [quoted in] Hutchinson's *History of Massachusetts.*

or taken away by any legislative act, I cannot accede to the argument that the Oireachtas cannot alter, modify or repeal them. The framers of our Constitution may have intended 'to bind man down from mischief by the chains of the Constitution', but if they did, they defeated their object by handing him the key of the padlock in Article 50.

Other Constitutions, e.g. that of the Kingdom of Serbs, Croats and Slovenes, and those of the Republics of Austria, Poland, Estonia and Czechoslovakia, have esteemed all or some of these rights and privileges so highly as to declare them to be 'fundamental', or 'constitutional', or 'guaranteed', and the Republic of Mexico has provided in its Constitution a unique and very remarkable judicial safeguard for affording immediate redress by the decree of an Independent Federal Tribunal when any of the fundamental rights of man secured by its Constitution have been infringed *by any authority whatsoever*, and for excusing the obedience of a law or decree which is *ultra vires* of the enacting legislature or judiciary. The 'personal guarantees' so protected include ten relating to criminal trials; no arrest except upon a previous charge founded upon evidence, or in cases of *in flagrante delicto,* no search of private houses except on a warrant issued by a judge specifying the place to be searched, the persons to be arrested and the objects sought; and an express proviso that 'No one shall be tried according to private laws or by special tribunals. Military tribunals shall in no case and for no reason extend their jurisdiction over persons not belonging to the army.' But the fact that the Constitutions of other countries prohibit such invasions of the rights of liberty and property, and such extraordinary innovations in the methods of administering justice in criminal cases as have been introduced into our Constitution by Amendment No. 17, affords no ground for condemning as unconstitutional in *this* country, or as contrary to any inalienable rights of an Irish citizen, an enactment which appears to have received the almost unanimous support of the Oireachtas, for we have been told that those of our legislators by whom it was opposed most vehemently as unconstitutional and oppressive, when it was first introduced, have since completely changed their opinions, and now accord it their unqualified approval. It is true that even a unanimous vote of the legislature does not decide the validity of a law, but it is some evidence that none of those whose duty it is to make laws see anything in it which they regard as exceptionally iniquitous, or as derogating from the standard of civilization which they deem adequate for Saorstát Éireann. Indeed it is possible that our Constituent Assembly may have followed too slavishly the constitutional models of other nationalities, and that, just as the constitutional safeguards of Freedom of Speech, Trial by Jury, Security of Person and Property, with others, were only introduced into the Constitution of the United States by way of amendment a year after the original Constitution had been adopted; so the amendments of our Constitution which have been enacted during recent years, whereby these and similar safeguards have been minimised or abrogated, more truly represent our national ideals. If this be so, we find the Briton's conceptions of liberty and justice set forth in his Magna Carta and his Bill of Rights; those of the American in his Declaration of Independence and his Constitution; while those of the Gael are enshrined in Amendment No. 17 (which is to prevail, in case of inconsistency, over everything in the Constitution except Article 1 and 2), and subsequent amendments. However this may be, I can find no justification for a declaration that there was some 'Spirit' embodied in our original Constitution which is so sacrosanct and immutable that nothing antagonistic to it may be enacted by the Oireachtas. This Court has no jurisdiction to express an opinion upon any questions other than the constitutionality of the amendments before us, and their correct interpretation, once the legislature has thought fit to enact them. Perhaps I may be permitted again to refer to a couple of American decisions upon similar questions. 'Courts cannot nullify an Act of State Legislature on the vague ground that they think it is opposed to a general latent spirit supposed to pervade or underlie the Constitution where neither the terms nor the implications of the instrument disclose any such restriction.'[43] 'Such a power is denied to the Courts, because to concede it would be to make the Courts sovereign over both the Constitution and the people, and convert the government into a judicial despotism.'[44]

The last contention of Mr Overend,[45] that every person who accepted citizenship of the Irish Free State when it was first established, or at any subsequent date, did so upon the faith of an undertaking, express or implied, on the part of the state, embodied in the Constitution, that no alteration of the Constitution to his detriment would thereafter be made, is so manifestly untenable upon any ground of law or principle, that I mention it only to show that it has not been overlooked.

Equally unfounded is the suggestion that the power of amendment introduced in Article 50 should be treated by analogy to a proviso in small print at the end of a fraudulent prospectus, or to a condition on

43 *Walker v. Cincinatti*. 24 Ohio 41.
44 *Golden v. Prince*. 3 Wash. C.C. 313.
45 Senior Counsel for the applicants, subsequently a judge of the High Court 1943–8.

the back of a railway ticket handed to an illiterate traveller. Such arguments show the desperate straits to which the appellants have been reduced. Article 50 seems to me to occupy its appropriate place, at the end of the group of clauses which deal with the creation, composition and powers of the legislature, and every person who became a citizen must be presumed to have been aware of the existence of Article 50, and to have accepted citizenship upon the terms therein set forth.

Fortunately it can never again be suggested that the Saorstát has obtained citizens by false pretences, now that the Oireachtas has promulgated *urbi et orbi*, to the Czechoslovak and the Mexican, to our kinsmen in the United States of America and throughout the British Commonwealth of Nations, and, above all, to our fellow countrymen in Northern Ireland, whose cooperation we profess to desire, as well as to all those who seek, or acquire, or have thrust upon them, rights under our new Irish Nationality and Citizenship Act, Amendment No. 17 as an integral part of our Constitution, setting forth in the clearest language, in the forefront of that document, the conditions under which liberty is enjoyed and justice may be administered in 'this other Eden, demi-Paradise, this precious stone, set in the silver sea, this blessed plot, this earth, this realm, this' Saorstát.

No. 34: [1935] IR pp 244–5

Extract from the opinion of Justice James Murnaghan in *The State (Ryan) v. Lennon*

Supreme Court, Dublin
19 December 1934

The consequences of a decision in favour of the extension of the period during which amendments may be made by way of ordinary legislation alone are grave and far reaching but it is the duty of the Court upon a point of construction to arrive at a conclusion irrespective of the consequences of the decision. I am ready to conjecture that when Article 50 was framed it was not considered probable that any such use of the power would be made as has been made but the terms in which Article 50 is framed does authorise the amendment made and there is not in the Article any express limitation which excludes Article 50 itself from the power of amendment. I cannot therefore find any ground upon which the suggested limitation can be properly based. It must also be remembered that in this country the Referendum was an untried political experiment and it cannot be assumed that the referendum should be incapable of alteration or removal. I feel bound by the words of Article 50 which allows amendment of the Constitution as a whole, of which Article 50 is declared to be a part. I am therefore of opinion that power was given to amend Article 50 and that consequently the period during which the Constitution may be amended by way of ordinary legislation has been validly extended to a period of sixteen years from the date of coming into operation of the Constitution. In my opinion the appeal should be dismissed.

I have already made some observations upon the manner in which the Constitution has been amended by the Special Powers Tribunal Act, 1931. The power of amendment is not a power of temporary suspension and as the Act of 1931 has been put into operation the Constitution must, I should imagine, be considered as amended so as not to be inconsistent with the provisions of the Act of 1931. To discover what the provisions of the amended Constitution now are is a matter of no small difficulty; and if the Act of 1931 should in the future cease to remain in force I fear that grave doubts will arise as to what the Constitution really is. It is therefore highly desirable that amendments of the Constitution should be made either by way of repeal of specific Articles or by the substitution of amended articles instead of those which it is desired to alter.

NO. 35: [1935] IR pp 472–87

Privy Council decision in *Moore v. Attorney General for the Irish Free State*

Whitehall, London
6 June 1935

The Judicial Committee of the Privy Council held:

1. That, as the Articles of Agreement for a Treaty between Great Britain and Ireland (hereinafter referred to as 'the Treaty') were given the force of law by 12 Geo. 5, c. 4, and as the Constitution of the Irish Free State (Saorstát Éireann) Act, 1922, was scheduled to 13 Geo. 5, c.1, both the Treaty and the Irish Free State Act formed parts of the statute law of the United Kingdom, each being part of an Imperial Act, and each derived their validity therefrom.

2. That before the passing of the Statute of Westminster, 1931, it was not competent for the parliament of the Irish Free State to pass an Act abrogating the Treaty because the Colonial Laws Validity Act, 1865, forbade a Dominion Legislature to pass a law repugnant to an Imperial Act.
3. That the effect of the Statute of Westminster was to remove the fetter on the Irish Free State Legislature imposed by the Colonial Laws Validity Act, 1865, and that Legislature could now pass Acts repugnant to an Imperial Act.
4. That accordingly the Constitution (Removal of Oath) Act, 1933, which would otherwise be invalid because it removed from Article 50 of the Constitution the condition that there could be no amendment of the Constitution unless it was within the terms of the Treaty, was valid by virtue of the Statute of Westminster.
5. And that the Constitution (Amendment No. 22) Act, 1933, was also valid by virtue of the same statute, though otherwise invalid because it was repugnant to Clause 2 of the Treaty, since it abolished the right to petition His Majesty in Council, that right being part of the law, practice and constitutional usage governing the relationship of the Crown and of the Imperial Parliament to the Dominion of Canada, and that law, practice and constitutional usage was by Clause 2 of the Treaty also to govern the relationship of the Crown or representative of the Crown and of the Imperial Parliament to the Irish Free State.

Performing Right Society v. Bray Urban District Council, [1930] IR 508, followed.

6. And that the said amendment effected by the Constitution (Amendment No. 22) Act, 1933, abolished the right to petition His Majesty in Council, was not invalid on the ground that it affected the King's prerogative in a matter outside the Dominion and outside the competence of the Parliament of the Irish Free State, because the King's prerogative in this respect and in this particular statute (i.e., the Statute of Westminster) was made matter of Parliamentary legislation so that it was *pro tanto* merged in the Statute, and the Statute gave powers of amending and altering the statutory prerogative.

Petition to have it declared that an amendment to the Constitution of the Irish Free State, enacted by the Constitution (Amendment No. 22) Act, 1933, (No. 45 of 1933), was no bar to the maintenance by the petitioners of their appeal before the Judicial Committee of the Privy Council.

The Petitioners had obtained special leave to appeal from the decision of the Supreme Court of the Irish Free State under the proviso to Article 66 of the Constitution of the Irish Free State, in the action brought by them against the Attorney General of the Irish Free State and others, claiming a declaration that they were entitled to a several fishery in the entire tidal portion of the River Erne, in the county of Donegal. (The decision of the Supreme Court is reported in [1934] IR 44)

[Matter omitted]

Counsel for the petitioners informed the Judicial Committee on 12 July 1934, when the appeal came before the Judicial Committee for hearing, that for the moment they were unable to proceed with their appeal, because they had been unable to get the record of the proceedings in the Supreme Court of the Irish Free State. It was necessary to file that record with the Registrar of the Privy Council before the appeal could be set in motion. And on 16 November 1933, the Parliament of the Irish Free State had passed the Constitution (Amendment No. 22) Act, 1933, providing that no appeal should lie from a decision of the Supreme Court of the Irish Free State to His Majesty in Council, and that it should not be lawful for any person, after the passing of that Act, to proceed with an appeal from any judgment or order of that Court. That on 24 November 1933, the Order in Council giving the petitioners special leave to appeal against the decision of the Supreme Court had been lodged with the Registrar of that Court, but the Registrar had returned the Order in Council to petitioners' solicitors, with an endorsement upon it to the effect that, having regard to the recent legislation amending Article 66 of the Constitution, he could not receive, or act on, this Order, without a direction of the Supreme Court which gave the decision appealed from.

After some correspondence with the Registrar of the Judicial Committee of the Privy Council, counsel stated the Registrar of the Irish Free State Supreme Court refused to transmit the record of the proceedings in that Court to the Privy Council. In these circumstances, the petitioners asked that they should not be precluded from proceeding with their appeal, but might have leave to deliver to the Registrar of the

Privy Council the necessary documents, and that such documents should be treated as the record required to be lodged.

Counsel therefore suggested that, as a preliminary, the Judicial Committee should decide as to the validity of the Act passed by the Parliament of the Irish Free State, so far as it related to the appeal. He submitted that it was desirable, for the reasons he had indicated, that the matter should first be dealt with as a preliminary issue. If that should be decided against the petitioners, it would end the matter, and the great expense of preparing the record would be saved. On the other hand, if it was decided in their favour, the appeal could proceed in the ordinary way. He thought the Constitutional issue would have to be decided in any event, and the most convenient course would be to discuss and decide it as a preliminary matter.

The Lord Chancellor [Viscount Sankey] said that they could not make any order to the effect desired by counsel, but they could advise His Majesty that the course suggested would be the most convenient one to take.

Counsel said there was also the possibility, when the matter came before their Lordships on the preliminary issue, that they would not have the assistance of the Attorney General of the Irish Free State or of counsel for the fishermen respondents. In these circumstances, great responsibility would be placed upon counsel for the appellants. Perhaps their Lordships would take the view that the Attorney General of England might be notified in order that they might have his assistance.

Lord Atkin suggested that it might be desirable to notify the Secretary for the Dominions.

After a private consultation by their Lordships, the Lord Chancellor announced that they would advise His Majesty to give direction that the petition be postponed, except that it be referred to the Judicial Committee of the Privy Council to determine the preliminary question as to the validity of the Irish Free State act, in so far as it affected the appeal of the petitioners, and that the hearing of this preliminary issue be fixed for 16 October following.

The hearing of this preliminary issue was not proceeded with on 16 October but it was proceeded with on 3 and 4 December, and on the latter day the hearing was adjourned pending the hearing of an appeal from Canada, in which the right of appeal to the Privy Council and the effect of the Statute of Westminster also arose.[46] The arguments were resumed on 9 April and were concluded on 11 April 1935.

[46] *British Coal Corporation and Others v. The King* [1935] IR 487.

Mr Wilfred Greene, K.C., Mr G.R.B. White (both of the English Bar), and Mr Arthur C. Newett (of the Irish Bar) appeared for the appellants, Moore and others. The Attorney General of England (Sir Thomas Inskip, K.C.) and Mr Wilfred Lewis (of the English Bar) were present to assist the Board. The Attorney General for the Irish Free State and the other respondents did not appear and were not represented.

The Lord Chancellor [Viscount Sankey], in giving the judgment of the Board, said: This is a petition to have it declared that an amendment to the Constitution of the Irish Free State—namely, Constitution (Amendment No. 22) Act, 1933—is no bar to the maintenance by the petitioners, who are the appellants, of their appeal before this Board. The petitioners claim to be owners of a fishery in the tidal waters of the River Erne, in Ireland. They had brought an action in the Irish Courts to enforce their claim and had succeeded before the trial judge. On appeal to the Supreme Court that judgment was reversed on 31 July 1933 by a majority. The petitioners then presented to the Privy Council their petition for special leave to appeal, the grant of which leave was, on 9 October 1933, advised by this Board, and on 10 November 1933 an Order granting such leave was made by the King in Council. But on 16 November 1933, an Act was passed by the Oireachtas of Saorstát Éireann, the Parliament of the Irish Free State, hereinafter called the Oireachtas, providing that no appeal should lie to His Majesty in Council from any Court in the Irish Free State. This enactment was also expressed to apply to appeals then pending. The petitioners thereupon brought this petition praying to have it declared the enactment was void and did not bar their appeal.

The Attorney General for the Irish Free State and the other respondents did not appear before this Board. The Attorney General for England did, however, appear and gave the Board his assistance on the law relevant to the questions at issue. For the decision of these questions it is necessary to consider the mode in which the Constitution of the Irish Free State was established.

On 6 December 1921 there were signed in London 'Articles of Agreement for a Treaty between Great Britain and Ireland'. The instrument will hereinafter be referred to as 'the Treaty'. It was signed by representatives of Great Britain, on the one hand, and of the Irish Free State (or what became of the Irish Free State) on the other. On 31 March 1922, an Act of the Imperial Parliament was passed. It was entitled the Irish Free State (Agreement) Act, 1922, and by section 1 (1) it provided that as from the date of that Act the Treaty, which was scheduled to it, should have the force of law. It was also provided by section 1 (2) that there should be elected certain members of a body to be called the House of the Parliament, to which the Provisional Government should be responsible, and which should have power, as respects matters within the jurisdiction of that Government, to make laws in like manner as the Parliament of the Irish Free State when constituted. The latter provision was expressed in order to give effect to Article 17 of the Treaty, which was in the following terms:

> By way of provisional arrangement for the administration of Southern Ireland during the interval which must elapse between the date hereof and the constitution of a Parliament and Government of the Irish Free State in accordance therewith, steps shall be taken forthwith for summoning a meeting of members of Parliament elected for constituencies in Southern Ireland since the passing of the Government of Ireland Act, 1920, and for constituting a provisional Government, and the British Government shall take the steps necessary to transfer to such provisional Government the powers and machinery requisite for the discharge of its duties, provided that every member of such provisional Government shall have signified in writing his or her acceptance of this instrument. But this arrangement shall not continue in force beyond the expiration of twelve months from the date hereof.

This Act gave no power to 'the House of the Parliament' to enact a Constitution for the Irish Free State.

In due course 'the House of the Parliament', which was a single chamber body, was elected and met on 9 September 1922. It proceeded to sit as a constituent assembly for the settlement of the Constitution of the Irish Free State. The measure which it so passed was scheduled to an Act of the Imperial Parliament entitled the Irish Free State Constitution Act, 1922, which received the Royal Assent on 5 December 1922, and which described the measure as the Constituent Act, and by section 1 provided as follows:

> The Constitution set forth in the First Schedule to the Constituent Act shall, subject to the provisions to which the same is by the Constituent Act so made subject as aforesaid, be the Constitution of the Irish Free State, and shall come into operation on the same being proclaimed by His Majesty in accordance with Article Eighty-Three of the said Constitution, but His Majesty

> may at any time after the proclamation appoint a Governor General for the Irish Free State.

The provisions to which the Constitution was made subject by the Constituent Act were recited in the Act and were as follows:

> The said Constitution shall be construed with reference to the Articles of Agreement for a Treaty between Great Britain and Ireland set forth in the Second Schedule hereto annexed (hereinafter referred to as the Scheduled Treaty) which are hereby given the force of law, and if any provision of the said Constitution or of any amendment thereof or of any law made thereunder is in any respect repugnant to any of the provisions of the Scheduled Treaty, it shall, to the extent only of such repugnancy, be absolutely void and inoperative and the Parliament and the Executive Council of the Irish Free State shall respectively pass such further legislation and do all such other things as may be necessary to implement the Scheduled Treaty.

Sections 4 and 5 of the Act were in the following terms:

> 4. Nothing in the said Constitution shall be construed as prejudicing the power of Parliament to make laws affecting the Irish Free State in any case where, in accordance with constitutional practice, Parliament would make laws affecting other self-governing Dominions.
> 5. This Act may be cited as the Irish Free State Constitution Act, 1922 (session 2), and shall be deemed to be the Act of Parliament for the ratification of the said articles of agreement as from the passing whereof the month mentioned in Article Eleven of the said articles is to run.

Thus the Treaty received the force of law, both in the United Kingdom and in Ireland, by reason of the passing of an Act of the Imperial Parliament; and the Constituent Act owed its validity to the same authority.

Before referring to the material clauses of the Constitution it will be convenient to quote Articles 1 and 2 of the Treaty, which are as follows:

> 1. Ireland shall have the same constitutional status in the Community of Nations known as the British Empire as the Dominion of Canada, the Commonwealth of Australia, the Dominion of New Zealand, and the Union of South Africa, with a Parliament having powers to make laws for the peace,

order and good government of Ireland and an Executive responsible to that Parliament, and shall be styled and known as the Irish Free State.

2. Subject to the provisions hereinafter set out the position of the Irish Free State in relation to the Imperial Parliament and Government and otherwise shall be that of the Dominion of Canada, and the law, practice and constitutional usage governing the relationship of the Crown or the representative of the Crown and of the Imperial Parliament to the Dominion of Canada shall govern their relationship to the Irish Free State.

The construction and effect of Article 2 were considered by the Judicial Committee in *Performing Right Society v. Bray Urban District Council.*[47] It was there held that the words of that Article specially ensured the right to petition His Majesty in Council, because that right was part of the law, practice and constitutional usage then governing the relationship of the Crown or representative of the Crown and of the Imperial Parliament to the Dominion of Canada. Their Lordships in the present case follow that decision.

Of the articles of the Constitution the following are so material in this matter that they should be set out here in full:

> Article 12: A Legislature is hereby created to be known as the Oireachtas. It shall consist of the King and two Houses, the Chamber of Deputies (otherwise called and hereinafter referred to as 'Dáil Éireann') and the Senate (otherwise called and herein generally referred to as 'Seanad Éireann'). The sole and exclusive power of making laws for the peace, order and good government of the Irish Free State (Saorstát Éireann) is vested in the Oireachtas.
>
> Article 50. Amendments of this Constitution within the terms of the Scheduled Treaty may be made by the Oireachtas, but no such amendment, passed by both Houses of the Oireachtas, after the expiration of a period of eight years from the date of the coming into operation of this Constitution, shall become law, unless the same shall, after it has been passed or deemed to have been passed by the said two Houses of the Oireachtas, have been submitted to a Referendum of the people, and unless a majority of the voters on the register shall have recorded their votes on such Referendum, and either the votes of a majority of the voters on the register, or

[47] [1930] IR.

> two-thirds of the votes recorded, shall have been cast in favour of such amendment. Any such amendment may be made within the said period of eight years by way of ordinary legislation and as such shall be subject to the provisions of Article 47 hereof.
>
> Article 66. The Supreme Court of the Irish Free State (Saorstát Éireann) shall, with such exceptions (not including cases which involve questions as to the validity of any law) and subject to such regulations as may be prescribed by law, have appellate jurisdiction from all decisions of the High Court. The decision of the Supreme Court shall in all cases be final and conclusive and shall not be reviewed or capable of being reviewed by any other Court, Tribunal or Authority whatsoever.
> Provided that nothing in this Constitution shall impair the right of any person to petition his Majesty for special leave to appeal from the Supreme Court to His Majesty in Council or the right of his Majesty to grant such leave.

It seems that the proviso to Article 66 of the Constitution was inserted to give effect in that particular regard to Article 2 of the Treaty, and hence under Article 50 of the Constitution that proviso could not be amended in the way in which it is sought to amend it by abolishing the right of appeal because such an amendment would not be within the terms of the Scheduled Treaty.

On 6 December 1922, there was issued a Proclamation of His Majesty announcing the passing and adoption of the Constitution, and thereafter the House of Parliament or Constituent Assembly or Provisional Parliament was in due course dissolved and a Parliament called the Oireachtas for the Irish Free State was elected in due course.

On 14 May 1929, the Oireachtas passed an Act, the Constitution (Amendment No. 16) Act, 1929, which substituted for the eight years specified in Article 50, as being the period during which amendment might be made without a referendum, a period of sixteen years. All the subsequent amendments which are referred to in this judgment were made without a referendum in accordance with this amendment. Mr Wilfred Greene, for the petitioners, rightly conceded that Amendment No. 16 was regular, and that the validity of these subsequent amendments could not be attacked on the ground that they had not been submitted to the people by referendum.

On 11 December 1931, the Statute of Westminster, hereinafter called the Statute, was enacted. It was the result of the proceedings at the

Imperial Conference, 1930, in which representatives of the Irish Free State took part, together with the delegates of the other Dominions. That fact is recorded in the first recital, and in the last recital it is recorded that the Irish Free State, with the other Dominions, had requested and consented to the submission of the measure to the Parliament of the United Kingdom. Section 1 includes in the expression Dominion (with the other Dominions) the Irish Free State. Of the other sections that which is most relevant in these proceedings is section 2, which is in the following terms:

> 2 (1) The Colonial Laws Validity Act, 1865, shall not apply to any law made after the commencement of this Act by the Parliament of a Dominion. (2) No law and no provision of any law made after the commencement of this Act by the Parliament of a Dominion shall be void or inoperative on the ground that it is repugnant to the law of England, or to the provisions of any existing or future Act of Parliament of the United Kingdom, or to any order, rule or regulation made under any such Act, and the powers of the Parliament of a Dominion shall include the power to repeal or amend any such Act, order, rule or regulation in so far as the same is part of the law of the Dominion.

Sections 3 and 4 also refer to the Irish Free State as being a Dominion within the meaning of the Statute.

On 3 May 1933, the Oireachtas passed an Act, No. 6 of 1933, entitled the Constitution (Removal of Oath) Act, 1933. That Act, by section 2, provided that section 2 of the Constitution of the Irish Free State (Saorstát Éireann) Act, 1922, should be repealed and, by section 3, that Article 50 of the Constitution should be amended by deleting the words 'within the terms of the Scheduled Treaty'.

Finally, on 15 November 1933, the Oireachtas, as already stated, enacted the Constitution (Amendment No. 22) Act, 1933, amending Article 66 of the Constitution so as to terminate the right of appeal to his Majesty in Council.

It is clear that, if this last-mentioned amending Act is valid, the petition must fail because the amendment of the Constitution embodied in that Act must bar the right of Appeal to the King in Council, if it is effective. But it cannot be effective unless the earlier Act (No. 6 of 1933) is also valid—namely, that which is directed to removing from Article 50 the condition that there can be no amendment of the Constitution unless it is within the terms of the Scheduled Treaty. On the construction of Article 2 of the treaty, which has been adopted above, Article 50, while it stands unamended, must prevent any amendment of the Constitution which would impair the right of appeal—that is, any amendment whereby the right of appeal to the King in Council is to be impaired.

Hence it must be determined whether that Act of the Oireachtas, No. 6 of 1933, was validly enacted.

Mr Greene, for the petitioners, has contended that this last-mentioned Act was not valid.[48] His argument was that the Constitution derived its existence not from any legislation of the Imperial Parliament but solely from the operations of an Irish body, the Constituent Assembly, which is called in Ireland the Third Dáil Éireann. This body, it is said, though mentioned in the Irish Free State (Agreement) Act, 1922, was in fact elected pursuant to a resolution passed on 20 May 1922, by the Second Dáil Éireann, an Irish Legislative Assembly. The Third Dáil Éireann was thus, it was alleged, set up in Ireland by election of the people of Ireland of their own authority as a Constituent Assembly to create a Constitution, and having accomplished its work went out of existence, leaving no successor and no body in authority capable of amending the Constituent Act. The result of that argument is that a Constitution was established which Mr Greene has described as a semi-rigid Constitution—that is, one capable of being amended in detail in the different articles according to their terms, but not susceptible of any alteration so far as concerns the Constituent Act, unless perhaps by the calling together of a new Constituent Assembly by the people of Ireland. Thus the articles of the Constitution may only be amended in accordance with Article 50, which limits amendments to such as are within the terms of the Scheduled Treaty. On that view Mr Greene argues that the law No. 6 of 1933 is *ultra vires* and hence that the amendment No. 22 of 1933 falls with it.

It follows from that argument, if accepted, that the right of appeal to the King in Council is preserved unimpaired. In support of his argument that the Constituent Act and the Constitution are subject only to what is called Irish law, and outside the authority of the Imperial Parliament, either in inception or in possibility of alteration save as provided therein, Mr Greene referred their Lordships to [a decision of] the Supreme Court of Ireland, *The State* (*Ryan and Others*) *v. Lennon and Others*, the judgment in which was delivered on 19 December 1934. In that case Chief Justice Kennedy is reported to have expressed a view which corresponds in substance to that contended for by Mr Greene.

[48] Wilfred Greene KC (1883–1952), counsel for the petitioners, subsequently Master of the Rolls and head of the English Court of Appeal (1937–49) and Law Lord (1949–52).

But their Lordships cannot accept these contentions. In their opinion, the Constituent Act and the Constitution of the Irish Free State derived their validity from the Act of the Imperial Parliament, the Irish Free State Constitution Act, 1922. This Act established that the Constitution, subject to the provisions of the Constituent Act, should be the Constitution of the Irish Free State and should come into operation on being proclaimed by His Majesty, as was done on 6 December 1922. The action of the House of Parliament was thereby ratified. Apart from such ratification that body had no authority to make a Constitution. All the authority it originally possessed was derived from the Irish Free State (Agreement) Act, 1922, section 1 (1) and (2) of which have been referred to above. Those subsections only gave the House of Parliament jurisdiction to make laws in respect of matters within the jurisdiction of the Provisional Government. It has been pointed out in the foregoing that in the Statute the Irish Free State was treated as one of the Dominions, the delegates of which took part in the Imperial Conference of 1930. The Irish Free State is, in their Lordships' judgment, bound by the Acts of the Imperial Parliament in the same way as any other of the Dominions. If it were not for section 2 of the Statute the Oireachtas would have had no power to amend or repeal an act of the Imperial Parliament, and has now such power only so far as any such Act is part of the law of the Dominion in virtue of section 2 of the Statute. Hence the Act No. 6 of 1933 and the Amendment No. 22 of 1933, and certain other Acts of the Oireachtas not here material which contain amendments of the articles which are not within the terms of the Treaty, are only valid Acts of the Oireachtas in virtue of the Statute. For the Statute alone gives to the Oireachtas power to repeal or amend the Constituent Act, which has the force of an Imperial enactment by reason that it is embodied in the Irish Free State Constitution Act, 1922.

Mr Greene has contended that these amendments cannot be deemed to be valid under the Statute because the Oireachtas in enacting these Acts was not purporting to proceed under the Statute, but was assuming to proceed solely under Irish law. But as what the Oireachtas was doing was in truth, as already stated, the repealing or amending of parts of an Imperial Statute—namely, the Irish Free State Constitution Act, 1922—what the Oireachtas did must, in their Lordships' judgment, be deemed to have been done in the way in which alone it could legally be done—that is, by virtue of the Statute, Article 66 of the Constitution has been validly amended, with the result that the proviso to that article is removed and appeals to the King in Council are now prohibited.

The position may be summed up as follows: (1) The Treaty and the Constituent Act form parts of the statute law of the United Kingdom, each of them being parts of an Imperial Act. (2) Before the passing of the Statute of Westminster it was not competent for the Irish Free State Parliament to pass an Act abrogating the Treaty because the Colonial Laws Validity Act forbade a Dominion Legislature to pass a law repugnant to an Imperial Act. (3) The effect of the Statute of Westminster was to remove the fetter which lay upon the Irish Free State Legislature by reason of the Colonial Laws Validity Act. That Legislature can now pass Acts repugnant to an Imperial Act. In this case they have done so.

It would be out of place to criticise the legislation enacted by the Irish Free State Legislature. But the Board desire to add that they are expressing no opinion upon any contractual obligation under which, regard being had to the terms of the Treaty, the Irish Free State lay. The simplest way of stating the situation is to say that the Statute of Westminster gave to the Irish Free State a power under which they could abrogate the Treaty, and that, as a matter of law, they have availed themselves of that power.

Mr Greene has finally contended that the amendment is invalid because it affects the prerogative of the King in a matter outside the Dominion and outside the competence of the Oireachtas. It might be possible to state many objections to this contention, but it is enough here to say that whatever might be the position of the King's prerogative if it were left as matter of the common law, it is here in this particular respect and in this particular enactment made matter of Parliamentary legislation, so that the prerogative is *pro tanto* merged in the Statute, and the Statute gives power of amending and altering the statutory prerogative. This objection also fails.

In the result their Lordships are of opinion that the petition should fail and be dismissed. They will humbly so advise his Majesty.

[Judicial Committee of the Privy Council: Viscount Sankey, L.C., Lord Atkin, Lord Tomlin, Lord Macmillan and Lord Wright.][49]

[49] See Chapter I for a discussion of the relevant Irish legislation. The Judicial Committee consisted of John Sankey, Viscount Sankey (1866–1948, Lord Chancellor, 1929–35); James Richard Atkin, Baron Atkin (1867–1944); Thomas James Chesshyre Tomlin, Baron Tomlin (1867–1935); Hugh Pattison Macmillan, Baron Macmillan (1873–1952) and Robert Alderson Wright, Baron Wright (1869–1964).

CHAPTER IV

DRAFTING A NEW CONSTITUTION, 1935

The first instructions for the heads of a draft Constitution were given by de Valera to the Legal Adviser in the Department of External Affairs, John Hearne, in late April 1935.[1] These instructions were given verbally by de Valera and the 'squared paper draft' appears to reflect those instructions.[2] Some of the key principles of the Constitution—the Preamble, the nature of the State, creation of the President, fundamental rights and the referendum—trace their origins back to this draft.

Yet it may be surmised that some of these instructions must reflect Hearne's own thinking. The 'squared paper draft' makes reference both to a Constitutional Court and 'organic laws', i.e., laws which the Oireachtas would be empowered to make to give effect to basic constitutional principles.[3] However, the idea of a Constitutional Court was then practically unknown in the English speaking world and no one but a specialist constitutional lawyer would have used the term 'organic laws' (itself a term used by constitutional lawyers versed in the continental legal tradition). This suggests that these ideas were imparted by Hearne to de Valera rather than the other way around.

A further clue may be found in the somewhat cryptic note 'Page 187—German Pres TFA'.[4] This was clearly a reference to the office of German

[1] A few months later de Valera, speaking at Ennis, gave his first public intimation of his plans when he announced that 'before the present Government left office they would have an Irish Constitution from top to bottom': *Irish Press*, 1 July 1935.

[2] See document no. 38. Hearne's memorandum of 17 May 1935 states that his draft was based on verbal instructions (see document no. 41). Given that the 'squared paper draft' uses legal and constitutional terms known only to constitutional specialists, these are quite possibly de Valera's own notes of conversations between Hearne and himself. Besides, it seems unlikely that instructions of this kind would be given in this informal fashion.

[3] Thus, for example, Article 16.7 provides:

> Subject to the foregoing provisions of this Article, elections for membership of Dáil Éireann, including the filling of casual vacancies, shall be regulated in accordance with law.
>
> A law which sought to regulate electoral law in accordance with these provisions would be an example of such an organic law in this sense.

[4] Apart from the reference to the German Presidency, it is not clear what the other letters refer to.

President under the 1919 Weimar Constitution. Article 41 of the Weimar Constitution provided that the President was directly elected by the German people and every German citizen who had completed their thirty-fifth year was eligible for office. Article 43 provided that the term was seven years, but that he could be re-elected. It also contemplated that the President could be removed from office by a two-thirds vote in the Reichstag which would then go to a referendum recall vote.[5] Rejection of the measure by the voters would act as a re-election of the President and cause the Reichstag to be dissolved. The President was not permitted to be a member of the Reichstag himself (Article 44);[6] he had supreme command of the armed forces (Article 47);[7] and he was invested with the right of pardon (Article 49).[8] The President further appointed the Chancellor and, on the latter's recommendations, the Ministers.[9] There was also a procedure in Article 59 whereby the President could be impeached before the State Court of Justice (Staatsgerichtshof), provided the original motion was supported by at least one hundred members of the Reichstag.[10] Given the similarity between these provisions and the corresponding provisions of Article 12 and Article 13 of the Constitution, it is hard to think that the Weimar model was not hugely influential:

> The office and functions of the President, which had to be devised from scratch in 1937, exhibit so many secondary resemblances to the office and functions of the President of the Weimar Republic under the Constitution of 1919 that a direct importation must be suspected.[11]

If the squared draft instructions further hint at the Weimar model, this suggestion seems more likely to have come in the first instance itself from Hearne rather than de Valera.[12]

[5] Interestingly, under the heading 'referendum' on the last page, one finds the single word 'recall'.
[6] Cf. Article 12.6.1° of the Constitution.
[7] Cf. Article 13.4 of the Constitution.
[8] Cf. Article 13.6 of the Constitution.
[9] Cf. Article 13.1 of the Constitution.
[10] Articles 12 and 13 of the Constitution likewise provided for an impeachment procedure for the President. At least 30 members of either House of the Oireachtas are required to sign the original impeachment motion (Article 12.10.3°) and Article 13.8.2° envisages that the Houses of the Oireachtas may establish a 'court, tribunal or body' to investigate the charge. It may be of interest to note that Article 61 of the German Baltic Law (1949) now provides that the German President may be impeached before the German Constitutional Court provided that the decision to impeach is supported by either two-thirds of the Bundestag or the Bundesrat.
[11] Kelly, *Irish Constitution*, 224–5.
[12] Further evidence for this contention comes from the Hearne drafts dealing with the powers of the President in document no. 40. These powers clearly follow the Weimar model. Article 5 of Hearne's draft required the President to swear an oath upholding the Constitution before Dáil Éireann, while Article 42 of the Weimar Constitution also required the President to swear his oath to protect the Constitution and the laws of the Realm before the Reichstag. There are also clearly echoes of the Weimar oath in Hearne's draft. Cf. Article 12.8 of the Constitution which requires the President to swear his oath 'to maintain the Constitution of Ireland and uphold its laws...in the presence of members of both Houses of the Oireachtas', the judiciary and 'other public personages'.

It is clear from the earliest drafts of the Constitution that de Valera was anxious to ensure that any constitutional changes strengthened and protected the fundamental rights of citizens. Not only was this a key concern of the 1934 Constitution Review Committee,[13] but Hearne's first preliminary drafts of the new Constitution lay considerable emphasis on these objectives. His explanatory memorandum (dated 17 May 1935) to accompany the draft Heads of a Constitution commenced by reciting de Valera's instructions:

> The Preliminary Draft of Heads of a Constitution which accompanies this memorandum is based upon verbal instructions given by the President on Wednesday, 30 April, and on Friday, 2 May. In general, the instructions of the President were to prepare a draft of the Heads of a new Constitution for Saorstát Éireann. In particular, the draft was
>
> A. to contain certain basic Articles guaranteeing fundamental human rights;
> B. to place the said Articles in a specially protected position, i.e., to render them unalterable save by the people themselves or by an elaborate constitutional process;
> C. to provide for the suspension of the said Articles during a state of public emergency only;
> D. to contain machinery for effectively preserving public order during any such emergency;
> E. to provide for the establishment of the Office of President of Saorstát Éireann, the holder of which would fulfil all the functions now exercised by the King and the Governor General in internal affairs; and
> F. to contain provision for the retention of the King as a constitutional officer of Saorstát Éireann in the domain of international relations.

The earliest drafts of the fundamental rights provisions reflected these concerns. The fundamental rights provisions of the May 1935 draft largely correlate to the corresponding provisions of the 1922 Constitution, save that three points of interest may be noted.

First, this draft repudiated the—quite unrealistic—guarantee which had been originally contained in Article 72 of the 1922 Constitution that 'no extraordinary courts shall be established'. In this respect Hearne

[13] See Chapter II of this volume.

drew on the earlier recommendations of the 1934 Committee inasmuch as the draft Article 43(b) provided that extraordinary tribunals 'may be established under this Constitution to deal with a state of public emergency proclaimed under this Constitution'. Article 46 also dealt with a state of emergency and was clearly a forerunner of Article 28.3.3°.

Secondly, the only conscious innovation in the fundamental rights provisions at this stage was contained in the draft Article 38 (which formed the basis for the present Article 40.1) which provided that: 'All citizens of Saorstát Éireann are equal before the law.' Although this innovation was plainly modelled on the equality guarantees contained in the Weimar Constitution (as well, perhaps, as the 'equal protection of the laws' provision contained in the fourteenth Amendment of the US Constitution), the final version of Article 40.1 later was to attract controversy on the ground that it was intended to be subversive of women's rights.[14] The fact that a provision which had been so obviously intended by Hearne to be progressive and egalitarian was objected to on this ground in its own way affords evidence of the extent to which the entire constitutional project was so little understood.

Finally, it ought to be noted that Hearne's draft was a largely secular one, in that it displayed almost none of the specifically Catholic influences to be found in the final version of the Constitution.[15] Hearne's Preamble was impressively drafted:

> In the name of Almighty God, We, the Sovereign Irish People through our elected representatives assembled in this Dáil Éireann sitting as a Constituent Assembly, in order to declare and confirm our constitutional rights and liberties, consolidate our national life, establish and maintain domestic peace on a basis of freedom, equality and justice, ensure harmonious relations with neighbouring peoples, and promote the ultimate unity of Ireland do hereby, as of undoubted right, ordain and enact this Constitution.[16]

The elegance of this draft, coupled with its vision for the State, is far removed from the 'Hibernia Irredenta' of which McElligott complained when reviewing the claim of right in respect of Northern Ireland

[14] See Chapter XI of this volume.

[15] Cf. the comments of Keogh:

> It is unfortunate that we have no record of John Hearne's reaction to the flood of documentation from [McQuaid]. One is tempted to speculate that he may have developed, as a consequence, a lifelong aversion to certain papal encyclicals, 'Church, State and Society', in Farrell (ed.), *De Valera's Constitution*, 121, n.19.

[16] See document no. 40.

contained in (the original) Article 2 and Article 3 some two years later.[17] It was, perhaps, asking too much of the Ireland of the 1930s to adopt a draft as noble, as fair-minded and as secular as this. As the drafting process went on, the provisions of the Constitution which were influenced by Catholic teaching were largely added on towards the end of the drafting process, either because they corresponded with de Valera's own personal wishes and political agenda or following representations from clerical or political sources. The basic point nevertheless remains true: the sub-structure of the Constitution was fundamentally liberal-democratic and secular in nature, with the religiously-inspired provisions superimposed upon this secular sub-structure. One way or another, Hearne's May 1935 draft remained the basic model for what was later to come. The fact that he produced such an elegant and comprehensive document single-handedly within such a short time frame is its own tribute to his skill and imagination as a constitution-drafter.

Hearne's drafts appeared to have lain fallow for a period of months. When first produced, however, it was not even fully clear whether there was to be a new Constitution at all or, alternatively, whether this draft was to be engrafted upon the existing Constitution.[18] However, speaking in the Dáil in May 1936 on the Constitution (No. 24) Bill 1934 (which provided for the abolition of the old Seanad), de Valera indicated his hope that a new Constitution would be presented to the House that autumn.[19] The British Government were then informed in June 1936 'as a matter of courtesy' that a new Constitution would be introduced over the course of the following months and that this document would make no provision for either the Monarch or the Governor-General.[20] It was at that point, following the abolition of the

[17] See document no. 158.

[18] See document no. 39.

[19] 62 *Dáil Debates*, Cols 1198–9 (28 May 1936).

[20] See document no. 61. See also Deirdre McMahon, *Republicans and Imperialists: Anglo-Irish Relations in the 1930s* (London, 1984), 172–9; Nicholas Mansergh, *The Unresolved Question: The Anglo-Irish Settlement and its Undoing, 1912–1972* (Yale, 1991), 291–2. Some months after the removal of the Crown from the Irish Free State Constitution in the wake of the Abdication crisis in December 1936, the British Government protested on 3 April 1937 (somewhat belatedly, it might be thought) that this constitutional amendment amounted to a breach of the 1921 Treaty, but they also indicated that they were prepared to treat this change as not amounting to a fundamental change in the status of the Irish Free State. The Irish Government responded on 27 April 1937, just before the publication of the new Constitution, by saying that:

> With regard to a departure from the provisions of the [1921 Treaty]...it need only be said that the evolution in the status of the Members of the Commonwealth which has taken place since the [Treaty was] signed has created an entirely new situation; [the Treaty has] been gradually replaced by legislation in the Irish Parliament based on declared principles of co-equality. It is on the basis of these principles also that the new Constitution about to be presented to the people has been drawn up. [The Treaty] postulated control of the Irish Parliament by the British Parliament. Until that situation was ended no approach to a final settlement between the peoples of the two countries could be made, NAI, DT S10463.

This diplomatic exchange set the scene for the ultimate British response to the new Constitution, for in a statement issued on 29 December 1937 (the date the Constitution came into force) that Government

Seanad and the establishment of the Second House Commission[21] that the stage was then set for a resumption in earnest of the drafting process.

No. 36: UCDA, P152/39

George Gavan Duffy to Eamon de Valera

Dublin
7 April 1935

Dear President,
In case you may not have seen President Salazar's new Portuguese Constitution, approved by national plebiscite on March 19, 1934, I want to call your attention to it, as it is highly original and most interesting in many respects.

With regard to the Second Chamber in particular I think the position may interest you: The legislative body is the National Assembly, but side-by-side with it is a Corporative Chamber, consisting of representatives of local authorities and representatives of 'social interests of an administrative, moral, cultural and economic character', chosen in manner prescribed by law.

The Corporative Chamber sits in secret—at least its sessions are not public—and it is its duty to give its view in writing on every Bill presented to the National Assembly before that body considers the Bill; it exercises no veto and passes no Bills.

Apart from the vocational representation in this Chamber, the remainder of its representation, deriving from the local authorities, is remarkable as being based on the family.

The Constitution undertakes to protect the family as the basic unit of the State; parish councils are elected by the families exclusively; above the parish councils there are municipal councils and above these provincial councils, and both sets of bodies are elected by the parish councils, representing the families, and by vocational and other guilds.

I have the Constitution in Portuguese, which Miss Austin, if she is still in External Affairs, could translate, and in an official translation in

[20] *contd.* indicated—with a sense of almost weary resignation—that it was also 'prepared to treat the new Constitution as not effecting a fundamental alteration in the position of the Irish Free State, in future to be described under the new Constitution as "Éire" or "Ireland", as a member of the British Commonwealth of Nations' (NAI, DT S10463). For more, see www.irishconstitution.ie.

[21] See Chapter V of this volume.

very bad French, and can lend you these documents. Excuse my troubling you in case you are already fully informed; I write on the off chance that you are not, as it would be a pity for you to miss a daring innovation and the whole Constitution repays perusal. A good deal, however, is left to the laws, of which I have not any particulars.

No. 37: UCDA, P152/39

Kathleen O'Connell to George Gavan Duffy

Dublin
15 April 1935

A Chara,
I am directed by the President to thank you for your letter. He would be very glad to have the loan of your copy of the Portuguese Constitution.

He desires me to say that at one time he was considering the possibility of a Vocational Council, but the difficulty is that here we have very few Vocational organisations.

No. 38: UCDA, P150/2370

'Squared Paper Draft'—Draft of heads of a Constitution, drawn up by Eamon de Valera on squared copybook paper

[May 1935]

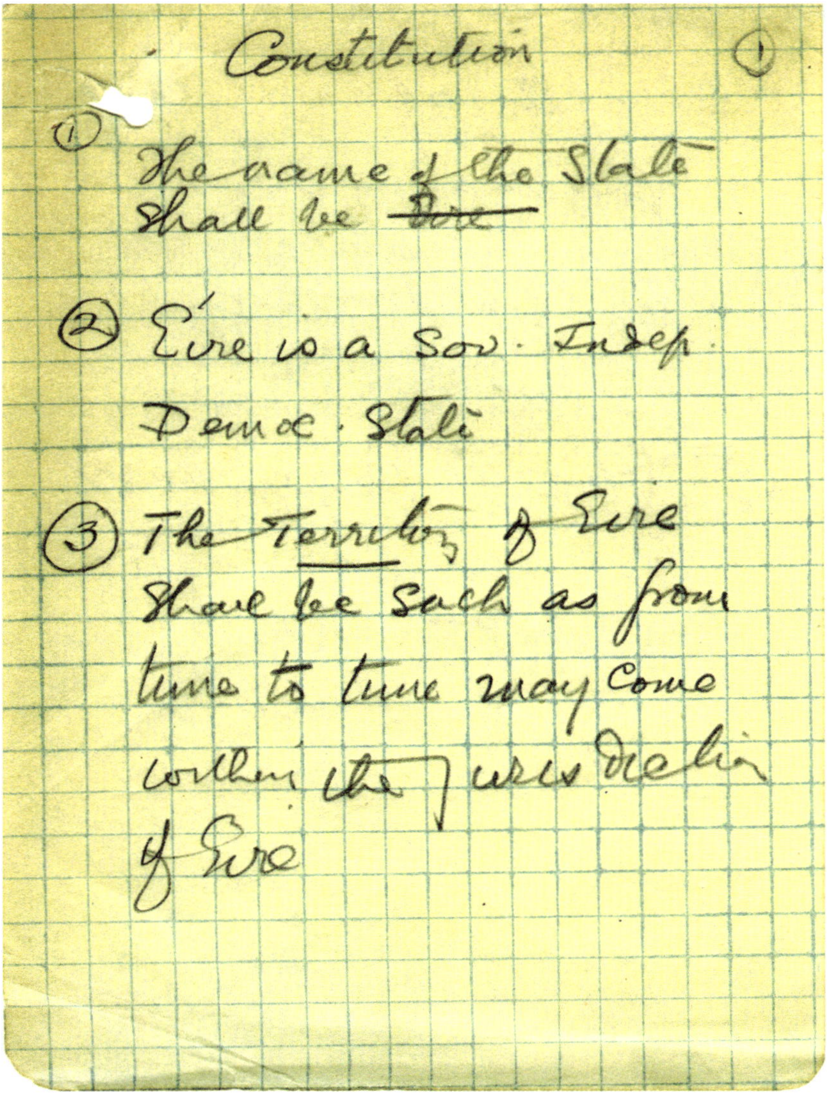

Constitution (1)

(1) The name of the State shall be ~~Eire~~

(2) Éire is a Sov. Indep. Democ. State

(3) The Territory of Éire shall be such as from time to time may come within the jurisdiction of Éire

(2)

(4) In Eire the ultimate Sov. power shall rest with the people who shall be the ultimate Court for deciding all national and political questions

(5) From the people under God all Governmental authority, legisl, Exe & Judicial shall be derived. These powers

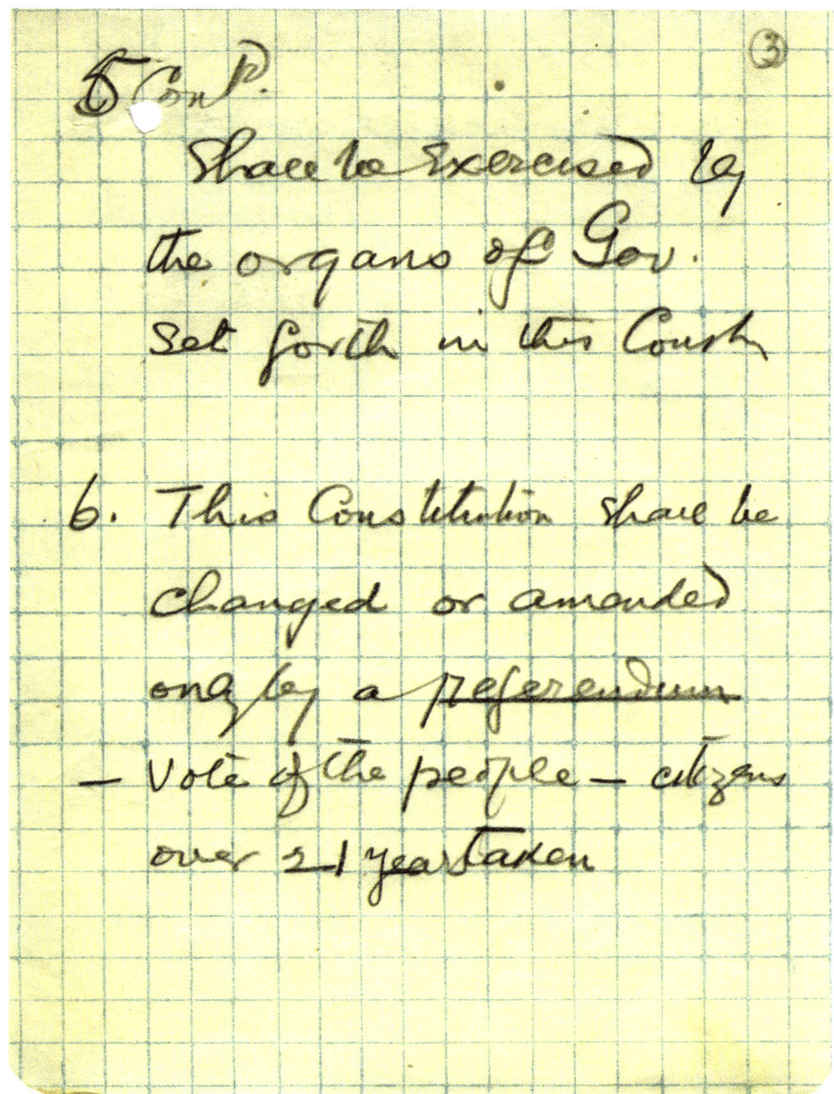

③

5 Cont.

Shall be Exercised by
the organs of Gov.
set forth in this Consti

6. This Constitution shall be
changed or amended
only by a referendum
— Vote of the people — citizens
over 21 years taken

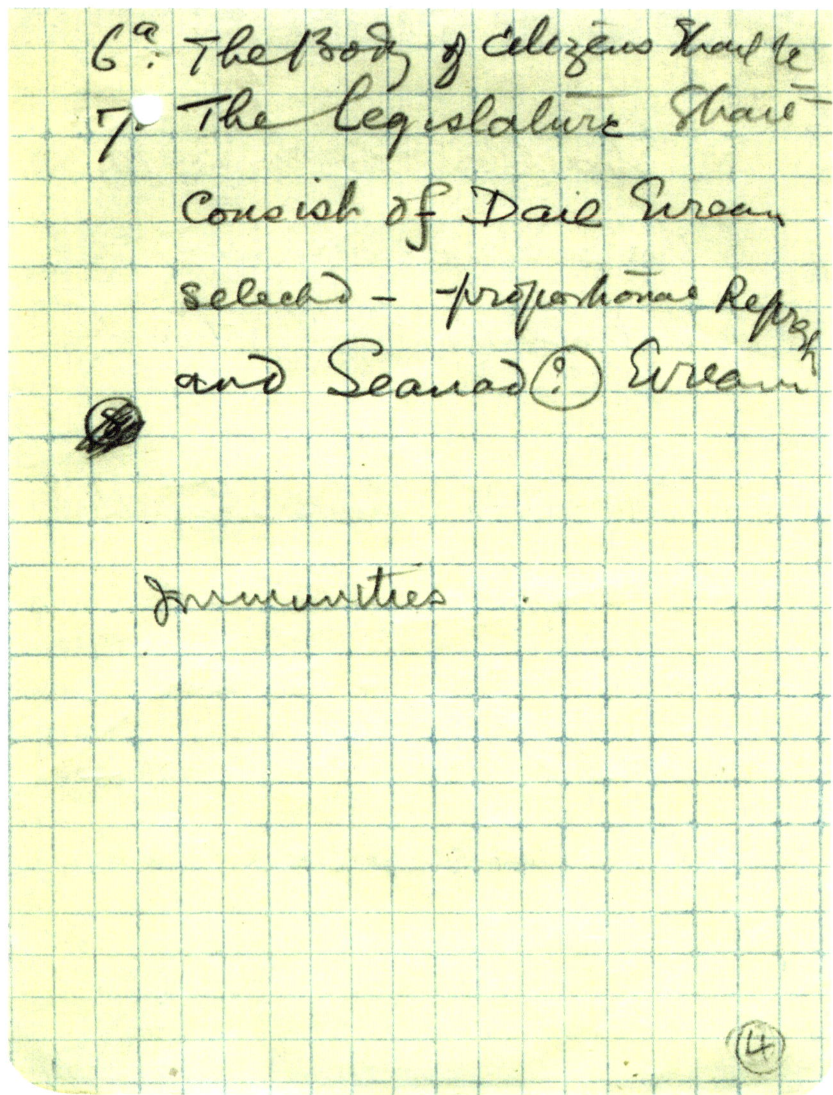
6a. The Body of citizens shall be
7. The Legislature shall consist of Dail Eireann selected – proportional Repr.
and Seanad(?) Eireann
(8)

Immunities.

(4)

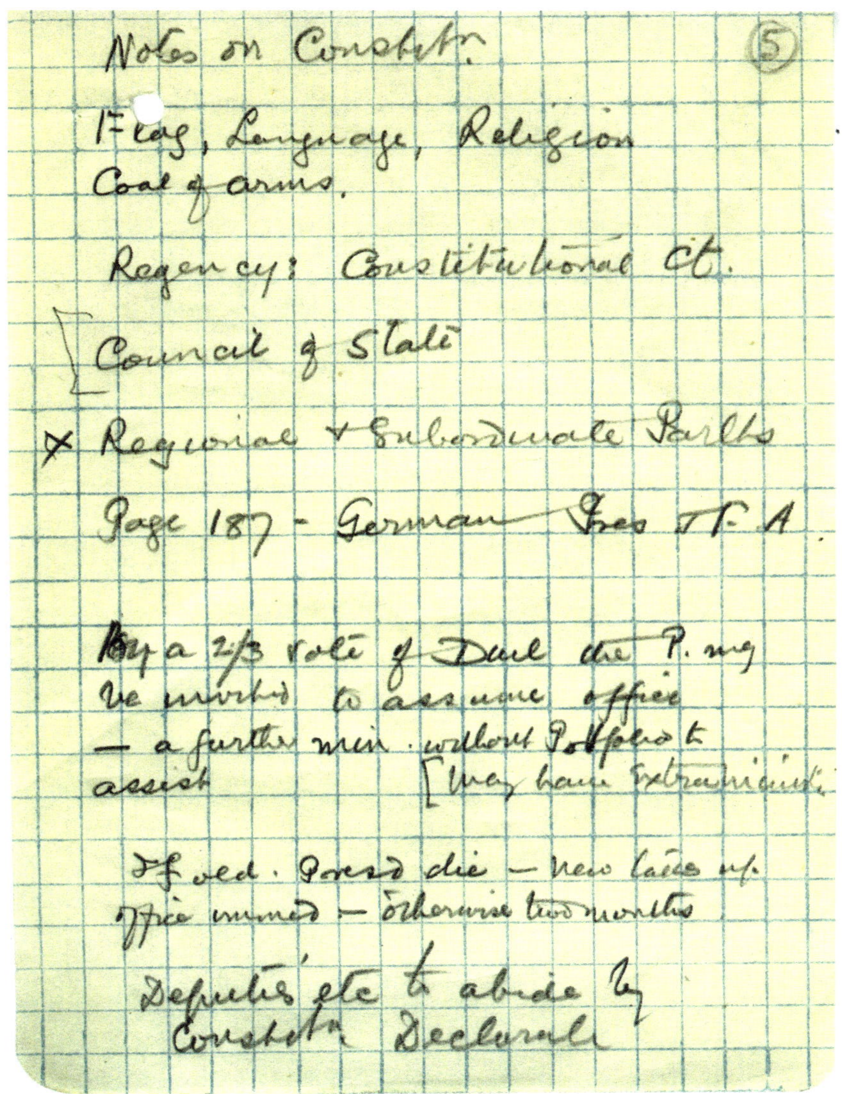

Notes on Constitn. (5)

Flag, Language, Religion
Coat of arms.

Regency: Constitutional Ct.

[Council of State

x Regional & Subordinate Parlts

Page 187 – German Pres & F. A.

By a 2/3 vote of Dail the P. may
be invited to assume office
– a further min. without Portfolio to
assist [may have extraordinary

If ved. Presd die – new Pres. up.
office immed – otherwise two months

Deputies etc to abide by
Constitn. Declaration

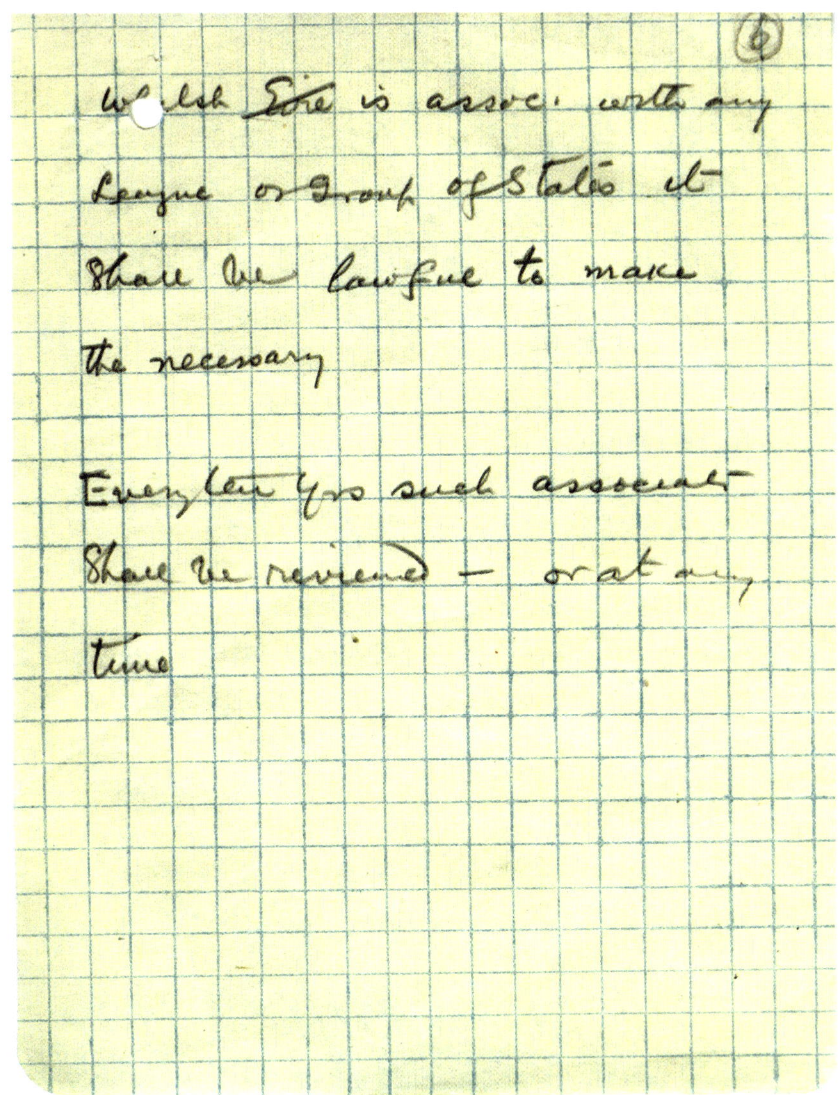
(6)

Whilst Eire is assoc. with any League or Group of States it shall be lawful to make the necessary

Every [illegible] yrs such associat shall be reviewed – or at any time

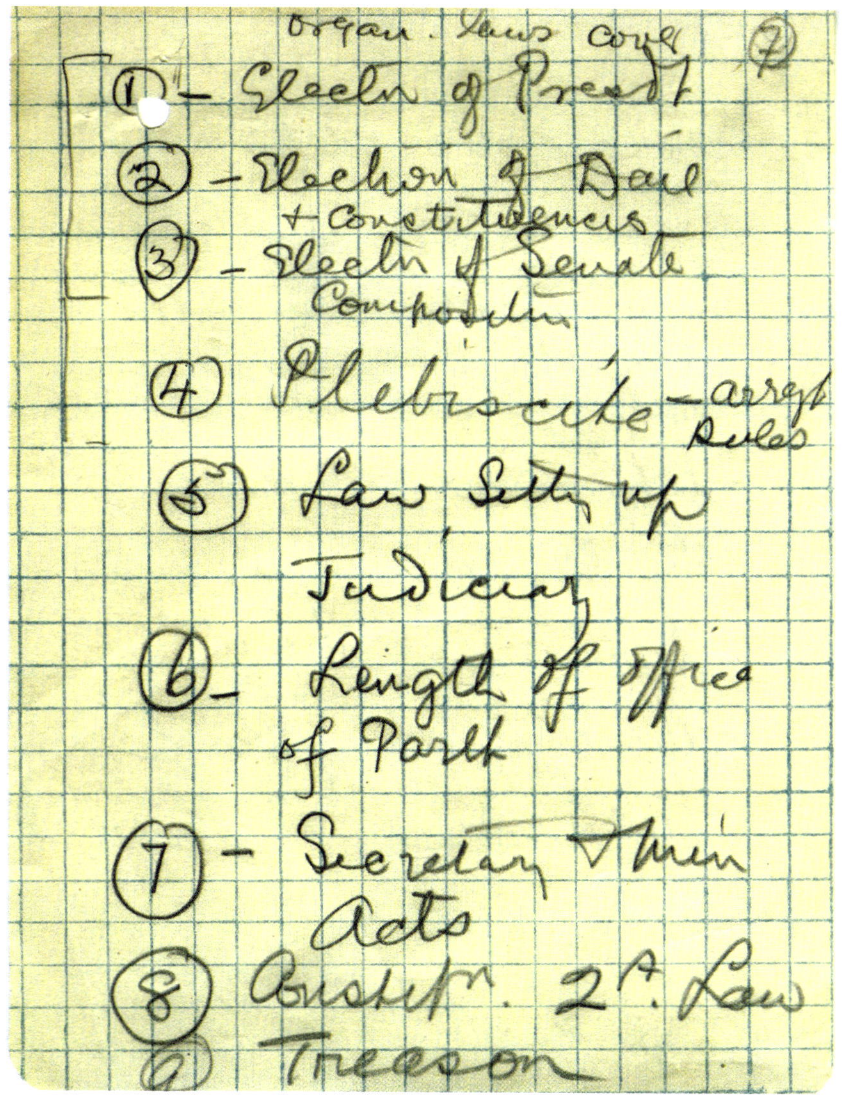

Organ. Laws Cons. (7)

(1) – Electn of Presdt

(2) – Election of Dail + constituencies

(3) – Electn of Senate Compositn

(4) Plebiscite – arrangt Rules

(5) Law setting up Judiciary

(6) – Length of office of Parlt

(7) – Secretary & Admin Acts

(8) Constitn. 2d. Law

(9) Treason

Preamble — The I. people acknowdg their dependn on almighty God, thanking him for the preservation of their nation & dedicatg themselvs to his Service, acceptg the ten comndts as fund law give themselvs this constitn, Fundamental so as to

① ② ③

See Proc. 1916, Decl. of Ind. 1919 & Dem. Prog.

Transitional (9)

1 The next parlt shall be at liberty to pass organic laws to have immed. effect — but must be ratified by referendum at time of next general election

—

(2) Existing laws carried over — (1) Election Boundaries
(2) Dail Elech
(3) Judiciary
(4) Ministers & Secs

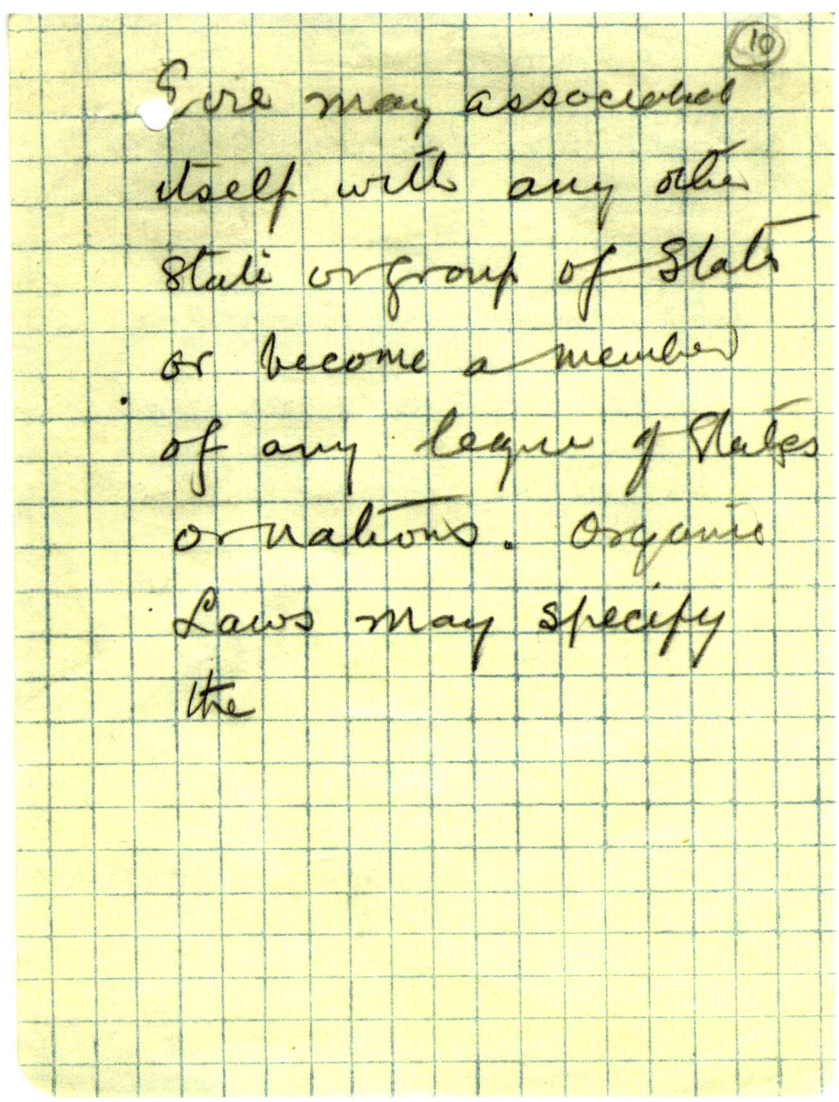

(10)

Eire may associate
itself with any other
State or group of States
or become a member
of any league of States
or nations. Organic
Laws may specify
the

Bor. (11)

1 ~~That~~ S.W.F note accepts the desapp & shows no real apprec. of ~~how I. often~~ the fundamentals in the problem

2. ~~In~~ def. as many times ptd out the I. people have no imperial interests or aspirations – They want to keep out of war.

(1) The only right they concede is that I. shd not be used as basis of attack on Britain

(2) When common threat invasion of the two islands – co-operation wd. come.

The State guarantees to all its citizens

To the family it guarantees etc

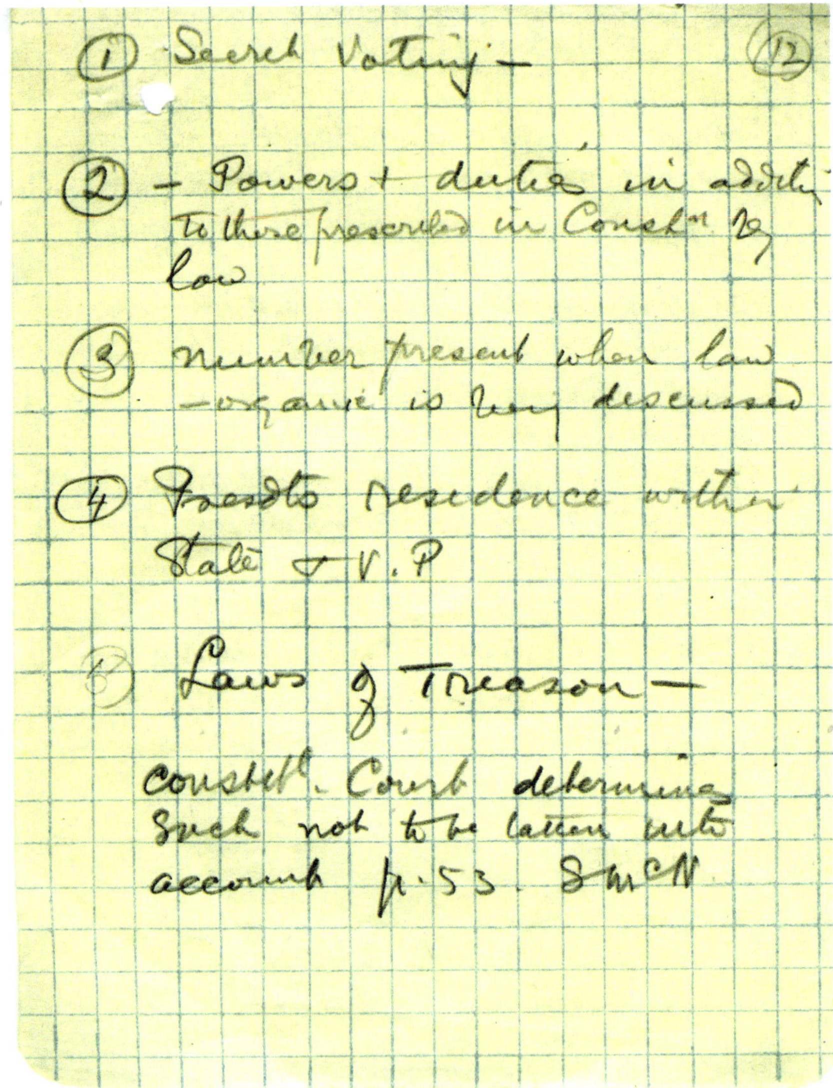

(1) Secret Voting — (12)

(2) – Powers + duties in addition to those prescribed in Constn by law

(3) number present when law – organic is being discussed

(4) Presdts residence within State + V.P

(5) Laws of Treason —

Constitl. Court determining such not to be taken into account p.53. SMcN

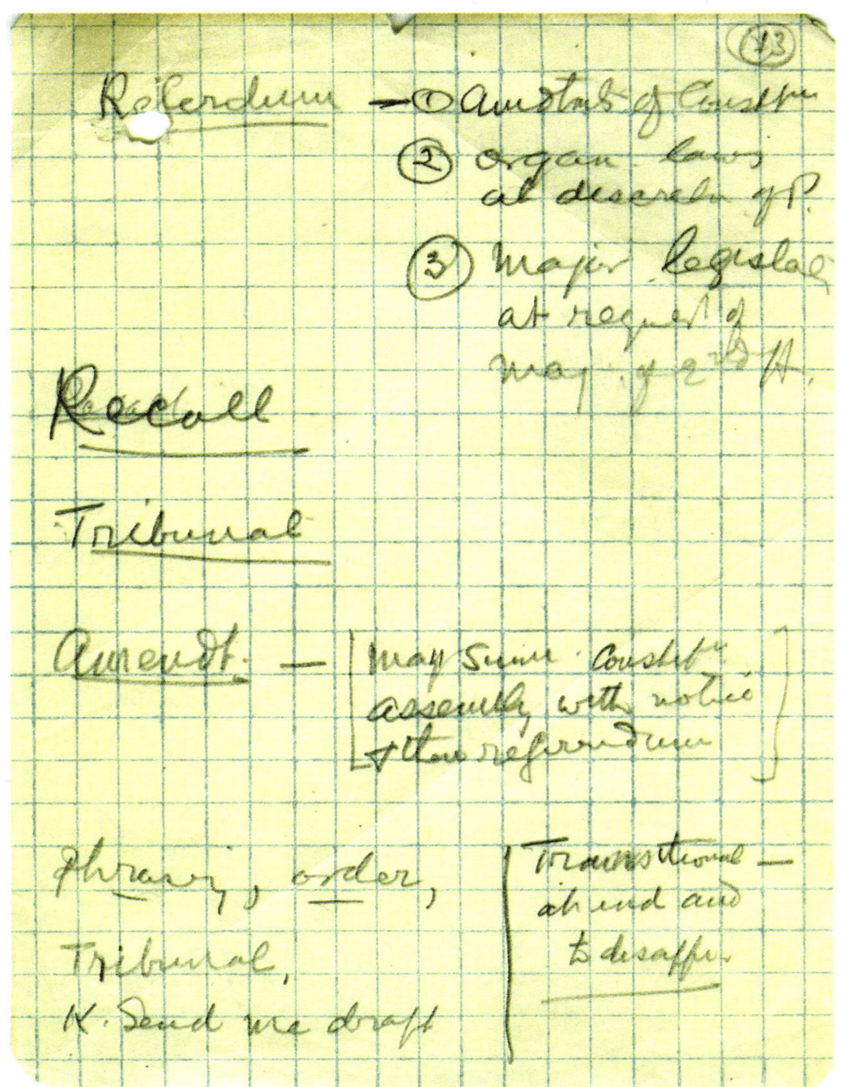

(13)

Referendum — ① amendt of Constn
② organic laws at discretion of P.
③ major legislation at request of maj. of 2nd H.

Recall

Tribunal

Amendt. — [may summ. Constit. assembly with notice & then referendum]

Phrasing, order,
Tribunal,
K. Send me draft

[Transitional — at end and to disappear]

No. 39: UCDA, P150/2370

John Hearne to Seán Moynihan

[Department of External Affairs]
18 May 1935

Secretary,
I now submit the draft of Heads of a Constitution which I have prepared on the verbal instructions of the President. I attach a short explanatory memorandum stating the scope of the President's instructions and giving the reasons for the preliminary method adopted in the preparation of the present draft.[22]

The next stage of the work would appear to be to recast those Articles of the Constitution of 1922 which it is intended to retain but which have been found defective in one way or another during the past twelve years.

The draft heads now submitted would, it is thought, form a suitable basis for a general discussion with the President at this stage on the scope of the project as a whole.

No. 40: UCDA, P150/2370

'Preliminary Draft of Heads of a Constitution for Saorstát Éireann'

17 May 1935

Preamble

In the Name of Almighty God, We, the Sovereign Irish People through our elected representatives assembled in this Dáil Éireann sitting as a Constituent Assembly, in order to declare and confirm our constitutional rights and liberties, consolidate our national life, establish and maintain domestic peace on a basis of freedom, equality and justice, ensure harmonious relations with neighbouring peoples, and promote the ultimate unity of Ireland do hereby, as of undoubted right, ordain and enact this Constitution.

Introductory

Article 1
Saorstát Éireann is an independent sovereign State.

[22] See document no. 40.

All powers of government and all authority, legislative, executive and judicial, derived from God through the people shall be exercised in Saorstát Éireann through the organisations continued or established by, or established under, and in accord with this Constitution.[23]

Citizenship
Article 2
The citizens of Saorstát Éireann shall be all persons who are citizens of Saorstát Éireann by or under the law in force at the date of the coming into operation of this Constitution or who hereafter become citizens by or under the said law or any future law.[24]

The National Language
Article 3
The Irish language is the National language of Saorstát Éireann. The English language shall (be equally)[25] recognised as an official language. Special provisions may be made by law for districts in which only one of the said languages is in general use.

The President
Article 4
The President of Saorstát Éireann (hereinafter referred to as 'the President')[26] shall be elected by the people of Saorstát Éireann.

Every citizen of Saorstát Éireann who has completed his thirty-fifth[27] year is eligible for the office of President.

The President shall hold office for seven years and shall be eligible for re-election. He shall remain in office until his successor is elected.

The President shall not be a member of the Chamber of Deputies established by this Constitution (hereinafter referred to as 'Dáil Éireann').

The first President shall be elected at an election at which the area of jurisdiction for the time being of Saorstát Éireann shall form one electoral area and the election shall be conducted in accordance with a law to be passed by the existing Legislature. The second and every subsequent President shall be elected in accordance with the said law or any future law passed by the Parliament of Saorstát Éireann created by this Constitution (hereinafter referred to as 'the Oireachtas').

Should the President die or resign during his term of office the election of a new President shall be held not later than two months from

[23] Annotated by de Valera: 'The name of the State shall be Éire'. Some of the annotations to this document which follow are elliptical in nature. They are presented exactly as found. All annotations to this document were made by Eamon de Valera, unless otherwise noted.
[24] Annotated: 'Put general clause born etc or who are'.
[25] Annotated: 'also be'.
[26] Annotated: 'Uachtarán'.
[27] Annotated with a question mark.

the date of such death or resignation and such election shall be conducted in accordance with the law for the time being in force relating to the election of President and the President so elected shall hold office for seven years and shall be eligible for re-election.

In the event of the President becoming ill or incapacitated for more than six months the Council of Ministers established by this Constitution (hereinafter referred to as 'the Council of Ministers') may, by a majority decision taken with three fourths of its members present, call upon Dáil Éireann to appoint a Deputy President who shall act until the President is able to resume his functions. The appointment of a Deputy President by Dáil Éireann under this Article shall be made by a Resolution of Dáil Éireann passed by a simple majority of the total membership thereof.

Article 5
The President when entering upon his office shall take the following oath before Dáil Éireann:

> 'I swear by Almighty God that I will maintain the Constitution of Saorstát Éireann and uphold its laws and that I will dedicate my powers to the service and welfare of the people of Saorstát Éireann and defend the State against all its enemies whomsoever domestic and external and fulfil my duties faithfully and conscientiously in accordance with the Constitution and the law. So help me God.'

Article 6
The supreme command of the defence forces of Saorstát Éireann is hereby vested in the President, who shall exercise the same in accordance with the law. All commissioned officers of the defence forces shall hold their commissions from him.

Article 7
The President shall, as hereinafter mentioned, represent Saorstát Éireann in international relations:

(1) He shall appoint the diplomatic representatives and consuls of Saorstát Éireann in other States and receive the diplomatic representatives of other States accredited to Saorstát Éireann.
(2) He shall negotiate and conclude treaties and conventions.
(3) He shall sign
  (a) The Letters of Credence and Recall of the diplomatic representatives of Saorstát Éireann accredited to other States,

(b) The Commissions of consuls appointed for Saorstát Éireann in other States,
(c) The full powers of plenipotentiaries empowered to conclude international treaties and conventions in the Heads of States form,
(d) The instruments of ratification of such treaties and conventions, and
(e) The exequaturs of consular representatives appointed in Saorstát Éireann.

Article 8

The right of pardon, and power to remit or commute sentences imposed, and to remit the legal consequences of verdicts given, by any courts exercising criminal jurisdiction are hereby vested in the President.

Article 9

The President (a) shall appoint the Prime Minister on the nomination of Dáil Éireann and (b) shall, on the nomination of the Prime Minister assented to by Dáil Éireann, appoint the other members of the Council of Ministers.

He shall appoint the judges of the Supreme Court, the High Court and all other Courts continued by or established under this Constitution.

Article 10

The Oireachtas shall be summoned and dissolved by the President.

Article 11

The President shall in accordance with this Constitution assent to and sign Bills passed by Dáil Éireann and presented to him for his assent and signature hereunder.

Article 12

The existing statutory powers and duties of the Governor-General shall cease to be exercisable and performable by the Governor-General and shall be exercised and performed by the President in accordance with this Constitution.

Article 13

The salary of the President shall be determined by law.[28]

Article 14

The powers and duties conferred and imposed on the President by this Constitution or by any Act of the Oireachtas shall not be exercisable and performable by him save only upon the advice of the Council of Ministers.[29]

[28] Annotated: 'Establishment?'.

[29] Annotated: 'Exceptions?'.

The Oireachtas

Article 15

A Parliament is hereby created otherwise called and herein generally referred to as the Oireachtas. The Oireachtas shall consist of the President and Dáil Éireann. The sole and exclusive power of making laws for Saorstát Éireann is hereby vested in the Oireachtas.

Article 16

The Oireachtas shall hold at least one session each year.

Article 17

The Oireachtas shall be summoned and dissolved by the President on the advice of the Council of Ministers. Provided, however, that the power of the dissolution shall not be exercisable on the advice of a Council of Ministers which has ceased to retain the support of a majority in Dáil Éireann.

Article 18

The sole and exclusive right to raise and maintain armed forces is hereby vested in the Oireachtas.

Article 19

The Oireachtas shall have no power to declare acts to be infringements of the law which were not so at the date of their commission.

Dáil Éireann

Article 20

There shall be a Chamber of Deputies (to be known and called and herein generally referred to as 'Dáil Éireann'). Every citizen who has reached the age of twenty-one years and who is not placed under disability or incapacity by this Constitution or by law shall be eligible to become a member of Dáil Éireann.

Article 21

All citizens of Saorstát Éireann without distinction of sex who have reached the age of twenty-one years and who comply with the provisions of the electoral laws from time to time in force shall have the right to vote for members of Dáil Éireann. It shall be composed of members who represent constituencies determined by law. The first Dáil Éireann to be elected after the coming into operation of this Constitution shall be composed of members representing the existing constituencies, and the election of the members of the said first Dáil Éireann shall be conducted in accordance with the provisions of the existing electoral law.

Article 22
Every member of Dáil Éireann shall, except in case of treason, felony, or breach of the peace, be privileged from arrest in going to and returning from, and while within the precincts of Dáil Éireann, and shall not, in respect of any utterance therein, be amenable to any action or proceeding in any Court other than Dáil Éireann itself.[30]

Article 23
All official reports and publications of Dáil Éireann and of the Oireachtas shall be privileged, and utterances made therein wherever published shall be privileged.

Article 24
Dáil Éireann shall make its own Rules and Standing Orders, with power to attach penalties for their infringement and shall have power to ensure freedom of debate, to protect its official documents and the private papers of its members, and to protect itself and its members against any person or persons interfering with, molesting or attempting to corrupt its members in the exercise of their duties.[31]

Article 25
Dáil Éireann shall elect its own Ceann Comhairle and Leas Ceann Comhairle and shall prescribe their powers, duties, remuneration, and terms of office. The member of Dáil Éireann who is the Ceann Comhairle immediately before a dissolution of the Oireachtas shall, unless before such dissolution he announces to Dáil Éireann that he does not desire to continue to be a member thereof, be deemed without any actual election to be elected in accordance with this Constitution at the ensuing general election as a member of Dáil Éireann for the constituency for which he was a member immediately before such dissolution or, in the event of a revision of constituencies having taken place, for the revised constituency declared on such revision to correspond to such first-mentioned constituency the number of members actually to be elected for such constituency at such general election shall be one less than would otherwise be required to be elected therefor.

Article 26
Subject to the right of the President to dissolve the Oireachtas in accordance with this Constitution Dáil Éireann shall fix the date of reassembly of the (Oireachtas),[32] and the date of the conclusion of the session of Dáil Éireann.

[30] Annotated: 'Presdt. Immunity'.
[31] Annotated: 'How to have comnds executed?—courts?'.
[32] Annotated: '? DE'.

Article 27
At a General Election for Dáil Éireann the polls shall be held on the same day throughout the country, and that day shall be a day not later than thirty days after the date of the dissolution of the Oireachtas. Dáil Éireann shall meet within one month of such day, and shall unless earlier dissolved continue for (six)[33] years or such shorter period as may be fixed by legislation from the date of its first meeting, and not longer.

Article 28
In case of death, resignation or disqualification of a member of Dáil Éireann, the vacancy shall be filled by election in manner to be determined by law.

Article 29
Dáil Éireann shall as soon as possible after the commencement of each financial year consider the Estimates of receipts and expenditure of Saorstát Éireann for that year, and, save in so far as may be provided by specific enactment in each case, the legislation required to give effect to the Financial Rcsolutions of each year shall be enacted within that year.

Article 30
Money shall not be appropriated by vote, resolution or law, unless the purpose of the appropriation has in the same session been recommended by a message from the President acting on the advice of the Council of Ministers.

The Council of Ministers
Article 31
There shall be a Council otherwise called and herein generally referred to as the Council of Ministers to advise the President on the government of Saorstát Éireann. The Council of Ministers shall be responsible to Dáil Éireann. Every Minister shall be a member of the Council of Ministers.

The number of Ministers and their respective powers, duties and functions shall be determined by law. Pending the enactment of laws determining their number, the Council of Ministers shall be composed of the same number of members as is the Executive Council in existence at the date of the coming into operation of this Constitution.

The existing Departments of State are hereby continued.

The President of the Council of Ministers shall be called and known as 'the Prime Minister', and the Vice-President of the Council of Ministers shall be called and known as 'the Deputy Prime Minister'.

[33] Annotated: 'Exceptions'.

Every member of the Council of Ministers shall be a member of Dáil Éireann.

The Prime Minister and the other members of the Council of Ministers shall be appointed by the President in accordance with the provisions of this Constitution.[34]

Subject as aforesaid, the law in force at the date aforesaid in relation to the Executive Council, the existing Departments of State and the rights, powers, duties and functions of the respective heads of the said Departments shall continue in force pending the enactment of further laws. References in the laws hereby continued in force to the Executive Council, the President and Vice-President of the Executive Council, and to any Minister, head of a Department of State, shall be construed and have effect as references respectively to the Council of Ministers, the Prime Minister and Deputy Prime Minister, and to the member of the Council of Ministers administering such Department as aforesaid.

The existing Department of External Affairs shall be called and known as the Department of Foreign Affairs and the Minister who is head of the said Department at any time after the enactment of this Constitution shall be called and known as 'the Minister for Foreign Affairs'.

Article 32

The Council of Ministers shall meet and act as a collective authority and shall be collectively responsible for all matters concerning the Departments of State administered by the members thereof. The Council of Ministers shall prepare estimates of receipts and expenditure of Saorstát Éireann for each financial year and shall present them to Dáil Éireann before the close of the previous financial year.[35]

Article 33

The appointment of a member of Dáil Éireann to be a member of the Council of Ministers shall not entail upon him any obligation to resign his seat as a member of Dáil Éireann.

The Judicial Power

Article 34

The judicial power of Saorstát Éireann shall, subject as hereinafter mentioned, be exercised and justice administered by the public Courts at present existing. Every judge or justice being a member of any such Court, holding office at the date on which this Constitution comes into operation, shall continue to be a member thereof and hold office by the

[34] This paragraph annotated: 'General Transition art'.

[35] Annotated: 'Co-ordinate these r.m'.

like tenure and upon the like terms as heretofore unless he signifies to the President his desire to resign. Future appointments of judges and justices of the existing Courts and appointments of judges and justices of any Courts hereafter established under this Constitution shall be made by the President.

Subject as hereinafter provided, the existing Courts shall for the time being continue to exercise the same jurisdiction as heretofore.

The exclusive original jurisdiction heretofore vested in the High Court to determine the validity of any law having regard to the provisions of the Constitution hereby repealed is hereby terminated. The said Court shall have exclusive original jurisdiction to determine the validity of any law having regard to the provisions of this Constitution. Every decision of the High Court on the question of the validity of any law shall be subject to the like appeal as that to which, at the date of the coming into operation of this Constitution, a decision of the said Court on the question of the validity of any law having regard to the provisions of the Constitution hereby repealed was subject.[36]

The Oireachtas may at any time reconstitute or reorganise the existing Courts or redistribute the jurisdiction of the said Courts or of the judges thereof or terminate the said Courts and establish other public Courts in lieu thereof. The Oireachtas may reconstitute or reorganise or redistribute the jurisdiction of any public Courts (or of the judges thereof) established hereunder. The public Courts of Saorstát Éireann shall always comprise Courts of First Instance and a Court of Final Appeal. The Courts of the First Instance shall always include a High Court invested with full original jurisdiction in and power to determine all matters and questions whether of law or fact, civil or criminal, and also Courts of local and limited jurisdiction with a right of appeal as determined by law.

The Court of Final Appeal shall with such exceptions (not including cases which involve questions as to the Validity of any law having regard to the provisions of this Constitution) and subject to such regulations as may be prescribed by law, have appellate jurisdiction from all decisions of the High Court.

Article 35

The judges and justices of the existing Courts and all judges and justices hereafter appointed to the said Courts or to any Courts established under this Constitution shall be independent in the exercise of their functions and subject only to the Constitution and the law. A judge or justice shall

[36] This paragraph annotated with a question mark.

not be a member of Dáil Éireann and shall not hold any other office or position of emolument.

The Comptroller and Auditor-General
Article 36
Dáil Éireann shall from time to time appoint a Comptroller and Auditor-General to act on behalf of Saorstát Éireann. He shall control all disbursements and shall audit all accounts of moneys administered by or under the authority of the Oireachtas and shall report to Dáil Éireann at stated periods to be determined by law.

Article 37
The Comptroller and Auditor-General shall not be removed from office except for stated misbehaviour and incapacity of a resolution passed by Dáil Éireann. He shall not be a member of Dáil Éireann.

Subject as aforesaid, the existing Comptroller and Auditor-General shall continue to hold office by the like tenure and upon the like terms as heretofore.

Fundamental Rights
Article 38
All citizens of Saorstát Éireann are equal before the law.

Article 39
Freedom of conscience and the free expression and practice of religion are, subject to public order and morality, guaranteed to every citizen, and no law may be made either directly or indirectly to endow any religion, or prohibit or restrict the free exercise thereof or give any preference, or impose any disability on account of religious belief or religious status, or affect prejudicially the right of any child to attend a school receiving public money without attending the religious instruction at the school, or make any discrimination as respects State aid between schools under the management of different religious denominations, or divert from any religious denomination or any educational institution any of its property except for the purpose of roads, railways, lighting, water or drainage works or other works of public utility, and on payment of compensation.

Article 40
The right of free expression of opinion as well as the right to assemble peaceably and without arms, and to form associations or unions is guaranteed for purposes not opposed to public morality. Laws regulating the manner in which the right of forming associations and the right of free assembly may be exercised shall contain no political, religious or class distinction.

Article 41
The liberty of the person is inviolable, and no person shall be deprived of his liberty except in accordance with law. Upon complaint made by or on behalf of any person that he is being unlawfully detained, the High Court and any and every judge thereof shall forthwith enquire into the same and may make an order requiring the person in whose custody such person shall be detained to produce the body of the person so detained before such Court or judge without delay and to certify in writing as to the cause of the detention and such Court or judge shall thereupon order the release of such person unless satisfied that he is being detained in accordance with the law.

Article 42
The dwelling of each citizen is inviolable and shall not be forcibly entered except in accordance with law.

Trial of Criminal Offences
Article 43
No one shall be tried save in due course of law and extraordinary courts shall not be established, save only

(a) Such Military Tribunals as may be authorised by law for dealing with military offenders against military law, and
(b) Such other extraordinary tribunals as may be established under this Constitution to deal with a state of public emergency proclaimed under this Constitution.

The jurisdiction of military tribunals shall not be extended to or exercised over the civil population save in time of war or armed rebellion or during a period of public emergency proclaimed under this Constitution, and for acts done during such time or period, and in accordance with law.

Article 44
A member of the defence forces of Saorstát Éireann not on active service shall not be tried by any Court Martial or other Military Tribunal for an offence cognisable by the Civil Courts, unless such offence shall have been brought expressly within the jurisdiction of Courts Martial or other Military Tribunal by any existing code of laws or regulations for the enforcement of military discipline or any such code which may be hereafter approved by the Oireachtas.

Article 45
No person shall be tried on any criminal charge without a jury save in the case of charges in respect of minor offences triable by law before a

Court of Summary Jurisdiction, charges for offences against military law triable by Court Martial or other Military Tribunal, and charges for offences triable before a Military Tribunal or other extraordinary court in time of war or armed rebellion, or during a state of public emergency proclaimed under this Constitution.

Emergency Powers
Article 46
If and whenever Dáil Éireann or, if Dáil Éireann is not sitting, the Council of Ministers is satisfied that a grave state of public disorder exists throughout Saorstát Éireann or in any specified area thereof and that the ordinary laws and civil courts are not adequate for the preservation of public order Dáil Éireann or the Council of Ministers (as the case may require) may, by proclamation, declare a state of public emergency in respect of the area to which such proclamation relates.

Whenever the Council of Ministers declares a state of public emergency under this article the President shall forthwith summon the Oireachtas. Upon the reassembly of the Oireachtas the proclamation of the Council of Ministers declaring a state of public emergency shall forthwith be laid before Dáil Éireann and if within seven days after such proclamation is laid before it Dáil Éireann passes a resolution annulling such proclamation such proclamation shall be annulled accordingly but without prejudice to the validity of anything previously done in pursuance thereof. A proclamation issued by Dáil Éireann or by the Council of Ministers under this Article declaring a state of public emergency may be expressed, and, if so expressed, shall operate to suspend temporarily the operation of such and so many of the Articles of this Constitution as may be specified in such proclamation.

The Oireachtas may enact such legislation establishing such extraordinary courts and investing such courts with such jurisdiction as may in the opinion of Dáil Éireann be necessary to deal with any such state of public emergency as aforesaid; but such legislation shall not come into operation unless and until a proclamation is issued under this Article declaring a state of public emergency, and then only for the period of such emergency.

Nothing in this Constitution or in any law continued thereby or passed thereunder shall be invoked to nullify any provision of this Article or of any legislation passed under this Article or to oust the jurisdiction of any Court established hereunder or to invalidate any act or thing done in pursuance of this Article or of any legislation enacted for the purposes thereof.

The decisions of any Court established under this Article shall not be subject to appeal to or review by any other court.

War and Defence
Article 47
Saorstát Éireann shall not be committed to war with any other State save only with the consent of Dáil Éireann.

In the event, however, of an invasion of the territory of Saorstát Éireann the President and the Council of Ministers shall take immediate measures for the defence of the State pending the enactment by the Oireachtas of such legislation as may be necessary for that purpose.

Exercise of Treaty-Making Power
Article 48
A treaty of alliance shall not be concluded with any other State save with the approval of Dáil Éireann signified by a resolution of Dáil Éireann passed before the ratification of such treaty.

Article 49
International agreements affecting the revenue shall not be binding unless and until approved by a resolution of Dáil Éireann.

Amendment of the Constitution
Article 50
The Oireachtas may amend any Article of this Constitution with the exception of the Articles relating to fundamental rights (namely, Article 38, Article 39, Article 40, Article 41 and Article 42) and this Article by way of ordinary legislation expressed to be an amendment of the Constitution.

The Articles relating to fundamental rights (hereinbefore expressly mentioned) and this Article shall not be amended by the Oireachtas unless and until the Bill containing the proposed amendment or amendments of any such Article, after it has been passed by Dáil Éireann and before being presented to the President for his assent, shall have been submitted to a Referendum and either the votes of a majority of the voters on the register or two thirds of the votes recorded shall have been cast in favour of such amendment or amendments.

Every Referendum shall be conducted in accordance with laws enacted by the Oireachtas for that purpose and for the time being in force.

State Seals
Article 51
The present Great Seal of Saorstát Éireann and any Great Seal of Saorstát Éireann hereafter established shall be in the custody of the President.

Neither the present nor any future Great Seal of Saorstát Éireann shall be affixed to any instrument save upon the advice of the Council of Ministers. Every such Seal shall be authenticated on every document to which it is affixed by the countersignature of the Minister for Foreign Affairs.

The present Signet Seal and any or other similar Seal hereafter established in lieu thereof shall be in the custody of the Minister for Foreign Affairs, and shall not be affixed on any document save on the advice of that Minister.

Repeal of Constitution of 1922 and Continuance of Laws
Article 52
The Constitution enacted and given the force of law by the Constitution of the Irish Free State (Saorstát Éireann) Act, 1922 is hereby repealed save in so far and so long as any provision or provisions thereof is or are continued in force by any Article of this Constitution. Every such provision so continued in force by this Constitution shall remain in force unless and until amended or repealed by the Oireachtas.

All other laws in force at the date of the coming into operation of this Constitution, save in so far as they are in conflict with this Constitution or any provision thereof, are hereby continued in force and shall remain in force unless and until amended or repealed by the Oireachtas.

Transitory Provisions
Article 53
So long as Saorstát Éireann remains associated as a Member of the British Commonwealth of Nations the following documents shall before being issued be countersigned by the Minister for Foreign Affairs of Saorstát Éireann, that is to say:

(a) The Letters of Credence and Recall of the diplomatic representatives of Saorstát Éireann accredited to other States.
(b) The Commissions of consuls appointed for Saorstát Éireann in other States,
(c) The full powers of plenipotentiaries empowered to conclude international treaties and conventions,
(d) The instruments of ratification of such treaties and conventions,
(e) The exequaturs of consular representatives appointed in Saorstát Éireann.

No. 41: UCDA, P150/2370

Explanatory Memorandum for Preliminary Draft of Heads of a Constitution for Saorstát Éireann

John Hearne, [Department of External Affairs]
17 May 1935

The Preliminary Draft of Heads of a Constitution which accompanies this memorandum is based upon verbal instructions given by the President on Wednesday, 30 April, and on Friday, 2 May. In general, the instructions of the President were to prepare a draft of the Heads of a new Constitution for Saorstát Éireann. In particular, the draft was to contain certain basic Articles guaranteeing fundamental human rights;

A. to place the said Articles in a specially protected position, i.e., to render them unalterable save by the people themselves or by an elaborate constitutional process;
B. to provide for the suspension of the said Articles during a state of public emergency only;
C. to contain machinery for effectively preserving public order during any such emergency;
D. to provide for the establishment of the Office of President of Saorstát Éireann, the holder of which would fulfil all the functions now exercised by the King and the Governor General in internal affairs; and
E. to contain provision for the retention of the King as a constitutional officer of Saorstát Éireann in the domain of international relations.

The draft Heads are an attempt to write down the President's instructions and insert them into the text of the existing Constitution rather than an effort to construct—at this stage—a completely new Constitution. This preliminary method has been adopted for the following reasons: 1) The task to be undertaken appears to be to effect a far-reaching Constitutional reform within the framework, as far as possible, of the existing State rather than to establish a new State with a constitutional system fundamentally different from that now obtaining. 2) The method adopted has, it is thought, the advantage of showing the precise extent to which the changes contemplated will modify the Constitution of 1922.

The President's proposals raise two major questions, namely:

1) Whether the new Constitution should (or could) be enacted by the existing Oireachtas, and, if not, whether a Constituent Assembly should be called and, if so, how?
2) Whether a new Constitution on the lines indicated in the President's instructions would be in accord with the constitutional provisions of the Treaty of 1921 or would involve a breach of that instrument.

Each of these questions will be examined in separate memoranda. The specially difficult problem of fitting the King as a constitutional officer for the purposes of international relations only into the framework of a State internally organised on a Presidential basis will fall to be discussed in the second of the separate memoranda referred to. The several alternative drafts of Articles 7 and 53 of the draft Heads will illustrate the complexity of the matter. But a formula may be devised which would obviate the necessity of inserting any specific provision in the written Constitution in relation to those functions of the King which it is intended to retain.

No. 42: UCDA, P150/2370

Memorandum from John Hearne to Eamon de Valera

[Department of External Affairs]
22 October 1935

The particular problem to which you referred in our recent conversations, namely, that of excluding the King from the internal constitution of the State, while at the same time continuing (with some modifications) the existing practice in the sphere of international relations is dealt with in Articles 7 and 53. There are five alternative drafts of those Articles, namely, one in the text itself and four others attached as Alternative Drafts A, B, C and Dd.[37] We are preparing further alternative drafts.

The document as a whole is being recast so as to be suitable for introduction in the present Dáil as an ordinary constitutional measure. The draft Constitution in its present form was prepared on the assumption that it would be passed by a Constituent Assembly.

[37] See document no. 40 for preliminary draft.

'Alternative Draft A of Articles 7 and 53'
Article 7: The President shall receive the diplomatic representatives accredited by other States to Saorstát Éireann. He shall sign (a) the Letters of Credence and Recall of the diplomatic representatives of Saorstát Éireann accredited to other States, (b) the Commissions of Consuls appointed by Saorstát Éireann in other States, (c) the full powers of plenipotentiaries empowered to conclude international treaties and conventions, (d) instruments of ratification of treaties and conventions, (e) the exequators of consuls appointed in Saorstát Éireann.

Transitory Provisions
Article 53: So long as Saorstát Éireann remains associated as a member of the British Commonwealth of Nations the Minister for Foreign Affairs shall countersign (a) the Letters of Credence and Recall of the diplomatic representatives of Saorstát Éireann accredited to other States, (b) the Commissions of Consuls appointed by Saorstát Éireann in other States, (c) the full powers of plenipotentiaries empowered to conclude international treaties and conventions, (d) instruments of ratification of treaties and conventions, (e) the exequators of consuls appointed in Saorstát Éireann.

'Alternative Draft B of Articles 7 and 53 (Jointly)
Article 7: The President shall receive the diplomatic representatives accredited by other States to Saorstát Éireann. The following documents, namely (a) the Letters of Credence and Recall of the diplomatic representatives of Saorstát Éireann accredited to other States, (b) the Commissions of Consuls appointed by Saorstát Éireann in other States, (c) the full powers of plenipotentiaries empowered to conclude international treaties and conventions, (d) instruments of ratification of treaties and conventions, (e) the exequators of consuls appointed in Saorstát Éireann, shall be countersigned by the Minister for Foreign Affairs.

(Note: This Article would not be accompanied by any Transitory Provisions; but should Saorstát Éireann become a Republic and should it then be decided that the President's function in international relations be inserted in the written Constitution the Constitution would have to be amended by the insertion of appropriate additional Articles. This would, in my view, be necessary, as the President would have no constitutional functions at all in international relations unless they were expressly given to him by the Constitution itself.)

'Alternative Draft C of Articles 7 and 53 (Jointly)'
Transitory Provisions
Article 53: So long as Saorstát Éireann remains associated as a Member of the British Commonwealth of Nations the King shall represent Saorstát Éireann in international relations. No act shall be performed or performable by the King in that capacity save upon the advice of the Council of Ministers communicated through the Minister for Foreign Affairs. In particular, the following documents, namely, (a) the Letters of Credence and Recall of the diplomatic representatives of Saorstát Éireann accredited to other States, (b) the Commissions of Consuls appointed by Saorstát Éireann in other States, (c) the full powers of plenipotentiaries empowered to conclude international treaties and conventions, (d) instruments of ratification of treaties and conventions, (e) the exequators of consuls appointed in Saorstát Éireann, shall be countersigned by the Minister for Foreign Affairs.

'Alternative Draft D of Articles 7 and 53'
Article 7: In the event of the withdrawal of Saorstát Éireann from membership of the British Commonwealth of Nations the President shall represent Saorstát Éireann in international relations. Pending such withdrawal all executive acts in relation to international affairs shall be performable save upon the advice of the Council of Ministers communicated through the Minister for Foreign Affairs.

(Note: This draft would not be accompanied by any Transitory Provisions).

No. 43: UCDA, P150/2370

Memorandum from John Hearne to Seán Murphy

Department of External Affairs
10 December 1935

I send you herewith the accompanying notes on the Constitutions of Czechoslovakia, Austria, Spain, Poland, the United States and France showing the machinery established to determine the validity of laws and to resolve e.g. conflicts between the administrative authorities and the Courts. It will be observed that in only three of those Constitutions is there provision for a Constitutional Court so called.

I enclose copy of an extract (bearing on the subject) from the Report of the Constitution Committee which reported on 3 July 1934.[38]

[38] Annotated by Murphy: 'President, herewith memorandum on Constitutional Courts in other countries which you asked for this morning'.

Memorandum on the methods for ensuring the constitutionality of legislation in other nations:

Constitutional Court of Czechoslovakia
The following are the Articles of the Constitution of the Republic of Czechoslovakia which relate to the Constitutional Court of that Country.

Article 1: Enactments which are in conflict with the Constitutional charter or with laws which may supplement or amend it are invalid.
The Constitutional Charter may be altered or amended only by laws specifically designated as Constitutional Laws.

Article 2: A Constitutional Court shall decide as to whether the laws of the Czechoslovak Republic…conform with Article 1.

Article 3:

1) The Constitutional Court shall consist of seven members, two of whom shall be members of and appointed by the High Court of Administration, and two shall be members of and appointed by the High Court of Justice; the remaining two members and the Chairman shall be nominated by the President of the Republic.
2) The appointment of representatives of the above-named Courts to the Constitutional Court, the sessions and procedure thereof, and the execution of its judgements shall be provided for by a special law.
(It is provided by Article 20 that a member of the Constitutional Court shall not be a member of the National Assembly).

Constitutional Court of Austria
The Austrian Constitution contains elaborate provisions (in eleven Articles) as to the jurisdiction of the Constitutional Court of Austria. Article 140 of the Austrian Constitution is as follows:

> 'The Constitutional Court shall give judgement in all questions as to the unconstitutionality of laws in the case of Provincial laws upon the motion of the Federal Government and in the case of Federal Laws upon the motion of the Provincial Government but ex-officio when the law presupposes a finding of the Constitutional Court.'

By Article 147, the Constitutional Court consists of 'a President, Vice-President and the requisite number of members and substitute members'. The President, Vice-President and one half of the members and deputy members are elected by the National Council (Lower House), and the other half of the members and deputy members by the Federal Council (i.e. Upper House), and they hold office for life. (Further provisions as to the organisation and procedure of the Court are prescribed by Federal legislation).

Spanish Tribunal of Constitutional Guarantees
Article 100 of the Spanish Constitution (1931) is as follows:

> 'When a Court of Justice is called upon to apply a law which it considers is contrary to the Constitution, it shall suspend its proceedings and address an application to the Tribunal of Constitutional Guarantees for the opinion of that Tribunal.'

The President of the Republic and the President of the Council and all Ministers of State are criminally responsible for infractions of the Constitution committed by them, and may be brought before the Court of Constitutional Guarantees. But the President cannot be brought before the Tribunal save upon the vote of three-fifths of the total number of members of the Chamber of Deputies.

Position under Polish Constitution
Article 86 of the Polish Constitution is as follows:

> 'A special Court shall be set up to decide on conflicts of jurisdiction as between the Administration and the Courts.'

There is no specific reference in the Constitution to a Constitution Court as such.

Position under the United States Constitution
Section 2 (1) of Article III of the United States Constitution vests jurisdiction to determine the validity of laws (under the Constitution) in the Judiciary. There is no special Constitutional Court distinct from the ordinary Federal Courts. If a State is party to the case the Supreme Court has original jurisdiction.

Position under the French Constitution
In cases of conflict between the Administrative Courts and the Ordinary Courts a Court of Conflict decides. The Minister of Justice acts as President. Three members are chosen by their colleagues from amongst the Councillors of State. Three others are chosen from the Court of Cassation (the Supreme Appellate Tribunal) in the same way. Two others are chosen by the other seven. They all hold office for three years and are eligible for re-election.[39]

[39] Appended to this memorandum is a copy of the observations of the 1934 Constitution Committee on Article 65 of the 1922 Constitution, for which see document no. 27, Appendix A.

CHAPTER V

THE ABOLITION OF THE SEANAD, 1936

Following the Treaty settlement in December 1921, Arthur Griffith promised representative Southern Unionists that the new Constitution would make provision for both a system of proportional representation and due representation for the Southern Unionists in a new Senate. The nature of this promise was explained to the Dáil by President W.T. Cosgrave in September 1922:

> The next part is a question of honour which affects the Government, and I should say the Party which supports the Government, having been made in much the same way as the Articles of Agreement with the British Government that is, the Agreement entered into with the representatives of the Southern Unionists on the one hand and Mr Griffith on the other—mainly Mr Griffith, although I believe the Minister for Home Affairs was also associated with him.
>
> It should be mentioned first that the adoption of the principle of Proportional Representation in the elections for the Dáil was one of the matters offered in the Draft Constitution itself as originally prepared, for the purpose of giving effect to President Griffith's Undertaking in his published statement on the subject. It is therefore a special safeguard for the representation of minorities, in what is known or called Proportional Representation. That is not mentioned in the Letters of Agreement, but I intend to

submit it for the sanction of the Dáil. The heads are as follows: '(1) The Senate to consist of 60 members, of whom two are to be selected by the National University of Ireland and two by the Dublin University. If the Six Counties remain in the Free State there would also be two members added from the University of Belfast. (2) The remaining 56 members of the Senate to be elected from a Panel consisting of three times the number of members to be elected, of whom two-thirds are to be nominated by the Dáil and one-third by the Senate, in each case voting according to principles of Proportional Representation; and also of persons who have at any time been members of the Senate and indicate their desire to be included on the Panel. (3) The Electorate for the Senate to be persons of thirty years and upwards. (4) The period between the first presentation of a Bill to the Senate and the date upon which it shall be deemed to be passed, whether the Senate agree or not, to be 270 days, as provided by Article 37 of the Draft. (5) Power to be given to three-fifths of the members of the Senate to require a referendum during the 90-day period mentioned in Article 46, without a petition as there provided, that is to say, a three-fifths majority of the Senate in Session and voting may call for a referendum, or, in the alternative, the petition there mentioned to remain. (6) Provision to be made for joint debate of the two Houses in case of disagreement, but not for joint voting (see end of Article 37). This provision, not be applied to a money bill. (7) Decision on a referendum to be final, without further delay. Voting at the referendum, to be by ballot. (8) The question whether any particular Bill is or is not a Money Bill to be certified by the Speaker of the Dáil, subject to appeal to a Committee of Privileges drawn equally from both Houses presided over by a Judge of the Supreme Court who shall have a casting vote, but no other vote.' That is to say of the twenty-eight Members who are nominated, fourteen will draw lots and fourteen successful Members will have twelve years of office, and the other fourteen will have six years of office. Of the elected Members the first fourteen elected will have nine years term of office and the last fourteen elected three years term of office. That would be for the first

Senate only. The nominated Members will be nominated by the President in the manner calculated to represent minorities of interest not represented adequately in the Dáil, and such nominations to be made on the advice of the following bodies:

Chambers of Commerce;
College of Physicians and College of Surgeons;
Benchers of King's Inns and Incorporated Law Society; and
The Corporations of Dublin and Cork.

The stipulation as to consultation not to be embodied in the Constitution but to be contained in an undertaking to be embodied in a resolution of the new Parliament. The text of the resolution to be submitted to the new Government was agreed between President Arthur Griffith, the Southern Unionists and the British Government and will be properly submitted when that portion of the Constitution is dealt with.

10. A matter which gave rise to considerable difference of opinion and was ultimately after much debate agreed to, was that the constituency for the election of Senators should be the Saorstát taken as a whole, that is the entire country was to be the constituency.

11. It was also agreed that the entire term of office of a Senator should be twelve years and that no person should be eligible for election who had not reached the age of 35 years.

12. The clauses in which these various headings of agreement are set out; first settled by the Law Officer on behalf of the Provisional Government and by Sir F. Greer and Sir F. Liddell on behalf of the British Government and the Southern Unionists and the texts were submitted at a conference and agreed to as they are now contained in the draft Constitution. All these matters are the subject of deliberate agreement between the Irish Government representatives and the representatives of Southern Unionists and the British Government; and the Irish Government is accordingly bound to pass all these provisions as Government provisions.[1]

[1] 1 *Dáil Debates*, Cols 355–7 (18 September 1922).

This was, therefore, a political commitment given at the time which the Government felt bound to honour. The arrangements regarding the Seanad did not, however, form part of the Treaty itself and so at all times the Oireachtas was free to amend these provisions, subject only to the referendum required.[2] The most important power enjoyed by the Seanad was the power to suspend the coming into force of Bills for a 270-day period, which was later extended to a maximum of eighteen months.[3]

Article 81 of the 1922 Constitution provided for special rules for the election of the First Seanad. Of the 60-member House, 30 were to be nominated by the President of the Executive Council who was required, in making such nomination, 'to have special regard to the providing of representation for groups or parties not then adequately represented' in the Dáil. The other thirty were to be elected by the Dáil, voting on principles of proportional representation. So far as the future elections were concerned, these were to be conducted on a country-wide basis with the elections held on the basis of proportional representation. Membership was confined to persons aged thirty-five years and over[4] 'who shall be proposed on the grounds that they have done honour to the Nation by reason of useful public service or that, because of special qualifications or attainments, they represent important aspects of the Nation's life'.[5]

Many of these provisions turned out to be unworkable[6] and these were extensively amended throughout the 1920s. The main change was that the electorate was now to be the members of the Oireachtas voting using proportional representation,[7] selecting from a panel of candidates formed in the manner prescribed by law.[8]

The first clash of substance between the Dáil and the Seanad came with the Constitution (Removal of Oath) Bill 1932, which was the first

[2] But, as we have seen already, by virtue of the provisions of both Article 50 (allowing for amendments by ordinary legislation for the first eight years of the Constitution's existence) and Constitution (Amendment No. 16) Act, 1929 (which extended that period for another eight years), the Constitution (including the provisions dealing with the Seanad) was susceptible of change by means of ordinary legislation for the entirety of the 1922 Constitution's existence.

[3] Article 38. This was later amended by the Constitution (Amendment No. 13) Act, 1928 which also introduced a new Article 38A. The effect of this change was that the Seanad could exercise a suspensory power in respect of all Bills (other than Money Bills) for a period of eighteen months from the date the Bill was first sent by the Dáil to the Seanad or the date of the re-assembly of the Oireachtas following a general election, whichever was the earlier, in which case the suspensory period was shortened to 60 days.

[4] Later reduced to thirty years by the Constitution (Amendment No. 8) Act, 1928.

[5] Article 30.

[6] The 1922 Constitution had contemplated a rolling system of election by the entire electorate every three years. The first such election saw candidates nominated by the Seanad and the Dáil, as well as nineteen out-going Senators who sought re-election. The result 'was a ballot paper several feet long, containing seventy-six names arranged in alphabetical order, from which nineteen new Senators had to be elected', O'Sullivan, *I.F.S. and its Senate*, 152.

[7] Article 32, as amended by Constitution (Amendment No. 6) Act, 1928.

[8] Article 33, as substituted by Constitution (Amendment No. 9) Act, 1928.

parliamentary measure introduced by de Valera's incoming Fianna Fáil Government. As the Seanad purported to insist on amendments to which the Dáil disagreed, the suspensory period of eighteen months was due to run from 19 May 1932[9] and would have expired on 18 November 1933, unless a general election intervened. Following the early general election in January 1933, the Removal of Oath Bill was again sent to the Seanad on 1 March 1933 and the Dáil subsequently disagreed with the Seanad's amendments. In the end, the enactment procedure provided for in Article 38A was invoked by the Dáil and the measure became law on 4 May 1933.

This clash between the Dáil and the Seanad on the Removal of Oath Bill was to prove to be the first of many such clashes between the Upper House and de Valera's Government. The suspensory power was subsequently invoked in respect of legislation dealing with agricultural produce, local government franchise, the wearing of political uniforms, university representation in the Dáil, the length of the Seanad's suspensory power and the abolition of the Seanad itself.[10] These clashes between the Lower and Upper Houses ultimately paved the way for the demise of the Seanad in May 1936 following the enactment of the Constitution (Amendment No. 24) Act, 1936.

As can be seen from de Valera's speech to the Dáil on 28 May 1936,[11] the abolition of the Seanad went in tandem with his plans for a new Constitution. While he was in two minds on the topic, he did say that:

> If it can be shown how we can constitute a Seanad which, practically, will be of value then certainly we will give such a proposition most careful consideration. If it cannot, then, the Constitution will be introduced with a Single Chamber Legislature.

With this in mind, on 9 June 1936 the Government appointed the Second House Commission whose terms of reference were to determine the powers, composition and method of election of a Second House 'in the event of its being decided to make provision in the Constitution for such Second Chamber'.[12] The 23-member commission was widely drawn with representatives from across the political spectrum,[13] the universities and the

[9] That is, the date the Bill was first received by the Seanad.

[10] See O'Sullivan, *I.F.S. and its Senate*, 622–5.

[11] 62 *Dáil Debates*, Cols 1198–9 (28 May 1936).

[12] See document no. 45.

[13] Thus, for example, members included William Norton, then leader of the Labour Party, and prominent non-party members of the Dáil, such as Frank McDermot, Dr Robert Rowlette and Professor William Thrift. There were no Fine Gael members, since 'it had refused to co-operate on the ground that there was no undertaking that a Second Chamber would, in fact, be established', O'Sullivan, *I.F.S. and its Senate*, 490.

legal profession. The heavyweight nature of the Commission is attested to by the fact that Chief Justice Hugh Kennedy acted as Chairman and the Attorney General, Conor Maguire, was Vice-Chairman. The membership not only included John Hearne, but also a leading Catholic intellectual, Professor Alfred O'Rahilly of University College, Cork, who had been a member of the original 1922 Constitution committee.

Speaking in the Dáil at the end of June 1936, de Valera indicated that he hoped to have the draft of a new Constitution ready by that autumn.[14] This clearly impacted on the timetable of the Second House Commission, which was required to report by the end of September 1936. The Commission duly reported at the end of September, having called no witnesses or heard from outside experts.[15] The majority report[16] was clearly hugely influential, as most of its recommendations form the basis for the Seanad created by the Constitution. The majority concluded that the Seanad should have no veto power, but simply a short suspensory power of three months' duration.[17] It likewise thought that even this suspensory power might be overridden where the President of the Executive Council[18] certified that the Bill was necessary on grounds of public safety or urgency.[19] Other recommendations as to the Seanad's powers were similarly accepted.[20]

So far as the election of the Seanad was concerned, the Committee recommended that one-third of that body be appointed by the Taoiseach.[21] It also envisaged that the elected members would be drawn from panels representing the national language, culture and the arts, agriculture and fisheries, industry and commerce, finance, health and social welfare, foreign affairs, education, law, labour and public administration with a limited franchise. This recommendation was closely followed in the drafting, with the Constitution opting for the panel system for electing forty-three Senators.[22] The Commission had hoped that:

> It might be possible by selecting a Panel of persons who had attained positions of responsibility and distinction in

[14] 63 *Dáil Debates*, Cols 242–3 (24 June 1936).
[15] O'Sullivan, *I.F.S. and its Senate*, 491.
[16] See document no. 47.
[17] See now Article 23.1.2° of the 1937 Constitution.
[18] That is, An Taoiseach.
[19] See now Article 24.1
[20] See, for example, that the Seanad should have no power to amend Money Bills (Article 20.1); that a Bill (other than a Money Bill) can be initiated in the Seanad (Article 20.2.1); that the Seanad should have an equal role in the judicial impeachment process (Article 35.4.1°); that members of the Government should have the right to be heard in both Houses (Article 28.8).
[21] Article 18.1 now provides that the number of nominated Senators is eleven.
[22] See Article 18.7. Apart from the eleven nominated senators, the other six senators would be elected by the University graduates.

> their own particular vocations or occupations to afford a wide choice of persons certainly qualified by their ability, character, knowledge and experience for Membership of the House, and that the selection of members might not be made on a political party basis.[23]

While the Commission's recommendations provided the blueprint for the Constitution's Second Chamber, the fond hopes of the Commission with regard to the panel system were ultimately dashed, since the political system would not pass up the opportunity to ensure that the vast majority of persons elected through the panel system were first and foremost party political politicians.

No. 44: 20 Seanad Debates, Cols 2433–6

Speech of Thomas Westropp Bennett, Chairman of the Seanad, on the last day of business prior to its abolition

Leinster House, Dublin
19 May 1936

We have finished our labours, and nothing remains to be done but to ring down the curtain. I think we may congratulate ourselves on having done the State some service. For my part, I owe a special debt of gratitude to you all for your sincere help to me during the many years in which I tried to fulfil with impartiality the duties of my office as your Chairman. On the 11 December, nearly 14 years ago, we met here in bleak December. We met in darkness. We emerge in light, conscious that we did our duty, and conscious that, in our every act, we tried to build and strengthen this infant State. We met, as I say, educated in different environments, animated by different political ideals and ambitions, possibly distrusting one another. Yet, in a few short years of contact, as Senator O'Farrell[24] said, we realised that each one of us, in our individual capacity, was working for the good of the State, that each was doing his best, playing his part, and pulling his weight in the boat. And so now we come to the end. No recriminations may or should be allowed. All I ask leave to do is to express the hope that we who have striven for the up-building of this State will continue to uphold this State so far as we can. If I might venture to express a hope, it would be that my voice, addressed from this Chair for the last time, would go out over our heads to the country at large in an appeal for respect for

[23] See document no. 47.
[24] John Thomas O'Farrell, member of Seanad Éireann (1922–36, 1948–51).

the law. The law is being made by our representatives for all of us. There is no safeguard for democracy but in the keeping of the law. I hope it will be kept. If we, who are in the sere and yellow leaf, are approached for our counsel, I hope we shall say: 'Work for the law, by the law, and with the law.' Thus only will democracy be preserved and strengthened. We met in darkness; we emerge in light—the light of May, before us the glory of summer and the hope of autumn, with the reaping of the harvest. The harvest will be reaped by some men of goodwill—a harvest which will be great, giving a return which will be bounteous. I was struck some little time ago by a poem written by a Northern lady. Perhaps it was the sadness of the poem that appealed to me. The authoress was attuning her mind to the various responses of Nature and she was struck by the robin. This is what she said:

> 'Maybe you mind the robin
> Sitting his lone on the thorn,
> Preening himself on days that are gone,
> Brave with a joy forlorn.
> 'Tis true, it is bleak December,
> And no Spring hopes has he;
> "Remember", he sings, "Remember", Ah, thon's the wee bird for me'.

I thank you all. We shall remember the contacts we made here. We shall remember our friends of different creeds, of different politics, of different ideals, animated by one desire—the advancement of this State. So far as God gave us light we fulfilled our duty, and we leave the stage conscious of our own rectitude. I thank you all, and I declare the Seanad adjourned *sine die.* [25]

No. 45: UCDA, P4/1278

Eamon de Valera to Hugh Kennedy

Dublin
9 June 1936

A chara,
The Executive Council today appointed a Commission consisting of:

> The Hon. Aodh Ua Cinneidigh, Chief Justice of Saorstát Éireann, Chairman

[25] The Seanad was actually abolished by means of the enactment of the Constitution (Amendment No. 24) Act, 1936. The Act was signed by the Governor General on 29 May 1936 and the Seanad formally stood abolished as of that date.

Mr Conor A. Maguire, Attorney General, Vice Chairman
Professor Daniel A. Binchy, MA, PhD, BL
Mr Samuel L. Browne, KC
Mrs Helena Concannon, MA, DLitt, TD
Mr Joseph Connolly
Mr George Gavan Duffy, KC
Dr Robert P. Farnan
Mr James Geoghegan, KC, TD
Mr John Hearne, BA, LLB, BL
Mr Thomas Johnson
Sir John Keane, Bart.
Mr Eamon Lynch
Mr Frank McDermot, TD
Professor William Magennis, MA
Mr Seamus Moore, TD
Mr John Moynihan
Mr William Norton, TD
Professor Alfred O'Rahilly, MA, BSc, PhD
Dr Robert J. Rowlette, TD
Professor Michael F. Tierney, MA, TD
Professor William E. Thrift, MA, TD
Mr Richard Wilson,

with the following terms of reference:

> To consider and make recommendations as to what should be the functions and powers of the Second Chamber of the Legislature in the event of its being decided to make provision in the Constitution for such Second Chamber and, further, to consider and make recommendations as to how in that event such Chamber should be constituted as regard number of members, their qualifications, method of selection and period of office, and what allowances (if any) should be made to such members.

Mr John Malone, Principal Clerk on the staff of the Oireachtas, will act as Secretary.

No. 46: UCDA, P4/1278

Hugh Kennedy to Eamon de Valera

Dublin
30 September 1936

Dear Mr President,
I have the honour to send you herewith the Report of this Commission with three minority reports and six separate memoranda from individual members.[26]

I am happy to be able to comply with your request that the Commission report to you before the first of October. This has only been possible by the diligence of the members and the sacrifices of time and effort they have made to this end, for which I have to express my personal indebtedness to them.

I have also to express to you my own gratitude and the gratitude of each and every member of the Commission for that you gave us the services of Mr Malone as Secretary. It is not only that it was invaluable to us to have his great efficiency and his knowledge and experience of parliamentary affairs always ready for our services, but his unstinted devotion and indefatigable labour, regardless of time or himself, have combined to make it possible to send to you within the time you named the results of our deliberations.

No. 47: NAI, DT S8642/8

Majority Report of the Second House of the Oireachtas Commission

30 September 1936

Mr President,

1. The Commission to consider and make recommendations with reference to a Second Chamber of the Legislature received its appointment by letter from you dated the 9 June, 1936, the terms of reference being:

   'To consider and make recommendations as to what should be the functions and powers of the Second

[26] Minority reports and separate memoranda not reproduced.

Chamber of the Legislature in the event of its being decided to make provision in the Constitution for such Second Chamber and, further, to consider and make recommendations as to how in that event, such Chamber should be constituted as regards number of members, their qualifications, method of selection and period of office, and what allowances (if any) should be made to such members.'

2. The Commission met on twenty-seven occasions, the Chairman or Vice-Chairman nominated by you presiding at each of its Meetings.
3. In accordance with your request that the Commission should report to you and the Executive Council on or before the first of October of the present year, the Chairman on behalf of the Commission now presents this Report. It will be recognised that in a body of so many members, there must be, as there has been, a considerable diversity of opinion as to various matters and as to detail, and it has not been found possible to unite all the views in a single Report, setting forth a single view throughout, but the Commission has thought the preferable course, in the circumstances, is to present a single consecutive Report as a whole, made up of majority opinions on the various individual issues.
4. It was ruled, as a matter of interpretation of the terms of reference early in our proceedings, that the Commission was not to consider whether a Second House should be established or not.
5. The Commission proceeded on the basis that the Constitution of Dáil Éireann and its constitutional position shall continue substantially as they are at present, subject only to such changes as may be entailed by the establishment of a Second House.
6. It was decided to recommend:
   (i) That the Second House should have power to elect its own Chairman, and that it should have power to regulate and control all its own business and for that purpose to make any Standing Orders which it might consider necessary or desirable;
   (ii) That the members should have the same immunities and privileges as are conferred by the Constitution on the members of Dáil Éireann;

(iii) That no Bill initiated in Dáil Éireann should be enacted into law until it has been sent to the Second House and an opportunity afforded to that House for consideration;

(iv) That the Second House should not have the power to impose a veto on any Bill sent to it by Dáil Éireann;

(v) That the Second House should return a Bill sent to it by Dáil Éireann, with its amendments (if any) within a term of three months from the date when it has been first sent to that House, subject to such term being extended by agreement with Dáil Éireann, and subject to the provisions for special matters hereinafter mentioned;

(vi) That the refusal of the Second House to pass a Bill (other than a Money Bill) or the passing of such Bill with amendments which Dáil Éireann does not accept, should not have the effect of delaying the enactment of such Bill beyond a date three months after the date on which it was first sent to the Second House: Provided that, in computing the term of three months, any Recess of Dáil Éireann of one month or upwards shall be excluded.

7. The majority of the Commission is of the view that a Bill (other than a Money Bill) may be initiated in the Second House.

8. The Commission is of opinion that the Government should have power, on the motion of a Minister, to initiate a Bill (other than a Money Bill) in the Second House. This power could be usefully exercised for the purpose of initiating Bills intended for the Consolidation of Statutes, a form of legislation of which, the Commission is informed, there is urgent need.

9. The Commission is of opinion that the examination of the Rules and Orders for giving effect to legislation also affords material for the special attention of the Second House, or of a Special Joint Committee of both Houses set up for the purpose.

10. The majority of the Commission is of the view that a Resolution for the removal of a judge, or for the removal of the Comptroller and Auditor-General, for stated misbehaviour or incapacity, should, in addition to being passed by Dáil Éireann, be passed also by the Second House, before it can become effective.

11. The Commission is of opinion that the Second House should not have power to reject a Bill conforming to the definition of a Money Bill; and, further, that the Second House should not have power to amend any Bill so as directly to impose or increase any charge on the State funds.

 The Commission proposes that a 'Money Bill', as referred to in these recommendations, shall be such a Bill as is certified to conform to the following definition:

> 'A Money Bill means a Bill which contains only provisions dealing with all or any of the following subjects, namely, the imposition, repeal, remission, alteration or regulation of taxation; the imposition for the payment of debt or other financial purposes of charges on public moneys or the variation or repeal of any such charges; supply, the appropriation, receipt, custody, issue or audit of accounts of public money; the raising or guarantee of any loan or the repayment thereof; subordinate matters incidental to those subjects or any of them. In this definition the expressions 'taxation', 'public money' and 'loan' respectively do not include any taxation, money or loan raised by local authorities or bodies for local purposes.'

12. The majority of the Commission recommends that in respect of a 'Money Bill' as defined in the foregoing paragraph:
 (i) The Second House, in regard to such Bill, shall have power only to make recommendations which may be accepted or rejected by Dáil Éireann;
 (ii). Any such recommendations shall be made to Dáil Éireann by the Second House within a period of twenty-one days after such 'Money Bill' has been sent to it.
13. The majority of the Commission is of opinion that, so long as there is no operative provision in the Constitution for a Referendum, it should be provided that the Second House should have the right, by a majority of the members of the whole House, to call for a Referendum to the people on any legislation involving an amendment of the Constitution in any respect, and that Dáil Éireann should be bound by the result of such Referendum.
14. Some members of the Commission were also of opinion that the Second House should have the right to call for the

submission of other major matters of legislation to the people by a Referendum for decision in case of a conflict of view between the two Houses, which it has been found impossible to reconcile by Conference or otherwise.

15. The majority of the Commission is of the view that every Minister should have the right to attend and be heard in the Second House.
16. The majority of the Commission recommends that, in cases in which the President of the Executive Council, on the introduction of a Bill, certifies by message to both Houses that the Bill, the subject of such message, is urgent and immediately necessary for the preservation of the public peace or safety, or is rendered necessary by the existence of a national emergency, whether internal or international, the time for consideration by the Second House should, by resolution of Dáil Éireann, be abridged to such period as the said resolution may determine: Provided that a Bill so certified shall as enacted (if the Second House so requires) contain a Clause limiting the duration of the Bill when enacted to a period of four months: Provided, also, that the time for consideration shall not be abridged to a period of less than seven days dating from the day upon which such Bill is sent from Dáil Éireann to the Second House.
17. There was substantial agreement amongst the members of the Commission that the number of members of such Second House should be 45.
18. In the recommendations put forward by the Commission for the constitution of the Second House the Commission had in mind that the Second House should be constituted of persons chosen on account of their ability, character, experience and knowledge of public affairs.

    The majority of the Commission is of opinion that a proportion of the persons nominated to the Second House, and of those nominated for election, should be persons with a competent knowledge of the national language.

    The majority, also, considers that it is important that some of the members of the Second House should be women.[27]

[27] On 28 September 1936, Helena Concannon, George Gavan Duffy, Joseph Connolly, James Geoghegan, Seán Moore, William Magennis and Hugh Kennedy submitted the following reservation to paragraph 18: 'We are strongly of opinion that it is due to the dignity of the National Language that effective provisions should be made at the outset to ensure and maintain the gradual predominance of Irish as the language of the Second House', NAI, DT S8642/8.

19. It was further agreed by the members of the Commission that there should be a minimum age qualification for membership, namely, the age of thirty-five years.
20. It was in regard to the method of selecting the members of the Second House that the greatest diversity of opinion prevailed. While the proposals made to the Commission—with one exception—included nomination as a method for obtaining a part of the membership of the Second House, the proposals differed as to the number to be so obtained, and, principally, as to the method by which the remaining members were to be selected. The main proposals for constituting the House—other than the proposals embodied in this Report—may be summarised as follow:
    (i) That the members of the Second House should be elected by a direct vote of the people;
    (ii) That the Second House should be, in part, nominated and, in part, elected—the election to be held in constituencies based on provinces;
    (iii) That it should be, in part, nominated, and, in part, constituted by dividing the elected First House—a certain number of members at each General Election being elected to Dáil Éireann in excess of those required to constitute that body;
    (iv) That it should be, in part, nominated, and, in part, elected by a system of Vocational Election;
    (v) That it should be, in part, nominated, and, in part, elected by Dáil Éireann from a Panel of persons actively concerned in certain specified public interests or services—the nominating authority to the Panel to be (among other suggestions) a Committee of Dáil Éireann;
    (vi) That it should be obtained, in part, by election by Dáil Éireann from a Panel prepared by a nominating authority having regard to the qualifications specified in paragraph 22, and, in part, by uncontrolled nomination, the nominating authority in both cases being the President of the Executive Council;
    (vii) That it should be obtained, in part, by controlled nomination, and, in part, by uncontrolled nomination, the nominating authority in both cases being the President of the Executive Council.

21. The majority of the Commission decided to recommend that one-third of the members of the Second House should be nominated, and that the nominating authority should be the President of the Executive Council.
22. The majority of the Commission is of opinion that the remainder of the members of the Second House should be selected from a panel of persons who then are, or have been, actively concerned in public interests or services to be specified, the panel being prepared for each election.
23. The majority of the Commission is of opinion that:
    (i) The selection of the panel from which members are to be elected should be made by a nominating authority or Committee of persons (not necessarily members of Dáil Éireann) elected for that purpose by Dáil Éireann on the system of proportional representation;
    (ii) The nominating authority should be required by its terms of reference to nominate for the panel not fewer than twice the number of persons to be elected having regard in each case to the qualifications set forth in Paragraph 22 and, as far as practicable, to the representation of the national interests and services indicated in paragraph 25;
    (iii) Any two members of the nominating authority should be entitled to make six nominations to the panel;
    (iv) The nominating authority should consist of seven persons, of whom one shall be Chairman.
24. The majority of the Commission is of opinion that the members of the Second House to be elected should be so elected by a College of Electors, to consist of every person who had been a candidate at the immediately preceding General Election for Dáil Éireann.

    The Election should be conducted in accordance with a scheme whereby each elector would be entitled in the Election for a Second House to cast one vote for every 1,000 first preferences he received at the Election for Dáil Éireann. A fraction of 1,000 exceeding 500 to be reckoned as 1,000.

    The Election to be by means of the Single Transferable Vote, and to be by Postal Ballot.

    The whole country should be a single constituency.[28]

[28] On 30 September 1936, John Hearne submitted the following reservation to paragraph 24: 'I dissent from the recommendation made by the majority of the members of the Commission in paragraph 24 of

25. The public interests or services referred to in paragraph 23 should cover such matters as: National Language and Culture, the Arts, Agriculture (in all its forms) and Fisheries, Industry and Commerce, Finance, Health and Social Welfare, Foreign Affairs, Education, Law, Labour, Public Administration (including Town and Country Planning).
26. The majority of the Commission is of opinion that the Second House should be reconstituted after each General Election.
27. A proposal which recommended itself to some members of the Commission was, that a proportion of the Second House be selected on the basis of vocations or occupations, but these members did not reach a scheme which satisfied a majority of the Commission to recommend to you.

    It is to be noted, however, that a selection of members of the Second House on a basis of vocations or occupations was not contemplated for the purpose of making the Second House a body to represent such vocations or occupations in the discharge of the functions and powers of the Second House, but rather that it might be possible by selecting for a Panel persons who had attained positions of responsibility and distinction in their own particular vocations or occupations to afford a wide choice of persons certainly qualified by their ability, character, knowledge and experience for Membership of the House, and that the selection of members might not be made on a political party basis. It is realised that the Second House is not to be contemplated as consisting of individual specialists in their own particular business, whose function would be in the nature of giving expert advice on their own particular subjects, but it is repeated, that it is suggested for the purpose of securing the selection of generally eligible persons to constitute the Second House who should be competent to deal with all its business whatever it may be.
28. The general view of the Commission was that membership of the Second House should carry the same allowances as those applicable to membership of Dáil Éireann.

[28] *contd.* the Report. The majority of the Commission—rightly in my view—rejected a proposal that the members of the Second House to be elected should be elected by a direct vote of the people. That a proportion of the members of the Second House should be elected was, however, generally agreed. In my view, the only practicable method of election is election by Dáil Éireann. I suggest, therefore, that the members of the Second House to be elected should be elected by Dáil Éireann on the system of proportional representation', NAI, DT S8642/8.

29. As I have said this Report is in the nature of a narrative. The decisions represent the majority opinions of those present on the particular occasions, sometimes a substantial majority, sometimes however only a bare majority. During the greater part of the time we sat, the average attendance was about seventeen. I may say that the views, whether of the majority or minority, were vigorously debated. It is in accordance with the general view that I present this Report. It is however accompanied by two minority Reports, each of which is a consistent whole differing substantially from this Report. One is signed by Professors O'Rahilly, Binchy and Tierney, Messrs Moynihan, MacDermot and ex-Senators R. Wilson and Sir John Keane, the other is signed by myself. These reports explain themselves and the reasons for putting forward independent views. Other members of the Commission entertain different opinions on various particular matters which however have not been committed to separate written statements, other than the several memoranda of reservation which I send herewith. Otherwise the members are satisfied that the Report be offered in its present form as a whole.[29]

[29] The Committee met on several occasions between June and September 1936. See NAI, DT S8642/1–8.

Chapter VI

Submissions from Religious Bodies and Discussions with the Churches

In September 1936 the Provincial of the Jesuit Order in Ireland appointed a committee 'to advise on certain matters connected with the Constitution'.[1] The Committee decided to draw up a preamble 'drawn up on the model of the preamble of the Polish Constitution', articles dealing with the family, education, marriage, religion, private property, freedom of speech and 'any other matters that may be suggested by a study of Concordats and existing Constitutions'. The Committee speedily produced a short but impressive document which contained a Preamble and articles on Religion, Marriage, The Family, Education, Private Property and Liberty of Speech. Many of these draft provisions were drawn from the Polish Constitution of 1921 and the Austrian Constitution of 1934,[2] as well as from prominent Papal Encyclicals.[3]

The driving force behind the Jesuit team was Fr Edward Cahill, a personal friend of de Valera. While the Jesuits themselves recognised that many of Cahill's views were 'rather singular',[4] he was nonetheless given permission to present the Committee's document to de Valera, provided that any additional recommendations which he made personally were also approved by other members of the Committee.[5] The Jesuit document proved to be enormously influential, albeit that in some

[1] See document no. 52. See also Seán Faughnan, 'The Jesuits and the Drafting of the Irish Constitution of 1937', in *I.H.S.*, 26 (1988), 79–102; Finola Kennedy, 'Two Priests, the Family and the Irish Constitution', in *Studies*, 87 (1998), 353–64.

[2] Although some provisions were modelled on the Belgian and Norwegian Constitutions.

[3] Principally Leo XIII's *Rerum Novarum* (1891), Pius XI's *Casti Connubii* (1930) and *Quadragesimo Anno* (1931).

[4] See document no. 53.

[5] See document no. 55.

respects it simply meant that translations of parts of the 1921 Polish Constitution (on which the Jesuit document heavily relied) found their way into the Constitution through this indirect route.

A good example here is the similarity between the Preamble to the 1921 Polish Constitution and the Preamble to the Constitution:

> The name of Almighty God!
> We, the Polish Nation, thankful to Providence for freeing us from a servitude of a century and a half; remembering gratefully the courage and steadfastness of the self-sacrificing struggle of generations which have unceasingly devoted their best efforts to the cause of independence; taking up the glorious tradition of the memorable Constitution of the Third of May; having in mind the weal of our whole, united, and independent mother country, and desiring to establish her independent existence, power, safety, and social order on the eternal principles of right and liberty; desirous also of ensuring the development of all her moral and material forces for the good of the whole of renascent humanity, and of securing quality to all citizens of the Republic, and respect, due rights, and the special protection of the state to labour, do enact and establish in the Legislative Sejm of the Republic of Poland this constitutional law.

The Preamble to the Irish Constitution provides:

> In the name of the Most Holy Trinity, from Whom is all authority and to Whom, as our final end, all actions both of men and States must be referred,
> We, the people of Éire,
> Humbly acknowledging all our obligations to our Divine Lord, Jesus Christ, Who sustained our fathers through centuries of trial,
> Gratefully remembering their heroic and unremitting struggle to regain the rightful independence of our Nation,
> And seeking to promote the common good, with due observance of Prudence, Justice and Charity, so that the dignity and freedom of the individual may be assured, true social order attained, the unity of our country restored, and concord established with other nations,
> Do hereby adopt, enact, and give to ourselves this Constitution.

The influence of the Jesuit draft here is obvious, as their draft Preamble provides:

> In the name of the most Holy Trinity and of our Lord Jesus Christ, the universal king, we, the people of Ireland, being the parent nation of the Irish race, mindful of the long centuries of persecution we have had to endure, and full of gratitude to God who has so mercifully preserved us from innumerable dangers in the past; hereby, as an independent Christian nation, establish this sovereign Civil Society of the Irish people.[6]

The first four lines of the Preamble closely follow the Jesuit (and, by extension, the Polish) model, with the final three lines drawing on Hearne's more secular May 1935 draft.[7] The Jesuit draft remained hugely influential to the end, albeit that de Valera was completely unmoved by Cahill's protestations regarding the lack of a general interpretation clause[8] or the acknowledgement of the Church of Ireland,[9] so that by the end of the process he had become a somewhat marginalised figure.[10]

The Jesuits were not alone among clerical figures in seeking to contribute to the drafting process. Certainly, de Valera's own friend and spiritual adviser, Fr John Charles McQuaid C.S.Sp., also played a major role.[11] McQuaid certainly peppered de Valera with letters and memoranda, particularly in the period from February to April 1937. There is no doubt but that McQuaid's influence was significant and extended broadly throughout key aspects of the draft Constitution,

[6] See document no. 58. As Dermot Keogh has argued:

> It may not be an accident that the topics on which the Jesuits wrote became Articles 41 to 45 of the new Constitution—even if the content was radically altered...That was undoubtedly where de Valera derived his inspiration for the final wording of what was to become Article 44; see 'Church, State and Society', in Farrell (ed.), *De Valera's Constitution*, 110.

[7] See document no. 40.

[8] In his letter to de Valera of 23 May 1937, Fr Cahill argued for a general interpretation clause to ensure that the personal rights provisions of Articles 40 to 44 would be interpreted in 'harmony with the dictates of the natural law as summarised in the social teaching of the Catholic Church'. Rather presciently, Fr Cahill argued that:

> The terms *justice* (Article 45.1), *personal rights* (Article 40.3.1), *property rights* (Article 40.3.2) and possibly others such as *capacity* (Article 40.1) convey different ideas to the student of Catholic social science [than] to those (including all or most of our judges, and lawyers, and possibly most of our public men) whose ideas are much influenced by the individualistic and liberal principles of English jurisprudence. Hence there is, I fear, *real danger* that the intentions aimed at in the draft Constitution may be frustrated, except it is made clear in the Constitution itself in what terms such terms are to be understood. See document no. 199.

[9] See document no. 199.

[10] De Valera wrote to Cahill on 24 May 1937 thanking him for his suggestions: see document no. 203. De Valera confessed that he did not know 'whether it will be possible to incorporate them at this stage', while regretting that it had not been possible 'to talk to you generally about the Constitution'.

[11] See John Cooney, *John Charles McQuaid: Ruler of Catholic Ireland* (Dublin, 1999), 94–103.

including aspects of what ultimately became Article 45.[12] There are certainly dozens upon dozens of items relating to the draft Constitution extant in the Dublin Diocesan Archives, which were plainly sent by de Valera to McQuaid in advance of its formal publication.[13] There is no doubt, therefore, but that there was an extremely close liaison between them in the period from February to April 1937. McQuaid certainly assisted with suggestions and numerous issues of phraseology and wording. Yet, in the end, one might query the extent of that influence.

Thus, for example, it has been suggested that de Valera 'had long and frequent discussions with McQuaid who actually provided the most satisfactory draft of the Preamble to the Constitution'.[14] But this does not seem correct. As we have seen, the first five lines of the Preamble find strong echoes in the earlier Jesuit draft, with the last four lines mirroring the earlier May 1935 Hearne draft. It is likewise true that aspects of the famous encyclicals, *Rerum Novarum* and *Quadragesimo Anno*, find reflection in Article 41 (Family) and Article 43 (Property) and it is equally true that McQuaid had brought these provisions to de Valera's attention.[15] But the Jesuits had already done this in a comprehensive fashion several months previously. De Valera also rejected some of McQuaid's more extreme demands in respect of contraception and the banning of secret societies, just as he had in the case of Fr Cahill.[16]

The discussions with the Churches

The draft Constitution as circulated on 16 March 1937 left blank what was to be become Article 44 dealing with religion, albeit that a religious article had been included in a preliminary draft of 10 March.[17] That earlier draft had been strikingly confessional in tone:

> The State acknowledges that the true religion is that established by Our Divine Lord, Jesus Christ Himself, which He committed to His Church to protect and propagate, as the guardian and interpreter of true morality. It acknowledges, moreover, that the Church of Christ is the Catholic Church.[18]

[12] See Cooney, *John Charles McQuaid*, 95–6. Note also Fr McQuaid's letter to de Valera of 8 March 1937 enclosing an amendment 'dealing with widows, orphans and the aged', which appears to echo what ultimately became Article 45.4.1° (document no. 84).

[13] Dublin Diocesan Archives (hereafter DDA), AB8/A/V/47–48, AB8/A/V/50–52, AB8/A/V/55–61.

[14] Cooney, *John Charles McQuaid*, 96; Farragher, *De Valera and his Alma Mater*, 173.

[15] See, for example, McQuaid's letter of 16 February 1937 to de Valera: document nos 74–5.

[16] Cooney, *John Charles McQuaid*, 98.

[17] NAI, DT S9715A. See www.irishconstitution.ie.

[18] 'Preliminary Draft, 10 March 1937', NAI, DT S9715A. See www.irishconstitution.ie.

At this remove, it is hard to say what prompted de Valera to include such a formula in the first instance and, indeed, what prompted him to have second thoughts. One possibility is that de Valera initially yielded to suggestions from McQuaid and other like-minded clerical figures[19] to include a provision along these lines.

Perhaps de Valera was so preoccupied with trying to ensure that the draft would not provoke a backlash from a variegated and volatile Catholic constituency that he failed to anticipate the reaction from some members of his own front bench and, most importantly, from other churches. The explanation may lie in the fact that de Valera accepted the ultramontane formula as conforming most closely to his own personal views. But when the political ramifications of such formula were pointed out to him, he immediately saw the public danger to his own personal position and to the Fianna Fáil government.[20]

In this regard it seems that some of the more republican members[21] of the Government may have objected to what they regarded as the disenfranchisement of the Protestant minority. Some of this thinking is doubtless reflected in the guidelines prepared for Joseph Walshe for his discussions with Vatican officials on the draft Article 44:

> 1. If the attempt were to be made to embody in the new Constitution the full Catholic ideal there would be an immediate outcry from the Protestant section of the population, and a bitter religious controversy might easily ensue.
> 2. In the present circumstances, such a controversy would in every way be disastrous…
>
> 10. The Government would further be charged with having raised a new barrier to the reunion of our country, and with having recklessly caused offence to a section of our countrymen whose ancestors produced many patriots whose names are revered in many a Catholic home, Wolfe Tone, Robert Emmet, Parnell etc…[22]

By 3 April 1937, de Valera was already in retreat and the draft shown to the Papal Nuncio, Paschal Robinson, showed a distinct move away from

[19] Such as the Archbishop of Armagh, Cardinal Joseph McRory: see Keogh, 'Church, State and Society', 113.
[20] Keogh, 'Church, State and Society', 111.
[21] Led, perhaps, by Seán MacEntee and Gerald Boland: see 'The Gerry Boland Story', *Irish Times*, 11 October 1968. Keogh observes (based on an interview with Seán MacEntee) that the Government had given de Valera: 'A free hand to conduct negotiations on the content of the religious article, provided the result did not establish any particular church', 'Church, State and Society', 121.
[22] See document no. 153.

the earlier drafts of March 1937.[23] There then followed extensive discussions with the various church leaders, including Archbishop Edward Byrne (Roman Catholic), Archbishop John Gregg (Church of Ireland), Rev. William Massey (Methodist)[24] and Dr James Irwin (Presbyterian).[25] In the end, de Valera moved back to the original (largely secular) formula which had been contained in Article 9 of the 1922 Constitution, along with the new 'special position' of the Catholic Church and the recognition of the other Churches formula. In the end, all of the Churches were satisfied with this, with the exception of the disaffected elements in the Catholic Church.[26]

How Catholic was the 1937 Constitution?

No one denies that the Constitution was influenced to some extent by Catholic teaching and doctrine. There are still express traces of this, most noticeably in the Preamble which:

> still conveys a very nationalist view of history in which unionists could not recognise themselves and along with many other areas of the Constitution, has a broadly Christian, often specifically Catholic, tone that does not match the political culture of the State as well as it did.[27]

In other cases:

> There is nothing visibly Catholic about the phraseology to the uninformed eye—only those familiar with Catholic social teaching would be able to identify the origins of the expression used.[28]

That, however, the Constitution was influenced by Catholic social teaching is surely unremarkable given the historical context of 1937. What is more remarkable, however, is the extent to which that document also reflected secular—one might almost say 'Protestant'—values of

[23] See document no. 123.

[24] William Henry Massey (1877–1937); President of the Methodist Church in Ireland (1936–7). The Editorial Board wishes to thank Rev. Robin Roddie of the Wesley Historical Society for providing biographical details for Rev. Massey.

[25] James Alexander Hamilton Irwin (1876–1954); ordained a Presbyterian minister in 1903; toured America with Eamon de Valera in 1920; member of the national executive of Fianna Fáil (1945–54).

[26] Thus there was objection in some quarters to the use of the term 'Church of Ireland': see the letter from Cahill to de Valera on 23 May 1937:

> I presume you know that the term 'Church of Ireland' which occurs in Art. 44.1.3° has aroused no end of criticism and surprise; for it really seems to be an authoritative approval of a piece of lying propaganda. I hope it will be changed; Document no. 199.

[27] Michael Gallagher, 'The Constitution and the Judiciary', in John Coakley and Michael Gallagher (eds), *Politics in the Republic of Ireland* (4th edn, London, 2005), 94.

[28] Gallagher, 'The Constitution and the Judiciary', 77–8.

liberal democracy, respect for individual rights and the separation of the Church and State and the extent to which *it does not* reflect Catholic teaching. This analysis, however, is but rarely reflected in non-legal commentaries.

Take, for example, the comments of Roy Foster:

> But the democratic, popular-sovereignty approach [of the Constitution] was combined with an assumption that the nature and identity of the Irish polity was Catholic, reflected in five articles defining 'rights'. These were much influenced by papal encyclicals and current Catholic social teaching. Divorce was prohibited; the idea of working mothers denounced; the Roman Catholic Church was granted a 'special position…as the guardian of the faith professed by the great majority of the citizens', though the rights of minority Churches were defined.[29]

This passage merits some extended analysis. Exhibit A in the Foster analysis is the provisions of the (now repealed) Article 44.1.2° and Article 44.1.3° dealing with the special position of the Catholic Church. These provisions provided that:

> 2. The State recognises the special position of the Holy Catholic Apostolic and Roman Church as the guardian of the Faith professed by the great majority of the citizens.
> 3. The State also recognises the Church of Ireland, the Presbyterian Church in Ireland, the Methodist Church in Ireland, the Religious Society of Friends in Ireland, as well as the Jewish Congregations and the other religious denominations existing in Ireland at the date of the coming into operation of this Constitution.

The similarity between Article 44.1.2° and the words of the preamble to 1801 Concordat between the Pope and Napoleon is striking: 'The Government of the Republic recognises that the Catholic, Apostolic and Roman religion is the religion of the great majority of the French citizens.'

In October 1955 de Valera wrote to Radio Éireann to controvert the statement made in a radio broadcast that the Napoleonic concordat provided the inspiration for Article 44.1.2°:

[29] R.F Foster, *Modern Ireland: 1600–1972* (London, 1988), 544.

> If there is any similarity in the phrases of the Constitution and those of the Concordat referred to—a document which, by the way, I have never seen—it is purely accidental; a mere coincidence and nothing more.[30]

Yet the similarity between the two documents is so striking that it can scarcely be entirely accidental. There was, moreover, a close similarity between the then Article 44.1.2° and Article 114 of the 1921 Polish Constitution:

> Art. 114. The Roman Catholic religion, being the religion of the preponderant majority of the nation, occupies in the state the chief position among enfranchised religions. The Roman Catholic Church governs itself under its own laws. The relation of the state to the church will be determined on the basis of an agreement with the Apostolic See, which is subject to ratification by the Sejm.
> Art. 115. The churches of the religious minorities and other legally organised religious communities govern themselves by their own laws, which the state may not refuse to recognise unless they contain rules contrary to law.

Given the French influence on Polish intellectuals, it seems not unreasonable to assume that the Napoleonic Concordat must have played some role in the drafting of Article 114 of the 1921 Constitution, not least given the similarity of the underlying idea and the language used.

One can compare Article 114 of the Polish Constitution with Article 1(b) of the Jesuit Draft of October 1936 on which it was expressly modelled:

> The Catholic Faith, which is the faith of the vast majority of the nation, and which is inseparably bound up in the nation's history, traditions and culture, occupies among religions in our country a unique and preponderant position.[31]

This draft clearly provided de Valera with a model for Article 44.1.2°. But while he clearly did not realise it, yet through one of these improbable accidents of legal evolution (involving the borrowing of the

[30] *Irish Times*, 14 October 1955.
[31] See document no. 58.

idea and language used by the Poles and the express use of the Polish draft by the Jesuits), the origins and language of Article 44.1.2° can probably be traced back to the Napoleonic Concordat.

In many ways, however, it is very difficult to see why these provisions gave rise to so much fuss. This very point was made by Professor Alfred O'Rahilly writing in the *Irish Independent* in May 1937:

> But nothing whatever follows from this alleged recognition; it does no good to us,[32] and it is sure to raise prejudice in others. The reason assigned for the recognition is not very theological: it is the Church of 'the great majority of the citizens'. The next clause is very curious. The State 'also recognises' several specified Churches and religious denominations existing in Ireland (Éire?) 'at the date of the coming into operation of this Constitution'. What about others not mentioned (e.g. the Baptists) or others not yet here? Presumably the answer is that they can do very well without this 'recognition', which does not seem to carry any implications.[33]

Some of the smaller denominations also sought recognition,[34] while the recognition of the Jewish Congregations in 1937 gave particular satisfaction.[35] Fr Cahill was deeply offended by use of the term 'Church of Ireland'.[36] Insofar as these provisions gave rise to any legal effects,[37] these were slight and affected marginal aspects of what might be termed lawyer's

[32] That is, Roman Catholics.

[33] See www.irishconstitution.ie. O'Rahilly elsewhere described the special position clause as 'nothing more but a piece of neutral scientific statistics expressed in fervent phraseology', *Thoughts on the Constitution* (Dublin, 1937), 65.

[34] See letters from Walter T. Scott to Patrick Little on behalf of the Christian Science Committee on 22 May 1937 and 3 June 1937 (document nos 198, 210). Maurice Moynihan responded on 17 June 1937, saying that he trusted that Scott would realise that:

> it would not have been feasible to specify by name all the religious denominations to which it applies. [De Valera] feels that the position of all religious denominations and of individual members thereof is adequately safeguarded by the provisions of the sub-section in question as it stands and by the general provisions of Article 44 as a whole (document no. 215).

[35] See document no. 172. See also the similar comments of Dr Massey on behalf of the Methodist Church in Ireland: document no. 149.

[36] See document no. 199.

[37] It is true, however, that in *Re Tilson*, [1950] IR 1, a majority of the Supreme Court declined to say—although they might easily have done—that these provisions conferred no privileged position on the Roman Catholic Church. In his dissent, Justice Black—the only Protestant member of the Court—stoutly denied that Article 44.1.2° admitted of 'any distinction as between persons of different religions'. He added:

> If I had thought it did, I could never have made a public declaration that I would uphold it; and if in fact it did, I imagine it would gain for us an unenviable distinction among the democratic peoples of the world.

See generally, John Whyte, *Church and State in Modern Ireland, 1923–79* (Dublin, 1980), 169–71 and Gerard Hogan, 'A Fresh Look at *Tilson's* case', *Irish Jurist,* 33 (1998) 311.

law, such as discrete aspects of the law relating to charities.[38] But this was as nothing compared to the situation in most other European countries (France here being the notable exception) in 1937, many of whom provided for some form of an established religion in one shape or another.

In the United Kingdom, for example, section 3 of the Act of Settlement (1701) provided that the Monarch and his or her spouse were required by law to join the Established Church on accession. The Monarch was further required to take an oath of office to uphold the supremacy of Protestantism:[39] bishops from the Established Church sat in the House of Lords and up to 1975 both the equivalent of the Chief Justice and the Minister for Justice were required to be members of the Church of England.

Nor was this approach confined to the United Kingdom. Thus, for example, Articles 2 and 4 of the Norwegian Constitution provide:

> Article 2: All inhabitants of the Realm shall have the right to free exercise of their religion.
> The Evangelical-Lutheran religion shall remain the official religion of the State. The inhabitants professing it are bound to bring up their children in the same.
> [Jesuits are not tolerated].[40]

[38] See Kelly, *Irish Constitution*, 2037–41. In one of the very few cases where these deleted provisions might be said to have had some legal impact, *Bank of Ireland Trustee Co. Ltd. v. Attorney General*, [1957] IR 257, 275, Justice Dixon said that:

> It was implicit in the terms of [the deleted provisions] that adherence to and practice of any of the religions there recognised may be presumed to be of public benefit.

But note the comments of Justice Geoghegan in *O Beolain v. Fahy*, [2001] 2 IR 279, 365:

> Long before [Article 44.1.2] was abolished by referendum the provision as to the special position of the Roman Catholic Church was not considered by constitutional lawyers to have any legal implications. It was merely reflecting what was perceived to be a fact on the ground at the time of the enactment of the Constitution.

Note also the comments of Justice Barrington in *Campaign to Separate Church and State Ltd. v. Minister for Education*, [1998] 3 IR 321, 355:

> The better opinion appeared to be that the recognition of the 'special position' of the Roman Catholic Church was merely a recognition of a fact and implied no privileged position at law. Nevertheless the term 'special position' was a source of misunderstanding. As long as it remained there was a latent suspicion that while all citizens were equal, Roman Catholics might, in some sense, be more equal than others.

[39] This was no mere historical anachronism, as King George VI took such an oath upon his coronation of 12 May 1937 as the Constitution was being debated in the Oireachtas. De Valera had earlier drawn attention to the religiously discriminatory character of the oath as justifying an attitude of 'detachment and protest' towards the whole coronation ceremony, 65 *Dáil Deabtes*, Col. 869 (24 February 1937). The question of whether the Vatican was going to attend the Coronation in an official capacity was also raised by Walshe during his trip to Rome in April 1937: see document no. 155.

[40] This provision of Article 2—which was extant in 1937—caused the Norwegians no little embarrassment during the diplomatic conference leading up to the signing of the European Convention of Human Rights in 1950. Following some controversy, the Norwegian Government originally proposed a reservation under Article 64 ECHR on the basis that Article 2 of the Constitution merely precluded the propagation of religious doctrine by the Jesuits and did not extend to precluding the admission of Jesuits to Norwegian soil. Following a parliamentary debate in the Storting in November 1956, the words in brackets in Article 2 were deleted and the reservation withdrawn: see Erik Møse, 'Norway', in Blackburn and Polakiewicz (eds), *Fundamental Rights in Europe, the ECHR and its Member States 1950–2000* (Oxford, 2001) with 625–6.

> Article 4: The King shall at all times profess the Evangelical-Lutheran religion, and uphold and protect the same. The relation of the state to such churches and religions will be determined from time to time by legislation after an understanding with their legal representatives.
> Article 116: The recognition of a new, or hitherto not legally recognised religion, may not be refused to religious communities whose institutions' teachings and organisation are not contrary to public order or public morality.[41]

Nor is this approach confined to pre-war constitutions. Thus, for example, Articles 7 and 8 of the Italian Constitution of 1948 provide:

> Article 7
> (1) State and Catholic Church are, each within their own reign, independent and sovereign.
> (2) Their relationship is regulated by the Lateran pacts. Amendments to these pacts which are accepted by both parties do not require the procedure of constitutional amendments.
>
> Article 8
> (1) Religious denominations are equally free before the law.
> (2) Denominations other than Catholicism have the right to organise themselves according to their own by-laws, provided they do not conflict with the Italian legal system.
> (3) Their relationship with the state is regulated by law, based on agreements with their representatives.

A similar approach is to be found in the 2001 Greek Constitution, Article 3 of which provides:

[41] It may be noted that a slightly modified version of this is found in Article 25 of the 1997 Polish Constitution:
(1) Churches and other religious organisations shall have equal rights.
(2) Public authorities in the Republic of Poland shall be impartial in matters of personal conviction, whether religious or philosophical, or in relation to outlooks on life, and shall ensure their freedom of expression within public life.
(3) The relationship between the State and churches and other religious organisations shall be based on the principle of respect for their autonomy and the mutual independence of each in its own sphere, as well as on the principle of co-operation for the individual and the common good.
(4) The relations between the Republic of Poland and the Roman Catholic Church shall be determined by international treaty concluded with the Holy See, and by statute.
(5) The relations between the Republic of Poland and other churches and religious organisations shall be determined by statutes adopted pursuant to agreements concluded between their appropriate representatives and the Council of Ministers.

1. The prevailing religion in Greece is that of the Eastern Orthodox Church of Christ. The Orthodox Church of Greece, acknowledging our Lord Jesus Christ as its head, is inseparably united in doctrine with the Great Church of Christ in Constantinople and with every other Church of Christ of the same doctrine, observing unwaveringly, as they do, the holy apostolic and synodal canons and sacred traditions. It is autocephalous and is administered by the Holy Synod of serving Bishops and the Permanent Holy Synod originating thereof and assembled as specified by the Statutory Charter of the Church in compliance with the provisions of the Patriarchal Tome of June 29, 1850 and the Synodal Act of September 4, 1928.
2. The ecclesiastical regime existing in certain districts of the State shall not be deemed contrary to the provisions of the preceding paragraph.
3. The text of the Holy Scripture shall be maintained unaltered. Official translation of the text into any other form of language, without prior sanction by the Autocephalous Church of Greece and the Great Church of Christ in Constantinople, is prohibited.

Finally, we may note that Article 9 of the Spanish Constitution of 1978 provides:

(1) Freedom of ideology, religion, and cult of individuals and communities is guaranteed without any limitation in their demonstrations other than that which is necessary for the maintenance of public order protected by law.
(2) No one may be obliged to make a declaration on his ideology, religion, or beliefs.
(3) No religion shall have a state character. The public powers shall take into account the religious beliefs of Spanish society and maintain the appropriate relations of cooperation, with the Catholic Church and other denominations.

From this (necessarily incomplete) survey, we can see a broad pattern emerging which was true both in 1937 and today: the Protestant states of northern Europe normally provided for an established Church. The Catholic countries accorded a variant of the 'special position' status to the Catholic Church, while also often expressly providing for a Concordat of some kind.

Of course, in one sense, Whyte was quite correct to say that the religious freedom provisions of Article 9 of the 1922 Constitution 'would have suited a country of any religious complexion'.[42] Those provisions of Article 9 were, however, so secular in character that they would, for example, have readily suited countries with a very strong tradition of the separation of Church and State such as France and the United States. It was, however, unrealistic to expect such entirely secular provisions to be adopted in a country such as Ireland in 1937 with a very different historical tradition,[43] especially where establishment or 'special provision' type-clauses were the norm throughout Europe.

None of this is to suggest for a moment that the 'special position' clause ought to have been retained. It is, however, to suggest, contrary to the implicit assumptions of commentators such as Foster and Whyte, that judged by the contemporary European standards of 1937—and even judged by the standards of today—there was nothing particularly exceptional about Article 44.1.2°. If anything, the only surprise was that the reference to Catholicism simply reflected the historical facts and that de Valera did not go further.

Of course, once the 'special position' provisions were deleted following the 1972 referendum, the underlying secular nature of the rest of Article 44[44] fully shone through. Freedom of conscience and free profession and practice of religion, subject to public order and morality, are guaranteed.[45] The State is precluded from endowing any religion[46] and Article 44.2.3° provides that the State shall not: 'impose any disabilities or make any discrimination on the grounds of religious profession, belief or status'. The Supreme Court has, moreover, held in *Campaign to Separate Church and State Ltd. v. Minister for Education*[47] that any UK-style establishment of a Church would of necessity 'be

[42] John Whyte, *Church and State in Modern Ireland: 1923–79* (Dublin, 1980), 51.

[43] As Ronan Fanning has argued:

> Neither should those who damn the Catholic triumphalism they so readily identify in the 1937 Constitution ignore the residual impact of ingrained anti-Catholicism that had so characterised British dealings with Ireland since the sixteenth century. Nor should they forget that an especially vicious form of anti-Catholic prejudice and discrimination was an outstanding feature of that part of Ireland still within the United Kingdom. Fanning, 'Mr de Valera Drafts a Constitution', 42.

[44] Article 44.1 excepted.

[45] Article 44.2.1° of the Constitution.

[46] Article 44.2.2° of the Constitution.

[47] [1998] 3 IR 321.

impossible to reconcile with the prohibition of religious discrimination in Article 44.2.3°.'[48]

It is, however, undeniable that, irrespective of constitutional theory or comparative constitutional law, the enactment of the Constitution came at a high price in terms of an accommodation with Northern Ireland. As the Constitution had de facto ended every link with the United Kingdom and the Commonwealth (save for the shadowy presence of the Crown permitted by Article 29.4.2°), asserted a *de jure* claim to sovereignty over Northern Ireland and was, moreover, demonstrably influenced in at least some of its provisions by Catholic social teaching, it was unlikely, to put it mildly, to contribute to such an accommodation.

The second contention made by Foster was that the Constitution assumed that the 'nature and identity of the Irish polity was Catholic, reflected in five articles [Articles 40 to 45] defining "rights".[49] These were much influenced by papal encyclicals and current Catholic social teaching.'

Of the five articles dealing with fundamental rights, Article 40 is by far the most important, guaranteeing equality before the law; the protection of life, person, good name and property; personal liberty; *habeas corpus* and *habeas corpus* procedure; the inviolability of the dwelling and the rights to free speech, assembly and association. The equality clause in Article 40.1 was borrowed from the equivalent clause in the 1919 Weimar Constitution. In addition, Article 40.3.1°—which roughly corresponds in this regard to the fourteenth Amendment of the US Constitution—imposes the general obligation on the State by its laws 'so far as practicable' to defend and vindicate the 'personal rights of the citizens'. Just as with the fourteenth Amendment, Article 40.3.1° has been the vehicle whereby the courts have subsequently held that a number of fundamental rights—not otherwise expressly enumerated elsewhere in the Constitution—are impliedly protected.

But, one might ask, what is so specifically Catholic about these provisions of Article 40? Writing over 50 years ago, Declan Costello (then a Dáil Deputy, but subsequently Attorney General from 1973 to 1977 and a judge of the High Court from 1977 until 1998) argued that,

[48] [1998] 3 IR 361, per Justice Keane. In his separate judgment, Justice Barrington noted that while section 5 of the Government of Ireland Act, 1920 had contained a ban on the establishment of any religion, this was not reflected in Article 16 of the Treaty nor Article 8 of the 1922 Constitution. He added:

> Why the express prohibition on the establishment of any religion was dropped is not quite clear. But presumably it was because the combined effect of the ban on the endowment of any religion and the prohibition of the granting of any preference on the grounds of religious belief or status was to make an express ban on establishment unnecessary; [1998] 3 IR 352.

[49] In passing, it seems curious that Professor Foster should refer to 'rights' in inverted commas, suggesting, perhaps, that these provisions were of little value. This gives no sense at all of the vast case-law which these provisions have subsequently generated. Thus, for example, the 2003 edition of Kelly, *Irish Constitution* devotes over 800 pages to a discussion of Articles 40 to 45.

in contrast to Article 41, Article 42 and Article 43, Article 40 derived from 'secular and rationalist theory'.[50] Indeed, one would be hard put to find *any* Catholic influences whatever in Article 40, unless it be the anti-abortion provisions of Article 40.3.3° inserted by referendum in 1983. Indeed, another distinguished historian, F.S.L. Lyons, writing some twenty years previously, had described Article 40 as being 'very much in the liberal, almost one might say, the egalitarian, tradition'.[51]

The provisions dealing with the family and education in Article 41 and Article 42 fall into another category and it is generally acknowledged that these provisions were influenced by contemporary Catholic social teaching. Taken in isolation, however, this statement might serve to create the misleading impression that these provisions were exceptional in themselves. Most continental constitutions contain similar provisions dealing with the protection of the family, as does Article 8 of the European Convention of Human Rights. A good example here is provided by Article 6 of the German Basic Law:

> (1) Marriage and family enjoy the special protection of the state.
> (2) Care and upbringing of children are the natural right of the parents and a duty primarily incumbent on them. The state watches over the performance of this duty.
> (3) Separation of children from the family against the will of the persons entitled to bring them up may take place only pursuant to a law, if those so entitled fail in their duty or if the children are otherwise threatened with neglect.
> (4) Every mother is entitled to the protection and care of the community.
> (5) Illegitimate children shall be provided by legislation with the same opportunities for their physical and spiritual development and their position in society as are enjoyed by legitimate children.

The special case of divorce aside, is there anything so different between these provisions of the German Basic Law and Article 41 of the Constitution?[52]

[50] Declan Costello, 'The Natural Law and the Irish Constitution', in *Studies*, 45 (1956), 403, 414.
[51] F.S.L. Lyons, *Ireland since the Famine* (London, 1972), 544.
[52] It is true that, in the one case where case-law based on Article 6 of the German Basic Law was relied on, *Murphy v. Attorney General*, [1982] IR 241, the Supreme Court rather tersely (and quite unconvincingly) said that this case-law did not assist the plaintiffs' contentions. In *Murphy* the plaintiffs had challenged the constitutionality of provisions of the Income Tax Act, 1967 which had aggregated the incomes of husbands and wives for tax purposes. Reliance was placed on a decision of the German Constitutional Court in 1957 which had held similar German legislation to be unconstitutional on the ground that it infringed Article 6(1), because it interfered with the right of married persons to make personal decisions, including

> 1. 1° The State recognises the Family as the natural primary and fundamental unit group of Society, and as a moral institution possessing inalienable and imprescriptible rights, antecedent and superior to all positive law.
> 2° The State, therefore, guarantees to protect the Family in its constitution and authority, as the necessary basis of social order and as indispensable to the welfare of the Nation and the State.
> 2. 1° In particular, the State recognises that by her life within the home, woman gives to the State a support without which the common good cannot be achieved.
> 2° The State shall, therefore, endeavour to ensure that mothers shall not be obliged by economic necessity to engage in labour to the neglect of their duties in the home.
> 3. 1° The State pledges itself to guard with special care the institution of Marriage, on which the Family is founded, and to protect it against attack.

Moreover, Article 41 equally reflects the thinking of the earlier Weimar Constitution of 1919:

> Article 119
> Marriage, as the foundation of the family and the preservation and expansion of the nation, enjoys the special protection of the constitution. It is based on the equality of both genders.
>
> It is task of both the state and the communities to strengthen and socially promote the family. Large families may claim social welfare. Motherhood is placed under state protection and welfare.
>
> Article 120
> It is the supreme obligation and natural right of the parents to raise their offspring to bodily, spiritual and social fitness; the governmental authority supervises it.

[52] *contd.* the right of the wife to decide whether she would devote herself to the home or work outside the home. As the legislature could not directly interfere with that right, the Court held that it could not do so indirectly by means of tax measures designed to penalise working wives.

But it is not easy to see why the Supreme Court so fleetingly dismissed this (very convincingly) reasoned German authority, especially as that Court has in other key decisions recognised that the autonomy of family decision-making from State interference is at the heart of Article 41: see, for example, *McGee v. Attorney General,* [1974] IR 284; *Re Article 26 and the Matrimonial Homes Bill 1993,* [1994] 1 IR 305, and *North Western Health Board v. HW,* [2001] 3 IR 622.

> Article 121
> Legislation has to create equal preconditions for children born out of wedlock, concerning their bodily, spiritual and social development, as they are given to legitimate children.
>
> Article 122
> Youth is to be protected against exploitation as well as against moral and spiritual dissipation, bodily neglect. State and communities have to take appropriate measures.
>
> Measures which interfere by the means of force in the parents' right to raise their children may only be taken if based on a law.

Given that other provisions of the Constitution appear to have been clearly adapted from the Weimar model,[53] it seems reasonable to assume that these provisions of the Weimar Constitution were at least examined by the drafters. The Jesuit draft dealing with the family and marriage—which was heavily influenced by the 1921 Polish Constitution and the 1934 Austrian Constitution[54]—was also itself very influential. With the exception of the special provisions of Article 121 dealing with children born out of wedlock, one could find a close fit between these provisions of the Weimar and Article 41 and, for that matter, much of Article 42. The reality probably is that the fundamental rights provisions of Article 40 to Article 44 reflect a diverse jumble of sources, ranging from common law tradition, papal encyclicals, Article 16 of the Treaty, the Jesuit draft, disparate provisions of the US Constitution, the 1919 Weimar Constitution, the 1921 Polish Constitution, the 1934 Austrian Constitution, the 1922 Constitution and the recommendations of the 1934 Constitution Review Committee.

It is, in any event, necessary to reflect on the scope and import of Article 41 itself. The whole object of Article 41 was to protect the autonomy and privacy of the family and to repose key decision-making with regard to the education and welfare of children in parents, subject to the right of the State—as provided for in Article 42.5—to intervene in the case of an objective failure on the part of parents. As Justice Hardiman pointed out in *North Western Health Board v. HW* this mode of thinking regarding the family is by no means confined to papal encyclicals:

> Professor Goldstein [a noted US family lawyer] suggests that the common law 'reflecting Bentham's view, has a

[53] See, for example, Article 12 and Article 13 dealing with the President, and Article 40.1 dealing with equality.
[54] The provisions of these constitutions themselves also drew on the Weimar model.

> strong presumption in favour of parental authority free of coercive intrusions by agents of the State'. I would endorse this as a description of the Irish constitutional dispensation, even if any reflection of the views of Jeremy Bentham is coincidental. I do not regard the approach to the issue in the present case mandated by Articles 41 and 42 of the Constitution as reflecting uniquely any confessional view.[55]

Of course, the Foster thesis proceeds on the implicit assumption that the fact that a particular constitutional right is inspired by Catholic social teaching is a sufficient objection in itself. But what surely matters is the inherent value of the right actually protected by the Constitution as distinct from its philosophical source or inspiration.[56] If one looks at the major constitutional issues raised in the contemporary case-law—such as the right of the parents to make their own decisions about medical tests for their children,[57] or the right of parents to obtain information about medical treatment administered to their children,[58] or the right of spouses and children of Irish citizens to remain in the State[59]—it is hard to say that anything turns on whether the constitutional right in question was inspired by the writings of Thomas Aquinas on the one hand or by Thomas Paine on the other.[60] In any event, the jurisprudence in respect of property rights under Article 43 has evolved to the point that, even if it be true that the provisions of Article 41 and Article 42 were rooted in specifically Catholic social teaching, 'the case law has long since broken loose of that particular inspirational source'.[61]

[55] [2001] 3 IR 622 (757).

[56] But cf. the comments of Aughey, 'Obstacles to Reconciliation in the South', in *Building Trust in Ireland* (*Studies Commissioned by the Forum For Peace and Reconciliation*) (Belfast 1996), 30: 'The source of Catholic social teaching *is* sufficient grounds for unionists to reject the Constitution and the content of the Constitution does *not* matter…because the common good it seeks may be admirable in itself but it is estranged from unionists'.

[57] *North Western Health Board v. HW*, [2001] 3 IR 622.

[58] *McK v. Information Commissioner*, [2006] 1 IR 12.

[59] *Fajujono v. Minister for Justice*, [1990] 2 IR 152; *Lobe v. Minister for Justice, Equality and Law Reform*, [2003] 1 IR 1; *Cirpaci v. Minister for Justice, Equality and Law Reform*, [2005] IESC 42.

[60] Of course, a separate question is whether Article 41 and Article 42 place undue weight on the protection of the autonomy of the family at the expense of the welfare of children: see generally *North Western Health Board v. HW*, [2001] 3IR 622; *N v. Health Service Executive*, [2006] IESC 60; [2006] 4 IR 374.

[61] Gerard Hogan, 'The Constitution, Property Rights and Proportionality' in *Irish Jurist*, 32 (1997), 396. It is true that in *Re Article 26 and the Health (Amendment) (No.2) Bill 2004*, [2005] 1 IR 105, 202, Chief Justice Murray described the right to property ownership as having 'a moral quality which is intimately related to the humanity of each individual', whose development 'represents the meaning of natural law language of Article 43.1.1° in a manner unprecedented in modern property rights jurisprudence': Rachel Walsh, 'The Constitution, Property Rights and Proportionality', in *Dublin University Law Journal*, 31 (2009), 7. This may well be so, but it is still a form of natural law which has moved well beyond any inspirational source derived from specifically Catholic social teaching.

No. 48: UCDA, P150/2393

Fr Edward Cahill to Eamon de Valera

Lisdoonvarna, Co. Clare
4 September 1936

I trust you will not take it ill or regard it as any indication of respect and esteem that I send you the enclosed papers in their present condition. I have been sent here some ten days ago unexpectedly by my superior and do not expect to be back in Dublin till the middle of next week or possibly later. The drafting of the suggestions which I had in mind took me much longer than I expected and is still far from satisfactory; but as the time is running on I think it better to send the papers to you as they are (I think that they are fairly legible) than to await my return when I could have them typed, and by consulting others have the suggestions themselves improved, amplified or possibly curtailed. I intended to give for each heading the reference to the pages of my book, in which the particular point is treated and in which the authoritative reference or citation are usually [given].[62]

The enclosed is really little more than a rough draft. Still it will give you an idea of what I have in my mind. Should you think it useful, I could after my return get the opinion of some few others of our fathers who are interested in the matter and [annex][63] the present draft. The one I send is the only copy I have. I hope that you yourself and Mrs de Valera and all the family are well, and that you are not overworking yourself.

No. 49: UCDA, P150/2393

Memorandum by Fr Edward Cahill 'Suggestions for Drafting a new Constitution'

Lisdoonvarna, Co. Clare
4 September 1936

In response to your kind invitation I am sending you some suggestions which I hope may prove useful in the drafting of the new Constitution.

[62] Word is obscured. 'Given' is the most likely possibility.
[63] Word is obscured. 'Annex' is the most likely possibility.

I am sorry for the long delay which I could not avoid and am sincerely grateful to you for giving me an opportunity of assisting even so little in a work which I look upon as by far the most important that has ever yet befallen the lot of an Irish administrator to undertake. The Government of which you are the head have now an opportunity which may never recur of giving to the Irish State (which will ultimately include all Ireland) a genuinely Christian Constitution. Such a constitution (our people being what they are) no succeeding administration could permanently alter at least in essentials. Its elevating influence would gradually make itself felt in almost every detail of public life and that influence would extend even beyond the geographical limits of the country.

Hence what I am principally interested in is that in the drawing up of the Constitution due consideration be given to the Church's teaching (which is very comprehensive) regarding the functions and duty of the State, as well as to the conclusion of traditional Catholic philosophy, and the general attitude of standard Catholic authors. I should like very much if you could find time to read over the passages in my book—*The Framework of a Christian State*—in which the matter in question is briefly treated in the light of Catholic teaching and tradition. The special passages to which I refer are the following:

Chap. IX, arts. 1, 3, 4 and 5 (105–7 and 113–23);
Chap. XXIII, arts 1 to 6 (451–86, and especially 465–75);
Chap. XXV, arts 2 and 3 (496–503);
Chap. XXVI, art. 1 (514–20) and finally
Chap. XXIX, art. 2 (607–13).

In another book of mine—*Freemasonry and the anti-Christian movement*—(of which also I sent you a copy at the time of its first publication 1929) a portion of Chap. VIII (viz. 153–7) may also be useful and suggestive. From reading these passages, with the citation which they include, you will I think easily see that the plea not unfrequently [sic] put forward (even sometimes by Catholics who have not had the opportunity of studying these matters seriously) that the nature of a Constitution makes little practical difference, is not only untrue, but is directly contrary to the teaching of the Popes and to the whole trend of Catholic tradition.

Hence I believe that it is of paramount importance in all the best interests of the country (and I am confident that it would be ardently welcomed by the overwhelming majority of the Irish people) that the new Constitution should make a definite break with the Liberal and non-Christian type of State. This latter, which has been forced upon us by a foreign, non-Catholic power is exotic, unnatural and quite foreign to the native tradition. It tends in innumerable ways to cramp and paralyse the free development of the people's Catholic life and culture. It causes lamentable and sometimes very dangerous confusion of thought upon public questions of the highest importance; and it leaves the door open to still graver dangers. To give a few examples of the anomalies that may and do occur as a result of this unnatural type of constitution: although the people of the Irish Free State are almost entirely Catholic, and probably amongst the best Catholics in Europe, a person or association may under the present Constitution, have a legally valid claim to the protection of the Executive in the propagation of the most anti-Christian of degrading or even blasphemous doctrines or practices or writings, provided he avoids offending against the few conditions laid down in the statutes, which he can easily manage to do. Again it is a well-known fact that a certain Judge of the Supreme Court recently gave a judgement in which he denied the existence of a Natural Law superior to all human enactments, and rejected the idea of indefeasible personal rights which no positive statutes can invalidate (*Irish Monthly*, April 1936, 247–53 or *Studies*, March 1936, 17–18). Again the name of the same Judge of the Supreme Court of the most Catholic State in Europe (the Irish Free State) is given in the Irish Freemason Calendar as a Freemason of one of the very highest degrees,[64] who consequently must have taken the impious and more or less blasphemous oaths which I refer to in my book on Freemasonry alluded to above (65–6) and must also have gone through the impious and more or less blasphemous ceremonies of initiation described in the same book (141–4). What is true of this judge is also true of one of the Official Censors of Publications appointed by the Government.

A Constitution of Ireland should be, if not confessedly Catholic (which may at present be not feasible) at least definitely and *confessedly Christian*. I do not believe and I should be very sorry to have to think that our Catholic people can have peace and contentment or true prosperity under any other system. The devine [*sic*] command, 'Seek ye first the Kingdom of God and his Justice and all other things shall be added unto you' applies to States as well as to persons; and its truth has probably never been more clearly exemplified than at the present day. This point is constantly stressed by the Popes especially by the two great

[64] The judge in question was Justice Gerald Fitzgibbon. The judgment in question was his decision in *The State (Ryan) v. Lennon*, for which see document no. 33.

Popes Leo XIII and our present Holy Father, Pius XI whose Encyclicals form the basis of modern Catholic Social Science. 'When men recognise', says Pius XI 'both in private and public life that Christ is King, society will then at last receive the great blessing of real liberty, well ordered discipline, peace and harmony'. All this is of special urgent importance at present, when the anti-Christian and disruptive forces of the world are apparently being mobilised for a determined effort to destroy the Church and what is still left of Christian civilisation; and change radically the whole system of life and thought which has developed under Christian influence and teaching. In Ireland there does not appear to be any solid justification for the introduction of a new Constitution that would be otherwise than Christian. All the Irish people, including those of the N. East counties, are with the exception of a negligible minority (such as the Hebrew element) professing Christians; and the overwhelming majority are not only professing but practical Catholics, whose religion is dearer to them than anything else on earth. It is a commonplace to assert that the English Protestant culture and the English economic and fiscal system which have been forced on Ireland will, unless eliminated, prove fatal obstacles to the real emancipation of the country from a foreign yoke. The same thing is true of the unchristian Liberalism which has been introduced from the same source into the public life of the Irish people. But political Liberalism contains within itself much greater danger than either English culture or individualistic capitalism. It is in fact the underlying philosophy and the unifying element of all the movements mutually antagonistic in many details, which are now making for the destruction of Christianity. Again, our people have never freely accepted the unchristian Constitution under which they have been forced to live since the English conquest. To accept such a Constitution now, when for the first time they are free to choose, would be a national disaster of the first magnitude. Hence it seems to me that if the present government of the Free State miss the opportunity which now presents itself, of giving the people at least a Christian Constitution, they will have betrayed in a very grave manner a sacred trust committed to them by providence and will deservedly suffer an irreparable loss of prestige in the minds of the best of their own people and of the Catholic people of Europe. Besides, considering the world-wide reputation which Ireland enjoys as a truly Catholic nation—a reputation which has been so well and worthily sustained on more than one occasion of late by the President—such a betrayal would be not only a grave injustice to their own people but also an injury and scandal to the whole Catholic world.

Finally, I am convinced that the want of due reverence for law and the suspicious attitude towards the legitimate civil authority which unfortunately are too prevalent amongst our people, who are in most other ways so good and virtuous are rooted mainly in the fact which they feel but usually do not correctly analyse that the character of the Constitution under which they live is not of a kind to merit their reverence or loyalty. Give them a Constitution which is in harmony with their ideals and convictions and of which they can be proud and the present regrettable attitude will gradually disappear and a new powerful element of harmony and national unity will be introduced into our public life. I beg your indulgence for inflicting this long letter on you, and for the frankness with which I state my views. My excuse is that I have the matter on which I write very much at heart and believe it to be of dominating and far-reaching importance.

N.B. The detailed suggestions which I send herewith refer only to the general principles upon which a constitution in harmony with the Natural and Divine Law must be based. These general principles are merely an application of the Papal teaching and of the conclusion of Catholic philosophy. They or most of them should I think be formally embodied in some shape or other in the written Constitution. Some such series of general principles or ideals is necessary even as a means of educating the people's representatives and unifying the social outlook. They should be taught even to school children. This latter point is of special and urgent importance with us in Ireland, where we have to deal with a deeply rooted tradition of unchristian Liberalism of some two centuries standing, and where the common law, if any such exists, is too often doubtful and unreliable owing to historical causes.

The special organisation of the government of the country which the Constitution must define is outside my present scope as we could have a Christian Constitution under any one of several possible systems. Personally, I should like that the Constitution provide for a *strong Executive* which at the present day (when a Christian country has to defend itself against disruptive forces from within and all around it), is of exceptional importance. Hence I should like to have a President of the State with a fairly long tenure of office, and elected not by the legislature but by the people; and an Executive which would be independent of the legislature, being appointed by the President or his Minister and *responsible only to him* (as in Portugal under the new Christian Constitution) with proper safeguards against the abuse of power by the Executive. In this system the Government would not go out of office if defeated in a bill which they had sponsored; and the unnatural party system would then disappear.

Suggestions regarding the General or Fundamental Principles of the Constitution:

I. The following are assumed as fundamental principles of the Constitution:
   i) God is the ultimate source of political authority, and of all valid rule.
   ii) Jesus Christ, the eternal Son of God, true God and true Man, is the Supreme King and Ruler of all States and nations, with whose laws all laws of the State must be in harmony.
   iii) The facts that man has been created by God to praise reverence and serve Him on earth and to be eternally happy with Him afterwards in Heaven; and that everyone has a personal responsibility and indefeasible right to work out his temporal well-being and his eternal happiness by the exercise of his free will are the necessary foundations of all civil rights and duties.
   iv) The family is the fundamental unit of Civil Society upon whose healthy vigour the good of the whole civic body depends.

II. Hence although freedom of religious worship is guaranteed within the limit of public order and morality, no legal enactment or administrative decree is to be accounted constitutional or valid, which may tend to impugn directly or indirectly the *supreme authority of God*, the *Divinity of our Lord Jesus Christ*, the *immortality of the soul*, the *freedom of the will*, the *indissolubility of the marriage tie or the responsibility and due authority of parents* in the upbringing and education of their children; and any public act or exhibition whether by word or writing or otherwise that would directly impugn any of these is to be accounted illegal and criminal.

III. Seeing that by the divine and natural law a valid marriage can be dissolved only by death the State has no power to dissolve a valid marriage and cannot recognise a supposed or attempted dissolution. Since by the Christian law the marriage contract is under the control of the Church, the State cannot recognise a supposed or attempted marriage which by the Christian law is invalid, nor refuse to recognise a marriage which is valid according to the Christian law. Hence in the case of a member of the Catholic Church the civil authority can recognise or register only such a marriage contract as has been made in accordance with the condition which the Catholic Church requires for validity. (Drafting not satisfactory or complete. This provision could have been copied from the Italian Constitution of which, however, I have not a copy.)

IV. Although the primary responsibility and control of the education of the young belong inalienably to the parents and the Church, it is a function of the State to assist where necessary and supplement their efforts as far as the public good may require.

V. Since religion and moral training is an essential and the most important element in all true education, the State cannot subsidise or assist any school or educational institution which does not include adequate religious training as an essential portion of its educational programme.

VI. Although it may be possible in exceptional circumstances, with the cooperation of the Ecclesiastical authorities to secure a certain degree of true religious education even in mixed or neutral schools, it will be the aim of the educational authorities to facilitate the provision of denominational schools for all.

VII. As the unity, stability and fecundity of the family, and the purity of family life are the first essentials for the prosperity of society, and the disintegration of the family a certain cause of ruin, it must be the primary object of State legislation to safeguard the unity and harmony of domestic life, the authority of parents over their children, the security of the family homestead and the stability of the hereditary property or estate.

(a) Since in the design of the Author of nature, the man and not the woman is meant to be the founder of the family, and the husband and father the breadwinner (while the wife and mother is mistress of the home) the aim and effect of a sound economic social policy must be to make it possible for every young man of adult age to found a family, and for every husband and father to support a family in decent comfort.

(b) Boys and girls who are minors may not be employed in gainful occupation without the consent of the father or guardian; and if so employed they will be under the control of the latter.

VIII. It is the essential function of the State to safeguard the common good in regard to the life, the liberty, the property, the morals and all the natural and justly acquired rights of each and all of the citizens, especially of the working classes and the poor, whose needs have the first claim; and to promote as far as possible not only their material well being but also their intellectual, moral and religious interest.

IX. The Government will take measures not only to secure as far as possible the safety and liberty of each person and of the nation at large against violent aggression, but also to safeguard the territory of the State against the economic, peaceful penetration of foreign capitalists and syndicates which may prove little less fatal to the people's real liberty and prosperity than foreign political or military control. Hence it will be a function of the Government to safeguard for the citizens of the State, the lands, the mines, the territorial waters, the harbours, the wharves, the waterways, the railways, the mills, the manufacturing and distributing industries, the theatres and places of amusement; and to free all these as soon as possible from foreign control wherever such control may exist.

X. For similar and still more urgent reasons it is a duty of the Government to secure that the issue of credit, which at the present day 'supplies as it were the lifeblood of the entire economic body' should not fall directly or indirectly under the control of foreign or international financiers, nor be abused in the interests of private individuals or syndicates to the injury of the common good.

XI. Seeing that civil society is meant by nature to be a quasi-organic body, composed of different parts, which while having each its own special function, dovetail into one another, co-operating for the good of the whole, it must be the policy of the legislature and executive of the State to strengthen the municipal bodies, and to foster and promote the growth of industrial and professional associations and guilds each of which should gradually assume more and more responsibility for the interests of its own members and gradually, be invested with widening powers in the management and control of its own special industry or profession.

XII. Since it is the essential purpose and function of the State (which it cannot validly abdicate or hand over even partially to another body not under its control) to safeguard and promote the temporal good of its members, it cannot tolerate within the body politic armed forces nor [*sic*] under the control of the Government nor industrial unions, which are under the jurisdiction of foreign or international Committees, nor associations secret or otherwise which are linked up or affiliated with foreign or international associations of a political or subversive character, nor secret oath-bound societies which are so dangerous to the peace and union or moral and religious interest of the people.

XIII. [65] Seeing that it is one of the functions of the State to safeguard the moral and religious interest of the citizens and the Christian culture of the nation at large in matters which the State alone can adequately control, and since the people of Ireland owing to the loss of their own native language are exposed in quite an abnormal degree to the influences of an alien culture, and of a moral code fundamentally different from their own, it is a duty of the Irish Government and of the municipal bodies to take effective measures to safeguard the people's faith and morals and native culture against the dangers coming from an imported Press and cinema of an irreligious, immoral or degrading tendency.

XIV. Since social peace and union between the different classes is essential to the stability of the State and to the common good; and as these are impossible where the citizens are split up into warring factions with opposing interests and ideals it is the duty of all—of the ruling authorities of the State, of the municipal bodies, of the industrial and

[65] This paragraph is mislabelled 'XII' in the original document, with each subsequent paragraph number affected. The correct numbering is given here.

professional associations and of each individual citizen—to co-operate in promoting peace and union among all different classes of the body politic. Since peace and union are impossible or unreal except they be founded on social justice, the Government, the municipal bodies, and all the different associations and members of the body politic must co-operate to eliminate as far as possible all reasonable causes of division and antagonism between the different classes and sections of the people. Above all effective measures must be taken on the one hand to secure for agricultural and industrial employees a just wage (implying at least a family wage for men of adult age), fair conditions of work, security against enforced idleness, and a due participation in the fruits of industry; and on the other hand to keep in check the activities of agitators who would sow disunion or discontent with the object of fermenting a destructive and unchristian class war.

XV. While communal or even State ownership (especially of public forests, town parks, parochial playgrounds, communal pasture lands, etc, and in exceptional circumstances even of certain productive industries) is not excluded, where it is found most suitable in the interests of the public good, the economic organisation of the country will rest eventually on private ownership of productive property as understood in Christian teaching; and it will be the aim of legislation and of government administration to encourage and facilitate an ever widening distribution of private property, and to enable and induce as many as possible to become owners.

XVI. Seeing that a very wide distribution of ownership of productive property is one of the best safeguards of personal liberty, and is practically essential for real democracy the legislature and administration of the State as well as the municipal bodies will encourage and assist industrial workers as well as agricultural labourers to acquire small plots of land. They must also take measures to safeguard small agricultural holdings as well as small firms and enterprises of every kind against absorption by the large and more powerful and give special protection and encouragement to co-operative industry.

XVII. Since the natural resources of the country such as the land, the mineral wealth, the fisheries, the waterways, etc, are the ultimate source from which the citizens of the State have to be maintained, it is a duty of the Government to prevent their being unjustly or unduly held up by private individuals or syndicates; and so to adjust property rights in regard to them as to secure that they be developed and utilised for the public good.

XVIII. Since the vigour and stability of the State rest mainly on the rural classes who are the custodians of the national traditions and the ultimate source from which all the other classes of the community have to be recruited (seeing that town families are unstable and tend to die out or disappear) it must be the policy of the legislature to safeguard by every feasible means the interests of the rural population, to uphold its political influence (for instance by securing that the basis of representation be territorial rather than mere density of population), to promote the multiplication of rural homes and discourage in every feasible way the tendency towards urbanisation, which is a sure sign and forerunner of national decay.

XIX. Since the working classes, including small farmers, agricultural labourers and industrial employees form by far the largest portion of the population, with whose interests the common good is mainly associated, every effort must be made to encourage and promote the due organisation of the workers in industrial unions; so to adjust the system of taxation that taxes fall as little as possible on the workers and small owners; to safeguard the poor against profit-eering and usury; and to provide a prompt and impartial administration of justice within easy reach of the poorest of the citizens.

XX. No member of the Government, whether of the legislature, the Executive or the Judiciary, nor any servant of the State belonging to any department whatsoever may belong to the Masonic order or to any other secret, oath bound society.

XXI. Every member of the Government and every servant of the State shall before entering upon office swear to uphold the Constitution of the State and be loyal to its President for the time being.

No. 50: JA, J55/64

Eamon de Valera to Fr Edward Cahill

Department of the President
19 September 1936

I am returning herewith your manuscript and a typed copy of it.[66] I have read it over carefully. It is very useful in indicating the principles which should inspire all governmental activity so as to make it conform with Catholic teaching. The difficulty is to decide how much can or should be embodied formally in the new Constitution.

I can see that some of the principles might be set forth in a preamble, but I fear there is not much that can be incorporated into the body of the Constitution, i.e., made Articles of it.

If you could find time to put into the form of draft Articles, with perhaps a draft preamble, what you think should be formally written into the Constitution, it will be very helpful. I could then arrange, when I had seen your draft, to have a chat with you about it.[67]

No. 51: UCDA, P150/2393

Fr Edward Cahill to Eamon de Valera

Milltown, Dublin
21 September 1936

My thanks for your letter of 19 September with enclosures. I will willingly do what you suggest. It may however take some time—some weeks as I would like to secure the advice and help of some others.

[66] Refers to document no. 49.
[67] A copy of this letter is also found at UCDA, P150/2393.

No. 52: JA, J55/65/1

Minutes of Jesuit Constitution Committee, first Meeting

Milltown, Dublin
24 September 1936

Session 1, 24 September 1936
A committee having been appointed by Fr Provincial to advise on certain matters connected with the Constitution, the first meeting of the Committee was held on Thursday, 24 September 1936 in Milltown Park, 10am.

There were present Fr [Patrick] Bartley (President), Fr [Edward] Cahill, Fr [Joseph] Canavan and Fr E[dward] Coyne. Fr [John] MacErlean (Secretary) was absent, being on retreat.

The following points were decided:

I. A preamble is to be drawn up on the model of the preamble to the Polish Constitution.

II. Articles are to be drafted on the following subjects: a) The rights of the family, particularly with regard to the education of the children; b) Religion to be taught in all schools, which are to be denominational whenever there is no insuperable difficulty; c) The State cannot dissolve a valid marriage; d) The relations between the Catholic Church and the State is [*sic*] to be defined by a Concordat; e) Freedom of religious worship; f) Ecclesiastical property; g) Private property; h) Freedom of speech and of the press, and the limitations of this freedom; i) Any other matters that may be suggested by a study of Concordats and existing Constitutions.

The meeting was adjourned to Thursday, 1 October.

P. Bartley, S.J.
1 October 1936

No. 53: JA, J55/65/2

Fr Patrick Bartley to Fr Laurence Kiernan

Milltown, Dublin
11 October 1936

My dear Fr Provincial,
We hope to bring the work of our Committee to a conclusion at our meeting on Thursday next. I propose then, with the approval of your Reverence, to hand over our suggestions to Fr Cahill, who will deliver them in the proper quarter. It is of the utmost importance that no time should be lost, if our recommendations are to be in before the official draft is completed.

Our work has been very harmonious so far. Fr Cahill is in full agreement with it, and has shown no desire to veto anything. If any difficulty of this kind should arise, it will have to be met with diplomacy: and I think it can be so met.

But there is another difficulty, and a very real one, that can only be met by the exercise of your Reverence's authority. It is this. Fr Cahill will almost certainly want to add recommendations of his own to those approved by the Committee. Now these recommendations, partly by their sheer bulk and partly by their singular character, are likely to bring discredit on the very solid findings of the Committee, especially if they are delivered at the same time as the Committee's findings.

Therefore, with all deference, I advise your Reverence to give Fr Cahill the two following instructions:

1) When he delivers the recommendations of the Committee, he is to add nothing that has not been specifically approved by the Committee.
2) Later, not very much later perhaps, but later, he will be free to send in additional recommendations, provided that these are approved by any two of those who have served on the Committee with him. The Committee by this time will have ceased to exist.

The kind of censorship I suggest in the second of these instructions is, I think, quite justified. The source of Fr Cahill's recommendations will be quite well known to a small number of very important people. The reputation of the Society will be involved: and the Provincial has the right to watch over that reputation.

What I have said about Fr Cahill's intentions is not pure conjecture. I know for certain that he is preparing voluminous recommendations and that some of them at least are rather singular.

Yours in Christ,
Patrick Bartley, S.J.

No. 54: JA, J55/65/3

Fr Patrick Bartley to Fr Laurence Kiernan

Milltown, Dublin
15 October 1936

My dear Fr Provincial,
Our Committee finished its collective labours today. We maintained our harmony to the end though I was prepared for some dissension in the last session.

I myself am preparing the final report: and Fr Cahill will type it. We shall meet for the last time on Sunday just to give this report a final look over.

I told Fr Cahill that we were authorised by your Reverence to deliver this report through him in the proper quarter. I told him also that I understood that your Reverence had some instructions to give him regarding this report. I did not profess to know the nature of these instructions.

I think you may send on the instructions at once. I am now more convinced than I was before that they are necessary. They should reach him on Saturday at latest.

Yours in Christ,
Patrick Bartley, S.J.

No. 55: JA, J55/65/4

Fr Laurence Kiernan to Fr Edward Cahill

Gardiner Street, Dublin
16 October 1936

My dear Fr Cahill,
I have heard with great pleasure that the committee appointed some weeks ago to draft suggestions for the new Constitution has been able to

do such good work, and I understand that its recommendations will be given your Reverence by Fr Bartley one of these days. Now, as that document will be the product of the best heads we have in matters of this kind, I think it would be well if it were presented as it stands by your Reverence to Mr de Valera.

It may be that you would like to add to some of the matters dealt with in this report, or possibly to suggest alternative recommendations. I have no objection to your doing this, but think 1) that this second document ought not to be handed in with the first or at least as not forming part of the first; and 2) that, since what you recommend will be regarded as emanating from the Society, and on the other hand in view of the extreme importance of the matter, I would ask you to submit for censorship to any two you may select of the committee members the document you may propose to hand Mr de Valera.

Finally, I wish to thank your Reverence very sincerely for all the good work you have done in this important matter.

With best wishes, devotedly yours in Xt.,
L.P. Kiernan, S.J.

No. 56: JA, J55/65/1

Minutes of Jesuit Constitution Committee, 5th Meeting

Milltown, Dublin
18 October 1936

Session 5, 18 October 1936
All members of the Committee were present at the meeting held at Milltown Park at midday, 18 October 1936, viz. P.P. Bartley, MacErlean, Cahill, Canavan, E. Coyne.

The preamble was slightly changed so as to read 'In the name of the Most Holy Trinity and of our Lord Jesus Christ, the Universal King, we the people of Ireland, etc, full of gratitude to God who has so mercifully preserved us from innumerable dangers in the past, hereby, as a united independent Christian nation, establish this sovereign society of the Irish people, etc. And so in accordance with the principles laid down, etc, we freely and deliberately to the glory of God and honour of Ireland, sanction this Constitution and decree and enact as follows:

Art. 1 Religion: 'may' substituted for 'will' in 'The relations of the state to other religious bodies 'will' be determined by an agreement', etc.

Religion in 4 (b): In Fr Canavan's alternative article the final words 'profess the Catholic faith' were changed to 'are members of the Catholic church'.

Art. 4 Education (b): Delete 'religious bodies' and say 'all citizens and all associations of citizens'.

Education (d): for 'subsidised wholly or in part' say 'maintained or subsidised'.

Education (e): Read 'schools maintained or subsidised by the state shall be in principle denominational, and except in special circumstances to be defined by law, boys and girls of adolescent age shall be educated separately'.

Education (f): Dele[te] 'as defined by law' and read 'Primary education is compulsory on all Irish citizens'.

Article 5. Private Property.

(a) Say 'The right of individual citizens and of associations of citizens to own private property in productive as well as non-productive goods is acknowledged, etc.'

(d) Say 'The state, etc, may not limit, etc, except when the law, etc'.

It was resolved unanimously that references to constitutions and concordats of Catholic states should be added to the various assertions made above, that those who have the task of drawing up the contributions may come to know what the Catholics of other Catholic European states have already secured.

No. 57: UCDA, P150/2393

Fr Edward Cahill to Eamon de Valera

Milltown, Dublin
21 October 1936

Enclosed herewith I send a typed copy of a draft Preamble, and of draft articles for the proposed Constitution. I have, in drawing them up, confined myself to the minimum that I would consider necessary to realise a Christian Constitution, as I feared to outstep the limits of what you asked me to do. I should like to send in addition, should you wish and consider it useful, some few other draft articles, which I believe would be really necessary, or which would certainly be very useful. In the draft articles which I am sending several essential matters are not touched on, some because they are left to be settled by a Concordat, such as the civil observance of Sundays and holydays, the juridical personality of religious Congregations and communities in regard to property, (at present religious houses of Congregations have no juridical standing, and their property is held in the names of individuals): others are omitted because there is no need to mention them, seeing that they are already fairly well attended to; such as the obligation of the State to provide for the moral and religious interests of all those under its charge, such as soldiers, prisoners, etc. Nevertheless, I realise how desirable it would be to have such things embodied in a Constitution, which is meant to be permanent.

Again, there are some other headings not pertaining directly to the matter of religion, which I should like to see included in the Constitution, as a portion of the general principles and guarantees. These I could send on, should you wish it, without much delay. These articles would refer to the State (its essential functions); the Citizens (their rights, etc.); associations, industrial and others; and the rural population. Under one of the last two headings would come a suggestion in which I am much interested, viz. the formation of parochial rural Councils or committees to be elected solely by the heads of families in the parish, (as is provided in the Portuguese Constitution of 1933), and which would be the nuclei of the social and cultural and economic life of the parish. If the principle were adopted in the Constitution, the detailed plan would serve to give a statutory recognition to the Christian family, such as is given in the Portuguese Constitution, marking a definite departure from the Liberal, unchristian ideal and a return to the solid Christian tradition.

I have, in drawing up the drafts I am sending you, availed myself of the advice and assistance of three or four others, some of whom have made a special study of these matters; others, although not specialists, are pretty well informed on them, and are men on whose judgement I have confidence.

I considered that it may be useful to indicate the sources which are relied on in making the drafts; and so I have had the references to the official ecclesiastical documents on which the particular section is based, written in, under each separate section; and in some cases references to the parallel articles in some of the Catholic Constitutions of European Catholic States, especially Austria (the Constitution of 1934) and Poland, both of which have non-Catholic minorities about as large as the non-Catholic minority of the 32 counties of Ireland. The further sections to which I refer above that I would like to send would be modelled largely on the Portuguese Constitution of 1933.

I hope sincerely that you will find all this or some of it helpful and useful in the arduous work you have on hand. If you consider that I can be of any further assistance, I shall be always at your service.

No. 58: UCDA, P150/2393

Jesuit Constitution Committee's 'Suggestions for a Catholic Constitution'

Milltown, Dublin
18 October 1936

Abbreviated References

A. Conc.—Austrian Concordat of 1934 (published in French in D.C. (vide infra), vol. 32, col. 1250, ff 1934).
A. Const.—Austrian Constitution of 1934 (published in D.C. (vide infra), vol. 32, col. 78).
C.I.C.—*Codex Juris Canonici*
C.S.G.—*Catholic Social Guild* (Oxford) publications, among which is the English translation of Pius XI's *Quadragesimo Anno.*
C.S.P.—*Code of Social Principles*. Published by C.S.G. (vide supra). This is a translation of the Original French *Code Social*, which is a summary of Catholic social principles, drawn up by the Malines International Union. This latter includes the leading specialists of Europe in Catholic Social Science.
C.T.S.—Booklets of the Catholic Truth Society, London, among which are English translations of the chief Papal Encyclicals issued 1928–31.
D.C.—*Documentation Catholique*, Paris, especially vol. 32 (1934).
F.C.S.—*Framework of a Christian State* by Rev. E. Cahill, Dublin.
Pol.—Polish Constitution of 1921, published in S.C.W. (vide infra).
Port.—Portuguese Constitution of 1933 (English translation, typed copy).
P.P.—*The Pope and the People*, a selection of Papal Encyclicals, in English, published by the C.T.S. (vide supra), London, 1931.
S.C.W.—*Select Constitutions of the World*. second edition, edited by Shiva Rao (Madras, 1934).

Preamble

In the name of the most Holy Trinity and of our Lord Jesus Christ the universal king, [68] we, the people of Ireland, being the parent nation of the Irish race, mindful of the long centuries of persecution we have had to endure, and full of gratitude to God who has so mercifully preserved us from innumerable dangers in the past; hereby, as an independent Christian nation, establish this sovereign Civil Society of the Irish people.[69]

Acknowledging that all supreme political and civil authority, legislative, executive and judicial, and all other moral powers of government come to us from God;[70] and recognising that for the just and efficient exercise of this authority and these powers it is necessary to transfer, separate and distribute them to such persons and bodies as are hereinafter described and set up in and by this Constitution; we declare that all such authority and powers shall be exercised only in accord with the precepts of the Divine Law, natural and positive, and that any other exercise of them is, and shall be null and void, and of no moral force, and in no way sanctioned by us.

With the sacred purpose and intention of maintaining social unity and order on the eternal principles of Justice, and Liberty, and of ensuring the development of all the moral, spiritual and material resources of our citizens and country,[71] we guarantee to all citizens of this state full equality before the law as human persons, and full recognition and protection by the state of all their personal and family rights.[72]

And so in accordance with the principles laid down in this Preamble and the following fundamental law; we freely and deliberately, to the Glory of God, and the honour of Ireland, sanction this Constitution, and decree and enact as follows:[73]

Article I (Religion)

(a) Freedom of religious worship (in public and in private) is guaranteed to all within the limits of public order and morality.[74]

(b) The Catholic Faith, which is the faith of the vast majority of the nation, and which is inseparably bound up in the nation's history, traditions and culture, occupies among religions in our country a unique and preponderant position.[75]

[68] Title: A. Const. in D.C. (1934), col. 77; Pol. preamble in S.C.W., 86; Pol. art. 54 (S.C.W., 92).
[69] Pol. preamble in S.C.W., 85.
[70] A. Const. preamble in D.C. (1934), col. 77.
[71] Pol. preamble (S.C.W., 85).
[72] Pol. preamble.
[73] Pol. preamble.
[74] Pol. art. 111 (S.C.W., 101); A. Const. art. 27 (D.C. [1934], col. 81).
[75] Pol. art. 114 (S.C.W., 101).

(c) The relations between the Catholic Church and the State, in matters that concern both Church and State, shall be determined by an agreement to be entered into with the Holy See. This agreement shall be ratified by the Oireachtas, and after such ratification shall have the force of law.[76]

(d) The relations to the State of other religious bodies within the nation may be determined by an agreement between the State and the official representatives [of] the bodies in question.[77]

(e) Every religious association recognised by the State may freely manage its own affairs, own and acquire movable and immovable property, administer and dispose of the same, possess and enjoy its revenues and endowments, and maintain institutions for religious, educational and charitable purposes.[78]

Article II (Marriage)

(a) The Civil Power cannot dissolve a marriage validly contracted.[79]

(b) The conditions required for the civil validity of the betrothals and marriages of Catholics shall be identical with those laid down in the Code of Canon Law of the Catholic Church. The competent authority of the Catholic Church shall, where a member of that Church is concerned, decide finally all questions as to the existence of the marriage bond. All such decisions, when they have been duly communicated to the State, shall be registered by it and given civil effect.[80]

Note: In case it should be found impossible to include paragraph (b) in the Constitution, the following is suggested as an alternative—(b) (Alternative) Seeing that the Catholic Church has its own marriage laws, the State shall, after agreement with the Holy See, bring its marriage laws into conformity with the Canon Law, where one or both parties to a marriage are members of the Catholic Church.

Article III (The Family)

The Family, being a natural society, and being the fundamental unit of Civil Society, possesses natural, inalienable, and imprescriptible rights,

[76] Pol. art. 114.

[77] Pol. art. 115 (S.C.W., 101); A. Const. art. 28, n. 5 (D.C. (1934), col. 82).

[78] Pol. art. 113 (S.C.W., 101); A. Const. art. 29 (D.C. [1934], col. 81).

[79] C.I.C., 118; Leo XIII, *Quod Apostolici Muneris*, 1878 (17–18); Leo XIII, *Arcanum Divine*, 1880 (31–3, 36–7).

[80] Italian Concordat, art. 34 of *Acta Apostolicae Sedis*, 1929, 290; Pius XI, *Casti Connubii*, 1930, (C.T.S., 64–5); A. Const. art. 7 (D.C. [1934], col. 1260) and protocol to art. 7 (A. Const. art. 7 col. 1271).

prior and superior to all positive law. Being moreover indispensable to the continuance, strength and well being of the Nation, the Family shall have its essential nature, its just dependence, and its rights respected and in a very special way protected by the State and its laws.[81]

Article IV (Education)

(a) It is the natural right as well as the duty of parents to provide, as far as in them lies, for the education religious, moral, physical and intellectual of their children. Parents may freely choose teachers for their children, and freely select the schools to which their children's education is to be entrusted.[82]
(b) All citizens and all associations of citizens have the right of founding, owning and administering schools and educational institutions, provided that they fulfil the conditions required by law relative to the welfare physical and moral of the children, and provided that they are well disposed to the State.[83]
(c) The State has the duty and the right to assist in the work of education, and to supplement private effort, as far as the public good requires.[84]
(d) The teaching of religion within school hours, and as a part of the curriculum, shall be obligatory in all schools, maintained or subsidised by the State. This teaching shall be under the direction of the religious body to which the pupils belong.[85]
(e) Schools maintained or subsidised by the State shall be in principle denominational; and, except in special circumstances to be defined by law, boys and girls of adolescent age shall be educated separately.[86]
(f) Primary education is compulsory on all Irish citizens.[87]

Article V (Private Property)

(a) The right of individual citizens and of associations of citizens to own private property, in productive as well as in non-

[81] Leo XIII, *Rerum Novarum*, 1891 (130–40); Pius XI, *Casti Connubii* (On Christian Marriage, C.T.S., 62–3; C.S.P., nn 10–17, 18–19).
[82] Pol. art. 94 (S.C.W., 98), and art. 117 (Pol. art. 94, 107; A. Const. art. 31 (D.C. [1934], col. 82); Belgium, art. 17 (S.C.W., 576); C.I.C., 1113, 1373; Pius XI, *Divini Illius Magistri*, 1929 (C.T.S., 13–16, On Christian Education).
[83] Pol. art. 117 (S.C.W., 102); A. Const. art. 31 (D.C. [1934], col. 82; C.I.C., 1375.
[84] Pius XI, *Divini Illius* (C.T.S., On Christian Education, 18–21); C.S.P., n. 22.
[85] Pol. art. 120 (S.C.W., 102); A. Const. art. 31 (D.C. [1934], col. 82); A. Conc. art. 6 (D.C. [1934], col. 1258); C.I.C., 1378.
[86] C.I.C., 1374; Pius XI, *Divini Illius* (C.T.S., On Christian Education, 32–3, 36–40).
[87] Pol. art. 118 (S.C.W., 102); Pius XI, *Divini Illius* (C.T.S., On Christian Education, 20).

productive goods, is acknowledged and guaranteed by this Constitution.[88]

(b) The right of property has, however, a double aspect, individual and social. Hence the State has the right and duty to see that neither the acquisition nor accumulation of private property, especially in land, takes place in such a way as to injure the common good. It is also the right and duty of the State to see that the use which owners make of their property, especially goods of a productive nature, is in accord with the common good and with social justice.[89]

(c) The State shall prevent by suitable laws the natural resources of the country, such as land, mines, fisheries, waterways, etc, from being unduly held up by private individuals or syndicates, and shall so adjust property rights as to secure that these are duly developed and utilised in the interests of the common good.[90]

(d) The State shall guarantee the protection of private property, and may not limit or abolish individual or collective private property, except when the law so provides for reasons of public utility and with fair compensation.[91]

(e) It shall be the aim of the State to promote a wide distribution of private property, especially in land.[92]

Article VI (Liberty of Speech, of the Press, etc.)
Liberty of speech and liberty of the Press, which are conceded to all within due limits, shall not extend to the utterance, publication or circulation of anything that is subversive of the Christian religion, of Christian morality, or of public order in the State. The law, when occasion demands, shall define more clearly the limits of these liberties.

The liberty accorded to the theatre, the cinema, the radio and such like is confined within the same limits, which shall, when necessary, be defined by law.[93]

[88] Pol. art. 99 (S.C.W., 99); Leo XIII, *Rerum Novarum* (P.P., 135–40); Pius XI, *Quadragesimo Anno* (C.S.G., 173; C.T.S., On the Social Order, 20).
[89] Leo XIII, *Rerum Novarum* (151–3); Pius XI, *Quadragesimo Anno* (C.S.G., 18–20; C.T.S., On the Social Order, 20–3); C.S.P., nn 77–8.
[90] Pius XI, *Quadragesimo Anno* (C.S.G., 18–20; C.T.S., On the Social Order, 19–20); C.S.P., nn 77–8.
[91] Pol. art. 99 (S.C.W., 99).
[92] Leo XIII, *Rerum Novarum* (158–9); Pius XI, *Quadragesimo Anno* (C.S.G., 23–5; C.T.S., On the Social Order, 27–9).
[93] A. Const., art. 26 (D.C. [1934], col. 80–1); Norway, art. 100 (S.C.W., 625); Pius VII, *Post tam diuturnas*, 1814 (F.C.S., 469–70); Leo XIII, *Officiorum si Munerum*, 1897 (*Officiorum si Munerum*, 470); Pius XI, *Casti Connubii*, 1930 (C.T.S., On Christian Marriage, 22–3).

It is worth noting that a copy of the Jesuit Constitution Committee's suggestions is found in the papers of Fr John Charles McQuaid (DDA, AB8/A/V/48). It is evident that de Valera passed a copy to McQuaid. However, there is no known reference to the document found in McQuaid's correspondence with de Valera, while the document found in McQuaid's papers, most unusually, has no annotation of any kind in McQuaid's hand.

No. 59: JA, J55/64

Fr Edward Cahill to Eamon de Valera

Milltown, Dublin
13 November 1936

I am sending herewith the further draft articles which I referred to in my letter of 21 October.[94] I have been delayed unavoidably much longer than I foresaw, and I hope that what I send may still be in time for your consideration in connection with the new Constitution.

When I came to draft the proposed articles in reference to the rights of citizens, I found that practically all the points which I had in mind, except those referring to the rights of association were included or implied in the draft articles already sent in. I found further that the whole matter of associations (already touched on in nn. XI, XII and XVIII of my previous letter of 4 August)[95] is so complicated and many sided, and would require so many draft articles that I considered it useless to handle it in my present state of ignorance as to how far you would be at present prepared to go in dealing with it, fundamental and important as it undoubtedly is.

I am not without hope that you may at least be able to do something towards realising my suggestion (contained in my letter of 21 October) in regard to the setting up of parochial rural committees. I believe that such parochial committees elected by the heads of families (and of which the principal ministers of any considerable religious body within the parish would be ex-officio members) would little by little open the way towards solving the (at present) almost hopeless problem of rural and agricultural organisation; and, being founded on the natural basis of the family and the parish, would be saved from the corruption and jobbery, which apparently prevailed in the previous rural councils, which were based on an artificial and individualistic basis, and from which the ministers of religion, who in the rural districts are practically the only well educated leaders, were excluded by law. If the proposed council [*sic*] had each a parish hall, with a playground, etc, in the neighbourhood of the church, the end would be substantially secured even if their powers were very limited.

The article concerning the denominational character of the public hospitals would if adopted serve to undo a very grave injury to our poor,

[94] See document no. 57.
[95] Cahill is almost certainly referring to his letter of 4 September 1936. See document nos 48–9.

practically all of whom are Catholics, and who naturally desire to have a proper religious environment when they are ill or dying. It would besides serve to anticipate the danger which has proved so real in continental countries of an undue ingérence of non-Christian aliens into the medical profession.

Hoping that what I send may be useful, and wishing you and yours all blessing, I have the honour to remain, your obedient servant in Christ.[96]

No. 60: UCDA, P150/2393

'Supplementary Suggestions for the New Constitution of the Irish Free State'

Fr Edward Cahill, Milltown, Dublin
13 November 1936

Supplementary to Article I (Religion)

(b) The State is bound to provide moral protection and religious ministration to citizens with whom it is directly concerned in public institutions such as educational institutions, barracks, hospitals, houses of detention, mental homes, etc.[97]

(g) Hospitals, mental homes, houses of refuge, etc, maintained or subsidised from public funds shall be in principle denominational.

Supplementary to Article III (The Family)

(b) The rural families as being the most important element of the population, and the element upon which the strength and welfare of the nation mainly depends shall be a special object of care of the State.

(c) The stability of the rural families shall be safeguarded by laws of inheritance, preventing the mortgaging or alienation of the family inheritance within limits to be fixed by law.

(d) The conditions of the employment of women and minors in industry shall be fixed by law, in accordance with the interests of the family and the common good.[98]

[96] A copy of this letter is also found at UCDA, P150/2393.
[97] Pol. art. 102 (S.C.W., 99–102).
[98] Leo XIII, *Rerum Novarum*, 1891 (P.P., 156); Pius XI, *Quadragesimo Anno*, 1931 (C.S.G., 27–8, 51).

Supplementary to Article V (Private Property)

(f) The voluntary subdivision of larger farms within the limits of economic proportions shall be encouraged and facilitated by subsidising the erection of suitable homesteads in newly formed farms.

(g) Special facilities shall be given to agricultural labourers to acquire independent homes with a specified minimum of land of sufficient extent to supply milk and vegetables for the labourer's family.

Supplementary to Article VI (Liberty of Speech, of the Press, etc)

(a) Public opinion, being of the highest importance as a social force, must be safeguarded from such factors as may lead it astray from truth, justice and the common good.[99]

(b) Liberty of speech, etc (as in Art. VI above referred to).

(c) The Press exercises a public function, and cannot refuse to publish such notes of reasonable dimensions as shall be issued to it by the Government.[100]

(d) The law shall secure to every citizen and recognised corporate body the right to insert free of charge, and without legal process, a vindication of character in any periodical in which such citizen or corporate body may have been injured or defamed.[101]

The Fundamental duties of the State

The following articles, summarising Catholic teaching regarding the general duties of government are adapted from the Portuguese Constitution of 1933. Whether or not quasi-abstract articles of that kind can be fitted into the proposed Irish Constitution the present writer does not know. They are put here on the chance that they may be useful or suggestive. They would be useful in the Constitution for educative purposes.

(a) (The State shall)[102] take all necessary measures to safeguard the common good, in regard to the life, liberty, property, morals, and all the natural or justly acquired rights of all the citizens, and to promote as far as possible their material, intellectual and moral interests.

[99] Port. art. 20.

[100] Port. art 21.

[101] Port, art. 8, sect. 2.

[102] 'It is the primary function of the State to' is written above these words, in manual hand.

(b) The State shall respect and safeguard the due autonomy of the family; and in due measure, the free and proper functioning of the lesser social units within the nation.

(c) It is the duty of the State, while encouraging the private initiative of individuals and organised bodies, to stimulate, assist and coordinate their activities; and where necessary to supplement and complete them; and to take measures that a just harmony of interests prevail, and that particular interests be subordinated to those of the community.

(d) It is the duty of the State to protect in a special way the interests of the poor and the less favoured social classes, that they may participate in the advantages of civilisation.[103]

The following eight articles, borrowed with certain adaptations from the Portuguese Constitution of 1933, may be of some use.

1) The territory of the Irish Free State includes all the land of Ireland and the adjacent islands; the territorial waters, the inland rivers, and the air above them.[104]

2) No portion of the national territory shall be acquired by a government or legal entity of another country, save for the setting up of diplomatic representation, when such other country affords reciprocal privileges to the Irish State.[105]

3) The Irish nation includes all Irish citizens residing within or without its territory and all these shall be regarded as dependents of the State, and subject to its laws save in as far as the provisions of international law shall require otherwise.[106]

4) All foreigners in, or residing in the Irish State, whether temporarily or permanently, are likewise subject to the laws of the Irish State, due regard being had to the provisions of international law.[107]

5) The Irish Free State is organised on the principles of equality of all its citizens before the law, and the free access of all classes of the community to the benefits of civilisation.

6) The state may grant honourable distinctions or recompense to those citizens who have become conspicuous by personal

[103] Port. art. 6. Cf. also C.S.P., nn 43–50.
[104] Port. art. 1. There is an echo of this in both the original and present version of Article 2 of the Constitution.
[105] Port.art. 2.
[106] Port.art. 3.
[107] Port.art. 3.

merit or by their civic or military achievements; and the law may establish orders, decorations, medals or diplomas for this purpose.[108]

7) No rights or goods of the State that affect either its own prestige or the greater utility of the nation may be alienated.[109]

8) Objects of artistic, historic or national value, officially recognised as such, are under the protection of the State, and may not be injured or alienated in favour of foreigners.[110]

Irish is the official language of the Irish State; but English shall also be recognised as an official language, except in those districts (to be determined by law) where Irish is the usual language of the home.

Every member of the government, and every servant of the State, shall before entering upon office swear to uphold the Constitution of the State.[111]

[108] Port. art. 37.
[109] Port. art. 51.
[110] Port. art. 51.
[111] Written in manual hand at the end of the document.

CHAPTER VII

EXTERNAL RELATIONS AND ABOLISHING THE OFFICE OF GOVERNOR GENERAL, 1936

The 1922 Constitution made no special provision for foreign affairs. This was scarcely surprising given that the focus of that Constitution was on internal, rather than external, sovereignty. Article 29 of the 1937 Constitution, dealing with international relations, was a conspicuous novelty which may fairly be ascribed to Hearne's influence and, indeed, to his general interest in matters of international law. Much of this was quite *avant garde* for its time. Thus, for example, Article 29.2 clearly reflects the terms of the Kellogg Briand Pact of 1928–9:[1] 'Ireland affirms its adherence to the principle of the pacific settlement of international disputes by international arbitration or judicial determination.'

Article II of the Kellogg Briand Pact had provided that:

> The High Contracting Parties agree that the settlement or solution of all disputes or conflicts of whatever nature or of whatever origin they be, which may arise from them, shall never be sought except by pacific means.

One aspect of Article 29 did, however, reflect domestic concerns. Article 29.5.2° provides that:

> The State shall not be bound by any international agreement involving a charge on public funds unless the

[1] The Pact was an international treaty signed by the United States, United Kingdom, Germany, Belgium, France, Italy, Canada, Australia, New Zealand, South Africa, India, Poland, Czechoslovakia and the Irish Free State renouncing 'war as an instrument of national policy'. It was named after the two statesmen who sponsored it, Frank Kellogg, then US Secretary of State and Aristide Briand, then French Minister for Foreign Affairs.

> terms of that agreement shall have been approved by Dáil Éireann.

De Valera had long objected to the terms of the 1923 financial settlement with the British Government which had never been laid before the Dáil and an early version of Article 29.5.2° appears in Hearne's May 1935 draft.[2]

The particular difficulty confronting the drafters with regard to international relations was, of course, the position of the Crown. In the explanatory memorandum which accompanied his May 1935 draft Hearne had acknowledged the:

> specially difficult problem of fitting the King as a constitutional officer for the purposes of international relations only into the framework of a State internally organised on a Presidential basis.[3]

Hearne's May 1935 draft anticipated both the External Relations Act, 1936 and the Republic of Ireland Act, 1948. Article 7 provided that the new President would 'represent Saorstát Éireann in international relations', and went on to provide that he would have the general power to conclude international treaties and to accredit diplomatic representatives. Article 53 was a Transitory Provision that provided:

> So long as Saorstát Éireann remains associated as a Member of the British Commonwealth of Nations [all relevant diplomatic documents] shall before being issued be countersigned by the Minister for Foreign Affairs of Saorstát Éireann.

By October 1935, Hearne had supplied alternatives of this draft. One further version of Article 7 did not give the President a role in international relations, but simply confined the role to accreditation of diplomats and signing the instruments of ratification of treaties. Hearne added:

> But should Saorstát Éireann become a Republic and should it then be decided that the President's function in international relations be inserted in the written Constitution, the Constitution would have to be amended by the insertion of appropriate additional Articles. This would, in my view, be necessary, as the President would

[2] Article 49 of that May 1935 draft provided: 'International agreements affecting the revenue shall not be binding unless and until approved by a resolution of Dáil Éireann'. See document no. 40.
[3] See document no. 41.

> have no constitutional functions at all in international relations unless they were expressly given to him by the Constitution itself.[4]

Another version provided:

> In the event of the withdrawal of Saorstát Éireann from membership of the British Commonwealth of Nations the President shall represent Saorstát Éireann in international relations.[5]

By June 1936 the Government was in a position to send a message to King Edward VIII indicating that it was their intention to 'introduce a Bill for the purpose of setting up a new Constitution' by the autumn:

> This Constitution will deal with the internal affairs of Saorstát Éireann, leaving unaffected the Constitutional usages relating to external affairs. Amongst the provisions of the new Constitution will be the creation of the office of a President elected by the people and abolition of the office of Governor-General.[6]

By the summer of 1936 Hearne had produced a draft of a Foreign Relations Bill with the new Constitution. Many of these provisions ultimately were reflected in Article 28 and Article 29. Hearne noted:

> Legislation in the terms of the draft Bill would throw the whole question of the Kingship for the purposes of external relations only into its proper context, namely, the context of the sovereignty of the State. It would demonstrate the minor place which the forms of the only instruments now issued through the agency of the several Monarchy occupy in the Constitutional system now to be established. And it places a ringing emphasis upon the authority and control of the people in every aspect of the external relations of the State.[7]

Events then took an unexpected turn which played directly into the hands of de Valera and Hearne. The Abdication Crisis broke in early December 1936 with the abdication of Edward VIII on December 10. The crisis which then erupted saw the Dáil hurriedly recalled to discuss

[4] 'Alternative Draft B of Articles 7 and 53 (jointly)': see document no. 42.
[5] 'Alternative Draft D of Articles 7 and 53': see document no. 42.
[6] See document no. 61.
[7] See document no. 63.

the Constitution (Amendment No. 27) Act, 1936 which provided for the disappearance of the Crown and the abolition of the office of Governor General. On the following day the External Relations Act, 1936 was enacted and provision was finally made for external association, i.e., that for so long as the Crown was 'recognized by those nations [of the British Commonwealth] as the symbol of their co-operation', the Crown would have the function of the accreditation of diplomats.[8] External association was by now a *fait accompli* and fate had thus unexpectedly removed another obstacle to the drafting of a new Constitution.

No. 61: UCDA, P150/2368

Memorandum from the Executive Council of the Irish Free State to Edward VIII

Government Buildings, Dublin
8 June 1936

The Government of Saorstát Éireann, in pursuance of their policy of establishing conditions for permanent peace and harmony amongst the Irish people and providing a more secure basis for friendship and co-operation with the people of Great Britain, intend, at the beginning of the Autumn session of parliament, to introduce a Bill for the purpose of setting up a new Constitution. This Constitution will deal with the internal affairs of Saorstát Éireann, leaving unaffected the Constitutional usages relating to external affairs.

Amongst the provisions of the new Constitution will be the creation of the office of a President elected by the people and the abolition of the office of Governor General.

Eamon de Valera, President of the Executive Council and Minister for External Affairs of Saorstát Éireann, begs to submit, for the information of Your Majesty, the attached memorandum [above] concerning the intention of the Government of Saorstát Éireann to introduce a Bill in Dáil Éireann for the purpose of setting up a new Constitution.

[8] See www.irishconstitution.ie. For the Abdication Crisis and the enactment of the External Relations Act, 1936, see O'Sullivan, *I.F.S. and its Senate*, 478–87; Sexton, *Ireland and the Crown, 1922–36*, 163–70.

No. 62: UCDA, P150/2370

Memorandum from John Hearne to Seán Moynihan

Department of External Affairs
6 September 1936

Secretary
I submit herewith a preliminary draft of the Foreign Relations Bill.[9] The scheme of the draft Bill follows the lines discussed with the President on the fourth instant.

The references in the draft Bill to 'the Constitution' are references to the new Constitution, not to the Constitution of 1922. The new Constitution will contain the following fundamental declarations.

1) A declaration that Éire is an independent sovereign (democratic) state,
2) A declaration that all the internal and external prerogatives of the State vest in the people of Éire,
3) A declaration of the right of the people of Éire to determine and control and [*sic*] manner and form in which the said prerogatives (or any of them) shall be exercised or exercisable.

The Constitution will also contain an enactment to the effect that the manner and form in which all or any of the prerogatives referred to shall be exercised or exercisable may be determined by law.

These provisions are all recited in the preamble to the draft Bill. The Bill itself when enacted will be the determination by law of the manner and form in which certain of the external (or foreign) prerogatives are to be exercised.

Legislation in the terms of the draft Bill would throw the whole question of the use of the Kingship for the purposes of external relations only into its proper context, namely, the context of the sovereignty of the State. It would demonstrate the minor place which the forms of the only instruments now issued through the agency of the several Monarchy occupy in the Constitutional system now to be established. And it places a ringing emphasis upon the authority and control of the people in every aspect of the external relations of the State.

[9] See document no. 63.

No. 63: UCDA, P150/2370

Draft Foreign Relations Bill

John Hearne, Department of External Affairs
6 September 1936

Draft of a Bill entitled An Act to make provision in accordance with the Constitution for the Exercise and performance of certain of the Constitutional rights and functions of Éire in the domain of foreign relations.

Whereas by Article 2 of the Constitution Éire is declared to be an independent sovereign state:

And whereas by Article 3 of the Constitution the prerogative of peace and war, the treaty-making power, the right of legation and all other the foreign prerogatives of the State are declared to belong to the people of Éire:

And whereas by the said Article 3 of the Constitution the right of the people of Éire to determine and control the manner and form in which the said prerogatives (or any of them) shall be exercised or exercisable is declared to be absolute and indefeasible:

And whereas it is enacted by Article 4 of the Constitution that the manner and form in which all or any of the said prerogatives shall be exercised or exercisable may be determined by law:

Be it, therefore, enacted by the Oireachtas as follows:

1. (1) A state of war between Éire and any other State shall not be declared save with the consent of Dáil Éireann.
   (2) In the event of any invasion or threatened invasion of the territory of Éire the Council of Ministers shall forthwith take all such measures as they may consider necessary for the protection of the State.
2. (1) The treaty-making power of Éire shall not be exercised or capable of being exercised save only by or on the authority or advice of the Council of Ministers.
   (2) Save in the case of treaties or conventions of a technical or administrative character, the text of every international engagement undertaken in behalf of the State shall be laid before Dáil Éireann.
   (3) The State shall not be bound by any treaty or convention which imposes a charge upon the Exchequer unless the

terms thereof shall have been approved by Dáil Éireann prior to the ratification of such treaty or convention.

3. The diplomatic and consular agents of Éire in other countries shall be appointed by or on the advice of the Council of Ministers.

4. (1) So long as Éire is associated with the (Association)[10] of States commonly called and known as the British Commonwealth of Nations the following international instruments, that is to say:

   Treaties and conventions in the Heads of States form, Full powers and instruments of ratification relating to such treaties and conventions, Letters of credence or recall of envoys extraordinary and ministers plenipotentiary, Consular commissions and exequators,

   may be made and issued respectively in such form or forms as are now or may hereafter be recognised from time to time by the Governments of the several States of the said Association for the purpose of the exercise by each of those States of its treaty-making power or its right of legation.[11]

   (2) Every such full power, instrument of ratification, letter of credence or recall, consular commission or exequatur as aforesaid shall be passed under the Great Seal of Éire and shall be countersigned by the Minister for Foreign Affairs.[12]

5. This Act may be cited as the Foreign Relations Act, 1936.

No. 64: NAI, DT S9429A

Extract from Cabinet Minutes

Government Buildings, Dublin
10 December 1936

Item 1: Abdication of King Edward VIII

The President reported that he had been advised that it was the intention of King Edward VIII to abdicate. It was decided that legislation should be introduced:

[10] Word is circled by de Valera and replaced by 'Group'.
[11] This paragraph is annotated by de Valera: 'On advice of Exec. Committee'.
[12] Annotated by de Valera: 'Authenticated by counter signature of M.F.A., Prime Mtr, Presdt'.

(a) To give effect to the abdication as far as the Saorstát was concerned;
(b) To delete from the Constitution all mention of the King and of the Representative of the Crown whether under that title or under the title of Governor General;[13]
(c) To make provision by ordinary law for the exercise by the King of certain functions in external matters as and when so advised by the Executive Council.[14]

It was further decided that the President should request the Ceann Comhairle to summon Dáil Éireann to assemble at 3pm on Friday 11 December 1936 for the purpose of dealing with this legislation as a matter of urgency.

No. 65: NAI, DT S9430

Memorandum by Michael McDunphy 'The drafting of Constitution (Amendment No. 27) Bill'

Department of the President
10 December 1936

The Department of the President though intimately concerned with the subject of this Bill, was not at any time consulted regarding it.

The Bill was introduced without even a copy being furnished to the Department of the President, except for the purpose of handing it to the Dáil, for which purpose it was in the hands of the Assistant Secretary for about ten minutes. There was no time to even read the Bill nor was any information given regarding it to enable comments to be made on its contents.

All action on the Bill was taken by the Department of External Affairs, who in this, as in many other matters, completely ignored the Department of the President.

[13] Accomplished by Constitution (Amendment No. 27) Act, 1936. See www.irishconstitution.ie.
[14] Accomplished by Executive Authority (External Relations) Act, 1936. See www.irishconstitution.ie.

No. 66: NAI, DT S9429A

'Note on legal considerations making the External Relations Act requisite'

James Geoghegan, Office of the Attorney General
11 December 1936

The Act, as distinct from the Constitutional Amendments, is necessary, because:

1. In the unprecedented situation created by the abdication, the Courts might (without the Bill) hold (a) either that King Edward VIII is still on the throne so far as Saorstát Éireann is concerned, or (b) that there is no Successor to him under the law of Saorstát Éireann to perform the functions in question; or (c) that the British Act is effective to set up a new King here; and the greatest confusion would ensue if the position were left in doubt.
2. The new constitutional position of the Monarch in relation to Saorstát Éireann is nowhere else defined.
3. The Bill shows (and it is essential that we should show) that a law of Saorstát Éireann itself is necessary to authorise the performance of any royal functions in relation to Saorstát Éireann.

Also, it is desirable that the new method of bringing a Bill into force should be put into effect immediately as it will be when this Bill is passed.

No. 67: NAI, DT S9430

'Notes for the President on the Constitution (Amendment No. 27) Bill and the Executive Authority (External Relations) Bill'

Michael McDunphy, Department of the President
11 December 1936

1. The purpose of the Constitution (Amendment No. 27) Bill is to bring to an end the functions of the British Monarch in relation to the internal affairs of Saorstát Éireann, that is to

say the functions hitherto exercised by the Governor General. The Article of the Constitution relating to the appointment, remuneration and establishment of the Governor General is being deleted, but for the moment it may be necessary to retain the present occupant of the position in office until other arrangements are made for the performance of certain routine functions performed on the advice of the Executive Council.[15]

2. The Executive Authority (External Relations) Bill is a corollary to the other measure. It gives authority for the continued exercise by the British Monarch, on the advice of the Executive Council, of those functions, in regard to external affairs which he has hitherto exercised on behalf of the Saorstát. This provision is evidence of the desire we have always expressed for co-operation with the States of the British Commonwealth in matters of common concern to us and them.
3. It will be seen that the Bills taken together anticipate to some extent the Constitutional proposals which the Government some months ago announced its intention to introduce. An event which could not have been foreseen has made it necessary to bring this part of the scheme before the House at the present time and in the present manner.
4. The situation created by the abdication of King Edward the Eighth made it necessary to pass legislation of some kind here. Failure to do so would result in an ambiguous position. It would appear on the one hand to imply acceptance of the British legislation providing for the abdication and succession as binding on the Saorstát, and, on the other hand, it would cause some uncertainty as to the validity of future Acts of this House.
5. Having, then, to introduce some legislation to deal with the situation, the Government had to decide between:
   (a) Formally conferring upon the new British Monarch all the functions exercisable by the Crown under the existing Constitution;
   (b) Giving him functions in relation to external affairs only;
   (c) Establishing a Republic for the Twenty-Six Counties.
6. To propose that the new Monarch should have formally conferred on him all the present royal functions would be entirely inconsistent with the known policy of the Government

[15] This document was probably prepared for Eamon de Valera for use in the Dáil.

and with the will of the Irish people. It would be a definitely retrograde measure which, in the opinion of the Government, would be deservedly regarded by the people as a national humiliation. To establish a Republic for the Twenty-Six Counties in an emergency situation without full consideration of the possible effects of such a course on the ultimate unity of the country would be an irresponsible proceeding. To do so without reference to the people would be a violation of the Government's election pledges.

7. There remained the course of limiting the functions of the Monarch, so far as the Saorstát is concerned, to external affairs. This is the course which the Government is proposing to the House. It does not claim that in doing so it is suggesting any revolutionary change. The present Bills will simply bring the law and theory into conformity with the realities of our position. All the functions which are now being withdrawn from the Crown have been in fact only nominal. In proposing their withdrawal the Government is asking the House to put an end to a fruitful source of irritation and of misunderstanding of the Constitutional facts, in this country, and to a constant obstacle to the establishment of friendly relations with Great Britain. If in relation to these measures, the British Government observes the attitude of respect for the independence of the Saorstát which we have a right to demand, I think we may say that the prospects of co-operation between the two countries in matters where co-operation is required by their common interests will have been greatly enhanced.
8. I know there are people who will think that we are not going far enough in these Bills, and some people will say it who do not believe it. My answer is that we are going as far as we think right at this stage, and we are putting no barrier in the way of anyone who wants to go further and is supported by the Irish people.

No. 68: NAI, DT S9425

Memorandum by Michael McDunphy 'The Office of the Governor General after Constitution (Amendment No. 27) Act'

Department of the President
16 December 1936

1. I understand that Mr John Hearne, Legal Adviser, Department of External Affairs, informed the President yesterday that he had now come to the conclusion that the abdication of the King had resulted in the position that the Governor General was no longer in office, on either or both of the following grounds:
   A. That the manner in which the succession of the Crown from Edward VIII to George VI had been effected did not constitute a demise of the Crown within the meaning of the Demise of the Crown Act, 1901, and that consequently the Governor General's term of office had been terminated by the removal from the throne of the King by whom he had been appointed;
   B. That the amendment of Article 51 of the Constitution deprived the King of his position as repository of the executive authority of the State.
2. Mr Maurice Moynihan and I discussed the matter together today, but found ourselves unable to agree with the conclusion arrived at by Mr Hearne. We discussed the matter at length with Mr Philip O'Donoghue, Assistant to the Attorney General, and he is to examine the matter more fully in the light of our conversation.
3. With regard to A, it would appear that there is a misconception as to the meaning of the phrase 'demise of the Crown'. It is popularly but erroneously taken as meaning the death of the King, because of the fact that the death of a King is one of the means by which a Crown can be demised or transferred
4. The correct meaning of the phrase is the uninterrupted transfer of the crown and of the Sovereignty from one King to his successor.

5. As a result of the Saorstát statute, the Executive Authority (External Relations) Act, 1936, which became law on the 12th instant, the Crown in its relation to the Saorstát was transferred from Edward VIII to his brother George VI without interruption, and accordingly there was a demise of the Crown.
6. In these circumstances the position with regard to the Governor General is covered satisfactorily by section 1 (1) of the Demise of the Crown Act, 1901, which reads as follows:

   'The holding of any office under the Crown, whether within or without His Majesty's Dominions, shall not be affected, nor shall any fresh appointment thereto, be rendered necessary by the demise of the Crown.'

   So that the Governor General's position remains unaffected by the change in the occupancy of the throne.
7. The view that the correct meaning of 'demise of the Crown' is 'transfer of the Crown' is supported by the fact that Section 1 of the British Act dealing with the abdication, viz., 'His Majesty's Declaration of Abdication Act, 1936 (1 Edward VIII, c.3) provides inter alia '...that there shall be a demise of the Crown'.
8. If the popular interpretation of the words 'demise of the Crown' were to apply, the meaning of this phrase would be '...that there shall be a death of the King'. This is obviously absurd.
9. If the insertion of the word 'demise' in the Act were intended to make the 'Demise of the Crown Act' applicable to the situation, the phrase used would have been somewhat as follows:

   'There shall be *deemed to be*, for the purposes of the Demise of the Crown Act, 1901, a demise of the Crown.'
10. With regard to B in Mr Hearne's argument, it would appear according to British constitutional theory at least, that the prerogative is vested in the King and flows from him to the Executive, and not from the Executive to the King, and can only be taken from him by specific enactment expressly worded to that effect. If this theory be accepted, the King still retains, in spite of the amendment in Article 51 of the Constitution, all prerogative rights and powers formerly vested in him which have not been specifically taken from

him by Statute, so that the basis of the creation of the office of Governor General and of the appointment of the present holder has not been disturbed.

11. In spite of the doubt raised therefore by Mr Hearne under the two heads discussed, there appears to be very strong ground for holding that the present Governor General is still in office and is capable of performing all functions which have not been expressly taken from him by Statute.
12. Apart from the conclusion set out in the preceding paragraph, it must be accepted that unless there is an overwhelming case to the contrary, no reasonable judge would seek to give an interpretation which would result in a disturbance of the stability of the State. There must always be a presumption of Constitutionality in matters of this nature, and the onus of proof to the contrary must lie upon those who would challenge it.

No. 69: NAI, DT S8946

Memorandum by Michael McDunphy 'Abolition of the Office of Governor General'

Department of the President
December 1936

1. On the 11 December, 1936, an Act entitled 'Constitution (Amendment No. 27) Act, 1936' became law, which removed from the Constitution all specific mention of the King and of the Governor General, whether under that title or that of representative of the Crown. It was believed at the time of its introduction that its effect, as far as the Governor General was concerned would be to remove from him the specific functions mentioned.
2. After its passage into law, however, the President was advised by the Department of External Affairs that the amendment to that Act, by deleting Article 60 of the Constitution, had abolished the office of the Governor General.

CHAPTER VIII

DRAFTING RESUMED, SEPTEMBER 1936–MARCH 1937

Following the abolition of the Seanad in May 1936, the way was clear for the drafting of a new Constitution. It is clear from the statements made in the Dáil in June 1936[1] that de Valera had hoped to present a new Constitution during the course of the autumn. Yet deliberations appear to have begun in earnest on the new Constitution only in August with Hearne's work on what was to become Article 29 (international relations) in August 1936.[2] What then seems to have happened is that, treating his own May 1935 draft as the framework document, Hearne shouldered much of the subsequent drafting up to the point of formal publication and circulation to Ministers on 16 March 1937[3] and a formal drafting committee was appointed only at the end of that month.[4] It seems clear that Hearne liaised directly with de Valera all during this period, although by February and March 1937, the parliamentary draftsman, Arthur Matheson, had also worked on the draft, as de Valera had asked him to see 'whether any provision could be shortened by leaving the subject-matter thereof to be dealt with by ordinary law'.[5] The Department of Finance appears to have been the only Department consulted during this particular stage of the process and even then its contribution was confined to a consideration of the financial articles of the 1922 Constitution.[6]

The drafting of the fundamental rights provisions was, of course, heavily influenced by the Jesuit submission of October 1936 and by the subsequent numerous submissions made by McQuaid.[7] Yet, in some

[1] See www.irishconstitution.ie.
[2] See Chapters VII–IX.
[3] See John Hearne to Kathleen O'Connell, 17 February 1937 (document no. 77). See also www.irishconstitution.ie.
[4] See document no. 120.
[5] Arthur Matheson to Eamon de Valera, 4 March 1937 (see document no. 82).
[6] See document no. 73.
[7] See Chapter VI of this volume.

ways, this entire period is, perhaps, the least documented part of the drafting process. There are, of course, a proliferation of actual drafts (many in different type faces and with different hands), but memoranda explaining the course of the drafting or explaining the reasons for certain changes are in short supply. Thus, for example, decisions appear to have been made during this period that the Constitution would define the extent of the national territory; provide for a Second House; provide for a ban on divorce; that it could only be amended by referendum; to drop the idea of a special Constitutional Court and to provide for a general obligation to protect fundamental rights via Article 40.3. But no documentation has been located which explains the rationale for any of these decisions or when or how or by whom they were taken.

As is clear from the May 1935 draft, Hearne's own drafting style was a model of elegance and economy. While he plainly favoured a short, simple document, this method of drafting could not have accommodated the wishes of those such as the Jesuits and McQuaid who favoured a document heavily influenced by Papal Encyclicals:

> There is likely to have been a real tension between those like Hearne who wanted a relatively short document and McQuaid who wished to convert the document into a Catholic document rooted in the Papal Encyclicals and in Thomistic philosophy.[8]

In the end, a form of drafting dialogue regarding the wording of the fundamental rights guarantees seems to have taken place, with the Jesuits and McQuaid making suggestions and Hearne endeavouring to see that some of these ideas were reflected in formal drafting language which the legal system could ultimately accommodate.[9]

But as early as October 1936, a draft Article 34 contained the precursor of the present Article 41 dealing with the family.[10] Later drafts of Article 34.2.3° contained a ban on contraception and Article 34.2.4° contained a ban on divorce. The ban on divorce survived, but the provisions dealing with contraception[11] were ultimately left to ordinary legislation.[12]

[8] Dermot Keogh and Andrew McCarthy, *The Making of the Irish Constitution, 1937* (Cork, 2007), 121.

[9] Keogh and McCarthy, *Irish Constitution*, 109–10.

[10] It should be noted that Professor Alfred O'Rahilly (a member of the drafting Committee of the 1922 Constitution) had circulated a draft ('Draft C') at the time which sought to protect marriage 'as the basis of family life and national well-being'. Article 41.1.2° echoes this draft, with its guarantee to protect the family 'as indispensable to the welfare of the Nation and the State'.

[11] A version of this prohibition survived as late as January 1937. Article 34.2.3° of that draft provided: 'Contraception and advocacy of the practice of contraception are prohibited and the possession, use, sale and distribution of contraceptives shall be punishable by law, UCDA', P150/2385.

[12] Criminal Law (Amendment) Act, 1935, s.17. It may be somewhat ironic in the circumstances, but this provision (banning the importation of contraception) was subsequently held to be unconstitutional by the Supreme Court in *McGee v. Attorney General*, [1974] IR 287.

By November 1936, the general outlines of the Constitution were plainly visible. A summary prepared for de Valera at this time thus summarised the key provisions of the fundamental rights guarantees:

> Constitutional Guarantees
> The following fundamental Constitutional rights shall be guaranteed to all citizens: equality before the law, freedom of conscience and freedom of expression and practice of religion, subject to public order and morality, the right to free expression of opinion, subject to public order and morality, the right to assemble peaceably and without arms, the right to form associations and unions, liberty of the person, and inviolability of the dwelling. Power will be taken in the Constitution to enact laws for the purpose of preventing or controlling meetings which are calculated to cause a breach of the peace or be a menace or a nuisance to the public. Religious associations will be guaranteed the right of assembly for the conduct of religious services in public and in private, subject to public order and morality. No religion shall be endowed by law. Legislation providing for State aid for schools will contain no discrimination against the schools under the management of a particular religious denomination. The property of any religious denomination will not be diverted save for the purpose of works of public utility and on payment of compensation.
>
> Special recognition will be given to the family in the State as the basis of social discipline and ordered society.
>
> The right to private ownership of property will be affirmed as a natural human right and the protection of private ownership of property will be guaranteed, subject to the law.
>
> All citizens will be guaranteed the right to free elementary education.[13]

This list corresponded to that previously drawn up by Hearne in May 1935, save that the protection of the family and property rights were now added for the first time.

Much of the initial detailed drafting seems to have been done by Hearne in November and December 1936, even if some of this work had to be interrupted to deal with the Abdication Crisis.[14] One draft

[13] See document no. 72.
[14] See Chapter VII of this volume.

which appears to date from early December 1936[15] contains what is by now a fully worked out version of Article 1 to Article 20, in both English and Irish. The English version was labelled by de Valera in his own hand 'second draft (a). Original English. Latest from Hearne.' The Irish version was also labelled by de Valera as 'second draft' and in an unknown hand the words 'Cóip an Uachtaráin'[16] are also written. This version also has handwritten corrections in ink (by one of the principal translators, Risteard Ó Foghludha) and in pencil by de Valera.

This version represents a considerable advance on the outline of the Constitution dating from just a couple of weeks previously.[17] By this stage, the Articles which had been so drafted were more fully formed and complex, with tighter language and more defined legal and political concepts. The lay out was as follows:

> Part I: The State. Articles 1–6, detailing the name of the state, its political format, sovereignty of the people, national flag, national language, citizenship requirements.
> Part II: The President. Articles 7–8, detailing status, duties, powers and functions.
> Part III: The National Parliament. Articles 9–20.

It is interesting to note that at this point not only had the Second House featured as a definite constituent part of the legislature, but also the name Seanad has been settled upon.

The other document was prefaced by a glossary of English words and their Irish equivalents. The Senate was translated as An Seanad, but Prime Minister is translated as Árd Aire,[18] while Deputy Prime Minister is translated as Leas Árd Aire.

By early January 1937, another fully worked out version of six Articles was available, containing advanced versions of what are now Article 14 (Presidential Commission), Article 26 (Reference of Bills to the Supreme Court), Article 27 (Reference of Bills to the People), Article 28 (Government), Article 31 and Article 32 (Council of State).[19] The first document is a typescript English text of (what were then) Articles 21–7 (undated), with holograph corrections by Hearne. The second document is an amended and corrected holograph Irish version of the same, in the hand of Mícheál Ó Gríobhtha.

[15] UCDA, P150/2378. This copy of the draft Constitution is marked 'checked to date 1/12/1936'.
[16] 'President's copy'.
[17] UCDA, P150/2375.
[18] The use of the term 'Taoiseach' was to come later.
[19] UCDA, P150/2380. While this document is undated, it seems in all probability from December 1936. The UCDA descriptive list for the de Valera papers dates it to December 1936/early 1937.

This was followed by a complete worked out draft in both English and Irish, one version of which appears to have been taken by de Valera with him on his trip to Zürich on 11 January 1937.[20] In the English version, the Articles are grouped under the following headings:

Part I: The State (Articles 1–6);
Part II: The President of E. (Articles 7–8);
Part III: The National Parliament (Articles 9–11);
Part IV: The Government (Article 12);
Part V: The Council of State (Articles 13–16);
Part VI: The Courts (Articles 17–23);
Part VII: The Comptroller and Auditor General (Article 24);
Part VIII: Amendment of the Constitution—The Referendum (Articles 25–31);
Part IX: Constitutional Guarantees (Articles 32–8);
Part X: Economic Life (Articles 39–43);
Part XI: Power to Suspend Certain Constitutional Provisions (Article 44);
Part XII: General (Articles 45–9);
Part XIII: Transitory Provisions [Blank].[21]

Some features of this latter draft call out for special attention. First, the draft Article 18 vested the High Court with full original jurisdiction to determine constitutional questions, whereas earlier drafts had contemplated that there would be a Constitutional Court. Hearne's draft from October 1936[22] envisaged that the Constitutional Court would enjoy an exclusive jurisdiction to determine the constitutionality of any law. It further contemplated a Constitutional Court of seven members, with two members appointed by the judges of the High Court, a further two members appointed by the Supreme Court, with the Chairman and two other members to be appointed by the President. De Valera's handwritten notes on the side of the document contemplated variations on this theme, including a court consisting of four serving judges, the Attorney General and two members nominated by the Dáil. A constitutional court along continental lines would certainly have represented a radical proposal for a common law jurisdiction such as Ireland and

[20] UCDA, P150/2385.
[21] An advanced version of what became the Transitory Provisions of the Constitution (i.e. those provisions preserving and carrying over the existing institutions and obligations of the (old) Irish Free State into the new State) was furnished by John Hearne on 19 February 1937: see note from Hearne to Kathleen O'Connell on 19 February 1937, UCD P150/2385 (not published).
[22] UCDA, P150/2373. It seems fairly certain that this draft was prepared by Hearne, given that he had previously prepared a memorandum on continental constitutional courts: see document no. 43.

while drafts as late as early January 1937 make reference to the existence of that Court, Article 32 of the first circulated draft of 16 March 1937[23] transferred these functions exclusively to the Supreme Court and de Valera was persuaded to give these functions back to the High Court only during the course of the Dáil debates on the Constitution.[24] This was clearly a matter which exercised the drafters and provides some evidence for the proposition that they foresaw a greater role for judicial review than is sometimes allowed. If that were not so, then the suggestion that there should be a Constitutional Court would surely not have been seriously entertained.

Second, not all of the subsequent changes were necessarily an improvement. Thus, for example, the draft Article 35 dealt with the rights of property in terms which were probably less convoluted than what ultimately became Article 43 of the Constitution:

> 1. The right to private ownership of property is hereby affirmed to be a natural human right and a basic principle of ordered human society.
> 2. The State guarantees protection of their private property to all citizens and all bodies corporate and unincorporate within the State, and no such property shall be limited or acquired by the State save for general utility purposes and upon payment of compensation. Nothing in this Article shall operate to prevent the seizure or forfeiture of property under an order of a court in accordance with law.

[23] See www.irishconstitution.ie.

[24] 67 *Dáil Debates*, Cols 1490–5 (2 June 1937). De Valera had previously expressed some unease at the prospect of giving the Supreme Court an interpretative role with regard to the drafting of the Constitution and the following comments reflect the earlier discussions he had with Hearne on the subject of a Constitutional Court:

> This matter of the Constitution is going to be interpreted, ultimately, by the Courts. The Supreme Court is going to be the body to decide on its interpretation. I know that a number of people would prefer to get some other body to be the judge in such matters, and I do not want to say, for one moment, that, if I could get another body to deal with the interpretation of the Constitution, and which could decide such matters just as well as the Supreme Court, I would not be in favour of having some body other than the ordinary courts. I know that in other countries, courts are set up, known, roughly, as constitutional courts, to deal with such matters, which take a broader view—again, I do not wish to be hurtful—which take a broader view, or not so narrow a view, as the ordinary courts which, strictly interpreting the ordinary law from day to day, have to take. If I could get from anybody any suggestion of some court to deal with such matters, other than the Supreme Court, then I would be willing to consider it, and, if it were feasible, to adopt the suggestion. I confess, however, that, as I confessed on another occasion with regard to the Senate, I could not get any other body that would be satisfactory. At that time, I could not get a satisfactory Seanad, and so I confess now that I have not been able to get anything better than the Supreme Court to fulfil this function. However, if it were possible to find a better body to deal with these matters, and if the lawyers would help me to put into this an indication whereby it could be suggested to the court that, in constitutional matters, the court should not take a narrow, or, what might be called, a strictly legalistic view, then I would do that; but again that is a course that I found too difficult to put down here and to reduce to practice.
> 67 *Dáil Debates*, Cols 53–4 (11 May 1937).

This version had the merit of making clear that legal persons (such as companies) enjoyed constitutional protection. Neither the text of Article 40.3.2° nor Article 43 makes this clear and it was left in the end to the courts to imply this conclusion.[25] Likewise, the test articulated in the second paragraph as to the circumstances when the State could intervene to regulate property rights through legislation ('save for general utility purposes and upon payment of compensation') is more definite and less vague than the 'exigencies of the common good' test contained in Article 43.2.2°.[26]

Third, the drafting style here remains unmistakably that of Hearne alone. Much of the language of the May 1935 draft remains unaltered and that which is new seems to have been done in his own particular style. In this regard, Hearne endeavoured to reflect in his own concise manner some of the ideas and suggestions advanced by others. However, the most significant change of all seems to have come about almost by accident. The draft of January 1937 contained no provision corresponding to the present Article 40.3:

> 1. The State guarantees in its laws to respect and, so far as practicable, by its laws to defend and vindicate the personal rights of the citizen.
> 2. The State shall, in particular, by its laws protect as best it may from unjust attack and, in the case of injustice done, vindicate the life, person, good name and property rights of every citizen.

The first version of Article 40.3 appears to have been drafted by Hearne in early February 1937. Labelled 'Early draft', it provided that:

> The State guarantees to respect, defend and vindicate the personal rights of each citizen.
>
> Accordingly, the State shall take all necessary measures to prevent any violation of these rights, enforce respect for social order and punish offenders ~~against its laws~~.

Having re-stated the equality guarantees and the prohibition on the creation of titles of nobility, the draft then continued:

> In particular, the State shall protect, as best it may, from unjust attack, and, in case of injustice done, ~~to~~ vindicate

[25] *Iarnród Éireann v. Ireland*, [1996] 3 IR 321.

[26] The language here is an echo of Article 44.2.6° (which draws its provenance from Article 16 of the Treaty), which provides that the property of a religious body or educational institution cannot be 'taken save for necessary works of public utility and on payment of compensation'.

> the person, life, ~~and good name of its citizens~~ and ~~their right of ownership~~ of every citizen.[27]

A slightly different version, probably dated 16 February, read as follows:

> 1. The State guarantees to respect the rights of every citizen and to defend and vindicate those rights.
> 2. The State shall therefore do everything necessary to protect those rights against violence; it shall enforce respect for social order, and punish those who transgress its laws.
> ...
> 6. The State guarantees
> 1° To protect as best it may the person, life and good name of its citizens against unjust attack, and in the case of injustice to vindicate the right.[28]

A later version drafted by Hearne read as follows:

> The State guarantees to respect, defend, and vindicate the personal rights of each citizen.
> The State shall, accordingly, take all necessary measures to prevent any violation of these rights, enforce respect for social order, and punish offenders.
> The State shall, in particular, protect, as best it may, from unjust attack, and, in case of injustice done, vindicate the person, life, good name and property rights of every citizen.[29]

De Valera then manually amended this draft, to read as shown above.[30] However, by mid-March 1937, the first official published version of the Constitution contained a clause which is worded almost exactly the same as the present Article 40.3.

Article 40.3 is, perhaps, the single most important provision in the entire Constitution. It has given rise to a colossal volume of litigation and the contrasting phrasing of Article 40.3.1° and Article 40.3.2°[31] have

[27] UCDA, P150/2387. This version of the present Article 40.3 is found in an undated, typescript text of Articles 24–49. The first page is marked 'Continuation' in green ink by de Valera. The emendations noted in the text above were made to the original typescript draft by de Valera.

[28] UCDA, P150/2392. This draft is undated but probably constitutes a literal English translation of the Irish draft, dated 16 February, found at UCDA, P150/2391.

[29] UCDA, P150/2387. This version of Article 40.3 (then numbered 38) is also found in the undated, typescript text of Articles 24–49, immediately preceding the 'Early draft'. However, it was clearly drafted at a later date.

[30] See document no. 78.

[31] Much judicial emphasis has been placed on the fact that the words 'in particular' appear in Article 40.3.2° and are absent from Article 40.3.1°. As Justice Kenny said in *Ryan v. Attorney General*, [1965] IR 287, 313:

lead the courts to determine that there is a range of 'unenumerated rights' in the former provision not elsewhere expressly spelt out in the Constitution which fail to be protected: these rights include the right to fair procedures, the right to earn a livelihood and the right to privacy.[32] Yet, remarkable as it may seem, there appears to be no documentary material which explains the thinking behind this provision and which the Department of Finance was later to consider potentially 'dangerous'.[33] While many have doubted whether the unenumerated rights doctrine had ever been foreseen by the drafters,[34] the language of Hearne's first draft of what was to become Article 40.3 provides some—admittedly fragmentary—evidence to suggest that it was intended to protect a category of rights other than those actually identified in the text ('...those that are inalienable, indefeasible and antecedent to positive law, as well as those that have been by law granted and defined...'). In the absence of more concrete evidence, it seems impossible to go further than this. All of these drafts certainly assume that the State was to be placed under a general duty to defend and vindicate the citizen's personal rights. It seems unlikely from the general wording of these drafts that this obligation was to be confined to the rights expressly set out in the Constitution.

But from whence did this sub-section originate and what was the original rationale behind the inclusion of such an important provision? Some have suggested the fourteenth Amendment of the US Constitution to which Article 40.3 has been judicially compared in its scope and effect.[35] Others have suggested that Article 40.3 was influenced by an extract from the encyclical, *Rerum Novarum*, an extract of which had been sent by McQuaid to de Valera:

> Rights must be religiously respected wherever they exist, and it is the duty of the public Authority to prevent and to punish violation of rights, and to protect every one in the possession of his own...wherever the general interest or any particular class suffers or is threatened with mischief which can in no other way be met or prevented, the public Authority must step in to deal with it.[36]

[31] *contd.*

> The words 'in particular' shows that [Article 40.3.2°] is a detailed statement of something which is already contained in sub-section 1 of the general guarantee. But [Article 40.3.2°] refers to rights in connection with life and good name and there are no rights in connection with these two matters specified in Article 40. It follows, I think, that the general guarantee in [Article 40.3.1°] must extend to rights not specified in Article 40.

[32] See generally, *Ryan v. Attorney General*, [1965] IR 287, and Kelly, *Irish Constitution*, 1389–1534.

[33] See document no. 104.

[34] See, for example, the comments of Justice Keane in *IOT v. B*, [1998] 2 IR 321, 369–70.

[35] See, for example, the comments of Justice O'Hanlon in *S v. S*, [1983] IR 68, 73.

[36] UCDA, P150/2411; Keogh and McCarthy, *Irish Constitution*, 111.

It is true that this extract appears to have been sent around the time when the first versions of Article 40.3 were drafted, but unlike, for example, aspects of Article 41 dealing with the family, there is no close fit between the language of this extract from *Rerum Novarum* and Article 40.3.

Once again, a newly enacted Constitution drawn from the civil law tradition appears to have provided the model for Hearne's draft. Article 6 of the Portuguese Constitution of 1933 had provided that:

> The State shall take all necessary measures to safeguard the common good in regard to the life, liberty, property, morals and all the natural or justly acquired rights of all of the citizens and to promote so far as possible their material, intellectual and moral interests.[37]

Hearne would seem clearly to have drawn on this model to provide for the State's general duty to protect personal rights and the reference in Article 40.3.1° to 'life, person, good name and property rights' seems to be a direct echo of the language of Article 6 of the Portuguese Constitution. Nor was this some chance coincidence, since Edward Cahill had enclosed these very provisions in the document 'Supplementary Suggestions for the new Constitution of the Irish Free State' in November 1936.[38] While Cahill had wondered whether 'quasi-abstract articles of that kind can be fitted into the proposed Irish Constitution', Hearne's consummate drafting skills showed once again that this was possible. It meant that, whether de Valera realised it or not and whether this had come about through accident or design, as the draft Constitution headed towards its first publication and restricted circulation on 16 March 1937, it now reflected legal thinking and influences drawn from a variety of sources, including the Weimar Constitution (1919), the Polish Constitution (1921), the Austrian Constitution (1934), the Portuguese Constitution (1933) and Papal Encyclicals, as well, of course, as constitutional law and theory drawn from the US and British traditions.

[37] George Gavan Duffy had already drawn de Valera's attention to this new Constitution and its corporatist character in a letter of 7 April 1935. De Valera expressed his wish in his reply of 15 April to have a copy of that Constitution, noting that 'at one time [I] was considering the possibility of a Vocational Council, but the difficulty is that we have very few vocational organisations': see document nos 36–7.

[38] See document no. 60. In the draft that he took with him to Zürich in January, de Valera had marked 'United States, Czechoslovakia, Portugal' on the cover. This seems to suggest a reference to the constitutions of those countries.

No. 70: UCDA, P150/2370

'Plan of Fundamental Constitutional Law'

John Hearne, Department of External Affairs
20 August 1936

'Plan of Fundamental Constitutional Law'

A. The Preamble3[9]

B. The State
Articles 1 and 2
Article 1: Name of State.
Article 2: Independence and democratic nature of State.[40]

C. The Sovereignty of the People
Articles 3, 4 and 5
Article 3: All powers of Government vested in the people. Form of the State determinable by them. Their absolute right to decide the manner in which powers of government are to be exercised.
Article 4: Organic laws to provide and regulate manner in which certain powers of government are to be exercised.
Article 5: Power to alter the Constitution vested in the people.

D. The National Language
Article 6: Irish language to be the national language.

E. The National Flag
Article 7: The National Flag to be the tricolour.

F. The Body of Citizens
Article 8: Definition of body of citizens.

G. Fundamental Rights of Citizens
Articles 9, 10, 11, 12 and 13
Article 9: Equality of citizens before the law.
Article 10: Freedom of conscience.[41]

[39] In the margins, de Valera has written: 'Source of Auth. national life. People. Family, [protect?]: 1916, 1921. Give themselves this Const'.
[40] In the margins, de Valera has written: 'Sov. indep. democ'. Before the start of Section C, the word 'Territory' has also been written by de Valera.
[41] The word 'tolerate' has been written in the margin by de Valera.

Article 11: Right of assembly and association. Right of free expression of opinion.

Article 12: Liberty of the person.

Article 13: Inviolability of the dwelling.

H. The Parliament

Article 14: To consist of the President and Dáil Éireann. Organic laws may provide for creation and constitution of a Second House of Parliament and may, subject to this Article, regulate the power and functions of any Second House that may be created to be defined in this Article.

Sole power of making laws to be vested in the Parliament.

I. The President

Articles 15 to 26 inclusive

Article 15: Creation of office.

Article 16: Election.

Article 17: Eligibility for office.

Article 18: Duration of office.

Article 19: Oath of office.

Article 20: Power to summon and dissolve Parliament.

Article 21: Promulgation of laws by the President.

Article 22: Appointment of Prime Minister, Ministers and Judges by the President.

Article 23: Supreme command of the Defence Forces.

Article 24: Right of pardon.

Article 25: Salary.

Article 26: Powers and duties of President performable only on advice.

J. The Council of Ministers

Articles 27 to 30

Article 27: Creation of the Council of Ministers.

Article 28: The Prime Minister and the Deputy Prime Minister.

Article 29: The number of members of the Council.

Article 30: Appointment of the Prime Minister on nomination of Dáil Éireann. Appointment of other Ministers.

K. The Judicial Power

Articles 31 to 33

Article 31: Establishment of the Constitutional Court.

Article 32: Jurisdiction.

Article 33: Continuance of existing Courts of First Instance and Court of Final Appeal.

L. The Comptroller and Auditor General
Article 34: Continuance of existing office and functions.

The State
Article 1: The name of the State shall be E.

Article 2: E. is a sovereign independent democratic state.

Sovereignty of the People
Article 3: All powers of government, legislative, executive and judicial in E. belong under God to the people of E. and are exercisable only through the organs established by the People of E.

The right of the People of E. to determine the form of the State and to decide the manner in which the said powers of government (or any of them) shall from time to time be exercised or exercisable is hereby declared to be absolute and indefeasible.

Article 4: The manner in which all or any of the powers of government shall be exercised or exercisable may be regulated by organic laws.

Article 5: This Constitution shall not be altered except as provided by this Article.

Every proposal for the amendment of this Constitution or any of the provisions thereof (including the provisions of this Article) shall in accordance with regulations to be made by the Oireachtas be submitted by Referendum to the decision of the people.

Every citizen who has reached the age of twenty-one years shall be entitled to vote at every such Referendum.

No such proposal as aforesaid shall become law unless (1) it shall have been passed by Dáil Éireann or, should a Second House of the Oireachtas be established, by both Houses of the Oireachtas and (2) upon its being submitted as aforesaid to a Referendum a majority of the voters on the Register shall have recorded their votes on such Referendum and either the votes of the majority of the voters on the register or two-thirds of the votes recorded shall have been cast in favour of such a proposal.

The National Language
Article 6: The Irish language is the national and official language of E. The English language shall be equally recognised as an official language. Special provisions may be made by law for districts in which only one of the said languages is in general use.

The National Flag

Article 7: The National Flag shall be the tricolour (Note: suitable heraldic description to be inserted).

The Citizens

Article 8: The citizens of E. are all persons who are by law citizens of Saorstát Éireann at the date hereof or who become citizens of E. by or under any law.

Fundamental Rights of Citizens

Article 9: All citizens are equal before the law.

Article 10: Freedom of conscience and the free expression and practice of religion are, subject to public order and morality, guaranteed to every citizen.

No legal disability shall be imposed by reason of religious belief or status.

No religion shall be endowed directly or indirectly by law.

Legislation providing for State aid for schools shall contain no discrimination against schools under the management of a particular religious denomination.

The property of any religious denomination shall not be diverted save for the purpose of works of public utility and upon payment of compensation.

Article 11: The following rights are guaranteed to all citizens subject to public order and morality: (1) the right of free expression of opinion, (2) the right to assemble peaceably and without arms and (3) the right to form associations and unions.

Laws may be passed to prevent or control open air meetings which are calculated to interfere with normal traffic or otherwise become a nuisance or danger to the general public.

Article 12: The liberty of the person is inviolable and no person shall be deprived of his liberty except in accordance with law.

Article 13: The dwelling of each citizen is inviolable and shall not be forcibly entered except in accordance with law.

The Parliament

Article 14: The Parliament shall be called and known as the Oireachtas. It shall, subject as hereinafter provided, consist of the President of E. and a Chamber of Deputies (herein generally referred to as Dáil Éireann).

Organic laws may provide for the creation, constitution and, subject to the provisions of this Article, the powers and functions of a Second

House of the Oireachtas. (Note 1. Insert provision defining powers and functions of any Second House created by organic law. [Note] 2. Insert provision continuing the existing Dáil as the Chamber of Deputies for the purposes of this Article).

The sole and exclusive power of making the laws of E. is hereby vested in the Oireachtas as constituted from time to time.

The President

Article 15: The office of President of E. is hereby created. The President of E. (herein generally referred to as 'the President') shall exercise and perform the powers and duties conferred and imposed on him by this Constitution or by any amendment thereof or any law enacted thereunder, but the said powers and duties shall not be exercisable or performable by him save upon the advice of the Council of Ministers.

Article 16: The President shall be elected by the people of E. in the manner provided by law.

Article 17: Every citizen of E. who has completed his thirty-fifth year shall be eligible for the office of President.

Article 18: The President shall hold office for seven years and shall be eligible for re-election. He shall remain in office until his successor is appointed.

Article 19: The President shall, when entering upon his office, take and subscribe the following oath before Dáil Éireann:

> 'I swear by Almighty God that I will maintain the Constitution of E. and uphold its laws and that I will dedicate my powers to the service and welfare of the People of E. and defend the State against all its enemies whomsoever domestic and external and fulfil my duties faithfully and conscientiously in accordance with the Constitution and the law. So help me God.'

Article 20: The Oireachtas shall be summoned and dissolved by the President: provided however that the Oireachtas shall not be dissolved on the advice of a Council of Ministers which has ceased to retain the support of a majority in Dáil Éireann.

Article 21: The President shall promulgate laws passed or deemed to have been passed by both Houses of the Oireachtas.

Article 22: The President shall, on the nomination of the Prime Minister assented to by Dáil Éireann, appoint the members of the Council of Ministers other than the Prime Minister.

He shall appoint the judges of the Supreme Court, the High Court and all other the Courts of E.[42]

Article 23: The supreme command of the Defence Forces of E. is hereby vested in the President, who shall exercise the same in accordance with the law. All commissioned officers of the Defence Forces shall hold their commissions from him.

Article 24: The right of pardon, and power to remit or commute sentences imposed, and to remit the legal consequences of verdicts given by any courts exercising criminal jurisdiction are hereby vested in the President.

Article 25: The salary of the President shall be determined by law.

Article 26: The powers and duties conferred and imposed on the President by this Constitution or by any future law shall not be exercisable or performable by him save only upon the advice of the Council of Ministers.

The Council of Ministers (Comhairle na nAirí)

Article 27: There shall be a Council, otherwise called and herein generally referred to as the Council of Ministers or (in Irish) An Comhairle na nAirí, in which the executive authority of E. shall be and is hereby vested. The Council of Ministers shall be responsible to Dáil Éireann. Every Minister shall be a member of the Council of Ministers and shall be a member of Dáil Éireann.[43]

Article 28: The President of the Council of Ministers shall be called and known as the Prime Minister ('an Príomh Aire'), and the Vice-President of the Council of Ministers shall be called and known as the Deputy Prime Minister ('Leas-Phríomh Aire').

Article 29: The Council of Ministers shall be composed of the same number of members as may be determined by law. (Note: The laws in force relating to the Executive Council as constituted at the date of the coming into operation of this Constitution will be continued in respect of the Council of Ministers. The same applies to existing Departments of State).

Article 30: The Prime Minister shall be elected by Dáil Éireann.

All the other members of the Council of Ministers shall be appointed by the President on the nomination of the Prime Minister with the assent of Dáil Éireann.

[42] The words 'Dáil E.' have been written in the margins by de Valera beside this article.

[43] A question mark has been placed in the margin by de Valera opposite the last sentence of this article.

No. 71: UCDA, P150/2374

Draft Constitution used at Cabinet Discussions

20–22 October 1936

Part I: The State

Article 1: The name of the State is E.

Article 2: E. is a sovereign, [independent], democratic state.[44]

Article 3: All powers of Government, legislative, executive and judicial in E. (~~emanate from~~) are vested in the people.[45] (~~, and~~) They are exercisable only through the Organs established by this Constitution or established or recognised by Organic laws made (~~thereunder~~) under the Constitution.

Article 4: ~~The national flag of E. is a tricolour in green, white and orange.~~[46]

Article (~~5~~) 4: The Irish language is the official language of E. The English language is recognised as a second official language. [Special provision may be made by law for the recognition of only one of the said languages as the official language in districts or areas in which that language only is in general use.][47]

Article (~~6~~) 5: The following are of Irish nationality and are (entitled to the rights of)[48] citizens of E.

1. All persons born in Ireland.
2. All persons born outside of Ireland of Irish parentage or descent as defined or limited by law.
3. All other persons on whom Irish nationality is conferred by naturalization in accordance with law.
4. ~~Irish nationality shall not be conferred by naturalization upon any person who disbelieves in or is opposed to organized government or is a member of or affiliated with any society or organisation entertaining or teaching disbelief in or opposition to organized government.~~[49]

[44] The word 'independent' has been placed in handwritten square parentheses.
[45] Words in parentheses have been crossed out, with 'They' preceding 'are exercisable', along with 'under the Constitution' added manually.
[46] Article 4 has been crossed out in its entirety, with each subsequent article renumbered manually.
[47] Square parentheses have been added manually.
[48] Words in parentheses added manually.
[49] Part 4 has been manually crossed out in its entirety.

5. The conditions governing the (acquisition)[50] loss of Irish nationality shall be regulated by law.

Part II: The President of E.

Article (~~7~~) 6: (Creation and Tenure of Office)[51] Office of President

1. The President of E. is hereby *created*.[52] The President of E. (hereinafter called 'the President') shall exercise and perform the powers and functions conferred on the President by this Constitution or by Organic Laws made thereunder.
2. The President shall be elected by direct vote of the people.[53]
3. The President shall hold office for seven years from the date upon which he enters upon his office (unless he previously dies, resigns, becomes permanently incapacitated, or is removed from office) and shall be eligible for re-election.[54]
4. Every person of Irish nationality who has completed his thirty-fifth year of age, who has ordinarily resided in Ireland during the ten years immediately preceding his nomination and who is nominated by not less than twenty members of the Oireachtas shall be eligible (for election)[55] for the office of President. A member of the Oireachtas shall not be entitled to participate in the nomination of more than one candidate for the office of President in respect of the same election.[56]
5. Elections to the office of President by direct vote of the people shall, subject to the provisions of Section 4 of this Article, be regulated by Organic Laws.[57]
6. The President shall not be a member of either House of the Oireachtas and shall not, save as provided by this Constitution, hold any other office.
7. The President shall enter upon his office on a date (to be fixed) not later than two calendar months after the date of his election.[58]

[50] Word in parentheses has been added manually.
[51] Section in parentheses has been circled manually, with 'Office of President' written in the margin.
[52] 'Created' has been manually underlined, with a question mark in the margin, followed by the words 'There shall be a President of E. who'.
[53] 'Proportional representation here or below' has been written beside Section 2.
[54] 'Certify?' has been written in the margin opposite 'permanently incapacitated'. 'Retiring President' and 'bankrupt' have also written opposite section 3.
[55] Words in parentheses have been added manually.
[56] 'Nomination' has been written in the margin opposite section 4.
[57] 'Proportional Rep.' has been written opposite section 5.
[58] 'To be fixed' has been added manually.

8. The President shall enter upon his office by taking and subscribing publicly (before the members of both Houses) the following oath before the Chief Justice of E.:

   'I swear by Almighty God that I will maintain the Constitution of E. and uphold its laws, ~~that I will defend the State against all its enemies whomsoever domestic and external,~~ that I will fulfil my duties faithfully and conscientiously in accordance with the Constitution and the law, and that I will dedicate my powers to the service and welfare of the people of E. So help me God.'[59]
9. The President shall not leave E. during his term of office save with the consent of the Council of Ministers.[60]
10. In the event of the temporary incapacity or absence from E. of the President, the functions of the office of President shall be discharged by a Commission which shall consist of such (~~two or more~~)[61] three members of the Council of State as, after consultation with the said Council, the President shall appoint for that purpose.[62]
11. The President shall be removed from office on impeachment (~~by~~)[63] before Dáil Éireann for (violation of the Constitution),[64] treason, bribery or other high crimes or misdemeanours and on conviction thereof by two-thirds of the total membership of both Houses of the Oireachtas at a joint session thereof.[65]
12. In the event of the removal from office of the President or of his death, resignation or permanent incapacity to discharge the functions of the office an election to fill the office shall be held within two calendar months after such event as aforesaid. Pending the entry upon his office of the President so to be elected the functions of the office of President shall devolve upon an acting President who shall be elected for that purpose by Dáil Éireann. An acting President shall enter upon his office by taking and subscribing the oath required by Section 8 of this Article to be taken by the President and he shall hold office for a period not exceeding four months from

[59] Crossed out manually.

[60] 'Govmt?' written opposite this Section, with 'Council of Ministers' underlined and annotated with 'hereinafter'.

[61] 'Two or more' crossed out manually, with 'three' written above.

[62] 'Who is to judge? Suppose he was unconscious' written in the margin opposite Section 10.

[63] 'By' deleted manually, with 'before' written above.

[64] 'Violation of the Constitution' added manually.

[65] Several discrete phrases are written in the margin opposite Section 11: 'originate'; 'date to'; 'cease to be President'; 'President dying in interval'; 'office vacant'.

the date upon which he enters upon his office as acting President.[66]

13. The President shall take precedence over all other persons in the State.
14. The President shall have an official residence, an official staff and secretariat and shall receive such emoluments and allowances as may be determined by law. The emoluments and allowances of the President shall not be diminished during his term of office.

Article (~~8~~) 7: Powers and Functions of the President

~~1.~~ The President shall summon and dissolve the Oireachtas on the advice of the Prime Minister: Provided, however, that the Oireachtas shall not be dissolved on the advice of a Prime Minister (who has ceased)[67] to retain the support of a majority in Dáil Éireann.[68]

~~2.~~ The President shall promulgate laws in the manner provided by Article [blank] of this Constitution.

~~3.~~ The President shall exercise the functions in relation to the Referendum conferred on him by the provisions of Article [blank] of this Constitution.

~~4.~~ The President shall exercise the functions in relation to the suspension of the provisions of Article [blank] of this Constitution conferred on him by Article [blank] hereof.

~~5.~~ The supreme command of the Defence Forces of E. is hereby vested in the President. The manner in which the President shall exercise this command shall be regulated by Organic Laws.

~~6.~~ All commissioned officers of the Defence Forces of E. shall hold their commissions from the President.

~~7.~~ The President shall, on the nomination of Dáil Éireann, appoint the Prime Minister, and shall, on the nomination of the Prime Minister, and with the previous approval of Dáil Éireann, appoint the other members of the Council of Ministers. A member of the Council of Ministers may be removed from office by the President acting on the advice of the Prime Minister.[69]

[66] The following has been written in the margin opposite Section 12: '[?] unto 3 members of C. of S. and in [contingency?] C.S. nominates 3 of members'. A separate annotation reads: 'First President'.

[67] Words in parentheses have been underlined, with 'whose govmt' written in the margin.

[68] Beneath Section 1 the following two annotations have been written: 'use his discretion'; 'whose Gov has recently sustained a'.

[69] The following annotations have been written opposite Section 7: 'en block' [*sic*]; 'wording' (opposite 'may be removed from office'); 'shall relinquish office'.

~~8.~~ The judges of the Supreme Court, the High Court and all other the Courts of E. shall be appointed by the President.

A judge of the Supreme Court, or the High Court, or the Circuit Court shall be removed from office by the President upon his being notified in the manner hereinafter provided that resolutions calling for the removal of such judge on the ground of stated misbehaviour or incapacity have been passed by both Houses of the Oireachtas. ~~The Chairman of Dáil Éireann shall notify the President of any such resolution as aforesaid passed by Dáil Éireann by sending a copy of such resolution signed by him to the President. The Chairman of the Second House shall similarly notify the President of any such resolution passed by the Second House.~~[70]

~~9.~~ The right of pardon, and power to remit or commute sentences imposed, and to remit the legal consequences of any verdicts given by any courts exercising criminal jurisdiction are hereby vested in the President.

~~10. The President may, at the request of the Council of Ministers and with the concurrence of Dáil Éireann, become chairman of a national government during a period of national crisis or emergency whether internal or external.~~[71]

~~11.~~ 10. Upon the reassembly of the Oireachtas after a dissolution thereof and on such other occasions as he may consider it right so to do the President may communicate with the Houses of the Oireachtas by message or address on such matters of national or public importance as, after consultation with the Council of State, to him shall seem meet.

~~12.~~ 11. Additional powers and functions may be conferred on the President by Organic Laws, and such powers and functions shall be exercised by him in accordance with such Laws.

~~13.~~ 12. The President shall not be held answerable in any court of law or equity for the exercise of the functions of his office or for any act done or purporting to be done by him in pursuance thereof. No action at law or in equity or other legal proceeding shall lie against the President in his private capacity during his tenure of office.[72]

[70] Sentence manually crossed out. The annotation 'Question of appointing an' has been written below paragraph 2 of Section 8.

[71] Section 10 manually crossed out, with subsequent sections renumbered.

[72] At the end of Section 12, 'Criticism in Dáil or Senate' has been written.

(President shall be notified immed. of all dec. of the Council of Ministers and shall be apprised in advance of all important matters on which a gov. decision is to be taken.)[73]

Part III: The National Parliament

Article 9:[74]

1. The National Parliament of E. shall be called and known (and is herein generally referred to) as the Oireachtas. The Oireachtas shall consist of the President and two Houses, the Primary House or Chamber of Deputies (otherwise called and herein generally referred to as 'Dáil Éireann') and the Second House (otherwise called and herein generally referred to as 'S').
2. The Oireachtas is the supreme legislative authority of E. No other ~~legislative~~[75] authority whatsoever has powers to make laws for E.
3. The Oireachtas shall hold at least one session each year.[76]
4. The right to raise and maintain armed forces is vested exclusively in the Oireachtas.

   No armed force (other than armed forces raised and maintained by the Oireachtas) shall be raised or maintained in E. for any purpose whatsoever.[77]
5. The State shall not declare or participate in any war without the assent of the Oireachtas, provided, however, that in the case of actual invasion the Council of Ministers may take such steps as they may consider necessary for the protection of the State.
6. The Oireachtas shall have no power to declare acts to be infringements of the law which are not so at the date of their commission.
7. Organic Laws may provide for the creation of subordinate legislatures and for the powers and functions thereof.
8. Each House of the Oireachtas shall elect its own Chairman and Deputy Chairman and shall prescribe their powers, duties, remuneration and terms of office.[78]
9. Each House shall make its own Rules and Standing Orders, with power to attach penalties for their infringement and shall

[73] Sentence in parentheses has been appended manually to Part II.
[74] Original article number sequence resumes here.
[75] Manually crossed out.
[76] Annotated: 'DE and Sen meet once a year [?]'; 'Define session?'; 'Taxation?'.
[77] Annotated: 'Defence law'.
[78] Section 8 is annotated: 'order business'; 'Justice?'.

have power to ensure freedom of debate, to protect its official documents and the private papers of its members, and to protect itself and its members against any person or persons interfering with, molesting or attempting to corrupt its members in the exercise of their duties.

10. Sittings of each House of the Oireachtas shall be public. In cases of special emergency either House may hold a private sitting with the assent of two-thirds of the members present.
11. All matters in each House shall, save as otherwise provided in this Constitution, be determined by a majority of the votes of the members present other than the Chairman or presiding member, who shall have and exercise a casting vote in the case of an equality of votes. The number of members necessary to constitute a meeting of either House for the exercise of its powers shall be determined by its Standing Orders.
12. All official reports and publications of the Oireachtas or of either House thereof shall be privileged and utterances made in either House wherever published shall be privileged.[79]
13. Every member of the Oireachtas shall, except in case of treason as defined in this Constitution, felony, or breach of the peace, be privileged from arrest in going to and returning from, and while within the precincts of either House, and shall not, in respect of any utterance in either House, be amenable to any action or proceeding in any Court other than the House itself.
14. No person may be at the same time a member of both Houses of the Oireachtas, and, if any person who is already a member of either House is elected to be a member of the other House, he shall forthwith be deemed to have vacated his first seat.
15. The Oireachtas shall make provision for the payment of its members and may in addition provide them with free travelling facilities in any part of E. and such (~~free postal~~)[80] other facilities as the Oireachtas may determine.

Dáil Éireann

Article 10:

1. Every person of Irish nationality who has reached the age of twenty-one years and who is not placed under disability or incapacity by law shall be eligible for membership of Dáil

[79] 'Privileged' has been manually underlined, with 'positive' written in the margin.
[80] 'Free postal' has been manually crossed out, with 'other' written above.

Éireann. Every person of Irish nationality who has reached the age of twenty-one years and who complies with the provisions of the Organic Laws relating to the election of members of Dáil Éireann shall have the right to vote for members of Dáil Éireann.

2. Dáil Éireann shall be composed of members who represent constituencies determined by Organic Laws. The number of members shall be fixed from time to time by such Laws, but the total number of members of Dáil Éireann shall not be fixed at less than one member for each thirty thousand of the population, or at more than one member for each twenty thousand of the population: Provided that the proportion between the number of members to be elected at any time for each constituency and the population of each constituency, as ascertained at the last preceding census, shall, so far as possible, be identical throughout the country. The members shall be elected upon principles of Proportional Representation, the election to be by means of the Single Transferable Vote. No Organic Law shall be enacted whereby the number of members to be returned for any constituency shall be less than three. The Oireachtas shall revise the constituencies at least once in every (~~ten~~)[81] fifteen years, with due regard to changes in distribution of the population, but any alterations in the constituencies shall not take effect during the life of Dáil Éireann sitting when such revision is made.

3. A general election for members of Dáil Éireann shall take place not later than thirty days after a dissolution of the Oireachtas.[82]

4. Polling at every such election shall take place on the same day throughout E.

5. The member of Dáil Éireann who is the Chairman of Dáil Éireann immediately before a dissolution of the Oireachtas shall, unless before such dissolution he announces to Dáil Éireann that he does not desire to continue to be a member thereof, be deemed without any actual election to be elected in accordance with this Constitution at the ensuing general election as a member of Dáil Éireann for the constituency for which he was a member immediately before such dissolution

[81] Manually crossed out, with '15' written in the margin.
[82] Section 3 has been annotated: 'Omission 28?'.

or, in the event of a revision of constituencies having taken place, for the revised constituency declared on such revision to correspond to such first-mentioned constituency. Whenever a former Chairman of Dáil Éireann is so deemed to have been elected at a general election as a member for a constituency the number of members actually to be elected for such constituency at such general election shall be one less than would otherwise be required to be elected therefor.

6. Subject to the foregoing, provision shall be made by Organic Laws for the following matters that is to say:
   (a) The number of members of Dáil Éireann;
   (b) The creation and revision of constituencies, and
   (c) The election of members of Dáil Éireann, including provision for the filling of casual vacancies, and
   (d) The payment of members of Dáil Éireann and the provision of travelling (and other)[83] facilities for such members.
7. Dáil Éireann shall have legislative authority exclusive of S. in relation to Money Bills as hereinafter defined.[84]
   A Money Bill means a Bill which contains only provisions dealing with all or any of the following subjects, namely, the imposition, repeal, remission, alteration or regulation of taxation; the imposition for the payment of debt or other financial purposes of charges on public moneys or the variation or repeal of any such charges; supply, the appropriation, receipt, custody, issue or audit of accounts of public money; the raising or guarantee of any loan or the repayment thereof; subordinate matters incidental to those subjects or any of them. In this definition the expressions 'taxation', 'public money' and 'loan' respectively do not include any taxation, money or loan raised by local authorities or bodies for local purposes.
8. (Insert provision for certification of Money Bill as heretofore).
9. As soon as possible after the commencement of each financial year Dáil Éireann shall consider the Estimates of receipts and expenditure of the State for that year, and, save in so far as may be provided by specific enactment in each case, the legislation required to give effect to the Financial Resolutions of each year shall be enacted within that year.

[83] Words in parentheses added manually.
[84] Sentence is annotated with a question mark.

10. Money shall not be appropriated by vote, resolution or law, unless the purpose of the appropriation has in the same session been recommended (to P.)[85] by a message in writing from the Council of Ministers signed by the Prime Minister.

The Second House ('S')

Article 11:

1. The number of members of S. shall be forty-five.
2. Every person of Irish nationality who has reached the age of thirty-five years and who is not placed under disability or incapacity by law shall be eligible for membership of S.
3. Provision as to term of office of members of S. (Decision to be taken).
4. Provision as to method or methods of selection of members of S. (Decision to be taken).
5. Every Bill initiated in Dáil Éireann shall (whether before or after its passage by Dáil Éireann) be sent to S. and shall be considered by S.
6. S. may amend any Bill (other than a Money Bill) sent to it by Dáil Éireann. Every such amendment shall be considered by Dáil Éireann.
7. S. shall return a Bill sent to it by Dáil Éireann with its amendments (if any) not later than ninety days after the date on which the Bill was sent to S., or such longer period as may be agreed to in respect of such Bill by both Houses.[86]
8. In the event of the failure of S. to pass a Bill (other than a Money Bill) sent to it by Dáil Éireann within the said ninety days (or any such longer period as aforesaid) or its failure to pass such Bill within the said ninety days (or such longer period) with amendments to which Dáil Éireann agrees such Bill may, at the expiration of the said ninety days (or such longer period), be sent to S. a second time. Should S. fail to pass such Bill within a period of ninety days from the date on which such Bill is so sent to it a second time or fail within the said period to pass such bill with amendments to which Dáil Éireann agrees such Bill shall if Dáil Éireann by a resolution passed at the expiration of the said period so declares be deemed to have been passed by both Houses.[87]

[85] Words in parentheses inserted manually, presumably meaning 'to President'.
[86] 'Withdrawal of Bill' written in the margin.
[87] 'Overriding period within which?' written in the margin.

9. If and whenever the Prime Minister on the introduction of a Bill certifies by message in writing addressed to both Houses that such Bill is urgent and immediately necessary for the preservation of the public peace and security, or is rendered necessary by the existence of a national emergency, whether internal or international, the time for consideration of such Bill by S. may by resolution of Dáil Éireann be abridged to such period as shall be specified in that behalf in such resolution.
10. S. shall have no power to reject or amend a Money Bill, but shall have power to make recommendations to Dáil Éireann with regard to every such Bill. Every such recommendation shall be made not later than twenty-one days after the date on which the Money Bill to which they relate is sent to S. by Dáil Éireann.
11. A Bill (other than a Money Bill) may be initiated in S. by a member of the Council of Ministers or a member of S.

Part IV: The Government

Article 12:

1. The Government of E. shall consist of a Council (herein generally referred to as 'the Council of Ministers). The Council of Ministers shall exercise and perform the powers and functions conferred on the Council of Ministers by this Constitution or by Organic Laws made thereunder.
2. The President of the Council of Ministers shall be called and known as 'the Prime Minister', and the Vice-President of the Council of Ministers shall be called and known as 'the Deputy Prime Minister'.
3. The Council of Ministers shall be composed of not less than nine and not more than fifteen members.
   The Prime Minister, the Deputy Prime Minister and the member of the Council of Ministers who is in charge of the Department of Finance, shall be members of Dáil Éireann. Not more than two of the other members of the Council of Ministers may be a member of S. Every member of the Council of Ministers who is not a member of S. shall be a member of Dáil Éireann.
4. The Prime Minister, the Deputy Prime Minister and the other members of the Council of Ministers shall be appointed respectively in the manner provided by section 7 of Article Eight of this Constitution.

The Deputy Prime Minister shall act for all purposes in the place of the Prime Minister should the Prime Minister die, resign, or become permanently incapacitated until a new Prime Minister shall have been appointed. The Deputy Prime Minister shall also act in the place of the Prime Minister during his temporary absence.

5. The Council of Ministers shall meet and act as a collective authority and shall be collectively responsible to Dáil Éireann concerning any Departments of State administered by the members of the Council of Ministers.
6. The Council of Ministers shall prepare Estimates of the receipts and expenditure of E. for each financial year, and shall present them to Dáil Éireann before the end of the previous financial year.
7. Every member of the Council of Ministers shall have the right to attend and be heard in each House of the Oireachtas.
8. A member of the Council of Ministers may resign from office by placing his resignation in the hands of the Prime Minister. The Prime Minister may at any time, for reasons which to him seem sufficient, request a member of the Council of Ministers so to resign, and, in the event of the failure of such member to comply with such request, the appointment of such member may be terminated by the President on the advice of the Prime Minister.
9. In the event of the Prime Minister ceasing to retain the support of a majority in Dáil Éireann, the Prime Minister and the other members of the Council of Ministers shall retire from office but shall continue to carry on their duties until their successors shall have been appointed.
10. The members of the Council of Ministers shall receive such remuneration as may from time to time be determined by law, but the remuneration of any Minister shall not be diminished during his term of office.

No. 72: UCDA, P150/2375

'Summary of Main Provisions of the Constitution [No. 2]'

5 November 1936

The general scheme of the Constitution will be as follows.

First there will be a Preamble acknowledging that all lawful authority comes from God and setting forth the ideals of the Nation and the purposes of the people in establishing this ~~new~~ Constitution.[88]

Articles will be grouped in a number of Sections or Parts. The First Part will contain declarations relating to the Nation, the national territory, the national language, and the sovereignty of the Irish people.

The national territory will be declared to be the whole of Ireland and the territorial seas of Ireland, and the right of the Nation to the whole of the national territory will be declared to be absolute and indefeasible.

The declarations relating to sovereignty will be to the effect that sovereignty resides in the people, that the people have the right to determine the form of government and of the institutions of government under which they desire to live, and also the right to determine the extent of the co-operation of the State with any other State or any league or group of States. The people will be declared to be the ultimate arbiters on all disputed issues of national or public policy.

The State

The State will be declared to be a sovereign, independent, democratic State. The powers of government will be exercisable only through the organs established by the Constitution.

The flag will be the tricolour of green, white and orange.

The official language of the State will be the Irish language. The English language will be recognised as a second official language.

Irish nationality and citizenship will be defined in relation to the Nation and the State.

The President

There will be a President of the State who will be elected by direct vote of the people, and he will hold office for seven years. The powers and functions of the President will in general be as follows: to summon and dissolve the National Parliament, to promulgate laws, to appoint and terminate the appointment of Ministers, Judges, etc., to hold the supreme

[88] 'New' is manually crossed out.

command of the Defence Forces, to exercise the right of pardon, and to exercise any additional powers and functions conferred on the President by law.

Save where otherwise provided by the Constitution, the powers and functions of the President will be exercisable by him only on the advice of the Government.

There will be a Council of State consisting primarily of certain officers of State whom the President must consult before exercising those of his functions which he exercises on his own responsibility. The President will, e.g., have the right after consultation with the Council of State to communicate by message or address with Parliament or with the nation on matters of national or public importance.

Three members of the Council of State will exercise the functions of the President in the event of his death, resignation, etc., until a new President takes office.

The National Parliament

The National Parliament ('the Oireachtas') shall consist of the President and two Houses, a Primary House or Chamber of Deputies ('Dáil Éireann'), and a Second House.

The Oireachtas shall be the supreme legislative authority of the State, and no other legislative authority shall have power to make laws for the State. The Oireachtas shall have the exclusive right to raise and maintain armed forces and no armed forces other than those so raised and maintained shall be raised in the State for any purpose whatsoever. The State shall not declare or participate in any war except with the consent of the Oireachtas. The Oireachtas shall hold at least one session in each year.

Each House of the Oireachtas shall elect its own Chairman and control its own procedure. Official reports and publications of the Oireachtas shall be privileged.

Dáil Éireann

Dáil Éireann shall be constituted as heretofore.

The Government

The Government of the State shall consist of a Council to be called the Council of Ministers. The President of the Council of Ministers shall be called the Prime Minister and the Vice-President will be called the Deputy Prime Minister. All the members of the Council of Ministers must be members of the Oireachtas, two may be members of the Second House.

The Council of Ministers will act as a collective authority and will be collectively responsible to Dáil Éireann concerning any Department of State administered by the members of the Council.

The Prime Minister and the other members of the Council of Ministers will retire from office in the event of the Prime Ministers ceasing to retain the support of a majority in Dáil Éireann.

The Courts

Justice will be administered in public courts by judges appointed in the manner provided by the Constitution. The judges will be independent in the exercise of their functions, subject only to the Constitution and the law. The jurisdiction and organisation of the Courts and the tenure of office of the judges thereof will generally be the same as heretofore.

The Comptroller and Auditor-General

There will be a Comptroller and Auditor-General with a tenure of office and functions as heretofore.

Constitutional Guarantees

The following fundamental constitutional rights shall be guaranteed to all citizens: equality before the law, freedom of conscience and freedom of expression and practice of religion, subject to public order and morality, the right to free expression of opinion, subject to public order and morality, the right to assemble peaceably and without arms, the right to form associations and unions, liberty of the person, and inviolability of the dwelling. Power will be taken in the Constitution to enact laws for the purpose of preventing or controlling meetings which are calculated to cause a breach of the peace or be a menace or a nuisance to the public. Religious associations will be guaranteed the right of assembly for the conduct of religious services in public and in private, subject to public order and morality. No religion shall be endowed by law. Legislation providing for State aid for schools will contain no discrimination against the schools under the management of a particular religious denomination. The property of any religious denomination will not be diverted save for the purpose of works of public utility and on payment of compensation.

Special recognition will be given to the family in the State as the basis of social discipline and ordered society.

The right to private ownership of property will be affirmed as a natural human right and the protection of private ownership of property will be guaranteed, subject to the law.

All citizens will be guaranteed the right to free elementary education.

Power to Suspend Certain Provisions of the Constitution
Provision will be made for the suspension during a grave state of public disorder or threatened public disorder of certain of the constitutional guarantees just mentioned, for example, that relating to the liberty of the person and the inviolability of the dwelling.

Amendment of the Constitution
Certain provisions of the Constitution will be declared to be fundamental and changes in those Articles will not be made unless the amendment is approved by the people in a Referendum held for that purpose. The Referendum will be regulated by law.

Miscellaneous
There will be a part containing miscellaneous provisions, provision, e.g., for trial by jury (except in certain cases) and the repeal of the Constitution of 1922.

Transitory Provisions
There will be a number of transitory provisions. These provisions are necessary to provide for the continuance of certain laws of an administrative character pending the full working of the new Constitution. There will, of course, be a provision containing laws generally subject to the new Constitution

Note: Side by side with the Constitution and subject to it a law will be enacted that so long as the State is associated with the States of the British Commonwealth of Nations certain functions heretofore exercised in the domain of external affairs by the constitutional monarchy recognised by those States will continue to be exercised on behalf of the State, but only on the advice of the Government.

No. 73: NAI, DT S9481

Seán MacEntee to Eamon de Valera

Department of Finance
2 January 1937

Dear Mr President,
I annex a memorandum on the Financial Articles of the existing Constitution which contains some suggestions for their amendment.

The present Articles have worked well in practice and have not been seriously attacked in public. In my Department, however, it has long been recognised that in matters of phraseology some of the Articles are not in every respect consistent with one another and that their meaning is occasionally doubtful or obscure; and the memorandum accordingly sets out suggestions for amendment on some points of detail, which I hope will commend themselves to you.

The Articles concerned are Nos 35, 36, 37, 54 and 61. The text of each Article (except No. 35) is quoted in its appropriate place in the memorandum.[89]

Memorandum on Financial Articles of the 1922 Constitution[90]

Article 35

This Article has been deleted from the Constitution by Constitution (Amendment no. 24) Act, 1936, but as it contains a definition of 'Money Bill' and as there may be a Second Chamber, it is presumed that a definition of 'Money Bill' will be required; and it is suggested that the definition in the deleted Article should be adopted as it stands.

Careful consideration has been given to the question whether any amendment in connection with the use of the term 'public monies', which is contained in the definition of 'Money Bill', should be made, having regard to the discussions in the Committee of Privileges set up under Article 35 in relation to the certification of the Land Purchase (Guarantee) Fund Bill, 1935, just a year ago. The view, however, is strongly held that any attempt to define the term with greater precision than at present will raise more difficulties than it solves.

Articles 36 and 54

These are as follows:

Article 36:

'Dáil Éireann shall as soon as possible after the commencement of each financial year consider the *Estimates* of receipts and expenditure of the Irish Free State (Saorstát Éireann) for that year, and, save in so far as may be provided by specific enactment in each case, the legislation required to give effect to the *Financial Resolution* of each year shall be enacted within that year.'

Article 54:

'The Executive Council shall be collectively responsible for all matters concerning the Departments of State administered by members of the Executive Council. The Executive Council shall prepare Estimates of the receipts and expenditure of the Irish Free State (Saorstát Éireann) for

[89] A copy of the memorandum was sent to John Hearne on 5 January, NAI, DT S9481.

[90] Drafted by Arthur Codling, see NAI, DFA 247/25.

each financial year, and shall present them to Dáil Éireann before the close of the previous financial year. The Executive Council shall meet and act as a collective authority.'

1. The subject matter of the second sentence of Article 54 is clearly linked directly with the substance of Article 36. It, therefore, seems highly desirable that they should be dealt with in a single Article.
2. In the original draft of Article 36 put before the Dáil the word 'Budget' appeared twice but the Dáil, after considering a Report by a special sub-committee, dropped the word and substituted the more precise phrases 'Estimates' and 'Financial Resolutions'. Article 54, which was new, also used 'Estimates'.

   There is no reason to alter these two terms, but the time limits imposed by the Articles have proved awkward.

   (a) 'Estimates of receipts and expenditure' have in practice signified the White Paper which is presented under Article 54 and covers, on the receipts side, Revenue (Tax and non-Tax) borrowings, repayments, etc., and on the expenditure side covers Central Fund Services, Supply Services and capital. But (i) the Estimates of revenue have to be based on the current rates of tax, etc., and not the rates contemplated for the new financial year, and (ii) it has been found most difficult to comply with the requirement that the Estimates shall be presented 'before the close of the previous financial year'. As often as not, compliance with the Article in this regard has not been effected.
   (b) As 'Estimates of...expenditure' might well be held to include the Volume of Estimates of Supply Services which is presented to the Dáil in February or March each year, as well as the Estimates of expenditure included in the White Paper just referred to, Article 36 seems to exclude consideration of the Volume of Estimates in the year preceding that to which they relate, although a partial consideration would often be convenient and although a Vote on Account has to be taken and Central Fund Act passed in relation to that year before 31 March.
   (c) It is desirable that the preparation and presentation of the Volume of Supply Estimates, as distinct from the White

Paper, should be incapable of being represented as outside the Constitution, when in point of fact it is one of the most important functions of the financial year.

3. Further, the Executive Council does not prepare any Estimates, either of receipts or expenditure, that function pertaining to the Minister in charge of the Department of Finance, who is mentioned in Article 52. This becomes clearer under Section 1 (ii) of the Ministers and Secretaries Act, 1924, which lays down that 'the Department of Finance...shall comprise the administration and business generally of the public finance of Saorstát Éireann and all powers, duties and functions connected with the same'.

   It therefore seems desirable to make the constitutional provision somewhat clearer and to bring it into greater accord with the actual facts, by mentioning the Minister for Finance.
4. It is therefore suggested that the amalgamated Article should run as follows:

   'The Executive Council, acting through the Minister for Finance, shall prepare Estimates of the receipts and Estimates of the expenditure of the Irish Free State (Saorstát Éireann) for each financial year and shall present them to Dáil Éireann which shall consider the said Estimates as soon as possible *after their presentation*; and, save in so far (follow as in Article 36).'

   This should get rid of the unnecessary restrictions mentioned above, and should give the Executive Council perfect flexibility in handling, through the Minister for Finance, Estimates of receipts and Estimates of expenditure either separately or together, as seems most advantageous and should permit of the presentation, if that were thought desirable, of Estimates of receipts based on the new rates of taxation, as well as Estimates based on the current rates.

Articles 37 and 61

Article 37 now runs as follows:

> Money shall not be appropriated by vote, resolution or law, unless the purpose of the appropriation has in the same session been recommended by a message from the Executive Council signed by the President of the Executive Council.

It was at first numbered Article 36 and down to and including the word 'message' is in its original form. Mr Kevin O'Higgins stated in explanation: 'That is simply the ordinary constitutional practice in the countries that our Constitution is in certain respects modelled on.'[91] In the Department of Finance, however, the Article has given rise to much difficulty in interpretation, having regard to our practice of appropriation by means of the Appropriation Act which is passed annually and is considered to carry out the intention of Article 61, which is as follows:

> All revenue of the Irish Free State (Saorstát Éireann) from whatever source arising, shall, subject to such exception as may be provided by law, form one fund, and shall be appropriated for the purposes of the Irish Free State (Saorstát Éireann) in the manner and subject to the charges and liabilities imposed by law.

The Articles, taken together, seem inconsistent, one contemplating that appropriation can be effected by 'vote, resolution or law', and the other that it can be effected only by law. It is unnecessary, for present purposes, to set out all the considerations which have been weighed and the interpretation which has been adopted in order to harmonise the two Articles and to justify existing financial procedure as being within the Constitution. It may be stated, however, that that procedure seems legal and that the Vote on Account may, most probably, be properly regarded as an appropriation of a bulk sum for specified services, while the Appropriation Act allocates specified sums for specified services. Nevertheless, on this construction of the Constitution it is not possible to give to the term 'appropriation' a single strict definition.

Various amendments have been considered, the simplest of which is to change the phrase 'shall be appropriated' in Article 61 to 'shall be *finally* appropriated'. But this would still leave two degrees of appropriation recognised by the Constitution, viz., Interim Appropriation and Definitive Appropriation.

The root of the difficulty is that a 'vote' or 'resolution' regarding the spending of money is not a final and conclusive act and should not be so regarded. It looks forward to another act of the legislature which will be final and definitive: it is only a preliminary to a law.

The best solution seems to be to recast Article 37 slightly, so that it will read:

> The Dáil shall not pass any vote, resolution or law for the appropriation of revenue or other public moneys unless the

[91] 1 *Dáil Debates*, Col. 1162 (4 October 1922).

purpose of the appropriation has been recommended *to it* by a message, etc.

This form would bring the Article more into accordance with the corresponding Articles in the Constitutions of Canada, Australia and South Africa.

The phrase 'revenue or other public moneys' may need some comment, as only 'money' is used in the existing Article 37. The Constitutions of both Canada and South Africa have the phrase 'public revenue or of any tax or impost', while that of Australia has 'revenue or moneys'. The latter seems better for our purpose, especially as 'impost' might call for definition; but 'public moneys' is more accurate than 'moneys'. Further, 'revenue', though mentioned in Article 61, does not seem, by itself, comprehensive enough to cover necessarily such departmental receipts as are authorised by the Appropriation Acts to be appropriated in aid of the expenditure of the several departments concerned. It has also to be remembered that the Revenue Departments (Revenue Commissioners and Department of Posts and Telegraphs) do not pay all their receipts into the Exchequer, but intercept sufficient to meet their current expenses. So the phrase 'revenue or other public moneys' seems the safest to adopt.

Again, the omission of 'in the same session' is suggested because of the ambiguity of the word 'session'. In practice, 'session' has been held, for the purposes of the Article, to mean 'Dáil', despite the opening sentence of Article 24.

To prevent, however, a 'message' from the Executive Council to one Dáil holding good without limit of time, the insertion of the words 'to it' is suggested. It is an inference from Article 28 that there is a succession of Dáils, so that the amendment would entail that a 'message' would have virtue only during the lifetime of the Dáil to which it was sent.

Article 54

The middle portion of this Article has been dealt with above in connection with Article 36. The remainder of the Article does not deal with finance.

Article 61

This has been dealt with in connection with Article 37. No amendment is suggested, if Article 37 is amended on the lines indicated.

Article 62

No amendment of this Article is suggested. It is suggested that Articles 61, 62 and 63 should, if convenient from the point of view of drafting, be placed earlier in the Constitution (say after Articles 36 and 37).[92]

No. 74: UCDA, P150/2395

Fr John Charles McQuaid to Eamon de Valera

Blackrock, Co. Dublin
16 February 1937

I am very glad to be able to enclose a most interesting and useful criticism of the French Constitution of 1814 by Pius VII.[93] I also send three new paragraphs for private property section. I hope they are according to the idea you had in mind.[94] At least they are accurate, for I spent the day on an analysis of *Quadragesimo Anno* and *Rerum Novarum*—which proved extraordinarily helpful to me, in my understanding of the Pope. I have here two copies of the *Codex* and it will give me great pleasure if you kindly accept both. The small one has a better index—I feel—and is very handy on a desk: the larger has a bold type and can fit into your library at the office. When you want me for discussion, I am at your full service.

No. 75: UCDA, P150/2395

Draft notes by Fr John Charles McQuaid concerning an article on Private Property

Blackrock, Co. Dublin
16 February 1937

1. The State…*temporal* goods.

4.1° The State shall use its best endeavour to provide that the material resources of the nations may be so distributed among private individuals

[92] This memorandum was prepared by Arthur Codling in December 1936. It is essentially a distillation of a longer memorandum on the financial provisions of the 1922 Constitution, submitted by Codling to Seán MacEntee on 12 December 1936, NAI, DFA 247/25. Hearne evidently requested a copy of this original memorandum from Codling, for on 19 January1937 Codling sent Hearne a copy, with the following cover note: 'As promised last week I enclose two copies of the Memorandum I prepared for my Minister in connection with the Financial Articles of the present Constitution. On one of the copies I have made notes in manuscript which briefly indicate some matters which arose on the consideration of the Memorandum and the reasons for two or three slight amendments in the draft Articles set out therein'.
[93] Enclosure not found.
[94] See document no. 75.

and the various classes of the population as adequately to procure the common good of the community as a whole.

4.2° The State, while acknowledging that the work of body and mind is an honourable means of virtuous and creditable living, shall aim, by this just distribution of material resources, at aiding all the citizens to attain that higher level of prosperity and culture which is more consonant with human dignity.

No. 76: UCDA, P150/2395

Fr John Charles McQuaid to Eamon de Valera

Blackrock, Co. Dublin
17 February 1937

I beg to enclose a draft of the paragraphs on free competition, etc, which, after much thought, I feel to be more logical and compact.[95] I hope the correction will not prove inconvenient. In the paragraph on 'share in the land', I have recast the third reason, making it more accurately represent the famous passages in *Quadragesimo Anno* and also *Rerum Novarum*. With O'Rahilly's draft,[96] I feel very disappointed; but, I suppose it was hasty and was all that could be done at the time.

[95] Enclosure not found.

[96] A reference to the draft Constitution drawn up by Alfred O'Rahilly in 1922. De Valera sent a copy of this Constitution to McQuaid in early 1937. See DDA, AB8/A/V/47.

No. 77: UCDA, P 150/2387

John Hearne to Kathleen O'Connell

17 February 1937

ROINN GNOTHAI COIGRICHE
DEPARTMENT OF EXTERNAL AFFAIRS

BAILE ÁTHA CLIATH
DUBLIN

Miss O'Connell,

Herewith Articles 46 to 50 inclusive: Trial of offences, and Repeal of Constitution of Saorstat Eireann and Continuance of Laws. Two copies.

It only remains to send you the draft of the Transitory Provisions

John J. Hearne

17·2·37.

No. 78: UCDA, P150/2387

Draft Article 38[97]

[John Hearne, Department of External Affairs]
[February], 1937

Personal Rights and Social Policy

Personal Rights:
Article 38[98]

1. 1° The State acknowledges that all citizens are as human persons equal before the law.
   2° The State shall, however, in its enactments have due regard to individual differences of capacity, physical and moral, and of social function.
   3° Titles of nobility shall not be conferred; Orders of Merit may (however) be created.[99]
2. 1° The State guarantees to respect, defend, and vindicate the personal rights of each citizen. ~~The State shall, accordingly, take all necessary measures to prevent any violation of these rights, enforce respect for social order, and punish offenders~~.[100]
   2° The State shall, in particular, protect, as best it may, from unjust attack, and, in case of injustice done, vindicate the person, life, good name and property rights of every citizen.
3. 1° No person shall be deprived of his personal liberty save in accordance with law.
   2° Upon complaint being made by or on behalf of any person that he is being unlawfully detained, the High Court and any and every judge thereof shall forthwith enquire into the same and may make an order requiring the person in whose custody such person shall be detained to produce the body of the person so detained before such court or judge without delay and to certify in writing as to the cause of the detention and such Court or judge shall thereupon order the release of such

[97] This draft Article is undated, with all emendations made manually by de Valera.
[98] Article 40.1 to 40.6 of the present Constitution.
[99] Word in parentheses added manually.
[100] Manually crossed out.

person unless satisfied that he is being detained in accordance with the law.

3° Nothing in this Article, however, shall be invoked to prohibit control or interfere with any act of the defence forces of Éire during the existence of a state of war or armed rebellion.

4. The dwelling of a citizen shall not be forcibly entered save in accordance with law.
5. The State shall permit the exercise ~~by the citizens~~[101] of the following rights, always provided that the exercise of these rights shall not conflict with true morality or social order.

1° The State shall permit citizens to express freely their convictions and opinions.

The education of public opinion being, however, a matter of such grave import to the common good, the State shall see to it that the organs of public opinion, such as the Radio, Press and Cinema, while preserving their rightful liberty of expression, shall not be used to undermine social order or right morality, or, especially in times of war, the authority of the State.

The publication or utterance of blasphemous, seditious, or indecent matter are offences punishable by law.

2° The State shall permit citizens to assemble peaceably without arms.

Laws (however) may be passed to prevent or control meetings which are calculated to cause a breach of the peace or to be a danger or nuisance to the general public.[102]

Open air meetings shall be subject to police regulations and control so as not to interfere with public convenience or normal traffic.

3° The State shall permit citizens to form associations and unions.

Laws regulating the manner in which the right of forming associations and unions and the right of free assembly may be exercised and shall contain no political, religious or class discrimination.

[101] Manually crossed out.
[102] Word in parentheses added manually.

No. 79: UCDA, P 150/2382

Transcription from Oxford English Dictionary Definition of 'vindicate' in Article 40.3

[February], 1937

VINDICATE (Definition from Large Oxford Dictionary)

f.L. vindicat, ppl. stem of vindicare to claim, to set free, to punish etc., f. vim acc. sing. of vis force + dic stem of dicere to say.

1. (a) To exercise in revenge
   (b) To avenge or revenge (a person, cause, wrong etc.)
   (c) To punish; to visit with punishment.

2. To make or set free; to deliver or rescue.

3. To clear from censure, criticism, suspicion or doubt, by means of demonstration; to justify or uphold by evidence or argument.

4. To assert, maintain, make good, by means of action, esp. in one's own interest; to defend against encroachment or interference,

5. To claim as properly belonging to oneself or another; to assert or establish possession of (something) for oneself or another.

No. 80: UCDA, P150/2397

Memorandum from Arthur Matheson to Eamon de Valera 'The Constitution'

Parliamentary Draftsman's Office
1 March 1937

The Constitution
As requested by you on Saturday, I send you herewith a suggested draft of Article 10 of the new Constitution.

In preparing this draft I have been guided chiefly by a desire to avoid the numerous defects which experience has disclosed in the wording of Article 11 of the existing Constitution.

The Theory underlying the old Article 11 and the new Article 10 is that all natural resources should belong to the State and should be exploited for the benefit of the people and not for the private profit of individuals; that theory has no application to land because all land is the subject of private ownership, and in so far as the State owns land it does so in the same way as a private individual. Therefore natural resources and land must be dealt with separately in the Article. Therefore the Article should vest in Éire *all* natural resources (subject to existing private interests) and there is no reason for limiting it to the natural resources which were vested in Saorstat Éireann; on the other hand the Article should not vest any land in Éire except so far as is necessary for continuing State ownership where it actually exists at the coming into operation of the new Constitution.

I would submit that all matters of management and alienation should be left to ordinary law; experience with the existing Article 11 has shown that any attempt to control by the Constitution the management and alienation of State property is undesirable.

I would submit that land acquired by the State in the future should be expressly mentioned.

I would submit that inland waters should be grouped with land, as they are the subject of private ownership in the same way as land is; but the territorial waters of the sea should be grouped with natural resources, because there is no private ownership in the sea.

As the air and all forms of potential energy are specifically mentioned in the existing Article 11, I would submit that they should be mentioned in the new Article 10, so as to prevent erroneous deductions being made from their omission.

'The Parliamentary Draftsman's suggested draft of Article 10'
All mines, minerals and other natural resources (including the air and all forms of potential energy) within the (~~national territory~~ jurisdiction of the Gov. and Parlt.),[103] and all royalties and franchises in that territory, and also the territorial waters of Éire belong to Éire subject to all estates and interests therein lawfully vested in private persons immediately before the coming into operation of this Constitution. All land and inland waters which belonged to Saorstat Éireann immediately before the coming into operation of this Constitution belong to Éire to the same extent as they then belonged to Saorstat Éireann. Provision shall be made by law for the management of the property vested in Éire by this Article and for the control of the alienation, whether temporary or permanent, of that property. Provision shall also be made by law for the management of land and inland waters acquired by Éire after the coming into operation of this Constitution and for the control of the alienation, whether temporary or permanent, of the land and inland waters so acquired.

No. 81: UCDA, P150/2397

Memorandum from Arthur Matheson to Eamon de Valera

Parliamentary Draftsman's Office
2 March 1937

[Articles 13 and 32 in this note correspond with Articles 15 and 34.4.3° in the published Constitution.]

Article 7:
The full details of the flag must be prescribed somewhere, but it might be better to prescribe them by ordinary law instead of in the Constitution. It has been suggested to me that the Article might stand in its present form with the substitution of 'a tricolour' for 'the tricolour'; I agree, but it would be safer to word the Article as follows:

> 'The national flag of Éire is a tricolour of green, white and orange in such form as shall be defined by law.'

Article 12:
In Section 2, I would submit for consideration the following subsection instead of the present Subsection 2°, viz:

[103] Section in parentheses has been amended by de Valera to read as shown.

'2° The President may refuse to dissolve the Oireachtas on the advice of a head of the Government who has ceased to retain the support of a majority in Dáil Éireann.'

Article 13:
In Section 8, I think the word 'session' in Subsection 1° is unobjectionable; there seems no doubt that it is equivalent to 'sitting' or 'meeting' and does not bear the technical meaning which it carries in relation to the British Parliament. The same remark applies to the word 'sessions' in Subsection 4°.

In Subsection 14°, I would recommend the omission of the word 'felony'.

Article 14:
In Section 2, Subsection 3°, I would suggest that the expression 'so far as is possible' is too strict, and the expression 'so far as is practicable' would be better.

Article 17:
In Section 3, I am afraid that the possibility of a dissolution of the Oireachtas before the completion of the general election for Seanad Éireann consequent upon a previous dissolution will give rise to a number of problems and require rather elaborate provisions; for instance, what is to happen to the pending general election for Seanad Éireann? Is it to be dropped and a new general election begun? I would suggest a provision to the effect that when the Oireachtas has been dissolved it shall not again be dissolved until after the completion of the general election for Seanad Éireann; such a provision would be the easiest way out of the difficulty and would not appear to have any political objections.

Article 18:
I think this Article is slightly unsure in regard to casual vacancies: I would suggest:

(a) confine clause 1° to general elections;
(b) preserve clause 2° as it is;
(c) add a further clause as follows: '3° The method of filling casual vacancies in the number of the elected members of Seanad Éireann shall be regulated by law'

[Matter omitted]

Article 32:
In Section 4, Subsection 4°, the last line will require modification as there are some cases (e.g., workmen's compensation cases) in which there

is an appeal from the Circuit Court direct to the Supreme Court; I would suggest that the following words should be added after the words 'High Court', viz:

> 'and shall also have appellate jurisdiction from such decisions of other Courts as shall be prescribed by law'.

Article 33:
The Circuit Court is not established by the Constitution and is not mentioned in any other Article; I would submit that it should not be mentioned in this Article; or alternatively that it should be mentioned and its equivalent provided for in Article 32.

No. 82: UCDA, P150/2397

Memorandum from Arthur Matheson to Eamon de Valera

Parliamentary Draftsman's Office
4 March 1932

The Constitution
In pursuance of your direction, I have examined the draft Constitution up to the end of Article 24 with a view to seeing whether any provision could be shortened by leaving the subject-matter thereof to be dealt with by ordinary law, and I send you herewith suggestions for a re-draft on those lines in three cases in which it appeared to me to be practicable, viz., the re-election of the Ceann Comhairle, the reference of a Money Bill to a Committee of Privileges, and the reference of a Bill to the Supreme Court.

In the last mentioned case, it should be considered whether the expression 'advisory opinion' should be retained or deleted in favour of the word 'decision' or the expression 'advisory decision'.

I would submit for your consideration whether sections 4 and 5 and Article 12 (relating to the duties of the President) are really necessary.

I will examine the remainder of the draft Constitution with a view to seeing whether any other similar shortening is practicable.

'Suggestion by the Parliamentary Draftsman for a re-draft of section 6 of Article 14 (pages X21 and X22)'
Provision shall be made by law to enable the member of Dáil Éireann who is the Chairman of Dáil Éireann immediately before a dissolution of the Oireachtas to be deemed without any actual election to be elected if he so desires at the ensuing general election as a member of Dáil Éireann.

'Suggestion by the Parliamentary Draftsman for a re-draft of section 2 of Article 15 (pages X24 to X26)'
2.1° The Chairman of Dáil Éireann shall certify any Bill which, in his opinion is a Money Bill, to be a Money Bill.
2.2° Every such certificate shall be final and conclusive subject only to a reference to a Committee of Privileges under the subsequent provisions of this Article.
2.3° [Provision shall be made by law enabling Seanad Éireann][104] to have the question whether a Bill, certified by the Chairman of Dáil Éireann to be a Money Bill, is or is not a Money Bill referred to a Committee of Privileges consisting of an equal number of members of Dáil Éireann and of Seanad Éireann and a Chairman who shall be a judge of the Supreme Court.
2.4° The decision of the Committee of Privileges shall be final and conclusive.
[2.4° The P[resident] may, having heard the C[ouncil] of S[tate], refuse or reject the petition.
2.5° The decision of the Committee of Privileges shall be final and conclusive.][105]

'Suggestion by the Parliamentary Draftsman for a re-draft of Article 23 (pages X38 to X40)'

Article 23

1. This Article applies to any Bill passed or deemed to have been passed by both Houses of the Oireachtas other than a Money Bill, a Bill expressed to be a Bill to amend this Constitution, or a Bill in respect of which a resolution shall have been passed by Dáil Éireann under section 6 of Article 20 of this Constitution.
2. Provision shall be made by law enabling the President, after consultation with the Council of State, to refer any Bill to which this Article applies to the Supreme Court for an advisory opinion as to whether such Bill is repugnant, in whole or in part, to this Constitution and enabling the President to postpone signing and promulgating the Bill until the Supreme Court has given its opinion, and requiring the President to decline to sign or promulgate the Bill if the Supreme Court advises that it is repugnant, in whole or in part, to this Constitution.

[104] The words in square parentheses have been manually added by de Valera, with the annotation 'S.E. may petition the Presdt to have' in the margin.
[105] Section in square parentheses added manually by de Valera.

No. 83: UCDA, P 150/2387

Pre-circulation printed version of Articles (38) 40 and (39) 41 and (40) 42*

[March, 1937]

PERSONAL RIGHTS AND SOCIAL POLICY. 36

PERSONAL RIGHTS AND SOCIAL POLICY.

Personal Rights.

Article 38.

1. 1° The State acknowledges that all citizens are as human persons equal before the law.

2° The State shall, in particular, in its laws have due regard to individual differences of capacity, physical and moral, and of social function.

3° Titles of nobility shall not be conferred. Orders of Merit may, however, be created.

2. 1° The State guarantees to respect, defend, and vindicate the personal rights of each citizen.

2° The State shall, however, protect, as best it may, from unjust attack, and, in case of injustice done, vindicate the person, life, good name and property rights of every citizen.

3. 1° No citizen shall be deprived of his personal liberty save in accordance with law.

2° Upon complaint being made by or on behalf of any person that he is being unlawfully detained, the High Court and any and every judge thereof shall forthwith enquire into the same and may make an order requiring the person in whose custody such person shall be detained to produce the body of the person so detained before such court or judge without delay and to certify in writing as to the cause of the detention and such Court or judge shall thereupon order the release of such person unless satisfied that he is being detained in accordance with the law.

3° Nothing in this Article, however, shall be invoked to prohibit control or interfere with any act of the defence forces of Éire during the existence of a state of war or armed rebellion.

4. The dwelling of a citizen shall not be forcibly entered save in accordance with law.

5. The State shall permit the exercise by the citizens of the following rights, always provided that the exercise of these rights shall not conflict with true morality or social order.

1° The State shall permit citizens to express freely their convictions and opinions.

* Handwritten annotations by de Valera.

Article 38 *(continued).*

The education of public opinion being, however, a matter of such grave import to the common good, the State shall see to it that the organs of public opinion, such as the Radio, Press and Cinema, while preserving their rightful liberty of expression, shall not be used to undermine social order or right morality, or, especially in times of war, the authority of the State.

The publication or utterance of blasphemous, seditious, or indecent matter are offences punishable by law.

2° The State shall permit citizens to assemble peaceably and without arms.

Laws, however, may be passed to prevent or control meetings which are calculated to cause a breach of the peace or to be a danger or nuisance to the general public.

Open air meetings shall be subject to police regulations and control so as not to interfere with public convenience or normal traffic.

3° The State shall permit citizens to form associations and unions.

Laws regulating the manner in which the right of forming associations and unions and the right of free assembly may be exercised shall contain no political, religious or class discrimination.

The Family.

Article 39.

1. 1° The State recognises the Family as the natural primary and fundamental unit of Society, and as a moral and juridical institution possessing inalienable and imprescriptible rights, antecedent and superior to all positive law.

2° The State, therefore, guarantees to protect the Family in its constitution, authority and government, as the necessary basis of social order and as indispensable to the welfare of the Nation.

3° In particular, the State recognises that by her life within the home, woman gives to the State a support without which the common good cannot be achieved. The State shall, therefore, endeavour to secure that women, especially mothers and young girls, shall not be obliged to enter avocations unsuited to their sex and strength.

Article 39 *(continued).*

2. 1° The State pledges itself to guard with special care the institution of Marriage, on which the Family is founded, and to protect it against attack.

2° No law shall be passed which shall impair its essential properties of unity and indissolubility.

3° No person whose marriage has been dissolved under the civil law of any other State shall be capable of contracting a valid marriage in Éire during the lifetime of the other party to the marriage so dissolved.

Education.

Article 40.

1. The State acknowledges the Family as the primary and natural educator of the child, and guarantees to respect the inalienable right and duty of the parents to provide, according to their means, for the religious and moral, intellectual, physical and social education of their children.

2. Parents shall be free to provide this education in their homes or in private schools or in schools [established by the State.]

3. The State pledges itself not to oblige parents, in violation of their conscience and lawful preference, to send their children to Schools [established by the State.]

4. The State, however, as guardian of the common good, shall require in view of actual conditions a certain minimum education, intellectual and moral, physical and social.

5. The State shall aid and supplement private and corporate educational initiative, particularly by providing free primary education and, when the public good requires it, other institutions, with due respect, however, for the rights of parents, especially in the matter of religious and moral formation.

6. In exceptional cases, where the parents [for physical or moral reasons] fail in their duty towards their children, the State as guardian of the common good, by appropriate means shall supply the place of the parents, but always with due respect for the natural and imprescriptible rights of the child.

No. 84: UCDA, P150/2395

Fr John Charles McQuaid to Eamon de Valera

Blackrock, Co. Dublin
8 March 1937

I beg to enclose the amendment dealing with widows, orphans and the aged. It will be noted that I have retained the word *support*, qualifying *just claims*, because it is unfair to expect, as so many do, that the State will do everything. It devolves on the family to support—where it can—its own aged members, in a spirit of charity. Further, we have, at no point, met the most potent form of social agitation: the unsettled strike. A great deal of the venom of Communism could be neutralised, if, where strikes do occur, a mode of settlement, fair to both sides, could be found. I venture, therefore, to suggest a small paragraph—which is both correct in social doctrine and capable of averting [?] evils.

When next we meet, perhaps, we could discuss the paragraph, unless you see fit to incorporate it at once.[106]

N.B. The Bishop of Waterford has a very interesting comment on this latter question and advocates a remedy similar to that suggested (Pastoral letter of Lent, 7 February 1937). You will have noted that last year we had the Train strike and this year we are to be given a huge building strike. We are thus being kept in a state of social unrest, with intervals of quiet.

No. 85: NAI, DT S9710

Seán MacEntee to Eamon de Valera

Department of Finance
9 March 1937

Dear Mr President,
I have discussed with the Controller of the Stationery Office the arrangements which must be made for a General Election this year, and I understand that this presents no difficulty, that so far as an Election is concerned the Stationery Office is quite ready to deal with one at any time now.

[106] Neither of the enclosures mentioned found in UCDA.

In connection with the Constitution, however, the Controller is in great difficulties, as he has no official knowledge that a Referendum on it will in fact be taken. If one is to be taken it will be necessary for the Stationery Office in connection with it to make special arrangements for Referendum Forms, ballot boxes, etc., etc. It is therefore desirable that the Executive Council, as soon as possible, should take a formal decision as to whether a Referendum will in fact take place, and should communicate this fact to the Departments concerned, which in addition to the Department of Finance and the Stationery Office will, no doubt, also include the Department of Local Government and Public Health, which Department, I understand, will be responsible for the conduct of the General Election and, presumably, will also be responsible for the conduct of the Referendum.

I presume that your Department will take the initiative in submitting the question to the Council and making arrangements with the Departments.

No. 86 UCDA, P150/2373

Department of External Affairs
Undated

Article on the Courts and a Constitutional Court

[John Hearne, Department of External Affairs]
[Undated]

Article XVI[107]
The Courts

Section 1.
Justice shall be administered in public courts established by the Oireachtas ~~by~~. [The] judges [shall be] appointed in the manner provided by this Constitution.

All judges shall be independent in the exercise of their functions and subject only to the Constitution and the law.

The Courts shall comprize Courts of First Instance, a Court of Final Appeal, and a Constitutional Court.

Section 2.
The Courts of First Instance shall include a High Court invested, subject as herinafter provided, with full original jurisdiction in and power to determine all matters and questions whether of law or fact, civil or criminal.

[107] The document has been transcribed so as to incorporate de Valera's handwritten amendments. De Valera's deletions are shown by a line through the text, while his additions are included in square parentheses. Handwritten amendments to punctuation have been added silently.

The High Court shall not have jurisdiction to entertain or determine the question of the validity of any law, [but may refer question to Constitutional Court].[108]

The Courts of First Instance shall also include Courts of local and limited jurisdiction with a right of appeal as determined by law.

Section 3.
The Court of Final Appeal shall be called the Supreme Court.

The Supreme Court shall, with such exceptions and subject to such regulations as may be prescribed by law, have appellate jurisdiction from all decisions of the High Court. The decision of the Supreme Court shall in all cases (not involving val[idity] of a law) be final and conclusive.

Section 4.
The Constitutional Court shall have exclusive jurisdiction to determine the question of the validity of any law having regard to the provisions of this Constitution. The decision of the Constitutional Court on every such question shall be final and conclusive.

The Constitutional Court shall consist of seven members who shall be appointed as follows:

The Chairman and two other members shall be appointed by the President.

Two members shall be appointed by the judges of the Supreme Court.

Two members shall be appointed by the judges of the High Court.[109]

Section 5.
The judges of the High Court, the Supreme Court and the Constitutional Court[110] shall not be removed except for stated misbehaviour or incapacity and then only by a resolution passed by Dáil Éireann, or, in the event of a Second House of the Oireachtas being established, by resolutions passed by both houses.

Section 6.
The remuneration of any of the judges referred to in the preceding Section of this Article shall not be reduced during his continuance in office.

[108] Annotated 'state case' in the margins.

[109] There are two annotations in the margins relating to Section 4. The first reads as follows: 'Be presided over by the C.J. and shall consist of the C.J. and one other; the Pres. of the H.C. and one other; the C. Comh.; Cathaoirleach; the A.G.; and [Presidents?]. 4 Judges, 1 A.G., 2 Dáil, 3 persons by P[resident] E[executive Council]'. The second annotation reads: 'Chief Jus. (Pres.); Pres. H.C.; C.C. and Cath.; A.G. 2 nom. by P., 1 by S[upreme] C[ourt]; 1 by H[igh] C[ourt] (each year? Or for each case?). P. constitutes court. Remuneration of those nom. by P'.

[110] Constitutional Court has been manually placed in parentheses by de Valera and annotated with a question mark.

Section 7.
No judge shall be eligible to sit in the Oireachtas or to hold any other office or position of emolument.

Section 8.
Subject to the foregoing, the following matters may be regulated by Organic Laws and Rules of Court made thereunder, that is to say:

The number of judges of the Supreme Court, the High Court, and all other Courts (other than the Constitutional Court) established under this Constitution.

The constitution and distribution of business and jurisdiction among the said Courts and judges.

The organization and procedure of the said Courts and of the Constitutional Court.

The terms of appointment of the judges of the Courts aforesaid.[111]

No. 87: NAI, DT S9715A

Draft Constitution, privately circulated[112]

10 March 1937

See www.irishconstitution.ie.

[111] It is of interest to compare this draft with Article 3 of the Czechoslovak Constitution of 1920, (see also document no. 43).

In many respects, the correspondence is striking. Both Constitutional Courts were to consist of seven members. The two other principal courts (in our case, the High Court and the Supreme Court) were to have the right to choose two members each, with the Chairman and the other two members chosen by the respective Presidents of the State. Likewise, both texts provided for the enactment of a special law regulating the organization and procedure of the Constitutional Court. While in both cases there was a judicial majority of "ordinary" judges, it is not clear that it was necessarily envisaged that the other members would be judges - or perhaps even lawyers.

De Valera put brackets around the words "and the Constitutional Court" with regard to the standard guarantees in respect of tenure which suggests that he may have envisaged that these other members of the Court would not be judges in the ordinary sense of that term. If such proposals had prevailed, then any Irish Constitutional Court might ultimately have evolved much like the French *Conseil Constitutionnel* with a mixture of judicial and political members.

De Valera also seems to have toyed with the idea of whether personages such as the Attorney General and the Ceann Comhairle might not be *ex officio* members of the Constitutional Court. There are, of course, echoes of this in Article 31.2.i of the Constitution which provides that the Chairman of Dáil Éireann, the Chairman of Seanad Éireann and the Attorney General are *ex officio* members of the Council of State. A further question raised by de Valera in the margin was whether the Presidential nominees were to receive remuneration and queried whether such nominees were to appointed for "each year or each case?" The proposal does not appear to have been taken much further. There was a passing reference to a Constitutional Court in a later draft in early January 1937, but thereafter there was really to be only one question: would the power of judicial review be vested in the High Court at first instance (as with Article 65 of the 1922 Constitution) or would this jurisdiction be vested exclusively in the Supreme Court?

The published draft originally provided that the Supreme Court would have such exclusive jurisdiction, but following representations both in the Dáil and elsewhere (see document no. 167), de Valera finally opted to give this jurisdiction to the High Court, with a right of appeal to the Supreme Court: see 67 *Dáil Debates* at 1492–1492 (2 June 1927).

[112] It is not clear to whom this draft was circulated, though it may be conjectured that it was only to de Valera's closest and most trusted advisers. The copy retained on file bears Joseph P. Walshe's name.

No. 88: NAI, DT S9710

Extract from Cabinet Minutes

Government Buildings, Dublin
12 March 1937

New Constitution
The following general procedure in regard to the enactment of the new Constitution was approved:

(a) the draft should be submitted to Dáil Éireann for approval, the procedure for its consideration by the Dáil being that applicable to a Bill;
(b) if approved by Dáil Éireann the draft should be submitted to a plebiscite of the people, to be held at the same time and in the same manner as the forthcoming General Election, provision being made for a simple affirmation or negative in respect of the whole draft;

should the draft be approved by a majority of the votes given at the plebiscite, the Constitution should be brought into operation by a resolution of Dáil Éireann passed for that purpose.

Authority was given for the preparation of the necessary legislation in regard to the plebiscite.[113]

[113] See Chapter XII below.

CHAPTER IX

OBSERVATIONS ON THE DRAFT CONSTITUTION, MARCH 1937

'In examining the draft of the Constitution, the Department of Finance has taken the line that it was not called upon to praise, but rather to point out possible defects and difficulties, so what follows is conceived in that spirit.'[1] These were the opening lines of the response of the deeply unhappy James J. McElligott on being presented with the draft Constitution, circulated on 16 March.[2] This draft was distributed to all Government Departments, along with the Ceann Comhairle and senior judges. Responses were to be prepared and returned by the end of that month. There were many important contributions to the ensuing debate, but the responses of McElligott and Stephen Roche call out for particular attention.[3]

McElligott prepared a lengthy memorandum which was sent to the Department of the President on 23 March 1937.[4] Among his key objections was the extent to which the draft Constitution provided for judicial review of legislation:

[1] See document no. 104.

[2] While various articles were redrafted countless times between 16 March and 1 May (the date of the official publication), there were four more drafts printed by Cahills before that latter date: 1st Revise (1 April), 2nd Revise (10 April), 3rd Revise (24 April) and 4th Revise (26 April). Beginning with the 10 March printing and ending with the version of the Constitution submitted to plebiscite, there were in total nine different printings of the Constitution. See www.irishconstitution.ie.

[3] For a profile of McElligott, see Ronan Fanning, *The Irish Department of Finance 1922–1958* (Dublin, 1978), especially 490–2.

[4] See document no. 104. This thirty-nine page memorandum was in many respects a devastating attack on the fundamental purposes and objects of the Constitution itself. But McElligott was noted for his 'readiness to present his political masters with what he knew was unpalatable advice couched in caustic and coruscating prose', Fanning, *Department of Finance*, 491. The Department of Finance memorandum was not generally circulated. It was communicated directly to the Department of the President, where it was seen by de Valera and the drafting committee. It seems unlikely that it was seen by many outside of this circle, if any at all.

> Apart from questions of complexity and expense involved in the Constitution, it seems that there will be a degree of uncertainty introduced into our legislative system by the extent to which recognition is given to the doctrine of repugnance.

Not surprisingly, McElligott was particularly troubled by the draft text of Article 43.[5] At this stage Article 43 not only dealt with property rights, but also included a number of additional sections, many of which ultimately appeared in Article 45. McElligott objected that such 'declaratory phrases' while 'individually unobjectionable as a statement of social policy' might 'if launched into the void in the draft Constitution, recoil like a boomerang on the Government of some future day in circumstances not anticipated by the originators'. The memorandum also argued that the draft Article 43 was:

> not of a kind usually enshrined in the Constitution. They will not be helpful to Ministers in the future but will provide a breeding ground for discontent, and so create instability and insecurity. They are consequently objectionable and even dangerous. Their provisions are too vague to be of positive assistance to any Government and are yet sufficiently definite to afford grounds for disaffection to sections of the Community, who might claim that the Government were not living up to the Constitution.
>
> The provisions are the more objectionable by reason of the earlier Articles relating to repugnance under which laws may be disallowed after reference to the Supreme Court or to a Referendum. Some of the provisions are too advanced, some too conservative and many cut across action taken daily by the Government, e.g., restrictions on private property and initiative.
>
> Further the provisions are most unnecessary. Distinct advances along the lines of social and economic policy outlined have already been made without the aid of these declaratory provisions, some of which are themselves, it should be noted, repugnant to present Government policy, e.g., we do not settle 'as many families as practicable' on the land.[6] 'Five acres and a cow' would suffice if that were the policy. We create economic holdings of twenty-five acres…

[5] Then numbered Article 41 in the 16 March 1937 draft.
[6] As now provided for in Article 45.2.v.

> Also, the provisions are contradictory. The State has established monopolies in important articles such as sugar, electricity, cement, tyres, oil etc.[7] The reference to the 'economic domination of the few in what pertains to the control of credit'[8] is not understood. In so far as one can attach any intelligible meaning to it, it is untrue, but it could easily be worked up by agitators as a weapon of attack on the Banks, the Agricultural Credit Corporation, the Industrial Credit Co., or against any large joint-stock concern.

These concerns were also reflected in the observations, circulated at around the same time, of the Department of the President[9] on the first draft. In essence, these particular observations appear to have constituted an Article by Article commentary with de Valera's own personal response to suggestions and comments which had been made by others on the first published draft. It seems clear from the comments on Article 43 that de Valera had already realised by this stage that it would be necessary to distinguish between fundamental rights (which would be justiciable in the courts) and certain types of socio-economic rights (which would not be so justiciable):

> The President's intention is that a number of these Sections are merely statements of moral principles and should not be created positive rights.
>
> I have accordingly suggested the following formula which should be inserted at the beginning of this portion of the Constitution:
>
> > 'The State shall be guided in its general policy by the principles embodied in this Article, but the said Article shall not of itself operate to confer rights.'[10]

Gavan Duffy made very similar comments in respect of the fundamental rights provisions in a note to de Valera on 2 April 1937:

[7] That is, the provisions of the present Article 45.3 notwithstanding. The Department of Industry and Commerce expressed similar concerns in a memorandum of 24 April1937: see document no. 160.

[8] A modified version of this phrase appears in the present Article 45.2.iv.

[9] That is, President of the Executive Council, corresponding to what would now be the Department of the Taoiseach. Moynihan had already anticipated this objection to the original version of Article 43, for, writing to all government departments on 16 March 1937, he had said that this provision:

> is still under examination with a view to having it placed in a special category in the Constitution. It is intended as an indication of the principles which should inform the policy of the social and economic laws of the State. The President [de Valera] would be glad to have the views of Departments on the principles contained therein; see document no. 90.

[10] See document no. 105. These observations had been written by McDunphy.

> The articles intended to carry with them *legal* redress for the citizen can be segregated from those which enunciate and [are] classified under some such separate title as '*Legal rights secured to the citizens*.' These principles might be entitled 'Guiding Principles of Social Policy' or '*Principles of Social Policy*', the term 'personal rights' being omitted to prevent confusion, as a 'right' implies legal redress.[11]

We see here the genesis of the preamble to the present Article 45[12] and the origins of the clear division that was ultimately drawn between the Fundamental Rights provisions on the one hand (Articles 40 to 44) and what became the Directive Principles of Social Policy (Article 45) on the other:

> The principles of social policy set forth in this Article are intended for the general guidance of the Oireachtas. The application of these principles in the making of laws shall be the care of the Oireachtas exclusively and shall not be cognisable by any Court under any of the provisions of the Constitution.

The language of the Preamble to Article 45 closely follows a draft suggested by Gavan Duffy on 2 April:

> The Oireachtas is the guardian of the Constitution. In fulfilling that trust the Oireachtas shall faithfully observe the guiding principles of social policy set down in Articles...

[11] UCDA/P150/2416 Italics underlined in the original. De Valera also received a personal letter from a John Finnerty dated 21 May 1937. Finnerty appears to have been a senior legal adviser to the Department of Transportation in Washington DC, who, along with a list of other prominent Irish-Americans, had been sent a personal copy of the draft Constitution by Kathleen O'Connell:

> Let me say that I particularly admire Articles 40, 42, 43 and 44 and perhaps especially the social provisions of Article 45. I assume that the provisions of the 1st paragraph of Article 45 excluding the courts from taking any cognisance of the operation of these principles is not without relevance to the experience we are now having with our own Supreme Court, NAI, DT S9852.

Hearne corresponded in early April 1937 with Charles Bewley, the Irish Minister to Berlin regarding the legal implications of section 5 of the Weimar Constitution 1919. These sections sought to guarantee a degree of social and economic justice, but Bewley replied on 5 April 1937 saying that these provisions were not juridicially enforceable, but that these provisions represented 'the expression of a hope that the legislature would act in a certain way': NAI DFA 147/2. See generally, Rachel Walsh, 'Private Property Rights in the Drafting of the Irish Constitution: A Communitarian Approach' *Dublin University Law Journal*, 33 (2011) 86-95.

[12] The Department of Finance was pleased with this change and as McElligott noted in his comments on the third revise on 24 April 1937:

> The Preamble which now introduces this Article deprives it of the character of a declaration of rights enforceable in the courts and to that extent it meets the objections urged by the Department of Finance; see document no. 158.

> The application of these principles in the making of laws shall be the exclusive care of the Oireachtas and shall not be cognisable by any court under any of the provisions of this Constitution.

Of course, the very fact that de Valera agreed to such an elaborate distinction being made at this point of the drafting process might suggest an awareness that the other fundamental rights provisions contained in Articles 40 to 44 would be justiciable and would form the basis for an attack on the constitutionality of enactments of the Oireachtas. Certainly, it is manifest from these comments that this distinction must have been to the forefront of the minds of the drafting committee at this time, not least in the light of the concerns—which had been so bluntly expressed—of McElligott and Roche.

This point had also excited the attention of two important commentators who themselves had been members of the 1922 Constitution Committee: James Douglas and Professor Alfred O'Rahilly.[13] The former had noted that:

> One important feature of the draft Constitution is the recital of a large number of 'Fundamental Rights' in Articles 40 to 44. Article 45 enumerates a number of principles of social policy which shall not be cognisable by any Court and which have therefore no constitutional validity. Articles 40 to 44 are presumably binding on the Oireachtas, and it would appear that the validity of any law may be challenged on the ground that it does conform to these articles. Whether or not it is wise to set out fundamental principles of government in the Constitution is a matter on which a difference of opinion existed in the original Constitution Committee. One of the drafts contained a statement of general fundamental rights not unlike those which appeared in President de Valera's draft.
>
> If the new draft Constitution is passed in its present form, we may look forward to some very interesting arguments in the Supreme Court when Constitutional cases are under consideration.
>
> For instance, it is difficult to see how a Court can decide whether any particular Act has respected 'as far as

[13] For Douglas, see J.A. Gaughan (ed.), *Memoirs of Senator James G. Douglas: Concerned Citizen* (Dublin, 1998). O'Rahilly has been described as 'the outstanding controversialist in the Ireland of his day, presenting trenchantly argued—if often idiosyncratic—views on virtually every topic of public debate', Louis McRedmond (ed.), *Modern Irish Lives: Dictionary of 20th Century Biography* (Dublin, 1996), 256.

> practicable' the personal rights of the citizen (Article 40.3.1°) or whether the State has 'endeavoured' to ensure that mothers should not be obliged by economic necessity to engage in labour to the neglect of their duties in the home (Article 41.2.2°). The reason for the constitutional distinction between Article 45, on the one hand, and Articles 40 to 44, on the other, is not clear to me.[14]

The distinction between justiciable and non-justiciable rights was also strongly emphasised by O'Rahilly. Speaking of Article 45, O'Rahilly admitted that:

> Mr de Valera is undoubtedly dealing with a real difficulty; but I think that he has dealt with it in the wrong place and in the wrong way.
>
> For outside [Article 45] the Draft lays down other social principles for the guidance of the Oireachtas; and these declarations he has left to be cognisable by the Supreme Court. For instance, according to Mr de Valera, the Court might be asked to decide whether such and such an Article has 'as far as practicable' respected the citizen's personal rights or whether in an enactment the State has really 'endeavoured' to prevent the economic exploitation of mothers.
>
> Why should the Court be bound to take cognisance of Articles 40 and 41 and be precluded from 'cognising' Article 45? I see no reason for this discrepant attitude towards different articles. Mr de Valera, who gives the Supreme Court power to determine the constitutionality of a law, is surely not logical in withdrawing some of the included social principles from the judge's cognisance. Personally, I reiterate, I am against giving this power to the Court. My chief reason is that we do not know what parameters of jurisprudence they will employ.
>
> Without being a lawyer I know enough of British jurisprudence and law principles—in which most of our legal men are saturated—to know that on many important points they differ from the presuppositions of Catholic sociology. Hence I see no use in registering new social principles (i.e., new in relation to British legalism) in the

[14] *Irish Independent*, 8 May 1937.

> Constitution and then allowing them to be pared down with the knife of an alien jurisprudence. But even I, holding this view which is apparently not generally shared, object to withdrawing part of the Constitution from the 'cognisance' of the Courts.[15]

These particular comments were also expressly drawn to the attention of the drafting committee.[16] But the concerns that were expressed in these Departmental observations did not relate solely to the property rights and social policy provisions. De Valera's own Department observed with respect to the fundamental rights provisions that: 'It is clear that as they stand many of them could be invoked so as to create very difficult situations.'[17]

The Secretary of the Department of Justice, Stephen Roche, also prepared a lengthy memorandum which, not surprisingly given his clear antipathy to judicial review of legislation, expressed serious concerns about the potential for judicial activism which the new Constitution would afford. Roche was thus, for example, unhappy with the major/minor offences distinction contained in Article 38.2:

> If the Oireachtas thinks proper to give [the District Court] summary jurisdiction in the case of attempted suicide, it should not be in the power of anybody to occupy the time of the Supreme Court for days with the argument that attempted suicide is not a minor offence.[18]

Similar concerns were expressed by the Department of Education about aspects of Article 42;[19] by the Department of Lands about the

[15] *Irish Independent*, 15 May 1937. See www.irishconstitution.ie.

[16] The drafting committee prepared a bulky file summarising a list of objections and comments made both in the press and elsewhere, NAI, DT S9882. The comments of both Douglas and O'Rahilly were summarised and included in this file.

[17] See document no. 105.

[18] See document no. 101. The question here, of course, was whether the Oireachtas could designate certain offences as truly 'minor' offences such as would enable them to be tried summarily, i.e. without a jury. This question has, indeed, occupied the time of the Supreme Court on many occasions, with several statutory provisions having been found unconstitutional on this account: see *Re Haughey*, [1971] IR 217, and Kelly, *Irish Constitution*, 1175–94.

[19] Thomas Derrig wrote to de Valera on 12 April 1937 expressing certain departmental concerns about Article 42, among them the question of whether Article 42.5 would provide sufficient constitutional authority for enactments such as the provisions of the Children's Act, 1929 (which allowed children to be sent to an Industrial School on the grounds of their parents' poverty. See document no. 138.) These fears were subsequently realised by decisions such as *In re Doyle*, Supreme Court, 21 December 1955. Here the Court held that s.10 of the Children's Act, 1941 (which allowed a Court to send a child to an industrial school where the parents were unable to support it) was invalid having regard to Article 42.1 and was not saved by reference to Article 42.5.

Of course, in line with the recommendations of the 1934 Committee, the obligation on the State previously contained in Article 10 of the 1922 Constitution had been changed in the new Article 42.4 from 'provide' free primary education to 'provide for' free primary education. The Department of Finance

constitutionality of the Land Commission;[20] by the Department of Local Government regarding aspects of Article 34;[21] by the Registrar of Marriages about aspects of Article 44;[22] and by the Revenue Commissioners about aspects of Articles 34 and 37.[23]

[19] *contd.* in their observations on the second revise (17 April 1937—see document no. 154) noted with satisfaction that the obligation contained in Article 42.4 had been somewhat diluted. McElligott nevertheless expressed concern that it was 'still open to the interpretation it places on the State an obligation to provide free books, etc., for children in primary schools'. (The Department of Lands expressed a similar concern lest Article 42.4 might impose additional financial obligations regarding the construction and maintenance of school buildings.) But while these precise concerns have not (at least to date) been shown to be well-founded, nevertheless the gist of Finance's fears—namely, that Article 42.4 would be interpreted in unexpected ways so as to place a heavy financial burden on the State—have been surely borne out by a series of remarkable decisions dealing with disadvantaged children. In *FN v. Minister for Education*, [1995] 1 IR 409, Justice Geoghegan held that the State's obligations under Article 42.5 meant that it was required 'as soon as reasonably practicable' to make 'suitable arrangements of containment with treatment' for the applicant, a young boy with severe behavioural problems. This was followed in quick succession by cases such as *DB v. Minister for Justice*, [1999] 1 IR 29; *Sinnott v. Minister for Education*, [2001] 2 IR 545); *TD v. Minister for Education*, [2001] 4 IR 259; *O'Carolan v. Minister for Education and Science*, [2005] IEHC, 296; *O'C v. Minister for Education and Science*, [2007] IEHC, 170 (where issues concerning the extent of the State's obligations to cater for children with special needs were discussed at length). It is a fair surmise that McElligott—whose major objective was to minimise the 'heavier bill presented by the new Constitution to the taxpayer'—would not have been pleased with all of these developments. At the same time, decisions such as *TD* demonstrated a judicial willingness to defer to executive decisions with financial implications and it is fair to say that the Supreme Court's reasoning in cases such as *TD* would have very much been to McElligott's liking.

[20] Similar concerns were expressed by the Department of Finance in their comments of 24 April 1937 on the third revise:

> No change has been made to meet the criticism that the use of compulsory powers of acquisition of property might be questioned under the section. Possibly the section is to be interpreted as merely prohibiting the abolition of the rights of property in general, but, as it stands, it seems to be capable of being applied to any particular act of expropriation, of the kind, for instance, being carried out every other day in the Land Commission. Those acts can hardly be called 'delimitations' of the exercise of the right of private property and are therefore not covered by [Article 42.1.2°] (see document no. 158).

It may be noted, however, that in *Fisher v. Irish Land Commission*, [1948] IR 3, the plaintiff conceded that property could be expropriated for public purposes, in this instance, the distribution of lands to necessitous farmers. The constitutionality of section 39 of the Land Act, 1939 was upheld, with Chief Justice Maguire observing tersely that it was not contested that the Legislature 'has the power to expropriate owners so as to make land available for public purposes'.

[21] In a memorandum dated 22 March 1937 the Department expressed concerns about Article 41: 'It is important that the existing powers of Local Bodies to acquire private rights to property for public purposes should not be weakened'. See document no. 99.

[22] In a memorandum dated 13 May 1937 the Assistant Registrar General drew attention to the fact that the Marriage Acts (which prescribed different rules for marriages depending on the religious denomination of the celebrants) appeared to be inconsistent with the non-discrimination provisions contained in Article 44.2.3° (see document no. 185). While similar arguments have been advanced by other commentators (see, for example, Kelly, *Irish Constitution*, 2068), this point does not yet appear to have been litigated. However, in the light of cases dealing with Article 44.2.3° religious discrimination (such as, *M. v. An Bord Uchtála*, [1975] IR 81) it is hard to see how, given a suitable case, such a challenge might not succeed.

[23] In a memorandum dated 7 April 1937 the Revenue Commissioners expressed concern lest Article 34.3.1° (which vests the High Court with a full original jurisdiction to determine all matters and questions, whether law or fact) might be interpreted as conferring a right of appeal on questions of fact from decisions of the Special Commissioners (now Appeal Commissioners) for Income Tax. They were also concerned that the limitation contained in Article 37, confining the vesting of limited judicial functions to non-judicial personages to civil matters only, might affect aspects of tax collection and revenue penalties. They accordingly suggested that it might be desirable if the reference to 'matters other than criminal matters' were to be deleted (see document no. 126). This memorandum presciently anticipated arguments which were subsequently to be advanced in cases such as *Melling v. O Mathghamhna*, [1962] IR 1, and *McLoughlin v. Tuite*, [1989] IR 82.

While the drafting committee sought to respond to these concerns by, for example, seeking advice from the Attorney General's Office on some of the issues raised,[24] the fundamental objection on the part of many Departments—concern that they would not be able to live up to the new Constitution's new guarantees and the consequential possibilities for judicial review—were, for the most part, simply brushed aside. Thus, in a letter dated 13 April 1937 enclosing the Department of Justice's response to the second revise Roche urged McDunphy to think again about the entire project.[25] Not surprisingly, therefore, the Departmental submission of the same date commenced with the following frank statement:

> Generally the Department [of Justice] felt that the draft Constitution went too much into detail, whereas the Department's feeling is that the shorter and more general the Constitution is the less likely it is that the maintenance of law and order will be impeded by limitations on the power of the Dáil and by conflicts between the judiciary and the executive. The Departmental view on these particular matters and on the general principle remains unchanged, but presumably a decision has been taken in favour of the opposite point of view and there is nothing to be gained by re-opening the matter.

It will be seen from these comments that Roche evidently considered that the drafting committee was so determined to enshrine the system of judicial review of legislation coupled with fundamental rights guarantees that further resistance was futile. It will be seen, therefore, from the general departmental reaction that the key Departments—Finance, Justice and, not least, that of the President of the Executive Council—realised at an early stage the potential importance of the fundamental rights provisions in general and of judicial review of legislation in particular. The Department of Justice had, through Roche, argued

[24] In a memorandum prepared by Philip O'Donoghue on 26 May 1937, the Attorney General's office sought to reassure the Revenue Commissioners with regard to Articles 34 and 37. O'Donoghue argued that it was necessary for Article 37 to permit the delegation of certain limited judicial functions to non-judicial personages:

> It is absolutely necessary in order to give effect to much of our present day legislation that the Commissioners in the Land Commission, the Minister for Industry and Commerce, County Registrars, Referees (to mention but a few) shall be entitled validly to carry out certain functions of a judicial or quasi-judicial kind. While persons affected by such decisions are not debarred from bringing proceedings in the courts [to challenge such decisions on vires grounds], Article 37 merely attempts to establish that the rulings of such quasi-judicial bodies shall not be upset on purely technical grounds, namely that they were not judges. This is mischievous. (See document no. 206).

[25] See document no. 140.

strongly against the entire project. If, therefore, de Valera had not intended to give such a prominent role to the courts in relation to these matters, it cannot be said that he had not received adequate advance warning about the direction which the draft Constitution might have been taking.

Some Specific Constitutional Provisions

This point is also borne out by a more detailed examination of a number of key constitutional provisions.

Article 15.2.1°

Article 15.2.1°. provides that: 'The sole and exclusive power of making laws for the State is hereby vested in the Oireachtas: no other legislative authority has power to make laws for the State.' The object of this provision is generally regarded as being to declare in emphatic terms the legislative independence of the Oireachtas and to guard against any suggestion that the Westminster Parliament might enjoy any residual legislative authority.[26] Of course, in modern times, this provision has assumed enormous importance since it is the very mechanism whereby the courts ensure that the Oireachtas has not abdicated its law-making powers to the executive, although, of course, the force of this provision has been diluted considerably given the huge volume of legislation which either derives from or gives effect to European Union obligations. But here again doubts have been expressed as to whether the drafters ever intended that Article 15.2.1° should be used in this way. As Justice Ronan Keane said in *Laurentiu v. Minister for Justice*:

> Historically, this article can be seen as an uncompromising reassertion of the freedom from legislative control by the Imperial Parliament at Westminster of the new State. But it is also an essential component in the tripartite separation of powers which is also the most important feature of our

[26] Article 12 of the Irish Free State Constitution had provided that: 'The sole and exclusive power of making laws for the peace, order and good government of the Irish Free State (Saorstát Éireann) is vested in the Oireachtas'.

But, of course, that Oireachtas was subject to the legislative shackles which had been imposed by section 2 of the Constitution of the Irish Free State (Saorstát Éireann) Act, 1922 (which gave the Treaty the superior force of law) and it might be argued that the Oireachtas only acquired full legislative independence with the passing of the Statute of Westminster 1931. D.G. Morgan has noted that the 'peace, order and good government' formula was:

> Typically used in constitutions for 'dominions' at a time when this expression was current (see, e.g., South African Act, 1909, s.59) or colonies. However, in spite of this unwelcome association, the expression seems not to have indicated any substantial curtailment of legislative power, see Roberts-Wray, *Commonwealth and Colonial Law* (1966), 369–70; D.G. Morgan, *The Separation of Powers in the Irish Constitution* (Dublin, 1997), 262–3.

> constitutional architecture which is enshrined in general terms in Article 6.[27]

D.G. Morgan has very helpfully outlined the background to the drafting of Article 15.2.1° and has presented impressive evidence that the drafters were principally concerned with potential interference by the Westminster Parliament:

> However, there is good historic evidence that the principal—and probably the only—body which the Founding Fathers had in mind, in 1922 and again in 1937, was the former colonial power, in particular the Imperial Parliament at Westminster...Nor, seen with the eye of the time, was there anything strange in this pre-occupation. The Imperial Conferences of 1926 and 1930 and the Statute of Westminster were still in the future and the Imperial Parliament retained the power (substantially restricted, by convention only) to legislate for the dominions. And writing in the 1930s, Dr Kohn and Professor Mansergh each accept, in the most matter-of-fact way, that the provision is directed against the supposed power of the British Parliament to super-legislate over the Dominion Parliaments. Likewise in the future, was the fear of delegated legislation, popularised by Chief Justice Hewart in 1929.[28]

Morgan continued by observing with regard to Article 15.2.1°:

> This shows two changes in comparison with its precursor in the 1922 Constitution. First, the formula 'for the peace, order and good government' was dropped...Secondly, another part was added on to the provision, namely: 'no other legislative authority.' Although this matter was not discussed by the [Dáil] of 1937, it seems likely that this additional part was designed to bar the door even more strongly (albeit at the cost of repetition) against the Imperial Parliament: for the phrase 'other legislative authority' is surely more apt to refer to the Westminster Parliament than the Irish Minister for (say) Agriculture.[29]

There can be no doubt whatever but these considerations were uppermost in the minds of the drafters, but the contemporary

[27] [1999] 4 IR 26, 83.
[28] Morgan, *Separation of Powers*, 262–3.
[29] Morgan, *Separation of Powers*. 262.

documentation demonstrates that these were not the only considerations. The issue of the potential relevance of Article 15.2.1° to statutory instruments was first raised by Gavan Duffy in his notes of 11 April 1937:

> If the Oireachtas has the sole and exclusive power to make laws, what of statutory rules and orders and by-laws which, if they are not 'laws' are waste paper? Article 50 presumably means to continue them as 'laws' in force. It seems to follow that Art. 15 must say that nothing therein contained shall prevent the delegation of legislative powers by the Oireachtas for the purpose of carrying its laws into effect.[30]

These comments were transmitted to the drafting committee and O'Donoghue argued trenchantly in response:

> 1. It has been suggested that Article 15.2 is deficient in omitting to refer to Statutory Rules and Orders. This Article is drawn in the same terms as the corresponding Article 12 of the existing Constitution. No difficulty or inconvenience has been caused under the present Constitution by reason of the absence of any saving provision for Statutory Rules and Orders. I am definitely of opinion that the present Article 15 is completely satisfactory in this regard and that no reference should be made to any Statutory Rules or Orders.
> 2. If any saving clause is added to this Article it must take away from the sole and exclusive powers vested in the Oireachtas. In other words, [it would] lend support to the view that Ministers and Departments can also legislate in respect of certain matters. I submit that this would be mischievous and I would call attention to the fact that, largely through the vigilance of the Parliamentary Draftsman, the criticism of legislating by Order is much less in volume than in Great Britain where the Lord Chief Justice frequently calls attention to the pernicious tendency of delegated legislation.
> 3. Statutory Rules and Orders, as the title suggests, are intimately related with legislative enactments. They are considered part of the law and have the force of law but

[30] See document no. 134.

alone do not constitute legislation. They must always be referred back to the enabling statute under which they are made. Very little consideration will indicate the abuses which would grow up if the legislature contented itself with enacting loose and indefinite principles adding that the Minister could give effect to such principles by rules and regulations.

4. The principles of legislation must be definitely enacted in the statute. Statutory Rules and Orders may prescribe such matters as the form, time and manner of carrying into effect the objects of the statute but any such rule which would seek to depart from the scope of the statute, impose new obligations or confer new rights, would be clearly *ultra vires* under the statute and could properly be set aside by the Courts. This position is clearly understood by lawyers and, in my opinion, it is a position that should be strenuously defended.[31]
5. It will be said that the only object of mentioning Statutory Rules and Orders in the new Article will be to give them a claim to be considered legislation. As I have said, alone they do not constitute legislation and cannot be considered apart from the statutes under which they are derived. It is definitely in the public interest that the legislature should make itself explicit and clear in its enactments and that no encouragement should be given to slovenly or imperfect statutory provisions while relying on Statutory Rules and Orders to complete what the legislature itself should have done.[32]

This drew the following response from Patrick Lynch on 16 April:

> I have carefully considered this question, and thoroughly agree with the opinions expressed in the above minute. The suggestion that to have an addition to Article 15.2 in the terms indicated must have been made under a misapprehension. Statutory Rules and Orders, as the term itself shows, must be something necessary to enable the carrying out of the statute and for that purpose must be in conformity with it strictly and literally. A statement in a

[31] This principle is reflected in the key decisions of the Supreme Court on this point: *City View Press v. AnCO*, [1980] IR 381; *Laurentiu v. Minister for Justice, Equality and Law Reform*, [1999] 4 IR 1; *Leontjava v. Director of Public Prosecutions*, [2004] 1 IR 534.
[32] See document no. 150.

> statute, and particularly in an Article of the Constitution, that legislation should be subject to, or varied or read subject to, Statutory Rules and Orders to be made by some other person or body than the legislature, is a contradiction of terms. It would certainly be not permitted to be incorporated in any piece of considered legislation by anyone who has had to study the subject. I am not aware that the Article in the existing Constitution proved to be in any way at variance with the opinion I have expressed.

McDunphy noted on the margin of Gavan Duffy's comments that 'Mr Matheson is satisfied that there is no point in [Gavan Duffy's argument].'

Article 15.4
Article 15.4 provides:

> 1. The Oireachtas shall not enact any law which is in any respect repugnant to this Constitution or any provision thereof.
> 2. Every law enacted by the Oireachtas which is in any respect repugnant to this Constitution or to any provision thereof shall, but to the extent only of such repugnancy, be invalid.

Article 15.4 was an innovation and it clearly imposes an obligation on the Oireachtas to take strict cognisance of the limitations on its legislative power imposed by the Constitution. Not surprisingly, the courts have fastened on to this provision in order to justify the general presumption of constitutionality of an Act of the Oireachtas:

> The presumption of constitutionality which operates in favour of an Act of the Oireachtas is based on the presumption [and is] an expression of the 'respect which one great organ of State owes to another' that the Oireachtas has obeyed the injunction of Article 15.4.1°.[33]

Article 15.4.1° has also been expressly cited by way of justification for the exercise of the powers of judicial review.[34] But it is quite clear that de Valera's own Department had reflected on the possible implications of this provision at drafting stage:

[33] Kelly, *Irish Constitution*, 269. The internal quotation is taken from the judgment of Justice O'Byrne in *Buckley v. Attorney General*, [1950] IR 67, 80.
[34] See *National Union of Railwaymen v. Sullivan*, [1947] IR 77, 100, per Justice Murnaghan; *Buckley v. Attorney General*, [1950] IR 67, 83, per Justice O'Byrne.

> A Bill containing provisions for the amendment of the Constitution is, until it becomes law, repugnant to the Constitution and the question might be considered whether this section requires any amendment in the light of this consideration.[35]

Although no action was taken on foot of this suggestion, it was not until some sixty years later that the issue was ultimately disposed of with the Supreme Court's ruling in *Riordan v. An Taoiseach* (*No.1*)[36] to the effect that a Bill to amend the Constitution was not a 'law' for the purpose of Article 15.4.1°. While the issue, is perhaps, a minor one, it provides further evidence of the extent to which these provisions were carefully examined and the foresightedness of the drafting team.

Article 26 and the plan for a Constitutional Court

The other innovation as far as the power of judicial review is concerned was contained in Article 26. This provides that the President, following consultation with the Council of State, may refer Bills prior to signature to the Supreme Court for adjudication as to their constitutionality.[37] It is worth spending some time examining the drafting of Article 26, since this provision was at the heart of the drafters' plans for judicial review of legislation. As we have already seen, the 1934 Constitution Review Committee could not agree on whether the functions of the ordinary courts in constitutional matters should be transferred to a special Constitutional Court.[38] The very first draft heads of a new Constitution submitted by John Hearne on 17 May 1935 had envisaged that the power of judicial review of legislation would continue to be vested in the High Court. However, on 10 December 1935, Hearne had prepared

[35] See document no. 105.

[36] In *Riordan v. An Taoiseach* (*No. 1*), [1999] 4 IR 325, the plaintiff claimed that the 15th Amendment of the Constitution Act, 1995 was unconstitutional, but Justice Barrington held (339–40) that an Act to amend the Constitution, duly passed, was not a 'law' for the purposes of Article 15.4 and, by extension, it also would seem that it is not a 'law' for the purpose of Article 34.3.2°:

> There can be no question of a constitutional amendment properly placed before the people and approved by them being itself unconstitutional. That is why the President has no power to refer to the Supreme Court a Bill containing a proposal to amend the Constitution for an opinion on its constitutionality. A proposed amendment to the Constitution will usually be designed to change something in the Constitution and will, therefore, until enacted, be inconsistent with the existing text of the Constitution, but, once approved by the People under Article 46 and promulgated by the President as law, it will form part of the Constitution and cannot be attacked as unconstitutional…Such 'law' is in a totally different position from the 'law' referred to in Article 15.4 of the Constitution which refers only to a law 'enacted by the Constitution'.

[37] However, Money Bills, Bills the time for which have been abridged by the Senate and Bills to amend the Constitution are excluded from the scope of Article 26. For the Article 26 procedure see Kelly, *Irish Constitution*, 398–417; Casey, *Constitutional Law in Ireland*, 332–9.

[38] See document no. 27.

a memorandum on the functions of Constitutional Courts in other countries and this memorandum was seen immediately by de Valera.[39] While the memorandum was purely factual, Hearne's introductory minute is nonetheless of interest:

> I send you herewith the accompanying notes on the Constitutions of Czechoslovakia, Austria, Spain, Poland, the United States and France showing the machinery established to determine the validity of laws and to resolve, e.g., conflicts between the administrative authorities and the Courts. It will be observed that in only three of those Constitutions is there provision for a Constitutional Court so called.[40]
>
> I enclose a copy of an extract (bearing on the subject) from the Report of the Constitution Committee which reported on 3 July 1934.

Some nine months later on 20 August 1936 Hearne submitted what he described as a 'Plan of Fundamental Constitutional Law and Parliamentary Draft'. These draft heads sketched out the provisions relating to the courts as follows:

> Article 31. Establishment of the Constitutional Court.
>
> Article 32. Jurisdiction.
>
> Article 33. Continuance of existing Courts of First Instance and Court of Final Appeal.

The latest hint of this thinking may be found in the draft of 2 January 1937, where the draft Article 38.4 provided in relevant part that:

> The Supreme Court shall have *full original* jurisdiction *in and power* to determine questions *as to* the validity of any law having regard to the provisions of this Constitution.[41]

The draft Article 39 (the equivalent of the present Article 36) provided that, subject to the foregoing provisions of the Constitution relating to the courts, the following matters might be regulated by law, including: '(c) the procedure of the Courts of *Éire*, including the Constitutional Court.' A line was crossed through these words by Hearne and this

[39] The Assistant Secretary minuted to de Valera: 'Herewith memorandum on Constitutional Courts in other countries which you asked for this morning' (see document no. 43).
[40] The three countries in question were Czechoslovakia, Austria and Spain.
[41] UCDA, P150/2387. The italicised words were written by hand by Hearne.

appears to be the last reference to a Constitutional Court in any of the drafts. At this stage, however, it was considered that the Supreme Court would perform the work of a Constitutional Court in that it was to be given exclusive jurisdiction to determine the constitutionality of laws. Side by side with this, Hearne's first drafts of Article 26 bore a striking similarity in both style and structure to that provision as it was ultimately enacted. There were, however, some very important differences. Hearne's first draft envisaged that the President would refer the Bill to the Supreme Court upon the petition of two-fifths of the members of the Dáil or a majority of the Seanad. While the petitioners were required to state the ground or grounds of alleged unconstitutionality on which the petition was based, the President was given no independent discretion in the matter, since the draft Article 26.4 provided that:

> 4. Upon receipt of a petition addressed to him under this Article the President shall forthwith refer the question raised by the petition to the Supreme Court for an advisory opinion thereon.

The draft Article 26.5 also envisaged that the Supreme Court would give what was described as an 'advisory opinion' not later 'than seven days after the date of such reference'. This draft also provided for the 'one judgment' rule on Article 26 references. By the date of the fourth (pre-publication) draft of the Constitution—prepared by Hearne on 3 February 1937—Article 26 was even closer to its ultimate form in that the discretion as to the reference was now vested in the President following consultation with the Council of State.[42]

The new Article prompted a number of different observations from those to whom the draft was shown. The Parliamentary Draftsman, Arthur Matheson, had been asked to review the existing drafts 'with a view to seeing whether any provision could be shortened by leaving the subject-matter to be dealt with by ordinary law' and Article 26 was among those provisions which Matheson had sought to shorten.[43] Matheson's draft sought to enable provision to be made by legislation subsequently enacted by the Oireachtas for the reference of Bills to the Supreme Court and, in the end, this particular draft was not adopted. Several suggestions of Matheson regarding the Article 26 procedure did, however, prove to be influential. In a letter of 4 March 1937 to de Valera, Matheson queried whether: 'the expression "advisory opinion" should be retained or should be deleted in favour of the word "decision" or the

[42] UCDA, P150/2387. Numbered as Article 21 in this draft.
[43] See document no. 82.

expression "advisory decision".'[44] This wording is now reflected in the provisions of Article 26 itself which refers to the 'decision' of the Supreme Court, i.e., not simply non-binding advice from the Court to the President.

By early March 1937 the draft of Article 26 envisaged that at that stage the Supreme Court would form an opinion as to the constitutionality of the Bill. Matheson noted that:

> In sub-article 5, is the Court entitled to hear argument, and, if so, argument by whom? If the Court is entitled to hear argument, then the bill is correctly stated to be referred to 'the Court'; but if the Court is to arrive at a decision in private, then the bill should be stated to be referred to 'such of the judges of the Supreme Court as are able to act', and subsequent references should be to 'the judges and not to 'the Court'.[45]

Article 26.2.1° now requires the Court to arrive at its decision having heard arguments 'by or on behalf of the Attorney General and by counsel assigned by the Court' and this change appears to have been prompted by Matheson's comments. The related issue as to the number of judges who might sit on Article 26 was queried by Finance in their comments on the Second Revise in mid-April, but this was firmly rebuffed by McDunphy who noted in handwriting on the submission: 'This has been carefully considered and decided on. The Court must be a court of five judges.'[46]

Comments were also received from Conor Maguire, George Gavan Duffy and Gerald Fitzgibbon on the subject of Article 26. Maguire made two interesting points, the first of which appeared to raise doubts about the desirability of this provision:

> This Article may have the effect of placing the Court in conflict with the Dáil. The parties before the Court will in practice be (on the one side) the President and Council of State and on the other the Dáil.

[44] See document no. 82.

[45] McDunphy noted in his observations that, having spoken to de Valera, it was agreed that Article 26 should be amended so that the 'Attorney General should be entitled to be heard by the Court' (see document no. 105).

[46] See document no. 154. In a letter which Hearne wrote to Michael Rynne (his successor as Legal Adviser in the Department of External Affairs and who was a member of the 1940 Constitution Review Committee) on 4 May 1940, NAI, DT S10299, he explained that the object of the five judge requirement was to ensure that there 'is little likelihood...of a Supreme Court which had decided, on a reference to them under Article 26, that a Bill is valid, holding that the same Bill when enacted into law is invalid'. Article 34.3.3° (inserted by the Second Amendment of the Constitution Act, 1941) copper-fastens this by providing for an immunity from subsequent constitutional challenge in respect of a Bill the constitutionality of which has been upheld by the Supreme Court on an Article 26 reference.

> If the Article is to stand, consideration might be given to providing for a presumption of constitutionality so as to put the onus on the Counsel who alleges unconstitutionality. Is there not a danger in asking the Court to decide a matter around which fierce controversy will have raged at a moment when the controversy will probably be at fever heat?[47]

These comments have found echoes in subsequent controversies. Thus, in the first two Article 26 references in 1940[48] and 1943[49]—which took place with Chief Justice Timothy Sullivan presiding in the Supreme Court—counsel on behalf of the Attorney General supporting the Bill went first and with counsel appointed to oppose the Bill replying. This practice—appropriate to the order followed if a law had been found to be unconstitutional in the High Court—suggested that the very fact that the Bill had been referred by the President under Article 26 was sufficient to create an aura of unconstitutionality. Interestingly, the practice was discontinued during the course of the third Article 26 reference in 1961, *Re Article 26 and the Electoral (Amendment) Bill*[50] when the Supreme Court directed that the ordinary practice should prevail and counsel opposing the Bill should proceed first.[51] It may be just co-incidental that Chief Justice Conor Maguire (as he had by this stage become) was presiding in the Supreme Court for this reference, but the change in practice was certainly consistent with the expression of his views some twenty-four years earlier. Moreover, despite frequent attempts to persuade the Supreme Court to the contrary, it has consistently adopted

[47] Conor Maguire to Eamon de Valera, 23 March 1937, UCDA, P150/2416; Similar concerns were expressed by Deputy John A. Costello in an article written in the *Irish Independent*, 5 May 1937:

> The system which it is proposed to set up conferring consultative jurisdiction on the Supreme Court at the instance solely of the President is a novel one and which, it is imagined, may not commend itself to the judicial mentality which notoriously dislikes being consulted on hypothetical questions apart from concrete cases or past realities.
>
> The President may refer a Bill to the Supreme Court at the public expense in the teeth of the wishes of the Prime Minister or of the Dáil. Apart from the consideration of hypothetical cases being considered by the courts, it is not easy to see the justification for these proposals. It is not easy to see the necessity for allowing the President so to involve the public in expense at his own particular will and fancy.

[48] *Re Article 26 and the Offences against the State (Amendment) Bill, 1940*, [1940] IR 470. For a detailed discussion, see Chapter XIV below.

[49] *Re Article 26 and the School Attendance Bill, 1942*, [1943] IR 334.

[50] [1961] IR 169.

[51] Chief Justice Maguire noted:

> Although in the two earlier cases of a reference of a Bill to the Court under the Article counsel for the Attorney General opened the argument, it was agreed by counsel that owing to the nature of the provisions contained in this Bill it would be more convenient if counsel assigned by the Court should open the argument and state the grounds on which it would be submitted that the Bill was repugnant to the Constitution. This procedure was approved by the Court. [1961] IR 179.

the view that a Bill passed by the Houses of the Oireachtas enjoys the presumption of constitutionality.[52]

The other comment made by Maguire was an immensely practical one: 'seven days is much too short a time in which to obtain a considered decision on such an important question. It should *at least* be one month.'[53] This suggestion was acted upon and in the draft Constitution as published the time period was extended to thirty days. But even this was considered by some to be too short and on the day of publication of the draft Constitution, Fitzgibbon wrote to de Valera with cogent arguments regarding the difficulties which even the thirty-day time limit might involve:

> It will be necessary to take steps to get together a Court of five judges to hear the question. The question must be referred within four days of the passing of the Bill. The reference might be at a moment when the judges were on Circuit under the Courts of Justice Act. There might be delay in assembling five judges to hear the case. In any event, the Attorney General must make up his case, and still more, the Court at its first sitting might find it necessary to assign counsel to argue against the Attorney General, as provided by the Article itself. Such counsel must have some reasonable time to make up an argument in a case which would be, in the nature of things, one of the first importance, and there is no telling how long the argument might take.
>
> I fully realise the vital importance of an early decision, and I am profoundly conscious of the dissatisfaction which has been occasioned, on at least two occasions, by long delays on the part of the Supreme Court in delivering their judgment in important cases,[54] and I have no objection to offer to a proposal that judgment should be given within

[52] See *Re Article 26 and the Criminal Law (Jurisdiction) Bill 1975*, [1977] IR 129; *Re Matrimonial Homes Bill 1993*, [1994] 1 IR 305, and *Re Article 26 and the Illegal Immigrants (Trafficking) Bill 1999*, [2000] 2 IR 362. In the latter case the Court expressly rejected the invitation to overrule its earlier decisions, with Chief Justice Ronan Keane observing that the argument that a Bill did not enjoy the presumption of constitutionality gave 'entirely insufficient weight to the fact that the President, although doubtless an integral part of the Oireachtas, plays no part whatever in the purely legislative function of the Oireachtas'.

[53] Gavan Duffy was to make a similar point as late as 11 April 1937 in his 'Notes on the Final Draft Constitution': 'The argument may be lengthy and 14 days from the close of the argument would be more satisfactory than a fixed time after the date of the reference' (see document no. 134).

[54] This is presumably a reference to the on-going Erasmus Smith Schools case, the delays in respect of which had caused the Court not a little embarrassment. The Supreme Court had heard the appeal in this matter in 1933, but no judgment had been given by the date of Chief Justice Kennedy's sudden death in December 1936. Although the Supreme Court offered to re-hear the appeal, the parties had had enough of the delays and a settlement was announced to the Supreme Court on 23 June 1937: see the *Irish Times*, 24 June 1937.

> a stated period after the arguments have concluded. The judges who have heard a case might well be directed to make up their minds within even a shorter period than one month, but I feel very strongly that injustice might be caused, and a proper consideration of an important constitutional question might be prejudiced, if a hard and fast law were to be passed that all the preliminaries and all the argument must be prepared and a decision pronounced, irrespective of the magnitude and complexity of the questions involved, within thirty days of the reference of the matter by the President, who must himself act within four days of the decision of the Oireachtas.
>
> That decision might conceivably be made shortly before Christmas, or Easter or while the courts were closed in summer, and many judges are away on vacation, and the thirty days would be running irrevocably all the time.
>
> Provide, if you will, that the question shall be referred to the Supreme Court of five judges who shall proceed to hear it *at the earliest opportunity* and shall pronounce their decision within a month, or a week, if you will, of the conclusion of the *hearing*, but modify the provision that the decision must be given, even though the case be unheard, within a month from the date of the reference.[55]

These suggestions were accepted and Article 26.2.1° now requires the Supreme Court to pronounce judgment as soon as may be, but, in any case, within sixty days from the date of the reference.[56] Even this time limit may be too onerous and the Constitution Review Group recommended in 1996 that the period be extended to ninety days.[57]

Gavan Duffy's first comments on Article 26 appear to date from the second half of March 1937. His observation was:

> It would hardly be fair for the President to ask the Court, nor practicable for the Court to answer such a question as

[55] See document no. 168, emphasis in original. De Valera replied on the same day, thanking Fitzgibbon warmly for his comments and assuring him that his observations would receive 'careful consideration'.

[56] In fact, Article 26.2.1° as originally published provided for a 30 day limit. This was changed to 60 days at Committee Stage in the Dáil following a Government amendment to this effect. As de Valera said:

> The purpose of that amendment is to give a longer time to the courts to hear a case and to arrive at a decision. It is hoped, of course, that the court will do it as soon as possible, but it has been represented to me that to fix the time that we have in the Draft as 30 days might make it difficult for the court to examine fully the questions involved, and consequently we are extending the period from 30 to 60 days, 67 *Dáil Debates*, Col. 1490 (2 June 1937).

[57] *Report of the Constitution Review Group* (Stationery Office, Dublin, 1996), 85. See www.irishconstitution.ie for this report.

> 'Can you find anything unconstitutional in this Bill?' The practical way of making the Court consultative is to enable the Government to inquire whether or not a Bill is for specified reasons, or in specified requests, unconstitutional, or to limit the inquiry to a specified clause or clauses.
>
> If this view is accepted, some re-drafting of Article [26] is necessary. I have not attempted this in the absence of more definite information as to the intention of the Article. But the objection above noted to its present form will be felt, and no doubt voiced, very strongly by lawyers. The alternative way suggested would seem to give the Government all that it really needs and to give a very useful power to consult the Court.[58]

These suggestions were echoed by the President's own comments which were made in respect of the draft of 16 March 1937:

> The President is of the opinion that where possible a definite question should be referred to the Court in each case, that is to say, that the Court should not be asked whether a Bill is unconstitutional but whether a specific provision to be specified by the President is or is not constitutional. I understand this is the view of the President of the High Court.[59]

Although McDunphy minuted that it might be best to 'leave this to practice', the drafters ultimately took note of these suggestions, since the final version of Article 26.1.1° permits the President to refer specified parts of the Bill:

> The President may, after consultation with the Council of State, refer any Bill to which this Article applies to the Supreme Court for a decision on the question as to whether such Bill or any specified provision or provisions of such Bill is or are repugnant to this Constitution or to any provision thereof.

In fact, of the fifteen Article 26 references to date, in only three cases has the President exercised the option of referring only a specified provision. This first occurred in 1943 with the reference of the School Attendance Bill, where President Hyde referred only one section of the

[58] See document no. 114.
[59] See document no. 105, observations on Article 22.

Bill for consideration by the Court.[60] President McAleese also availed of this power twice in 2000 when she referred Part V of the Planning and Development Bill 1999 and sections 5 and 10 of the Illegal Immigrants (Trafficking) Bill 1999 to the Supreme Court.

In other cases there have been clear signs of judicial unease where the entirety of very large Bills have been referred to the Court, most recently with the Employment Equality Bill, 1996, where the entirety of the Bill had been referred by the President. In its decision in that reference, *Re Article 26 and the Employment Equality Bill, 1996*, the Court was confronted with a very substantial Bill which raised a miscellany of constitutional issues.[61] The Court drew attention to these difficulties towards the start of a very long judgment:

> The form of reference in this case has raised certain practical problems for the Court...When one considers that the Bill consists of 74 sections and either amends or refers to 33 other statutes one can see that the task confronting the Court is a formidable one. The task is not made lighter by the fact that the Court is constitutionally obliged to give its decision on the Bill within 60 days of the date on which the Bill was referred to the Court by the President. Within this time the Court must assign counsel, give them time to prepare their written submissions, hold an oral hearing at which the issues are debated in open court, make its decision and deliver its judgment. It would have been possible for the President to specify some specific provision or provisions of the Bill on which she needed the Court's decision but she was not obliged to do that.[62]

To some extent, these comments may be seen as almost an implied criticism of the President for having referred the entirety of such a large Bill. But why have Presidents to date generally refrained from availing of the option to refer only a specified provision of the Bill? Two reasons may be advanced. The first is probably that it has often been felt to be impossible to isolate what may often be inter-locking statutory provisions. The second concern probably stems from the wording of Article 34.3.3°:

> No Court whatever shall have jurisdiction to question the validity of a law, or any provision of a law, the Bill for

60 [1943] IR 334.
61 [1997] 2 IR 321.
62 [1997] 2 IR 331.

> which shall have been referred to the Supreme Court by the President under Article 26 of the Constitution, or to question the validity of a provision of a law where the corresponding provision in the Bill for such law shall have been referred to the Supreme Court by the President under the said Article 26.[63]

Although it seems relatively clear from this provision that the finality attributed thereby to a finding of validity by the Supreme Court in an Article 26 reference only applies to the sections actually referred by the President, the matter is, perhaps, not completely free from doubt.

An issue which was closely related to the Article 26 jurisdiction was whether the Supreme Court should have an exclusive original jurisdiction in constitutional matters, as had been proposed by the early 1937. This prompted a very interesting submission from Nicholas Barron:

> Because the Supreme Court is granted exclusive and original jurisdiction of such a matter, the lower Court must, upon the raising of such a question, proceed according to either of the following methods:
>
> A. Refuse to determine the issue of a pending cause until the constitutionality of the law is determined by the Supreme Court.
>
> This would result in such a matter being referred first to the Supreme Court to determine the constitutional question only (because it has original jurisdiction only to determine that question and no other.) If the law is held to be constitutional it will be necessary to again refer the matter back to the Court of First Instance for a hearing on the other issues—a most expensive procedure.
>
> B. Try all other issues and deliver judgment thereon; then it would be necessary to proceed to the Supreme Court by way of a Writ of Certiorari, or some similar procedure, to determine the constitutional question.
>
> This seems to be an unnecessary division of jurisdiction, especially when an issue of patent unconstitutionality is considered. It is also a most expensive way of dealing with the problem. Both of the methods allowable under the section as it now stands

[63] As inserted by the Second Amendment of the Constitution Act, 1941.

> would act as hardships to many, especially when a law violated their constitutional rights in smaller matters.

Barron then went on to offer two alternative suggestions. The first was that where a constitutional question was raised, the Supreme Court would have jurisdiction to the exclusion of all other courts. His first alternative draft provided that:

> The Supreme Court shall have full original jurisdiction in and power, exclusive of all other courts, to determine any and all matters, civil or criminal, and any and all issues of law and fact arising therein, when a question or questions are raised in such matters as to the validity of any law having regard to the provisions of the Constitution.

He added that:

> A provision of this nature would place completely in the hands of the Supreme Court the determination of all of the issues in such a case. It would concentrate the matter in one court only.

The other alternative suggested by Barron involved a devolution of power to determine the constitutional issue to the lower courts, save that such determination would only bind the parties to the case and would not have *erga omnes* effect:

> The courts of first instance shall have jurisdiction to determine the validity of any law having regard to the provisions of the Constitution, when such validity of such law has not previously been determined by the Supreme Court, provided, however, that such a determination by a Court of First Instance shall not be generally binding, but binding only in so far as the particular matter under consideration is concerned. An appeal from such Court of First Instance direct to the Supreme Court shall be allowed on such question of the validity of a law.

Barron's commentary on this proposal is especially revealing:

> Under these provisions litigants would be facilitated in protecting their constitutional rights in petty as well as in major matters. The extent of the jurisdiction of the lower courts in such constitutional questions is limited and a decision of unconstitutionality by one of these courts

> would not invalidate the law insofar as the general public and State officials and representatives are concerned. The law would be to them a constitutional law until declared otherwise by the Supreme Court.
>
> A citizen should be entitled to full constitutional protection at all times and before all the courts. A very important part of the protective force of the fundamental law is that no statute can be passed in derogation of its provisions. A citizen should be entitled to plead the protection of the Constitution before any court in the land and in any matter no matter how unimportant.[64]

These were very sensible suggestions. While all of Hearne's initial drafts and thinking on this topic—a Constitutional Court, 'abstract' judicial review via the Article 26 procedure and an original constitutional jurisdiction for the Supreme Court—appear to have been heavily influenced by the constitutional structure in civilian countries, the vesting of an original jurisdiction in the Supreme Court would probably not have been practicable.

For a start, that Court's overall function is best discharged as an appellate court, where it reviews the legal conclusions of the High Court and lower courts on the basis of primary facts found by the court of trial. Given that at least some right of appeal is generally regarded as fundamental to the proper functioning of a legal system, it would scarcely have been ideal if the Supreme Court had operated as a court of first and last instance in constitutional matters, particularly in lengthy cases where the hearing of evidence would have been protracted.[65] Barron's views were not immediately accepted and the Constitution as originally published on 1 May 1937 vested the Supreme Court with an exclusive and original jurisdiction in constitutional matters.

This aspect of the draft was subjected to sustained criticism from the legal community. For example, in a thoughtful article written by 'A Lawyer' it was argued that:

> Most lawyers will probably agree that the Article depriving the High Court of jurisdiction to hear a case involving the constitutional validity of any law and transfer that jurisdiction solely to the Supreme Court is a grave blunder.

[64] See document no. 167.

[65] Thus, in *Ryan v. Attorney General*, [1965] IR 294, 65 days were occupied with the hearing of complex scientific evidence directed towards the issue of whether or not the fluoridation of the public water supply system violated her constitutional right to bodily integrity.

> The real value of a Court of Appeal (as the Supreme Court is) lies in the fact that it has presented to it a case by counsel who have already prepared, argued and been questioned on every aspect of it by a competent court, and that the Court of Appeal has before it also the judgment of that Court and the reasons for that judgment. With such material before it the task of the Court of Appeal is enormously lightened. Now it is proposed to deprive the Supreme Court of this material and to throw upon it the duty of hearing the case for the first and last time, and that in respect of the most onerous task of a court—namely, the determining whether or not the legislature has exceeded its powers.[66]

Writing in the same newspaper a few days later, Deputy John A. Costello also made a similar point:

> But surely it cannot have been intended by the framer of the Constitution to deprive a citizen of his right to *habeas corpus* when he is illegally detained in virtue of a law which is, or is alleged to be, unconstitutional.
>
> That, however, is the effect of the draft as it stands. A law is passed which appears to be unconstitutional, and under that law a person is deprived of his liberty. If he applies to a judge of the High Court for relief by way of *habeas corpus*, on the ground that he is illegally detained by virtue of the unconstitutional provisions of a law, the High Court judge must refuse his application until the Supreme Court has determined the question by whatever machinery may be devised to enable the Supreme Court to decide on the constitutionality or unconstitutionality of the law. In the meantime the person remains,

[66] *Irish Independent*, 3 May 1937 (see www.irishconstitution.ie). The comments of Justice O'Flaherty in *Best v. Wellcome Foundation Ltd*, [1993] 3 IR 421, illustrate this point rather well, albeit in a different context. Here the Supreme Court was asked to review on appeal an inference from a primary fact by the trial judge in a complex medical negligence case and Justice O'Flaherty's comments (485) illustrate the value of the sifting process conducted by the High Court in any complex civil action:

> In a sense we approached this case with certain advantages over the trial judge. We have had the advantage of seeing the case laid out before us in its entirety, with the findings of the trial judge in place. A number of issues debated at the trial have disappeared from the scene before us…It is true that the scientific evidence was traversed extensively once more but while the trial judge had to grapple with it as it emerged in a raw condition it was well-matured when it came before us. The trial judge had to wrestle with a welter of documents in the course of the case and while they did not diminish before us they appeared well-contained and ordered. At the end of the day we were left in a position where the spotlight was allowed to shine brightly on the single, great issue in the case: the credibility of the [plaintiffs].

> perhaps illegally and unconstitutionally, deprived of his liberty.[67]

These were telling criticisms of an innovative proposal. At all events, in response to opposition suggestions, the Government agreed to an amendment at the Committee Stage of the Dáil debates on the Constitution whereby the power was transferred to the High Court with a right of appeal to the Supreme Court.[68]

The key point in all of this is that whatever the merits and demerits of the structure of judicial review which the drafters were considering (such as a Constitutional Court, the Article 26 procedure and the plan for an exclusive constitutional jurisdiction for the Supreme Court), this entire protracted debate would surely have been an empty exercise had not the drafters been serious about the potential impact of judicial review of legislation.

Article 40.3.1° and Article 40.3.2°

The personal rights provisions contained in Article 40.3 are probably the most important single clauses in the entire Constitution.[69] As we have already noted, much of modern constitutional law traces its origins to the decision of Justice Kenny in *Ryan v. Attorney General* to the effect that Article 40.3.1° protected fundamental rights not expressly enumerated elsewhere in the Constitution. In recent times, the correctness of this decision and the very legitimacy of the jurisprudence which it has subsequently engendered has been a matter for fervent debate.[70]

[67] *Irish Independent*, 6 May 1937.

[68] The following exchange took place between de Valera and Professor O'Sullivan at the Committee Stage:

> **Eamon de Valera (Fianna Fáil):** There is something to be said for that inasmuch as you have the same court dealing with constitutional matters all the time.
>
> **Professor John Marcus O'Sullivan (Fine Gael):** Unless a judge of the High Court can take into account the constitutionality of a law, a citizen of this State who was arrested under a law the constitutionality of which he contested, could not apply to a judge of the High Court for a *habeas corpus*...
>
> **Eamon de Valera (Fianna Fáil):** That was not the point on which we were deciding...We were dealing with the general question as whether it is better that the High Court should have the initial jurisdiction as regards the constitutionality of laws, with an appeal to the Supreme Court, or whether you should have the Supreme Court being the first court to deal with it and have no further appeal. Much could be said on both sides and it was not easy to make up one's mind as to which was the better. The point brought out by the Deputy is undoubtedly an extra reason why it is well to have the High Court having the original jurisdiction in that case. 68 *Dáil Debates*, Cols 1492–5 (12 June 1937).

[69] During the drafting of the Constitution, Article 40.3 was not assigned that number until the draft Constitution was submitted to the Dáil. The various numbers assigned to the article prior to this were as follows: 38.2 in the drafts of 10 and 16 March; omitted from the 1st Revise (1 April); 41.3 in the 2nd Revise (10 April); 39.3 in the 3rd and 4th Revises (24 and 26 April).

[70] For this debate, see Gerard Quinn, 'Reflections on the Legitimacy of Judicial Activism in the Field of Constitutional Law', in *Dlí*, 29 (1989); Gerard Hogan, 'Constitutional Interpretation' in Frank Litton (ed.), *The Constitution of Ireland, 1937–1987* (Dublin, 1988), 173–91; Gerard Hogan, 'Unenumerated Personal Rights: Ryan's Case Re-evaluated', in *Irish Jurist*, 25–7 (1990–2), 95; Richard Humphreys, 'Constitutional Interpretation', in *Dublin University Law Journal*, 59 (1993), 15; Humphreys, 'Interpreting Natural Rights' in *Irish Jurist*, 28–30 (1993–5), 221; A. Kavanagh, 'The Quest for Legitimacy in Constitutional Interpretation', in *Irish Jurist*, 32 (1997), 185.

What, therefore, do the drafting papers tell us about this debate? There appears to have been no counterpart to Article 40.3 in Hearne's original 1935 draft or in the drafts from the autumn of 1936. However, by mid-February 1937, the fourth pre-publication draft was ready. At this stage, the key provisions of the draft Article 38 (now Article 40) read as follows:

> 1. The State guarantees to respect and defend the personal rights of each citizen [including] those that are inalienable, indefeasible and antecedent to positive law, as well as those that have been by law granted and defined. Accordingly, the State shall take all necessary measures to prevent abuses, enforce respect for social order and punish offenders against its laws.

A line was then drawn through the first sentence and a note from Hearne read as follows: 'The State guarantees to respect, defend and vindicate the personal rights of each citizen.'[71]

This re-casting of the language was of some importance and perhaps even Hearne probably did not then appreciate its potential significance. It is particularly unfortunate that there appears to have been no memorandum prepared by him which sought to explain the objectives of this provision. This omission notwithstanding, this re-drafting would nevertheless seem to provide some evidence that the personal rights referred to in Article 40.3.1° had not been not intended—by Hearne, at least—to be confined to those rights actually enumerated elsewhere in the Constitution. It is clear from the language of the earlier draft (with its reference to the protection of rights which were expressed to be 'inalienable, indefeasible and antecedent to positive law', as well as those rights 'that have been by law granted and defined') that it was here intended to protect all rights deemed to be sufficiently fundamental by the courts, irrespective of whether such rights were elsewhere expressly enumerated in the Constitution. It is perhaps also noteworthy that an extended dictionary definition of the word 'vindicate'—a vital word which is used in both Article 40.3.1° and Article 40.3.2°—was reproduced in printed form for de Valera's attention.[72] The clear

[71] A line was also drawn through the word 'abuses' and an accompanying note from Hearne in the margin: 'any violation of these rights' ('Article 38—Personal Rights and Social Policy', UCDA, P150/2387).

[72] See document no. 79. By what can only be described as a remarkable coincidence, in *Grant v. Roche Products* [2008] 4 IR 679 [2008] IIESC 35, the Supreme Court had recourse to the very same Oxford English Dictionary definition (albeit in a later version) of the word 'vindicate' in construing the obligations of the State under Article 40.3.2°, with Justice Hardiman observing:

> It will first be noted that the obligation to 'vindicate' the life of the citizen arises 'in the case of injustice done'. Accordingly, the word 'vindicate' has to be construed if possible in a manner

inference here is that the drafters regarded the actual language of Article 40.3 as being at least potentially significant.

In addition, the draft Article 40.3.2° (then numbered Article 38.4) provided that:

> The State guarantees to protect, as best it may, from unjust attack, and, in the case of injustice done, to vindicate, the person, life and good name of its citizens and their right of ownership.

The only further contemporary insight into the thinking of the drafters may be gleaned from the reaction of the various Departments to these provisions. Not surprisingly, this reaction was generally adverse. While the precise future significance of these provisions may not have been identified by many of the departmental commentators, their unease about the potential implications was palpable. From the Department of Justice, Roche characteristically expressed unhappiness about the breadth of the guarantees contained in Article 40.3.2°:

> The guarantees given in section 2 of the Article are very widely worded and may have unexpected results. For example, under [Article 40.2.3°], if a man is slandered, is the State really bound to vindicate his good name? Is that guarantee carried out by the existing device of providing a Court in which he can, at his own risk, sue his slanderer?[73]

Finance had similar objections. McElligott queried whether Article 40.3.2° could be interpreted:

> to oblige the State to take the initiative in libel actions, proceedings for the recovery of debts, and actions for damages in cases of personal injury? This might be a straining of the sense, but greater clarity would be desirable.

[72] *contd.* which connotes an appropriate response to an 'injustice'. That injustice is alleged to be the bringing about of the death of the deceased by an act of 'wrongdoing', to quote the statutory phrase. There is in fact no difficulty in so construing the term, if one has regard to the ordinary and natural meaning of the word 'vindicate' as set out in the Oxford English dictionary. There, the word, which is a transitive verb, is said to derive from the Latin *vindicare,* which is defined as meaning to claim, to set free, to punish, or to avenge. The English term is given the following meanings:

- avenge, revenge;
- take revenge (on a person) for a wrong;
- claim, assert, or establish the possibility of;
- clear of blame, justify by evidence or argument;
- establish, assert, or maintain;
- defend against encroachment or interference.

[73] See document no. 101. Numbered Article 38.2.2° in the draft of 16 March, referred to here by Roche.

McElligott was even more concerned about Article 40.3.1°: 'It is still thought that they are dangerous and there still remains obscurity as to what practical obligations they impose on the State.'[74] McDunphy was unimpressed. He wrote 'policy' beside McElligott's comments on Article 40.3.1° and, in response to the latter's concerns regarding the extent of the obligations imposed on the State by Article 40.3.2°, he minuted: 'The Law Officers are satisfied.'

The Irish language text

At some point in either late September or early October 1936, it was decided that work should begin on the Irish text of the Constitution. It has been suggested that this process was begun with the secondment of Mícheál Ó Gríobhtha from the Department of Education on 19 October 1936.[75] However, in a letter dated 12 October 1936, Risteárd Ó Foghludha informed de Valera, 'Do chonnac on chló-script, fé chlúdach, ag Mícheál agus bhí sé go deas',[76] suggesting that Ó Gríobhtha had begun work on the Irish text from at least the first week of October; at the time, Ó Foghludha was working with the Irish legation in Paris, from where he wrote the letter.[77] In any event, Ó Gríobhtha was seconded from the Department of Education on 19 November and given an office in Government buildings, close to de Valera.

Ó Gríobhtha worked alone on the Irish text until 11 November, when he was joined by Ó Foghludha, whose job was to edit and revise the drafts submitted by Ó Gríobhtha. The surviving drafts in the de Valera papers suggest that Ó Foghludha was a demanding editor. According to Breandán Mac Giolla Choille, Ó Gríobhtha's drafting was intended to translate precisely the legal wording of the English version, with Ó Foghludha rendering this translation into more natural or legible Irish prose.[78]

Although Ó Gríobhtha and Ó Foghludha were occasionally assisted by Professor Tomás Ó Máille during the first months of 1937, the two men worked practically alone to prepare the first Irish text, printed on 25 March 1937. For the purpose of revising this draft, a committee was established on 3 April to bring the Irish text into conformity with 'the

[74] See document no. 154. Numbered Article 41.3.1° and 41.3.2° in the 2nd Revise, referred to here by McElligott.
[75] Breandán Mac Giolla Choille, 'I dtaobh an tsaothair sin na Gaeilge ar an mBunreacht', in *Feasta* (October 1988), 64; Micheál Ó Cearúil, *Bunreacht na hÉireann: A Study of the Irish Text* (Stationery Office, Dublin, 1999), 2–3.
[76] This may be translated as follows: 'Mícheál showed me the manuscript on a confidential basis and it was very fine'.
[77] UCDA, P150/2373.
[78] Mac Giolla Choille, 'I dtaobh an tsaothair', 64.

practice of the Oireachtas Translation staff'.[79] Two of the Oireachtas Translation Section's senior translators, Liam Ó Rinn and Tomás Page, were seconded to join Ó Gríobhtha and Ó Foghludha. According to Maurice Moynihan, their work was extremely demanding:

> During the four weeks ended Saturday, 30 April, 1937, all these officers were working at high pressure. During the greater part of that time it was necessary for them to return to the office in the evening and to work until a late hour, often until midnight or later. In addition, they worked on Saturday afternoons and Sundays, and Mr Ó Gríobhtha and Mr Ó Foghludha worked on public and privilege holidays during Easter.[80]

During April, Professor Tomás Ó Rathaille also consulted with the committee, contributing, in Maurice Moynihan's estimation, a total of five days' work to the translation, during which he 'revised generally the entire text and also contributed a certain amount of original translation'.[81] The Irish committee's work was no doubt made all the more difficult by the constant redrafting of several articles of the English text that occurred during April 1937, necessitating constant revision of the Irish text.[82]

On 14 June 1937, during Dáil debates on the Constitution, W.T. Cosgrave labelled the Irish text 'a mere translation of the English', going on to note that:

> The Irish text was prepared hurriedly by competent people who suffered from the disadvantage of being a Committee, of having to deal with a badly prepared English text, and with an author incapable of giving them any assistance in Irish.[83]

In response, de Valera defended the method of drafting of the Irish text:

> I want to tell those who suggest that the Irish was only an afterthought, a mere translation of the English, that the Irish drafting has gone on *pari passu* almost from the beginning, when the fundamental ideas that were accepted

[79] Mauricc Moynihan minute, 24 August 1937, NAI, DT S9965A.
[80] Maurice Moynihan minute.
[81] Maurice Moynihan minute.
[82] Several of the translators received remuneration for their work. Ó Gríobhtha received £50, Ó Foghludha received £40, Ó Rinn received £15, Page received £5 and Ó Máille received £30. Ó Rathaille refused remuneration, informing Moynihan that 'his pleasure in being of assistance and the expression of the President's appreciation...were sufficient recompense', NAI, DT S9965A.
[83] 68 *Dáil Debates*, Col. 351 (14 June 1937).

for the Constitution were being put in draft form. It is true that, as far as the literal drafting of the Constitution was concerned, it has been largely left to one person...But that does not mean that that Draft was not criticised. It does not mean that that Draft was not changed from its original form to the form in which you have it now, finally. It was changed a number of times...The Irish has gone side by side with that. We got the most competent people we could find for the Irish. This Constitution has been criticised and examined closely by language experts, and just as we have had no real serious criticism of the document itself from the practical point of view, or of its principles, we have not had, as far as the Irish language is concerned, any criticism that was worth while. Therefore, as far as the Irish version is concerned, it is a document of which we can be proud.[84]

In remarking that 'the most competent people' were consulted with for the Irish text, de Valera referred not just to Ó Gríobhtha, but also to Ó Foghludha, Ó Rinn, Page, Ó Maille and Ó Rathaille. On 4 May, Maurice Moynihan wrote to the Department of Finance seeking their approval for the establishment of a committee to 'make recommendations as to any changes that may be desirable, by way of simplification, in the spelling of Irish in the Draft Constitution'.[85] The committee was chaired by Eoin MacNeill,[86] with ten ordinary members, including Ó Rathaille, Ó Máille and Ó Foghludha.[87] Having met on four occasions between 7 and 21 May, the committee produced a majority and minority report, which were submitted on 25 May.[88]

It has been argued that, once the translation of the English into Irish had begun, it was the Irish text that provided the basis for further revision of the Constitution, with the English text standing essentially as a translation of the Irish.[89] There is little evidence to support this assertion. As Micheál Ó Cearúil has comprehensively demonstrated, the Irish text of the 1937 Constitution is no 'mere translation'.[90] It may equally be

[84] 68 *Dáil Debates* Col. 413 (14 June 1937).
[85] Maurice Moynihan to J.J. McElligott, 4 May 1937, NAI, DT S9859A.
[86] Eoin McNeill (1867–1945), Minister for Finance (1919), Minister for Industries, (1919–21), Minister for Education (1922–5), TD (1919–27).
[87] For a full list of committee members, see document no. 195.
[88] For the reports, see NAI, DT S9859A. It is notable that one of the signatories of the minority report (for which there were four signatories) was Tomas Ó Rathaille.
[89] T.P. Ó Neill and Pádraig Ó Fiannachta, *De Valera* (2 vols, BÁC, 1970), ii, 327.
[90] For a comprehensive study of the drafting of the Irish text of the 1937 Constitution, see Micheál Ó Cearúil, *Bunreacht na hÉireann: A study of the Irish Text* (Dublin, 1999). A copy is available at http://www.constitution.ie/publications/irish-text.pdf. See also Ó Cearúil, *Bunreacht na hÉireann: Divergences and Inconsistencies? Neamhréireachtaí agus Easpa Leanúnachais?* (BÁC, 2003); Ó Cearúil, *Bunreacht na hÉireann: Two Texts or Two Constitutions?* (Dublin, 2002).

said that the English text is no translation of the Irish, but rather formed the basis from which the teams of Irish translators worked to produce a complementary text, identical in principle, if not in language, with only occasional lack of correspondence between the two texts.[91]

Conclusions

What, then, does the material from March and April 1937 tell us about the drafting process? Clearly, the first draft had engendered considerable unhappiness on the part of the Department of Finance and the Department of Justice. The concerns of the former were, to some extent, assuaged by the moving of the socio-economic rights provisions to a new non-justiciable Article 45. While some of the concerns of the latter were also taken into account, Roche seems to have remained dissatisfied, expressing his dislike of:

> the whole idea of tying up the Dáil and the Government with all sorts of restrictions and putting the Supreme Court like a watch-dog over them for fear that they may run wild and do all sorts of indefensible things.[92]

While significant drafting changes took place at all stages throughout the drafting process, by the end of March 1937, the overall structure of the Constitution had taken shape. De Valera was now in a position to appoint Moynihan, McDunphy, O'Donoghue and Hearne as members of the drafting committee.[93] The fact that the drafting committee consisted entirely of pro-Treaty supporters[94] helped to ensure continuity with the 1922 Constitution, but also, generally speaking, probably operated as a moderating force. As Keogh has observed, the Committee members:

> were of a liberal disposition [and were] all people of wide culture. They were wholly free of the stridency associated with certain vociferous elements in the Irish Catholic Church

[91] See generally, Kelly, *Irish Constitution*, 386–97.

[92] See document no. 142.

[93] This seems largely to have been a formality, since they, together with Arthur Matheson, had been heavily involved in the drafting of the Constitution prior to this appointment, even if Hearne had done much of the actual drafting up that point.

[94] John Hearne was a Waterford Redmondite. As a student in University College, Dublin in 1919 Hearne had shared with James Dillon (later Minister for Agriculture) the role of defending the 'old unfashionable order' of the Irish Party: see Maurice Manning, *James Dillon: A Biography* (Dublin, 1999), 27. Maurice Moynihan supported the terms of the Treaty, but said later that he kept his opinions to himself in his republican family: see Deirdre McMahon, 'Maurice Moynihan (1902–1999)—Irish Civil Servant', in *Studies*, 89 (2000), 71–2. Philip O'Donoghue had been appointed a District Judge in 1923 and Michael McDunphy was appointed Assistant Secretary in the Department of the President of the Executive Council in the same year. It is difficult to see how O'Donoghue or McDunphy could have been appointed to either position unless they were thought to have pro-Treaty sympathies.

> in the 1930s. All...had broad intellectual horizons. None were the victims of then fashionable ideological phobias.[95]

De Valera was fortunate in his drafting team, for if he did not have the benefit of such a skilled and broad-minded committee, it is more likely that both the content and design of the Constitution would have suffered accordingly. In the hands of others, it is likely that the Constitution would have been fatally damaged through the influence of confessional, right-wing, authoritarian thinking. While the Constitution contained some elements of this thinking (e.g., the ban on divorce, the tone and content of the Preamble), the drafters also ensured—possibly by virtue of reliance on the continental constitutions—that the Constitution contained as much of the thinking of Paine as much as it did of Catholic social teaching. The fact that the Constitution has not only survived but has thrived in the totally different Ireland some seventy five years later provides its own testament to the ability of the drafters to influence de Valera's thinking and to produce a document which substantially transcended the cultural values of Ireland of the 1930s.

But, even before the Constitution could be published or the debate take place in the Dáil, de Valera had to deal with the most sensitive issue of all, the treatment of religion in Article 44.

No. 89: NAI, DT S9715A

Draft Constitution circulated to Government Departments

16 March 1937

See www.irishconstitution.ie.

No. 90: NAI, DT S9715A

Maurice Moynihan to P.J. Ruttledge

Department of the President
16 March 1937

A Chara,

1. I am directed by the President to refer to the copies of the draft Constitution sent to you for your consideration today.

[95] Keogh, *Church, State and Society*, 106.

2. The President would be glad to have the observations of your Department on the Constitution generally, and in particular on the following Articles:
   Article 9—Nationality and Citizenship
   Articles 32, 33, 34 and 35—The Courts
   Article 36—Trial of Offences
   Article 37—Treason
   Articles 38 and 39—Personal Rights and Family
   Article 43—Suspension of the Constitution
3. Articles 38 to 42 are not yet in their final form.
4. Article 41 is still under examination with a view to having it placed in a special category in the Constitution. It is intended as an indication of the principles which should inform the policy of the social and economic laws of the State. The President would be glad to have the views of Departments on the principles contained therein.
5. The President would be glad to have the preliminary observations not later than 23 March.

No. 91: NAI, DT S9715A

Maurice Moynihan to Seán MacEntee

Department of the President
16 March 1937

[Paragraphs 1, 3, 4 and 5 of this letter are identical with that at document no. 107 above.]

2. The President would be glad to have the observations of your Department on the Constitution generally, and in particular on the following Articles:
   Article 10 (relating to the vesting of certain property in the State)
   Those Articles in the parts dealing with the National Parliament and the National Government which relate to Money Bills, Submission of the Estimates to Dáil Éireann and the Consideration of the Estimates by Dáil Éireann.

Articles 30 and 31 (relating to the revenue and to the Comptroller and Auditor General).[96]

No. 92: UCDA, P150/2395

Fr John Charles McQuaid to Eamon de Valera

Blackrock, Co. Dublin
16 March 1937

I am deeply grateful for the draft. It is such a joy to see it in print; now it remains to see it enacted. It reads very well. I think I note already the few changes made. I beg to enclose a copy of the work I have been at: rummaging in the heads of the last few Popes! I hope it is what you want.

No. 93: NAI, DT S9715B

Memorandum from James Ryan to Eamon de Valera
Observations on first circulated draft

Department of Agriculture
18 March 1937

Dear Mr President,
I attach Memorandum covering some points in the Draft Constitution. I have purposely refrained from comments on Articles 38 to 41 inclusive because I have a great deal to say about these articles and I expect to have very much more when I have studied them more closely.

Observations

Article 8:
As drafted I am afraid it may not achieve the object in view. The word 'only' in the last line should be omitted. If not omitted I believe a person convicted at a Court held in Galway at the moment could appeal on the grounds that he did not get a fair trial as Irish is not the only language in general use in the district. If we could achieve the position in which Irish is permissible to anybody while English is only permissible in

[96] A similar letter to those sent to Finance and Justice was sent to each Department, with paragraphs 1, 3, 4 and 5 worded identically. Paragraph 2 asked for observations on the Constitution generally, as well as Articles that appeared to be relevant to a particular department. The same letter was also sent to the Ceann Comhairle. Of the government departments, only the Department of Industry and Commerce neglected to submit any observations or recommendations.

certain districts, we would reach the ideal. This might be done by deleting Section 3 and by adding to the end of Section 2 'in districts in which Irish is not in general use'.

Article 11:
Section 2 says 'the President shall be elected by direct vote of the people'. I would like to be sure under this Article that a candidate returned unopposed would be validly elected.
Section 3—Under this Article a President is eligible for re-election. I assume that this only applies to a President who has served his full term and it may be necessary to state that.[97]

Article 12.12:
I think this is the only case in which the President acts with the approval of the Government and, at the same time, has to consult the Council of State. I am not sure if it is wise that he should consult the Council of State on an occasion such as this.

Article 13.9:
Under this Section the remuneration of Chairmen and Deputy Chairmen is prescribed by each House. Under Section 16 of the same Article the remuneration is fixed by law. This would appear to be overlapping.[98]

Article 14.2.4°:
It is provided here that constituencies must be reviewed at least every fifteen years. The old provision of ten years appears to me to be preferable because it compels the Oireachtas to take note of the census on every occasion.

Article 15.2.3°:
I think it is a most invidious task for the President to select members of the Dáil and Seanad for the Committee of Privileges. It would be much better in my opinion to allow each House to nominate one member to sit with the Judge as prescribed.

Article 16.3:
I think it would be well to make it clear that the Taoiseach does not nominate his members until the elected members are first elected.

Article 17:
A very awkward situation may be created under this Article if a Dáil is elected in which a Government cannot be elected. As the Article stands

[97] Annotated in margin 'If he resigns?'. All annotations to this document were made by McDunphy.
[98] Annotated in margin 'No. Section 16 deals with allowances to members'.

the Dáil would have to carry on until a new Seanad is elected. They would then obviously dissolve, have a new Dáil formed and again a new Seanad elected. It would be better to provide that the new Seanad must be elected within ninety days from the dissolution unless, in the meantime, the Dáil has again dissolved.

Article 20.7.3°:
It is provided here that a Public Safety Act cannot remain in force for more than three months unless both Houses agree to a longer period at the time of its passing. I think it would be well to give both Houses the opportunity of extending the law within the three months if they so desire.

Article 23.2.2°:
I think it would be well to provide that a majority of the Judges of the Supreme Court present should be sufficient for this purpose. If, for instance, two of those Judges are absent through illness during an epidemic, a majority verdict would possibly be very difficult to obtain.

Article 23.3:
As drafted, the President gets very little time to study the Bill and to consult the Council of State. I think it would be wise to change six days to eight days in this Section.

Article 24.4.2°:
This throws a very heavy burden on the Taoiseach. If we have a conscientious or pernickety President the position of Taoiseach will become almost impossible.

Article 29.1.1°:
The President can only appoint a commission during his temporary absence from Éire. I think it would be better to leave out the words 'from Éire' so that the President would be enabled to appoint a Commission if absent through illness or convalescence or perhaps through bereavement.

No. 94: NAI, DT S9715A

Memorandum from Michael McDunphy to Maurice Moynihan

Department of the President
19 March 1937

Secretary,

1. Consideration will require to be given to the question of the procedure to be adopted in considering Departmental comments on the draft Constitution.
2. As far as I am concerned, I have no comment to make on the draft as a whole, and my observations will, therefore, be directed towards individual articles or sections. This will probably be the case with other Departments also.
3. With a view to easy reference, I am devoting a separate page to each article or section on which I have any observations to make, and if this were done by each Department all the comments on a particular article or section could be assembled in this Department so as to facilitate consideration by the Executive Council. Judging from the material which I have already written, the task of consideration by the Executive Council is likely to be a fairly big one and for that reason it might be better that the comments should be examined, in the first instance, by a Committee rather than by the Executive Council as a whole.
4. I would suggest that you raise this with the Executive Council today.[99]

No. 95: NAI, DT S9715A

Maurice Moynihan to all Ministers and Frank Fahy

Department of the President
19 March 1937

A Chara,

With reference to my letter of the 16th instant in regard to the draft Constitution, I have to inform you that it would greatly facilitate this

[99] Annotated by McDunphy on 19 March to the effect that his suggestion on the format which each department should submit their observations was agreed to by Moynihan, but that Moynihan felt that the formation of a separate committee was not necessary at that time.

Department in collation of the material received from various Departments for consideration by the Executive Council, if the observations in respect of individual articles or sections thereof are entered on separate pages.

I shall be glad, therefore, if arrangements may be made accordingly, fifteen copies being furnished to this Department so that a copy may be available for each Minister, etc.

No. 96: UCDA, P150/2395

Fr John Charles McQuaid to Eamon de Valera

Blackrock, Co. Dublin
21 March 1937

I enclose the few emendations suggested last night.[100] It occurs to me, that for the interpretation of all this section one must presume as a canon of just interpretation:

a) That the natural sense of the words will be maintained;
b) That the mind of the legislator will be duly regarded;
c) That moral—not mathematical—possibility will be envisaged.

Otherwise, any private citizen—or indeed, jurist—could drive any law or interpretation of law to an impossible conclusion concerning the obligations of the State.

No. 97: UCDA, P150/2395

Fr John Charles McQuaid to Eamon de Valera

Blackrock, Co. Dublin
22 March 1937

I hope the enclosed will meet the case we discussed.[101] The statement is a combination of two more Papal pronouncements! So we are in good company. You will note that I have put in the rational and Christian concept of work. I am continuing the dossier.

[100] Enclosure not found. It is not quite clear to what section of the Constitution McQuaid is referring in this letter.
[101] Enclosure not found.

No. 98: NAI, DT S9715B

Memorandum from the Department of Defence
Observations on first circulated draft

22 March 1937

Article 12.6 and 12.7.1°:
It is suggested that a provision be inserted in Section 6 to the effect that the command of the forces in time of war should be delegated to a military officer.

The regulation by law of the President's powers and functions in relation to the supreme command will be provided for in the Defence Bill now in draft. That Bill, however, may not become law until some time after the coming into force of this Constitution. In the interval it will be necessary that these powers and functions should be determined. It is suggested that an Article be inserted in the Transitory Provisions, providing that during such interval the President shall exercise such functions of command as have hitherto been vested in the Executive Council up to the date of the coming into force of this Constitution.[102]

Article 12.11:
It is suggested that, as a matter of military necessity, the power of remitting, commuting, or suspending sentences of military tribunals for the enforcement of military discipline must be vested in the authorities more immediately concerned with military discipline.[103]

Article 13.6:
It is suggested that this Article be amended to read as follows:

1° The right to authorise and regulate the raising and maintenance of military or armed forces is vested exclusively in the Oireachtas.

2° No military or armed force other than a military or armed force the raising and maintenance of which is authorised and regulated by the Oireachtas, shall be raised or maintained for any purpose whatsoever.[104]

[102] Annotated by McDunphy: 'Covered'. All annotations to this document were made by McDunphy, unless otherwise specified.
[103] Annotated: 'Covered'.
[104] Annotated: 'Now [Article] 15. Covered'.

Article 26.3:
It is suggested that the following words be inserted after the words 'summary jurisdiction':

> 'or a courtmartial or other military tribunal for the enforcement of military discipline.'

Article 36.1.2°:
In at least two classes of cases it will be shown that the jurisdiction of courtsmartial must extend to persons who at the time of trial have civilian status.

Firstly, a provision is necessary in the Defence Act to meet the case of a person who commits an offence against the Act while subject to it, and who then ceases to be subject to it. Reservists and Volunteers continually so change their status. If the offence is a purely military one the civil courts have no jurisdiction to try it. The jurisdiction of courtsmartial must, therefore, be extended to cover such cases. Section 194, Defence Forces Act, 1923, purports to do so.

Leaving aside the status of Reservists and Volunteers when not in training, a man discharged from the Army, and with the full status of a civilian cannot be tried as a 'military offender against military law'.

Secondly, in connection with legislation at the moment being drafted for the establishment of an Irish Red Cross Society, a difficulty of a similar nature would be encountered due to the wording of this Article. Any Voluntary Aid Society in the nature of a National Red Cross is, as the name implies, auxiliary to an Army and not part of it.

Article 10 of the Geneva Convention reads:

> 'The personnel of Voluntary Aid Societies, duly recognised and authorised by their Government, who may be employed in the medical units and establishments of armies, is placed on the same footing as the personnel referred to in the preceding Article, provided always that the first-mentioned personnel shall be subject to military law and regulations.
>
> Each State shall notify to the other, either in time of peace or at the commencement of, or during the course of hostilities, but in every case before actually employing them, the names of the Societies which it has authorised, under its responsibility, to render assistance to the regular medical service of its armies.'

To bring the personnel of the proposed Irish Red Cross Society under 'military law and regulations' when on active service so as to conform to the Geneva Convention, a provision accordingly has been included in the Defence Bill.

In order, therefore, to cover the types of cases above referred to it is suggested that the last line of Article 36.1.2° be deleted and the following substituted:

> 'of offences against military law alleged to have been committed by persons while subject to military law'.[105]

Article 36.2:
The word 'expressly' in the fourth line of this section also appears in Article 71 of the existing Constitution. Its presence gave rise to certain difficulties in drafting the Defence Forces Acts. It is suggested that the word 'expressly' be omitted and that the section be amended to read as follows:

> 'A member of the Defence Forces of Éire not on active service shall not be tried by any courtmartial or other military tribunal for an offence cognisable by the civil courts unless such offence is within the jurisdiction of courtsmartial or other military tribunal in accordance with any law or regulations for the enforcement of military discipline.'[106]

Article 36.3.3°:
It would appear from the position of this Subsection that the word 'section' should be substituted for the word 'Article'.[107]

Article 38.5:
The following addendum to the section is suggested:

> 'In the interests of discipline, military law may restrict for members of the Defence Forces, the rights conferred by this section.'

[105] Annotated: 'Covered'.
[106] Annotated: 'Covered'.
[107] Annotated: 'Covered. Leave the word Article'.

No. 99: NAI, DT S9715B

Memorandum from the Department of Local Government and Public Health
Observations on first circulated draft

22 March 1937

Article 11:
Elections for the office of President are to be regulated by law. If such law provides for petitions in a similar manner to that governing elections to Dáil Éireann, the result of any election so questioned may not be known until the new period of office has started. In that event the Commission under Article 29 will apparently have to function.

In Subsection 2 (ii) of Section 4 of this Article it would be well to insert the words 'administrative counties or county boroughs'. Tipperary County contains two administrative areas. It would be also necessary to ensure that the power rests with the elected Councils in the case of County Boroughs where the managerial system is in force. Perhaps the position would be met by the insertion of the word 'elected' before Councils.

It is presumed that the law regulating the election for the office of President will also regulate the manner in which elected Councils will act in making a nomination.

Article 13:
In the first paragraph of Subsection 12 it is suggested that after the word 'present' there be inserted the words 'and voting on the question'.

Article 14:
Subsection 6 of Section 2 of this Article should be read subject to the provisions of Section 6 of the Article. The Chairman of Dáil Éireann may be returned originally by a three-member constituency. It should also be made clear that this clause does not regulate the filling of casual vacancies.

Section 4 of this Article must not invalidate a General Election if owing to an emergency, such as a storm, the polling at a particular place was not held on that day. This has happened at a General Election and provision was made for the holding of the poll at a later day under a special provision of the Electoral Act dealing with emergencies and difficulties.

Article 16:
In connection with Subsection 3 of Section 7 of this Article attention is drawn to Section 44 of the Prevention of Electoral Abuses Act, 1923. The Attorney General is required to institute prosecutions where corrupt and illegal practices have prevailed at elections. Also to Section 7 if a corrupt practice is proved to have been committed by or with the knowledge and consent of any candidate at such election the candidate is for ever incapable of being elected to or being a member of the Oireachtas—if by the agent of a candidate, the candidate is disqualified for seven years. Where an illegal practice has been committed there are corresponding but shorter period penalties.

The provisions of this Section should be modified to except persons subject to legal incapacity of the class mentioned here for membership of the Dáil.

The expression 'general election' must be taken to mean, in the event of an election in a constituency at a general election being quashed, the subsequent election held pursuant to the decision on the petition. It is submitted that this is a question that could not be settled by legislative enactment.

Article 17:
As regards the terms of Section 2 of this Article this is a postal Ballot and the poll will be open for several days. The expression 'day of the poll' really means 'the close of the poll' and it would be well to substitute a more precise definition.

Article 40:
In Section 5 the words 'particularly by providing free primary education' might imply the provision by the State of the full cost of such education, including free books and the full cost of erection of schools, etc.

Article 41: (Private Property)
The Local Government, Public Health and Housing Codes contain provisions whereby a local authority may be empowered to acquire land and other rights compulsorily for the purposes of their powers and duties. The procedure is controlled by the Minister for Local Government and Public Health. An appeal lies to the Circuit Court. It is important that the existing powers of Local Bodies to acquire private rights to property for public purposes should not be weakened.

As regards social policy it is thought that a statement of leading principles would tend to greater elasticity and provide sufficient guide for subsequent legislation on social matters. The reference to particular aspects of social policy contained in the sub-paragraphs of Section 5 of this Article are somewhat vague. The first sub-paragraph refers to a sufficient wage for domestic needs, present and future. The working classes to-day desire a higher standard of living and higher rates of wages not alone for domestic needs but for their requisite personal and conventional needs. The third sub-paragraph of Section 5 would involve legislation. As indicated by the opening words 'by attempting to regulate' the underlying principles would not be susceptible of easy application.

Sections 4, 5 and 6 might be combined into one Section setting out the leading principles which should guide the State in promoting the economic welfare of the people and in establishing an economic order regulated according to social justice.

Section 7 of Article 41 refers to 'the less favoured classes of Society', a somewhat vague expression. It also pledges the State to contribute to the support of the infirm, the widow, the orphan, and the aged poor who are past their labour. At present the State does not directly contribute to the support of the infirm or the aged poor, unless they are over 70 years of age. Assistance is provided by Boards of Assistance for these classes. Would the pledge of the State be met by the assistance given by Local Bodies out of local funds, or would it involve direct provision by the State out of State funds?

Widows and orphans receive assistance on certain conditions. Non-contributory pensions are subject to a means test. It is not clear that Section 7 (1) contemplates any such test.

The State contributes to the welfare of the blind over 30 years of age. Assistance is also provided for this class by Local Bodies. The State also contributes to School Meals and other social services administered by Local Bodies. As in the case of Section 5 references to particular aspects of social policy might be omitted from Section 7. In the second line of the first sub-paragraph of this Section the word 'welfare' (or 'interests') might be substituted for the word 'rights'.

It would appear to be inadvisable to include a rigid provision on the lines of Section 10 of this Article without a full examination of the method of forming vocational groupings and some experience of the working of such a system.

Article 46:

As regards Section 3 of this Article the earlier provision relating to a General Election to Dáil Éireann restricts a voter to one vote. The existing electoral provisions for Dáil Franchise permit either of a 'residence' or 'business premises' qualification. It can happen that a person may be registered twice, although a second vote is open to challenge at the polling at a Dáil Election. In the absence of a restriction here to one vote at a referendum it could be inferred that such a restriction was not intended, and that a voter could take advantage of a mistake (or failure to remove a duplicate entry). See Article 14.2 relating to elections to Dáil Éireann.

It is also submitted that citizens should not be allowed to vote at a referendum without regard to legal incapacity. Corrupt Practices at Dáil Elections are bribery, personation, treating, undue influence, aiding, and abetting, counselling or procuring the commission of the offence of personation, and knowingly publishing a false statement of the withdrawal of a candidate at an election. One of the penalties is incapacity for seven years from being a Dáil or Local Government Elector, or voting at a Dáil Election or Referendum. This existing incapacity seems inconsistent with the absolute right here given.

No. 100: NAI, DT S9715B

Memorandum from Arthur Matheson to Patrick Lynch
Observations on first circulated draft of Constitution

Parliamentary Draftsman's Office
22 March 1937

Attorney General,

In accordance with your request, I have gone carefully through the printed draft of the proposed new Constitution and have to submit the following observations thereon.

Article 10:

In section 3, there is a slip which is my fault; the word 'vested' is not appropriate because the two previous sections state that certain property 'belongs' to Éire but they do not actually vest any property in Éire; I would submit that in the said Section 3 the words 'property vested in Éire in this Article' should be deleted and that either the words 'property which belongs to Éire by virtue of this Article' or the words 'property which is declared by this Article to belong to Éire' should be substituted.

Article 12:

In Section 4, I would suggest that the word 'Oireachtas' should be substituted for the word 'Parliament' in the three places in which the latter word occurs.

In Section 13, the effect of Subsection 3° is to prevent legal proceedings against the President only during his term of office; that paragraph does not prevent legal proceedings being brought against the President *after* the expiration of his term of office in respect of things done by him during his term of office.

Article 14:
In Section 3, at the end of Subsection 2°, the word 'Oireachtas' should be deleted and the expression 'Dáil Éireann' substituted.

Article 20:
Section 4, in Subsection 2°, the case of a bill being returned by Seanad Éireann within twenty-one days without any recommendation is not provided for; I would suggest that, after the words 'twenty-one days' in the third line, the words 'either without any recommendation or' should be inserted.

Article 24:
In Section 6 provision should be made for members of the Government retaining office during a dissolution of Dáil Éireann; a member of the Government could not comply with this section as it stands because, during a dissolution, there would be no Dáil Éireann. I would also suggest that it should be made clear whether, when the same Government returns to power after a dissolution, the Taoiseach and the other members of the Government require re-appointment.

Article 29:
Section 2; the duty of convening a meeting of the Council of State should be imposed on some suitable person, as for instance the Taoiseach; the only existing provision for summoning a meeting of the Council of State is section 8 of Article 27, but that section would not apply because there would be no President in office.

Article 34:
In clause (i), the reference to the declarations to be taken by the judges should be deleted as those declarations are fully provided for by articles 32 and 57.

No. 101: NAI, DT S9715B

Memorandum from Stephen Roche to P.J. Ruttledge
Observations on first circulated draft

Department of Justice
22 March 1937

Minister for Justice,[108]
I attach some observations as I have been able to prepare in the available time.

I must ask your indulgence for errors, omissions, and inelegancies. The work was done, as you know, in extreme haste, out of the office, mainly during St Patrick's Day and the weekend, 20th and 21st. When I describe my commentary as very imperfect I am not doing so in any conventional way but am stating a regrettable fact of which I am afraid there will be ample evidence.

In particular, I have not been able to make any attempt to revise the typing of my original manuscript.

I would respectfully suggest that a round-the-table discussion between a Cabinet Committee and officials is essential if this long and most important document is to receive anything like adequate examination in the short time available. Even with that precaution, I have serious fears that the time is too short to give reasonable security against error.

Article 8:
The declaration in Section 1 of this Article that 'The Irish language is the official language of Éire' requires careful consideration in the light of the actual facts. In practice, English is the almost universal language both of official and of non-official life here; less than 15 per cent of our officials know Irish and the percentage amongst the general public is less than that. The percentage that actually *uses* Irish is still smaller.

Attention is directed to the possibility that the words quoted may be interpreted as meaning that any official whose duty it is to convey information or advice to another official or to a Minister or to a member of the public (possibly *urgent* information or advice) discharges this duty sufficiently by conveying such information in Irish—*the* official language—although the person to whom he is addressing himself does

[108] It would appear these observations were drafted by Stephen Roche for P.J. Ruttledge, who thought fit to forward them to the Department of the President as they stood.

not understand him. This is not merely a fanciful idea, the thing has already occurred in practice.

It is not the Government's fault that the great majority of Irishmen do not understand Irish and the Government will have nothing to apologise for in recognising that fact as a fact. The use of Irish as a device for obstruction and irritation does no good to the language. Part 3 of the Article should be modified accordingly—it is not a question merely of 'districts'.

Article 9:
It is not possible to give any assurance that this Article, operating in conjunction with the existing law, will not give rise to difficulties. The matter is very complicated, and any summary statement of the law is dangerous. On the other hand, so far as I have been able to consider the question in the time available, I see no definite objections to this Article except those suggested in the following two observations, viz:

1. Is it safe to say, without qualification, that *all* persons born in Ireland should thereby become citizens: e.g. a child born in the French Legation, the parents being members of the staff of French visitors? (The 'extra-territorial' doctrine maybe a complete answer to this: I am not sure).
2. Section 3 ('Love of Motherland', etc) is really outside the scope of official criticism, but I venture to question whether it serves any useful purpose.

Article 11.4.2° (ii):
County Councils are not fundamental organisations: they are an administrative device created by ordinary (British) law; they may be varied or abolished by ordinary law. It has even been suggested that such a course should be adopted. It seems inelegant that a non-permanent, non-Constitutional organisation should be specifically mentioned in the Constitution as an essential factor in the election of the highest officer of the State. The particular mention of 'County Boroughs' emphasises this 'descent into particularity—'No County Borough…no President'!

Article 12.2.2°:
When has a Taoiseach 'ceased to retain the support of a majority in Dáil Éireann'? What is the test? Might it not be well to avoid any possibility of disagreement on that point? One possible way would be that the Taoiseach should first get a motion carried in the Dáil such as: 'That in the opinion of the Dáil it is advisable that the Dáil be dissolved'.

But there may be better ways, or there may be no real necessity for saying more than the text says.[109]

Article 12.7.8°:
Would it not be sufficient to stipulate that the President should appoint the Judges of the two Courts which are mentioned by name in the Constitution, viz, the Supreme Court and the High Court, leaving the ordinary law to deal with appointments of minor Judges, Justices, Commissioners, etc?

Article 12.11:
This will require careful consideration.
Is it intended as an *exclusive* prerogative? (If so, hundreds of trivial remissions will have to be submitted by the Minister for Justice to the Government and by the Government to the President).

Is it intended that the prerogative shall extend to the remission of 'legal consequences' which are at present *never* remitted, e.g. the forfeiture of a public house licence, in pursuance of express statutory provision, on a third conviction? Or to the remission of costs or compensation directed by the Court to be paid to an injured citizen?

If the prerogative is *not* intended to be *exclusive*, but is to be exercisable in certain cases, as at present, by a Minister, (or some other person, lower than the President), two alternatives suggest themselves viz.:

(a) Power to the President, on the advice of Government, to delegate the prerogative (but not, it is suggested, in capital cases)

Or

(b) To say, in effect, that the law may provide for remission, etc., by some other authority to any extent which the Oireachtas may think proper.

Article 12.13, paragraph 3:
The wording might be reconsidered: the separate mention of 'equity' seems a little detailed and pedantic: query, use some broader phrase such as 'The President shall not be answerable to any process at law, civil or criminal, during the term of his office'.

[109] Roche here raised an issue about which there is still no completely satisfactory answer. If the Taoiseach is defeated on a vote of confidence in the Dáil, he has quite obviously lost that support. But suppose a Taoiseach pre-empts a certain defeat in the Dáil by asking the President for a dissolution in advance of that vote. Is the President *obliged* to accede to this request or can he or she form the view that the Taoiseach has evidently lost that support and thus decline to grant such a dissolution? Note, of course, that the President is obliged to accede to the request for a dissolution *unless* the Taoiseach has lost the support of the Dáil, in which case the President has a discretion in the matter. To date, no President has ever refused such a request.

As to the *substance* of the paragraph, is it deliberately intended to ignore the *possibility* of a President being guilty of some serious crime in his private life—e.g. fraud or murder—quite unconnected with his conduct as President but so grave that public opinion calls for action? Or is it considered that impeachment under Section 10 of Article 11 covers this possibility?

(These observations are made by way of anticipation of the point being raised in the Dáil: the writer would personally be quite prepared to agree that the risk is negligible.)

Article 13.2
The wording seems capable of improvement: there are three statements following closely on one another viz.,

1. The Oireachtas is the *supreme* authority (implying *other* authorities).
2. There is *no other* authority.
3. Other authorities may be created.

The meaning is clear but the verbal clashes are rather harsh. See also Article 15.1, paragraph 1, which creates *another* supreme legislative authority.

Article 13.5, paragraph 1:
Is this first paragraph necessary? Is not paragraph 2 sufficient?

Article 13.6:
Is it correct to speak of the Oireachtas raising or maintaining an Army? Is not the proper phrase 'save as authorised by the Oireachtas' or something like that?

Article 13.7, paragraph 1:
This is merely a negative provision. *Who* is to declare war should the necessity arise?

Article 15.1, paragraph 1:
This paragraph rather clashes, verbally, with Article 13.2…see preceding note on that Section.

Article 15.4:
In the first line query make it clear that 'vote or resolution' is qualified by the words following the word 'law' in the next line.

Article 16.4
The specific mention of the two Universities offends against the theory that the Constitution should not be dependent on non-essentials: see

remarks on Article 11.4, paragraph 2: 'No Dublin University—No Constitution' will not do as a motto!

Article 20.5
Is 'sub-section' (at the end of line 6) used advisedly as the best word? (I have nothing against it but just take the opportunity of drawing attention to the desirability of getting an agreed, standard, system of reference, so as to avoid uncertainty in the use of such words as 'section', 'sub-section', 'clause', 'paragraph'. In this connection, the use of the Arabic figures with a distinguishing small circle is objectionable to the extent that it may cause confusion in references, particularly when a typewriter is used for copying).

Article 20.7, paragraph 2:
This paragraph is capable of giving the impression that the Bill becomes law *whether the Dáil passes it or not*. That impression will not survive analysis but query make the meaning clearer on the view by inserting such words as 'if passed by the Dáil' after the word 'Bill'.

Article 21.4, paragraph 5:
The full implications of this paragraph are not clear to me. Is there to be any authoritative text in *English*?

Articles 32, 33, 34, 35 and 36
(Courts and the Administration of Justice):
The Department of Justice view is that the fewer limitations imposed on the legislature in this matter the more satisfactory the position will be found in practice.

In particular, the following points need consideration:

1. The title 'Judge' (see Article 32.1) should be reserved for the higher Courts: nothing should be inserted in the Constitution which would entitle, say, District Justices to call themselves Judges as of right.
2. Beyond a general declaration that everybody entrusted by law with the exercise of judicial discretion shall in the exercise thereof be subject only to the Constitution and the law, nothing specific should be said in the Constitution about any Court lower than the High Court.
3. Article 34 requires careful consideration. The more general its terms are, the better. The specific mention of Rules of Court is probably dangerous: it might for instance exclude Ministerial orders under Statute not being Rules of Court.

4. Article 35 is of course a great improvement on the present position, but it, taken together with Article 36, is open to the objection, from the Department of Justice point of view, that the trial of criminals without a jury (except in the case of minor offences) is definitely barred, except during an 'emergency'. Some time ago a committee of which I was a member,[110] was asked by the President to report on certain questions connected with the Constitution. One of the recommendations made was that, in addition to any provision which might be made for emergencies, there should always be available a Special Tribunal to deal with offenders of a certain type—the type, shortly, to secure whose acquittal, jurors are habitually intimidated.

   I still adhere to that recommendation, because I desire to avoid the situation which may otherwise arise that political crimes will go unpunished until they become as frequent and serious as to constitute an emergency so that we will have a perpetual cycle of (a) unpunished crime and (b) emergency.
5. There are some minor objections to Articles 35 and 36 which may be worth noting for consideration, viz:
   (a) Is 'limited' in Article 35 a safe expression?[111]
   (b) Are a Peace Commissioner's functions as regards criminal matters covered by Article 35?
   (c) In Article 36, section 3, it should be made clear that when the law gives the summary court jurisdiction the summary court *has* jurisdiction. For example, if the Oireachtas thinks proper to give Justices summary jurisdiction in the case of attempted suicide, it should not be in the power of anybody to occupy the time of the Supreme Court for days with the argument that attempted suicide is not a minor offence.

[110] A reference to the 1934 Constitution Committee: for proceedings and report see Chapter II.
[111] The reference here is to what became Article 37.1 of the Constitution. This provision allows the Oireachtas to confer 'limited' judicial functions in non-criminal cases on non-judicial personages and it had no counterpart in the Constitution of the Irish Free State. The 1934 Constitution Review Committee had recommended a change along these lines 'so as to meet the present position in which judicial or quasi-judicial functions are necessarily performed by persons who are not judges within the strict terms of the Constitution, e.g. Revenue Commissioners, Land Commissioners, Court Registrars, etc.'. See document no. 27.

The phrase 'limited' judicial functions is not without difficulty. Does it mean 'limited' in the sense of the number of functions conferred? Or does it refer to the potential implications of the exercise of the power in question? The Supreme Court opted for the latter construction in *Re Solicitors Act, 1954*, [1960] IR 239, where it held that key parts of the Solicitors Act, 1954 were unconstitutional insofar as it enabled the Disciplinary Committee of the Law Society to strike off a solicitor. These provisions were held to constitute judicial powers which were not 'limited' for the purposes of Article 37.1.

Article 38:
The guarantees given in Section 2 of the Article are very widely worded and may have unexpected results. For example, under 2.3°, if a man is slandered, is the State really bound to vindicate his good name? Is that guarantee carried out by the existing device of providing a Court in which he can, at his own risk, sue his slanderer?

In Section 5, the words 'true Morality' are used in page 36 and 'right morality' on page 37. Either expression is open to the charge of having no definite meaning at all, in law. In practice, the Supreme Court Judges are being authorised to pronounce finally on a question not of law but of ethics.

The wording of the clauses about blasphemy and public meetings requires consideration from the point of view which may be expressed by the question: 'Are we here creating definite offences and conferring definite powers on the police, or are we merely authorising the Oireachtas to do so'?[112]

Articles 43 and 44
(Emergency Provisions):
On a necessarily hasty consideration, these provisions are quite satisfactory from the Department of Justice point of view. They appear to give the Oireachtas power, if it desires to do so, to re-enact Article 2A of the existing Constitution. This is in accordance with the Department's view. If anything, the text goes too far: I doubt if power to suspend Articles of the Constitution (Article 43) is necessary at all, having regard to the effect, in practice, of laws made under Article 44.

See however my observations on Articles 32–6 as to the desirability of having the ordinary Courts supported *permanently* by a Special Tribunal.

[112] The reference here to blasphemy is that which ultimately became the saving clause in Article 40.6.1°.i:

> The publication or utterance of blasphemous, seditious or indecent matter is an offence which shall be punishable in accordance with law.

As Roche pointed out, it is not clear from these words whether this provision *obliges* the Oireachtas to create such offences. As it happened, this matter lay fallow until *Corway v Independent Newspapers (Ireland) Ltd.*, [1999] 4 IR 484, when the Supreme Court effectively held that the common law of blasphemy had not survived the enactment of the Constitution, given that it was based on the tenets of Christian (and, specifically, Anglican) doctrine only. It appears that successive Attorneys General advised subsequently that Article 40.6.1°.i created a duty upon the Oireachtas to legislate on the topic: see the comments of Dermot Ahern (Minister for Justice, Equality and Law Reform) on the Report Stage of the Defamation Bill 2008, 196 *Seanad Debates*, Col. 1019 (9 July 2009).

Section 36 of the Defamation Act, 2009 now creates an offence of blasphemy. The maximum penalty is a fine of €25,000. Section 36(2) provides that 'a person utters blasphemous matter if (a) he or she publishes or utters matter that is grossly abusive or insulting in relation to matters held sacred by any religion, thereby causing outrage among a substantial number of the adherents of that religion, and (b) he or she intends, by the publication or utterance of the matter concerned, to cause such outrage'.

Section 36(3) provides that it shall be a defence for the defendant to prove 'that a reasonable person would find genuine literary, artistic, political, scientific or academic value in the matter to which the offence relates'. Section 36(4) provides that the section does not apply to cults.

No. 102: NAI, DT S9715B

Memorandum from Patrick Lynch to Maurice Moynihan
Observations on first circulated draft

Office of the Attorney General
23 March 1937

I send herewith some observations on the draft Constitution. The time available does not enable a complete analysis of the document to be made and there are probably points which have been overlooked.

Observations of the Attorney General (22 March 1937)
It will be appreciated that the ideal of a sovereign national parliament can only be approached by reducing to the narrowest limits any constitutional restrictions. It follows from this that the greater the number of matters expressly covered in the constitution, the greater will be the consequent limitation on the powers of the legislature under that constitution. This is merely mentioned because of the probability of acute criticism in the Dáil which renders it more necessary to be guarded in one's criticism of the draft Constitution. For example, it would be competent for the Oireachtas to make any legislative enactment without hindrance on any matters on which the existing Constitution is silent but in respect of which there is express provision made in the new draft, while in future the exercise of this power will be controlled by such provisions.

Article 10:
It does not appear why the word 'inland' is inserted in clause 2 and twice in clause 4 of Article 10 having regard to the absence of restriction on Article 11 of the present Constitution in the use of the word 'waters'. It is suggested that the word 'inland' be omitted from the three places mentioned in Article 10.

Article 12.11:
Article 12.11 as appearing in the draft is capable of being read as merely recognising, but not expressly conferring, any right to pardon. I would imagine this power is now to be expressly conferred rather than derived from any previous possessor of the prerogative of mercy. Perhaps the words 'vested in and exercised by the President' would express what is intended.

Article 22:
The new Article 22 provides for obtaining the authoritative opinion of the majority of the Supreme Court on the possible repugnancy of a Bill. It is wisely provided that minority opinions will not be stated on these occasions. It is worthy of consideration whether a similar provision should not apply to the decision of the Supreme Court in the exercise of its original jurisdiction under Article 32.4.3°. It appears to me that it is desirable in the public interest that while recourse must be had to a Constitution Court in certain contingencies that anything like encouragement should not be given to persons or organisations to raise questions of constitutionality when they may be disposed to do so in order to cause embarrassment or delay. Citizens should as far as possible be free from doubt or uncertainty about the validity of their constitutional rights and duties as laid down in day-to-day legislation. One can visualise wealthy federations or robust trade unions thinking it profitable to speculate on the chance of obtaining a minority judgment in their favour or even delay by assailing legislation on the ground, for example, that it infringed the respective provisions of Article 41.

Article 26:
There has been from time to time some criticism as to the use in legal proceedings of the word 'The State' on the ground that it was meaningless. It is to be found in law reports in cases of mandamus and the like, and the phrase is an inelegant effort to provide a successor for the King. This has never been covered by the Criminal Justice Administration Act which makes the Attorney General prosecutor by name in most cases. There is a good deal to be said for having proceedings of a criminal kind and, in fact, all State proceedings brought in the name of 'the people of Éire'.

Article 27:
It would be well to consider whether under Article 27 the Chief Justice and the President of the High Court may not be somewhat embarrassed when adjudicating in Court in respect of any issue arising on a matter that has come previously before them as members of the Council of State. Perhaps this question could be solved by ascertaining whether the present holders of these judicial offices would be willing to act on the Council of State.

Article 34:
Article 34 does not mention that the terms of appointment of Circuit Judges and District Justices 'shall be such as are or may be regulated by law'.

Article 43:
The suspension of constitutional guarantees in a time of grave emergency may not be lightly undertaken but when such procedure is invoked it should not fail to achieve its purpose because of regard for any constitutional niceties. Therefore it is suggested that the *Habeas corpus* provision should also be suspended as well as the setting up of Military Courts.

This objection may be got over by the insertion of the words 'and of the *Habeas Corpus* Act' in line 5 after the word 'Constitution'.

Article 44.1.1°:
Add after the word 'jurisdiction' the words 'and making such other provisions'.

I would suggest that consideration be given to inserting a clause with a view to limiting the jurisdiction of the Tribunals proposed to be established by a term or condition that such Tribunals would not have power to inflict the death penalty.

Suggested general alterations:

[Matter omitted]

Article 38.3: The word 'lawful' before 'associations'.

[Article 41.3]: The word 'to' before the word 'be'. In line 3 instead of the word 'lawfully' before the word 'delimit' insert the words 'by law' after the word 'use'.

No. 103: NAI, DT S9715B

Memorandum from Thomas Derrig to Maurice Moynihan
Observations on first circulated draft

Department of Education
23 March 1937

In reply to your letter dated 16th instant, in which you request the observations of my Department on the Constitution generally and in particular on those Articles containing provisions which appear to be of special concern to my Department, I desire to inform you that the general principles of the Draft Constitution and in particular of those Articles which relate specially to my Department are approved both by me and by my Department.

I note that Article 38 to 42 are not yet in their final form and that Article 41 is still under examination.

I desire to make the following observations:

Article 40.2:
The words 'established by the State' should be omitted and the words 'aided or recognised by the State' substituted therefore.

Article 40.3:
The words 'established by the State' should be omitted and the words 'to which parents object on religious grounds' substituted therefore. The word 'schools' in this Section should not begin with a capital letter.

Article 40.4:
The order of the adjectives in the last line might be changed to read as follows: 'moral and physical, intellectual and social'.

Article 41.2:
Perhaps the words 'of external goods' might be inserted at the end of this Section.

Article 41.5:
Substitute the word 'inform' for the word 'imbue' in the fourth line.
Article 41.5, Subsections 1, 2, 3 and 4 might begin 'shall endeavour', 'shall provide', 'shall attempt', 'shall ensure'.

Article 41.5.1°:
After the word 'wage' perhaps it might be well to insert the word 'and living conditions'.

Article 41.5.3°:
Perhaps the word 'scales' might be preferable to the word 'scale' in line 3.

[Matter omitted]

Article 25:
Perhaps the word 'itself' might be inserted after the verb 'to avail' second line.

[Matter omitted]

No. 104: NAI, DT S9715B

Memorandum from James J. McElligott to Maurice Moynihan Observations on first circulated draft

Department of Finance
22 March 1937[113]

1. In examining the Draft of the Constitution the Department of Finance has taken the line that it was not called upon to praise but rather to point out possible defects and difficulties, so what follows is conceived in that spirit.
2. The observations of the Department on the Constitution generally, as well as on particular Articles, have been asked in the minute of the 16th instant from the President's Office and these are supplied. Complying also with this request views are expressed on matters which are more properly the province of other Departments. Further, a number of obvious points are mentioned, such as the need for implementing legislation or for consideration by other Ministries. It is realised that these are not likely to be overlooked, but, in view of the limited time available, some of them might escape notice.
3. The observations furnished are not exhaustive as only a short period has been allowed to examine a long and complicated document of which some of the Articles are not yet in final form and some, viz., those relating to religion, Church and State, have not yet been furnished. It is presumed that all the various Departments and sub-Departments of State will be called in to advise where necessary so as to reduce the risk of error. The Department of Finance has accordingly omitted to deal with quite a number of matters which fall within the province of other Ministries.
4. Apart from questions of complexity and expense involved in the Constitution, it seems that there will be a degree of uncertainty introduced into our legislative system by the extent to which recognition is given to the doctrine of repugnance. Under Article 22 and 23 bills passed by both Houses of the Oireachtas may be referred by the President, after consultation with the Council of State, to the Supreme

[113] Submitted to Moynihan on 23 March.

Court; or, after presentation of a petition by a majority of members of the Senate and 4/9s of the members of the Dáil, may be referred by the President to a Referendum. If Articles 38 to 41 dealing with personal rights and social policy are retained, it is conceivable that many efforts will be made to upset bills properly passed and this would be undesirable.

5. In numerous Articles the phrase occurs 'provision shall be made by law' for the implementing of the Article. It is not clear whether Article 49, dealing with the continuance of laws to the extent to which they are inconsistent with the Constitution, provides the means of enabling the administration to be carried on and the various powers under existing laws to be exercised in all their fullness. In this connection the point also arises whether the words 'by law' which occur in various Articles cover existing enactments. An enormous mass of consequential legislation will necessarily follow the adoption of the Constitution and will occupy the attention of the Parliamentary Draftsman's Office and of Government Departments for a year or two, to the almost total exclusion of other business, and certainly to the detriment of their daily administration. If this view is accepted it may be possible to provide that those parts of the existing Government machine which have worked efficiently should be preserved, and with them the laws under which they operate. The point is further referred to later where the need for preserving existing Departments and distribution of functions is dealt with.
6. The possibility of reprisals of an economic or other character following the enactment of the Constitution have not been dealt with. It is conceivable that it may be held to deprive us automatically of any preferences we enjoy in the British and Dominion markets. Even if no consequence of the kinds mentioned were to follow it may be necessary for us to undertake the entire cost of our own defences by sea, on the coast and otherwise, and this would add considerably to what will, in any case, be a heavier bill presented by the new Constitution to the taxpayer.

Articles 1 to 3:

These Articles, dealing with the Nation as distinct from the State, (a distinction which many political scientists would not admit), seem rather to vitiate the Constitution, by stating at the outset what will be described, and with some justice, as a fiction, and one which will give offence to neighbouring countries with whom we are constantly protesting our desire to live on terms of friendship.

Having been at such pains to expel fictions from the existing Constitution and to bring theory into line with practice, it seems inconsistent now to import an even greater fiction.

Further, from the point of view of international law, it is not clear whether we are on safe ground in claiming sovereignty and jurisdiction over land recognised internationally, *de jure* and *de facto*, as belonging to another country.

The doctrine of repugnance finds a place in our Constitution, and this doctrine may be used against us by the countries referred to and may expose us to the risk of adverse judgment from international bodies such as the League of Nations or the Hague Court. A rebuff from such authorities would be rather wounding to the national pride, and would set back the cause which we wish to advance.

From the practical point of view, apart from the fear of consequences, these Articles will not contribute anything to effecting the unity of Ireland, but rather the reverse. Besides they will impose an additional and more severe strain on our relations with the numbers of the British Commonwealth of Nations, relations which are already difficult enough, and which coming events, apart from the Constitution, will make even more difficult.

It is not usual in a Constitution to define the national boundaries.

Query: does the expression 'The Irish Nation' not include all Irishmen whether living in or outside Ireland.

Article 4:

The adoption of the name of Éire will, presumably, entail the alteration of Currency and Bank Notes, Coinage, Seals of State and of Government Departments, and all kinds of Government Stationery, e.g., Postal Orders, Old Age Pensions Orders, etc. This is going to be expensive if we are not allowed to do even after the coming into force of the Constitution. The latter is stated to become operative within six months after its approval by the people. In the case of coinage and bank notes, for example, the minimum stocks held are for two years, and these are costly to manufacture.

The adoption of the name 'Éire' may be quite justifiable from the traditional and scholarly points of view, but from a realistic point of view it seems a mistake. This land is generally known internationally as Ireland or one of the derivatives of that name, and so there will probably be a long period of confusion and misunderstanding before the unaccustomed name conveys a definite meaning to educated people throughout the world.

Article 6.2:
This Section refers to 'the Organs of State established by this Constitution'. No subsequent Article formally establishes Organs of State. It is presumed the reference is to legislative, executive and judicial organs although not so stated. Possibly there would be less apparent need for defining Sections if the word organs were printed without a capital letter, or a colourless phrase, such as bodies, institutions, or authorities, introduced.

Article 9
It is not clear how far these provisions represent a departure from the existing law in regard to nationality and aliens but presumably this will be examined in the Department of External Affairs and the Department of Justice. It would seem as if the provisions of the Irish Nationality and Citizenship Act, 1935, (No. 13) and the Aliens Act, 1935, (No. 14) would have to be reviewed to bring them into line with this Article.

Article 9.3:
Is this not so fundamental and inherent in nationality as not to require inclusion in the Constitution?

Article 10:
The provisions of this Article appear to be generally satisfactory so far as the Department of Finance is concerned. It provides the power of alienating State property without distinction as to the date of its acquisition by the State and it removes the Constitutional restriction limiting such alienation to a maximum of 99 years. The Article will, however, involve the enactment of fresh legislation to govern the control, alienation and management in future of State property. It is possible also that the Article as drafted may have some effect on existing Statutes, such as the State Lands (Workhouses) Act, 1930 (No. 9), the Mines and Minerals Act, 1931 (No. 54) and the Foreshore Act, 1933 (No. 12). The necessity for the revision of the Statutes quoted is, however, a matter for the consideration, in the first instance, of the Department of Local Government and Public Health, and the Department of Industry and Commerce, respectively.

Article 10.1:
'Lawfully vested in private persons'—does this include property vested in public bodies and companies e.g. quarries belonging to County Council? If not, amendment is necessary.

Article 11.7:
Who are 'public personages' under the Constitution? Perhaps this should read 'citizens'. (c.f. Art. 38.1.1°).

Article 11.10.1°:
It is open to doubt whether the impeachment should not be taken on the initiative of Dáil Éireann and the tribunal to the Seanad. Presumably impeachment will be in the nature of a safety valve at some time of popular excitement so that the drive for impeachment would more naturally be expressed through the popular assembly; whilst the calm and judicial atmosphere necessary for a tribunal would be more likely to be found in the Seanad than in the Dáil.

Article 11.10.3°:
Perhaps the President should be entitled to appear, as well as to be represented.

Article 11.12.2°:
'The President and his official staff shall receive such emoluments and allowances as may be determined by law.' It is not desirable that the staff and secretariat should be included in this provision as they will, presumably, be members of the Civil Service, Army, etc., whose remuneration will be otherwise determined.

Article 12:
Various powers hitherto exercised by the Executive Council or other Bodies are transferred to the President, particularly the appointment of Judges of the Supreme Court, the High Court, and all other Courts and Tribunals established by law, and the right of pardon and of commuting sentences imposed by the Courts. Presumably the Departments concerned will advise as to the desirability or otherwise of the changes.

Article 12.1:
As an tUachtarán 'appoints' the members of the Government under Subsection 2°, the introduction of the terms 'remove from office' in Subsection 3° might necessitate a description of the steps constituting removal. It is suggested that the last line of that sub-Section should be altered to: 'Cancel the appointment of any member of the Government'.

Article 12.2:
Subsection 2° is not a new provision but merely a qualification of 1°. It is suggested that 1° and 2° should be linked together as one Subsection by the word 'but'.

Article 12.6:
Vests the supreme command of the Defence Forces in the President. This involved a departure from the existing situation in which the command-in-chief reposes in the Executive Council but is exercised through, and in the name of, the Minister for Defence (Section 5 of the Defence Forces (Temporary Provisions) Acts, 1923). It also involves a departure from a recent decision of the Executive Council (S.7359 of 3 April, 1935)[114] in relation to the terms of the proposed permanent Defence Forces Bill to the effect that no change should be made in the provisions of the existing Defence Acts in relation to the command of the Forces. There are, nevertheless, ample precedents in other countries (e.g., U.S.A., France, Germany and Poland, which are Republics, and Italy and Great Britain, which are Monarchies) for vesting the supreme command in the person who is recognised as Head of State and holds precedence over all other persons in the State. No objection is, therefore, seen to the provision which, it is noted under Section 7, will involve fresh legislation.

Article 12.8 and 12.11:
In these two Sections the President appears to be given unfettered power to appoint Judges and to exercise the right of pardon and remission in respect of sentences imposed by the Courts. In this respect the Sections differ rather strikingly from other Sections under the same Articles, which are careful to indicate by whose advice or on whose nomination the President must act. Presumably, however, the exercise of the President's functions under Sections 8 and 11 are governed by the provisions of Section 14 of the same Article.

Article 12.11:
It is clear that no saver is required for the statutory powers of remission of the legal consequences of verdicts given by the Courts in respect of offences against e.g. the Revenue laws, which are vested in the Revenue Commissioners? Similarly as regards certain powers of remission of the Minister for Justice. These powers, so far as the Revenue Commissioners, at any rate, are concerned, should be maintained. They are of importance from the administrative point of view, but not sufficiently important to call for the intervention of the President.

Article 12.13.3°:
The phraseology of this Subsection raises the question whether proceedings can be taken against the President retrospectively after he has ceased to hold the office in relation to matters which took place during

[114] Refers to NAI, DT S7359.

his tenure of office. In this respect the intention of the Section is not quite clear on the face of it.

Article 13:
Though the definition of 'Oireachtas' includes the President, at times it denotes only the two Houses (13.1.3°; 13.8).

Article 13.2.2°:
'No other authority whatsoever has power to make laws for Éire.' Does this render *ultra vires* the making of statutory rules and orders?

Article 13.5:
Here subsection 1° and 2° seem inconsistent; 1° telling the Oireachtas it is not to do it, and 2° saying what is to happen when the Oireachtas does it.

Article 13.7.2°:
Would attack from the sea or from the air, without any landing force, constitute 'actual invasion' within the meaning of the subsection?

Article 13.9
The remuneration of Chairman and Deputy Chairman of each House should be fixed by law as in the case of the President (11.12.2°), Ministers (24.12.v), and Attorney-General (26.7).

Article 13.16:
This Section involves a widening of the provisions of the similar Article 23 of the existing Constitution in that it provides for, in addition to free travelling facilities, 'such other facilities in connection with those duties (as public representatives) as the Oireachtas may determine'. This extension of the provisions of the existing Constitution may involve additional expenditure if the facilities are intended to cover matters like postage facilities and access to the services of a staff of Secretaries, Typists, etc. Such extension would require fresh legislation.

Article 14.1.1°:
Do the words 'by law' which occur here and elsewhere in the draft Constitution cover existing enactments?

Article 14.2.6°:
This Article runs 'no law shall be enacted whereby the number of members to be returned for any Constituency shall be less than three'. Presumably the object of this sub-section is to allow scope for proportional representation to operate. It would, however, be ineffective in the case of a Constituency of three members where one of them is the

Chairman of Dáil Éireann and is deemed under the provisions of Articles 14.6 to be elected a member of Dáil Éireann at the ensuing General Election without any actual election.

Article 14.6:
The terms of this section do not appear to be as clear and definite as the second part of the corresponding Article 21 of the existing Constitution.[115]

Article 14.7:
This provision apparently involves the enactment of fresh legislation.[116]

Article 15.2.2° and 3°:
The introduction of the President, with a possible veto, is an innovation, the necessity for which is not apparent. The matter of procedure regarding the question whether a Bill is or is not a Money Bill might well be left to the two Houses of the Oireachtas.

Article 15.3.1°:
(See also Article 24.3.3°) The phraseology is intended to cover the preparation and presentation of the Volume of Estimates for Supply Services as well as the White Paper relating to Receipts and Expenditure, but the Draftsman might consider whether it is necessary to make specific provision in relation to the Volume of Supply Estimates.

Article 15.3.2°:
It might be considered by the Draftsman whether the passing of the Central Fund Act and the Appropriation Act is adequately covered by this sub-section. Perhaps it would be better to omit it as like Article 36 of the present Constitution, it appears to make the passing of the Central Fund Bill in March, with its provision for expenditure in the *following* year, unconstitutional. If it is to be retained it should be so modified as to enable that Bill to be taken before the commencement of the appropriate financial year. Presumably the word 'year' in the subsection is intended to mean 'financial year'.

Article 16:
The election of members of Seanad Éireann will involve the enactment of fresh legislation embracing the regulation of practically all matters covered by the provisions of Article 16 as a whole. Subsection 1° of Section 7 does not state who will actually draw up the list of names on

[115] Annotation unclear.
[116] Annotated by McDunphy: 'Of course'. All annotations to this document were made by McDunphy unless otherwise specified.

each of the five panels, presumably the Government, with or without some outside Assistance. To preserve the non-party character of the Second Chamber some outside assistance would seem to be necessary.

Article 20:
Section 7 which provides for the curtailment of the Seanad's normal time for consideration when a Bill is certified as urgent, would be improved if the Certificate of Urgency were made subject to the assent of the President. As the Section stands it is open to abuse, and any abuse of it would adversely affect public confidence.

Article 21.4.1°:
It might be considered whether this sub-section might not read: 'Every Bill shall become and be the law of Éire as on and from the day on which the Bill shall be signed by the President.'

Article 21.4.2°:
Similarly this sub-section might read: 'Every Act shall come into operation on the date on which it is signed by the President…'

Article 21.4.4°:
It is not clear to what 'copy' alludes and it is suggested that the words 'the document so signed' should be substituted for 'such signed copy' in the second line and the word 'document' substituted for the word 'copy' in the penultimate line.

Article 21.4.5°:
The issue of authoritative texts in the English language is essential if the work of administration and ordinary business is to be properly carried out and if a mass of useless litigation is to be avoided. It is suggested that Subsection 5° should be amended so as to require 'the Clerk of Dáil Éireann or such officer as aforesaid' to cause to be issued an authoritative version in the English language of every law enacted by the Oireachtas. For many years to come, this will be absolutely essential for the use of Statutes by Departments, as well as by members of the public if hopeless confusion is to be avoided. Further, a limitation of the requirement to the issue of an authoritative text in the Irish language appears to be at variance with the provisions of Article 8.2 of the draft Constitution, wherein 'the English language is recognised as a second official language'.

Article 22.2.2°:
Presumably the opinion of a majority of the *sitting* Judges is intended.

Article 23.2 and 23.3:
The President may have only two days in which to summon the Council of State, consider their representations and arrive at his decision on the question of a referendum on a Bill. There seems no logical reason why the period should not be extended by another day as he is allowed seven days within which to sign Bills.

Article 23.4.2°:
If action under this Subsection is to be taken, it would appear to be necessary for the President to be required at some stage in the proceedings described in the preceding Subsection to return to the Taoiseach the Bill which he declines to sign, otherwise how can the Taoiseach comply with the terms of the Subsection by presenting the Bill to the President for his signature?

Article 24.1
It is noted that no upper limit has been fixed to the number of members who constitute the Government. The provision differs in this respect from the similar provision in Article 51 of the existing Constitution, which prescribes that the Executive Council shall consist of not more than twelve not less than five Ministers. On financial grounds the absence of an upper limit appears undesirable.

Article 24.6.1°:
It is urged that the Minister for Finance should in all cases, hold the office of Tánaiste, in which event he would be ex officio a member of the Council of State. Alternatively, the Minister for Finance should in his own right be a member of the Council of State in view of the importance of his special functions and of his general supervisory powers over State expenditure of all kinds. As the Article stands the Tánaiste may hold any Ministry or may even be a member of the Government without portfolio.

Presumably it is not the intention of 1°, as might be inferred from the section, that the Taoiseach, Tánaiste and Minister for Finance should ex officio be members of Dáil Éireann.

Article 24.9.2°:
The terms of this Subsection appear to contain a certain obscurity. On a strict reading it might be interpreted to limit the duration of office to ten days from the date of the first meeting of Dáil Éireann next held after appointment and to preclude the possibility of the temporary holder of the appointment being appointed to fill the permanent

appointment. The Subsection would be free from all obscurity if it were phrased as follows: 'A temporary appointment of this nature shall not be held for longer than ten days from the date, etc.'

Article 24.12:
This Section will apparently involve the re-enactment of some Measure corresponding to the existing Ministers and Secretaries Acts and it is for consideration whether such legislation is, on general principles, desirable as it may involve the upsetting of inter-Departmental relations which are at present, on the whole, working smoothly.

The remarks previously made about the maintenance of existing State organisations and existing laws, where they have been functioning efficiently, apply also here. If all the machinery set up by the Ministers and Secretaries Acts is to be dismantled and the organisation and distribution of business among Departments of State to be re-considered, great waste of time and energy will be involved, with corresponding detriment to other more useful activities of Government.

Article 25:
In the absence of an explanatory Memorandum, the various reactions and repercussions of this change are difficult to understand and it is suggested that External Affairs should furnish information as to the precise significance of this Article and its probable effects on our relations with external Governments. In certain eventualities serious economic and financial consequences may follow, and even if the latter could be averted no preparation to avert them can be made unless the precise intention of this Article as regards our international position is known.

Article 25.5:
So far as the provisions of this Section are understood they appear to involve the re-enactment of the Constitution (Amendment No. 27) Act, 1936 (57 of 1936) providing for the appointment of Diplomatic and Consular Agents abroad and the conclusion of International Agreements.

Article 25.6 25.7:
The operation of these Sections may have consequences which possibly have not been visualised. In practice the State subscribes to quite a number of international institutions and organisations under agreements, the terms of which are never laid before and formally approved by Dáil Éireann. It is questionable also whether the need for compliance with the Sections might not cramp the style of Departments in the matter of negotiation for International Agreements. An illustration

would be the negotiation with a British Department of State for the transfer of certain services or officers connected with services about to be transferred. The Sections seem to be drawn far too tightly.

Article 26.6.5°:
Is there not need for a safeguard similar to that in Article 24.11? It would be supplied by the addition of words 'but the Attorney General retiring in such circumstances shall continue to carry on his duties until his successor shall have been appointed'.

Article 26.7:
The provisions of this Section would probably involve the enactment of new legislation establishing the Attorney General's Department as one distinct from the Ministerial Departments of State, i.e., he will come out of the Ministers and Secretaries Act. (*Vide* Article 55.4) There appears to be no need for this distinction.

Article 27:
This deals with the Council of State, and it is not clear whether members of that body, other than those who hold official positions, are to be paid, nor how a meeting is to be held if the President is unable to convene it.

Article 27.2.i:
The Comptroller and Auditor-General is declared to be an ex-office member of the Council of State. It is suggested that his place should be taken by the Minister for Finance unless the suggestion previously made is accepted, viz: that the Minister for Finance should always occupy the post of Tánaiste. Failing the adoption of either of these suggestions, the Article ought, in the opinion of the Department, expressly include that Minister as a member of the Council of State. His inclusion would increase his prestige and his effectiveness as Minister and it would bring to the Council a fuller and more general knowledge of the work of administration and of the financial and economic affairs of the State than any of the ex-officio members named in the Article, with the exception of the Taoiseach, could possess. His special experience of the conduct of Parliamentary business and especially of Money Bills make him a more suitable ex-officio member of the Council of State than the Comptroller and Auditor General.

For the sake of consistency and for the purpose of encouraging the use of the Irish forms, it might be well, even in the English translation of the Constitution, to give the titles of officers of State in Irish only. The use of the forms 'Chairman of Dáil Éireann' and 'Chairman of

Seanad Éireann' seems unnecessary as the public is already familiar with the Irish forms of those titles.

Article 30:
This Article should stand independently and not be under the heading of the Comptroller and Auditor General. It might perhaps be inserted after Article 10. The words 'of Éire' in the third line might perhaps, be displaced by 'and'.

Article 31 (and Article 12.10 and Article 55.3):
The provisions of this Article and the others mentioned above in brackets will probably involve the revision of the Comptroller and Auditor General Act, 1923 (No. 1), owing to the change in procedure as regards appointment to and removal from the Office. Article 55.3 is probably intended in a general way to include the officials of the Audit Office amongst those whose tenure is safeguarded by the provisions, but there is some doubt whether such staff are existing Officers of the Government of Saorstát Éireann. *Vide* latter comments on the provisions of Section 35.3.

Article 31.2.1°:
The Comptroller and Auditor General 'shall not hold any other office or position of emolument'. Presumably this means office of emolument or position of emolument as the officer in question is to be an ex-officio member of the Council of State. A similar expression is used in regard to the President (Article 11.6.3°) and Judges (Article 33.2).

Articles 32, 33 and 34:
The provisions of these Articles will involve the revision of the existing Courts of Justice Acts—a matter primarily for the consideration of the Department of Justice.

Occasion might be taken to reconsider the advisability of the retention of the phrase 'any other office or *position of emolument*' in Section 2 of Article 33, the interpretation of which has given rise to some doubts in relation to the receipt of public moneys by a District Justice in respect of fees for publication of work in Irish under An Gúm.

Article 32.3.1°:
It is not clear whether this extends the right to appeal from the Circuit to the High Court to points of law and fact in all cases. If so, is it desirable?

Article 32.5.1° and 2°:
Is this declaration necessary in view of the declaration prescribed by the Courts of Justice Act, 1924, and of Article 34? The procedure prescribed

is extremely inconvenient and possibly productive of delay. For example, the Chief Justice might be absent from Éire or temporarily incapacitated by illness. It is unnecessarily expensive to require the attendance in Dublin of Circuit Judges and District Justices from all parts of the country. Would it not suffice for the Supreme Court and High Court Judges to make and subscribe the declaration in open court before a number of their colleagues, and for the Circuit Judges and District Judges to make and subscribe the declaration publicly in open Court? Under the existing Constitution the nature of the declaration and the method of making it are regulated by Statute.

The above remarks apply with equal force to the provisions of Sections 3, 4 and 5 of Article 57.

Articles 38 to 41:

In this and the three succeeding Articles 39, 40 and 41 there are a number of mandatory provisions making it compulsory on the State to do a number of vague and undefined things, e.g. 'to have due regard to individual differences of capacity, physical and moral, and of social function' to imbue 'all the institutions of public life' with social justice and 'social charity', etc.

These Articles are not of a kind usually enshrined in a Constitution. They will not be helpful to Ministers in the future but will provide a breeding ground for discontent, and so create instability and insecurity. They are consequently objectionable and even dangerous. Their provisions are too vague to be of positive assistance to any Government and are yet sufficiently definite to afford grounds for disaffection to sections of the community, who might claim that the Government were not living up to the Constitution.

The provisions are the more objectionable by reason of the earlier Articles relating to repugnance under which laws may be disallowed after reference to the Supreme Court or to a Referendum. Some of the provisions are too advanced, some too conservative and many cut across action taken daily by the Government, e.g. restrictions on private property and initiative.

Further, the provisions are mostly unnecessary. Distinct advances along the lines of the social and economic policy outlined have already been made without the aid of these declaratory provisions, some of which are themselves, it should be noted, repugnant to present Government policy, e.g. we do not settle 'as many families as practicable' on the land. 'Five acres and a cow' would suffice if that were the policy. We create economic holdings of twenty-five acres. No doubt, the Land

Commission will offer its views on this point, and the Department of Industry and Commerce on the provisions dealing with labour conditions, the economic rights of the less favoured classes, and the ruralisation of industry, while the Department of Local Government will, presumably, deal with the provision relating to the support of the infirm, the widow, the orphan and the aged.

Also, the provisions are contradictory. The State has established monopolies in important articles such as sugar, electricity, cement, tyres, oil, etc. The reference to the 'economic domination of the few in what pertains to the control of credit' is not understood. In so far as one can attach any intelligible meaning to it, it is untrue, but it could easily be worked up by agitators as a weapon of attack on the Banks, the Agricultural Credit Corporation, the Industrial Credit Co., or against any large joint-stock concern.

These various declaratory phrases are of an idealistic tendency which, while individually unobjectionable as a statement of social policy, may, if launched out into the void in the draft Constitution, recoil like a boomerang on the Government of some future day in circumstances not anticipated by the originators. For example, the difficulty of the Government at present in dealing with the claim for compensation lodged by Mr More O'Ferrall whose son was murdered and whose family have been forced to emigrate would be greatly increased if the provisions of Section 2.2° of Article 38 were included in the existing Constitution.

It is quite open to the State in any legislation which it enacts to give effect to the ideals expressed in these declaratory passages without being bound to do so by the express terms of the Constitution. For example without any commitment to the pledge affirmed in Article 41.7.1° the State has already in numerous Acts like the Old Age Pensions Acts, the Army Pensions Acts, the Blind Pensions Acts, the Widows and Orphans Pensions Acts, given effect to the ideals underlying the provisions of this Subsection, and there is nothing to stop further legislative progress in the same direction without putting in the hands of enthusiasts for any particular cause an unnecessarily powerful instrument of agitation which it is feared might be freely used in support of all sorts of unreasonable and impracticable proposals for further social legislation. Some of the declaratory subsections appear to be highly dangerous, e.g. Article 41.6.2°, (already referred to) 'the economic domination of the few', which, by reason of the very general character of its terms can be interpreted by everyone according to his individual outlook on life and could easily be worked up to lead people astray, or Article 41.6.1°, which could easily be utilised in conjunction with Article 41.9 by critics as a condemnation per the Constitution of the action of the present Government in establishing practical monopolies in the manufacture of tyres, sugar, industrial alcohol, cotton yarn, the refinement of crude oil, certain forms of transport, and retention of a monopoly in the manufacture of electricity and the carriage of postal material. Article 41.8 might offer a lever in agitation to extend the scope of land division when the present amount of land available for distribution is exhausted and when the only means of extension of this process would be by compulsory subdivision of the holdings already distributed, which might be contrary to the principle of Article 41.2, but might be reconcilable with the provisions of Article 41.3.

Some of the declaratory Subsections, as already stated, are obscure in their object and meaning, e.g. Article 38.1.2° and Article 39.1.3° and in any case it is difficult to see how practical effect can be given to them by legislation. If the latter provision has for its object the restriction of the low-paid employment of women and children (but not necessarily overtaxing their sex and strength), to the exclusion of many fathers of families who badly need the employment, it would be welcome to many interested in contemporary social problems. This particular problem is further dealt with in Article 41.5, i, ii and iv. Practically every one of these declaratory passages is capable of different interpretations and being utilised for different objectives by different individuals, e.g., fixing of minimum wages, of appropriate scales of wages, the control or the decontrol of industry and manufactures, etc.

In Sections 4 and 6 of Article 40 but particularly Section 5 it is suggested that the use of the word 'shall' is dangerous, and the word 'may' would be distinctly preferable. The insertion of the word 'may' appears to be at least desirable after the word 'necessary' in Section 9 of Article 41.

In connection with Article 39.2.2°, if the prohibition of the future passage of a law which might impair the unity of marriage carries with it the corollary of abrogating any existing law of the same tendency, it would be necessary to repeal existing law in the Saorstát which provides for judicial separation.

In Article 38.5.1° the words 'sec to it' read curiously. No doubt the Irish version is suitably phrased and a more happy rendering than the present one could be inserted.

What is the distinction between 'true' morality and 'right' morality?

Article 40:
The corresponding Article 10 of the present Constitution reads 'All citizens of the Irish Free State (Saorstát Éireann) have the right to free elementary education', and there is some doubt whether it does not commit the State to the provision of school books and other school requisites free to pupils of public primary schools. Section 5 of Article 40 of the Draft Constitution seems to be capable of a similar interpretation and perhaps an amendment is necessary.

Article 41.2:
'Attempting' is not good. It is suggested that 'purporting' or 'proposing' should be substituted. Our use of 'compulsory powers' in various spheres may be questioned under this Section.

[Matter omitted]

Article 41.8:
'Traditional preference' is open to doubt. The Irish emigrants to the U.S.A., for instance, have shunned rural life. Generally the wording seems vague, colloquial and lacking in precision.

Article 43:
The Article, which provides the Constitutional foundation for the establishment of an emergency Court such as is at present provided under Article 2A of the existing Constitution by the Constitution (Special Powers) Tribunal, will almost certainly involve the immediate enactment of legislation of a similar character which may be the subject of acutely controversial discussion in the Oireachtas. Its consideration is, however, mainly for the Departments of Justice and of the Attorney General.

Articles 47 and 49:
Reference to the above mentioned Articles appears to provide the appropriate opportunity to suggest enquiry from the Law Advisers as to what becomes of the protection afforded to Transferred Officers of their rights under Article X of the Treaty, which are safeguarded expressly under the present Constitution by the provisions of Article 78. No doubt Article 49 keeps in force the Civil Service (Transferred Officers) Compensation Act, 1929, but apparently only to the extent to which it is not inconsistent with the draft Constitution. If the Scheduled Treaty which includes Article X disappears with the repeal of the existing Constitution, with it there appears to go the entire substructure of the Act of 1929 which is expressed to confirm a certain agreement interpreting and supplementing that Article. Presumably the intention

is not to abolish the rights of the Transferred Officers, now reduced to a limited number of able and willing officers of the State. It would be desirable however to have the position elucidated and to see by what means, if any, these rights are preserved in the draft Constitution. If the matter has been overlooked in the general repeal of the existing Constitution, it is suggested that it should receive immediate attention with a view to the avoidance of unnecessary apprehension on the part of an important section of the Civil Service and of many persons at present drawing allowances of compensation already awarded and to which the State is fully pledged. Possibly it will involve the express incorporation in the Constitution of the terms of Article X of the Scheduled Treaty suitably amended. Another possible alternative would be to add at the end of Article 55.3 a clause somewhat in the following form:

> 'and every such existing Officer who has transferred from the British Government by virtue of a transfer of services shall on transfer to the service of the Government of Éire hold office on the same conditions as to compensation on discharge from or retirement from office as those which applied to him immediately before the coming into operation of this Constitution.'

Article 48.1:
The interpretation of this Section is difficult for any person who is not a legal expert. It would appear to be highly desirable (and particularly so in the case of the Department of Finance in relation to the many matters in which the powers and functions it has exercised since 1922 have been derived traditionally from Treasury practice through the channel of the Transfer of Functions Order of 31 March 1923) if the powers, functions, rights and prerogatives of Ministers, exercised through their Departments immediately before the 11 December, 1936, were declared to belong to the corresponding Ministers comprising the Government of Éire. To illustrate the foregoing observation the authority for the grant of Marriage Gratuities to established Women Civil Servants on retirement lies not in any Statutory provision but in Treasury Minutes of 1894 and 1895. The bonus system at present in operation in Saorstát Éireann, but no longer in operation in Great Britain, has its origin not in Statute but in Resolutions of the British House of Commons and was brought into effect by means of Treasury Circulars prior to the Transfer of Functions in 1922. Many Regulations in full force and observance in the Service Departments have their origin in old decisions of the Treasury whose accepted successor is the Department of Finance. The draft

Constitution should, in some express way if possible, provide support for the continuance of all this Treasury practice and tradition.

Article 55.3:
This Section is take[n] to be intended to secure the continuity of tenure of every existing Civil Servant. But doubts are felt as to whether for example a member of the Staff of the Oireachtas, or of the Audit Department, or of one of the Bodies governed by Trustees (e.g. National Gallery and National Library) or of one of the Boards governed by Commissioners (e.g. Revenue Department, and possibly Land Commission and Board of Works) is described with sufficient accuracy in the Section as 'an existing Officer of the *Government* of Saorstát Éireann'.

If this doubt is shared by the Attorney General's Department, which has had experience of similar doubts expressed in connection with the preparation of Section 24 of the Superannuation Act, 1936, the remedy would appear to lie in extending the expression to cover:

(a) Oireachtas Staff,
(b) Comptroller and Auditor-General's Staff (either in this Article or in Article 58),

And

(c) Officers of all Statutory Boards of Commissioners and other Statutory Boards and Bodies exercising any function of government or discharging any public duties in relation to public administration in Saorstát Éireann and also of any Board of Commissioners established by order of the Executive Council under Section 7 of the Adaptation of Enactments Act, 1922.

See also notes under Article 31 and Articles 47 and 49.

Article 56:
The Commission to exercise the presidential functions during the period before the election of the first President is to consist of the Chief Justice, the President of the High Court and the Chairman of the Chamber of Deputies. It is conceivable that vacancies might occur in one or both of the two judicial offices mentioned or that one or more of the persons named in the Article might be temporarily incapacitated or might refuse to act. Is it necessary to limit the choice of personnel so rigidly? The three members of the Commission could be selected, for example, by the persons who are to be ex-officio members of the Council of State from their own number.

Article 57.3:
This appears to conflict with the procedure contemplated in the Executive Powers (Consequential Provisions) Bill, Clause 3(1).
See also note re this Article under Article 32.

Article 59:
This Article in conjunction with Article 12, Sections 6 and 7 will involve the revision of the Defence Forces (Temporary Provisions) Acts. This is mainly a matter for consideration by the Department of Defence.

The Department of Justice will no doubt consider whether it involves also the revision of the Police Code in relation to the appointment of the Commissioner and other Officers heretofore appointed by the Executive Council.

Article 60:
In view of all the preparations, legislative and otherwise, that have to be made and of the effect which the Constitution will have in increasing expenditure, it is suggested that it should not be brought into operation within such a short period as six months after its approval by the people, and that in any case it should start to operate as from the beginning of a financial year. The necessary Budgetary provision, etc., could then be made.

No. 105: NAI, DT S9715B

Memorandum by Michael McDunphy
Observations on 1st circulated draft[117]

Department of the President
23 March 1937

Article 1:

A. Do the words 'within the national territory' restrict us in any way from passing laws with extra-territorial effect?[118]
B. In the reference to the development by the Irish nation of its own life, free from external interference, is the omission of 'cultural' intentional?

[117] Nearly all annotations to this document, detailing the effect of each observation, were made in red typescript. Where this is not the case, it is recorded in the footnote. Annotations were added by McDunphy. It seems that McDunphy presented his observations not to Moynihan, but to de Valera himself.

Article 6:
Does the right of final appeal connote a right on the part of the people to a referendum on any question of national policy, even where not specifically provided for in the Constitution? If so, how is this right to be exercised, and on whose initiative or through what channel?[119]

Article 8:
The President, after consultation with the Executive Council today, wants this Article further considered with the greatest care. The exact relative positions of the two languages in the State as a whole and in any particular area affected by legislation under Section 3, e.g. the six counties or the Gaeltacht, requires special attention.[120]

Article 9:
The exact relation between the expressions Irish Nationality, Irish Citizenship, Citizens of Éire, is not clear. This, however, is a matter for the Departments of Justice and External Affairs. The provisions in the Article as a whole require examination in the light of the existing law dealing with nationality and citizenship. Their implications in relation to other Articles of the Constitution dealing with the rights etc. of citizens, e.g. Article 38.2 would appear to require special consideration.[121]

Article 10.1:

A. The expression 'sources of potential energy' might be better than 'forms of potential energy'.
B. The expression 'all estates and interests therein lawfully vested in private persons' might be replaced by the expression 'all lawful private interests existing'.[122]

Article 11.3.1°:
If the President wishes to resign, to whom does he tender his resignation and how does it become effective?[123]

Article 11.3.2° and 11.7:
The date of entering upon office is rigidly fixed by both sections but on different bases. It might not always be practicable to secure co-incidence. The President [of the Executive Council] favours the amendment of Section 7 so that it shall read: 'The President, on entering upon his office, shall take and subscribe…'

[119] Annotated: 'No. Leave as it is'.
[120] Annotated: 'Article to be completely amended'.
[121] Annotated: 'Article to be amended'.
[122] Annotated: 'Whole article to be amended'.
[123] Annotated: 'No change to be made'.

I think, however, that Section 7 should be the governing section and that the taking of the declaration should determine the entering on office. The matter is to be discussed further.[124]

Article 11.4:
Is the stipulation as to residence in Ireland during the ten years immediately preceding nomination sufficiently definite? Is there no possibility that it might be open to interpretation as *any time during* such period, or is it clear beyond doubt that it means for the *whole* of that period?[125]

Article 11.6.3°:
The President [of the Executive Council]'s view is that the President of the State should not hold any office of emolument whether under the State or outside. If the subsection requires amendment to make this clear this should be done.[126]

Article 11.7:
The expression 'other public personages' requires definition, otherwise there could be no evidence that this condition of the section has been fulfilled.[127]

Article 11.9:
'and' in the second line should be 'or'.

Article 11.10:

A. A President might refuse to sign a Bill properly entitled to enactment, or otherwise neglect or refuse to comply with specific provisions of the Constitution.[128]
B. He might, moreover, behave in a manner calculated to bring his high office into contempt or disrepute, e.g. by gross intemperance, indiscretion, etc., or otherwise make the ordered administration of the State difficult.[129]

Provision should be made to cover such a contingency, if necessary, by power of removal.

Article 11.10.2°:
Change 'investigate' into 'enquire' into.

[124] Annotated: 'Section 3 is to be amended so as to provide that the President shall enter as soon as may be after the date of termination of office of his predecessor. Section 7 is to stand and to be the governing factor'.
[125] Annotated: 'Section amended to make this clear'.
[126] Annotated: 'Leave as it is'.
[127] Annotated: 'Leave as it is'.
[128] Annotated: 'This will be covered by an Amendment of Article 29 re Commission to act for President in his absence'.
[129] Annotated: 'It is felt that a situation of this nature need not be provided for in the Constitution. It could be dealt with suitably if it arose'.

Article 11.10.3°:
'to appear and to be represented at'.

Article 11.11:
The determination of the President's 'permanent incapacity' should rest with some authority presumably the Council of State. This is provided for in other Articles but it is not clear that it applies here.[130]

Article 11.12.2°:
The expression 'determined by law' should perhaps be 'determined in accordance with law'. It is undesirable that the salaries and emoluments of particular members of any State staffs should be governed by *ad hoc* statute.[131]

Article 12.1.2°:
It should be made clear that it is the nomination of the Taoiseach which requires approval by Dáil Éireann and not the appointment of the members of the Government by the President.[132]

Article 12.2.1°:
The President should be required to consult the Council of State before refusing to dissolve Dáil Éireann under this Subsection.[133]

Article 12.8:
Include Justices of the District Courts by the words 'Justice'.

Article 12.11:
The use of the word 'exercised' suggests that the right of pardon vests with some authority other than the President.

The President [of the Executive Council] is satisfied that the words 'vested in' should be inserted before the word 'exercised'.

1. Mr Kinnane of Justice, is very worried about this Article. If the President *alone* can pardon or remit, and there is no power of delegation, the position will be *impossible*.

   At least 20 minor cases, now dealt with by the M[inister of] Justice at his own consideration, pass through Justice each day. If all these have to go to the President, through the Govt., the position can be imagined.
2. What about rights of third parties. Can these be cancelled by the President? Why not omit this Article altogether, Article 48.2 is adequate and much more practical.[134]

[130] Annotated: 'Leave as it is'.
[131] Annotated: 'Agreed. Change made'.
[132] Annotated: 'Agreed. Change to be made'.
[133] Annotated: 'No. Absolute discretion'.
[134] Annotated: 'Redrafted and approved in its final form by the President (26 March 1937)'.

Article 12.13.3°:
This Subsection should be extended by words to the following effect: 'or at any time in respect of any action or function performed by him in his official capacity during his term of office', reserving, of course, the right of impeachment under Article 11.10 of the Constitution.[135]

Article 12.14:

1. It should not be essential for every advice to the President to be sent by the Taoiseach. In practice such advice where in writing will normally be sent over the signature of a senior official at the Taoiseach's Department. If the Article as it stands conflicts with this, it should be amended accordingly. The point might be met by the omission of the words 'by the Taoiseach'.
2. There are some Articles or Sections of the Constitution in respect of which the application of this section is not definitely clear. It should, if necessary, be amended so as to remove any room for doubt. In particular, it should be provided that in respect of matters in which the President is entitled or bound to consult with the Council of State, there is no question of his being obliged to act on the advice of the Government.[136]
3. Provision should be made for countersignature by the Taoiseach of all instruments signed by the President on the advice of the Taoiseach or of the Government. It is a question, however, whether this is a matter for the Constitution.[137]

Article 12.15:
It is regarded as undesirable that additional powers should be conferred on the President by ordinary law. The matter is of sufficient importance to justify amendments of the Constitution for this purpose.[138]

Article 13.1.3°:
'The Oireachtas' in this subsection should read 'the House of the Oireachtas'. As a corollary the expression 'it may determine' should perhaps read 'the Oireachtas may determine'.[139]

Article 13.2.2°:
It should be made clear that this Subsection does not preclude the making of byelaws, etc., by non-legislative bodies.[140]

[135] Annotated: 'Leave as it is, but change the expression "tenure of office" to "term of office".'
[136] Annotated: 'Each Article affecting the powers of the President to be specific as to advice or otherwise on whom they are exercised. Article 12.14 is to be omitted (25 March 1937).'
[137] Annotated: 'Not a matter for the Constitution'.
[138] Annotated: 'No, to be by *law*'.
[139] Annotated: 'Agreed. Change made'.
[140] Annotated: 'Agreed that this section should remain as it is'.

Article 13.5.1° and 2°:

1. Would it not be better if these two sub-sections were combined. Separated as they are, one or other of them has the appearance of being unnecessary. Probably Subsection 2 would be sufficient.
2. A Bill containing provisions for the amendment of the Constitution, is, until it becomes law, repugnant to the Constitution, and the question might be considered whether this section requires any amendment in the light of this consideration.

Article 13.6.2°:
The effect of this section when enacted will be such that the presence of British Forces at present at our ports will be a breach of the Constitution. The position, perhaps, might be met by amending the subsection so as to read 'maintained by or with the permission of the Oireachtas', etc.

If this be done it will of course be necessary that legislation to give effect to this provision should be enacted concurrently with the Constitution.

Article 13.7.1° and 2°:
The powers conferred on the Government under Subsection 2 should be rigidly limited to those necessary to deal with an actual invasion and to provide against the recurrence. It should not be possible for a Government to take advantage of such an action to commit the State, without the consent of the Dáil, of participation in a war which might conceivably involve the country to an extent and for a period far beyond that necessary to deal with the invasion.

Subsection 1 should, therefore, be made absolute, and Subsection 2 be made definitely subordinate to it.[141]

In my opinion Subsection 2 is dangerous. As it stands it would permit a Government to avail of the mere fact of invasion to declare war and so commit the State to an extent far beyond that necessary.

I think it should be made definitely subject to Subsection 1, and that the prohibition of declaring war without the consent of the Oireachtas should be made absolute and should extend to all occasions whatsoever.[142]

Article 13.9:
It should be made clear that:

[141] Annotated: 'To be amended. Dáil to be summoned forthwith'.
[142] Annotated: 'We discussed this matter at length with the President. He thinks it will be sufficient to provide in Subsection 2 that the Dáil shall be summoned forthwith'.

A. A Chairman may hold office only for so long as he is a member of the House by which he is elected, and
B. That he ceases to be chairman on the dissolution of that House.[143]

Article 13.11.1° and 2°:
The two subsections appear to be contradictory. The insertion of the word 'however' after 'emergency' in Subsection 2 would clarify the position.[144]

Article 13.13.1°:
'present and voting'.

Article 13.15:
The automatic vacation of a seat in one of the Houses on election to a second House should extend to *nomination* as a member of the Seanad.[145]

Articles 14–17: Dáil and Seanad
Arrangement of Articles
The President desires that the provisions relating to the Dáil and Seanad, respectively, should, as far as possible, be arranged in the same logical sequence, and grouped in the same number of articles corresponding generally in scope.[146]

Article 14.1.2° and 3°:
Subsections 2 and 3 as they stand appear to be mutually contradictory.[147]

Article 14.2.1°:
The President wants it made clear that members of Dáil Éireann shall be representatives and not delegates and that they should be representative of the country as a whole and not merely of constituencies.

Article 14.2.3°:
The word 'identical' in the context appears too specific. Would not the word 'same' be more appropriate.[148]

Article 15.2.4°:

1. A time limit should be fixed within which the decision of the Committee of Privileges should be given.

[143] Annotated: 'Amendment made accordingly'.
[144] Annotated: 'To be done'.
[145] Annotated: 'Done'.
[146] Annotated: 'Mr Hearne is to do this'.
[147] Annotated: 'These Subsections are to be redrafted so as to remove the mutual contradiction'.
[148] Annotated: 'Change made'.

2. It should be provided that in the event of an inequality of votes, the Chairman should have a casting vote.[149]

Article 15.2.5°:
The President should be required to consult with the Council of State before deciding not to accede to the request.[150]

Article 15.3.2°:
As this section is being removed from its association with Money Bills, the President considers that it should be amended so as to read as follows:

> 'Save in so far as may be provided by specific enactment in each case a Bill required to give effect to the financial resolutions of each year shall be passed so as to enable it to become law within that year.'[151]

Article 15.4:
For the same reasons as in the case of Article 15.3.2°, the words 'enact any law' should be altered to read 'pass any Bill'.[152]

Article 16.3:

A. Can a person nominated by the Taoiseach to be a member of Seanad Éireann refuse to accept that nomination.
B. Can a Taoiseach secure or reinforce his majority in the Dáil by appointing members of the Opposition to be members of the Seanad.[153]

Article 16.6:
This section appears to be unnecessary having regard to the provisions of section 1 of Article 18.[154]

Article 17.1:
The person or authority charged with the duty of convening the Seanad after a general election should be stipulated.

Should there not be a provision fixing the latest date for re-assembly after a general election.[155]

[149] Annotated: 'Decided 26 March 1937: Section to be redrafted on lines of provision in present Constitution, subject to (a) right to demand reference to be restricted to Seanad and by resolution only, (b) one member of each House to be appointed and (c) President to appoint'.
[150] Annotated: 'Out. Not agreed to'.
[151] Annotated: 'Agreed to and decided (26 March 1937)'.
[152] Annotated: 'Agreed to and decided'.
[153] Annotated: 'Decision: Section to be amended so as to provide that the Nomination must be subject to the prior consent of the person nominated'.
[154] Annotated: 'To be deleted'.
[155] Annotated: 'President to convene and to fix date (26 March 1937)'.

Article 17.3:
The object of this section is not clear and the President considers that it might be deleted.[156]

Article 19:
President has decided that this is to read: 'Provision may be made by law for the direct election by any functional or vocational group or association of so many members, etc'.

Article 20.7.1°:
I have suggested and the President agrees that there should be only one message to the President and that a copy thereof should be sent by the Taoiseach to the Chairman of both Houses.[157]

Article 20.7.2°:
Dáil must have passed Bill.[158]

Article 20.7.3°:
There should be power to extend the period after the passing of the Bill.[159]

Article 21.2.2°:
It should be clear that there should be only one communication to the President, namely that from the Government, and that the Seanad should not be entitled to send a message of concurrence separately to him.

The position might be met by the insertion of the word 'prior' before 'concurrence'.[160]

Article 21.4.4°:
The Bill after signature should be sent back by him to the Taoiseach so that the latter may have direct notice of its signature as at present.

The Subsection as worded might be interpreted as requiring or authorising the President to return the Bill direct to the Clerk of the Dáil.[161]

Article 21.4.5°:
Provision in respect to legislation in English should be made for Bills passed in Irish.[162]

[156] Annotated: 'Deleted, but consult Matheson (26 March 1937)'.
[157] Annotated: 'The President subsequently directed that the text of the original Article should be restored'.
[158] Annotated: 'Agreed'.
[159] Annotated: 'Agreed'.
[160] Annotated: 'This has been done'.
[161] Annotated: 'Better omit the provision [sending] the Bill back (that is mere procedure), and amend the Subsection to read: "As soon as may be after the President has signed any Bill (and promulgated it as law) the Clerk of Dáil Éireann…purpose, shall…In other words, omit "such signed copy shall be returned to" and "who" after the word "purpose".'
[162] Annotated: 'Text has been amended'.

Article 22.1.1°, 2° and 3°, and 22.2.1° and 2°:

1. The Court should be the whole of the Supreme Court, any absentee therefrom being replaced by a Judge of the High Court nominated for that purpose by the Chief Justice.
2. The President is of the opinion that where possible a definite question should be referred to the Court in each case, that is to say, that the Court should not be asked whether a Bill as a whole is unconstitutional but whether a specific provision to be specified by the President is or is not Constitutional. I understand that this is the view of the President of the High Court.
3. Where a Court decided that a provision in a Bill is repugnant to the Constitution they should be required to state the respect or respects in which it is so repugnant and their reason for so deciding.[163]

Article 22.2.1° and 2°:
The Attorney General should be entitled to be heard by the Court.[164]

Article 24.1:
Should there be a maximum number of Ministers?[165]

Article 24.4.2°

1. What machinery is contemplated to give effect to this section? Is it intended that written reports will pass between the Taoiseach and the President.
2. In the event of conflict between the President and the Taoiseach, it would be open to the President to create a very difficult situation by insistence upon frequent reports, particularly if they had to be in writing.
3. If the President is to be kept informed of decisions taken on matters of domestic and international policy by the government, that means in essence that the President will be entitled, and can claim to see all Cabinet Minutes. The practical objections to this are serious.
4. It would of course be possible to send to the President a copy after every meeting, but this is most undesirable. Unless the staff of the President and of the Taoiseach are identical in personnel, and this does not seem to be contemplated, such a

[163] Annotated: 'Notes 2 and 3. Leave to practice'.
[164] Annotated: 'Amended accordingly'.
[165] Annotated: 'Maximum to be 15'.

position would create a position in which the custody of confidential cabinet records would pass out of the control of the Government.

5. I suggest that this subsection should be worded much more generally, and that the use of the word 'reports' should be avoided. All words after the word 'policy' in the second line might well be deleted.[166]

Article 24.6.1° and 2°:
During a dissolution the Ministers are not members of the Oireachtas. This should be covered.[167]

Article 24.9.1° and 2°:
Why is this section brought in[?] The appointee is already a member of the Government. This is a matter for a Ministers and Secretaries Act. See section 12 which provides for the distribution of portfolios by ordinary law.[168]

Article 24.10:
It would seem from this subsection that a Government which secures a majority in the Dáil can remain in office without any time limit.

Although not specifically provided for in the last Constitution it was always the practice that a new Government should be elected after the reassembly of the Dáil consequent on a general election.

Apart from the desirability of this on general principles, it had the advantage from the point of view of the Head of the Government that he could get rid of a member of his Government simply by omission to reappoint him, whereas under the new Constitution the only way to get rid of a Minister who has outlived his usefulness would be to subject him to the ignominy of forcing him to resign.

Apart from the points mentioned above, the text of the subsection, owing to the succession of conditions, is somewhat difficult to follow.[169]

Article 25.4:

1. Does this section cover our association with members of the British Commonwealth? It seems to be straining the ordinary interpretation of international law if this is the case.

   An association of the Scandinavian or the Baltic or the South American states would scarcely be described as an

[166] Annotated: 'Executive Council on 24 March 1937 agreed to deletion of all words after "policy". Mr Hearne has amended the subsection accordingly'.
[167] Annotated: 'To be amended'.
[168] Annotated: 'Section to be omitted'.
[169] Annotated: 'To be left as it is'.

association for the purposes of international cooperation, and our position vis-à-vis Great Britain and the Dominions appears to be somewhat on the par.

2. A second point arises. Would it be possible for a pro-British Government in Éire to invoke this section so as to revert to Dominion status?[170]

Article 26.1:
Is it necessary that the Attorney General should be in the Constitution[?][171]

Article 26.3:

1. I would suggest that the words 'or authorised' should be substituted for the word 'appointed'.
2. Omit the words 'on his behalf'. (To cover a temporary vacancy in the office of Attorney General).[172]

Article 27.2:
It is difficult to see what contribution the Comptroller and Auditor General could make to the deliberations of the Council of State, or in what respect his experience or his functions would entitle him to be a member of that body.[173]

Article 27.2.3°:

1. It might be charged in the Dáil that it would be possible in certain circumstances for the President by exercising the power under this section to overload the Council of State in a particular direction.
2. There is room here for the setting up of a new element of conflict within the State and this is to be avoided at all costs.
3. If what is sought is a wider basis of advice, would it not be better to require him before making such additional appointments to consult with the existing Council of State.[174]

Article 29.1.1°:
What happens if:

A. There is a disagreement among the members of the Commission. Is this covered by Section 4? What if only two are available in these circumstances.
B. If two or all three are ill or otherwise unavailable.

[170] Annotated: 'The Article was subsequently amended and this section omitted'.
[171] Annotated: 'To be left in'.
[172] Annotated: 'Amendments agreed'.
[173] Annotated: 'To be deleted'.

C. If the Chairman is ill or for other reason unable to convene the Commission.[175]

Article 29.3:
The words 'or fails' should be inserted after the word 'unable'.[176]
Article 32.5.1°:

The stage at which a Judge should be obliged to make and subscribe a Declaration should be stipulated. I suggest that this section should read:

> 'Every person appointed a Judge under this Constitution shall, *before entering on his duties as such Judge*, make and subscribe such Declaration.'

In the absence of a definite provision of this kind there is no means of determining, for the purposes of Subsection 3, when a Judge has declined or neglected to make this Declaration. Neither is there anything to prevent him entering on his duties before complying with this provision.[177]

Article 32.5.2°:
Provide against absence of the Chief Justice by adding after the words 'Chief Justice' in the last line 'or senior available Judge of the Supreme Court'.

The words 'in open Court' will have to be put in some other place.

Article 34

1. Opening paragraph: Omit 'and rules of Court made thereunder'. This is restrictive and is in any case unnecessary.
2. In [part] i: Omit the words 'the declarations to be taken by the judges of the said Courts on appointment'. This conflicts with Article 32.5.
3. Add a new clause: 'The terms of appointment of Judges of all other Courts as prescribed by law'.[178]

Article 38.1. (unnumbered Subsection):

A. If the King, on the advice of the British Government, confers a title on one of our citizens, as frequently happens, does this constitute a breach of the Constitution, and, if so, what remedy is there.

[174] Annotated: 'The President thinks that there is no danger of the type mentioned. The maximum number to be so appointed is five'.
[175] Annotated: '[All] to be covered by suitable amendments'.
[176] Annotated: 'Done'.
[177] Annotated: 'The Article is to be amended accordingly'.
[178] Annotated: 'To be amended'.

B. Mexican Constitution, Article 12: 'No titles of nobility, prerogatives of hereditary honours shall be granted in the United States of Mexico, nor shall effect be given to those granted by other countries'.[179]

Articles 38–41: General
These sections deal with Social and Personal rights. It is clear that as they stand many of them could be invoked so as to create very difficult situations.

Article 43.2.1°:
This Article seems to contemplate independent actions by the President and by the Government, namely, the issue of a proclamation by the Government and the issue of an order by the President.

There should be a link between the two actions.

The Government should specifically advise the President of their intention to issue an order and the President's concurrence should be essential.

Alternatively, there should be only one instrument issued, either by the President on the advice of the Government, or by the Government with the concurrence of the President.[180]

Article 43.4:
The President's intention is that a number of these Sections are merely statements of moral principles and should not be created positive rights.

I have accordingly suggested that the following formula should be inserted at the beginning of this portion of the Constitution:

> 'The State shall be guided in its general policy by the principles embodied in this Article, but the said Article shall not of itself operate to confer rights'.[181]

Article 46.3:
Bring this into line with 14.1.2° re qualifications for voting at a general election for the Dáil.

Relate:

A. General election to Dáil 14.1.2°.
B. Election of President 11.2.

[179] Annotated: 'This whole Article is being revised'.
[180] Annotated: 'This Article is being completely altered'.
[181] McDunphy offered no personal observation on this Article. The comments transcribed above were clearly made following consultation with de Valera. They are recorded in the same red ink as all the other annotations which denote the outcome of the deliberations by de Valera and the Executive Council on McDunphy's observations.

C. Referendum on law and amdts. to Constitution 46.3.[182]

Article 49:
Add the following clause as suggested by Mr Matheson:

> 'Laws enacted before, but expressed to come into force after, the coming into operation of this Constitution shall, unless otherwise enacted by the Oireachtas, come into force in accordance with the terms thereof.'

Article 52.2:
Why not add a safeguarding proviso similar to that in Article 29.3.[183]

What are to be the exact functions of the Commission.

'May' in the fourth line should be 'shall'.

Article 54:
It is not clear why the phrase 'Chamber of Deputies in respect of the present Dáil' is used. The words 'Dáil Éireann' are used throughout the existing Constitution.

This point also arises in Articles 54 and 55.[184]

Article 55.1:
What happens if the Government is defeated between date of coming into operation of the Constitution and the appointment of a President. Who appoints the new Government.[185]

Article 57.4:
Why not before the Chief Justice as in Article 32.5.1°.

Article 57.5:
Change 'immediately upon the coming' into some phrase such as:

> 'Not later than thirty days after the coming into operation of this Constitution or such later date in respect of any individual judge as may be approved by the Chief Justice'.

The Article as drafted is unsatisfactory in view of 57.6.

Article 60.2
The words 'polling day' in second last line should be 'polling'.

1. What documentary evidence will be on record of the authentic text for future convenient reference?

[182] Annotated: 'Done'.
[183] Annotated: 'Executive Council agrees'.
[184] Annotated: 'No action'.
[185] Annotated: 'To be provided for'.

2. What is the authoritative text on which the plebiscite will be based?
3. Should there not be some document enrolled or placed in the State archives?

No. 106: UCDA, P150/2416

Memorandum from Conor Maguire to Eamon de Valera
Observations on first circulated draft

Four Courts, Dublin
23 March 1937

Article 5: Having regard to the detailed provisions as to the Constitution of the Legislature, the insertion of the adjective 'democratic' seems unnecessary.

Article 6: I personally dislike and disapprove of any theory of Government which places the elected Government under the immediate control of the people, e.g. by giving the right to a Referendum or by requiring a Government to confine itself to legislation for which it has a mandate. This Article appears to adopt such a concept of Government.

Article 10: This is an improvement on the old Article 11, Section 3. The use of the word 'alienation' seems inappropriate. I presume it refers to the creation of estates and interests in private persons in State property.

Article 12:

4. Seems needlessly full. It is hardly necessary to specify the functions conferred on the President.
5. Same comment as above.
8. The appointment of the President of the members of all tribunals seems to give too much importance to all statutory tribunals.
11. See below.
12. (1), (2), (3): The requirement that messages from the President must have prior approval of the Government means that in effect they will be Government pronouncements and will be regarded as such.

The words 'legal consequences of verdicts' seem inappropriate. Verdict usually refers to the finding of a jury. It only carries such consequences as a judge thinks proper. In minor Courts there is no verdict in the above sense. Presumably what is intended is that power to remit punishment or penalties imposed by any Court shall be given to the President.

Article 13.2.3°: Is it strictly correct to say that the Oireachtas sits. Should it not be sufficient to say that the two Houses should 'sit'.

Article 13.7.1°: Who is to declare war?

Article 13 (14): The House is described as a *Court*. Is it to have powers to punish members for utterances—If so they must be given in the Constitution.

Article 22: This Article may have the effect of placing the Court in conflict with the Dáil.

The parties before the Court will in practice be on the one side the President and the Council of State and on the other the Dáil.

If [the] Article is to stand consideration it might be given to providing for a presumptuous constitutionality so as to put the onus on the Counsel who alleges unconstitutionality. Is there not a danger in asking the Court to decide a matter around which fierce controversy will have raged at a moment when the controversy will probably be at fever heat?

Article 22.2.1°: seven days is much too short a time in which to obtain a considered decision on such an important question. It should be at *least* one month.

Article 23: I have already expressed my own view on the value of a referendum. The words fundamental national importance should be preceded by some word showing that it is *new* proposals which are covered. There seems no reason why ordinary legislation along accepted lines might not be of fundamental national importance. Presumably it is not intended that the referendum should apply to such proposals as these.

Article 24.3.2°: This section does not seem to be an improvement on the similar terms of Article 54 of the present Constitution.

Article 25:

3. 'Judicial decision' implies a Court with power to employ sanctions. No such Court exists at the moment nor is it likely to exist in the future.
2. The phrase agreed principles of international law seems to me not to have a clear meaning. Law implies 'sanction'. There is no

> sanction behind what is popularly described as International Law. Furthermore, law implies clearly defined principles. It seems loose to refer to '*agreed*' principles. By whom are they agreed?

Article 26: Seems needlessly elaborate. 2 and 5—Could I suggest be omitted. If 2 is to remain the words 'and legal opinion' should be omitted.

Article 27: I do not like the Council of State. It seems to be a purely ornamental body with no powers save as regards advising on Bills which are suggested to contain unconstitutional provisions.

Articles 32, 33, 34, 35: These Articles follow the lines suggested by some when I was Attorney General. For this reason I do not wish to comment on the important changes they make. Furthermore it may be better that I as a judge should not make comments on the policy contained in these Articles.

Article 32.5.1°: Taken from Courts of Justice Act. (a) a small point is that the President of the High Court is not mentioned elsewhere in the Constitution. (b) Justice presumably meaning District Justice is not elsewhere mentioned in the Constitution. The inclusion of Justice in this and later Articles will provide an argument in favour of their being judges in the [bill? fair?]. See opening words of the article.

Article 32: I do not like to comment on this Article as all the Judges may consider it improper.

Article 38.2.2: 'However' seems out of place.

Article 38.5.1: 'Convictions' seems unnecessary.

Article 38.5.2: 'Normal traffic' seems to be covered by public convenience.

Article 38.5.3: There seems no reason for substituting the word discriminate for 'distinction' used in the old Article 9.

The Family
This part of the Constitution is new to me. I cannot offer comment that would be useful. The following criticisms however occur to me.

Article 39.1.3: I do not understand what end is being aimed at. I do not know of any law *compelling* mothers or young girls to enter avocations unsuited to their sex.

Article 39.2.3: Is it intended that the marriage of persons who have been divorced elsewhere will be recognised as valid if contracted elsewhere than in Éire?[186]

Article 43 (5): This seems to me difficult to justify. If it is effective it enables the legislature completely to ignore the Constitution. Section 4.1° seems to be effective to provide for the establishment of extra-ordinary Courts. This section seems unnecessary.

Article 43.6°: This seems objectionable. I suggest it should provide that 'Legislation under this Article may provide that'.

The Referendum
Article 46:

1. Does not require any percentage of the electorate to vote.
2. 1° Seems to leave unprovided for the case of a bill being *negatived* by a majority of less than 35 per cent of the electorate. It can hardly be intended that in such a case the bill shall be held to be approved under 2°.

Article 57:
1° and 4° District Court of Justice mentioned although it is not mentioned in the Constitution.

No. 107: NAI, DT S9715B

Memorandum from Oscar Traynor to Maurice Moynihan Observations on first circulated draft

Department of Posts and Telegraphs
[?] March 1937

[Matter omitted]

Article 9.3:
Is this necessary or desirable? It is, of course, true, but it is the sort of truth which does not really need to be stated, and it looks like an attempt to make people patriotic by Act of Parliament.

If considered necessary to retain the Section should not the word 'political' be deleted?

[186] Annotated by de Valera: 'What is present position?'.

Article 11:
Section 9: For '*and* in the event' substitute '*or* in the event'.

Sections 10.1° and 2°: The reason of the limitation of this function to the body named in 1° is not clear, though I think the limitation of the corresponding function in 2° is sound. It seems to me that the function provided for in 1° might be exercised equally by either of the bodies referred to. There may, probably there is, good reason for the limitation, but it is not apparent.

Section 10.3°: Liable to be misread. Transpose 'At the investigation by Dáil Éireann the President shall have the right to be represented'.

Section 11: If President removed, dies, becomes incapacitated etc., will his successor remain in office for a full term of seven years or only for the unexpired period of office of the former President?

Article 12:

[Matter omitted]

Section 8: This seems to give the person named absolute power in himself, without consultation with any other person or body, to deal with these matters. But he might, in his own person, be quite unable to judge of the suitability or the fitness of the various persons who might be concerned. It is, of course, the case that he himself would be nominated to represent majority choice, but he would be nominated for reasons probably quite apart from the qualities which this article would demand.

Would it not be advisable to have these appointments made 'on the advice of the Taoiseach'?

Section 11: Add 'on the advice of the Taoiseach'.

[Matter omitted]

Article 13.8:
Should not this be altered to read: '*Each House of the Oireachtas* shall hold at least one session each year'?

Article 14:
Section 3.2°: Should not the word 'Oireachtas' be substituted by the words 'previous Dáil'?

Section 5: Should not the words 'and the results of which have been declared' be inserted after the word 'held'.

Article 15:
Section 2.2° and 3°: Is it necessary to make it clear that the time limit laid down in Article 20.4.1° and 2° for the return of Money Bills by An

Seanad applies to a Bill referred to a Committee of Privileges for determination as to whether it is a Money Bill?

Article 22:
This confines to one person alone the power to initiate the consideration of the legality of any Instrument. Presumably it is implicit in the Article that he shall consider specially this aspect of every Instrument submitted to him, especially where, during the proceedings antecedent to the submission of the Instrument to him, there has been discussion of this nature.

Article 25.7:
(Note [that] the observations on this Article were furnished by the Secretary, Department of Posts and Telegraphs).

This is the only Article which may have any reaction on the Post Office. It may possibly affect the method of dealing with the International Postal Telegraphic and Telephonic Conventions.

At present we are members of (a) The Universal Postal Union and (b) The International Telecommunications (i.e. Telegraph, Telephone and Radio) Convention. Membership of these bodies, which regulate the international control exchange and transit of mails, telegrams, telephone-calls and wireless, involves an annual payment by us towards expenses of about £600 a year, provided for in Sub-head B of the Estimates. These Conventions are revised every five years, and are then ratified afresh by the respective Governments. The Telecommunications Convention, for instance, will be revised next year, and the Postal one in the following year. Hitherto these agreements have not been laid before the Dáil at all, being purely technical and administrative. At present they are ratified by the Post Office obtaining, in the ordinary way, the sanction of the Department of Finance and Department of External Affairs to the arrangements. This new clause would, however, possibly involve these agreements being somehow laid before the Dáil—it depends, of course, on the interpretation of the phrase 'unless the terms of the agreement shall have been approved by Dáil Éireann', and they are very technical documents running into several hundreds of pages of folio printing of no general interest. The point would be met if the qualifying proviso in 25.6 were also added here, viz., 'this provision shall not however apply to international conventions of a purely technical and administrative character'.

There is also, it seems to me, another possibility arising out of this Article, that any agreement we might make with the British Post Office Administration on even a minor question of administrative detail involving finance might be held to be an 'international agreement' under this clause. At the present moment, of course, everything of this sort is scrutinised by Finance, by the Comptroller and Auditor General, and by the Dáil itself through the Public Accounts Committee.

This Article would probably affect other Departments also, and the point should be considered and elucidated by the Parliamentary Draftsman.

Article 27.1:
Would it not be desirable to make it clear that the Council of State is a purely advisory body whose advice the President is free to accept or reject? After Council of State *insert* 'an advisory body'.

What quorum is required for the Council of State.

Article 29:
Section 1.1°: In the event of disagreement among the three members of the Commission would it not be well to make provision for a decision? Suggest a new Section 6:

Section 6: In the event of the Commission appointed under this Article not being able to arrive at a unanimous decision on any matter referred to it the decision shall rest with the Chairman.

[Matter omitted]

Article 41:
Section 5: Par. (i)—Should 'their' be 'his'? Would it not be better for par. (iii) to become par. (i)?

Section 10: 'on the basis of the various forms of social activities'. Not clear as to meaning of this.

Article 43.6:
Would it not be desirable to make provision for appeal to or review by an existing Court say the Supreme Court?

After 'as may be' insert 'designated or'?

Article 46.1:
Would it not be well to insert the same provision as in Section 2.1° regarding the minimum percentage required to make the Amendment effective? Otherwise if people are apathetic the Constitution may be altered by the votes of a very small percentage of the electorate.

Article 50:
Section 1: Would it be desirable to make it more clear by the insertion of the words 'without a Referendum' after the words 'by the Oireachtas'?

[Matter omitted]

No. 108: NAI, DT S9715B

Memorandum from the Department of Lands to M. Moynihnan Observations on 1st circulated draft

[?] March 1937

Article 10 seems to raise a difficulty in construction. It appears to contemplate minerals being owned by Éire and at the same time by private individuals.

Article 11.3.2°:
The period of 30 days within the limits of which the election of President must be held appears from the administrative point of view to be too short. A wider limit might be advisable.

11.11:
The sixty-day period in this section seems to be too short for the purpose indicated. A period of three months might be allowed with a view to administrative case and efficiency.

Article 23.3:
Subsection 3 gives the President only six days in which to consult the Council of State and give his decision on the petition. This six-day period seems to be too short.

Article 29.2 and 29.3:
Is it not necessary to provide some machinery for the calling together of the Council of State in the absence of incapacity of the President? Who is to do it?

Article 35:
The Land Commission is affected by this Article and it is considered that it will be necessary to include specific reference to the exercise of 'judicial powers' by the persons or bodies covered by the Article. Certain of the Land Commission's functions come, without question, under the head of 'judicial powers', and might be held to be outside the scope of the Article which validates only '*limited functions* of a judicial *nature*'. In view of all that has been said by the Courts about 'judicial functions', 'judicial acts' and 'judicial powers' it seems to be necessary that 'powers' should be specifically mentioned in this Article.

The Legal Adviser to the Land Commission has made the following observations on this Article:

I note that the phrase 'Judicial Power' no longer occurs in the Constitution, Article 32.1 using, instead, the word 'Justice'. There is therefore not the necessity I thought there would be for the use of the phrase Judicial Power in Article 35; all the same I think it would be safer to have the word 'power' in this Article to prevent the argument being used that the 'exercise of judicial power' was another way of saying 'administration of justice'. I would venture to say just, therefore, that in lieu of the words 'limited functions of a judicial nature' the following words should be inserted: 'powers and functions of a judicial nature within a limited jurisdiction authorised by law'.

I also feel a difficulty about the concluding words of the Article: as it reads the functions may be exercised by a body, notwithstanding that the body is not a Court appointed or established under the Constitution. Supposing, however, that it is considered advisable to establish or rather to re-establish the Land Commission as a Court of limited jurisdiction, under Article 32.3.2°, we might be met by the old argument that the judicial functions referred to in Article 35 could not be exercised by any persons except Judges of the Courts of limited jurisdiction. My difficulty, which may have nothing in it, would be met by substituting for the words 'notwithstanding that' the words 'whether or not', and omitting the word 'not' in the following line.

What I am afraid of is that it could be argued and possibly decided that Article 35 had no reference to Courts of limited jurisdiction.

Henry Monahan

Article 38.5:
Is there any difference between the 'true morality' of page 36 and the 'right morality' of page 37? Is either adjective necessary?

Article 40.5 binds the State to provide 'free primary education'. At present a School Manager must find a fixed proportion of the cost of school buildings and must maintain them, keep them cleaned and heated, etc. Would the Article as worded provide an argument for additional claims on State financial assistance?

41.7.2°:

'The State shall endeavour to give to us as many families as practicable a share in the land'.

It is considered that this particular phrase in this section should not be allowed to stand as drafted. There can be few more dangerous suggestions, at the present juncture, when the State is expending its utmost efforts in taking over and re-distributing all the suitable land that is not adequately worked, than that it should be made the object of the State to give as many people as possible a share in the land. There is no easier way of distributing land than to give all comers a share; *but there is no more certain method of wasting and misusing a national asset.* There is no advantage to the community unless the land distributed is to be worked by competent agriculturists who will live on it without further assistance from the State and who will produce from it more than it has been producing and will maintain on it and out of it a greater number of human beings than have been maintained in the past. The subsection as it stands would compel a change in Land Commission policy. They would have to cast their net more widely than they do and to divide the lands acquired in smaller parcels and to many more people than they would regard as wise or profitable. The argument of the Constitution would be unanswerable; access to land would have to be given to the maximum number of families.

It is more strongly suggested that the subsection should be amended in such manner as the following: 'the State shall endeavour to place as many families as practicable in a position of economic security on the land.' This would give the approval of the Constitution to the ideal of raising the many poor, uneconomic holdings to an economic level and placing as many families as possible on small holdings capable of maintaining them in reasonable comfort.

No. 109: NAI, DT S9715B

Memorandum from the Ceann Comhairle, Frank Fahy to Maurice Moynihan
Observations on 1st circulated draft

[?] March 1937

Article 11.2.2°:

It is observed that the age qualification fixed by this sub-section is that a citizen must have *completed* the age of twenty-one years. In the cases, however, of Dáil elections (Article 14.3°)[187] and the Referendum (Article

[187] This appears to be a reference to Article 14.1.1°.

46.3) the Articles are phrased: 'Every citizen who has *reached* the age of twenty-one years' etc. The reason for the change in phraseology is not apparent, but it may be desirable that the phrasing should be uniform in all cases.

Article 11.7:
Presumably it is not considered necessary to prescribe a place where the declaration is to be taken and subscribed—for example, the Dáil Chamber.

Article 11.10 and Article 12.13.2°:
The matter of impeachment of the President arises in Section 10 of Article 11, and in Section 13, Subsection 2° of Article 12 and it may be convenient to put forward in one note, certain queries arising on both.

Those in connection with Section 10 are:

(a) Whether a supplementary law working out the form and process of impeachment is contemplated.
(b) If not, whether the impeachment is to be by way of Resolution for the passing of which a bare majority or casting vote (Article 13.12.1°) will suffice?
(c) If it is to be by Resolution, who will construe the offences which are 'other high crimes and misdemeanours'?
(d) Will the Dáil, for purposes of Section 13, Subsection 2°, be a Court—*vide* Article 13.14?
(e) Will removal from office be the only punishment for the offence of treason?

And that on Section 13, Subsection 2° of Article 12 is:

(f) The meaning attaching to the provision 'as is, in the opinion of the Chairman of Dáil Éireann necessary for the proper investigation of the charge'.

It is desired to preface the comments on the points raised by saying that one would prefer, if it were found practicable, to omit the impeachment provisions. It is recognised, however, that other Constitutions make provision in this regard, and in view, particularly, of the provisions contained in Section 13.3° of Article 12, it is presumed contingencies such as are covered by Section 10.1° of Article 11 must be provided for. In regard to the points raised:

(a) The answer would appear to be in the negative. But a supplementary law would, it is considered, be a preferable course. Procedure in such investigations appears to have been (and may be still) the subject matter of separate enactments in for example, France, Poland and Czechoslovakia. There are so many matters, which one can contemplate arising that some more detailed direction seems essential.

(b) If impeachment is to be by way of Resolution there would seem to be lack of perspective in stipulating that in such a serious matter a bare majority in a House of a quorum or over, or a casting vote, should suffice, particularly in view of the provision of Article 15.2.2°—which stipulates that for the decision of a minor matter such as the possible reference of a Bill to a Committee of Privileges, there must be a House of 35 members.

(c) Again, if impeachment is to be by Resolution it is considered that the construction of the expression 'other high crimes and misdemeanours' should not be left without further guidance to the Chairman of the House.

(d) This query is prompted by the consideration that Houses of Parliament when engaged on the trial of charges are treated as Courts of Record.

(e) If removal from office is to be the only punishment, it is feared that the proposal will provoke considerable criticism as being totally inadequate for the crime of treason as defined in the Draft Constitution. One may recall in this connection that the President will be a person elected to the highest office in the gift of the people by their votes. One further observes that in cases of conviction of impeachment in, for example, the United States, that the party convicted, in addition to removal from office and disqualification to hold and enjoy any office of honour, trust or profit under the United States, 'shall nevertheless be liable and subject to indictment trial, judgment and punishment, according to law' (Section 3 of the Constitution of the United States of America).

(f) Remarks somewhat similar to those offered in regard to the Chairman of the Seanad in sub-paragraph (c) apply also to this matter. If the function of the Chairman of the Dáil is to be simply to construe a Resolution of the Seanad from the point of view of relevancy and order in debate, then the matter would appear to be one for the Standing Orders of the Dáil which that House is empowered to make under Article 13.10. If, however, it is to be the Chairman's function to rule

> regarding admissibility of evidence and such matters, then the Chairman, on such an occasion should, it is considered, be a Judge of the Supreme Court. The Constitution of the United States of America provides that on the trial of the President of that country the Chief Justice presides.

Article 11.11.3°:
Presumably the President's emoluments will be charged on the Central Fund? If so, it might be well to insert a provision to this effect in this Subsection, even though [Article 12], Section 13.1° gives him protection from criticism in debate in the Dáil.

Article 12.1.1°:
The term 'Taoiseach' has acquired a military significance which might be considered objectionable. Would not 'Príomh-Aire' be a better term?

Article 12.4:
The descriptions in this section of Bills, as being 'Bills of the Parliament' seems unnecessary, if, indeed, not inaccurate in the case of Bills of the third category (reference to a Committee of Privileges). In the latter case the Bills have only passed one House, and, consequently, an inaccuracy in description is suggested. Furthermore, the description is not consistently applied, because in Article 45.2, there is a description of a Bill as 'a Bill of the Oireachtas'.

It is suggested that the words 'of the Parliament' should be omitted in Section 4 of Article 12, and the words 'of the Oireachtas' in section 2 of Article 45.

Article 12.8:
Tribunals have been established under the Tribunals of Evidence Act, 1921, for the investigation of such matters as the Pig Industry, Marketing of Vegetables etc. Would it be necessary under the terms of this section, that Chairmen of such Tribunals should, after the coming into operation of the Draft Constitution, be Judges?

Article 12.13.2°:
In regard to this Subsection, please see the comments offered on the subject matter of impeachment generally, on Article 11.10.

Article 12.13.3°:
This is another Subsection which, it is surmised, will provoke unfavourable criticism, when read in conjunction with the impeachment provision. Furthermore, it seems to embody a change in policy in regard to road traffic cases. After considerable pressure in the Dáil, the Minister

for Local Government and Public Health put forward, and had accepted, a section in the Road Traffic Bill of 1933, making liable the Minister for Finance for accidents caused by cars used by Officers of State. In view of that declaration of policy, and so recently, it seems illogical to exempt a car used by the President, and to continue liability in cases of cars used by the Taoiseach, the Tánaiste and other Ministers.

A personal view-point on the Subsection, as a whole, is that it is anachronistic.

The National Parliament

General:
Suggestions in regard to Articles 13 to 23 inclusive have already been supplied. The following further observations are offered:

Article 13.8:
It is observed that the description 'session' is retained, without definition. It has been previously suggested that description 'sitting' is, in view of the practice obtaining, more accurate. A session of the Dáil, for example is coterminous with the life of the Parliament. The House is adjourned over Recesses, and not prorogued. The practice has much to commend it.

Article 14.2.6°:
It was suggested that this Subsection should be deleted, for the reason that it was considered that a debate on the subject whether three member constituencies meet the requirements of P[roportional] R[epresentation] should not be dragged across the discussion of the Draft Constitution. One has as heard it stated by persons who consider themselves experts on the question that three member constituencies do not.

It is still considered that the subject should await the next Revision of Constituencies Bill.

Article 15.2.3°:
It is presumed that the questions of including time limits for the appointment of a Committee of Privileges, and for its report back—previously provided for in Article 35 of the Constitution—have been considered and that such provisions are found to be unnecessary.

Article 16.1:
I take it that the working out of the scheme adopted for electing a Seanad necessitates a revision to the 60 number Seanad, and overrules all arguments advanced against such a large and expensive Second Chamber.

Article 16.4:
Extraneous consideration probably makes it advisable to grant equal representation to both Universities. Could the question be considered in the abstract, it would seem reasonable to assign greater representation to the National University which has three constituent colleges and which enters more largely into the life of the nation.

Article 16.7.3°:
Provision will have to be made for early and authoritative returns of the number of first preference votes received by Dáil candidates.

Article 20.4:
A question arises on this section as to the position of a Bill, introduced as an 'Urgency Bill', under the terms of section 7.1°, which on its passage by the Dáil was found by the Ceann Comhairle to be a Money Bill, was so certified by him, was then sent to Seanad Éireann with a resolution abridging the time for consideration to a period lesser than the 21 days permitted under Section 4. If the period was 21 days or over, no question would arise, because the full constitutional period would be available, but if under 21, which section would apply? One can conceive of an 'Urgency Bill' as defined in Section 7.1°, being a 'Money Bill'.

If the point is considered one of substance, it is suggested that Section 4.1° might be amended by the insertion after the words 'Every Money Bill' of the words 'other than a Money Bill in respect of which a resolution shall have been passed by Dáil Éireann under Section 7 of this Article'.

Article 20.7.1°:
It has been represented that the words 'abridged to' in the second line on page 20 are unnecessary, since in respect of 'Urgency Bills', there will be no stated period—such Bills being excluded from the scope of Section 5. The suggestion is that the Subsection should conclude: 'shall, if Dáil Éireann so resolves be such period as shall be specified in the resolution'.

Article 21.2.2°:
Here, also, it is presumed that the concurrence of Seanad Éireann means the passing of a Resolution to that effect in a House of a quorum or over.

Article 21.3:
Should not Money Bills also be included in this section? The greater number of such Bills are purely formal Bills, e.g., Central Fund Bills, Appropriation Bills—in the full enactment of which time is a factor and—for the earlier signing of which resolutions of concurrence should not be necessary.

Article 21.4.5°:
The wording of this Subsection prompts a query as to how the Clerk of the Dáil can cause to be issued an *authoritative text* in the Irish language? What would be the authority—since presumably the Irish text will not have been the version before the Oireachtas? The Clerk can cause to be issued an authorised translation—which he had done up to the present—the authority being the Standing Orders.

Moreover, is not the implication in the Subsection that Bills will be enacted in the English language, and if that be so, is the provision a desirable one, from the Irish language point of view, to write into the Draft Constitution.

The suggestion is that the Subsection should be amended to read as follows: 'The Clerk of Dáil Éireann or such officer as aforesaid shall cause a translation to be made of each such law into the official language other than that in which the said Bill was signed.'

Article 24:
Presumably it has not been considered necessary to include in this Article provisions similar to those contained in Articles 58 and 59 of the present Constitution—appointment of a member as a Minister entailing no obligation upon him to resign his seat or to submit himself for re-election; and that the remuneration of a Minister shall not be diminished during his term of office.

The latter provision enabled the Ceann Comhairle to rule out of order motions on the Estimates that reduced sums payable as salaries, and was considered a useful provision. The alternative method was to move that the Estimate be referred back for re-consideration, and the view is held that under this method the attack on the Estimate was directed more on line of an administrative and political character than on a personal basis. That view may not be held generally, but if experience supports it, it is thought that the provision might be inserted.

The President's emoluments and allowances are not to be diminished during his term[s] of office (Article 11.12.3°).

Article 29.2.2°
Would the duty of signing and promulgating Acts devolve on the Chairman of such Commission? I observe (Section 4) that any two of the Commissioners may act.

Article 37: Treason
The definition appears to be isolated and insulated. Presumably it must be considered in relation to the statute law that prescribes the punishment for the offence.

Article 43.3.1°:
Under the Protection of the Community (Special Powers) Act, 1926, the proclamation was expressed to summon *the Oireachtas* 'to reassemble…on a convenient day…not less than three nor more than five days after the making of the proclamation'. Should not there be some time limit also fixed either in 1° or 2°?

Article 45.2:
The description 'Bill of the Oireachtas' has been commented in the note to Article 12.4.

Article 46.3:
Every citizen is to be entitled to vote, and subject to that and the other provisions, the Referendum is to be regulated by law. But presumably citizens disqualified under the prevailing electoral law will not be entitled to vote. The insertion after the word 'years' of the words 'and who complies with the provisions of the prevailing electoral laws' is suggested. In this connection, reference is made to the terms of Article 14 of the present Constitution.

Article 54.2:
It is observed that the Ceann Comhairle will be carried over as a member of the Dáil, but not as Chairman. It would seem, therefore, that the Chairman of the Chamber of Deputies, who will be a member of the Commission provided for in Article 56.2, will have to submit himself for re-election. It is considered that equally with the other Officers who will form the Commission, the Ceann Comhairle should also be carried over.

No. 110: NAI, DT S9715B

Maurice Moynihan to William T. O'Brien[188]

Department of the President
25 March 1937

A chara,

1. I am directed by the President to send you herewith three copies of the draft Constitution for your consideration.
2. Articles 38 to 42 are not yet in their final form.
3. The President would be glad to have, as soon as possible, the observations of the Revenue Commissioners on the

[188] William T. O'Brien (1872–1941), Chairman of the Revenue Commissioners (1923–39).

Constitution generally and in particular on those Articles containing provisions which appear to be the special concern of the Commissioners.[189]

No. 111: UCDA, P150/2395

Fr John Charles McQuaid to Eamon de Valera

Blackrock, Co. Dublin
25 March 1937

Herewith I send with great pleasure the remaining dossier, print by print, for the Family, Education and Private Property.[190] By tonight, I hope to have Church and State all typed. These are auspicious days for the work.[191]

No. 112: UCDA, P150/2395

Fr John Charles McQuaid to Eamon de Valera

Blackrock, Co. Dublin
25 March 1937

I am very sorry if I am somewhat late—and I hope I have not disappointed. I enclose the more useful excerpts connected with Religion.[192] There are a few more valuable ones, but they can follow.

No. 113: UCDA, P150/2395

Fr John Charles McQuaid to Eamon de Valera

Blackrock, Co. Dublin
26 March 1937

I enclose the last of my dossier: with the sincere hope that it will prove of some avail.[193] What of the Secret Societies clause? I hope you are not too tired after three nights of labour; and that all goes well.

P.S. Would a note on 'Law' and the 'Common Good' be of some use, I wonder? I can easily prepare them.

[189] For response see document no. 126.
[190] Enclosure not found.
[191] In 1937, Holy Thursday fell on 25 March.
[192] Enclosure not found.
[193] Enclosure not found.

No. 114: NAI, DT S10159

Memorandum by George Gavan Duffy
Observations on 1st circulated draft

Dublin
[Undated]

Article 10:
It is observed that land is left out. But from whom does the owner in fee simple hold, if not from the State? And what right has the State to claim escheat on failure of heirs, if it is not the ultimate owner on behalf of the people? Section 2 puts land in a different category from natural resources by limiting the ownership of Éire to whatever the Saorstát owned, thus suggesting that there was a difference between the State's right in land and in natural resources. Nobody knows what were the rights in land of Saorstát Éireann, and it might be agreed that the ultimate royal title thereto was never effectually got rid of, whereas section 1 is clear and definite. Existing private rights are preserved by Article 49, but the phraseology of the print would seem to give them a constitutional status, so that the State could not buy them out, even with compensation, nor could it abrogate any private right in the natural resources which may be a mere abuse today. The suggested amendment leaves the Oireachtas free to act in the public interest.

Article 13:
The Oireachtas may, however, provide for the delegation of subordinate legislative functions by the creation and recognition of legislative administrative and other subordinate authorities and bodies, with functions of a minor legislative character. Whenever a Minister makes a statutory order and whenever a local authority makes a by-law, they are really making laws; so much so, that these enactments are intended to be kept in force as 'laws' by Article 49.

Article 16.7:
(v. Public Administration, including local government, and (*from planning*) social services).

Planning is likely to be of tremendous importance during the next twenty years, to judge by the example of other countries, and seems well worthy of special mention.

Article 22:
It would hardly be fair for the President to ask the Court, nor practicable for the Court to answer such a question as 'Can you find anything unconstitutional in this Bill?'

The practical way of making the Court consultative is to enable the Govt. to inquire whether or not a Bill is for specified reasons, or in specified requests, unconstitutional, or to limit the inquiry to a specified clause or clauses.

If this view is accepted, some re-drafting of Article 22 is necessary. I have not attempted this in the absence of more definite information as to the intention of the Article. But the objection above noted to its present form will be felt, and no doubt voiced, very strongly by lawyers. The alternative way suggested would seem to give the Govt. all that it really needs and to give a very useful power to consult the Court.

Article 22.2.2°:
The silencing of dissenting opinions comes from the British Privy Council, where its purpose is to conceal dissent from India and African nations, and from the Court of Criminal Appeal, where the purpose is to conceal dissent from the criminal. Surely it would be most undemocratic to apply the same policy to judicial opinions on the Constitution, and the people are entitled to know what their judges think. This would give an artificial sanction to the opinion of 3 Judges against 2, and those 2 are fully entitled to be heard, especially as they may be right.

Article 26.8:
Provision may be made by law for constituting a Director of Public Prosecution to act under and on behalf of the Attorney General in the administration of the criminal law.

(Without this provision a constitutional amendment would be necessary. The underlying idea is that there should be another barrister to relieve the Attorney from all prosecuting business and leave him free for the more important work, especially for the undertaking of the extensive law reforms that we need and that require a great deal of time and thought.)

Article 28:
The powers of the Council of State under sections 2 and 3 of this Article may be exercised by a majority in number of the Council.

It seems necessary to provide that the whole Council need not meet to do a valid Act, especially as one or more of the members may at a critical moment be ill or abroad.

Article 32:
Under this enactment as it stands there will be an appeal from the High Court in every case until a *future* law otherwise determines. It was so held by the Supreme Court under the corresponding provision (Article 66) of the present Constitution. Consequently, I have suggested an amendment to Article 49 to preserve existing rights of appeal pending any new legislation. The mere continuance of existing jurisdictions under Article 57 would not otherwise continue a right of appeal, which is now to be prescribed by a new law of the new Oireachtas, over the new Supreme and High Courts as established. (Re. Warner, 1929, IR 582.)

I suggest coupling the President of the High Court with the Chief Justice in order to avoid a deadlock in case of the death or illness of the Chief Justice.

Article 36.1.1°:
The suggested amendment is to prevent internment without trial.

Article 36.4:
Courts of summary jurisdiction shall try and punish minor offences only.

The amendment would prevent the infliction of very heavy Customs and Excise penalties by a police court. A more responsible Court seems desirable for a severe penalty.

Article 37:
Addition to iv. 'And shall be cognisable by the courts, whether committed within or without the territory of Éire'.

The addition is suggested because at Common Law we cannot punish a crime committed abroad.

Article 38:
During vacation a condition order of '*habeas corpus*' may have to be made in a judge's home. Perhaps the proposed amendment to Article 32 may cover the point.

Article 40:
This amendment is suggested because the Courts are accustomed to acting in a child's best interest so that the phrase gives an easily ascertainable standard, while the phrase in the print is much more indefinable.

Article 43:
It is suggested that it should be made clear (if so intended) that the present Article 2A will not be continued in force, as an existing law under Article 49. It will be observed that one effect of this repeal would seem

to be that persons sentenced under Article 2A will be entitled to release upon the coming into force of this Constitution, unless provision be made to the contrary.

Article 49:
See note to Article 32.

Article 57:
The jurisdiction will not be quite 'the same' under the new policy.

No. 115: UCDA, P150/2395

Fr John Charles McQuaid to Eamon de Valera

Blackrock, Co. Dublin
27 March 1937

This letter is unusual from me: it is only one of good wishes for a peaceful Easter. I hope you will soon draw breath—whatever breath my friends, the jurists, will have left you.

No. 116: NAI, DT S9715B

Draft Article 45

Stephen Roche and Philip O'Donoghue
30 March 1937

Article 45: To take the place of Articles 43 and 44
Special Provisions For The Preservation Of Public Order

1. 1° The Oireachtas may enact legislation making special provision for the preservation of public order and, in particular, for the setting up of Extraordinary Courts with such jurisdiction and powers as may be thought necessary for the purpose.

   2° Every Bill for an Act to which it is intended that this Article shall apply shall be expressed to be 'An Act for the preservation of public order and in pursuance of the provisions of Article 43 of the Constitution'.
2. Nothing in Articles...of this Constitution shall be invoked to invalidate any provision of this Article or of any legislation

passed under this Article or to oust the jurisdiction of any court established by, or to nullify any act or thing done in pursuance of any such legislation as aforesaid.

3. Legislation enacted under this Article shall not come into operation unless and until a proclamation shall have been made by the President under this Article.
4. If and whenever the Government are satisfied that the ordinary laws and the Civil Courts are not adequate for the preservation of public order the Government may so advise the President who shall, forthwith, issue a proclamation declaring that the legislation enacted under this Article shall come into operation.
5. Upon the making of such proclamation the said legislation shall immediately come into operation and shall remain in operation until determined in the manner provided in this Article.
6. Every proclamation made by the President under this Article shall, forthwith, be laid before Dáil Éireann, if sitting, and if Dáil Éireann is not sitting at the sitting thereof which takes place next after such proclamation.
7. If Dáil Éireann is not sitting the President may, after consultation with the Council of State, and if so required in writing by not less than twenty Deputies, summon Dáil Éireann at the earliest practicable date.
8. The legislation shall remain in operation until its operation is determined either by a proclamation of the President on the advice of the Government, or, a resolution of Dáil Éireann without prejudice in either event to the validity of anything done thereunder.
9. The Oireachtas may at any time repeal or amend legislation enacted under this Article.

No. 117: NAI, DT S9175B

Draft Article 38

[Department of Justice?]
30 March 1937

1. 1° No person shall be tried save in due course of law.

2° Extraordinary courts shall not be established save only such extraordinary courts as may be established by law for dealing with a state of war or armed rebellion or in pursuance of Article 43 hereof and such military tribunals as may be authorised by law for the trial of offences against military law alleged to have been committed by persons while subject to military law.

2. A member of the Defence Forces of Éire not on active military service shall not be tried by any court martial or other military tribunal for an offence cognisable by the civil courts unless such offence is within the jurisdiction of courts martial or other military tribunal by any law or regulations for the enforcement of military discipline.
3. No person shall be tried on any criminal charge without a jury except in the case of offences triable by a court of summary jurisdiction, charges for offences triable by extraordinary courts during a state of war or armed rebellion or in pursuance of Article 43 hereof and charges for offences against military law alleged to have been committed by persons while subject to military law.
4. Extraordinary courts, military tribunals and court martials mentioned in this Article are not courts within the meaning of Articles 32 and 26.3.[194]

No. 118: NAI, DT S9734

Maurice Moynihan to all Ministers

Department of the President
30 March 1937

1. I enclose herewith copy of a letter addressed by the Parliamentary Draftsman to the Attorney General in regard to legislation which will be necessary consequent on the coming into operation of the Constitution.[195]
2. The President concurs in the suggestion of the Parliamentary Draftsman that in general such legislation should be enacted

[194] Attached to this document is a handwritten memorandum by Michael McDunphy, headed 'Constitution (1937)—Establishment of Extraordinary Courts', dated 26 March 1937. It reads: 'The attached memo has been approved by the President as an article of the Constitution relating to the preservation of order. Mr Roche will have the necessary legislation prepared. It will take the place of Article 2A of the present Constitution'. Revised drafts of Article 38 and a draft of Article 45, incorporating the suggestions of this memo, were prepared on 30 March 1937.

[195] See Chapter XII of this volume.

in the interval between the date of the determination of the result of the Plebiscite and the date of the coming into operation of the Constitution.

He will be glad, therefore, if arrangements may be made by Departments for the preparation of legislation on that basis.

3. It is expected that the final draft of the Constitution will be available about the 7th proximo.

No. 119: UCDA, P150/2395

Fr John Charles McQuaid to Eamon de Valera

Blackrock, Co. Dublin
31 March 1937

I think the enclosed is safe and sure.[196] 'Juridical' in English would mean 'presumed to exist in law' or 'duly registered as an institution'. I hope to report progress by night time.

P.S. Perhaps you will have the sheet of suggestions on Article 41 by this evening. I can work on them too.

[196] Enclosure not found.

CHAPTER X

REVISING THE DRAFT CONSTITUTION, APRIL 1937*

NO. 120: NAI, DT S9715B

Memorandum regarding the 1st Revise of the Draft Constitution

Michael McDunphy, Department of the President
1 April 1937

Following the receipt of Ministerial and Departmental observations, the President appointed the undermentioned as a committee to examine the draft Constitution in detail in constant consultation with him.

Mr Maurice Moynihan	Secretary to the Executive Council.
Mr M[ichael]. McDunphy	Asst. Secretary to the Executive Council
Mr Philip O'Donoghue	Legal Assistant, Attorney General's Department
Mr John Hearne, B.L.	Asst. Legal Advisor, Department of External Affairs

As a result of the work of this committee a revise [of the Constitution] was produced, and printed copies of this first revise were in the hands of the President on 1 April.

*For commentary on the documents reproduced here, see Chapter IX.

No. 121: NAI, DT S9746

1st Revise of Constitution

1 April 1937

See www.irishconstitution.ie.

No. 122: NAI, DT S9868

Memorandum from John Hearne to Eamon de Valera

Department of External Affairs
3 April 1937

The Courts
The provisions with regard to the Courts are briefly as follows. There will be a High Court, a Supreme Court and Courts of lesser jurisdiction as at present. The judges will be independent in the exercise of their functions, subject only to the Constitution and the law. Jurisdiction to determine questions as to the validity of laws is reserved to the Supreme Court alone. You will recall that under the existing Constitution that jurisdiction is vested in the High Court with an appeal to the Supreme Court. In a list before me of fifty two countries I find that the courts of fourteen of these countries have powers comparable to those of the Supreme Court of the United States to pass on the constitutionality of laws, that the courts of seventeen have limited powers in this regard, and that the courts of twenty-one have no power to pass on the question at all. Where the Constitution of a country is written down and the legislative powers of the Parliament are declared to be subject to the Constitution, there must be an authority to determine the question as to the constitutionality of laws. The view on which the arrangement proposed in the draft Constitution is that Constitutional issues should be determined expeditiously and finally on the authority of the highest judicial tribunal in the land.

No. 123: UCDA, P150/2419

'Documents shown to [Papal] Nuncio on first visit (A1, B1, C1)'

3 April 1937

(A1)[1]
Article 42: Religion

1. The State acknowledges the right of Almighty God to public worship in that way which He has shown to be His Will.
2. Accordingly, the State shall hold in honour the name of God and shall consider it a duty to favour and protect religion ~~and shall not enact any measure that may impair its credit.~~
3. The State acknowledges that the true religion is that established by our Divine Lord, Jesus Christ Himself, which He committed to His Church to protect and propagate, as the ~~guardian and interpreter of true morality. It acknowledges, moreover, that the Church of Christ is the Catholic Church.~~ (spiritual guide of men and the guardian of right morals).[2]
4. ~~The State recognises the Church of Christ as a perfect society, having within itself full competence and sovereign authority, in respect of the spiritual good of men.~~
5. ~~1° Whatever may be ranked under the civil and political order is rightly subject to the supreme authority of the perfect society, the State, whose function is to procure the temporal well-being, moral and material, of Society.~~
~~2° The State pledges itself, therefore, in virtue of this sovereign authority conferred on it by God within its temporal sphere to enforce respect, by its just laws, for the inalienable rights of the citizen and the family, and to preserve, as best it can, conditions of right social and moral well-being.~~
~~3° In cases where the jurisdiction of Church and State requires to be harmoniously co-ordinated, the State may come to a special agreement with the Church and other~~

[1] Annotated by de Valera: 'Copy shown Nuncio—3 April. Did not leave a copy'. All emendations made in the document were written by de Valera. It is unclear whether these emendations were made prior to, during or after the visit to the Nuncio.
[2] Section in parentheses added manually in the margin by de Valera.

~~Religious Bodies, upon particular matters, civil, political and religious.~~[3]

6. [renumbered as 4] The State guarantees to all its citizens freedom of religious conviction and liberty to practice their religion, in private and in public, having due regard however to ~~social~~ public order and ~~right~~ morality.
7. [renumbered as 5] 1° The State pledges itself not to impose any disabilities on the ground of religious conviction that would be contrary to natural rights and social justice. (2° In particular, the State shall raise no barrier to employment in the public service on such a ground.)[4]
8. [renumbered as 6] Every religious association, recognised by the State shall have the right to manage its own affairs, own, acquire and administer property, movable and immovable, and maintain institutions for religious and charitable purposes.
9. [renumbered as 7] The property of a religious denomination shall not be diverted, save for necessary works of public utility and on payment of just compensation.
10. [renumbered as 8] Legislation providing State aid for schools shall contain no discrimination against schools under the management of a particular religious denomination.

(B1)[5]

Article [blank]: Religion

1. The State acknowledges the right of Almighty God to public worship in that way which He has shown to be His Will.
2. Accordingly, the State shall hold in honour the Name of God and shall consider it a duty to favour and protect religion.
3. ~~The State acknowledges that the true religion is that established by our Divine Lord, Jesus Christ Himself, which He committed to His Church to protect and propagate, as the spiritual guide of men and the guardian of right morals.~~[6]
4. The State guarantees to all its citizens freedom of religious conviction and liberty to practice their religion, in private and in public, having due regard however to public order and morality.

[3] Sections 4 and 5 have been crossed out in their entirety by de Valera, with the note 'free exercise' written in the margin.

[4] Section in parentheses added manually in the margin by de Valera.

[5] Annotated by de Valera: 'This is a copy of Document shown to Nuncio on 3 April. Copy left with him'. All emendations are made manually by de Valera.

[6] Entire section has been crossed out.

5. The State ~~pledges itself~~ guarantees not to impose any disabilities on the ground of religious conviction that would be contrary to natural rights and social justice~~. In particular, the State~~, nor shall the State place any barrier to employment in the public service on such a ground.
6. Legislation providing State aid for schools shall contain no discrimination against schools under the management of a particular religious denomination.
7. Every religious association, recognised by the State, shall have the right to manage its own affairs, own, acquire and administer property, movable and immovable, and maintain institutions for religious and charitable purposes.
8. The Property of a religious denomination shall not be diverted save for necessary works of public utility and on payment of just compensation.

(C1)[7]

Bunreacht

IN THE NAME OF THE MOST HOLY TRINITY, from Whom is all authority and to Whom, as our final end, all actions both of men and States must be referred,

WE, THE PEOPLE OF ÉIRE, Motherland of the Irish Race,

HUMBLY ACKNOWLEDGING all our obligations to our Divine Lord, Jesus Christ, for Whose true worship our fathers have endured so many centuries of pain.

GRATEFULLY RECALLING their heroic and unremitting struggle, especially in these latter times, to regain the rightful independence of our Nation.

AND SEEKING to promote the common good by due observance of the Christian principles of Prudence, Justice and Charity, whereby the dignity and freedom of the citizens may be rightfully secured and true social order adequately established and maintained,

DO NOW CONFIRM, ENACT, and PROCLAIM this our CONSTITUTION.

[7] Annotated by de Valera: 'Copy of the Preamble shown to Nuncio 3 April. He was left copy'.

No. 124: UCDA, P150/2395

Fr John Charles McQuaid to Eamon de Valera

Blackrock, Co. Dublin
5 April 1937

I beg to enclose herewith an amendment of Paragraph 6—which seems to me better, for it more explicitly distinguishes between State—respect for *individual* choice in things religious and State; tolerance of differing forms of worship: two different aspects of religious tolerance.[8] The original was quite correct: this form is less open to an accusation of being inaccurate. And on this question very acute writing has been done.

No. 125: UCDA, P150/2419

'Copies of documents shown Archbishop [Edward] Byrne on first visit'

5 April 1937

BUNREACHT

IN THE NAME OF THE MOST HOLY TRINITY, from Whom is all authority and to Whom, as our final end, all actions both of men and States must be referred,

WE, THE PEOPLE OF ÉIRE, Motherland of the Irish Race,

HUMBLY ACKNOWLEDGING all our obligations to our Divine Lord, Jesus Christ, Who kept our fathers constant to His worship through centuries of trial,

GRATEFULLY RECALLING their heroic and unremitting struggle, to regain the rightful independence of our Nation,

AND SEEKING to promote the common good by due observance of the Christian principles of Prudence, Justice and Charity, whereby the dignity and freedom of the citizens may be rightfully secured and true social order established and maintained,

DO CONFIRM, ENACT, and Give to ourselves this Constitution.

[8] Enclosure not found.

Religion
Article [blank]

1. The State acknowledges the right of Almighty God to public worship in that way which He has shown to be His Will.
2. Accordingly, the State shall hold in honour the Name of God and shall consider it a duty to favour and protect religion.
3. The State guarantees to all its citizens freedom of religious conviction and liberty to practice their religion, in private and in public, having due regard, however, to public order and morality.
4. The State guarantees not to impose any disabilities on the ground of religious conviction that would be contrary to natural rights and social justice, nor shall the State place any barrier to employment in the public service on such a ground.
5. Legislation providing State aid for schools shall contain no discrimination against schools under the management of a particular religious denomination.
6. Every religious association recognised by the State shall have the right to manage its own affairs, own, acquire and administer property, movable and immovable, and maintain institutions for religious and charitable purposes.
7. The Property of a religious denomination shall not be diverted save for necessary works of public utility and on payment of just compensation.

The Family
Article [blank]

1. 1° The State recognises the Family as the natural primary and fundamental unit group of Society, as a moral institution possessing inalienable and imprescriptible rights, antecedent and superior to all positive law.

   2° The State, therefore, guarantees to protect the Family in its constitution and authority, as the necessary basis of social order and as indispensable to the welfare of the Nation and the State.
2. 1° In particular, the State recognises that by her life within the home, woman gives to the State a support without which the common good cannot be achieved.

   2° The State shall, therefore, endeavour to secure that women, especially mothers and young girls, shall not be obliged through economic necessity to enter avocations unsuited to their sex and strength.

2. 1° The State pledges itself to guard with special care the institution of Marriage, on which the Family is founded, and to protect it against attack.
   2° No law shall be passed which shall impair its essential properties of unity and indissolubility.
   3° No person whose marriage has been dissolved under the civil law of any other State shall be capable of contracting in Éire a valid marriage during the life-time of the other party to the marriage so dissolved.

Education
Article [blank]
The State acknowledges the Family as the primary and natural education of the child, and guarantees to respect the inalienable right and duty of parents to provide, according to their means, for the religious and moral, intellectual, physical and social education of their children.

Parents shall be free to provide this education in their home or in private schools or in schools recognised or established by the State.

The State shall not oblige parents in violation of their conscience and lawful preference to send their children to any particular type of school.

The State, however, as guardian of the common good, shall require in view of actual conditions that the children receive a certain minimum education, moral and intellectual, physical and social.

The State shall provide free primary education and shall aid and supplement private and corporate educational initiative and, when the public good requires it, provide other educational facilities, with due respect however for the rights of parents, especially in the matter of religious and moral formation.

In exceptional cases, where the parents for physical or moral reasons fail in their duty towards their children, the State as guardian of the common good, by appropriate means shall supply the place of the parents, but always with due respect for the natural and imprescriptible rights of the child.

No. 126: NAI, DT S9715B

Memorandum from William Denis Carey[9] to Maurice Moynihan
Observations on 1st circulated draft

Office of the Revenue Commissioners
7 April 1937

A Chara,
With reference to your letter of the 25 Márta, 1937, enclosing three copies of the draft Constitution for the consideration of the Revenue Commissioners, I am directed to offer the following observations.

Article 12 as revised:
Subsection 1, Section 11 of this Article requires careful consideration in order to ensure that the powers of the Revenue Commissioners under existing law are preserved. Section 33 of the Inland Revenue Regulation Act, 1890 (applied to Customs duties by the Excise Transfer Order, 1909) enables the Commissioners to mitigate or remit penalties and to order any person imprisoned for an offence against the Inland Revenue or Customs code to be discharged before the term of his imprisonment has expired. Section 76, Courts of Justice Act, 1936 (No. 48 of 1936), requires the Commissioners to discharge persons imprisoned at the expiration of six months from the date of committal for non-payment of a Revenue penalty.

No doubt arises in regard to persons imprisoned as a result of civil proceedings for non-payment of Revenue duties. The position, however, as to whether proceedings for the recovery of Revenue penalties are civil or criminal has become somewhat obscure and the result appears to be that in imposing a term of imprisonment for some offences against the Revenue, the Court would be exercising a civil and in others a criminal jurisdiction. In *Attorney General v. Casey*[10] the proceedings were held to be civil, but in *Attorney General v. Healy*[11] a prosecution for the recovery of penalties under the Customs Acts was held to be criminal. The question then arises, are the Commissioners' powers relating to the release of prisoners committed by a Court exercising criminal jurisdiction affected by the provisions of Subsection 1 of Section 11 of Article 12? There are

[9] Secretary to the Revenue Commissioners (1923–39); Chairman of the Revenue Commissioners (1939–44).
[10] [1930] 1 IR 163.
[11] [1928] 1 IR 460.

a great many cases of this kind which are hardly of sufficient importance to require the intervention of the President and administrative difficulties will arise if the existing powers of the Commissioners are not preserved.

Article 13:
It is for consideration whether Subsection 2 of Section 2 of this Article does not require qualification in order to put beyond doubt the validity of statutory regulations made by the Commissioners or of duties imposed by Emergency Orders under the Emergency Imposition of Duties Act, 1932.[12]

Article 26:
Under existing law various powers are vested in the Commissioners and their officers in connection with appeals and proceedings for the recovery of Revenue duties and penalties. The following are examples:

Section 149, Income Tax Act, 1918—Confers powers on the Inspector of Taxes in regard to statement of case for opinion of the High Court. Case taken in his name.

Section 56(6), Finance Act, 1920—Confers similar powers on Revenue Commissioners in connection with Corporation Profits Tax appeals. Case taken in their name.

Section 11, Finance Act, 1924—Authorises the Collector of Taxes to sue for Income Tax in his own name in the Circuit and District Courts.

Section 33(3) and Section 60(3), Finance (1909–10) Act, 1910—Authorises the Revenue Commissioners to nominate any person to consult with the Referee hearing appeals on questions of property valuation for Death Duty purposes.

Section 13, Stamp Act, 1891—Empowers the Commissioners to state case for opinion of the High Court.

Section 273, Customs Consolidation Act, 1876—Empowers Officers of Customs to conduct cases.

Section 27, Inland Revenue Regulation Act, 1890—Empowers officer of Inland Revenue to conduct cases.

Section 38, Finance Act, 1896—Authorises certain officers of the Commissioners to conduct cases in Circuit Court.

These laws are kept in force by Article 49, but it is feared that the provision in Article 26 requiring the Attorney General to represent the

[12] It may be noted that in *McDaid v. Sheehy*, [1991] 1 IR 1, the High Court held that Section 1 of the Imposition of Duties Act, 1957 contravened Article 15.2.1° of the Constitution in that it enabled the Government to vary tax rates by Executive Order and thus to legislate. This decision was set aside by the Supreme Court on the technical ground that it was not strictly necessary for the High Court to have arrived at that decision on the facts of the case. While the 1957 Act has never been repealed, the section has never since been used by the Government, presumably because the Attorney General has advised that the section would not survive constitutional challenge.

State in all legal proceedings for the enforcement of law may lead to litigation on the grounds that the Commissioners and their officers are acting unconstitutionally. In this connection it should be borne in mind that there is an increasing tendency on the part of taxpayers to rely on legal technicalities with a view to the evasion of Revenue duties. The necessity of preserving free from all doubt the existing powers cannot, therefore, be too strongly emphasised.

Article 32:
It is not clear whether Subsection 1 of Section 3 of this Article might be held to confer a constitutional right of appeal in tax cases from the Circuit Court to the High Court on questions of fact. Under existing law the right of appeal in such cases is limited to questions of law, and it is most important that this limitation should continue.

Article 35:
This Article saves the position of the Special Commissioners and the Referee in regard to the hearing of appeals. The question whether the Special Commissioners would be exercising a criminal or civil jurisdiction in imposing penalties under section 107 of the Income Tax Act, 1918, appears to be somewhat doubtful and it would be desirable if the words 'in matters other than criminal matters' could be deleted.[13]

General Observations
Alteration in name:

1. Double Taxation Relief arrangements.—It is a question for consideration by the Department of External Affairs whether the Agreements between the Irish Free State and Great Britain and Northern Ireland in relation to double taxation are affected by the change of name to Éire.

[13] The question of whether a tax penalty is to be as a criminal penalty is somewhat unclear. If it were so regarded, then legislation enabling the Revenue Commissioners or the Special Commissioners for Income Tax (as the Appeal Commissioners were then called) to impose such a penalty would appear to be unconstitutional, since this would entail a non-judicial personage exercising judicial powers in criminal matters, contrary to Article 37 (then numbered Article 35). This is, therefore, why the Revenue Commissioners suggested that Article 37 be widened to allow non-judicial bodies to exercise limited judicial functions in criminal as well as non-criminal cases.

There is, however, an isolated Supreme Court decision, *McLoughlin v. Tuite*, [1989] IR 82, which holds that such Revenue penalties are not criminal in nature. The reasoning in this case is, however, not altogether satisfactory and the result seems at odds with other case-law. The European Court of Human Rights has taken the opposite view in *Paykar Yev Haghtanak v. Armenia*, [2007], *European Court of Human Rights*, 1130, noting that:

> The purpose pursued by these measures is to exert pressure on taxpayers to comply with their legal obligations and to punish breaches of those obligations. The penalties are thus both deterrent and punitive. The Court considers that the above is sufficient to establish the criminal nature of the offence.

2. Seals, Dies and Plates.—The adoption of the name Éire will necessitate the provision of new dies and plates in the case of seals, stamps, postal orders, etc., in which the name 'Saorstát Éireann' at present appears. If the Constitution is to become operative within the financial year 1937/8 a supplementary estimate of about £6,000 will be necessary for this purpose.

In accordance with the terms of the telephone message received subsequent to your letter, the observations of the Commissioners have been confined to the Articles which appear to affect the Revenue.

I am to add that the Commissioners will be glad to be favoured with an opportunity of considering any amendments in the Articles herein referred to before they are finally approved.

No. 127: NAI, DT S9746

Minute by Michael McDunphy regarding revision of the draft Constitution

Department of the President
9 April 1937

The first revise of the Constitution, dated 1 April 1937, was examined by the Committee of four referred to on file S9715.[14]

For the purpose of this examination the observations of Departments were not asked as the first revise itself had been prepared in the light of Departmental observations. The examination of this revise was completed by the night of 8 April 1937, on which date it was given to the printers for the purpose of a second revise.[15]

No. 128: NAI, DT S10159

2nd Revise of Constitution.

10 April 1937

See www.irishconstitution.ie

[14] See document no. 120.

[15] There does not appear to be any record of the meetings of this committee. Later correspondence between John Hearne and Maurice Moynihan suggests that no records were kept by this committee, or of conversations held between Eamon de Valera and John Hearne during the drafting process. See Moynihan to Hearne, 24 October 1963, UCDA, P122/105; Hearne to Moynihan, 7 November 1963, UCDA, P122/105.

No. 129: NAI, DT S10159

Maurice Moynihan to William T. O'Brien, Patrick Lynch, Frank Fahy and all Ministers inviting observations on 2nd Revise.

Department of the President
10 April 1937

A chara,

1. I am directed by the President to send you herewith, for your consideration, a revised draft of the Constitution.
2. He would be glad to have, at the earliest possible date, your comments and those of your Department on this draft, and in particular on those provisions which appear to be the special concern of your Department.
3. The observations received in connection with the first draft have been exhaustively examined, but if it be thought that any point raised in those observations has not been sufficiently covered in the accompanying text, special attention should be drawn to that fact.
4. The President would be glad if you would regard this matter as extremely urgent.
5. He desires that any copies of the first draft not yet returned to him should be forwarded to this Department.[16]

No. 130: UCDA, P150/2395

Fr John Charles McQuaid to Eamon de Valera

Blackrock, Co. Dublin
10 April 1937

I beg to enclose a further addition to the dossier—this time, mainly an argument from reason. I also send a very useful little work—the title of which is rather misleading, because it is really an excellent treatise in Civics.[17] I delayed, in order to have the latest edition. The author is a friend of mine, who worked with me in Rome. He was already a barrister

[16] Oscar Traynor replied to say that the Department of Posts and Telegraphs had no observations to make on the 2nd Revise, NAI, DT S10159.
[17] Enclosure not found.

and Doctor of Civil Law, and had been through the war, before doing his doctorate in Theology and Canon Law studies. I hope that all goes well.

No. 131: UCDA, P150/2395

Fr John Charles McQuaid to Eamon de Valera

Blackrock, Co. Dublin
[April] 1937

I have compared very carefully the draft—and attach two notes.[18] It reads very well. Have you in Art. 45 fixed yet the term 'other Christian'? I have been thinking much about it. Of course, they claim the title, but as so very many in all these Churches deny the divinity of Christ, unlike their ancestors, they have truly ceased to be Christian. Very often they are only ethical. But you may have already settled the question.[19] I am sure you will be relieved to have it all printed.

No. 132: UCDA, P150/2395

Fr John Charles McQuaid to Eamon de Valera

Blackrock, Co. Dublin
[April] 1937

I beg to enclose some interesting and, perhaps useful, examples drawn from other Constitutions, illustrating the use of general statements.[20]

No. 133: UCDA, P150/2395

Fr John Charles McQuaid to Eamon de Valera

Blackrock, Co. Dublin
[April] 1937

I think there can be no doubt that in the Papal pronouncements the word State means both civil society organised as a political unit and then

[18] Enclosure not found.

[19] The reference here to 'other Christian' appears to be a reference to the question of whether Article 44 (as it ultimately became) would simply refer to 'other Christian churches' or even 'other Christian bodies', so that the various Protestant denominations would not have to be separately enumerated in what ultimately became Article 44.2.3°. This appears to have been a matter of some sensitivity: see document no. 199 for Cahill's objections to the use of the term 'Church of Ireland'.

[20] Enclosure not found.

more particularly, that through which civil society speaks and functions, the Prince or the Government. Hence the society and the Government ought per se to progress the true faith and legislate in accord with it: *per accideus* it may not be prudentially possible to have that public admission. This seems to me the meaning of Leo XIII. Of course, once the State acknowledges God's right to public worship, it cannot be *secular*, even if it be not Catholic. And when the State legislates according to natural law, of necessity, it legislates according to Catholicity, because the latter is the guardian of the natural law.[21]

No. 134: NAI, DT S10159

Observations by George Gavan Duffy on 2nd Revise

11 April 1937

'Notes on Final Draft Constitution'

Article 13.3:
The President's successor should take office soon after his term ends; if he dies or resigns, this will not be after a 'period of seven years'. Article 13.10 should follow Article 13.3.[22]

Article 14.6:
The President might appoint the Judges on the advice of, or after consultation with, the Council of State.[23]

Article 15.2:
If the Oireachtas has sole and exclusive power to make laws, what of statutory rules and orders and by-laws, which, if they are not 'laws' are waste paper? Article 50 presumably means to continue them as 'laws' in force. It seems to follow that Article 15 must say that nothing therein contained shall prevent the delegation of legislative powers by the Oireachtas for the purpose of carrying its laws into effect.[24]

Article 18.7.3°:
As to the Seanad electorate the end of the clause is not quite clear; instead of the last two lines (from 'who complies' to end) why not say: 'and who

[21] Document nos 131–3 bear no date. It has been decided to include them here as a group.
[22] Annotated by McDunphy: 'Good point. Agreed'. All annotations to this document made by McDunphy.
[23] Annotated: 'No'.
[24] Annotated: 'Mr Matheson is satisfied that there is no point in this. No change'.

is otherwise qualified by law to vote at an election of members of Seanad Éireann', if this is the actual meaning?[25]

Article 25.1.1°:
It is submitted that the question ought to be whether the Bill or clause is repugnant *on specified grounds*. Such a decision must have much more weight than a general, pious opinion in favour of a Bill. The American precedents might be consulted; they are noted at 52 of Borchard's *Declaratory Judgments*[26] which is in the A.G.'s library. See also Holdsworth's *History of Eng. Law*, (1924, v, 350, 428 and 438).[27] The decision is not usually made final and conclusive, because the Court in giving it is not strictly acting in a judicial capacity; but it may generally be assumed that it will adhere to such a decision.[28]

Article 25.2.1°:
The argument may be (lengthy)[29] and fourteen days from the close of the argument would be more satisfactory than a fixed time after the date of the reference.[30]

Article 25.3.1°:
The President should decline to sign so much only as is condemned, not necessarily the whole Bill.[31]

Article 29.1:
I think this Article makes the A.G. cease to represent the *community*, a valuable protection against litigious persons; cp. the recent Listowel rates case. His functions as protector of charities are gone too. And the Oireachtas has no power to delegate his criminal functions, if it wants to do so.[32]

Article 32.2.3°:
Unless otherwise provided, the entire Council of State must meet to exercise these powers.

Article 34.1:
Justice cannot always be done in public courts. The interests of justice sometimes demand privacy, *e.g.* when the President is sitting for Infants and the Children's Court in the big cities, and *habeas corpus* in the Judge's

[25] Annotated: 'No. The present text is covered. No change'.
[26] Edwin Borchard, *Declaratory Judgments* (1st edition, Cleveland, 1934).
[27] William Searle Holdsworth, *History of English Law* (12 vols, London, 1903–38).
[28] Annotated: 'Not agreed. Leave as it is'.
[29] The word in parenthesis is annotated: 'Unlimited power of delay'.
[30] Annotated: 'No'.
[31] Annotated: 'No'.
[32] Annotated: 'Altered'.

home when the Courts are not sitting. The law should be competent to make exceptions, where the interests of justice so require.[33]

Article 34.4:
Provision will, no doubt, be made for excluding judicial interference in matters of policy enshrined in the Constitution.[34]

Article 32.2:
Should not the Council act for the President while he is being impeached?[35]

Article 38.1:
A law for internment without trial is not forbidden.[36]

Article 39:
Treason committed abroad will hardly be an offence, if the Constitution does not expressly make it so.[37]

If it is intended to take power to deport our own citizens under extradition agreements, surely it is desirable that the Constitution should say so in express terms.[38]

Transitory Provisions
Article 51.2:
Should not a Bill to amend the Constitution be so entitled, to prevent questions as to amendment by implication during the first three years?[39]

Article 58.1:
There seems to be no provision to continue the Land Commission and other quasi-judicial bodies.[40]

Article 61:
'Plebiscite held in accordance with law'—Is this the law of Saorstát Éireann? It cannot be the 'law' of the Constitution before the Constitution is in force and seems to need definition.[41]

[33] Annotated: 'Public Courts need not necessarily *sit* in public. See [Article] 36.iii. Procedure may be governed by law'.
[34] Annotated: 'Canon of interpretation'.
[35] Annotated: 'No. Policy, but not agreed'.
[36] But this did not prevent Gavan Duffy from subsequently reaching the conclusion in December 1939 that Part VI of the Offences against the State Act, 1939 (which did provide for internment) was unconstitutional: see document no. 279.
[37] Annotated: 'Why? It is not excluded'.
[38] Annotated: 'No. If not forbidden it is permitted'.
[39] Annotated: 'Yes. See Article 46.3'.
[40] Annotated: 'Covered by Article 56'.
[41] Annotated: 'No point'.

No. 135: UCDA, P150/2419

'Copies of documents taken by Sean T. [O'Kelly] to the [Papal] Nuncio, who was to submit them to the Cardinal (A3, B3, C3)'

11 April 1937

(A3)[42]

Proposed Preamble
IN THE NAME OF THE MOST HOLY TRINITY, from Whom is all authority and to Whom, as our final end, all actions both of men and States must be referred,
WE, THE PEOPLE OF ÉIRE,
HUMBLY ACKNOWLEDGING all our obligations to our Divine Lord, Jesus Christ, Who sustained our fathers through centuries of trial.
GRATEFULLY REMEMBERING their heroic and unremitting struggle to regain the rightful independence of our Nation.
AND SEEKING to promote the common good, with due observance of Prudence, Justice and Charity, so that the dignity and freedom of the individual may be assured, true social order attained, the unity of our country restored, and concord established with other nations,
DO HEREBY ADOPT, ENACT, and Give to ourselves this Constitution.

(B3)

Religion
Article [blank]

1. The State recognises that public worship is due to Almighty God. It shall hold His Name in reverence and shall respect and honour religion.
2. The State recognises *the special position* of the Catholic Church as the guardian of the Faith professed by the great majority of the citizens.[43]
3. The State also recognises the Church of Ireland, the Presbyterian Church, the Methodist Church, the Hebrew Congregation, and the other religious denominations existing at the date of the coming into operation of this Constitution as the guardian of the Faith of their respective communities.

[42] Annotated by de Valera: 'Copies of documents A, B, C taken by S.T. to the Nuncio for submission to the Cardinal, April 11, 1937. The Nun. to meet Cardinal at some point on our territory this Sunday afternoon'.
[43] Italics underlined by de Valera. See reference to this in Note 2 of Document C3.

4. Freedom of conscience and the free profession and practice of religion are, subject to public order and morality, guaranteed to every citizen.
5. The State guarantees not to endow any religion, and shall not impose any disabilities or make any discrimination on the ground of religious profession, belief or status.
6. Legislation providing State aid for schools shall not discriminate between schools under the management of different religious denominations, nor be such as to affect prejudicially the right of any child to attend a school receiving public money without attending religious instruction at that school.
7. Every religious denomination shall have the right to manage its own affairs, own, acquire and administer property, movable and immovable, and maintain institutions for religious or charitable purposes.
8. The property of any religious denomination or any educational institution shall not be diverted save for necessary works of public utility and on payment of compensation.

(C3)[44]
'Notes'

1. The lawyers have not yet seen the draft, and may want some changes in the phrasing, for example, the word denomination may be regarded as unsuitable, but the substance would be unchanged. The phrasing of the sections from 3 to 8 are those of [Article 8 of] the Constitution of 1922. Section 7 is new.
2. The principal bodies mentioned in Section 3 may refuse their consent unless the words underlined in Section 2 [of 'B3'] are omitted. In this case the question to be decided will be; whether Sections 2 and 3 are to be retained as modified, or go altogether.
3. There are very strong reasons for getting into the Constitution explicit mention of the Churches, with the Catholic Church in the premier position—the opportunity may not recur. The combined influence of the Churches will be united against atheism; the Church of Ireland and the Presbyterian Church are, like the Catholic Church, all-Ireland bodies in their organisation, and are powerful aids to prevent partition from being made complete or permanent.

[44] A duplicate of this document, also found at UCDA, P150/2419, carries the following annotation by de Valera: 'Notes shown to the Cardinal. Further points given verbally to Sean T.'.

4. The foregoing reasons urge that we should be willing to make some sacrifice if they become the *sine qua non* of agreement.
5. To insert Sections 2 and 3 without agreement would stir up a whole sea of troubles: a religious controversy at this time would be most unfortunate.
6. As regards the Preamble, many are sensitive because of its religious character. The mention of our Divine Lord's name they think is more suited to a Church document than to a Constitution, and fear that it may give rise to hypocrisy or pharisaism. This could all be met if it were generally known that the competent ecclesiastical authorities had approved of the religious part.

No. 136: UCDA, P150/2419

'Copies of documents shown to Archbishop [John] Gregg, to Rev. William Henry Massey, and taken by Dr [James] Irwin to be shown to the Moderator and Moderator Designate of the Presbyterian Church (A4, B4, C4)'

11 April 1937

(A4)
[Document A4 was untitled. It consisted of Sections 1, 2 and 3 of Document B3. A4 is annotated by de Valera: 'This actual copy given to and returned by the Presbyterians']

(B4)
[Document B4 was also untitled. It consisted of Sections 4 to 8 of Document B3.

(C4) 'Proposed Preamble'
[Document C4 was identical to A3, above].

No. 137: NAI, DT S10159

Draft Article on religious provisions[45]

12 April 1937

Freedom of conscience and the free profession and practice of religion are, subject to public order and morality, guaranteed to every citizen.

The State guarantees not to endow any religion, and shall not impose any disabilities or make any discrimination on the ground of religious profession, belief or status.

Legislation providing State aid for schools shall not discriminate between schools under the management of different religious denominations, nor be such as to affect prejudicially the right of any child to attend a school receiving public money without attending religious instruction at that school.

Every religious denomination shall have the right to manage its own affairs, own, acquire, and administer property, moveable and immovable, and maintain institutions for religious or charitable purposes.

The property of any religious denomination or any educational institution shall not be diverted compulsorily save for necessary works of public utility and on payment of compensation.

No. 138: NAI, DT S10159

Thomas Derrig to Eamon de Valera
Observations on 2nd Revise

Department of Education
12 April 1937

Dear President,

The only point in the new draft of the Constitution to which my Department wishes to draw attention is one arising under Subsection 5 of Article 43 which gives the State power to take the place of the parents where the latter 'for physical and moral reasons' fail in their duty towards their children. Under the Children's Act, 1929, which amends a

[45] The provenance of the draft is unknown. It is annotated by McDunphy: 'To be got in final form—[Parliamentary] Draftsman to see and compare with the article in Constitution of 1922. Approved by P[arliamentary] D[raftsman], 12 April 1937'.

subsection of the Children Act, 1908, 'poverty' is added to the reasons which would justify the State in sending a child to an Industrial School. The consent of the parent is necessary, in the latter case, as regards the committal of the child, but not as regards the retention of the child, once it has been committed. As 'poverty' can hardly be said to fall under the term 'physical and moral reasons', it might be argued that, when the Constitution is in force, the 1929 Act will be unconstitutional, in so far as it gives the Minister power to retain a child in an Industrial School on a ground ('poverty') which is not one of these mentioned in the Act and may therefore be held to be implicitly excluded. The point is a small one but the legal advisers might think it worth looking into. It could be met by amending the 1929 Act so as to take away from the Minister the power to retain a child at an Industrial School because of the poverty of its parents. Since the consent of the parent is necessary for the committal of the child, if the ground of the committal is destitution, it would seem to follow that the Minister should not have the power to retain such children in Industrial Schools against the parents' wishes and that the best way to meet the situation would be by the amendment of the 1929 Act.

With regard to the observations furnished by my Department in connection with the first draft, I should like to call attention to the fact that its comments on the phrase 'schools established by the State' were intended to make clear that the practice in this country was definitely opposed to the establishment of Primary or Secondary Schools by the State. In this respect the attitude of the Church in this country and the practice that has arisen, as a result of this attitude, has been narrower than the official Catholic position as defined in the 1929 Encyclical, since in the latter it is stated, as regards the position of the Church or family in Education, that the State 'should supplement their work, whenever this falls short of what is necessary, *even by means of its own schools and institutions*'.

This definite statement of the official position of the Church should be a sufficient defence of the inclusion in the Bunreacht of the phrase 'established by the State', as applied to schools, if it is considered desirable that the phrase should be retained. Moreover, since the more restricted rights accorded to the State by Catholic opinion in Ireland apply chiefly, if not entirely, to the establishment of Primary or Secondary schools, a further defence of the phrase 'schools established by the State' might be that it is intended only to apply to Schools of a Vocational nature of which there are already various types in existence in Saorstát Éireann under both the State and the Local Councils. Of the former type, namely schools established by the State and completely controlled by it, there are three in existence, The Metropolitan School of Art, The Irish Training School of Domestic Economy at Kilmacud and the Killarney School of Housewifery. These schools were established by the State under the British regime and the State still retains complete control of them. The Church has no connection of any sort with these schools, except that it either provides or supervises religious instruction in the Kilmacud and Killarney Schools.

In the case of all other schools established by the State, namely the Preparatory Colleges and the Model Schools, the Church has been made either the sole manager or the joint-manager and its guidance was sought when it became evident that the State would have to take the initiative in establishing the Preparatory Colleges. The reason for the different treatment of these latter schools was that they dealt with General Education, not with Vocational Training in the narrower sense, whereas the Metropolitan Schools of Art and the Schools of Domestic Economy and Housewifery at Kilmacud and Killarney are purely Vocational Schools of the same type as the Technical and other Vocational Schools which are established by the Vocational Educational Committee without producing any opposition on the part of the Church.

In the case of Vocational schools the Encyclical indeed seems to give the State the right to 'reserve to itself' their establishment and direction, 'provided it be careful not to injure the rights of the Church or of the family in what pertains to them'. The section of the Encyclical which deals with this is as follows: 'The State may therefore reserve to itself the establishment and direction of schools intended to prepare for certain civic duties and especially for military service' (page 16 of the English version).

We have never exercised the latter right, although we have occasionally been pressed to restrict vocational training to the Technical and Vocational Schools set up by the State and by other Public Bodies.

The above observations, I think, cover completely the issues that may be raised in connection with Article 43 of the Constitution which seems to be the only one that is the special concern of the Department.[46]

[46] Much of Derrig's letter repeats the observations made by Joseph O'Neill, Secretary of the Department of Education, in a letter written by O'Neill to de Valera on 8 April, UCDA, P150/2416. O'Neill evidently presented these observations to Derrig, who included them in the above.

No. 139: NAI, DT S10159

Memorandum from the Ceann Comhairle, Frank Fahy, to Maurice Moynihan Observations on 2nd Revise

Dáil Éireann
13 April 1937

Urgent
A Chara,

1. I am in receipt of copy numbered 29 of the revised draft of the Constitution, forwarded with your letter of the 9th instant.[47]
2. I still remain of the view, expressed in my previous observations, that the impeachment provisions might be omitted. Seeing, however, that the matter has received exhaustive examination and that it has been decided to retain the provisions, I am of opinion that the Draft Constitution should afford some guidance on the following points:
   (a) By whom the charge will be preferred before Dáil Éireann and in what manner?
   (b) By whom will the President be represented? Presumably by Counsel.
   (c) Presumably the Resolution for removal will be moved by a Minister?
   (d) What is to be the procedure, subsequent to the passage of the Resolution, for removal from office?[48]
3. The following further observations regarding the draft now under consideration are offered:

Article 14.2.3°:
Heretofore, non-emergency meetings of the Dáil (for the purpose, for example, of considering amendments of the Seanad to Bills which had been passed by the Dáil before adjourning) were convened by the Ceann Comhairle, at the request of the President of the Executive Council, under the power conferred by Standing Order No. 16. The Seanad could

[47] See document no. 129. Fahy evidently meant Moynihan's letter of 10 April.
[48] Paragraph 2 is annotated by McDunphy: 'I spoke to Mr [Seán] Malone today on behalf of the Ceann Comhairle. He is satisfied and will so advise the C.C. that mechanism for the impeachment should not be in the Constitution. 14 April 1937'.

also, under the provisions of a Standing Order (No. 19 (2)) of that House be convened by the Cathaoirleach.

If it is contemplated that in normal circumstances, these powers could still be the subject matter of Standing Orders, the Subsection, it is suggested, might be amended to deal only with the occasions envisaged in Article 27.3.2° and Article 40.7.

Article 20.2.1° and 20.3.1°:
Seeing that Subsection 2.1° prohibits the initiation of a Money Bill in Seanad Éireann, it may not be considered necessary to retain Section 3.1° particularly, as a Bill cannot be certified to be a Money Bill until after it has passed all amendment stages in the Dáil. To describe a Bill as a Money Bill before initiation would seem to be presumptive of the judgment of the Ceann Comhairle in this regard.

Article 24.4.4° and 24.4.5°:
In its present form, Subsection 4° prompts the query, upon whom will devolve the duty of transmitting the signed text for enrolment.

Under whose direction, also, will the official translations provided for in Subsection 5° be prepared and issued?[49]

[Matter omitted]

No. 140: NAI, DT S10159

Memorandum from Stephen Roche to Michael McDunphy Observations on 2nd Revise

Department of Justice
13 April 1937

Dear McDunphy,
Attached copies may be used by you as you think proper—or not at all!

Yours,
S.A. Roche[50]

[49] Annotated by McDunphy: 'Not for the Constitution. This will be governed by [?]'.
[50] The attached observations, drafted by Stephen Roche, were titled 'Departmental observations for the consideration of the Minister for Justice'. It is not clear if these observations received clearance from the Minister for Justice before being passed on to McDunphy. It is possible that Roche was acting on his own authority by forwarding them.

General Observations:
In commenting on the earlier draft the Department raised objections to a number of points, such as:

1. The lack of provision of any form of trial except trial by jury for serious political offences unless and until a definite state of emergency exists;
2. The conferring of the title 'Judge' equally on members of the Supreme Court and members of the lowest Summary Court.

A fairly large number of other criticisms were made, mostly of minor importance.

On the two points specifically mentioned and on the majority of the other points, nothing has been done to meet the views expressed by the Department. Generally the Department felt that the Draft Constitution went too much into detail, whereas the Department's feeling is that the shorter and more general the Constitution is the less likely it is that the maintenance of law and order will be impeded by limitations on the power of the Dáil and by conflicts between the judiciary and the executive. The Departmental view on these particular matters and on the general principle remains unchanged, but presumably a decision has been taken in favour of the opposite point of view and there is nothing to be gained by re-opening the matter.

On Particular Articles:
Article 2:
This is a new Article. Its legal effect is not understood: there seems to be some danger of its leading to confusion. Are there to be three classes of people, viz: Citizens, People 'belonging to the nation', and Aliens? What is the legal position of people who 'belong to the nation' but who are not citizens?[51]

Article 9:
There does not seem to be anything in this Article to avoid the difficulty mentioned in the earlier Departmental notes, viz., that as a practical proposition the use of Irish as an official language is not merely a question of 'areas'.[52]

Article 10:
This is an improvement on the previous draft because it is more general, but is the whole existing law as regards citizenship to lapse on the coming

[51] Annotated by McDunphy with a question mark. All annotations by McDunphy.
[52] Annotated: 'Amended to cover selected circumstances'.

into force of this Constitution? Or are all existing citizens of Saorstát Éireann to become citizens of Éire automatically and are the existing laws as regards the acquisition and loss of citizenship to apply, until amended or repealed, to citizenship of Éire?[53]

Article 14:
Section 9 of this Article, though better than the previous draft, is not quite what the Department of Justice would recommend. In practice, the Minister for Justice should have power to remit or reduce sentences of imprisonment where he thinks the case is clear and not important, without going to the Government or to the President. An unnecessary multiplication of papers and formalities is undesirable.[54]

Article 40:
The reference in Section 2 of Article 40 to the Article itself (40) seems to be a mistake.

Article 41:
In Section 6, paragraph (ii); is it intended to confer powers on the police directly without the interposition of law? Are the police regulations for the control of meetings to be made directly under the authority of this Article of the Constitution?[55]

Article 43.5
Cases are not uncommon in which the inability of parents to control their children is not due to failure in duty by the parents but to other causes. Is it the meaning of this provision of the Constitution that an incorrigible child shall not be sent to a reformatory until it has been proved that the child's bad conduct is due to a failure in duty by its parents?[56]

Article 58:
The Department of Justice doubts whether there is anything to be gained by making the Circuit Judges and District Justices take the new declaration. Apart from this, it might perhaps be prudent to modify Sections 5 and 6 a little so as to provide for the case of a Judge and Justice who genuinely and without malice overlooks the matter; for instance, a man who has been ill and on resuming duty after the passing of the Constitution does not comply with the Section. Would it not be reasonable that before deeming a Judge to have vacated office he should

[53] Annotated: 'The article containing laws, combined with a new adaptation of [?] Act will cure this'.
[54] Annotated: 'The section as amended is now satisfactory'.
[55] Annotated: 'Amended'.
[56] Annotated: 'Being considered'.

be definitely reminded of his obligation and required to carry it out and should be removed from office only if he persists in not carrying out his obligation after such reminder and direction?[57]

No. 141: NAI, DT S10159

Michael McDunphy to William Denis Carey

Department of the President
13 April 1937

Dear Carey,
Herewith, as arranged, are revised drafts of Articles 14.9 and 29 of the Constitution.

As regards 14.9 the word 'sentence' in the printed draft has been altered to 'punishment' and a new clause has been added after the word 'President'.

As regards Article 29, Sections 1, 2 and 4 have been deleted and replaced by a new Section 1.

Section 3 has now become Section 2, and has been amended by the insertion of a phrase after the word 'court' in the first line to meet a point raised by the Department of Defence in regard to trials by Courts Martial.

Sections 5, 6 and 7 have been re-numbered 3, 4 and 5.

Revised Draft of Article 14.9:

> 'The right of pardon and the power to commute punishment imposed by any court exercising criminal jurisdiction are hereby vested in the President but such power of commutation may, except in capital cases, also be conferred by law on other authorities.'

Revised Draft of Article 29:

Section 1 'There shall be an Attorney General of Éire, in this Constitution referred to as the Attorney General, who shall be the adviser of the Government of Éire in matters of law and legal opinion, and shall exercise and perform all such powers functions and duties as may be conferred or imposed on him by this Constitution or by law.'

[57] Annotated: 'Amended'.

Section 2	'All crimes and offences prosecuted in any court constituted under Article 34 of this Constitution, other than a court of summary jurisdiction shall be prosecuted in the name of the people and at the suit of the Attorney General or some other person authorised in accordance with law to act for that purpose.'
Sections 3, 4, 5	[These are identical with sections 5, 6, and 7 in the 2nd Revise dated 10.4.37.][58]

No. 142: NAI, DT S10159

Memorandum from Stephen Roche to Michael McDunphy 'New Constitution'

Department of Justice
13 April 1937

Mr McDunphy,

New Constitution
As you know, I dislike the whole idea of tying up the Dáil and the Government with all sorts of restrictions and putting the Supreme Court like a watch-dog over them for fear they may run wild and do all sorts of indefensible things, but if this theory is to prevail, as apparently it is, I think that there is a serious inconsistency in the present Draft Constitution, as there is also (from this point of view) in the existing Constitution. We solemnly guarantee that a man shall not be tried except in due course of law and the trial must be by jury, except in the case of minor offences. Obviously the idea is to protect the citizen against the malice of the Government in power. But if the Government in power has the support of a majority in the Dáil and in the Senate it can pass any legislation it likes, within the Constitution. Suppose that the Government in power is determined to deprive the whole front Opposition Bench of liberty and to treat them as criminals. Is there anything in the old Constitution or in the new Draft Constitution to prevent the enactment of a law saying specifically that:

[58] The revised articles here sent to the Revenue Commissioners were revisions of the draft Constitution distributed on 10 April, demonstrating the speed with which the drafting committee worked. As can be seen from document no. 126, the Revenue Commissioners' observations on the first draft of the Constitution had not been received until 7 April, by which time the drafting committee had almost completed their second revision of that original draft (see document no. 127). On 14 April, the Revenue Commissioners replied that they had no further observations on the revised articles, NAI, DT S10159.

> 'the persons named in the Schedule to this Act shall forthwith be apprehended and lodged in Portlaoighise Prison where they shall be detained in the same manner as if they had been sentenced to seven years' penal servitude'?

Or, if the Government does not wish to be quite so brutal, cannot the unpopular members be at least removed, by express law, to the Aran Islands? Or cannot a law be passed saying that any Inspector of the Garda Síochána may detain any person who appears to him not to support the Government politically and lodge him in prison until he, the Inspector, is satisfied that the man's political outlook has changed.

In all these cases, the victim would be detained 'in accordance with law', so *habeas corpus* would be no use to him and since he would not be tried at all the provisions as to trial by jury would not apply.

You may remember that under Mr Cosgrave's administration a law was passed providing for the internment of citizens without trial. I was surprised at the time that this could be done within the Constitution, but I was informed on high legal authority that while a man could not be tried without a jury, there was nothing in the Constitution to prevent him from being locked up for the rest of his life without any trial at all *if the law so provided.*

This aspect of the matter seems to me to throw an interesting light on the value of Constitutional guarantees.

No. 143: NAI, DT S10159

Memorandum by the Department of Local Government and Public Health
Observations on 2nd Revise

13 April 1937

Article 47:
The persons who are to vote at a Referendum (and at the Plebiscite on the Draft Constitution) are the persons who have the right to vote at an election of members to Dáil Éireann.

Section 5 of the Electoral Act, 1923 enacts that no member of the Police Force on full pay may vote at any Dáil election.

It is a question for consideration whether the particular circumstances which give rise to this legal incapacity at a Dáil election apply with equal force to the Referendum (and to the Plebiscite). In any case if the incapacity is removed for the purposes of Article 47 it should also be removed for the purposes of the Plebiscite.[59]

No. 144: NAI, DT S10159

Memorandum from Arthur Matheson to Michael McDunphy
Observations on 2nd Revise

Parliamentary Draftsman's Office
14 April 1937

Mr McDunphy,
As requested by you I have read the Transitory Provisions in the print of the Constitution (No. 49, dated 10 April, 1937) which you handed to me and I have the following suggestions to make in regard thereto.

Article 56:
This Article should be re-drafted as follows:

1. On the coming into operation of this Constitution, the Government in office immediately before the coming into operation of this Constitution shall become and be the Government of Éire for the purposes of this Constitution and the members of that Government shall, without any appointment under Article 14 thereof, continue to hold their respective offices of the corresponding offices as if they had been appointed thereto under the said Article 14.
2. The members of the Government of Éire in office on the date on which the first President shall enter upon his office shall receive official appointments from the President as soon as may be after the said date.
3. Every person holding any office or employment under the Government of Saorstát Éireann immediately before the coming into operation of this Constitution shall, on the coming into operation of this Constitution, become an officer or employee of the Government of Éire in the same capacity and with the like tenure and on the same terms as immediately before the coming into operation of this Constitution.
4. On the coming into operation of this Constitution, the several Departments of State of Saorstát Éireann shall become and be

[59] Annotated by McDunphy: 'Policy. Better not make exceptions'. A later annotation states: 'President does not agree'.

respectively Departments of State of Éire and shall, until otherwise determined by law, have the like functions as they respectively had immediately before the coming into operation of this Constitution.

Article 57:
Section 3 of this Article should be re-drafted as follows:

3. Wherever the Commission is incomplete by reason of a vacancy in an office, the holder of which is a member of the Commission, the Commission shall, during such vacancy, be completed by the substitution of the senior judge of the Supreme Court who is not already a member of the Commission, in the place of the holder of such office, and likewise in the event of any member of the said Commission being, on any occasion, unable to act, his place shall be taken on that occasion by the senior judge of the Supreme Court who is available and is not already a member, or acting in the place of a member, of the said Commission.

Article 58:
Section 1: In the 5th line, delete 'on the said date' and substitute 'immediately before the coming into operation of this Constitution'; in line 3, should not 'heretofore' be theretofore'?

Before Article 59 a new article should be inserted as follows:
On the coming into operation of this Constitution, the person who is the Attorney-General of Saorstát Éireann immediately before the coming into operation of this Constitution shall, without any appointment under Article 14 of the Constitution, become and be the Attorney-General of Éire as if he had been appointed to that office under the said Article 14.

Article 59:
This Article should be re-drafted as follows:
On the coming into operation of this Constitution, the person who is the Comptroller and Auditor-General of Saorstát Éireann immediately before the coming into operation of this Constitution shall, without any appointment under Article 14 of this Constitution, become and be the Comptroller and Auditor-General of Éire as if he had been appointed to that office under the said Article 14.

Article 60:
This Article should be re-drafted by substituting the following section for Section 1 and paragraph 1° of Section 2, and making Section 2 consist only of the present paragraph 2°:

1. On the coming into operation of this Constitution, the Defence Forces and the Police Forces of Saorstát Éireann in existence immediately before the coming into operation of this Constitution shall become and be respectively the Defence Forces and the Police Forces of Éire, and every member of either of those Forces shall continue to be a member thereof with the same rank, duties, tenure, and terms as theretofore, and in particular every person who is a commissioned officer of the Defence Forces of Saorstát Éireann immediately before the coming into operation of this Constitution shall become and be a commissioned officer of corresponding rank in the Defence Forces of Éire as if he had received a commission therein under Article 14 of this Constitution.[60]

No. 145: NAI, DT S10159

Memorandum by the Department of Lands
Observations on 2nd Revise

14 April 1937

Article 11.1: The Department of Lands wish to call attention to their previous note on this Article (No. 10 of first Draft). Can minerals owned by private individuals be expressed as belonging to Éire? Perhaps wording could be amended to provide for overriding authority in the State to deal with such minerals as are privately owned.

Article 37: In view of the Department of Lands the words 'or powers' are desirable after the word 'functions' in the fourth line.

[60] Document annotated by McDunphy: 'Changes made. 17 April 1937'.

No. 146: UCDA, P150/2416

Conor Maguire to Eamon de Valera
Observations on 2nd Revise

Dublin
14 April 1937

Dear President,
The only point which occurs to me as regards the enclosed draft of the Constitution is whether the provisions for enacting it are authorised by the Constitution at present in force.

I imagine this has been considered and that you are advised as to whether it will be necessary to make provision for the method of enactment proposed by a preliminary amendment of the present Constitution.

The Chief Justice to whom I mentioned this point promised to mention it to you at your meeting with him last night. I should perhaps also mention that in a case at hearing before me today strong criticism was passed by counsel on the failure of the Oireachtas to provide facilities for dissolution of marriage in the full sense for those who believe in the right of persons to remarry. It will probably be reported in tomorrow's paper.

I do not suppose it will alter your views but it gives a hint of the likelihood of there being strong objection to Article 49 by the minority.

No. 147: UCDA, P150/2395

Fr John Charles McQuaid to Eamon de Valera

Blackrock, Co. Dublin
15 April 1937

I beg to enclose some suggestions on the work of last night, which I trust may prove useful in some way.[61] It was kind of you to 'phone and I am very grateful. At the time, I was surrounded by people and could not say more than I did, in a bald way. I do not judge myself so indulgently as you have done. I was clearly at fault and I am sorry for it.

[61] Enclosure not found.

No. 148: UCDA, P150/2395

Fr John Charles McQuaid to Eamon de Valera

Blackrock, Co. Dublin
15 April 1937

Kindly pardon my sending you another note. I fear my many notes and papers must have only bothered you these last ten days. But it occurred to me as I said mass this morning that last night, I may have so shown my disappointment as to seem wanting in courtesy. If I did in the least way, I am very sorry for it.

Should I be able to serve, now or in the future, even to a small degree, I should like to think that you will not hesitate to ask me and to believe that I bow willingly to those who are placed above and who give their decisions.

P.S. I shall work at the Property section today and if anything occurs to me, I shall send it across.

No. 149: UCDA, P150/2419

William Henry Massey to Eamon de Valera

Dublin
15 April 1937

My dear President,
I have now had the advantage of consulting two of our most prominent and influential men, and reporting to them, in confidence, the subject matter of our interview. I also showed them the typed copies of draft of certain sections in the proposed new Constitution. They both confirm my own opinion expressed in our interview. We find nothing either in the substance or wording of the sections submitted to which we could fairly take exception.

As to the phrase 'the Catholic Church', we are not sensitive on the matter. We are quite satisfied that it should be used as the official title of the Church of the great majority in this country, so long as it is not used in any deliberately exclusive sense. The succeeding paragraph in the draft copy in which the other 'Churches' in this country are 'recognised' as such removes any doubt on this point.

May I point out that the official title of the Church, of which I have the honour to be the Head, is 'The Methodist Church in Ireland'.

As President of this Church, I greatly appreciate the courtesy and fairmindedness shown by you in arranging for our interview, and seeking to understand our point of view, and where necessary to meet, if possible, our reasonable wishes.

No. 150: NAI, DT S9823A

Memorandum from Philip O'Donoghue to Patrick Lynch
Observations on Article 15.2

Office of the Attorney General
16 April 1937

Príomh Aturnae,

1. It has been suggested that Article 15.2 is deficient in omitting to refer to Statutory Rules and Orders. This Article is drawn in the same terms as the corresponding Article 12 of the existing Constitution. No difficulty or inconvenience has been caused under the present Constitution by reason of the absence of any saving provision for Statutory Rules and Orders. I am definitely of opinion that the present Article 15 is completely satisfactory in this regard and that no reference should be made to any Statutory Rules or Orders.
2. If any saving clause is added to this Article it must be to take away from the sole and exclusive powers vested in the Oireachtas. In other words to lend support to the view that Ministers and Departments can also legislate in respect of certain matters. I submit that this would be mischievous and I would call attention to the fact that, largely through the vigilance of the Parliamentary Draftsman, the criticism of legislating by Order is much less in volume in this country than in Great Britain where the Lord Chief Justice frequently calls attention to the pernicious tendency of delegated legislation.
3. Statutory Rules and Orders, as the title suggests, are intimately related with legislative enactments. They are considered part of the law and have the force of law but alone do not constitute legislation. They must always be referred back to the enabling

Statute under which they are made. Very little consideration will indicate the abuses which would grow up if the legislature contented itself with enacting loose and indefinite principles adding that the Minister could give effect to such principles by rules and regulations.

4. The principles of legislation must be definitely enacted in the Statute. Rules and Orders may prescribe such matters as the form, time and manner of carrying into effect the objects of the statute but any such rule which would seek to depart from the scope of the statute, impose new obligations or confer new rights, would be clearly *ultra vires* that Statute and could properly be set aside by the Courts. This position is clearly understood by lawyers and, in my opinion, it is a position that should be strenuously defended.
5. It will be said that the only object of mentioning Statutory Rules and Orders in the new Article will be to give them a claim to be considered legislation. As I have said, alone they do not constitute legislation and cannot be considered apart from the Statutes under which they are derived. It is definitely in the public interest that legislature should make itself explicit and clear in its enactments and that no encouragement should be given to slovenly or imperfect statutory provisions while relying on Statutory Rules and Orders to complete what the legislature itself should have done.

I have carefully considered this question, and thoroughly agree with the opinion expressed in the above minute. The suggestion to have an addition to Article 15.2 in the term indicated must have been made under a misapprehension. Statutory Rules and Orders, as the term itself shows, must be something necessary to enable the carrying out of the Statute, and for that purpose must be in conformity with it strictly and literally. A statement in a statute, and particularly in an Article of the Constitution, that legislation should be subject to, or varied or read subject to, statutory rules and orders to be made by some other person or body than the legislature, is a contradiction of terms. It would certainly not be permitted to be incorporated in any piece of considered legislation by anyone who has had to study the subject. I am not aware that the Article in the existing Constitution proved to be in any way at variance with the opinion I have expressed. (Signed) Patrick Lynch

16 April 1937

No. 151: UCDA, P150/2419

Memorandum by Eamon de Valera
'Negotiations with the Churches'

[16] April 1937

On Saturday, 3 April, went to the Nunciature, took with me the documents marked A, B, C;[62] explained that I was being urged to put in something 1 of A, but it would be quite impossible; that I wished to as far as it was at all practicable, but could only go that far. 1 and 2 would cause no difficulty in Document B. 3 was a suggestion but would leave the matter still in the air but would inevitably be pushed either backwards or forwards. Was personally in favour of leaving it out. The Nuncio agreed. I indicated that I proposed seeing the Archbishop of Dublin. The Nuncio said the Cardinal was coming to town on Monday for Standing Committee Meeting of the Bishops on Tuesday, 6 April. Agreed to see the Cardinal, Monday evening, 5 April, at 6. Saw the Cardinal. He felt that omission of any mention of the position of the Catholic Church would cause considerable difficulty and cause me to be attacked. He would himself not attack, as he understood the difficulties. Had a draft drawn representing about 93 per cent of the population, but I pointed out the difficulties of such a draft.

Went to Archbishop's House. He liked the preamble immensely, and with the preamble was prepared to see, if I thought it necessary, omission of the Catholic Church as such. Next day, thinking over the matter it occurred to me that we might put in a clause recognising the fact that the Catholic Church was the guardian of the faith of the majority of the citizens.

Saw Dr Irwin, 10 April;
11th, Nuncio at Sean T.'s;
12th, called on Archbishop Gregg
12th, called to see Nuncio
12th, Dr Irwin comes to see me;
13th, phoned Nuncio;
13th, saw Reverend Mr Massey, Head Methodist Church;
14th, saw Dr Irwin;
16th, saw Dr Irwin and Moderator and Mod. Designate, Belfast;

[62] See document no. 123.

16th, Saw Nuncio at Sean T.'s, *J.P.W[alshe]. went to Rome (Friday evening).*
22nd, Called on the Nuncio.
23d, Nuncio phoned to say the Cardinal approved Christian Churches.
24th, Saw Nuncio and Cardinal.
26th, M. Moynihan saw Arch. Gregg, and D. Robinson got letter from Gregg to D'Arcy. (G. Satisfied)[63]
27th, Robinson goes to see D'Arcy.

On 10 April, saw Nuncio, who agreed to go next day to the Cardinal with documents [blank]. Next day Nuncio saw Cardinal. Reported that Cardinal quite pleased but disliked the last three lines of 3 and suggested they should be omitted. I argued with Nuncio over the difficulties. Pointed out that we must have the other person's point of view. Next day saw Archbishop Gregg, the Nuncio, and Dr Irwin in the evening.[64]

No. 152: UCDA, P150/2419

Memorandum by Eamon de Valera 'Instructions for Mr [Joseph P.] Walshe'

16 April 1937

1. General approval for religious part.
2. To get the official name of the Catholic Church.
3. To get permission to phrase ARTICLE [i.e. Section] 3 so as to include the phrase 'The State also recognises the other Christian Churches, namely, Church of Ireland, etc., as well as the Jewish Congregations and the other religious bodies existing in Éire at the time of the coming into operation of this Constitution'.

[63] Section in parentheses added manually by de Valera.
[64] This document is an amalgamation of two separate documents found at UCDA, P150/2419. The text in italics is from a document obviously compiled at a later date, presumably at the end of April. This later document simply lists dates, beginning with the visit to the Nuncio on 3 April, ending with the entry for 27 April. It does not include de Valera's personal notes, as found in the earlier document and reproduced here. For a fuller account of these discussions and negotiations, see Keogh, 'The Irish Constitutional Revolution: An Analysis of the Making of the Constitution', in Litton (ed.), *The Constitution of Ireland 1937–1987* (Dublin, 1988), 39.

No. 153: UCDA, P150/2419

Memorandum by Eamon de Valera
'Pro Memoria': Guidelines for Joseph P. Walshe for his discussions with the Vatican on the religious article

16 April 1937

1. The accompanying documents [blank] are drafts of proposed Articles in the new Constitution which it is hoped to publish on 24 April.
2. The lawyers may desire some changes in form or phrasing, but the substance is likely to remain unchanged, except in the case of document [blank] which presents the difficulty of reducing Catholic theory to a practical form.
3. The Articles concerning religion are not the Catholic ideal as regards the relationship between Church and State. In the actual conditions, however, it is not deemed possible to go farther than is provided.
4. About one fourth of the population of Ireland is Protestant. Until recently, in all State relations the Protestant Churches were the dominating influence.
5. The 'Church of Ireland' was until 1869 the State Church here, and the Protestant religion the State religion.
6. The Protestant Churches in this country are closely associated with the corresponding churches in Great Britain, in which there are over 40,000,000 Protestants. With this strength so close to hand, and with the recollections of their past supremacy, the Protestant members of our population find it hard to accept a second and subordinate place.
7. If the attempt were to be made to embody in the new Constitution the full Catholic ideal there would be an immediate outcry from the Protestant section of the population, and a bitter religious controversy might easily ensue.
8. In the present circumstances, such a controversy would in every way be disastrous. The Government would be charged by a large section even of its own supporters with having needlessly caused this controversy and with having wilfully disturbed the present religious calm in this part of Ireland.

9. The Government would likewise be charged with having provided the occasion for a renewal of the bitter attacks on our fellow countrymen in Belfast and in the rest of that part of Ireland in which Catholics are a minority.
10. The Government would further be charged with having raised a new barrier to the reunion of our country, and with having recklessly caused offence to a section of our countrymen whose ancestors produced many patriots whose names are revered in many a Catholic home. Wolfe Tone, Robert Emmet, Parnell, etc.
11. On the other hand the recognition of the Protestant Churches, even though they are put in a subordinate place, will produce considerable appeasement, will lead to better feeling and understanding between the different religious bodies here and may also lead to the desired political reunion of our country.
12. The effect of the recognition will, I am convinced, secure the united influence of all the Christian bodies against Atheism which present world conditions seem to indicate to be the enemy now most dangerous.
13. The premier and special position accorded to the Catholic Church as 'guardian of the Faith of the great majority of the citizens' will mean in practice that the Catholic Church will be the Church associated with the State on all public occasions.
14. Under our democratic Constitution the vast majority of the Ministers of State are certain to be Catholic, who will profess their religion openly and will attend religious functions in a Catholic Church on all occasions in which a manifestation of religious belief is called for.
15. In the past Ministers in a body have annually attended Mass on St Patrick's Day at the Catholic Pro Cathedral; the Government and members of Parliament have attended a special Mass on each occasion in which a new Parliament meets after the dissolution; at the Eucharistic Congress the State was officially represented by all Ministers.
16. The proposed draft will have the tacit, if not the expressed and explicit approval of the religious bodies mentioned in paragraph 3.
17. His Eminence, the Cardinal, and His Grace, the Archbishop of Dublin, as well as His Excellency, the Apostolic Nuncio, having regard to all the conditions, see no cause to disapprove.

18. It is requested that the above considerations be placed before the Holy Father with a view to obtaining his approval and blessing before publication.[65]

No. 154: NAI, DT S10159

Memorandum by James J. McElligott
Observations on 2nd Revise

Department of Finance
17 April 1937

Dréacht Bhunreacht na hÉireann
Notes on Revised Draft (2nd Revise):[66]

1. The numbering of Articles and Sections corresponds with those in the Revised Draft.
2. It is presumed that the Department of the President has approached the Revenue Commissioners directly for their views on the Revised Draft. The Minister for Finance agrees with the views of the Commissioners as set forth in their letter of 7th instant to the President's Department.[67]

Articles 1-4:
The Nation
These Articles take the place of Articles 1 to 3 and Article 9.1 of the previous version. The revised articles are less emphatic and aggressive in tone and to that extent they are perhaps less likely to arouse antagonism in the two neighbouring countries. But the claim to territory which does not belong to Saorstát Éireann still subsists in Articles 3 and 4 and therefore the general criticism contained in our previous observations on this part of the Draft Constitution still stands. It gives a permanent place in the Constitution to a claim to *Hibernia Irredenta*. The parallel with Italy's historical attitude to the Adriatic Seaboard beyond its recognised territory is striking, and as in that case it is likely to have lasting ill effects on our political relations with our neighbours.[68]

[65] Document annotated by de Valera: 'Copy given J.W. as a reminder'. A revised version of this document, also dated 16 April 1937, is found at UCDA, P150/2419. It has been decided not to include this version as it does not carry any annotation to imply that it was the version taken by Walshe to Rome. It may simply have been written by de Valera as an attempt to further refine his own thinking.
[66] All annotations to this document were made by McDunphy.
[67] See document no. 126. Annotated: 'Yes. Revenue Commissioners are satisfied'.
[68] Annotated: 'This is a matter of *Policy*. The previous comments, however, contain a certain amount of common sense'. As John Bowman has noted, 'McElligott's broadsides proved futile, no trace of their

Article 2:
This Article claims all persons born in Ireland, including exiles who may have acquired citizenship in another State, as 'belonging to the Irish nation'. It is not clear whether it confers and imposes the rights and duties of Irish nationality and citizenship on all such persons. If it does, it may have some inconvenient results; if it does not, it is largely meaningless. At all events, the intention should be made clear.[69]

Article 5:
This Article (No. 4 in previous version) remains unchanged.

The adoption of the name of 'Éire' will, presumably, entail the alteration of Currency and Bank Notes, Coinage, Seals of State and of Government Departments, and all kinds of Government Stationery, e.g., Postal Orders, Old Age Pensions Orders, etc. This is going to be expensive in any case, and it will be still more expensive if we are not allowed to exhaust any existing stocks, which, it is argued, we should be allowed to do even after the coming into force of the Constitution. The latter is stated to become operative within six months after its approval by the people. In the case of coinage and bank notes, for example, the minimum stocks held are for two years, and these are costly to manufacture.

The adoption of the name of 'Éire' though quite justifiable from the traditional and scholarly points of view, may from a realistic point of view be a mistake. This land is generally known internationally as Ireland or one of the derivatives of that name, and so there will probably be a period of confusion and misunderstanding before the unaccustomed name conveys a definite meaning to educated people throughout the world.[70]

Article 7:
Section 2: The terms 'organs of State' is still used. The word 'organs' is now printed with a small initial letter, as suggested. Some definition would still seem desirable.[71]

Article 9:
Section 1: It is doubtful whether the introduction of the phrase 'as the national language', which is argumentative, is properly in place in a sub-Article which is declaratory.

[68] *contd*: thinking being incorporated into the Constitution when published': *De Valera and the Ulster Question 1917–1973* (Oxford, 1982), 148. Yet to modern eyes, McElligott's critique was ultimately fully vindicated by the enactment of the 18th Amendment of the Constitution Act, 1998 in the wake of the Good Friday Agreement and the replacement of the (old) Article 2 and Article 3 by a new version of these provisions.

[69] Annotated: 'This section has now been deleted'.

[70] Annotated: 'This is a matter of *Policy*. Personally I favour the name Ireland, but it has been decided otherwise'.

[71] Annotated: 'Deliberately loose'.

Section 3: Is there any need for the word 'special' before the word 'provision'?[72]

Article 10:
Section 1 deals only with *future* acquisition and loss of nationality and citizenship. It does not say who are to be citizens on the enactment of the Constitution—that point being, presumably, regarded as covered by Article 2.[73]

The phrase 'are determined' seems to close the door against any amending legislation. More comprehensive phrasing would be: 'are and may be determined' or 'are determinable'.[74]

Article 11:
The point in our observations on Section 1 of the previous version has been fully met and the revised Article on the whole represents an improvement and is satisfactory.

Article 13:
Section 1: On line 2 there is an obvious misprint of 'caller' for 'called'.
Section 2.3°: Proportional representation can only apply where more than two candidates for the Presidency are nominated. Subsection 4.5° provides specifically for the eventuality of there being only one candidate nominated. Should there not be provision for the occasion when only two candidates have been nominated?[75]

Section 3.1°: It is suggested that 'unless within that period he dies' should be substituted for 'unless he previously dies'.[76]

Section 4.2° (i): Supposing that the election of a President is an urgent requirement and that Dáil Éireann happens at the period in question to be dissolved, the conditions prescribed in this Subsection cannot be fulfilled. To meet such a possible emergency, would it be well to provide for the inclusion amongst those eligible to nominate persons who had been members of the Dáil Éireann so dissolved?[77]

Section 4.4°: This Subsection gives any *former* President the unqualified right to nominate himself as a candidate to fill a Presidential vacancy. Section 10 provides for the holding of a new election in the event of the

[72] Annotated: 'Section 1: 'The statement that Irish is the national language is not "argumentative". It is incontrovertible fact. Section 2 has been redrafted, the word "special" has been omitted'.
[73] Annotated: 'Read *Article 50*. There will be an adaptation of Enactments Act to make the present Nationality Act fully operative'.
[74] Annotated: 'I agree that the word "are" might be better replaced by "may be" or "shall be".'
[75] Annotated: 'Wilfred Brown is satisfied'.
[76] Annotated: 'Amended to meet the point'.
[77] Annotated: 'If the Dáil is dissolved, General Elections must take place not later than 30 days after dissolution. *It might be well to cover this point*'.

removal of a President from office on impeachment or of his permanent incapacity to discharge the functions of his office. Should, therefore, the right of such a former President to nominate himself remain unqualified in the draft Subsection?[78] The chances are, admittedly, entirely against such an emergency arising—but million to one chances are coming to pass regularly in every Dublin Sweepstake and the emergency might be provided against by an amendment as follows:

> 'Retiring Presidents or former Presidents other than one who had been removed from office under Section 9 of this Article or who had become permanently incapable to discharge the functions of his office may become candidates on their own nomination.'

Section 10: It is suggested that this Section would come more appropriately if it were placed to follow immediately after Section 3.2° of this Article (say as Subsection 13.3.3°).[79]

Article 14:
Section 2: The power given to the President to convene the Oireachtas is, presumably, to be exercised only on the advice of the Government. Why, then, is he required to consult the Council of State? Such consultation implies that he may refuse to act on the Government's advice.[80]

Sections 6 and 9: The power to appoint Judges and the right of pardon are presumed to be exercisable by the President only on the advice of the Government.[81]

Section 9: This is a revision of Section 11 of Article 12 of the former version. It is not clear whether the revision saves the statutory powers of the Revenue Department. It is noted, however, that the President's powers of pardon and commutation are not expressed to be exclusive.

It should be made quite clear in the Constitution that the powers of the President do not take away the existing powers vested in the Revenue Commissioners. In Revenue cases, the Courts are sometimes regarded as exercising criminal jurisdiction and sometimes, merely civil jurisdiction.[82]

Section 11.3° still seems to permit legal proceedings against an ex-President for acts done during his tenure of office. Taken in conjunction with Article 13.9, it leaves both the State and an aggrieved individual

[78] Annotated: 'Policy'.
[79] Annotated: 'No. This has been done in a revised draft'.
[80] Annotated: 'Section 2.3° should be made clearer. The intention is that the President should not in this case act on the advice of the President'.
[81] Annotated: 'Yes. Perhaps 12 is still not clear'.
[82] Annotated: 'The section has now been revised, and the Revenue Commissioners are quite satisfied'.

without any means of redress against a President who is, for example, a drunkard or a defaulting debtor (unless drunkenness and non-payment of debts are 'high crimes and misdemeanours').[83]

Article 15:

Section 11, which is new, declares that members of the Oireachtas shall act as public representatives of the country and not as delegates of particular constituencies or interests. The principle underlying this declaration is excellent, but how is it to be enforced? Will Deputies no longer be allowed to interfere, for example, in Old Age Pension claims or even to press for relief grants or the establishment of new industries for their constituencies? If that is intended and can be carried out, the effect on public life will be very beneficial.[84]

Section 16: This Section corresponds to Section 16 of Article 13 of the former version. The retention of the words 'such other facilities (if any)' rather invites extension of the facilities at present available and alone permissible under the existing Constitution.

Article 16:

The words 'by law' still occur in several sections and it is not clear whether they cover existing legislation.[85]

Section 2.6°: This Section remains identical with Section 2.6° of Article 14 of the former version. It still remains open to the technical objection which was raised in our previous observation on that Section.[86]

Section 6: This Section remains identical with Section 6 of Article 14 of the previous version and our criticism on that Section still stands. It is useful to compare the terms of the draft Section with those of Article 21 of the existing Constitution, which are as follows:

Dréacht-Bhunreacht	Existing Constitution
Article 14	Second Part of Article 21
Section 6: Provision Shall be made by law to enable the Member of Dáil Éireann who is the Chairman immediately before a dissolution of Dáil Éireann	The member of Dáil Éireann who is Chairman of Dáil Éireann immediately before a dissolution of the Oireachtas shall, unless before dissolution he

[83] Annotated: 'Yes. In respect of [?] actions can be taken after the President's tenure of office. But [?] the Statute of Limitations'. The word 'drunkard' has also been underlined by McDunphy, with the note: 'The President is not disposed to provide against this'.

[84] Annotated: 'This may be omitted altogether. It obviously cannot be enforced'.

[85] Annotated: 'Yes'.

[86] Annotated: 'three-member Constituency where the ex-Ceann Comhairle is returned'.

to be deemed without any actual election to be elected a member of Dáil Éireann at the ensuing General Election.	announces to Dáil Éireann that he does not desire to continue to be a member thereof, be deemed without any actual election to be elected in accordance with this Constitution at the ensuing General Election as a member of Dáil Éireann for the Constituency for which he was a member immediately before such dissolution or in the event of a revision of Constituencies having taken place, for the revised Constituency declared on such revision to correspond to such first-mentioned Constituency. Whenever a former Chairman of Dáil Éireann is so deemed to have been elected at a General Election as a member for a Constituency the number of members actually to be elected for such Constituency at such General Election shall be one less than would otherwise be required to be elected therefore.

It is not appreciated on what grounds the shorter phraseology of the draft Constitution is preferred to the perfectly clear and precise provisions of the existing Constitution. Our financial interest in the matter lies in avoiding the possibility of one extra Deputy resulting from the lack of precision of the proposed Section. The words of the existing Constitution have been deliberately framed to provide for an emergency which has already arisen, and to pass them by would seem to be turning our back on the accumulated wisdom and experience of previous Parliaments.[87]

Article 17:
Section 1.1° is substantially as before. It was suggested that the Draftsman might be asked to consider whether specific provision was necessary in relation to the volume of Supply Estimates.

[87] Annotated: 'The above columnar comparison shows clearly *why* the present brief provision, which must be implemented by law, has been chosen'.

Section 1.2° (Financial Resolutions) is unchanged. It was suggested that it appeared to make the enactment of the Central Fund Bill in March unconstitutional.[88]

Article 18:
Section 7.1°: Presumably it is not intended to require a candidate to have knowledge of all the matters indicated. Accordingly, it is suggested that the words 'one or more of' should be inserted after 'experience of' in line 3.[89]

Article 20:
Section 5.1°: The words 'within not more than' might be substituted for the words 'at a period not longer than', or substitute 'later' for 'longer' or insert 'the end of' after 'at'.[90]

Section 2°: Provision should apparently be made fixing the precise date when the Bill shall be deemed to have been passed by those Houses.[91]

Article 21:
Section 2: The machinery for deciding whether or not a Bill is a Money Bill seems unduly complicated. The matter could adequately and appropriately be dealt with by the two Houses and a Committee of Privileges.[92]

If the Subsection be retained in its present form, the Uachtaráin and his Council of State are required to consider whether the question raised shall or shall not be referred to a Committee of Privileges and they must, therefore, go with a reasonable amount of care into the issues involved. If they decide to make a reference, that fact can hardly fail to prejudice the issue in the minds of the Committee of Privileges, even if only unconsciously,[93] seeing that the President and Council of State, constituted in accordance with Article 30.2, are of infinitely greater weight than a Committee of Privileges constituted under Article 21.2.3°.

Section 2.3°: It is suggested that there should be substituted for the words 'consisting of an equal number of members of Dáil Éireann and of Seanad Éireann' the words 'consisting of equal members...Seanad Éireann, respectively' or 'consisting of a number of members of Dáil Éireann and an equal number of members of Seanad Éireann'.[94]

[88] Annotated: 'I understand that Finance are now satisfied on both points'.
[89] Annotated: 'Drafting. J[ohn] H[earne] might see if the point need be met'.
[90] Annotated: 'The words "the expiration of" have been inserted before [quotation] opened, but perhaps the drafting might be improved. "Not later than twenty one" might be better'.
[91] Annotated: 'Perhaps the words "On the expiration of the said twenty one days" ought to be added to the end'. McDunphy has later added the annotation 'Done' beside this point.
[92] Annotated: 'No. It affects the powers of the Seanad'.
[93] Annotated in the margin at this point: 'Not necessarily'.
[94] Annotated: 'Drafting point. Seems ok'.

Article 24:
Section 4.5°: The amendments made here were possibly intended to meet the suggestions of the Department of Finance. It is doubtful, however, whether they actually do so. What will be the status of an 'official' translation? Can it be cited in the Courts as a document carrying any authority?[95] Possibly the same objection could be made to the term suggested—'authoritative'—in the context. If a law is passed in Irish, any translation issued by the Clerk cannot have the same authority as the original. It will be an interesting and, if accurate, useful document, but in the last resort it will always be necessary to go beyond it to the original.[96]

It seems desirable to designate the persons to be responsible for enrolling the signed text and for issuing the authoritative translations of laws.[97]

Article 25:
Section 2.2° has been amended by dropping the prohibition on the expression of an opinion by dissenting members of the Supreme Court. The amendment suggested by this Department—the insertion of the word 'sitting' to qualify 'majority of the judges'—has not been accepted.[98]

Article 26:
Section 1: The assent of one-third of the members of Dáil Éireann to a petition is now made sufficient. Four-ninths was the proportion stipulated previously.[99] The last part of the section—'a proposal of such national importance, etc.'—is not happily phrased. It might be considered whether it should read somewhat as follows: '...a proposal of vital national importance on which the will of the people has not been clearly ascertained and which ought not to be made law until it has been specifically referred to them'. The same remark applies to Section 4.1°.[100]

Section 3: The time allowed to the President to arrive at a decision on the question of a referendum has been extended as suggested.

Section 4.2°: The amendment suggested by the Department of Finance has not been made. In our observations on Section 4.2° of Article 23 of the previous version we called attention to an apparent gap in the

[95] Annotated: 'No'.
[96] Annotated: 'Yes'.
[97] Annotated: 'Leave to law'. The word 'authoritative' in this sentence has been underlined manually by McDunphy, with the annotation: 'Not "authoritative"—simply official'.
[98] Annotated: 'This has been carefully considered and decided on. The court must be a court of 5 judges'.
[99] Annotated: 'Policy'.
[100] The proposed alteration in wording has been annotated: 'This is not an improvement. Rather the contrary'.

machinery concerned with the completion of Bills which have been presented for the expression of the will of the people. Section 4.2° of Article 26 of the new version still presents the same technical difficulty. It is suggested that this might be overcome by the deletion of the words after 'Seal' on the 6th line of Section 4.1°. and the substitution therefore of the following words:

> '...and shall return such Bill which he shall decline to sign and promulgate as a law unless and until etc.'[101]

Article 27:

Section 1: An upper limit has now been set to the number of members of the Government, namely, fifteen. This is unnecessarily high.[102] Perhaps it is the intention to set a lower maximum by law.[103]

Transposition of Sections 4 and 3 is suggested.

Sections 6.1° and 7.1°: The suggestion that the Minister for Finance should hold the position of Tánaiste has not been adopted. The Department desires to press strongly the suggestion made in connection with the previous Article 24.5.1° that the Minister for Finance should hold the office of Tánaiste. Any other member of the Government (except the Taoiseach) can have only a very incomplete and, therefore, unbalanced knowledge on the work of Government Departments as a whole and is, therefore, essentially less fitted to act as deputy for the Taoiseach; whereas the Minister for Finance has, by virtue of his office, to obtain a general knowledge of the work of every Department of State and, in particular, a full acquaintance with the work of the central Department.[104]

On Section 7.1° this Department raised the question whether it was intended that the Taoiseach, Tánaiste and Minister for Finance should be *ex-officio* members of Dáil Éireann. The wording of the section has not been changed, and any doubt there may have been on this point remains. In view of the terms of *Article 16*, however, there does not seem to be any serious reason for doubt.

It is suggested that the word 'shall' should be replaced by 'must' as in Subparagraph 2°.[105]

Section 12: As this section now reads, it does not of itself seem to require new legislation. A general Adaptation of Enactments Act will, no doubt, become necessary in consequence of the enactment of the Constitution.

[101] Annotated: 'This is silly: of course the Bill must be sent back, but there is no need to put this in the Constitution'.
[102] Annotated: 'Policy'.
[103] Annotated: 'This could be done'. A later annotation states: 'No. Decided'.
[104] Annotated: 'Policy. Decided in the negative'.
[105] Annotated: 'Done'.

Article 28:
This Article is Article 25 of the previous version unchanged in substance. We are still without certainty as to its precise significance. The need for an explanatory Memorandum from the Department of External Affairs is more urgent than before.[106]

Section 4.2°, as amended, does not seem to make necessary the re-enactment of Constitution (Amendment No. 27) Act, 1936. It appears to supersede that Act, and legislation will only be necessary if it is decided to place limitations on the exercise of the power which it gives to the Government.[107]

The amendments to Section 5 appear to meet the points raised by this Department, but it is suggested that the words 'the State' in paragraphs 1° and 2° should be replaced by Éire, which is used elsewhere throughout this Article.[108]

Article 29:
Section 6.5°: There is still no provision for the carrying on of the duties of Attorney General in the interval between the resignation of one Taoiseach and the appointment of another. The addition of words 'but the Attorney General retiring in such circumstances shall continue to carry on his duties until his successor shall have been appointed' was suggested in our previous observations.[109]

Section 7: The provisions of this Section would probably involve the enactment of new legislation establishing the Attorney General's Department as one distinct from the Ministerial Departments of State, i.e., he will come out of the Ministers and Secretaries Act. (Vide Article 56.4). There appears to be no need for this distinction.[110]

Article 30:
Section 2: The Comptroller and Auditor General is no longer included among the *ex-officio* members of the Council of State. We have suggested that his place should be taken by the Minister for Finance or alternatively that the Minister for Finance should always occupy the post of Tánaiste.[111] Failing the adoption of either of these suggestions, the Article ought, in the opinion of the Department, expressly include that Minister

[106] Annotated: 'Get E[xternal] A[ffairs] to furnish a memo'.
[107] Annotated: 'Changed to as to require a law to be passed'.
[108] Annotated: 'No'.
[109] The initial annotation to this point read: 'Discussed with P[arliamentary] D[raftsman]. He and Mr [Philip] O'Donoghue are satisfied with present draft'. This annotation was later crossed out and replaced with 'Amended'.
[110] Annotated: 'Why?'.
[111] Annotated: 'No'.

as a member of the Council of State. His inclusion would increase his prestige and his effectiveness as Minister and it would bring to the Council a fuller and more general knowledge of the work of administration and of the financial and economic affairs of the State than any of the ex-officio members named in the Article, with the exception of the Taoiseach, could possess. His special experience of the conduct of Parliamentary business and especially of Money Bills make him a particularly suitable ex-officio member of the Council of State.[112]

This Article contains no reference to payment of members and provides no means of convening meetings when the President is unable to convene them. The omissions in the earlier draft were referred to in our notes.[113]

Article 33:
Section 2 is unchanged. It seems that the word 'office' in the last line is qualified by the words 'of emolument'.[114] This question was previously raised.

No amendment has been made in Article 56.3 (previously 55.3). Unless the expression 'existing officer of the Government of Saorstát Éireann' applies to an officer of the Audit Office, no provision is made for the security of tenure of the Audit Office staff.[115]

Article 34:
This Article corresponds to Article 32 of the previous version. Our previous point on Section 5.1° and 2° of that Article still holds good in relation to Section 5.2° of this Article. Our point about avoiding the necessity for the formal making of the declaration by Circuit Court Judges and by District Justices in the presence of the Chief Justice has been met to a certain extent by the introduction of the words 'or the senior available Judge of the Supreme Court in open Court' but the Section will still involve the attendance in the Supreme Court of a Circuit Judge or a District Justice on first appointment. It seems an unnecessary piece of punctilio in the Constitution in relation to Circuit Judges and District Justices. Presumably the idea underlying its retention is that a Barrister appointed to be a Circuit Judge or a District Justice will be in Dublin in any case and his appointment will not be seriously delayed. In certain circumstances, however, it might involve a new appointee in avoidable expenditure.[116]

[112] Annotated: 'President has definitely decided against this'.
[113] Annotated: 'Not now necessary. There is a permanent [committee?]'.
[114] Annotated: 'Of course'.
[115] Annotated: 'Mr [Philip] O'Donoghue is to discuss with the P[arliamentary] D[raftsman]'. A later annotation reads: 'Now covered by new draft'.
[116] Annotated: 'Policy. I think it highly desirable that *all* judges should conform to this procedure'.

Does the requirement apply to Deputy Judges and Deputy or Assistant Justices?[117]

Article 36:
This Article corresponds to Article 34 of the previous version and provides that the following matters shall be regulated by law and Rules of Court made there-under, that is to say:

Former version	Revised version
i. The number of Judges of the Supreme Court, the High Court, and all other Courts of Éire, the declarations to be taken by the Judges of the said Courts on appointment, the remuneration, age of retirement, and pensions of said Judges.	i. The number of Judges of the Supreme Court and of the High Court, the remuneration, age of retirement and pensions of such Judges. ii. The terms of appointment of the Judges of all other Courts.

Why have the words '*and all other Courts of Éire*' been eliminated from the original draft? Their inclusion seems necessary and their elimination rather suggests the possibility of the President being empowered to appoint as many Circuit Judges and District Justices as he wishes.[118]

Article 38:
Section 1.2° and Section 3: Is the reference in these Sections to Article 45 of the Constitution correct?[119]

Article 40:
Section 1.2°: Is the reference to Article 45 in this Section correct? Should it not be to Article 40? In this Section the use of the word 'every' before Bill rather conveys the idea of the possibility of there being many such Bills and the use of the word 'any' in substitution is suggested as preferable.

Section 2: Is the reference to Article 40 correct?[120]

Article 41:
Section 1: This Section corresponds to Section 1.1° and 2° of Article 38 of the previous version. The meaning and object of the second part of this Section still remain obscure.

[117] Annotated: 'If they are judges, yes'.
[118] Annotated: 'This is a valid point. (ii) might read: "The number of judges of all other courts, and their terms of appointment"'.
[119] Annotated: 'No. The article is being completely redrafted'.
[120] Both points are annotated: 'Being redrafted'.

Section 2.2°: This Subsection is new. There can be no question of any person, or body of persons, within the confines of Éire having the right or power to confer a title of nobility of honour in the future. Therefore, the objective aimed at by the Subsection can only be some outside Government or Potentate, such as the Pope (e.g. Orders conferred on the present Lord Mayor of Dublin, Mr Cosgrave, *Count* McCormack, the *Marquis* McSwiney), the British Monarchy (e.g. Birthday or New Year Honours which, in actual practice, have ceased to be conferred on Irish citizens resident in the Free State since 1922), or the French Republic (e.g. the Legion of Honour, or the educational honour of the violet ribbon). It is submitted that there is nothing obnoxious per se to the granting of these honours and that, generally speaking, they give pleasure to the Nation in seeing the public work, or an act of gallantry, of one of its citizens recognised by such an international gesture. But, even if there were, is a provision in the Constitution, which is not in itself binding on any outside granting authority, the correct channel of communicating the fact that the Irish Government desires to be first consulted? Would not this matter be better left to diplomatic usage and settled outside of the Constitution in accordance with whatever views are prevalent at the time?[121]

Section 3.1° and 2°: These Sections are more or less the same as Sections 2.1° and 2° of Article 38 of the previous version. It is still thought that they are dangerous and there still remains obscurity as to what practical obligations they impose on the State.[122]

Section 3.2°: Could this Subsection be held to oblige the State to take the initiative in libel actions, proceedings for recovery of debts, and actions for damages in cases of personal injury? This might be a straining of the sense, but greater clarity would be desirable.[123]

Section 4.2°: There is an obvious misprint of 'offer' for 'Order' in line 4.[124]

Article 43:

This article corresponds more or less to Article 40 of the previous version. Generally speaking, Section 4 in the revised version is an improvement on the old Section 5 and also on Article 10 of the existing Constitution. Possibly the obligations which the Article as a whole imposes on the State to provide education in various forms, or to endeavour to provide it, are counter-balanced by its assertion of the duty

[121] Annotated: 'Cf. Article 5 of the 1922 Constitution. Policy'.
[122] Annotated: 'Policy'.
[123] Annotated: 'The law officers are satisfied'.
[124] Annotated: 'Corrected'.

which lies on parents to provide according to their means for the education of their children. It is still thought, however, that the word 'may' should be inserted before the word 'provide' in line 4 of Section 4. As the Section reads at present it is not clear whether its intention is to carry forward the word 'shall', or the words 'shall endeavour to' join up with the word 'provide' in line 4. In the context the word 'may' would be best of all. The words 'shall endeavour to' would do but the word 'shall' would be dangerous from the financial point of view.[125]

Section 4 has been amended, but is still open to the interpretation that it places on the State an obligation to provide free books, etc., for children in primary schools.[126]

Article 44:
This Article, now in blank, presumably takes the place of the previous Article 41 relating to private property, which was the Article amongst those dealing with fundamental rights which was most open to criticism. It is to be hoped that the previous Article has been dropped for good as being too controversial, contradictory and dangerous.

We are still without the Article dealing with *Religion, Church and State*. It is most important that as much time as possible should be available for consideration of its terms.[127]

Articles 48 and 50

Article 48 is unchanged and there has been only a verbal alteration in Article 50. The effect of these Articles on transferred officers is still under consideration.[128]

Article 49:
The points raised by this Department have not been met. It was stated that the interpretation of this Section is difficult for any person who is not a legal expert. It is highly desirable (and particularly so in the case of the Department of Finance in relation to the many matters in which the powers and functions it has exercised since 1922 have been derived traditionally from Treasury practice through the channel of the Transfer of Functions Order of 31 March 1922) if the powers, functions, rights and prerogatives of Ministers, exercised through their Departments immediately before 11 December, 1935, were declared to belong to the corresponding Ministers comprising the Government of Éire. To

[125] Annotated: 'Consider'. A later annotation reads: 'President adheres to "shall"'.
[126] Annotated: 'Cf. Article 10 of present Constitution'.
[127] Annotated with an exclamation mark.
[128] Annotated: 'This matter as I understood has definitely been settled and the existing text accepted by the Department of Finance. In the circ[umstance]s the above comment is mischievous'.

illustrate the foregoing observation, the authority for the grant of Marriage Gratuities to established Women Civil Servants on retirement lies not in any Statutory provision but in Treasury Minutes of 1894 and 1895. The bonus system at present in operation in Saorstát Éireann, but no longer in operation in Great Britain, has its origin not in Statute but in Resolutions of the British House of Commons and was brought into effect by means of Treasury Circulars prior to the Transfer of Functions 1922. Many Regulations in full force and observance in the Service Departments have their origin in old decisions of the Treasury whose accepted successor is the Department of Finance. The draft Constitution should, in some express way if possible, provide support for the continuance of all this Treasury practice and tradition.[129]

Article 56:
Section 3: The observations submitted in our previous Memorandum on the corresponding Section 3 of Article 33 of the previous version still hold good and the phraseology of the present Article remains open to our criticism. The difficulty referred to might be overcome by the substitution of the phrase 'Civil Servant' for the phrase 'officer of the Government of Saorstát Éireann' in line 1.

The observations in our previous Memorandum on Articles 47 and 49 of the previous version still hold good, and with additional force, because what may at first have been due to oversight pure and simple now has the appearance of being the result of deliberate consideration. It is understood unofficially that Article 10 rights are regarded as preserved to Transferred Officers sufficiently in the provisions of Article 50 which, inter alia, will keep in force the provisions of the Civil Service (Transferred Officers) Compensation Act, 1929. The point has been discussed with Mr O'Donoghue of the Attorney General's Office and it has been stressed that the express abrogation of Article 78 of the existing Constitution leaves the Transferred Officers in future without express protection in the new Constitution. This Department has also stressed another point, namely, the psychological advantage of meeting the reasonable fears of the Transferred Officers by some express phrase in relation to compensation on removal from office even if it is desired to avoid an express reference to Article 10 of the existing Constitution. It is understood that the whole question is being further considered.[130]

[129] Annotated: 'The Attorney General's Department is satisfied'.
[130] Annotated: 'Mr [Philip] O'Donoghue is to discuss this whole question with the P[arliamentary] D[raftsman]'.

Section 56.4: Has the use of the expression 'Department of the Attorney General' in Section 4 any special significance? The Attorney General's Office is not a Department under the Ministers and Secretaries Acts.[131]

Article 57:
Section 3 provides that the place of any member of the Commission to exercise the Presidential functions who may be unable to act shall be taken by the 'next senior judge of the Supreme Court available'. (What is to happen if one of the officers designated as a member refuses to act)[132] or (if the Chief Justice, the President of the High Court or the Chairman of the Chamber of Deputies dies in the rather long interval between the coming into operation of the Constitution and the entry of the first President upon his office?)[133] Although it is provided that the Commission may act by two of its members, (the question arises whether the loss of one member would not automatically terminate the existence of the Commission or deprive it of its right to function),[134] in view of Section 2 which refers to 'a Commission consisting of the following persons, etc.' One of these persons is the 'member of the Chamber of Deputies (Dail Éireann) who is immediately before the said repeal'—i.e. of the present Constitution—'Ceann Comhairle'. He is unique and irreplaceable. The others are persons holding officers to which appointment is by the President or a validly constituted Commission to exercise the Presidential functions.[135]

Article 58:
It is observed that there is no precise provision to the effect that the Chief Justice of Saorstát Éireann shall become and be the Chief Justice of Éire such as has been inserted to cover the transfer under Article 56.4 of the Department of State, under Article 59 the transfer of the Comptroller and Auditor General, and under Article 60 the transfer of every Commissioned Officer of the Defence Forces. Without such express provision it is not quite clear how the Chief Justice of Saorstát Éireann becomes the Chief Justice of Éire and yet he has got to function in such office under Article 57.2 before the entry of the first President to his office.[136]

Dréacht-Bhunreacht na hÉireann
Notes on Revised Draft

[131] Annotated: 'The reference to the A.G.'s Department has been deleted'.
[132] Annotated: 'Unthinkable'.
[133] Annotated: 'Their successors will act'.
[134] Annotated: 'See new text'.
[135] Annotated: 'The Commission will always be complete'.
[136] Annotated: 'This seems to be a valid point. The Article might be amended similarly to 56—see P[arliamentary] D[raftsman] first however. He has passed this section'.

The attached note dealing with the effect of Articles 48, 50 and 58.3 on the position of Transferred Officers entitled to the benefit of Article X of the Treaty is supplementary to the Notes furnished on the 17th instant on the Articles mentioned and has particular reference to Mr P[hilip] O'Donoghue's minute of the 16th instant addressed to an Runaí, Roinn an Uachtaráin.[137]

Articles 48, 50 and 58.3:

1. It is accepted without question that the carrying over of the Civil Service (Transferred Officers) Compensation Act, 1929, by the draft Constitution preserves the statutory rights of Transferred Officers to compensation and the machinery for determining them.
2. In this limited respect the position will be in no way different from what it has been since the enactment of the Constitution (Removal of Oath) Act, 1933.
3. As matters stand, however, so long as the existing Constitution remains unrepealed, the rights of the Transferred Officers are enshrined not only in the Act of 1929 but also in the specific provisions of Article 78 of the Constitution, and if a Government were to repeal the Act of 1929, the Transferred Officers would be able to fall back upon the protection of Article 78, under which their rights would be for determination not by the Statutory Compensation Board, but by the High Court. It follows that a Government which desired to wipe out Article X Rights could not do so merely by the repeal of the Act of 1929 but would also have to repeal Article 78 of the Constitution. This would be, for the Government, quite feasible in practice until the expiration in 1938 of the period of 16 years within which (under Article 50 of the Constitution) it is competent to amend the Constitution by ordinary legislation without specific appeal to the People by Referendum.
4. Under the draft Constitution a future Government which looked with disfavour on the continued retention of rights to compensation by a particular section of the Civil Service could abrogate these rights entirely by simple repeal of the Act of 1929: if, however, the rights of the Transferred Officers were

[137] Annotated: 'Noted by President. He is not prepared to make any special provision in the Constitution for Article X Civil Servants. They are adequately protected by law. 22 April 1937'. The comments on Articles 48, 50 and 56 were submitted on 22 April, after the main body of McElligott's observations. They have been included here so as to keep all of the Department of Finance's observations together.

recognised specifically in a provision in the draft Constitution corresponding in substance to the terms of the existing Article 76, these rights could be abrogated (after the preliminary three year period) only by an amendment of the Constitution supported by an expression of the Will of the People.

It follows from the foregoing observations that, on the basis of the normal working of the Constitution, the position of the Transferred Officers under the new Constitution as drafted would be less secure than it is under the existing Constitution.

5. The present Government has definitely stated (vide the President's speech on 19 May, 1932, on the Report stage of the Constitution (Removal of Oath) Act, 1933—Debates Columns 2107 and 2108) that there is no intention whatever of interfering with the rights of Transferred Officers. In the observations in this minute there is, of course, no question of impugning the good faith behind that assurance. The absence of express provision in the draft Constitution on the lines of existing Article 76 will almost certainly evoke criticism which will inevitably lead to the repetition by the President of that assurance. In this connection it must be pointed out that such an assurance does not bind the successors of the Government that gives it, and that there would be no legal or moral barrier to prevent a future Government, by simple repeal of the Act of 1929, wiping out Article X Rights altogether. It seems inevitable that this view will not escape the notice of members of Dáil Éireann and that the Government, if it gives that assurance, will be pressed to accept an amendment giving it permanent form in the Constitution and will find it difficult to give adequate reason for not doing so. In these circumstances the Departmental view is that it would be better to anticipate Parliamentary pressure and from the very outset to have the point covered in the draft presented to the House. It should be practicable to draft a paragraph embodying the substance of Article 78 without reference by name to the Treaty. From the Departmental point of view the circumstances of the case would be adequately met by the addition at the end of Section 3 of Article 35 of some such words as the following:

> 'and shall retain such rights (if any) to compensation on retirement or discharge from office as he had immediately before that date'.

No. 155: UCDA, P150/2419

Memorandum from Joseph P. Walshe to Eamon de Valera 'Secretary's report on his visit to Rome'

Rome
22 April 1937

I arrived in Rome by air on Saturday 17 April about 4.30pm, having left Dublin by the Holyhead boat the previous morning. Macaulay[138] arranged an interview with Monsignor Pizzardo[139] the Assistant Secretary of State for midday Sunday.

Monsignor Pizzardo received us with his usual cheerfulness, and when I explained the object of my visit he said that he saw no difficulty in getting the desired approval. This, as things happened, proved to be excessive optimism. He arranged an interview for us with the Cardinal Secretary of State[140] for Tuesday. Meanwhile, I left with him, for the Cardinal's information, the first three sections of Article 45.

The Cardinal was most amicable. He kept us over an hour, well into lunchtime, as he did also on the two following days. I gave him an [exposé?] of the background, historical and religious, in which the new Constitution came to be written, and I emphasised particularly the aspect of the 'appeasement' which you desired to bring about, not only amongst our own people of all religious and political beliefs but also between our people and the British people. He was deeply interested in all I had to say about the aims you had set before you to accomplish, and he asked me endless questions.

I thought it well to say at a very early stage that you fully realised that the sections of the Constitution under discussion did not correspond with the complete Catholic ideal. You would like to have the approval of the Vatican insofar as it could be given. At any rate you wished to have the satisfaction of having let the Cardinal Secretary and the Holy Father see the sections relating to the Church before putting them before Parliament. Cardinal Pacelli expressed his great joy that you had done so. You should understand that whatever he and the Holy Father might say they were in the fullest sympathy with you and the Government in your difficulties, and they appreciated how great a task it was to achieve

[138] William J. Babbington Macaulay (1892–1964), Irish minister to the Holy See (1934–40).
[139] Monsignor Giuseppe Pizzardo (1877–1970), Papal Under Secretary of State, 1937.
[140] Cardinal Eugenio Pacelli (1876–1958), Cardinal Secretary of State (1930–9), elected pope, taking the name Pius XII (1939–58).

anything like the Catholic ideal in the special circumstances. Nevertheless, he would say with complete frankness and friendliness what he felt bound to say—though of course that would not detract from his good wishes and those of the Holy Father to you in your task.

He said that he had had a preliminary chat with the Holy Father, but would of course see him again the following (Wednesday) morning, in order to report to him the *apercu historique* which I had just given him. He felt however that the 'special position' given to the Catholic Church had no real value so long as there was not a formal acknowledgement of the R.C. Church as the Church founded by Christ. Moreover, its importance was based on numbers only (as far as the text was concerned) and the recognition given to the other Churches nullified any advantage which might have been derived from exclusive recognition. He thought we should use the word 'tolerates' in regard to them. He could see no juridical consequence flowing from the text used which could confer advantages on the Catholic Church not equally conferred on the other bodies. Ireland was *the* Catholic country of the world, and he thought we should have made a very special effort to give to the world a completely Catholic Constitution.

I told him I quite realised how important the form of the Constitution was in the mind of the Vatican, but from what I had already said he would appreciate that we had abstained from using the forms in order to be able to keep the realities. In our case the full Catholic framework would destroy absolutely the building we desired to construct. We had to take the long view in order to reconcile the most hostile religious opinions, and to get all our people to work for our common country.

Catholic forms in the rigid sense incorporated into our Constitution now would defeat that purpose, and would also certainly defeat the purpose which he and the Holy Father had in mind, namely the establishment of permanent peace with G.B. (an almost exclusively Protestant country). Above all they would hinder the growth and influence of the Catholic Church in Ireland and Great B., and would revive all the old accusations of intransigence and intolerance. In real truth, in our Constitution, we were being more Catholic than the Church because we were assuming the ultimate success of the aims of the Church, while the Cardinal's suggestion might well destroy all chance of ever attaining them.

The Cardinal all the time insisted that he was talking as a Church man must talk, and he never once departed during all our conversations from his attitude of the greatest possible friendliness. From the beginning he made me feel free from any sense of embarrassment whatsoever, and he encouraged me to be as frank with him as he was with me. I think that I did not omit any explanation or argument which could reasonably be offered.

But it became clear at a very early stage of our conversations that we should not succeed in getting any expression of approval of the text from the Vatican. From the nature of things they have to stake their full claim, and formal or indeed informal approval was not to be given to a text which did not come down completely on the side of strict Catholic doctrine. The Cardinal told me with a smile, but quite truthfully, that according to the strict teaching of the Church we were heretics to recognise any church but the one true church of Christ. Again I reminded him of the danger of seeing only the form, and he assured me at once that the Church would not take our heresy too seriously.

It did not shake him when I contrasted the expressly Christian character of our new Constitution with the liberalism (continental sense) of the old, though he recognised the great change for the better. He promised to have a long talk with the Holy Father and to obtain his blessing for [the Government] for having done so well in such difficult circumstances. It was clear when saying this that the Cardinal did not realise that the Holy Father was going to adopt the negative attitude which he made known to me the following day. Indeed he gave me the very clear impression that having said all *he* could say, he was going to get the Pope to bless the Government for the effort they had made to meet the Catholic viewpoint—without making any reference to the Constitution.

I need hardly say therefore that I was very disappointed when I received from the Cardinal yesterday the exact text of the words used by the Holy Father: '*Ni approvo ni nondisapprovo—taceremo*'. And the Cardinal did not leave me any doubt as to the meaning. I had asked him to ensure at least that the Holy Father would not disapprove. The answer was: 'I do not approve, neither do I not disapprove—we shall maintain silence'. I tried to translate the evil out of this double negative but the Cardinal held me to the sense. He went on to show that the Holy Father was doing quite a lot in saying that he would maintain silence. It was an attitude of complete neutrality. He might have taken the text without bearing in mind all the implications of the explanations I had given, because the text after all was what counted, but he refrained from disapproving. He would not say 'I approve' and while he would not say

'I do not disapprove' he took the middle position of keeping silence. So argued the Cardinal and while he clearly wanted to give us a crumb of consolation, he had to maintain that the Pope went to the extreme limit to which his position allowed him to go.

On the question of marriage which they regard as one of the supreme tests of the Catholicism of a State the Cardinal said we were also heretical. Cases of nullity and of *naturam et non consummatum* (in the case of marriages celebrated in the Church) are within the exclusive domain of the Church and must be formally declared so to be. I told him of the difficulties of taking that attitude in a country of mixed religions where divorce was forbidden to all. The non-Catholics could justifiably complain that a way of escape lay open to Catholics which was not available to them. I touched lightly on the difficulties *nature scandali* which could arise from cases in which evidence relating to defective intention for example might satisfy the ecclesiastical but not the lay mind. The Cardinal pointed out that the Yugoslav Government had recently concluded a Concordat with the Holy See formally accepting the full Catholic doctrine.[141] I suggested that as the Concordat was the subject of very serious quarrels between the Catholic Church and the Government the latter might not be able to ratify it against the will of the majority of their people, and that in the end it may prove to have been a grave mistake to insist on the full pound of flesh. The Cardinal admitted this, but he seemed to regard the displeasure of the Orthodox Church with a certain amount of satisfaction.

I insisted again and again that we regarded the fundamentally sound position of the Church in the hearts of the people as an infinitely greater safeguard for Catholic doctrine than form in any documents whether constitutions or concordats—and that that conviction was never absent from your mind when drawing up the constitution. The Holy Father and the Cardinal would realise as our State evolved that we had acted in the best interests of the Church as well as of the people.

At the Cardinal's request we went back again to see him today, Thursday. He told me how very ill the Pope had been and that there were several ministers accredited to the Vatican whom he had never seen and who would be annoyed if they heard—and they would hear—that he had given a private audience to me. However, there were some people whom in the normal course he had to see on a Saturday, and he would like Mr Macaulay and myself to come with them. He would be able to give us his blessing and perhaps say a word to us.

[141] In the margin Walshe gives the text of Article XXXII of the concordat concluded between the Yugoslavian government and the Vatican.

The Cardinal then asked me about the Coronation and our attitude regarding it. I explained to him our general attitude and also the particular objection we had to the continuing anti-Catholic character of the ceremony as stated publicly by you. I took the opportunity of saying that there were rumours in Ireland that the Legate was to attend the ceremony at Westminster, but that we naturally did not believe it. He assured me with great emphasis that they had never contemplated allowing the Legate to be present. 'If that happened', he said, laughing heartily, 'your Government would certainly be *plus Catholique que l'eglise*' and they would be right. Attendance as a spectator was of course permissible even for a Legate but the *natio scandali* was an all sufficient and compelling reason for abstention.

I thanked the Cardinal for his great kindness. He asked to be warmly remembered to you and to thank you for your courtesy in having sent me.

I wish to add that the position of influence with the Cardinal which is held by Mr Macaulay and his wife and the great friendship which he has for them made my task very easy and pleasant. The Cardinal's attitude from the first moment and I must repeat that he could not have been more friendly.

The Cardinal on Tuesday expressed himself as very pleased that you intended to use the full official title of the Church which he compared carefully with the Lateran Treaty. He said that the Holy Father would of course also be very pleased. I did not ask him a second time about the title as he was clear beyond misapprehension the first time. I am sorry that my telegram was not sufficiently clear about this point. 'Other Christian Churches' he could not formally approve of, but let it go without taking any responsibility for it. He thought 'Bodies' would be more appropriate. Again I had to explain that in using the word Church we were following the [bear? sic bare?] custom and doing only what ordinary courtesy required. We did not intend to imply—and nobody in our country would regard us as attempting to imply that there was any church in the strict sense—other than the one true church. He gave me a long and very interesting discourse on the oneness of the Church and the impossibility of having a plurality of them, and he quoted a good deal from an encyclical of the present Pope (6 January 1928) which immediately struck me as being a superb and very beautiful statement of the position.[142]

To conclude this scanty and hastily written report, I want to express my great regret at not having been able to do what I was sent out to do.

[142] Pius XI, *Mortalium Animos: On Religious Unity* (6 January 1928).

But I have learned a great deal about the attitude of the Holy See to such matters—and I can assure you, most confidently, that at the back of their adherence to rigid forms and dogmas there is very sincere respect, and even gratitude for the extent to which you have been able to go in making our constitution Catholic, notwithstanding the very great difficulties which they understand better than they pretend to understand them. I will of course amplify this report *viva voce* on my return.

No. 156: NAI, DT S10160

Maurice Moynihan to all Ministers, Patrick Lynch, William O'Brien, Patrick Little and Joseph P. Walshe, enclosing drafts of Articles 42 (Private Property), 43 (Religion) and 44 (Social Policy).

Department of the President
23 April 1937

A chara,
I am desired by the President to transmit herewith copies of draft articles of the Constitution entitled as follows:

Private Property:	Article 42
Religion:	Article 43
Directive Principles of Social Policy:	Article 44

The President would be glad to have your observations on these Articles at the earliest possible moment. He desires that the annexed copies should be returned to him with your reply.

Article 42: Private Property

1. 1° The State acknowledges that man, in virtue of his rational being, has the natural right, antecedent to positive law, to the private ownership of external goods.
   2° The State acknowledges further that the exercise of this natural right is, for social reasons, absolutely necessary, and guarantees to pass no law attempting to abolish the right of private ownership or the general right to transfer, bequeath and inherit property.
2. 1° The State recognises, however, that the exercise of the rights mentioned in the foregoing provisions of this Article ought, in

civil society, to be regulated by the principles of social justice.
2° The State, accordingly, may as occasion requires, delimit by law the exercises of the said rights with a view to reconciling their exercise with the exigencies of the common good.

Article 43: Religion

1. [Blank]
2. 1° Freedom of conscience and the free profession and practice of religion are, subject to public order and morality, guaranteed to every citizen.
   2° The State guarantees not to endow any religion, and shall not impose any disabilities or make any discrimination on the ground of religious profession, belief or status.
   3° Legislation providing State aid for schools shall not discriminate between schools under the management of different religious denominations, nor be such as to affect prejudicially the right of any child to attend a school receiving public money without attending religious instruction at that school.
   4° Every religious denomination shall have the right to manage its own affairs, own, acquire and administer property, movable and immovable, and maintain institutions for religious or charitable purposes.
   5° The property of any religious denomination or any educational institution shall not be diverted save for necessary works of public utility and on payment of compensation.

Article 44: Directive Principles of Social Policy

The principles of social policy set down in this Article are for the general guidance of the Legislature. The application of those principles in the making of laws shall be the exclusive care of the Oireachtas, and shall not be cognisable by any Court under any of the provisions of this Constitution.

1. The State shall strive to promote the economic welfare of the whole people by securing and protecting as effectively as it may a social order in which justice and charity shall inform all the institutions of public life.
2. The State shall direct its policy towards securing
   (i) that citizens may through their occupations find the means of adequately meeting their domestic needs.
   (ii) that the ownership and control of the material resources of the State may be so distributed amongst private

individuals and the various classes of the community as best to subserve the common good.

(iii) that there may be established on the land in economic security as many families as in the circumstances shall be practicable.

3. 1° The State shall favour and, where necessary, supplement private initiative in industry and commerce.
2° The State shall endeavour to secure that private enterprise shall be so conducted as to ensure reasonable efficiency in the production and distribution of goods and to protect the public against unjust exploitation.
3° The State shall make it a duty so to restrain the operation of free competition that the resources of the State or a particular class of goods may not pass into the ownership or control of a few individuals save as may be determined by law for the common good.
4° In particular, the State shall take care that in what pertains to the control of credit the welfare of the people as a whole shall be the constant aim.

4. 1° The State pledges itself to safeguard with especial care the economic rights of the less favoured sections of the community, and, where necessary, to contribute to the support of the infirm, the widow, the orphan, and the aged.
2° The State shall endeavour to ensure that the tender age of children and the inadequate strength of women shall not be abused and that they shall not be forced through economic necessity to enter avocations unsuited to their strength and sex.

5. With a view to securing a more equitable social balance, the State shall, as circumstances permit, favour the due constitution of functional and vocational groupings, on the basis of the various forms of social activity.

No. 157: NAI, DT S9853

Memorandum from Philip O'Donoghue to Patrick Lynch

Office of the Attorney General
23 April 1937

Príomh Aturnae:

1. A question has been raised on the draft Article on fundamental rights clause 6 of which guarantees liberty for free expression of convictions and opinions subject to public order and morality. It is apprehended that in its present form and without further qualifying words difficulty may be experienced in the army, police forces and the civil service in maintaining discipline and that measure of control over the exercise of the any such rights on the part of members of these services, which is essential. It will be observed that similar words are found in Article 9 of the present Constitution and I am not aware that they have been found inadequate.
2. Entry into any of the three services mentioned is entirely voluntary and any member of them would be held to have expressly accepted the restrictions on his exercise of those rights prescribed by the controlling authority of such services. Any conduct on the part of a civil servant, policeman or soldier by way of exercising the right of free expression would be entirely incompatible with his position if it interfered with the maintenance of discipline in the respective services.
3. It is inconceivable to my mind that the right of free expression of opinion on the part of a soldier could be the same as that of a civilian member of the public.
4. In my opinion it is competent for the Government to restrict the right of free expression of opinion in the case of the services mentioned to the extent necessary to maintain discipline and secure efficiency in the public service. It may be necessary in some cases such as that of a soldier in effect to arrogate that right altogether. If challenged, the matter must be determined in the last resort by the Courts who would have regard to the paramount consideration of the public interest and the requirements of the particular service in arriving at a decision.

5. If any words were added to these introductory words 'public order and morality' such as 'the maintenance of discipline in the public services' (or like words) it would not, in my opinion, improve the legal position. The question as to whether any restriction was necessary for the maintenance of such discipline would still remain open for the courts, if any affected person thought well to raise it.[143]

No. 158: NAI, DT S10160

Memorandum by James J. McElligott
'Notes on Revised Draft of Articles 42–4'

Department of Finance
24 April 1937

Article 42:
Section 1.1°: The meaning to be attached to 'external goods' is not clear. Presumably even Soviet Russia recognises, without specific declaration, the implicit right of a man to own a hat or a chair. Does 'goods' include lands or ground rents or such intangible assets as rights of way or copyright?

Section 1.2° has been extended to include the right to transfer, bequeath and inherit property. The word 'attempting', on which comment was made in the memorandum from this Department, remains. No change has been made to meet the criticism that the use of compulsory powers of acquisition of property might be questioned under the Section. Possibly the Section is to be interpreted as merely prohibiting the abolition of the rights of property in general, but, as it stands, it seems to be capable of being applied to any particular act of expropriation, of the kind, for instance, being carried out every other day in the Land Commission. Those acts can hardly be called 'delimitations' of the exercise of the right of private property and are, therefore, not covered by Section 2.

Article 43:
Section 1: It is noted that this section is in blank.

Section 2: The provisions of Subsections 1°, 2°, 3° and 5° are, in substance, identical with those of Article 8 of the present Constitution.

[143] Annotated by Patrick Lynch: 'I have carefully considered this matter and I thoroughly agree. 24 April 1937'.

Subsection 4° is new. No objection is seen to any of the provisions of the Section, but it is suggested that Section 2.2°, which is declaratory, should read:

> 'No religion or form of religious worship shall be endowed by the State nor shall the State impose any disabilities or make any discrimination on the ground of religious profession, belief or status.'

It will no doubt be considered whether the State would not have to provide for full divorce (with the right to re-marry) for those who see no objection to it on religious grounds.

Article 44:
The preamble which now introduces this Article deprives it of the character of a declaration of rights enforceable in the Courts, and to that extent meets the objections urged by the Department of Finance.

Section 2: The declaration in the third paragraph regarding the establishment of families on the land is now further qualified by the insertion of the words 'in the circumstances' and is less open to objection than before.

Section 3.1°: This is old Section 9 of Article 41 and our previous statement stands as to the desirability of introducing the word 'may' before the word 'supplement'.

Section 3.2°: This Subsection is new and may prove a temptation to spur the State on to unlimited interference in private enterprise.

Section 3.3°: It is suggested that this should commence: 'The State shall so regulate the operation, etc...'

Section 3.4°: As reworded, this Subsection is somewhat less likely than before to be a cause of embarrassment. It will still, however, encourage the activities of one of the noisiest and most ill-informed elements of the population. The Department of Finance suggested in its comments on the previous draft that the provisions dealing with the 'economic rights of the less favoured sections of the community' (Section 4.1°) and the employment of women and children (Section 4.2°) were unnecessary and liable to be misconstrued. The provisions remain substantially as before.

It is strongly urged that the words 'in particular' should be omitted from Section 3.4°. The factors mentioned in the three immediately preceding Subsections are probably just as important, vis-à-vis the welfare of the people, as is the control of credit.

Section 4.1°: I suggested that this should run: 'The State shall safeguard…and, where necessary, shall contribute, etc…'

This Subsection is old Subsection 7.1° of Article 41 and is still subject to our previous comments on that Subsection. It will make more difficult the task of a future Minister for Finance in resisting any scheme for the extension of legislation in favour of the interests referred to.

Section 5: This is possibly too vague to merit inclusion in a constitution. It might be considered whether in Article 44 only Sections 3 (1°, 2° and 3°) and 4 are of sufficient practical application to warrant inclusion in the Constitution.

No. 159: NAI, DT S10160

Memorandum from Seán Lemass to Eamon de Valera

Department of Industry and Commerce
[24] April 1937

President,

Article 46 [sic 44]
Section 1: What exactly is meant by 'all the institutions of public life'? Should not the end of the section read 'justice and charity shall determine the relations between classes'?

Section 2.i: Could not this be read as follows: 'Citizens who are willing may find the means through their occupations and citizens who are not willing may find the means otherwise'. If 'willing' were substituted by 'able and willing' it would read better. I suggest that the use of the word 'adequately' is dangerous. When the State pays rural workers 24 shillings per week it enables them to provide for their needs but not adequately. I suggest the substitution of 'adequately meeting' by 'providing for'.

Section 2.ii: I suggest that the idea contained in this Subsection is repeated in Section 3 Subsection 3 and that the two could be amalgamated.

Section 3.4°: I suggest it should be left out but if it is desired to keep it in the concluding words might be changed from 'the aim kept constantly in view' to 'the primary aim to be served'.

Section 5: The meaning of the phrase 'a more equitable social balance' is not very clear. Should it not be 'better control of economic activities'?

No. 160: NAI, DT S10160

Memorandum by John Leydon, with cover letter from Seán Lemass Observations on Article 44

Department of Industry and Commerce
[24] April 1937

President,
Herewith are some notes by Leydon on Art. 44. It is clear he misunderstood the purport of Section 3.3° but its wording permits such misunderstanding.

I think this Section 3.3° might be left out. The two ideas in it are I think covered by 2.ii and 3.2°. If you do not agree I think it must definitely be re-worded. The phrase 'restrain free competition' will be read in the contrary sense to what you intend. 'Regulate' or 'control' free competition would be better. In any event the phrase 'that...a particular class of goods may not pass into the ownership...of a few individuals' appears all wrong. It should be 'control of the supply of a particular class' or 'ownership of a particular class'.

My definite suggestion is to leave the paragraph out. It is not necessary. If 2.ii is not in conflict with Article 10 it covers the idea.

[Signed] Seán Lemass

'Notes on Draft Constitution as further revised', 24 April 1937
[John Leydon]

Article 44.2.ii: This provision appears to be inconsistent with Article 10 which vests all natural resources in the State.

It might also be held that the present arrangement for financing the Electricity Supply Board is contrary to the principle laid down in this provision.

It is suggested that ownership and control of certain material resources may in some circumstances become so important that they should, in the public interest, remain under the ownership and/or control of the Government.

Article 44.3.1°: It may be pointed out that in certain cases, e.g., the generation of electricity, the manufacture of sugar, the organisation of civil air transport, etc., the State at present definitely discourages private initiative. In certain other cases, e.g., the manufacture of rubber tyres, etc., the exercise of private initiative is rather restricted.[144]

No. 161: NAI, DT S10160

Maurice Moynihan to all Ministers, Patrick Lynch, William O'Brien and Frank Fahy, enclosing 3rd Revise of the Constitution

Department of the President
24 April 1937

I am desired by the President to transmit herewith copies of a further revise of the Constitution dated [blank].

He is anxious that the text should be sent for final printing tonight, and he would like, therefore, to receive from you not later than 4 p.m. today observations on any matters of vital importance to which you consider his attention should be drawn.

The comments already received in connection with previous drafts have all been very carefully considered and decided on, and any suggestions or observations on the annexed revise should be confined to points of substance not hitherto covered.[145]

No. 162: NAI, DT S10160

3rd Revise of Constitution

24 April 1937

See www.irishconstitution.ie.

[144] The Department of Posts and Telegraphs and the Revenue Commissioners responded to say that they had no observations on draft articles 42–4. No other written responses were communicated to the Department of the President, perhaps due to the short time allowed for inspection, as well as the delivery of the 3rd Revise of the Constitution on 24 April.

[145] The Departments of Agriculture, Local Government and Public Health, Defence, Posts and Telegraphs, the Ceann Comhairle and the Revenue Commissioners all replied to McDunphy to say that they had no observations on the 3rd Revise. No other written replies were received, NAI, DT S10160.

No. 163: NAI, DT S10160

Revised draft of Subsections 2 and 3 of Article 13.11

[26?] April 1937

13.11.2°: Whenever, by reason of vacancies in offices the holders of which are, primarily or substitutionally, members of the Commission by virtue of the next preceding Subsection, or by reason of a dissolution of Dáil Éireann, there are less than three members of the Commission, the number of members of the Commission shall be brought up to three by the inclusion in the Commission, for so long as may be necessary, of the requisite number of judges (selected in order of seniority) of the Supreme Court who are available.

13.11.3°: Whenever a member of the Commission is on any occasion unable to act and his substitute mentioned in Subsection 1° hereof is also unable to act on that occasion, the place of such member shall on the said occasion be taken by the senior judge of the Supreme Court who is available and who is not already a member, or acting in the place of a member of the Commission.[146]

No. 164: NAI, DT S10160

4th Revise of Constitution

26 April 1937

See www.irishconstitution.ie.

[146] Both of these Subsections were incorporated, in a slightly altered form, as Article 13.11.2° in the 4th Revise of the Constitution, printed 28 April. The revisions are handwritten and annotated by McDunphy: 'Drafts of 13.11, Sections 2 and 3. Now Article 14. 28 April 1937'. The reference to Article 14 is misleading, though it indicates that between 24 April and 28 April substantial changes to article numbering and content were still under consideration.

Chapter XI

Reaction to the Constitution, May–July 1937

The third revise of the Constitution was ready by 24 April and the final text by 26 April. A few minor changes were made to what ultimately became Article 40.1, Article 40.3.1° and Article 40.3.2° in the draft of 1 April. By 8 April the final draft corresponded exactly to the present version of Article 40.1, Article 40.3.1° and Article 40.3.2°. At about the end of March a distinction was drawn for the first time between the fundamental rights provisions as such and the Directive Principles of Social Policy. In the first published draft of 16 March, the Fundamental Rights provisions were headed 'Personal Rights and Social Policy'. But in that version the draft Article 43[1] incorporated features of both the present Articles 43 and 45, i.e., it mixed elements of the property rights guarantees with some of the exhortatory statements contained in the present Article 45.[2] The Departmental observations—which generally expressed significant unease regarding the potential scope of judicial review—also tended to be highly critical of this approach in particular. The outline of the religious Article (Article 44) was also settled.[3] During this period, almost every Article saw drafting changes of one kind or another, some quite significant.

There was, however, one deadline. It had already been determined that the plebiscite would be held on the same day as the general election.

[1] Then numbered Article 41.

[2] Including, for example, what corresponds to the present Article 45.2.ii:

> That the ownership and control of the material resources of the community may be so distributed amongst private individuals and the various classes as best to subserve the common good.

[3] See document no. 156. Although the content of Article 44 was to all intents and purposes settled by mid-April, it was not circulated to Departments until 23 April.

The eighth Dáil had first met on 8 February 1933 and by the end of April 1937 the Dáil was well into its final months. There was, thus, an imperative to ensure that the Constitution was published and debated in the Dáil in advance of that election. But if that election was to be held during the summer, this in turn constrained the drafters in terms of timing.

At all events, the draft Constitution was available in the shops on the morning of Saturday, 1 May 1937.[4] There then followed a debate in the Dáil which commenced with the Second Reading on 11 May. The Committee Stage commenced on 1 June. The Constitution was approved by the Dáil on 14 June and the Dáil was dissolved on the same day. The Constitution was approved by a majority of the voters in a plebiscite held on 1 July along with the general election.[5] As no steps were taken by the new Dáil to bring the Constitution into force by means of a resolution passed under Article 62.ii, the Constitution came automatically into force on the day following the expiration of one hundred and eighty days after its approval by plebiscite, i.e., 29 December 1937. The new Constitution was duly enrolled in the Supreme Court on 6 February 1938.[6]

The Constitution's treatment of women

The Constitution's treatment of women was a matter of almost immediate controversy following publication and, indeed, remains so to this day. This was the single biggest policy issue which dominated much of the debate at the time both inside and outside the Dáil. The case against de Valera on this point is made most eloquently by T.P. Coogan in his excellent and provocative book, *De Valera: Long Fellow, Long Shadow.* The Coogan thesis on this point is as follows:

First, the 1937 Constitution 'did away with an existing guarantee' in Article 3 of the 1922 Constitution which provided that 'every person without distinction of sex...shall...enjoy the privileges and be subject to the obligations of such citizenship'.[7] Secondly, the combination of

[4] Following a radio broadcast by de Valera on the evening of Friday, 30 April: see document no. 166.

[5] By 685,105 votes to 526,945: see *Iris Oifigiúil*, 16 July 1937.

[6] The Department of the Taoiseach considered that there was some urgency concerning the enrolment procedure, since a memorandum dated 6 January 1938 prepared by Padraig Ó Cinnéide for Moynihan explained that:

> It may be the fact that we are being excessively careful in this matter but as it is most probable that sooner or later an effort will be made to upset the Constitution or at any rate portions thereof, it is better to be sure than sorry (see document no. 249).

[7] This view was often expressed during the course of the May and June 1937: see, for example, the letter of 20 May 1937 from Doreen M. Ditchburn (Secretary of the Irish Women Citizens' and Local Government Association) to de Valera (document no. 193); letter of 22 May 1937 from Katherine Hassard and A.M. Conan to de Valera (document no. 197).

Article 40.1 (of which more presently), Article 41.2 and certain provisions of Article 45 considerably weakened the position of women. Thirdly, despite protestations from leading feminists such as Louie Bennett and Dorothy McArdle, de Valera refused to change position.[8] A separate concern was also voiced following the publication of the Constitution that the draft Article 9 (citizenship) and Article 16 (franchise) 'might give power to limit the political rights of women'.[9]

Article 3 and Article 14 of the 1922 Constitution

The first thing to note is that Article 3 of the 1922 Constitution was entirely concerned with the entitlement to and the acquisition of citizenship. This is made clear by the full text of Article 3:

> Every person, without distinction of sex, domiciled in the area of the jurisdiction of the Irish Free State (Saorstát Éireann) at the time of the coming into operation of this Constitution, who was born in Ireland or either of whose parents was born in Ireland or who has been ordinarily resident in the area of the jurisdiction of the Irish Free State (Saorstát Éireann) for not less than seven years, is a citizen of the Irish Free State (Saorstát Éireann) and shall within the limits of the jurisdiction of the Irish Free State (Saorstát Éireann) enjoy the privileges and be subject to the obligations of such citizenship: Provided that any such person being a citizen of another State may elect not to accept the citizenship hereby conferred; and the conditions governing the future acquisition and termination of citizenship in the Irish Free State (Saorstát Éireann) shall be determined by law.

The reference to 'without distinction of sex' and 'either of whose parents was born in Ireland' in Article 3 was important because, prior to that point, citizenship was generally determined by the paternal line and the extent (if at all) to which females could acquire citizenship in their own right was unclear. All that Article 3 did was to guarantee females the same right to citizenship as men.[10] The words 'without distinction of

[8] T.P. Coogan, *De Valera: Long Fellow, Long Shadow* (London, 1993), 493–5.

[9] See, for example, Memorandum of Joint Committee of Women's Societies and Social Workers, May 24, 1937 (document no. 202). In addition to Article 3, Article 14 of the 1922 Constitution provided in relevant part:

> All citizens of the Irish Free State (Saorstát Éireann) without distinction of sex, who have reached the age of twenty one years and who comply with the provisions of the prevailing electoral laws, shall have the right to vote for members of Dáil Éireann and to take part in the Referendum and Initiative.

[10] As does Article 9.1.3° of the Constitution.

sex' had, in fact, been inserted at Committee Stage in the Dáil Debate on the 1922 Constitution in order to clarify the scope of Article 3:

> **Professor William Magennis** (Cumann na nGaedheal): The amendment in my name reads: 'Article 3. To introduce after the opening words "Every person" the words "without distinction of sex".' The first line will then read 'Every person without distinction of sex, domiciled', etc. In the original draft, it will be remembered, this clause ended with the words 'men and women have equal rights as citizens'. That, I take it, was in the nature of a definition, because as you are all aware, there are contexts in Statutes, on which Courts have been bound to hold that the proper interpretation was that 'person' meant a man. Now if we have no indication here that leaves it beyond all doubt that 'person' means both man and woman we shall have a number of anomalous positions created in the later Articles. For example, 'the dwelling of each citizen is inviolable'. Is a woman a citizen and is her dwelling inviolable? 'All citizens of the Irish Free State have a right to free elementary education'. Has a girl or woman the right to free elementary education? It is simply by way of definition that I propose you add those words. They add nothing, I think, in substance, because, I take it, the original draft represented the mind of the Ministry on the matter and so this will be acceptable
>
> **W.T. Cosgrave** (Cumann na nGaedheal): As far as I am concerned I would be prepared to accept this particular amendment, but I want to make it clear that in doing so, I do not accept some of the implications that have been put up in connection with the case that has been made for women having equal rights of citizenship. I think that was the original term that was knocked out. That has implications which, I explained at the Committee stage, and which, as far as I am concerned, I am not prepared to accept. I am not prepared to accept the proposition that if having once passed a single clause with regard to this matter in the Constitution that we have to set about searching the archives of Acts of Parliament, decrees and so forth, and to regulate the position according to what is found there. The interpretation we had was that no

> disability would be suffered by women as against men. We certainly had not in our minds the change of the Income Tax laws or other matters, such as a man's responsibility for the upkeep of his wife and children, and so on. Neither had we in our minds laws anticipatory of marriage settlements or anything like that. That is the position. We will agree to accept alterations so far as the ordinary acceptance of equal political rights, and rights of citizenship are concerned, but not of a position which will put us into a difficulty to pass certain laws to regulate this whole procedure. We are not accepting that, but on the lines of citizenship—that is, to make them citizens, as intended—I am prepared to accept that and nothing more.[11]

This doubtless was an important advance in 1922, but—contrary to the Coogan thesis—Article 3 was not some sort of entirely free standing equality guarantee as between men and women.[12] After all, much of the discriminatory legislation—such as the Juries Act, 1927[13]—was enacted during the period of 1922–37 when Article 3 was in force. If, as the opposition claimed during the Dáil debates in 1937, Article 3 amounted to such a guarantee, it might be asked why the Cumann na nGaedheal Government persuaded the Oireachtas to enact such legislation when they were in power and, moreover, why such legislation was not immediately challenged as being unconstitutional?[14] The reality, of course, was that the reference in Article 3 to enjoying 'the privileges' of citizenship was intended to refer to rights such as the right to a passport, to consular assistance and so forth and it could not be divorced from that particular context.

Article 14 of the 1922 Constitution was also intended to ensure that women had the equal right to vote as men:

[11] 1 *Dáil Debates*, Cols 1666–9 (18 October 1922).

[12] See Mohr, 'The Rights of Women under the Constitution of the Irish Free State', in *Irish Jurist*, 41 (2006), 20.

[13] Which was subsequently found to be unconstitutional by the Supreme Court in *de Burca v. Attorney General*, [1976] IR 38, as being contrary to Article 38.5 (right to jury trial) and Article 40.1 (equality before the law).

[14] De Valera made this very point in the Report Stage debate on Article 40:

> It is extraordinary that it is now Deputies on the other benches are discovering all these prohibitions that were [in Article 3] in the old Constitution. I take it that they accepted in 1924 and, particularly in 1926, when the matter was raised; this question of the discrimination between men and women in the public service, for example. They had the old Constitution and, nevertheless, they went ahead and made that difference, 68 *Dáil Debates*, Cols 173–4 (9 June 1937).

The same point was also made by an opposition deputy, Frank McDermott:

> Article 3 of the old Constitution, so far as women are concerned, does no more than to assure them the rights of citizenship on the same basis as men. It does nothing whatever to protect them against the kind of legislation which Deputy McGilligan now says he is afraid of, 68 *Dáil Debates*, Col. 171 (9 June 1937).

> All citizens of the Irish Free State (Saorstát Éireann) without distinction of sex, who have reached the age of twenty one years and who comply with the provisions of the prevailing electoral laws, shall have the right to vote for members of Dáil Éireann, and to take part in the referendum and initiative.

Again, this was an important breakthrough, inasmuch as at the time under the Representation of the People Act, 1918, only women who were aged 30 and who satisfied certain property criteria were entitled to vote.

Article 9 and Article 16

Article 9.1 as originally published on 1 May 1937 had provided:

> 1. The acquisition and loss of Irish nationality and citizenship shall be determined in accordance with law.[15]

Article 16.1.1° as originally published had provided:

> Every citizen who has reached the age of twenty-one years, and who is not placed under disability or incapacity by this Constitution or by law, shall be eligible for membership of Dáil Éireann.

Upon publication, these provisions immediately gave rise to a storm of protest. As Brigid O'Mullane, the Secretary of Old Cumann na mBan, put it to de Valera in her letter of 18 May: 'We are of opinion that Articles 9 and 16 unless "no discrimination of sex" is stated, could interfere with women in matters of citizenship and franchise.'[16] The argument here, of course, was either that a law might be enacted which in some way deprived Irish females of their entitlement to citizenship, which in turn would affect their entitlement to vote or that females as a class might be declared to be under an 'incapacity' by law.[17]

[15] Note how different this formulation was from that contained in Article 9 of the 16 March draft which envisaged that that 'All persons born in Ireland' would have Irish nationality and citizenship (see www.irishconstitution.ie). In his memorandum of 22 March 1937 Roche had queried whether all persons born in Ireland should be entitled to Irish citizenship, echoing a debate which was later to take place in 2004 (see document no. 101). The 18th Amendment of the Constitution Act, 1998 provided via the new Article 2 that all persons born on the island of Ireland were automatically entitled to Irish citizenship, but Article 9 was in turn amended by the 27th Amendment of the Constitution Act, 2004 to modify that automatic entitlement.

[16] See document no. 189.

[17] The following exchange took place at the close of the Second Reading on the Constitution:

> **Eamon de Valera (Fianna Fáil)**: The Article reads: 'Every citizen who has reached the age of 21 years, and who is not placed under disability or incapacity by this Constitution or by law, shall be eligible for membership of Dáil Éireann'. Who is disqualified by law! I suppose that is the point.

De Valera had explained his thinking in this regard in his opening speech on the Second Stage:

> I took out that phrase and I make no apology for this any more than I did for the other phrase about the inviolability of the person. I consider it is a phrase which meant nothing in the context, could not mean anything because it was patently untrue, so I took out that phrase 'without distinction of sex'. Why? Because I considered it altogether unnecessary. Since we have begun to make laws in any sense for ourselves we have made no distinctions as citizens between men and women, as far as political rights are concerned. There is none suggested here. Citizens are mentioned a number of times, and our citizen law clearly indicates what we understand to be citizens. There is no distinction made in this Constitution, in regard to political rights, between men and women. I took out that phrase 'without distinction of sex' because it had no meaning in

[17] *contd.*

John A. Costello (Fine Gael): 'Who is not placed under disability or incapacity by this Constitution or by law.' The law might place women under incapacity.

Eamon de Valera: Does this refer to women?

John A. Costello: I say that a law can be passed under Article 16 placing women under incapacity to vote.

Eamon de Valera: That applies to other people as well as women. This in itself is not directed against women. Will the Deputy admit that?

John A. Costello: Certainly, and I think it is very objectionable for that reason.

Eamon de Valera: The first point, then, that it is directed against women, is not sustainable.

John A. Costello: Certainly. But an ordinary law can be passed.

Eamon de Valera: The Deputy admits that there is no discrimination against women as women in this. Is not that fair? The Deputy is anxious to watch as the guardian of the women. He wants to see that there is no loophole by which Parliament could possibly interfere with women's rights.

John A. Costello: A constitutional guarantee.

Eamon de Valera: I completely share the Deputy's view. I do not want this Constitution to deprive women of any rights which in justice and in nature they should have. Undoubtedly by this as it stands nobody who is not disqualified by law is interfered with. The Deputy will understand that in our electoral laws and other laws there are classes of people who are disqualified. There are people of unsound mind. It is a common form in these laws. It is in the old Constitution too.

John A. Costello: You do not get this Article in the old Constitution. You left out the words 'without distinction of sex'…

[Col. 466]

Eamon de Valera: …I will have this examined. I think what has been suggested is absurd. I think it is something that will be altogether unlikely in the nature of things to happen—that we should go back now and try to deprive women of their votes or anything of that sort; but if it is capable of that I will meet it. I will be only too willing to do it. It is the sort of thing I want to discover. I have asked every Government Department to scan this draft before the Committee Stage to see if, from their knowledge, there is anything in this that if left in would make it a less perfect instrument than we want it to be. When it has gone through, I hope it will be regarded as the work, not of an individual or even of the group of men who helped me in this, but that it will be the offering of this Irish Dáil to the people as the instrument of fundamental law in this State; 67 *Dáil Debates*, Cols 464–6 (13 May 1937).

> the context of the Constitution, and in the general atmosphere in which we have been the whole time as far as women's rights politically are concerned.
>
> Somebody wants to put it back. They want to have the reminder that at one time there was a distinction made. If they would take my advice they would let things alone...There is nothing in it to suggest that they cannot vote for and become members of the Dáil, that they cannot vote for and be Senators, or that they cannot vote for and become President. There is nothing in this Constitution which will debar them from being President of the Supreme Court, from being Chief Justice or from holding any single office in the State. There is no distinction made whatever between men and women as far as the vote, the franchise, office or anything else is concerned.[18]

At Recommittal Stage de Valera also moved an amendment to Article 9.1.3° so that it now provides that: 'No person may be excluded from Irish citizenship by reason of the sex of such person.'[19] De Valera likewise moved an amendment to both Article 16.1.2° ('without distinction of sex') and Article 16.1.3° ('on grounds of sex') to eliminate any possibility whatever of gender discrimination so far as the right to vote or to stand for election was concerned.[20]

Article 40.1, Article 41.2 and Article 45.4.2°

The second argument was that a combination of Article 40.1, Article 41.2 and Article 45.4.2° considerably weakened the position of women. Article 40.1 provides:

[18] 67 *Dáil Debates*, Cols 64–5 (11 May 1937). Note also the commitments that de Valera had earlier given to a deputation of Women's Organisations at a meeting on 14 May 1937. Hearne noted that:

> After a long discussion, the President informed the National University Women Graduates that whilst he did not at all share their apprehensions, he would nevertheless give careful consideration to their desire to have a barrier set up against the possibility of the enactment of any law discriminating against women in the matters of citizenship and franchise. He had already indicated to Deputy Costello in the Dáil last evening that he was prepared, if it was necessary, to insert in Article 16 a provision which would prevent any law being passed which would disqualify women citizens as such from the franchise. In the same spirit he was prepared to consider the possibility of inserting in Article 9 a provision which would set up a constitutional barrier of an Act being passed discriminating against women in the matter of citizenship. See document no. 186.

[19] 68 *Dáil Debates*, Col. 120 (9 June 1937).

[20] 68 *Dáil Debates*, Cols 153–4 (10 June 1937). De Valera explained his thinking thus:

> This is to make explicit what I think was already implied in the draft which we had—the fact that there should be no law placing any citizen under disability or incapacity on the grounds of sex, or disqualifying any citizen from voting on that ground. It is simply to meet a point raised by one of the Deputies on the opposite benches in connection with Article 16. There was a general right that they would have irrespective of sex, and then there was a clause dealing with disqualifications to be made by law. It was thought important that those disqualifications could not be made on the grounds of sex.

> All citizens shall, as human persons, be held equal before the law. This shall not be held to mean that the State shall not in its enactments have due regard to differences of capacity, physical and moral and of social function.

It is, however, necessary, to trace the actual origins of this provision. The idea that the fundamental rights provisions should contain a stand-alone equality guarantee originated with John Hearne, reflecting the latter's broadly egalitarian, liberal outlook. His earliest draft of the Constitution in May 1935[21] contained the following equality clause which seems to have been inspired by the corresponding provisions of the fourteenth Amendment of the US Constitution or by Article 109 of the 1919 Weimar Constitution.[22]

Indeed, the available evidence suggests that Weimar provided the model for this innovation. Hearne's draft seems to have been almost a verbatim copy of the opening sentence of Article 109 of the Weimar Constitution: 'All Germans are equal before the law.'[23] We have seen elsewhere how the Weimar Constitution provided an important template for other constitutional innovations. Weimar was mentioned (in the context of the Presidency) in de Valera's 'squared paper' draft[24] and, given that the equality before the law concept featured in Hearne's own first draft some three weeks later,[25] the similarity between this draft and Article 109 seems too great to be a pure coincidence.[26] The key point

[21] See Chapter IV of this volume.

[22] Note, however, the comments of Oran Doyle:

> From the earliest drafts of the new Constitution, it is clear that Hearne and de Valera intended there to be an equality guarantee, formulated in terms of 'equality before the law'. Although this marked a departure from the 1922 Constitution, which...contained no equality guarantee, it conformed to the European constitutional trend...Nevertheless, the drafters of the 1922 Constitution had also been aware of that constitutional trend in continental Europe and had chosen not to include an equality guarantee. For this reason, one cannot conclude that the drafters of the 1937 Constitution were merely following a constitutional trend: one is entitled to assume that they were, albeit to an unascertainable extent, motivated by an egalitarian ideal. That said, their model for Article 40.1 was almost certainly that popular in continental Europe at the time; Oran Doyle, *Constitutional Equality Law* (Dublin, 2004), 52.

Doyle goes on to reject the argument that the drafters borrowed from the 14th Amendment, partly because they would not have been happy with a judicial interpretation of that clause by the US Supreme Court at that time, see *Plessy v. Ferguson* 163 US 537 (1896), which 'held that racial segregation was fully consonant with equality'.

[23] 'Alle Deutschen sind vor dem Gesetze gleich'.

[24] See document no. 38.

[25] See document no. 40.

[26] Cf. de Valera's somewhat cryptic remarks on the Second Stage:

> There is another Article with regard to the equality of all citizens before the law. I am not going into the history of that phrase or its origin, either here or on the Continent; 67 *Dáil Debates*, Col. 74 (11 May 1937).

Mohr has also noted that a number of pro-Treaty women sent a circular including the texts of the equality provisions of the (then) recently enacted German, Austrian and Polish Constitutions to the Dáil when Article 3 was being discussed in October 1922: see 'The Rights of Women under the Constitution of the Irish Free State', 34; 1 *Dáil Debates*, Col. 1671 (18 October 1922).

here is that this provision was certainly intended to operate as some form of general equality guarantee, at least so far as the traditional civic freedoms were concerned.

By late February 1937, however, the equality provision had been re-drafted and the draft Article 40.1 (then numbered as Article 38.2) read as follows:

> The State acknowledges that the citizens are, as human persons, equal before the law.
>
> It shall, however, in its enactments, have due regard to individual differences of capacity, physical and moral, and of social function.

By the end of March, the proviso to Article 40.1 read thus:

> This *shall not mean, however*, that the State shall not in its *laws* have due regard to individual differences of capacity, physical and moral, and of social function.

Hearne deleted the italicised words and replaced them with 'paragraph shall not be held to mean' and 'enactments' respectively, so that by 8 April the proviso to Article 40.1 read:

> This shall not be held to mean that the State shall not in its enactments have due regard to individual differences of capacity, physical and moral, and of social function.[27]

As de Valera explained to the Dáil, he had always intended Article 40.1 to be of a 'positive character', but that the object of the proviso was to provide that 'the first part of the section should not be stretched in a direction in which it was never meant to be stretched'.[28]

De Valera admitted in the same debate that he had considered dropping the proviso altogether, but that he had changed his mind having heard the interpretation of Article 40.1 articulated by some opposition speakers:

> I was not completely and absolutely convinced of the necessity for the second part until Deputy McGilligan went on to interpret the first part in a way altogether different from the manner in which it arose originally. I think Deputy Fitzgerald-Kenney, when he was speaking on this particular matter, restricted the use of that to equal justice in the courts. I have no doubt that was the original

[27] UCDA, P150/2413. For a fuller account of this, see Doyle, *Constitutional Equality Law*, 51–66.
[28] 68 *Dáil Debates*, Cols 165–6 (9 June 1937).

> intention, that when people came before the courts, where it was A or B, the case was investigated irrespective of who A or B was. Now, undoubtedly, it has stretched from that meaning to mean that in all law citizens should be regarded as equal, which would make all law impossible, because we have constantly to distinguish between classes. If we want to be just we have to do it. We have to distinguish in our laws between the functions in the community. Whatever doubts I had before, I am satisfied from the way in which Deputy McGilligan has interpreted the meaning of the first part of this that it is essential that we should have the second part.[29]

It is clear, therefore, that de Valera was essentially trying to achieve what Justice Walsh later said Article 40.1 had achieved by importing 'the Aristotelian concept that justice demands that we treat equals equally and unequals unequally'.[30] This is not the place to essay a full account of the effect of Article 40.1.[31] After a slow and (at times) uneven start, the case-law on Article 40.1 has nevertheless now developed to the point whereby the Supreme Court has stated that:

> The forms of discrimination which are, presumptively at least, proscribed by Article 40.1 are not particularised; manifestly, they would extend to classifications based on sex, race, language, religious or political opinions.[32]

Thus, while fully recognising that there have been many instances where plausible claims might have succeeded, but ultimately failed,[33] it is important to note that the legislation and common law rules which have been found to be unconstitutional as contrary to Article 40.1 include the effective exclusion of women from juries via the Juries Act, 1927;[34] a series of common law rules which favoured husbands (but not wives);[35] or which paternalistically assumed an inferior position on the part of women;[36] a provision of the Adoption Act, 1974 which inhibited

[29] 68 *Dáil Debates*, Cols 169–70 (9 June 1937).
[30] [1976] IR 38, 68.
[31] For which see Kelly, *Irish Constitution*, 1323–86 and Doyle, *Constitutional Equality Law*, *passim*.
[32] *Re Article 26 and the Employment Equality Bill 1996*, [1997] 2 IR 321, 347, per Chief Justice Hamilton.
[33] See, for example, *Somjee v. Minister for Justice*, [1981] ILRM 324 (differing arrangements for citizenship of foreign spouses depending on whether they married an Irish man or an Irish woman not unconstitutional); *Norris v. Attorney General*, [1984] IR 36 (where a majority of the Supreme Court held that legislation criminalizing male (but not female) homosexual conduct was not contrary to Article 40.1).
[34] *De Burca v. Attorney General*, [1976] IR 38. The decision was also partly based on the nature of the right to jury trial in Article 38.5.
[35] *CM v. TM (No. 2)*, [1990] 2 IR 56; *W v. W*, [1993] 2 IR 476.
[36] *The State (Director of Public Prosecutions) v. Walsh*, [1981] IR 412.

widowers (but not widows) from adopting;[37] legislation based on blood ties;[38] electoral legislation discriminating in practice against the socially disadvantaged;[39] legislation which provided for heavier penalties for sexual assaults on men as distinct from women;[40] and campaign finance legislation and practices which either favoured the Government in referendum campaigns or which discriminated against new candidates as opposed to existing members of the Oireachtas in general elections.[41] In the light of this case-law, is hard to see how Article 40.1 could possibly be said to have worsened the lot of women, contrary to what Coogan argued. On the contrary, and putting matters absolutely no higher, Article 40.1 may be said to have made at least a modest contribution to improving the status of women.

So far as Article 41.2 is concerned, it is, of course, objectionably paternalistic:

> 2. 1° In particular, the State recognises that by her life within the home, woman gives to the State a support without which the common good cannot be achieved.
> 2° The State shall, therefore, endeavour to ensure that mothers shall not be obliged by economic necessity to engage in labour to the neglect of their duties in the home.

Yvonne Scannell has eloquently summarized the arguments thus:

> There are two ways of looking at this Article. The first is to take de Valera at his word and to regard the first paragraph as a tribute to the work that is done by women in the home as mothers. The second paragraph, if it is to be regarded as anything other than a paternalistic declaration, can be read as a constitutional guarantee that no *mother* is to be *forced* by economic necessity to work outside the home to the neglect of her duties there. The mothers covered by this guarantee would include widows, unmarried mothers, mothers whose husbands are unable or unwilling to support their families, even relatively rich mothers with heavy expenses such as those necessitated by caring for ill or handicapped children.

[37] *O'G v. An Bord Uchtála*, [1985] ILRM 61.
[38] *Blascaod Mór Teo. v. Commissioners of Public Works in Ireland* (*No. 3*), [2000] 1 IR 6.
[39] *Redmond v. Minister for Environment*, [2001] 4 IR 61 (electoral deposits held unconstitutional).
[40] *SM v. Ireland* (*No. 2*), [2007] 4 IR 369.
[41] *Kelly v. Minister for Environment*, [2002] 4 IR 191.

> The second way of looking at Article 41.2 is different. To some, it is grossly offensive to the dignity and freedoms of womanhood. It speaks of woman's *life* within the home (not just her work there), implying that the natural vocation of woman (the generic is used here, so it means *all* women) is in the home. It is the grossest form of sexual stereotyping. It can be regarded as an implicit denial of freedom of choice to women in personal matters, a freedom taken for granted by men. It speaks of *mothers* neglecting their duties, but omits to mention the duties of fathers. It fails to recognise that a woman's place is a woman's choice.[42]

But no matter how one can be justly critical of de Valera's old-fashioned paternalism as reflected in Article 41.2, it does not justify some of the more tendentious criticism which has been levelled against both Article 40.1 in particular and Article 41 in general.

De Valera's response to the criticism

The third contention was that de Valera did not respond to the critique of the clauses dealing with women in the Constitution and refused to make any amendments in response to the criticism. Coogan cites in this regard a letter from Louie Bennett which was published in the *Irish Press* on 12 May 1937 regarding Article 45.4.2°, which she described as 'the most indefensible in the Constitution'. Coogan then sets out the *present* version of Article 45.4.2°:

> The State shall endeavour to ensure that the strength and health of workers, men and women, and the tender age of children shall not be abused and that citizens shall not be forced by economic necessity to enter avocations unsuited to their sex, age or strength.

But this was *not* the version of the clause to which Ms Bennett had objected in her letter of 12 May 1937. The *present* version of Article 45.4.2° was only inserted by de Valera at Recommital Stage on 10 June following an earlier amendment which had been moved by Deputy Robert J. Rowlette.[43] The version to which Ms Bennett had objected was the *original* published version of Article 45.4.2° which was in the following terms:

[42] Yvonne Scannell, 'The Constitution and the Role of Women', in Farrell (ed.), *De Valera's Constitution*, 124–5.

[43] 68 *Dáil Debates*, Cols 242–8 (9 June 1937); Cols 258–9 (10 June 1937). For the earlier discussion of the merits of the Rowlette amendment, see 67 *Dáil Debates*, Cols 1896–7 (4 June 1937).

> 2°. The State shall endeavour to ensure that the inadequate strength of women and the tender age of children shall not be abused, and that women or children shall not be forced by economic necessity to enter avocations unsuited to their sex, age or strength.[44]

However, the final version (as enacted) of Article 45.4.2° read:

> 2°. The State shall endeavour to ensure that the strength of women and health of workers, men and women, and the tender age of children shall not be abused, and that citizens shall not be forced by economic necessity to enter avocations unsuited to their sex, age or strength.

Whatever one thinks of the *present* Article 45.4.2°, it is nonetheless clear that it represented a considerable advance over the *original* version and the reference to 'workers, men and women' went some way to contra-indicating the suggestion that women had no right to work outside the home. At Recommittal Stage de Valera further amended Article 45.2.i—again in response to a promise made to Deputy Rowlette—to insert therein the words 'all of whom, men and women equally, have the right to an adequate means of livelihood'.[45] Indeed, Bennett wrote to thank de Valera for their meeting on Saturday, 22 May 1937, adding:

> We are much reassured to know that Article 45.4 will be amended in the sense of the latter part of our proposed amendment (of which we gave you a copy, and which Dr Rowlette has tabled.[46]

Siobhán Mulcahy—echoing the earlier argument of Coogan—has claimed that: 'Deletion of Articles 40, 41 and 45, as demanded by women's organisations was never considered or debated by the Dáil. These arcane articles remain today.'[47]

It is, of course, strictly correct to say that the Dáil never considered deleting these provisions, but given the centrality of Article 40 in

[44] Diarmaid Ferriter notes that the Joint Committee of Women's Societies and Social Workers wrote to the Government on 24 May 1937 (see document no. 202) objecting to the use of the phrase 'the inadequate strength of women' in the original version of Article 45.2.i on the grounds that:

> The question of the adequacy or inadequacy of strength for any particular work is one which arises in the case of men, as much as in the case of women…much of the heaviest work done by women is in the home, or on the farm; Ferriter, *The Transformation of Ireland: 1900–2000* (London, 2004), 421–2.

Ferriter does not, however, mention the fact that these words were ultimately omitted from Article 45.2.i.

[45] 68 *Dáil Debates*, Col. 298 (10 June 1937).

[46] Bennett was, however, still exercised by the potential effects of the proviso to Article 40.1:

> We do not believe that the clear, reassuring statement contained in the first paragraph of this Article is capable of being misinterpreted in such a sense as to preclude special legislation to meet the needs of different groups of people. See document no. 201.

[47] Siobhán Mulcahy, 'Women, the Constitution and the Law', in *Village*, 26 August 2005.

particular as the key source of fundamental rights such as life, liberty, property, good name, equality, association and assembly, the dwelling and *habeas corpus*, this is scarcely surprising. It is, however, quite incorrect to suggest—insofar as Mulcahy seems to imply—that the Dáil never debated or considered the concerns of women's organisations. Quite the contrary—these concerns were forcefully and frequently articulated by key opposition Deputies. As we have seen, Article 9.1.3°, Article 16.1.1°, Article 16.1.2°, Article 45.4.1° and Article 45.4.2° were all amended in response to these concerns and a good deal of time on the Report and Recommittal Stages of the debate on the Constitution was taken up with these issues. It will be seen, therefore, that by these amendments de Valera went at least some distance towards meeting the concerns of the women's organisations, even if, of course, he did not go as far as either they then or we now would like.

No. 165: NAI, DT S9852

Memorandum by Michael McDunphy 'Constitution: Distribution'

Department of the President
29 April 1937

In addition to being circulated to Deputies in connection with the enactment of the Constitution, and to the press, the President has instructed that copies be sent to a) the Cardinal, b) the Archbishops, Bishops of the Catholic Church in Ireland, c) heads of other denominations, e.g. Church of Ireland, Presbyterian Church, Methodists, Society of Friends and the Jewish Congregation, d) certain persons in the United States and elsewhere, particulars of whom will be furnished by Miss O'Connell.

The despatch of copies to all these persons is to take place on the evening of Friday, 30th instant so that as far as possible they will be in their hands on Saturday morning simultaneously with the publication of the text in the press.

I have instructed Mr Murt O'Connell of the Dáil Staff, that the despatch of copies to Deputies should be so arranged that they will reach them on the morning of Saturday, 1st proximo, *but not earlier*.

He undertook that this would be done.

No. 166: NAI, DT S9868

Transcript of radio broadcast by Eamon de Valera

Dublin
10.45pm, 30 April 1937

I have come to the microphone tonight to say a few words by way of introduction to the Draft Constitution which has been published this evening. In the course of the coming weeks this Draft will be the subject of detailed discussion in the Dáil, and upon the conclusion of its examination it will be submitted for the people's approval in a national plebiscite. May I express the hope that it will be studied carefully and critically in every home in the country.

If our State is to be governed on the democratic principle, it is essential that the fundamental law should be thoroughly understood and deliberately approved of before it is enacted. Never before have our people been given an opportunity such as this. When in January 1919 the Dáil set up the Republic, it adopted a Constitution which provided the framework immediately necessary to enable the Government to be carried on in what was fundamentally a war situation. The people were not at any time asked to sanction its provisions. Only the broad question—the character of the State itself—was made an issue with the electors. On the other hand, the Draft Constitution of 1922 was published only on the morning of the General Election. No time was given to the people for examination or discussion. When the draft, somewhat amended, was passed later by the Assembly that met in September of that year it was not again submitted to the people before its enactment. The Constitution adopted on that occasion suffered from the fatal defects that it was framed not altogether by Irish hands and that it was made subject to a treaty admittedly imposed by the threat of force. Such a Constitution could have but one fate. I have in my hands a copy of it as it now stands, having been amended by no less than twenty-seven Statutes in less than half that number of years—seventeen passed by our predecessors, ten passed during the period of office of the present Government. Of its seventy-two original Articles, (omitting the transitory provisions) only thirty-one remain intact. The law relating to the Parliament, the law relating to the Executive Government, the law relating to the Judiciary, the law relating to the method by which the Constitution itself could be amended—in other words, the whole fundamental framework of the constitutional system—was radically changed within a comparatively short period of time.

I draw attention to these facts, not for the purpose of criticising the policy of our predecessors but simply to illustrate the state of our fundamental law at the present time and to point out the necessity on that ground, if on no other, for a new Constitution.

The Constitution now before the country has been drawn up from a severely practical point of view. It is not an essay in the application of the political or legal theories of any particular school. It is designed to provide a firm foundation for an ordered life and peaceful political development within the community, but the ideals which ought to inspire and direct that development are rightly emphasised. I know that there are many theorists who take the view that a written Constitution should contain nothing more than the legal machinery necessary for the establishment and control of the organs of State. Whilst agreeing that a Constitution should be as simple as possible, I cannot altogether share that view. In my judgment a Constitution ought to do more than define the character of the legislative, executive and judicial regime, and if it be based on the democratic principle it ought to do more, for example, than prescribe how the representative institutions should function, how the parliamentary responsibility of the Executive is to be secured, the independence of the Judiciary maintained, or the principle of universal suffrage applied. It should inspire as well as control, elicit loyalty as well as compel it. Every citizen should see in the basic public law of his country the sure safeguard of his individual rights as a human being—God-given rights which even the civil power must not invade. The protection of those rights means more in the long run to the integrity and continuance of organised society itself than the organisation of the institutions by which it is ruled. The time at my disposal this evening does not permit of more than a passing reference to the great institutions of the family, of marriage, and of private property, or to the place which they occupy in a Christian polity. There never was a time in which all these rights and institutions to which I have referred were so widely challenged as they are challenged today. In these circumstances, it is altogether appropriate that the attitude of our people should be made unmistakably clear.

I turn now to the provisions of the draft Constitution relating to the sovereign power and the establishment of the organs of State. Article 1, declares the right of the Nation to choose its own form of Government, to determine its relations with other nations, and to develop its life, political, economic and cultural, in accordance with its own genius and traditions. The Constitution is frankly based on the democratic principle. That principle runs right through the draft Constitution published today. By the votes of the people the President of the State will be chosen, by them the House of Representatives will be elected, and on the nomination of that House the responsible Government will be appointed. By the people only, through the Referendum, can the National Constitution be amended. The sovereignty resides in them as their inalienable and indefeasible right. Every elector who casts his vote in favour of the adoption of this Constitution will in effect be subscribing his name to the proposition that in this country the people and the people alone are the masters.

The proposal with regard to the National Parliament is that it should consist of the President and two Houses, a House of Representatives constituted as at present and a Second House consisting of sixty members. Eleven members of the Second House will be nominated by the Taoiseach, that is, the head of the Government; three will be elected by each of the Universities on franchises to be defined by law, and forty-three, whom I will refer to as panel members, will be elected from panels of candidates. The panel members will be elected from five panels broadly representing the following public services and interests, namely: (1) Education (including professional interests), (2) Agriculture and Fisheries, (3) Industry and Commerce, (4) Labour, and (5) Public Administration and Social Services. The intention is to set up a Second House roughly on a vocational basis, as recommended in one of the Reports of the Senate Commission which sat last year under the chairmanship of the distinguished lawyer who is no longer with us, the late Chief Justice Kennedy. The draft provisions with regard to the composition of the Second House will enable laws to be enacted providing for the direct election of members of the Second House by functional or vocational groups or associations should they at any time be established. The members so elected would be in substitution for an equal number of the panel members.

The relations between the two Houses of Parliament are clearly defined. A reasonable period of time will be afforded to the Second House for its consideration of Bills, but the Second House will have no power to veto or unduly delay legislation passed by the people's representatives in the Primary House.

The President will be elected by direct vote of the people, and will hold office for a period of seven years. The President will on the advice of the Government, or the head of the Government, summon and dissolve Parliament, sign and promulgate laws, appoint the judges. He will appoint the members of the Government on the nomination or with the approval of the House of Representatives. He will hold the command in chief of the Defence Forces, and the exercise of that command will be regulated by law. In addition, the President will have power to refer Bills to the Supreme Court for decision on the question of their constitutionality, and will also have power at the instance of a specified proportion of the members of the Houses of the Oireachtas to refer certain Bills to the people. These powers are undoubtedly great powers, and will call for the exercise of a wise discretion. The due exercise of these powers will, however, provide a safeguard for the Constitution itself and a protection for the people against legislation contrary to the public interest.

The proposals with regard to the Referendum contemplate the submission to the people of two classes of Bills: (1) Bills containing proposals for the amendment of the Constitution and (2) Bills raising major issues of national policy on which the will of the people has not already been pronounced. Here again the will of the people is the deciding factor on political issues. The Constitution cannot be amended save by an express vote of the majority of the people cast in favour of the amendment.

With regard to the provisions relating to the reference of other Bills to the people by the President at the instance of the Houses of the Oireachtas, the principle there embodied is that the authority of the people's representatives is to be maintained unless the people themselves definitely veto the proposal in question.

These and the other provisions of the draft Constitution you will, I hope, study for yourselves. The detailed exposition of the text I must leave for another time and another place.

No one, I hope, expects that with the adoption of this Constitution the national goal has been reached. There are many injustices in the existing political situation which this Constitution cannot directly remove—the partition of our country, the occupation by Great Britain of positions on our ports, the exaction by British of money which we hold not to be due, and legitimate dissatisfaction with these injustices will remain, different parties will continue to propose different policies for dealing with them. But the aim in drafting this Constitution has been so to design it that all these controversies will be outside the Constitution—so that the Constitution itself will not stand in the way of any remedies that may be proposed.

The Constitution as drafted will fit and will not prejudge whatever policies the people decide to adopt with regard to these matters. Within its framework domestic peace can be assured, and, in the words of its Preamble, the unity of our country restored, and concord established with other nations.[48]

No. 167: UCDA, P150/2416

Memorandum from Nicholas Barron to Eamon de Valera
Observations on the draft Constitution as published

[May 1937]

Constitution
Art. 34, Sec. 4 Par. 3 and Art. 34, Sec. 3 Par. 1: re Courts of Justice
The above provisions do *not* limit the power of the lower courts to determine the constitutionality of any Official *Act* or *Act* of an official.[49] Therefore their power to do so is presumed from the context of the provisions.

The result of Section 4 Paragraph 3, when a question of a law's validity arises before the Courts, is as follows:

Because the Supreme Court is granted EXCLUSIVE and ORIGINAL jurisdiction of such a matter, the *lower Court* must, upon the raising of such a question, proceed according to either of the following two methods:

A. Refuse to determine the issue of a pending cause until the constitutionality of the law is determined by the Supreme Court. This would result in such a matter being referred first to the Supreme Court to determine the constitutional question ONLY (because it has ORIGINAL jurisdiction only to determine that question and no other). If the law is held to be constitutional it will be necessary to again refer the matter back to the Court of First Instance for a hearing on the other issues—A most expensive procedure.
B. Try all other issues and deliver judgment thereon; then it would be necessary to proceed to the Supreme Court by way of a Writ of Certiorari, or some similar procedure, to

[48] Document has been annotated: 'Broadcast given by President de Valera at 10.45 p.m. on Friday, 30 April, 1937, and published in the press on Saturday, 1 May'.
[49] Both instances of the word 'Act' have been manually underlined, with the following note written in the margin: 'Act means here a human act, not a *statute* or law'.

> determine the constitutional question. This seems to be an unnecessary division of jurisdiction, especially when an instance of patent unconstitutionality is considered. It is also a most expensive way of dealing with the problem.

Both of the methods allowable under the section as it now stands would act as hardships to many, especially when a law violates their constitutional rights in smaller matters.

Suggestions: I have two alternatives to offer in place of Section 4 Paragraph 3.

First: Amend the Section and paragraph to read as follows:

> The Supreme Court shall have full original jurisdiction in and power, exclusive of all other Courts, to determine any and all matters, civil or criminal, and any and all issues of law and fact arising therein, when a question or questions are raised in such matters as to the validity of any law having regard to the provisions, etc.

A provision of this nature would place completely in the hands of the Supreme Court the determination of *all* of the issues in such a case. It would concentrate the matter in one court only.

Second: Amend the section to read:

> The Supreme Court shall have full, final and GENERALLY BINDING jurisdiction in and power to determine questions of the validity of any law, etc.

And add the following provision:

> The courts of first instance shall have jurisdiction to determine the validity of any law having regard to the provisions of this constitution, *when such validity of such law has not previously been determined by the Supreme Court*, PROVIDED, HOWEVER, THAT SUCH A DETERMINATION BY A COURT OF FIRST INSTANCE SHALL *NOT BE GENERALLY*, but BINDING ONLY in so far as the particular matter under consideration is concerned. An appeal from such Court of First Instance direct to the Supreme Court shall be allowed on any such question of the validity of a law.

Under these provisions litigants would be facilitated in protecting their constitutional rights in PETTY as well as in major matters. The extent of the jurisdiction of the lower courts in such constitutional questions is limited and a decision of unconstitutionality by one of these courts would not invalidate the law insofar as the general public and State officials and representatives are concerned. The law would be to them a constitutional law until declared otherwise by the Supreme Court.

A citizen should be entitled to full constitutional protection at all times and before all courts. A very important part of the protective force of the fundamental law is that no statute can be passed in derogation of its provisions. A citizen should be entitled to plead the protection of the constitution before any court in the land and in any matter no matter how unimportant.

Under Article 31 the Members of the COUNCIL OF STATE are *NOT* required to take an oath to UPHOLD THE CONSTITUTION, WHY? Art. 40, Sec. 4 Par. 1: What about his LIFE and PROPERTY? Nor is there anything guaranteeing due process of law in matters of Life and Property in Article 43.

Articles 43 and 44: Note Par. 5 Sec. 2 [of] Article 44. Why guarantee compensation to schools and religious bodies and preserve the right to 'DELIMIT' private property rights without mentioning compensation?

Article 50, Sec. 2: Should not this section commence with the same sentence as the first section of this Article (50)?

No. 168: NAI, DT S9856

Gerald Fitzgibbon to Eamon de Valera

Dublin
1 May 1937

Confidential

Dear Mr President,
I have received this morning a draft of the new Bunreacht, for which I am much obliged.

I hope that I am correct in assuming that it was sent to me with the intention that I might put forward for consideration any suggestions which occurred to me.

I suspect that the Judges may be summoned to consider in consultation those provisions which directly affect them or their office, and I am anxious not to forestall or prejudice any observations which my colleagues may offer. There is, however, one point which I think should be considered at once:

Article 26.2.1° proposes to enact that 'The Supreme Court…shall pronounce its decision on such question…not later than thirty days after the date of such reference…' I respectfully submit that the words 'the hearing' should be substituted for 'the date'.

It will be necessary to take steps to get together a Court of five judges to hear the question. The question must be referred within four days of the passing of the Bill. The reference might be at a moment when the Judges were on circuit under the new Courts of Justice Act. There might be delay in assembling five judges to hear the case. In any event, the Attorney General must make up his case, and still [?], the Court, at its first sitting might find it necessary to assign Counsel to argue against the Attorney General, as provided by the Article itself. Such Counsel must have some reasonable time to make up an argument in a case which would be, in the nature of things, one of the first importance, and there is no telling how long the arguments might take.

I fully realise the vital importance of an early decision, and I am profoundly conscious of the dissatisfaction which has been occasioned, on at least two occasions, by long delays on the part of the Supreme Court in delivering their judgment in important cases,[50] and I have no objection to offer to a proposal that judgment should be given within a stated period after the arguments have concluded. The judges who have heard a case might well be directed to make up their minds within even a shorter period than one month, but I feel very strongly that injustice might be caused, and a [?] consideration in an important constitutional question might be prejudiced, if a hard and fast law were to be passed that all the preliminaries must be gone through and all the arguments must be prepared and heard and a decision pronounced irrespective altogether of the magnitude and complexity of the questions involved, within thirty days of the reference of the matter by the President, who must himself act within four days of the decision of the Oireachtas.

That decision might conceivably be made shortly before Christmas, or Easter, or while the Courts were closed in summer, and many judges away on vacation, and the thirty days would be running irrevocably all the time.

Provide, if you will, that the question shall be referred to the Supreme Court of five judges who shall proceed to hear it *at the earliest opportunity*, and shall pronounce their decision within a month, or a week, if you will, of the conclusion of *the hearing*, but modify the provision that the decision must be given, even though the case be unheard, within a month from the date of the reference.

[50] One of the cases to which Fitzgibbon here alludes is presumably the *Erasmus Schools* case.

Dublin.

Confidential. 10 Merrion Square.

May 1. 1937.

Dear Mr President,

I have received this morning a draft of the new Bunreacht, for which I am much obliged.

I hope that I am correct in assuming that it was sent to me with an intention that I might put forward for consideration any suggestions which occurred to me.

I expect that the Judges may be summoned to consider in consultation those provisions which directly affect them or their office, and I am anxious not to forestall or prejudice any observations which my colleagues may offer.

There is, however, one point which I think should be considered at once.

Article 26. 2. 1° proposes to enact that "The Supreme Court .... shall pronounce its decision on such question ..... not later than thirty days after the date of such reference."

I respectfully submit that the words "the hearing" should be substituted for "the date".

It will be necessary to take steps to get together a Court of five judges to hear the question. The question must be referred within four days of the passing of the Bill. The reference might be at a moment when the Judges were on Circuit under the new Courts of Justice Act. There might be delay in assembling five Judges to hear the case. In any event, the Attorney General must make up his case, and still more, the Court, at its first sitting might find it necessary to assign Counsel to argue against the Attorney General, as provided by the Article itself. Such Counsel must have some reasonable time to make up an argument in a

case

case which would be, in the nature of things, one of the first importance, and there is no telling how long the arguments might take.

I fully realise the vital importance of an early decision, and I am profoundly conscious of the dissatisfaction which has been occasioned, on at least two occasions, by long delays on the part of the Supreme Court in delivering their judgement in important cases, and I have no objection to offer to a proposal that judgement should be given within a stated period after the arguments have con:cluded. The judges who have heard a case might well be directed to make up their minds within even a shorter period than one month, but I feel very strongly that injustice might be caused, and a proper consideration of an important constitutional question might be prejudiced, if a hard and fast law were to be passed that all the preliminaries must be gone through and all the arguments must
EH be prepared and heard, and a decision pronounced, irrespective altogether of the magnitude and complexity of the questions involved, within thirty days of the reference of the matter by the President, who must himself act within four days of the decision of the Oireachtas.

That decision might conceivably be made shortly before Christmas, or Easter, or while the Courts were closed in Summer, and many Judges away on vacation, and the thirty days would be running irrevocably all the time.

Provide, if you will, that the question shall be referred to the Supreme Court of five Judges who shall proceed to hear it at the earliest opportunity, and shall pronounce their decision within a month, or a week, if you will, of the conclusion of the hearing, but modify the provision that the decision must be given, even though the case be unheard, within a month from the date of the reference.

Yours respectfully Gerald FitzGibbon.

No. 169: NAI, DT S9856

Eamon de Valera to Gerald Fitzgibbon

Dublin
1 May 1937

Dear Mr Justice Fitzgibbon,
I have received your letter of today's date regarding the submission of bills to the Supreme Court before signature, under the new Constitution. I am grateful for your observations which will have my careful consideration.

No. 170: UCDA, P178/64

James Hogan[51] to Alfred O'Rahilly

Cork
[May 1937]

My dear O'Rahilly,
I had intended to give you my criticisms of the Constitution but on going carefully over it I find that they are very few. In many ways it seems to me a decided improvement on the last Constitution. It makes no bones about being the Constitution of a Catholic people, and in the present bad and mad world that is something to be thankful for. Personally I am not a bit afraid of the powers given to the President. They are no more than is necessary if the Constitution is not to become a football to be kicked about by the political parties as happened with the last Constitution. However, I do not understand why the social clauses of the Constitution having been stated to be fundamental should be withdrawn from the cognisance of the courts and their interpretation left entirely to the Oireachtas which may interpret them Heaven knows how in future time.

It is some gratification to see that our rulers are at last waking up to the existence of a Catholic social philosophy, and in this connection also it is satisfactory that provision should have been made for a direct functional representation which leaves open the way towards the gradual articulation of a functionally organised economic life in the state.

[51] James Hogan (1898–1963), Professor of History, University College Cork. Founder member of the Irish Manuscripts Commission and the Army Comrades Association.

This part of the Constitution is excellent in so far as it makes it possible to take a step in the direction of a functional democracy. Unfortunately, it seems to me that most of the good is taken out of the provision by the fact that representatives of vocational groups are to be substituted for those elected by TDs and would be TDs. We all know how slow people are to let go of any powers they may have, and I do not think it likely that TDs will be capable of the sort of self-denying ordinance by which representatives of functional or vocational groups would be directly elected. Unless a spirit of altruism by no means conspicuous up to the present takes possession of TDs in the future, it is not likely that they will let go their right to elect the 43 representatives to the Seanad for which the Constitution provides. If this be so there is no use talking about direct functional representation. It will remain a dead letter, I believe, unless definite provision is made for direct functional representation as soon as the necessary conditions in the way of the functional organisation of an industry or profession are fulfilled.

It is unfortunate that the Constitution should have used Éire instead of Ireland because of the ambiguities it creates. The whole world knows the meaning of Ireland but in the North and in England Éire will probably be taken to mean the present area of jurisdiction of the Saorstát. If this Constitution is meant to be a Constitution for the whole of Ireland and is meant to convey that meaning to people in the North and outside Ireland, then the term Ireland is preferable to Éire, and in fact the latter seems to me to be an evasion calculated to produce a false attitude towards a Constitution which purports *de jure* to deal with the whole of Ireland.

The point has already been put to me and I think there is a great deal of truth in it that the Constitution contains one fundamental omission—it omits to state what Éire is, whether it is a kingdom or a republic or what it is. It is not enough to say that 'Éire is sovereign, independent and democratic'. Is Éire a sovereign, independent and democratic Republic or is Éire a sovereign, independent and democratic monarchy? That is the most fundamental point and it has not been settled, and around that point will continue to rage the chief political controversies of the future. In other words, what purports to define the fundamental character of the Irish state omits the most important definition of all, namely whether Ireland belongs to the category of democratic republics or to the category of democratic monarchies or what else. What kind of state is Éire? In the absence of a Constitutional definition of this fundamental point the present Constitution is on a par with Hamlet without the Prince of Denmark. The old and now sterile controversy about the form of the state goes on. We are no clearer or better off than we were before. For my own part for a variety of reasons into which I am not going to enter I think that there was never a better time than the present for constitutionally clearing up the issue. The solution I favour is the simple and direct one, and I feel sure in the long run is the wisest one too. Take John Bull by the horns by announcing in Constitutional form that Éire or better still Ireland is a 'sovereign, independent and democratic' Republic.

No. 171: UCDA, P178/65

Michael Tierney to Alfred O'Rahilly

Dublin
4 May 1937

Dear O'Rahilly,
This is a hasty note to catch you before you have committed your views to paper.

In general I don't think the Constitution too bad. Apart from Dev's inevitable 'Year 1' business, it is, as the *Manchester Guardian* says, a conservative instrument.

My own ideal being a tripartite division of functions (= King, Lords and Commons), I am not at all opposed to the President. There may be room to argue about his election and powers (I don't think the latter large) but it sounds queer to me to have Cosgrave and Co. object to him on 'democratic' grounds. I thought 1932–4 had given us enough 'democracy' for a lifetime. What I should really like would be a system giving President and Senate power to block all legislation if agreed against Dáil. Of course the method of election is another matter.

Johnson's brainwave has been embodied in our Senate proposals, and the result is queer. However, remember it only means an enlargement of our proposed constituency.

My only two urgent objections are to Éire and the Taoiseach, both of which I think resemble the army's new Merry Widow dress uniforms. If he doesn't like Saorstát, why not Ard-Ríoghacht Éireann? If used, Éire will necessarily mean only the 26 counties.

Please don't object to *powers* for President or Senate. It is the Platonic and Medieval Christian tradition!

No. 172: NAI, DT S9852

Rabbinate Committee of the Dublin Jewish Community to Eamon de Valera

Dublin
4 May 1937

Rabbinate Committee of the Dublin Jewish Community.
ועד הרבנות בעיר דובלין
Dublin. 4.5.37.

Eamonn De Valera, Esq., T.D.,
President of the Executive Council,
Dail Eireann,
Leinster House.

The Rabbinate Committee beg to acknowledge with many thanks due receipt of a copy of the Draft of the New Constitution, which was addressed to Dr. Joshua Baker, with the compliments of the President.

They note with the greatest satisfaction and due appreciation that the "Jewish Congregations" are included in the clause giving equal recognition to the Religious Bodies in Eire: and they respectfully tender congratulations on the production of such a fair and just document.

Jacob Slotover
Hon. Sec.,
Shamrock Lodge,
159 Rathmines Rd.

No. 173: NAI, DT S9859A

Maurice Moynihan to Arthur Codling

Department of the President
4 May 1937

1. [Matter omitted] I am directed by the President to state that he proposes to set up a Committee with terms of reference of which the following is a translation:

   'To make recommendations as to any changes that may be desirable, by way of simplification, in the spelling of Irish in the Draft Constitution.'
2. The committee will consist of about eleven members, who will be persons of reputation in Irish scholarship and literature. Dr Eoin MacNeill will be Chairman and the other members will include Colm Ó Murchadha, Clerk of the Dáil, Shan Ó Cuiv, Department of the President, and Risteárd Ó Foghladha, Department of Education. The remaining personnel has not so far been finally determined, and a further communication will be addressed to you in due course in that regard.
3. It is proposed, with the concurrence of the Clerk of the Dáil, that Mr Séamus D'Altún of the Oireachtas Translation Staff should act as Secretary of the Committee.
4. It is anticipated that the report of the Committee will be presented not later than the 31st instant.
5. I am to request the sanction of the Minister for Finance to the appointment of the proposed Committee.[52]

No. 174: NAI, DT S9852

Archbishop Edward Byrne to Eamon de Valera

Dublin
4 May 1937

My dear President,
Allow me to express my sincere thanks for the Draft Copy of the Constitution which you have sent me by the Secretary of the Department

[52] See document no. 195.

for External Affairs. I have noticed that the Holy Catholic Apostolic and Roman Church still retains its special position.[53]

No. 175: NAI, DT S9965A

León Ó Broin to Maurice Moynihan

Department of Finance
5 May 1937

Dear Muiris,
For the sake of concord, you will please conceal the authorship of the annexed letter from the translators.[54]

Dear Muiris,
You may be interested in my first impressions of the Irish version of the draft Constitution. The translation is no doubt, on the whole, an accurate rendering of the English, but it contains many exasperating things, viewed from the angle of one who has learned 'official Irish', and who has to make use of Irish in official circles day-in-day-out.

The first general observation I would make is that too often the translators have departed from the terms and construction used by the Leinster House people and to which users of official Irish have become accustomed. Starting with Article 8, for instance, I think it is absurd at this hour of the day to translate the 'English language' by 'Sacs-Bhéarla'. Similarly, it is wrong, I feel, to introduce at this stage a new rendering for common phrases and words such as 'subject to', 'provisions', 'proposal', 'procedure', 'shall', 'may', etc. These are standard phrases and constructions in English. They had, we thought, become standardised in Irish also, and it is, I suggest, a mistake to make a change now. The confusion will be considerable, doubt will be thrown on the correctness and legality of things already done, and usually quite well done, and the changes will help to break the spirit of people with a limited knowledge of the language who have to pass examinations in Irish and whom we are exhorting to use Irish more and more in their official work. It is perhaps particularly noticeable and disastrous when we find Industry and Commerce which everybody had come to recognise in its Irish form as Tionnscal agus Tráchtáil as Tionnscal agus Ceannaidheacht. Again 'riarachán' becomes 'riarachas', reachtachan' becomes 'reachtaideacht', 'cánacha' becomes 'cánachas' etc.

[53] The Bishops of Cork; Ardagh and Clonmacnoise; Waterford and Cloyne also wrote to de Valera to express gratitude for the receipt of copies of the draft Constitution, NAI, DT S9852.
[54] These first lines are transcribed from a cover note attached to the main letter.

Well known titles such as An Dlí-Oifigeach and An tÁrd Scrúdóir are being dropped, I notice. This would be bad enough if express provision were made for the substitution of the new title for the old in the existing statute law, but that is not being done, I think. The existence of the two titles for the one post will add to the confusion. This multiplication of Irish variants, in my opinion, is a greater obstacle to progress than the former situation when we had no Irish equivalents at all for most of these technical terms. In an atmosphere that is often not very appreciative of the difficulties in the way of adapting Irish to current conditions, this business can become very unpleasant for people trying to 'push' Irish. And what can one say of the revival of the -ughadh ending, and its effect on unfortunate Civil Servants who for six years have been directed to use a certain simplified spelling which would not tolerate 3adh or 4adh even, although God knows they look innocent enough.

Article 22 on Money Bills when contrasted with the old Article 35 and Article 11 *vis a vis* the old Article 61 illustrate what I have in mind. Words and constructions given concrete meanings in 1922 have been carried over into all Finance legislation since and now in 1937 wholesale changes are made, all of them quite unjustifiably. I am not, of course, here concerned as to which is the better translation; that is I feel at this juncture quite beside the point. The important thing is that there should be no change for the sake of change, and that where a word or phrase, though originally perhaps a bad choice, has been accepted and is in common use, it should not be displaced.

I give on the annexed sheet some other things in the translation that brought me to a halt as I read them.[55]

If it is not too late I would strongly advise that an effort be made to bring the translation more into line with the Leinster House tradition.

No. 176: NA, DT S9902

Fr Edward Cahill to Eamon de Valera

Milltown, Dublin
8 May 1937

I am very sorry that I have been prevented by illness from acknowledging sooner your very kind message of 1 May—the inscribed and autographed

[55] Document not included. For a discussion of Ó Broin's comments, and a transcript of his observations, see Micheál Ó Cearúil, *Bunreacht na hÉireann: Divergences and Inconsistencies?*, 54–8.

copy of the new Constitution. I appreciate your over kind thoughtfulness, and am sincerely grateful for the gift, which I shall treasure, on account of the donor, and the inscription.

I congratulate you very sincerely on the Constitution. It is an honour to Éire; and is worthy of her. I do not think any other existing constitution 'professes the Lord' so plainly and uncompromisingly. Whatever carping critics may say or pretend, I do not think that our people will have that profession with all its implications changed or weakened.

You will I hope indulge me in making a few remarks which are needed if my letter be fully frank:

1) I am sorry that you were not able to embody in the Constitution the principle of *denominationalism in education.* It is at the very core of the antagonism between Christianity and Liberalism; and although it may be said that our primary and secondary schools are denominational in actual fact, the universities are not so, neither are the so-called technical or vocational schools. There is a very sinister phenomenon which 'strikes one in the eye' and needs explanation. This is the fact that Catholic Ireland of the 20th Century has given and still gives to the world a seemingly unending stream of apostate and semi-apostate writers, who in varying degrees have used and use their undoubtedly high literary gifts to excel in pornography, and in bitter contempt for the Catholic Faith (cf. Joyce, O'Flaherty, Austin Clarke, Conal O'Riordan, Con O'Leary, Francis Hackett, etc.). Our *non-denominationalism* is I believe somewhere very near the root cause.
2) In Article 40, section 6, 1° (end of 84) 'Shall not be used to undermine' would it be possible to insert here the word 'religion'? It is one of the duties of the State to safeguard religion.
3) In the same article and section, in the last paragraph of it, in the words 'the publication and utterance of blasphemous', etc, could the word 'circulation' be inserted before 'publication'? In Ireland there is little or no fear of a publisher or author publishing blasphemous or obscene matter. What is of very practical importance is the *selling* or circulation of such matter usually published in England.

Again offering hearty congratulations and [receiving] my sincere thanks: and wishing you and yours all blessings.

P.S. I am *very much* pleased at the institution of the President, and hope that his powers will not be curtailed. The making of a special *electorate* for Senate is ingenious and *effective* and still completely democratic. Prosit!

No. 177: NAI, DT S9856

Memorandum from George Gavan Duffy to Eamon de Valera

Dublin
8 May 1937

A Uachtaráin,
May I suggest the following points for your further consideration in the dréacht-Bhunreacht?

Article 29: Extradition powers are not mentioned.

Article 34: As under the present Constitution, the Courts will have no express power to sit *in camera*, where the interests of justice so require, but justice can be done only in public courts.[56]

Article 39: Treason by a citizen abroad is not included.

Article 51: If an amendment of the Constitution within three years need not be expressly described in the title as such, difficult questions will continue to arise as to alleged amendments by implication.

Article 58: There may be dangerous implications in giving the present Courts the *same* jurisdiction as under the 1922 Constitution; the jurisdiction under the new Constitution will hardly be the same, though it will be analogous or similar or 'the like'.

[56] Gavan Duffy's suggestion for change was ultimately accepted, albeit not immediately. The Second Amendment of the Constitution Act, 1941 deleted the original version of Article 34.1 and inserted the present version of Article 34.1 in its place. This provides for the administration of justice in public, 'save in such special and limited cases as may be prescribed by law'. Thus, the Oireachtas can, exceptionally, legislate to allow for *in camera* hearings, such as in family law matters. In addition, the courts have held that they enjoy an inherent jurisdiction to direct that some or all of a case can be heard otherwise than in public where this is necessary and essential to protect the constitutional rights of litigants: see *Re Ansbacher* (*Cayman*) *Ltd*, [2002] 2 IR 517; *Doe v. Revenue Commissioners*, [2008] 3 IR 328.

The new courts contemplated by Article 34 of the Constitution were not in fact established until 1961: see Courts (Establishment of Constitution) Act, 1961. In *Sullivan v Robinson*, [1954] IR 161, the Supreme Court held that Article 58 should be interpreted liberally so that on this interpretation the Court held that 'the reference of Bills to the Supreme Court [under Article 26] was contemplated as something that might be done during the transition period before the Courts were set up under the Constitution', 174.

No. 178: NAI, DT S9880

W.R. O'Hegarty[57] to Eamon de Valera

Joint Committee of Women's Societies and Social Workers, Dublin
8 May 1937

A Chara,
The [Joint Committee of Women's Societies and Social Workers] has appointed a deputation to wait on the leaders of the three Parties with regard to the status of women under the draft Constitution. I should be grateful if you would let me know at your earliest convenience when and where you can receive the deputation.[58]

No. 179: NAI, DT S9852

Cardinal Joseph MacRory to Eamon de Valera

Armagh
9 May 1937

My dear President,
I was away from home in the past week on a Confirmation tour, and only this morning noticed that a copy of the new Constitution had come to me 'with the compliments of the President'. I am very grateful and regret that I have not acknowledged it sooner.

On various occasions I heard it discussed by the Priests and in every instance the comments were favourable.

It must be a great relief to you to have had it launched, and I congratulate you sincerely.

No. 180: UCDA, P150/2395

Fr John Charles McQuaid to Eamon de Valera

Blackrock, Co. Dublin
10 May 1937

It is a great pleasure to send the enclosed ammunition.[59] Even though I had before me the actual texts, yet for complete safety, I submitted my

[57] Honorary Secretary of the Joint Committee of Women's Societies and Social Workers.
[58] See document nos 182, 186, 202.
[59] Enclosure not found.

text to Dr Lucey for criticism. His answer was, 'it is impeccable'. As he is an expert, I think we are safe, on this knotty question. I have been at the 'capacity and social function' passage. The Ennis speech reads very well indeed. Any time you want me, I am available.

No. 181: NAI, DT S9880

Mary J. Hogan[60] to Eamon de Valera

University College Dublin
11 May 1937

Dear Sir,
At a meeting of [the National University Women Graduates' Association] held last evening it was unanimously decided, and I was instructed to ask you to receive a deputation of the following Members from our Association: Professor Mary Hayden Professor Agnes O'Farrelly, Professor Mary Macken, Mrs McCarvill, Mrs Kane, Mrs Young, and Miss O'Carroll. To discuss the position of women under the proposed new Constitution consequent on the withdrawal of Article 3 of the Free State Constitution, and the provisions contained in some of the clauses of articles 40, 41, 45 of the proposed new Constitution.

No. 182: NAI, DT S9880

Maurice Moynihan to W.R. O'Hegarty

Department of the President
13 May 1937

A Chara,
With reference to your letter of the 8th instant, requesting the President to receive a deputation from your Committee relative to the status of women under the Dréacht-Bhunreacht, I am to say that the President will receive the deputation in his room in Government Buildings at 4 p.m. on Friday, the 14th instant.

In reply to a similar request the National University Women Graduates' Association has been informed that the President will receive a deputation at the same time on Friday next. It is understood that the

[60] Honorary Secretary of the National University Women Graduates' Association.

Association is represented on the Joint Committee of Women's Societies and Social Workers.[61]

No. 183: NAI, DT S9880

Lucy Kingston[62] to Eamon de Valera

National Council of Women of Ireland, Dublin
13 May 1937

A Chara,
At a meeting of above Council which took place yesterday, I was requested to express to you the earnest desire of our members that Article 3 may be restored to the new Constitution; and also that Articles 40, 41 and 45 may be deleted.

It was felt strongly that if this were done the whole tone of those Clauses which have reference to women would be more in keeping with the spirit of the Republican Proclamation of 1916.

No. 184: NA, DT S9856

Fr Edward Cahill to Eamon de Valera

Milltown, Dublin
13 May 1937

As I am deeply interested in the religious and social aspects of the new Constitution (which alone concern me) I am presuming to send another suggestion for your consideration. It would I believe be very desirable in the first place to *disassociate the Constitution completely* from the approaching general election; and secondly to give the people and all those concerned a *considerable time* to discuss and study it at leisure and apart from ephemeral political considerations. I fear that the association of the Constitution with a general election will do much to injure its prestige in the people's minds; and will tend to embitter opposition. A matter of such far-reaching importance for all the best interests of the country should be studied and discussed at leisure and as far as possible in an atmosphere of quiet and detachment. That will I fear be impossible, if it is taken up now, and finished with before the election,

[61] See document nos 178, 186.
[62] Honorary Secretary of the National Council of Women of Ireland.

and voted on by the people on the day of the election. Again if a few or even six months' interval is allowed to elapse between the election and the completion of the final draft of the Constitution it is (or seems to me to be) quite certain that even you yourself will receive many new lights, and possibly invaluable suggestions from various quarters, unfriendly as well as friendly (through articles in reviews, public lectures, etc) which will enable you to make the document much more valuable, and probably to forestall unforeseen difficulties.

Praying God to direct and assist you in the arduous work you have on hand, and wishing you and yours all blessings.

P.S. I do not expect a reply to this letter. I merely wish to send the suggestion.

No. 185: NAI, DT S9903

Michael G. Dowling[63] to J. Hurson

General Register Office
13 May 1937

Article 44.3
Mr Hurson,
The expression 'Church of Ireland'. If the Church of Ireland was disestablished by the Irish Church Act of 1869, did it not cease to be the Church of Ireland? The difficulty of correctly naming this denomination has always been felt in this office and a way out has often been found in the expression 'late established church of Ireland'. While such a description would not now be appropriate in view of the length of time which has elapsed since disestablishment, it is suggested that a true description of the church would be 'the Protestant Episcopalian Church in Ireland'.

The Irish Marriage Act of 1844 (7 and 8 Victoria, c.81) describes the Irish Protestant Church as 'The United Church of England and Ireland' (not United *Churches*)

This is also the description given in the Marriage Law (Ireland) Amendment Act, 1863 (26 Victoria, c.27).

The Irish Church Act of 1869 provides for the dissolution of the Union between the *Churches* of England and Ireland and that the 'Church of Ireland as so separated should cease to be established by law'.

[63] Assistant Registrar General, General Register Office.

This Act is to be cited for all purposes as the Irish Church Act, 1869 (Preamble and Section 1). In the remaining sections of this Act the Church is referred to as the 'said Church' or the 'said Church *in* Ireland' but not as the Church *of* Ireland except in Section 69 which is as follows:

> 'In all enactments deeds and other documents in which mention is made of the United Church of England and Ireland, the enactments and provisions relating thereto shall be read distributively in respect of the Church of England and the Church of Ireland, but as to the last mentioned Church, subject to the provisions of this Act.'

I would submit that this section does not authorise the use of the term 'Church of Ireland' after the date of the coming into force of the Act, as the Act disestablished the Church of Ireland as a term in itself expressive of an established or state church.

I think it is obvious from the wording of Marriage Acts passed subsequently to the Act of 1869 that there was a difficulty in giving a definite legal appellation to this Church. In the preamble to the Matrimonial Causes and Marriage Law Amendment Act, 1870 (33 and 34 Victoria, c.110) this difficulty is got over by calling it 'the said Church', thus:

> 'Whereas...it was enacted that on and after...that the said church of Ireland, in the said Act referred to as "the said Church" should cease to be established.'

Throughout the remainder of this Act it is referred to as the 'said Church', but in section 38 a clergyman of this Church is described as a 'Protestant Episcopalian clergyman' and not as a 'clergyman of the said church' nor 'a clergyman of the Church of Ireland'. The same description appears in Sections 39 and 40.

Article 44.2: 'The State guarantees not to endow...and shall not...make any discrimination on the grounds of religious profession, belief or status.'

Under this section the Slaughter of Animals Act would appear to be contrary to the Constitution. In this Act there is a plain discrimination against Christians, since Jews and Mahomedans, on the grounds of their religious beliefs, are privileged to slaughter animals in a way not permitted to Christians.

Article 44.4: 'Every religious denomination shall have the right to manage its own affairs', etc.

Under the Marriage Laws at present in force certain powers and functions are vested in the Minister for Local Government and Public Health and in the Registrar General. For instance a Bishop of the Protestant Church may licence churches for the celebration of marriages with the approval of the Minister. He may appoint licensing ministers who must enter into a bond with the Registrar General in the sum of £100 for the due and faithful execution of their office.

The appointment of Presbyterian Licensers must be approved by the Minister for Local Government and Public Health and they also must enter into a bond with the Registrar General in the sum of £100 for the due and faithful execution of their office as licensers of marriages.

Would it be possible that the provisions of Article 44 (4°) might be construed as handing over to the various churches the management of their own affairs in the matter of marriages to the exclusion of the Minister for Local Government and Public Health and the Registrar General.[64]

No. 186: NAI, DT S9880

Memorandum relating to the reception of deputations from Women's Organisations

John Hearne, [Department of External Affairs]
14 May 1937

The President to-day received two deputations representing women's organisations, The Joint Committee of Women's Societies and Social Workers, The Standing C[ommi]ttee on Legislation affecting women, and the National University Women Graduates Association, who desired to place before him their views on certain articles of the Draft Constitution.

After a long discussion, the President informed the National University Women Graduates Association that whilst he did not at all share their apprehensions, he would nevertheless give careful consideration to their desire to have a barrier set up against the possibility of the enactment of any law discriminating against women in the matters of citizenship and franchise. He had already indicated to Deputy Costello in the Dáil last evening that he was prepared, if it was necessary, to insert in Article 16 a provision which would prevent any law being

[64] For further correspondence on the title 'Church of Ireland', see document nos 199, 209.

passed which would disqualify women citizens as such from the franchise. In the same spirit he was prepared to consider the possibility of inserting in Article 9 a provision which would set up a constitutional barrier against the possibility of an Act being passed discriminating against women in the matter of citizenship.

No. 187: NAI, DT S9880

Memorandum from Stephen Roche to Maurice Moynihan

Department of Justice
15 May 1937

Dear O'Muimhneachain,
I see in this morning's papers that it is probable that an amendment will be put down to Article 9 of the draft Constitution to provide that there shall be no discrimination as to sex in connection with the acquisition and loss of citizenship.

I think it as well to put on record the fact that there is at present such discrimination and we think here that discrimination is almost inevitable. A foreign woman who marries an Irish citizen can be naturalised without any qualifying period of residence while a foreign man who marries an Irish woman must reside here for two years before a Certificate can be granted to him. The reasons for the discrimination are obvious. A foreign woman who marries a national and proposes to reside here does not in the ordinary way enter the labour market. A foreign man will usually intend to take up employment of some sort.[65]

There is also the point to which, however, it might not be advisable to draw too much attention that in the case of children born abroad Saorstát citizenship is transmitted through the father and not through the mother.

[65] A variant of this legislation that provided for more onerous naturalisation requirements in the case of foreign males marrying Irish females was challenged unsuccessfully in *Somjee v. Minister for Justice*, [1981] ILRM 324. The legislation was rendered gender neutral by section 3 of the Irish Nationality and Citizenship Act, 1986, but has now been replaced by section 5 of the Irish National and Citizenship Act, 2001: see Kelly, *Irish Constitution*, 164–5.

No. 188: NAI, DT S9880

J. Walshe to Eamon de Valera

Ulster Bank Buildings, Dublin
15 May 1937

My Dear President,
I am sorry to observe that you are disposed to take the clamour of those Suffragettes so seriously. In this attitude you are wholly misinterpreting the mind of the country. No doubt you have concluded that the agitation has been worked up by two or three women who are by no means disinterested in the matter of political limelight. As one who has had some experience in sensing the mind of the ordinary man or woman I can positively say that the most popular thing you could do, as well also as the very best thing nationally, would be to make it known that your desire was to send women back to the home where they belong.

That there is general regret if not resentment at the intrusion of women in the spheres of men is not an exaggeration. In Brazil, for instance, no women are permitted in industry except such indispensable occupations as Stores stocking women's garments. Even typists are males everywhere except in certain foreign establishments with the result that there is no unemployment whatever.

I would beg of you to take a strong stand in this matter and you will have the support of the people. You will solve the male unemployment problem at once if you direct that definite occupations must employ men and men only. Meanwhile take those young lads who now hang around the corners and put them into Labour Camps under military tutelage and make men of them. If they get the same conditions as privates in the National Army I can't see where the grievance would come in.[66]

[66] The author of this letter is not to be confused with Joseph P. Walshe, Secretary of the Department of External Affairs.

No. 189: NAI, DT S9880

Brigid O'Mullane to Eamon de Valera

Association of Old Cumann na mBan, Dublin
18 May 1937

A chara,
The Association of above has directed me to inform you that we have discussed the Articles of Bunreacht na h-Éireann regarding the status of women; but find that we cannot accept them in their present form.

We are of opinion that Articles 9 and 16 unless 'no discrimination of sex' is stated, could interfere with women in matters of citizenship and franchise.

Articles 40.1, 42.2 and 45.2 are, we believe, open to a wide interpretation that could lead to legislation affecting women in industrial life in a prejudicial manner. The past material conditions of life have gone and labour is easier, calling to-day, more for mental activity and intellectual quickness rather than for muscular strength of women is quite unnecessary and particularly hurtful to us who in the various phases of the struggle for National Independence, were so frequently called on by the I.R. Army, both in the Anglo-Irish and Civil wars to undertake tasks entailing heavy muscular toil, with the added risk of discovery and capture by the enemy. One of our proudest achievements is that we conveyed safely from place to place machine guns, heavy explosives and rifles, not to mention smaller arms, without any loss or capture of same in transit.

Already we have bitter experience of the inequality between men and women as testified in the Military Service Pensions Act, 1934, where women were degraded to the lowest ranks, and even then every possible obstacle placed in the way of women qualifying for pensions. Our attitude on this question is clearly defined in the attached statement which we sent to the Press in defence of our rights.[67]

The Proclamation of Easter Week 1916 gave to us women equal rights and equal opportunities in simple language that no legislation could change or tamper with, and on that Declaration of Independence did Cumann na mBan base its Constitution.

We now ask that Articles 40, clause 1, 41, clause 2, and 45, clause 2 be deleted from Bunreacht na h-Éireann and the clause of the Easter Week 1916 Proclamation according 'equal rights and equal opportunities to all citizens' be inserted instead.

[67] Statement not included here.

No. 190: NAI, DT S9880

Louie Bennett to Eamon de Valera

Irish Women Workers' Union, Dublin
18 May 1937

Dear Mr President,
My Committee are very anxious to have amendments made to the proposed Constitution which would enable them to support it.

We gather that you are prepared to modify the Sections dealing with strictly political issues in such a way as to secure equal political rights for women. But my Committee are very particularly concerned with Sections affecting the economic position of women. You will agree that they are rightly so concerned as these Sections affect working class women only.

My Committee urgently desire that their representatives *may have an interview* with you for the purpose of discussing these Sections, and they have instructed me to ask you if you would grant such an interview to our President, Mrs Kennedy, a working woman, Miss Elizabeth O'Connor one of our officials with a life-long experience of working class life, and myself.

We desire an informal discussion, not to be used for publicity beyond what you may expressly permit. The Sections proposed for discussion are: Articles 16.1; 40.1; 41.2 and 45.4. We shall esteem it a very great favour if you will consent to meet us.[68]

No. 191: NAI, DT S9856

Memorandum by the Department of Education 'Note on Article 16 of the Constitution'

19 May 1937

Article 16.1.2°:
'Every citizen who has reached the age of twenty-one years *who is not disqualified by law* and complies with the provisions of the law relating to the election of members of Dáil Éireann, shall have the right to vote at an election for members of Dáil Éireann.'

These are probably the most vital words in the Constitution. They are

[68] A deputation from the Irish Women Workers' Union was received by de Valera on 22 May. See document no. 201.

in fact with Articles 12.2.2° and 47.3 the foundations on which the whole structure rests.

It is a matter of common knowledge that the wider the franchise became the more certain became the attainment of the National ideal.

For this reason it is desirable that no loophole be left by which the people can be thwarted in the expression of its will.

The italicised words 'who is not disqualified by law' should, therefore, be closely examined and weighed.

The persons intended to be disqualified are presumably persons such as Civic Guards, people in confinement, etc.

Under the words as they stand new disqualifications could, however, be created by ordinary legislation, if the qualifying age of twenty-one years as such were left unchanged.

There is, hence, a danger that a reactionary government, desirous of retaining power, might use the loophole afforded to limit the franchise.

At the best the validity of any such new disqualification would be a matter to be determined by the Supreme Court.

The Parliamentary franchise was originally a franchise for freeholders. It was only in 1885 that it was extended to householders, and only in 1918 that the property qualification was removed.

If ordinary legislation were enacted to declare that a citizen, not being a £10 rated occupier, would be disqualified from voting at an election for members of Dáil Éireann, it is doubtful, to say the least, whether such legislation would be declared invalid.

The effect of such legislation on the register of electors can easily be imagined. The bulk of the young voters would disappear, and incidentally the woman voter would practically be wiped out.

No. 192: NAI, DT S10239A

J.B. Whelehan[69] to Michael McDunphy

Stationery Office
19 May 1937

Dear McDunphy,

Further to our phone conversation yesterday, I now send you the following particulars re. sale of the Draft Constitution.

The Sale Office, Nassau St, disposed of 416 copies, while there were 16 copies sold at the Spring Show, R.D.S.

[69] Controller of the Stationery Office.

Of the 416 copies sold at Nassau St 6 copies went to the United States of America, and 21 copies went to England. There were no large orders by the Trade, the largest received was one for 24 copies from a Limerick Bookseller. Only 3 copies went to Cork.

The purchases were largely confined to the Dublin area and were made principally by Insurance Offices, Solicitors, a few societies and by those interested in Education, it being remarked that Christian Brothers were large purchasers. Only two members of the Irish Hierarchy purchased copies.

While the demand for the Draft Constitution would appear disappointing, it must be remembered that wide publicity was given it in the entire press of the country.

The total number of copies printed was 2,200, of which 1,485 were taken for Official use. After sales to date, we have a balance of 283 copies on hand.

With regard to a further printing of the Draft as amended or approved by the Dáil, and assuming only reasonable alterations, I give for your information some costings taken out by us.

1,000 copies, cost £24. Schedule sale price 9d per copy (allowing Agents discount). 2,000 copies, cost £33. Sale price 6d per copy. 5,000 copies, cost £60. Sale price 4d per copy.

From these you will appreciate that the cost will not be prohibitive by any means, still as the document will only be an 'approved draft', until subsequent to the Plebiscite, a further printing, involving amendments of title, etc., will be essential.

We realise that the document as submitted to the people should be readily available to voters for a reasonable period prior to the date of the Plebiscite, and perhaps it is not out of place that we should suggest that copies be made available for inspection at all Post Offices and Garda Barracks, and Offices of District and Circuit Courts. These copies should be suspended, as is done with the Electors Lists and Register of Electors, and be not removable. Such an arrangement should be advertised in *Iris Oifigiúil* and the Press. This procedure should meet any reasonable objection on the grounds of publicity. Five thousand copies would amply cover distribution on the lines I suggest and would allow two copies to the Post Offices of larger centres of population.

I am, therefore, of the considered opinion that 6,000/7,000 copies would abundantly meet requirements for the issue of the approved draft.[70]

[70] Annotated by McDunphy: 'This would provide 1,000/2,000 copies for sale and the sale price would be 4d per copy. 19 May 1937'. On 21 June, the Stationery Office wrote to McDunphy to inform him that 30,000 copies of the Constitution, as approved by Dáil Éireann, had been ordered: 16,000 were to be

No. 193: NAI, DT S9880

Doreen M. Ditchburn[71] to Eamon de Valera

Irish Women Citizens' and Local Government Association, Dublin
20 May 1937

Dear Sir,
The following resolution was passed unanimously at a meeting of the Committee of the Irish Women Citizens' Association on Wednesday 19 May:

> 'That, in our view, Article 3 of the Constitution of 1922, in which it is expressly stated, that there shall be equal rights and opportunities for all citizens without distinction of sex, should be retained in the new Constitution. And Clauses 2 and 4.2° of Articles 41 and 45 respectively, should be deleted from the draft Constitution.'

The I.W.C.A. feel that the position of women in Saorstát Éireann has deteriorated in recent years from the ideal implicit in the Proclamation of 1916 and the Constitution of 1922, and that therefore it is necessary to retain Article 3 explicitly.

While realising that in the proposed Constitution it is intended to give women a certain protection, we believe that the only real protection for women in industry is to adopt the principle of equality and give equal pay for equal work.

In our opinion it would be quite impossible to carry out Clause 2 of Article 41 without subjecting women to an irritating supervision and interference; and, as has already been pointed out, if Clauses 1 and 2 of Article 45 are put into practice, this Clause is superfluous.

We feel that Articles 41 and 45 might be used by a reactionary Government to justify legislation which would exclude women from well paid occupations, thereby forcing them to undertake ill paid work involving heavier manual labour. We realise that such a misuse is far from the intentions of those who have drafted the proposal, but we feel that the position of women would be safer without the Clauses referred to

[70] *contd.* distributed to Post Offices. 2,000 were to be delivered to various booksellers, with the remainder earmarked for public libraries and Garda stations. Sale price was to be 2d. In a report published 10 Feburary 1938, the *Irish Press* noted that 52,000 copies of the Constitution had been sold up to that point, with 20,000 of those purchased by Fianna Fáil.

[71] Honorary Secretary of the Irish Women Citizens' and Local Government Association.

above in these Articles, and that instead the new Constitution should specifically guarantee to women equality of both political and economic opportunity.

No. 194: NAI, DT S9880

Dorothy Macardle to Eamon de Valera

London
21 May 1937

Dear President de Valera,
I want to write to you personally rather than write at length in the newspapers about the clauses on women.

Many of the attacks on these seem to me unreasonable, but I find myself in absolute agreement with Miss Louie Bennett's published letter to you. The real crux is the question of employment. The language of certain clauses suggests that the State may interfere to a great extent in determining *what opportunities* shall be open or closed to women, and there is no clause whatever to counterbalance that suggestion or to safeguard women's rights in this respect.

If, as I trust you do, you wish to be fair to women in the economic as well as in the political and civic spheres I think that a clause could be inserted in Article 45 which would at least exercise a good directive influence. I suggest:

> 45.4.3° 'The State shall endeavour to secure that neither in opportunities for employment nor in conditions of employment shall women suffer unfair discrimination on the sole ground of sex.'

The 'unfair' spoils it from the point of view of ideal justice, but to omit that would require the abolition of parts of the recent Conditions of Employment Act and that is too much to hope for, I know. This 'unfair' permits the process of reform to be gradual and leaves the way open for the establishment of a tribunal or Court of Appeal.

The phrase 'sole grounds of sex' permits discrimination on grounds of possession of other sources of income, functions and occupations (such as of motherhood), and necessity for supporting dependants.

I think this should do something to satisfy the legitimate fears of both men and women for the moment, imperfect as the provision might be, and would leave the way open for advanced legislation.

As the Constitution stands, I do not see how anyone holding advanced views on the rights of women can support it, and that is a tragic dilemma for those who have been loyal and ardent workers in the national cause.

No. 195: NAI, DT S9859A

Memorandum from Maurice Moynihan to Arthur Codling

Department of the President
21 May 1937

1. With further reference to my minute of the 4th instant[72] in regard to the setting up of a Committee to make recommendations as to any changes that may be desirable, by way of simplification, in the spelling of Irish in the Draft Constitution, I have to inform you that the personnel of the Committee was officially decided as follows:

Chairman:	An t-Ollamh Uas.	Eoin MacNeill
Members:	Cú Uladh	[Peadar T. Mac Fhionnlaoich]
	An Seabhac	[Pádraig Ó Síochfhradha]
		Risteard Ó Foghludha
		Shan Ó Cuiv
		Colm Ó Murchadha
		Micheal Breathnach
	An t-Ollamh Uas.	Tomás Ó Rathaille
	An t-Ollamh Uas.	Tomás Ó Máille
	An t-Ollamh Uas.	Osborn Bergin
	An t-Ollamh Uas.	Seamus Ó Searcaigh

2. Mr Seamus Dalton of the Staff of the Oireachtas was appointed as Secretary.
3. The first meeting of the Committee was held on the 7th instant, and, as previously stated, it is anticipated that the Committee will present its report not later than the 13st instant.
4. Apart from the question of a gratuity for the Secretary, it is not anticipated that the work of the Committee will entail any separate expenditure out of State funds.
5. The requisite stationery, etc., is being supplied by this Department.[73]

[72] See document no. 173.
[73] The Committee on Spelling of Irish submitted its report on 25 May 1937, NAI, DT S9859A.

No. 196: NAI, DT S9856

Memorandum from James G. Douglas to Michael McDunphy

Dublin
21 May 1937

Dear McDunphy,
With reference to our conversation yesterday afternoon I enclose a memo on certain amendments to the Constitution which I would like to see introduced. I did not send these to the President as I did not realise until my talk with you that suggestions from persons in public positions of responsibility would be welcomed. Although I am out of politics now and since the abolition of the Senate, have not studied any of the Bills which have been passed, I am very much interested in the new Draft Constitution and intend to vote for its acceptance.

I have to go to the Continent on business this evening and will be away for a week. I had not time yesterday evening to elaborate or give my reasons in full for my suggestions. If any interest is taken in them and if it is not too late when I return I would gladly set out my reasons in more detail. I may say that you are the only person with whom I have discussed these suggestions. You are at liberty to show them to the President or not as you think wise.[74]

Suggested Alterations In Draft Constitution

1. Provision that additional powers may be given to the President by law. I consider this is too drastic a power to give to a Parliamentary majority and suggest that any Bill giving additional powers to the President should not come into operation until 60 days after the next general election after the bill is passed. This would prevent dictatorial powers being given without the consent of the people. Alternatively the power to increase the President's functions by law should be restricted to acts done on the advice of the Executive but I prefer my first suggestion as it is less restrictive and allows for chance provided the people do not object.[75]
2. Council of State: I don't like the creation of seven councillors of State by the President who has power to remove them. I think the position of Councillor of State should be a life

[74] Letter is annotated by McDunphy: 'Considered by President, 22.5.37'. All annotations by McDunphy.
[75] Annotated: 'Done'.

appointment and be an honour which the Executive Council should be able to give persons irrespective of party who have given good service to the country. I think the choice of persons to have this honour should be in the hands of the Executive. The total number to hold the title might be restricted to 50 but I do not regard this as important. The President, instead of appointing 7 Councillors of State should nominate 7 *Acting* Councillors of State from amongst all the persons who hold the title. These persons would remain *Acting* Councillors for the term of the President's appointment unless removed by him and he would only summon the seven plus the Ex Officio Councillors of State. I believe a scheme like this would add dignity to the State and give the Executive a method of recognising service without creating titles.[76]

3. Seanad: I think the eleven nominated members of the Seanad should be chosen *before* the elections take place for the rest of the Seanad. This will enable the Taoiseach to choose good representative men as I believe either President de Valera or Mr Cosgrave would wish to do. If it is possible to wait until after the elections there is a danger that party pressure may make it difficult for the Taoiseach to avoid nominating defeated candidates which would be, to my mind, unfortunate.[77]
4. Seanad Panel: I think the Constitution should state the number of Senators for each Panel. I further think that once the method of nomination to panels has been fixed that any law altering these panels should not come into effect until after the next election to the Seanad. This would prevent a party, which did not expect to be re-elected with a majority in the Dáil, altering the panels so as to give them a majority in the next Senate.[78]
5. I believe it would be much wiser to retire only one half of the Seanad at each election. This would not apply to the University members or to the nominees of the Taoiseach. The number of the latter could be altered to 10 or 12 so as to provide 42 or 44 elected from panels with 21 or 22 each time. This would make Senators less dependent on parties and help to create a Seanad which was not a replica in political complexion of the Dáil.[79]
6. Article 15.7: This should read 'The Oireachtas shall meet at least once a year'. To the best of my belief 'Session' has a

[76] Annotated: 'President will consider this. I have given him a draft, 22.5.37'.
[77] Annotated: 'No. 22.5.37'.
[78] Annotated: 'No. Min and Max numbers fixed'.
[79] Annotated: 'No'.

definite meaning for private bill purposes. The difficulty [has] been got over but why not put it right when you have a new Constitution.[80]

No. 197: NAI, DT S9880

Katherine Hassard and A.M. Conan[81] to Eamon de Valera

Dublin University Women Graduates' Association,
Trinity College Dublin
22 May 1937

Dear Sir,
We have been asked by the Dublin University Women Graduates' Association, which Association includes nationals all over Saorstát Éireann, to write to you with reference to sections 40, 41.2.1°, 2°, and 45.4.2° of the Draft Constitution at present before the Oireachtas.

The Dublin University Women Graduates' Association wish strongly to urge the extreme inadvisability of embodying in the Constitution any distinction of sex. They feel that any such distinction, however well meant, will inevitably tend to make it easier to treat women unequally and unjustly in the various employments, and they wish to remind you of the declarations of the Irish Republican Proclamation in 1916, and of the 1923 [sic] Constitution of Saorstát Éireann (Clause III), in both of which the principle of equal citizenship for men and women is embodied, and to urge that this principle should be retained, and *clearly reaffirmed*, in any new Constitution to be promulgated in this country. Any variation from this principle would, in the opinion of the Dublin University Women Graduates' Association, be a retrograde step.

No. 198: NAI, DT S9928

Walter T. Scott to Patrick Little

Christian Science Committee on Publication for County Dublin
22 May 1937

Sir,
The enclosed memorandum is submitted in the spirit of perfect goodwill for consideration by the Executive Council.

[80] Annotated: 'No'.
[81] Joint Honorary Secretaries to the Dublin University Women Graduates' Association.

I should be gratefully pleased to hear at the earliest possible moment the result of their deliberations thereon.

If it is decided that the recommendations made in the memorandum cannot be accepted, would you kindly agree to receive a deputation for further discussion on the matter? The deputation would consist of myself and Sir George Mahon, acting as official representatives of both The Mother Church, the First Church of Christ, Scientist, in Boston, Mass., and of local Branch Churches.

Memorandum on behalf of the Christian Science Denomination on Article 44 of the Draft Constitution

It could be argued, at some future time, as regards Section 1, Subsection 3 that there was no official or legal knowledge of the existence of the Christian Science denomination in Ireland at the date of the coming into operation of the Constitution.

It could also be argued that Section 2, Subsection 1, should be construed subject to Section 1, Subsection 3, and the free practice of religion be thereby restricted to the denominations deemed to have existed in accordance with the said Section 1, Subsection 3.

The sincerity of the present Government is fully recognised and appreciated. In view, however, of the restrictions on the free profession and practice of religion by a certain type of Government in Europe at the present time, and in view of the approval of that type of government by some sections of political thought in the Free State today, it is felt that it should be placed beyond all doubt that the new Constitution recognises the Christian Science denomination.

Therefore it is respectfully submitted for the consideration of the Executive Council that the words 'The Church of Christ, Scientist', be inserted in Section 1, Subsection 3, after the words 'the Religious Society of Friends in Ireland'.[82]

No. 199: NAI, DT S9856

Fr Edward Cahill to Eamon de Valera

Milltown, Dublin
23 May 1937

I trust that you will not find my letters to you on the draft Constitution troublesome or importunate. I am deeply interested, as you know in

[82] Little formally acknowledged receipt of the letter on 1 June, having previously forwarded it, along with the enclosed memorandum, to de Valera on 29 May, NAI, DT S9928. For further correspondence regarding the Christian Scientist denomination, see document nos 210, 215.

certain aspects of it, and have given the matter very serious thought. I have besides discussed it with some others, who, besides being very well informed, are also much interested. With this preface I wish to bring under your notice some points that seem to me to be of special importance:

1) I agree with the underlying idea (though not with the way of putting it or with the terminology) of Pakenham's[83] critique of the draft Constitution (see Pakenham's article in the *Irish Independent*, 13 May, in the two paragraphs headed respectively 'An interesting question' and 'Matter for Atheistic propaganda'). In other words I believe that the *individual* aspect of private ownership is unduly stressed to the detriment of the counterbalancing or *social* aspect; and that this fact, especially when taken in conjunction with the individualism, which is so deeply embedded in our current jurisprudence, may (contrary to the manifest aim intended in the Constitution) render very difficult, if not impossible the long desired reorganisation of our economic and social regime in harmony with the Papal Encyclicals.

   Hence I would suggest that Article 43.2, should be so strengthened as to convey the properly balanced Catholic concept of property rights, as contained in the Papal Encyclicals; and stress more the duty of the State in their regard. Thus Article 43.2.1° could read somewhat as follows:

   > The state however recognises that, as the material goods of the world have been created for the benefit of all, the institution of private ownership is only a *means* to secure in an orderly manner consonant with man's rational nature the attainment of that end. Accordingly the exercise of the rights mentioned in the foregoing provisions of this article *must* in civil society, etc.

   Again in Article 43.2.2° the word 'shall' should, I believe, be substituted for 'may'. For the State is bound to provide for the common good; and it is patent that in modern times and especially in countries like Ireland the legal delimitations referred to are essential.
2) The term *social justice* (cf. Article 43.2.1°) which is so often used in the Encyclicals of Pius XI, and has for the student of

[83] Francis Aungier ('Frank') Pakenham (1905–2001), 1st Baron Pakenham and 7th Earl of Longford. Author of *Peace by Ordeal* (London, 1935) and, with T.P. O'Neill, *Eamon de Valera* (London, 1970).

Catholic social science a clear and definite meaning, is probably quite unknown in our current jurisprudence, or, if known, has a meaning different from its meaning in the Papal Encyclicals. Also the terms *justice* (Art. 45.1), *personal rights* (Art. 40.3.1°), *property rights* (Art. 40.3.2°), and possibly others such as *capacity* (Art. 40.1) convey different ideas to the student of Catholic social science, and to those (including all or most of our judges, and lawyers, and possibly most of our public men) whose ideas and mentality are much influenced by the individualistic and Liberal principles of English jurisprudence. Hence there is, I fear, *real danger* that the intentions aimed at in the draft Constitution may be frustrated, except it is made clear in the Constitution itself in what sense such terms are to be understood. Besides, considering the false ideas sometimes put forward by men who are supposed to be well educated, as well as by the more powerful sections of the Press it would be of the greatest importance to give Catholic social teaching (which of course does not go beyond the dictates of the natural law) a *legal* standing, as it were, in the fundamental law of the State. Accordingly I would suggest that some such provision as the following be inserted, say immediately after Art. 45.1, or immediately after Art. 44.1.2°:

> Accordingly the State shall by suitable enactments as occasion demands, bring its system of jurisprudence, and its legal code into harmony with the dictates of the natural law, as summarised in the social teaching of the Catholic Church, in the sense of which this article (viz. Art. 45) as well as Articles 40–4 are to be interpreted.

3) I am in complete agreement with the matter contained in enclosed letter;[84] and I believe that it touches upon the very root of those economic evils, which even still threaten the very life of the historic Irish nation, viz., *bachelorship*, *depopulation of the countryside*, and *emigration* especially of the young women. Hence I believe that Art. 45 should be so amended as to render it *mandatory*, perhaps by omitting the p*reamble*, and adding the provision which I suggest above (viz., in the preceding paragraph of this letter).

[84] The letter referred to was written by B.B. Waters and printed in the *Irish Times*, 22 May 1937. Copies are found at UCDA, P150/2393 and NAI, DT S9880.

4) I am quite convinced (and that too is the teaching of the Encyclicals) that effective social reconstruction along Catholic lines—especially such a reconstruction as will solve the Gaeltacht problem, and save our rural population—is impossible without *monetary reform*; and although you may not yet be convinced of that, or see your way to it, I would consider it very imprudent to allow anything in the Constitution to close the door against it. Now it seems to be generally admitted that a law or decree embodying such a reform has to be issued *unexpectedly*, or *rushed through* the legislature. Otherwise the manipulation of the financiers, or public panic will either render it ineffective or make its operation extremely difficult, or ruinously costly to the country. Hence I believe that a sufficiently wide loophole should be left in the Constitution to allow such a measure to be quite feasible, if or when the government decides that it should be taken.

P.S. I presume you know that the term 'Church of Ireland' which occurs in Art. 44.1.3° has aroused no end of criticism and surprise; for it really seems to be an authoritative approval of a piece of lying propaganda. I hope that it will be changed.[85]

No. 200: NAI, DT S9880

Mary Hayden[86] and Mary Hogan to the Executive Council

National University Women Graduates' Association, Dublin
23 May 1937

Gentlemen,
We are directed by the National University Women Graduates' Association to lay before you a statement of their views on the Status of Women under the proposed new Constitution. We are Members of a University in which perfect equality of rights and opportunities has been enjoyed by women both in theory and practice since its foundation in 1908.

While our anxieties with regard to Articles 9 and 16 have been met by the assurances of the President given to our deputation, we still view with alarm the Articles in the Constitution which appear to us to menace

[85] A copy of this letter is also found at UCDA, P150/2393. There is also a very rough draft found at Jesuit Archives, J55/64. For further correspondence relating to the title 'Church of Ireland', see document nos 185, 209.
[86] President of the National University Women Graduates' Association.

the citizen's right to work in whatever legitimate sphere he or she may deem suitable. We regret to find clauses in the Constitution which might be a directive to future Governments to pass legislation worsening the economic and social status of women.

In the following Article 40:

> 'All citizens shall, as human persons, be held equal before the law. This shall not be held to mean that the State shall not in its enactments have due regard to differences of capacity, physical and moral, and of social function.'

We object to this clause because it leaves it open to the legislature and the Courts to restrict the legitimate liberties of any citizen or group or class of citizens. We ask either for the deletion of this clause or for the insertion of a safeguard such as provided; there is no discrimination merely on the grounds of class, sex, or religion.

While the Women Graduates welcome the proposal that mothers be not forced to engage in labour to the neglect of their duties in the home, they regard with the strongest misgivings the provisions of Article 41.2.2°:

> 'The State shall, therefore, endeavour to ensure that mothers shall not be obliged by economic necessity to engage in labour to the neglect of their duties in the home',

which suggest interference on the part of the State with the affairs of the family. We consider that the husband and wife, knowing best what is necessary for the support and happiness of the family, should decide what work is necessary to these ends.

The same objections apply to Article 45.4.2:

> 'The State shall endeavour to ensure that the inadequate strength of women and the tender age of children shall not be abused, and that women or children shall not be forced by economic necessity to enter avocations unsuited to their sex, age or strength',

in so far as it refers to women. If the Constitution is aiming through these clauses at remedying the unemployment of men and the exploitation of women, we suggest that the application of the fundamental principle of social justice, equal pay for equal work, would go far to maintain a satisfactory balance.

As we regard a Constitution as a Charter of the rights of the citizen which in normal circumstances is inviolable, we appeal to you to give our proposals your favourable consideration.[87]

[87] See document nos 181, 182, 186.

No. 201: NAI, DT S9880

Louie Bennett to Eamon de Valera

Irish Women Workers' Union, Dublin
24 May 1937

Dear Mr President,

Mrs Kennedy and Miss O'Connor wish to join with me in thanking you very sincerely for giving us so much of your valuable time on Saturday forenoon and in expressing our appreciation of your willingness to give thought to our point of view on certain Sections of the Draft Constitution.

We are much reassured to know that Article 45.4 will be amended in the sense of the latter part of our proposed Amendment (of which we gave you a copy and which Dr Rowlette has tabled). But we feel bound to reiterate once more our profound dissatisfaction with the second paragraph of Article 40.1. It is impossible to dissociate from that paragraph suggestions of class and sex discrimination, and it seems to us deeply regrettable that a phrase should remain in the Constitution which carries interpretations offensive to a large section of the community and fundamentally different from your own intention. We do not believe that the clear, reassuring statement contained in the first paragraph of this Article is capable of being misinterpreted in such a sense as to preclude special legislation to meet the needs of different groups of people.

But if you are unwilling to delete the whole sentence as we strongly urge, it should surely be possible to amend it in such a way as to avoid an ambiguous use of the words 'differences of physical and moral capacity and of social function'. Or failing that, to add a sentence to the effect that there is here no intention to discriminate against any citizen on the sole ground of sex or of class.

In country homes, the housewife often finds it necessary to keep the house door open, but it is usual then to put up a half door as a safeguard against unwelcome intrusions. If you must keep this particular door in the Constitution open, put up a guard against Fascist intrusions.[88]

[88] See document no. 190.

No. 202: NAI, DT S9880

W.R. O'Hegarty to Maurice Moynihan

Joint Committee of Women's Societies and Social Workers, Dublin
24 May 1937

A Chara,
Would you kindly present enclosed memorandum to the members of the Executive Council. As the matter is urgent, we should be obliged if you would do so as soon as possible.[89]

Memorandum of the Joint Committee of Women's Societies and Social Workers
Gentlemen,
We beg, respectfully, to present to you a memorandum on the claims of the Joint Committee of Women's Societies and Social Workers relative to the status of women under the new Constitution, and on our reasons for objecting to certain articles in the Draft Constitution. We feel that these articles would enable a reactionary Government to pass class legislation against women.

The articles to which we object are Articles 40.1.2°; 41.2.2°; 45.4.2°.

With regard to Articles 9 and 16, we think that they, as at present worded, might give power to limit the political rights of women, but an assurance has been given by President de Valera that these clauses will be amended in such a way as to guarantee no interference with women's political rights or status. We, therefore, in this memorandum, direct your attention only to those clauses which we fear might interfere with our economic rights.

In Article 40.1, we ask that the second paragraph, beginning 'This shall not be held to mean…', be deleted, on the grounds that it would give the State dangerous power of passing enactments on sex or class lines. We hold that this paragraph is dangerous to men as well as to women.

Article 41.2.2° touches on a problem which already exists, but how would this problem be solved? It is difficult to believe that this would be possible on account of the extent of the need, and, even if it were, the question would arise as to who would decide whether the economic necessity in a household was such as to oblige the mother to do outside

[89] Annotated: 'Çopies circulated'.

work, or not. Would there be an enquiry into the needs and finances of the household, and, if so, would such an enquiry not be resented? If it would not be a question of doles, would the solution of the problem lie in providing work for the fathers, and, if so, how would this work be provided? Women fear that this article may foreshadow an extension of such legislation as Section 16 of the Conditions of Employment Act, legislation which would limit the opportunities of women in the economic field, and which could be passed under Article 40,1, second paragraph.

In this connection we would point to the constant propaganda here, and in other countries, in recent years, directed towards securing that, in obtaining employment, men shall have priority of claim to women, not on grounds of superior qualifications, but on grounds of sex. Whatever may be the aim of such discrimination, we hold that any legislation on these lines would be unjust, and likely to lead to grave abuses, and we re-affirm our belief in the principles of equal opportunities for both sexes, and equal pay for equal work.

In Article 45.4.2°, we ask for the deletion of all references to women, firstly, because we object to the phrase 'the inadequate strength of women'. The question of the adequacy or inadequacy of strength for any particular work is one which arises in the case of men, as much as in the case of women. Secondly, we fear that this article could be used to limit women's legitimate choice of occupation, on the grounds that their strength is inadequate. Further, the same difficulty arises here as in Article 41.2.2°. Who is to judge whether the strength of women is adequate for any particular employment, or not? Much of the heaviest work done by women is in the home, or on the farm. In industry, mechanisation has practically done away with heavy work. Women fear that this article may only be employed in cases where they come into competition with men, and will not be of any practical use to those who are doing the really arduous work above mentioned.

In view of the ambiguity of the above articles, and the objections made to them from many quarters, we ask that, instead of them, a clear and unequivocal statement of women's rights should be made in the new Constitution, such as is contained in Article 3 of the present Constitution, or in the Proclamation of 1916.

In urging your serious consideration of our arguments and objections, we would point out that women form, approximately, half of the population, and that they have made a long and arduous fight, involving many sacrifices and hardships, to win equality of status under the Constitution. We would further point out the danger of sex antagonism arising out of legislation restricting women's right to work. In Ireland, men and women have worked together freely and loyally, as comrades, in the national movement. Anything that would menace that pleasing relationship, and engender friction and discord between men and women, as workers, would, in our opinion, be disastrous.

No. 203: JA, J55/64

Eamon de Valera to Fr Edward Cahill

Dublin
24 May 1937

Dear Fr Cahill,
I received your letters of the 8th and 13th, and letter delivered by hand yesterday, the 23rd.[90] I am bearing your suggestions in mind, but do not know whether it will be possible to incorporate them at this stage. I need hardly say how grateful I am for them. I regret that it has not been possible to talk to you generally about the Constitution. I hope your health is continuing to improve. With kind regards. Sincerely yours,

(Signed) Eamon de Valera[91]

No. 204: NAI, DTS9902

Memorandum from Philip O'Donoghue to Maurice Moynihan

Office of the Attorney General
25 May 1937

Mr Moynihan,
With reference to the question raised as to the possible need to add the words 'circulation' or similar word to the words 'publication or utterance' at the end of page 84, Article 40, I have now looked up the meaning of those words in a legal dictionary.

Utterance is defined as the act of uttering. Uttering means tendering, selling, putting into circulation, publishing.

[90] See document nos 176, 184, 199.
[91] A copy of this letter is also found at UCDA, P150/2393.

It will thus be seen that the addition of the word 'circulation' would not add anything which is not already in the section and, therefore, no amendment on this ground is necessary.[92]

No. 205: UCDA, P150/2395

Fr John Charles McQuaid to Eamon de Valera

Blackrock, Co. Dublin
25 May 1937

I think that with the previous sheet, dealing with *donation* and *designation* theories of [power?], this one should answer [Professor Alfred] O'Rahilly.[93] Leo XIII is very explicit in not calling the designation theory by the strange names that Professor O'Rahilly found to fit it.

No. 206: NAI, DT S9924

Memorandum by Philip O'Donoghue

Office of the Attorney General
26 May 1937

[It was proposed by John A. Costello and Patrick McGilligan to delete Article 37 in its entirety. The following two documents were composed by Philip O'Donoghue in defence of the provisions of Article 37.]

Article 37: Notes for the Committee Stage
Article 37 reads as follows:

> 'Nothing in this Constitution shall operate to invalidate the exercise of limited functions and powers of a judicial nature, in matters other than criminal matters, by any person or body of persons duly authorised by law to exercise such functions and powers, notwithstanding that such person or such body of persons is not a judge or a court appointed or established as such under this Constitution.'

This Article, which only applies to civil matters, is designed to avoid the difficulties and litigation which were experienced in the past when the

[92] See point raised by Fr Edward Cahill in document no. 176.
[93] Enclosure not found.

exercise of powers of a judicial or quasi judicial nature was challenged in the Courts on the grounds that these were matters reserved to the Courts.

The phrase 'judicial power' has been dropped in the draft Constitution which speaks instead of 'Justice being administered in public courts' (Article 34.1)

It is absolutely necessary in order to give effect to much of our present day legislation that the Commissioners in the Land Commission, the Minister for Industry and Commerce, County Registrars, Referees (to mention but a few) shall be entitled validly to carry out certain functions of a judicial or quasi judicial kind. While persons affected from such decisions are not debarred from bringing proceedings in the Courts Article 37 merely attempts to establish that the rulings of such quasi judicial bodies shall not be upset on purely technical grounds, namely that they were not judges. This is mischievous.

No. 207: NAI, DT S9904

Memorandum by Philip O'Donoghue on the amendment proposed to Article 37 by John A. Costello and Patrick McGilligan

Office of the Attorney General
28 May 1937

This amendment is exceedingly dangerous and, presumably, will not be accepted under any circumstances.[94] The deletion of Article 37, which is proposed in the amendment, would seriously hamper Ministers and their officials in the administration of the functions of their Departments. Several existing Acts give Ministers quasi-judicial powers, the validity of which would be open to question if the amendment were carried. The danger that they would be questioned would be enhanced as a result of the raising of this issue in the Dáil.

The amendment would, moreover, produce chaos in a large area of administration, as it would deprive, of their functions, the numerous Courts of Referees, Appeal Committees and Appeals Tribunals operating under such Acts as the Old Age Pensions Acts, National Health Insurance Acts and Unemployment Insurance Acts. County Registrars would also find some of their functions taken away.

[94] See 67 *Dáil Debates*, Cols 305–12 (12 May 1937); Cols 1511–23 (2 June 1937).

No. 208: NAI, DT S9856

Brian J. McCaffrey[95] and P.E. Maloney[96] to Eamon de Valera

Dublin
28 May 1937

Dear Mr President,
The Árd Comhairle of An Ríoghacht, while welcoming the Draft Constitution most cordially and congratulating you most sincerely on the Catholic spirit which animates it, wishes to call your attention to some points of detail which may be of importance.

Article 6.1: The clause 'whose right it is to determine the rulers of the State' might seem to incorporate in the Constitution a theological opinion which, though tenable, is hardly in accord with the general democratic trend of the Constitution. Some modern theologians hold that civil authority comes from God *direct to the rulers* of the State—the people's function being only to *designate the rulers*. The other opinion—more democratic and more in accord with the traditional Catholic view—is that authority come from God *direct to the people* themselves, who then transfer it to the rulers. Hence the Ard Comhairle would suggest the omission of the above clause.

Article 41.3: This Article deals with a very complicated question and should be so drafted as not to preclude legislation which experience may show to be necessary. In illustration of this we may note the following:

(a) The Catholic Church (namely, the Holy See) can, and sometimes does, grant divorce in two cases: firstly in the case of a *Matrimonium ratum sed non consumatum*, and secondly in accordance with the *Pauline Privilege*. In both of these cases the marriage is valid but it is dissolved by the Church. It might be held under the new Constitution the State could not recognise the dissolution even by a special law.

In another set of cases a marriage *apparently* valid, and registered as such by both Church and State, may be *apparently* dissolved by a *decree of nullity* declaring that no valid marriage had taken place in the beginning. Here again it might be held that the State could not recognise such a

[95] President of An Ríoghacht, League of the Kingship of Christ.
[96] Secretary of An Ríoghacht.

decree. This difficulty could perhaps be avoided by altering the wording of Article 41.3.2° to read 'The Civil power (or the State) cannot dissolve a marriage validly contracted'.

(b) The Draft Constitution makes no change in regard to supposed marriages such as those made between a Catholic and a non-Catholic in a registry office or in a Protestant Church. While known to all Catholics to be invalid and merely legalised concubinage such a union is accepted by the State as a valid marriage.

Seeing as the Catholic Church is accorded a special position of pre-eminence in the Constitution it might perhaps be possible for the State to have regard for the marriage laws of the Church in cases where Catholics are concerned.

Article 45: The last clause of the preamble to this Article 'and shall not be cognisable etc' seems to tone down the strength of the sections which follow and to deprive them of due sanction. It would seem to preclude all means of obtaining a decision that a law in violation of them is unconstitutional. Hence the Ard Comhairle would suggest that the above is omitted.

No. 209: NAI, DT S9903

Secretary, Representative Body of the Church of Ireland to Maurice Moynihan

Dublin
31 May 1937

Dear Sir,
I am directed by his Grace the Lord Archbishop of Dublin to inform you that in the month of September, 1885, a case was laid by Her Majesty's Government before the Law Officers of the Crown and the following opinion was given on the title of the Church of Ireland:

> 'We are of opinion that this matter has been practically settled by the Legislature, and that the title of the Disestablished Church in Ireland is the CHURCH OF IRELAND. We do not think it necessary to refer to any of the statutes prior to the "Irish Church Act, 1869", by which the establishment of the Church of Ireland was

put an end to. It will be observed that this Act is entitled "An Act to put an end to the Establishment of the Church of Ireland". It recites in the preamble that "it is expedient that the union created by Act of Parliament between the Churches of England and Ireland, as by law established, should be dissolved, and that the Church of Ireland as so separated should cease to be established by law". The second section provides that the union created between the Churches of England and Ireland should be dissolved, and that the said Church of Ireland, thereinafter referred to as "the said Church", should cease to be established by law'.

'By a subsequent section of the same Act it is provided that "In all enactments, deeds and other documents in which mention is made of the United Church of England and Ireland, the enactments and provisions relating thereto shall be read distributively in respect of the Church of England and the Church of Ireland." We find in this statute a clear indication by the Legislature that although the Church is to cease to be established, the name of the CHURCH OF IRELAND is to be preserved. This is recognised by subsequent statutes. The Act of 38 Victoria, c.11 recites in the preamble that it is expedient to extend certain benefits to the late established Church of Ireland, and throughout the statute the words used are either "the late established Church of Ireland", or "the said Church". Again, in a statute dealing with public and parochial records (38 and 39 Victoria, c.59) the expression "parochial officer" is by the interpretation clause defined to mean "any rector, vicar, curate, parish clerk, or other parish officers of the Church of Ireland". A statute passed in 1884 (47 Victoria, c.10) to amend the Irish Church Act, 1869, recognises the title by such phrases as the following: "having regard to the altered circumstances of the said Irish Church"; "or in any other manner for the benefit of the said Irish Church." Thus it will be seen that both in the Act of Disestablishment and in subsequent legislation, either dealing with or referring to the Disestablished Church, the Legislature has given or recognised a term "CHURCH OF IRELAND", or its equivalent, "the Irish Church", as that by which it is to be denominated'.

'We are, therefore, of opinion that THE CHURCH OF IRELAND is the legal title.'[97]

[97] For further correspondence on the title 'Church of Ireland', see document nos 185, 199.

No. 210: NAI, DT S9928

Walter T. Scott to Patrick Little

Christian Science Committee on Publication for County Dublin
Dublin
3 June 1937

Sir,
The enclosed supplementary memorandum is sent to indicate the purpose and extent of the Christian Scientist denomination.

Any further information that may be required I shall be happy to supply.

Memorandum supplementary to that handed to the Parliamentary Secretary to the President of the Executive Council on 22 May 1937, by the Christian Science Committee on Publications for County Dublin:

To aid the Executive Council in their deliberations on the request for specific recognition of the Christian Science denomination in Article 44 of the draft Constitution, the following information is respectfully submitted:

The Headquarters of the Christian Science denomination is The Mother Church, The First Church of Christ, Scientist, in Boston, Mass. Its branches, numbering nearly 3,000, are to be found in all parts of the civilised world.

There are now two churches in Dublin; one in Belfast and a Society in Cork. There are, besides, informal groups of Christian Scientists in Newry, Bangor and Enniskillen.

Christian Science 'stands for the inalienable, universal rights of men. Essentially democratic, its government is administered by the common consent of the governed, wherein and whereby man governed by his Creator is self-governed.' (Miscellany 247 by Mrs Eddy).

The Movement is responsible for The Christian Science Monitor, with which the President and other members of the Executive Council are no doubt acquainted. This is an international daily newspaper, devoted to constructive and impartial journalism; its object, as stated by its founder, Mrs Eddy, is 'to injure no man, but to bless all mankind'. (Miscellany 353 by Mrs Eddy).

In the United States of America, Christian Science is now recognised as one of the leading religious denominations.[98]

[98] The letter and memorandum were forwarded to Eamon de Valera by Little on 4 June, NAI, DT S9928. See document nos 198, 215.

No. 211: NAI, DT S9856

Louis J. Walsh to Eamon de Valera

Letterkenny, Co. Donegal
5 June 1937

My dear President,

I am very glad to see from the official debates that you have promised to consider dropping the word 'iustis' out of the Bunreacht where it occurs in Article 58 or elsewhere. I object to it on linguistic grounds. Why use a word imported from the Bearla when we have a word with such fine native associations as 'breitheamh'. [Hugh] Kennedy deliberately called us 'breithimh' in the Courts of Justice Act of 1924—there was a debate on the subject. Native speakers always use the word and our designation as 'breithimh d'en Chúirt Dúithche' has passed into the popular parlance. We want the Bunreacht to be a model of good Irish for all future generations and so should avoid foreign words. Apart from this, there is the point made by [John] Costello about the implication of status involved. The Irish word is important from that point of view too—though our position is quite well secured by the ordinary law. Still, I think that on principle it is well to emphasise by the fundamental law of the State that the poor man has the same security for an independent tribunal for him as the rich man has. The man who can go to the High Court will never be oppressed, as his money will protect him; but the poor can be and often are oppressed by the Courts before which they have often to appear without an advocate and with nothing but the sense of justice of the breitheamh to safeguard them.

It is the District Court that touches most intimately the life of the ordinary man and it is through it that the Executive operates all its coercive machinery in a modern grandmotherly state. In as much as the District Justices will, for the most part, not have the same standing—financial or professional—as the Judges of the Higher Courts, it is particularly necessary to protect them from financial or other pressure from a tyrannical executive or corrupt Officialdom.

By law we are in reality better protected as regards tenure than are the High Court Justices. It would be easier for a parliamentary majority to get a Bill through the Dáil and Senate than—as has to be done in our case—to get the consent of the Chief Justice, President of the High Court and the head of our profession (Attorney General) for the dismissal of a D.J.: because dog does not eat dog, and the Judges will take a more detached view than would a parliamentary majority, obeying party whips. For that reason I don't suggest that there should be any such amendment as would require a resolution of both houses to dismiss one of us. But what I do suggest you do is this. Make it clear that we are 'breithimh' by the retention of the old word and amend Article 35.5 to extend to any judge 'exercising jurisdiction in criminal matters': and, as you have wisely pointed out the need of laying down in the Bunreacht certain guiding principles, add to that subsection some such words: 'The independence and security of tenure of all such judges, subject to good conduct and capacity, shall be maintained by law'.

I regard the Bunreacht as a wonderfully well conceived instrument of Constitutional Law. The checks and balances which you have embodied in it are brilliant solutions of the special difficulties of our position. I am very much in favour of your conception of a President and have expressed this view in an article signed 'Fear Dlighe' in the *Irish Press*. A mere ceremonial Head would cut no ice in Ireland, where everybody would take him as a joke. He must have power to be respected, and I can see no other satisfactory check on the powers of a corrupt or stupid parliamentary majority.

Don't mind all the nonsense that is being talked about women. The ladies, who are so vocal, would not be elected to any office by their fellow women if the franchise was a purely feminine one. Surely, the mass of women are entitled to say what they want, and they don't want these ladies to ask for them—the duty of serving on juries in what are often our filthy courts.[99]

Beannacht Dé ort!

P.S. As an Ulster man I regret that you have not been able to get a word for the State as distinct from the nation. People are already beginning to call the 26 counties 'Éire' which, I think, is dangerous.

[99] Letter is annotated by McDunphy: 'Seen by President'.

No. 212: NAI, DT S9931A

J.W. Kelly to Eamon de Valera

Institute of Journalists, Dublin
8 June 1937

Sir,
I am instructed by the Committee of the Dublin and Irish Association District of the Institute of Journalists to forward the following resolution passed at a meeting held on 7 June, and respectfully to ask you to receive a deputation in regard to the provisions affecting the Press in the draft Constitution.

> 'We view with grave concern those provisions of Article 40 of the Draft Constitution which deal with the Press. In our opinion the proposals to empower the State to take steps ensuring that the Prcss "shall not bc uscd to undcrminc public ordcr or morality or the authority of the State" are dangerously wide, and ambiguous, and could be used as a cover to interfere with the rights of journalists and constitute a menace to the liberty of the Press.'[100]

No. 213: NAI, DT S9931A

Maurice Moynihan to J.W. Kelly

Department of the President
9 June 1937

A chara,
I am directed by the President to acknowledge the receipt of your letter of 8th instant requesting him to receive a deputation representing the Dublin and Irish Association District of the Institute of Journalists in regard to the provisions affecting the Press contained in Article 40 (Section 6, paragraph 1) of the Draft Constitution.

In reply I am to state that the President regrets that it is not practicable for him at this stage to receive the proposed deputation. As you are aware, the Report Stage of the Draft Constitution will be in progress in Dáil Éireann today.

[100] See document no. 213.

No. 214: NAI, DT S9880

Betty Archdale[101] to Eamon de Valera

The Six Point Group, London
14 June 1937

Dear Mr de Valera,
I hope you will excuse the Six Point Group writing to you on a primarily Irish Free State matter, but as we have had such help from you in Geneva we felt we could not let this matter pass without approaching you. We also feel that inequalities to women concern all women wherever they may be.

When the I.F.S. adopted her 1923 [sic] Constitution women felt elated at the recognition of the equality of men and women in Article 3. For many years at Geneva the I.F.S. has been an invaluable supporter of the women in their efforts to raise the status of women by international means.

You can, therefore, imagine our sense of dismay at the clauses in the draft constitution, particularly clauses 40, 41.2 and 45.4.ii. These clauses are based on a fascist and slave conception of woman as being a non-adult person who is very weak and whose place is in the home. Ireland's fight for freedom would not have been so successful if Irish women had obeyed these clauses. You who have fought all your life for the freedom of your Country can surely not wish to deprive Irish women of the freedom for which they also have fought. If you would only help women to be free instead of clamping these tyrannous restrictions on them you would be doing a great service to women and to Ireland.[102]

No. 215: NAI, DT S9928

Maurice Moynihan to Walter T. Scott

Department of the President
17 June 1937

A chara,
I am desired by the President to refer to your letters of the second ultimo and third instant addressed to his Parliamentary Secretary, Mr Little,

[101] Chairman of the Six Point Group.
[102] For a draft reply, see document no. 218.

and to inform you that the terms of Subsection 3 of Section 1 of Article 44 of the Draft Constitution were settled after the most careful consideration, and that he trusts that you will realise that it would not have been feasible to specify by name all the religious denominations to which it applies. He feels that the position of all religious denominations and of individual members thereof is adequately safeguarded by the provisions of the Subsection in question as it stands, and by the general provisions of Article 44 as a whole.

Owing to the pressure of Parliamentary business, it was not possible for Mr Little to receive a deputation from your Committee as suggested in your letter of 22nd ultimo.

I have to apologise for the delay in sending you this reply.[103]

No. 216: JA, J55/64

Maurice Moynihan to Fr Edward Cahill

Dublin
25 June 1937

A Athair, a chara,
I have been directed by the President to thank you, on his behalf, for your letter of the 8th ultimo on the subject of the Draft Constitution.

With regard to the provisions of Article 40, Section 6, Sub-section 1°, in respect of blasphemy, the President was advised that 'utterance', as used in that Article, includes tendering, selling, putting into circulation and publication, and that there was no need, therefore, to make special reference in the Article to circulation.

With regard to other matters covered by your letter, I am to say that it was not considered feasible to include in the Constitution provisions on the lines which you suggested.

[103] See document nos 198, 210. Scott replied on 14 July acknowledging receipt of the letter, and conveying his thanks to de Valera 'for the expression therein of his opinion on Article 44 of the Constitution', NAI, DT S9928.

No. 217: NAI, DT S9880

Margery Corbett Ashby[104] to Eamon de Valera

International Alliance of Women for Suffrage and
Equal Citizenship, London
7 July 1937

Sir,
Having studied with great care the text of the Draft for the new Constitution of Ireland, now before your Legislature, on behalf of the International Alliance of Women for Suffrage and Equal Citizenship I venture to express the hope that in the text finally adopted there shall not appear in Articles 41 and 42 any wording which may subsequently be interpreted as permitting discriminations against the woman citizen.

In Article 41 a. (2), the phrases 'The State shall endeavour to ensure that mothers shall not be obliged by economic necessity to engage in labour' could undoubtedly in future legislation be used as a basis for limiting the free right of a married woman to earn her livelihood. It is an absolute right of every human being to decide what constitutes a necessity to engage in paid labour, and it is impossible for the State, while endeavouring to ensure a living wage for the family, to assess individual needs.

In Article 45, as amended in the Dáil, the reference to occupations unsuited to the sex of a worker, again opens the way for legislation discriminating against women as workers on the ground of sex.

Lastly, there would seem to be a possibility that so long as these references to women differentiating them as workers from men remain in the Clauses of the Constitution, Article 16.1 (1 and 2) dealing with electoral rights for those 'not placed under disability or incapacity by this Constitution or by law' might at some future date be invoked against the free and equal participation of women in elections and as candidates for seats in the legislature.

We therefore reiterate our earnest hope that in the Constitution as finally adopted there shall not appear in measures designed to safeguard the interests of the family or the workers as a whole, any wording which may at some subsequent time permit of any discrimination against the woman citizen in the free exercise of her economic or her political rights.

[104] President of the International Alliance of Women for Suffrage and Equal Citizenship.

No. 218: NAI, DT S9880

Draft letter from Eamon de Valera to Betty Archdale

Department of the President
28 September 1937

Dear Madam,

1. I have to acknowledge the receipt of your letter of the 11th instant in which you enquire whether the President has yet had time to consider your letter of the 14 June last on the subject of the position of women under the new Constitution.
2. The view conveyed in the statement that certain clauses of the Constitution 'are based on a fascist and slave conception of women' is evidently based on a misinterpretation of the particular clauses referred to, and of the Constitution as a whole, so far as the position of women is concerned.
3. In fact, complete equality of the sexes is presumed throughout the Constitution. Women have equal civil and political rights with men. It is expressly provided (Article 9.1.3°) that no person may be excluded from Irish nationality and citizenship by reason of the sex of such person, and by Article 16.1.1° and 3° distinction of sex is prohibited in the determination of eligibility for membership of Dáil Éireann.
4. In the matter of the parliamentary franchise express provision is also made against any distinction of sex (Article 16.1.2° and 3°).
5. There is no barrier to the holding by women of any office in the State. A woman may be President, Prime Minister, Chief Justice, Attorney General, or hold any other office.
6. The Irish citizenship law may fairly be claimed to be one of the most liberal in the world in regard to women and this law is being carried over by the Constitution.
7. Where special reference is made to women, as it is in one or two places in the Constitution, such reference is made to safeguard them against being the victims of some of the defects of the existing social system. For example, it is declared in Article 41.2.2° that the State shall 'endeavour to ensure that mothers shall not be obliged by economic necessity to engage

in labour to the neglect of their duties in the home.' It is clear that the words 'obliged by economic necessity' in this declaration have a definite meaning. Your organisation will, no doubt, agree that economic necessity does force mothers against their will to leave their home duties and become the breadwinners whilst their husbands are idle and unable to work. It can scarcely be suggested that the status of women is lowered because the State sets itself to remedy this evil.

8. In Article 45.4.2°, it is set down as a directive principle of social policy that 'the State shall endeavour to ensure that the strength and health of workers, *men and women*, and the tender age of children shall not be abused and that citizens shall not be forced by economic necessity to enter avocations unsuited to their sex, age or strength'. It is assumed that your organisation does not consider it wrong that the State should endeavour to ensure this. No barrier is imposed to the voluntary choice by women of any vocation. The clear intention is that economic pressure should not be allowed to compel men, women or children to engage in injurious occupations against their will.[105]

[105] Annotated: 'Not issued'. On the following day, 29 September 1937, a letter was issued to Ms Archdale with a simple acknowledgement of the receipt of her correspondence, NAI, DT S9880. See document no. 214.

CHAPTER XII

PREPARING TO IMPLEMENT THE CONSTITUTION, MAY 1937–JUNE 1938

The Constitution was approved by 685,105 votes to 526,945 at a plebiscite held on 1 July 1937 (the same day as the general election), pursuant to the Plebiscite (Draft Constitution) Act, 1937.[1] Accordingly, by virtue of Article 62.i, the Constitution came into force 180 days after its approval by the people, namely, Wednesday, 29 December 1937. There were, in addition, over 100,000 ballot papers 'rejected as invalid as being unmarked or void for uncertainty'.[2]

But by late June consideration was being given to the new legislation which was or which might be necessary when the Constitution came into force. By July the Parliamentary Draftsman, Arthur Matheson, had identified five items of legislation which ultimately were enacted as the Interpretation Act, 1937, Presidential Elections Act, 1937, Seanad Electoral (Panel Members) Act, 1937, Seanad Electoral (University Members) Act, 1937, and the Electoral (Chairman of Dáil Éireann) Act, 1937.[3] Matheson rejected the suggestion that legislation was necessary with regard to the Council of State, as he concluded that it had 'without any legislation, full power to regulate its own procedure'.[4] Matheson also raised the question, in the context of the discussions of the Constitution

[1] See minute by Michael McDunphy, 10 July 1937 (document no. 225) and *Iris Oifigiúil*, 16 July 1937.
[2] See letter from the Returning Officer, Wilfred Browne, to Michael McDunphy on 11 August 1937 (document no. 228). It should be recalled that this was the first ever referendum held in Ireland and the high number of spoiled votes may reflect an unfamiliarity with the process on the parts of many voters.
[3] See document no. 226. There were two other consequential items of legislation enacted in late 1937: the Constitution (Consequential Provisions) Act, 1937 and the Local Government (Nomination of Presidential Candidates) Act, 1937.
[4] See letter from Matheson to Moynihan, 28 August 1937 (document no. 233).

(Consequential Provisions) Bill 1937, as to whether some of the residual powers of the Governor General might be transferred to the President of Ireland 'acting on the advice of the Government; such transfer would appear to be authorised by sections 10 and 11 of Article 13 of the Constitution'.[5] McDunphy thought that this might include judicial appointments and the making of certain statutory instruments.[6] Nevertheless, both McDunphy and Moynihan advised against any such change,[7] as the former thought it unwise at this juncture 'until we have had some practical experience of the working of the new Constitution' to do 'anything so fundamental as to confer additional powers on the President, particularly in view of the controversy which this whole subject has aroused in the Dáil and outside'.[8]

The Constitution duly came into force on 29 December 1937 and with that the Irish Free State came to its end.[9] The most immediate priority was to arrange for a signed copy of the Constitution to be enrolled with the Office of the Supreme Court in accordance with Article 63 of the Constitution, 'in view of the possibility of the institution of court proceedings involving the validity of the Constitution or portions thereof'.[10] The Constitution was duly enrolled with the Registrar of the Supreme Court on 18 February 1938.[11]

No. 219: NAI, DT S9734

Memorandum from Arthur Matheson to Patrick Lynch

Parliamentary Draftsman's Office
4 May 1937

Attorney General,
On the 24th day of March, 1937, I sent you a minute in regard to legislation to complete the machinery of the State under the new

[5] See document no. 230.
[6] That is, other than to the High Court and Supreme Court which were already provided for in Article 35.
[7] De Valera agreed with this advice: see document no. 231.
[8] This was a reference to the concerns raised by the opposition in the Dáil—foolish as they now seem to us—that the office of the President might be used as a means of creating a quasi-dictator style figure. Article 13.10 provides that additional powers may be conferred on the President by law, but Article 13.11 requires that any such powers 'shall be exercisable or performable by him save only on the advice of the Government'. In fact, the powers conferred on the President by law are strictly limited and largely ceremonial in character. Thus, for example, the President is *ex officio* President of the Irish Red Cross (s.1 of the Red Cross Act, 1944). For further instances, see Kelly, *Irish Constitution*, 223–4.
[9] For the details of the religious ceremonies to mark the day, see document nos 240–3, 245, 250.
[10] See document no. 246.
[11] See document no. 249.

Constitution, and I annexed to that minute a schedule of the legislation which appeared to me to be necessary for that purpose. The draft Constitution having now been published, it appears to me to be proper to submit an amplification of that schedule; I therefore annex to this minute a schedule containing detailed submissions in regard to the legislation mentioned in my previous minute.

I assume that the Dáil will be dissolved early in June, the general election and plebiscite will take place towards the end of June, and that the Dáil will meet about the second week in July.

The more urgent legislation is unfortunately the heaviest and most difficult; I think that it would be possible to have the legislation relating to the Seanad and the Presidential elections ready for introduction about the middle of July, provided I am enabled to start on it immediately and to give it absolute priority to everything else; the Interpretation Bill and the Adaptation of Enactments Bill could probably be ready about the same time. From my point of view it would be very much better to have only a formal meeting of the Dáil in July and to postpone all the Constitutional legislation until the autumn; by the end of September the whole of that legislation could be ready for introduction.

I would ask that you should obtain for me from the President instructions as to whether the preparation of the Constitution legislation is to be undertaken now and, if it is to be undertaken now, directions as to its priority in regard to other legislation.[12]

Schedule referred to in the foregoing minute

1. An Act to amend the Interpretation Act, 1923
   This is a matter with which this office alone is concerned and for which I will require only formal instructions; the form of the Bill is under consideration and the drafting of it will be taken in hand as soon as the present pressure of work ceases.
2. An Adaptation of Enactments Act
   This is primarily a matter for this office, and I would recommend that in the first instance only formal instructions

[12] This memo from the Parliamentary Draftsman was effectively an updated version of a memo sent by him to the Attorney General on 25 March. In the memo of 25 March, Matheson raised the issue of consequential legislation being required to give full effect to the new Constitution. Matheson's proposal was to use the interval of time between the projected passing of the Constitution by plebiscite, and the coming into operation of the Constitution, to pass some of the more necessary legislative measures required. A copy of Matheson's memorandum of 25 March was passed to each department on 30 March, with the request that departments would prepare all legislation necessary to implement the Constitution. Moynihan's covering letter stated that 'it is expected that the final draft of the Constitution will be available about the 7th proximo'. However, it appears that none of the departments responded to the first memo, necessitating this second memo from Matheson which was communicated to all departments, NAI, DT S9734.

should be given; I will then have a draft bill prepared in this Office which can be circulated to all Departments for their comments. I am not at present in any opinion as to the contents of this Bill, but I am having the subject investigated in this Office; the actual drafting will present no difficulty, but the determination of the matters to be dealt with in the Bill and the manner in which they are to be dealt with will require much careful consideration.

3 (a). An Act regulating the election of the President

This is a matter on which I shall require full instructions, and presumably the elections branch of the Department of Local Government and Public Health should have charge of it. The Bill will necessarily fall into two main parts, viz., (i) the nomination of candidates; this will be wholly new and I do not think there is any existing enactment which would be of the slightest assistance; (ii) the election; this will presumably be modelled on Part IV (Seanad Elections) of the Electoral Act, 1923, and does not appear to present any difficulty.

The bill as a whole will be rather long, but the drafting of it will be laborious rather than difficult.

3 (b). An Act providing for the President's salary, establishment, and secretariat

This will be a short and simple Bill from the drafting point of view; presumably the Department of Finance will furnish detailed instructions in due course.

4. Seanad elections legislation

This will be a long, difficult, and very laborious task and will take at least a month, and probably much more, to complete.

The legislation for the elections of the six University members will presumably follow closely the existing legislation in regard to the University members of Dáil Éireann, and therefore I will require only formal instructions in regard to it. The formation of the panels is a wholly new matter and I will require full instructions in regard to it; I will also require instructions as to the number of votes which each voter is to have and as to whether the panels are or are not to be kept separate for voting purposes.

Apart from the foregoing matters, I will be able to work out a preliminary draft without detailed instructions.

A separate bill will be necessary in regard to bye-elections; until I know how casual vacancies are going to be filled I cannot express any opinion as to the legislation which will be necessary. I presume however that a casual vacancy amongst the University members will be filled by a bye-election on the same lines as a casual vacancy amongst the University representatives in Dáil Éireann is filled at present.

5. An Act to secure the re-election of the Ceann Comhairle
   This will be a short and simple Bill presenting no difficulty and for which I will need only formal instructions.
6. An Oireachtas (Payment of Members) Act
   This is a matter on which I will have to be given full instructions; from the drafting point of view it presents no difficulty. Presumably the Department of Finance will furnish me with detailed instructions in due course.
7. A Ministers and Secretaries Act
   I think that this is primarily a matter for this Office; it is to some extent linked up with the Adaptation of Enactments bill, and I am not at present able to express any opinion in regard to it; I am however having it looked into in this Office.
8. A State Lands Act
   This is a matter for the Department of Finance, and I have no observations to make in regard to it.

No. 220: NAI, DT S9734

Maurice Moynihan to all Ministers

Department of the President
12 May 1937

A chara,

1. I enclose herewith copy of a memo, with enclosure, addressed by the Parliamentary Draftsman to the Attorney General under date of 4th instant, in regard to the preparation of legislation necessary to complete the machinery of the new Constitution.[13]
2. The proposal that these Bills should be given absolute priority in drafting appears to be reasonable, but before giving authority to that effect, the President would like to have the

[13] See document no. 219.

views of Ministers, with special reference to any measures of an urgent nature on which your Minister may require the services of the Parliamentary Draftsman.

No. 221: NAI, DT S9957

Memorandum by Michael McDunphy 'Constitution 1937: Enrolment in the Supreme Court'

Department of the President
19 June 1937

1. I have discussed with Mr Joyce of the Parliamentary Draftsman's Office, the exact manner in which the record copy of the Constitution is to be signed, as provided in Article 63 of the Constitution.
2. I think the signatures should be preceded by words somewhat as follows: 'Signed by us at Dublin this...day of...1937', this inscription being followed by the signatures and official offices of the signatories.
3. Mr Joyce will discuss the matter with the Parliamentary Draftsman on his return from holidays.
4. The question as to whether the date 1937 should not also appear on the front of the Constitution will also be considered.

No. 222: NAI, DT S9855A

Memorandum from Maurice Moynihan to Arthur Matheson

Department of the President
21 June 1937

Dear Mr Matheson,
In connection with the preparation of legislation consequential on the enactment of the Constitution, perhaps you will consider whether there should be an act to regulate, and provide proof of, the proceedings of the Council of State, particularly as regards to Article 14.4, which confers on it positive functions as distinct from the right of mere expression of opinion.[14]

[14] See document nos 229, 232.

No. 223: NAI, DT S9734

Memorandum from James O'Connor[15] to Maurice Moynihan

Department of Justice
22 June 1937

Secretary,
In reply to your communication of the 12th ultimo (and relevant enclosures) upon the subject of the arrangements to be made for the preparation of legislation consequent on the adoption of the new Constitution, I am directed by the Minister for Justice to state that, so far as his Department is concerned, the matter upon which the services of the Parliamentary Draftsman will be most urgently required is the preparation of legislation to replace Article 2A of the existing Constitution and to amend the Treasonable Offences Act, 1925. In the Minister's view the preparation of such legislation, in regard to which he will shortly be in a position to indicate his proposals, should be given a reasonable degree of priority.

No. 224: NAI, DT S9711

Memorandum from Michael McDunphy to Maurice Moynihan

Department of the President
9 July 1937

1. According to the figures in the *Irish Press* of the 7th instant, the total votes, including those spoiled, cast at the Plebiscite and at the General Election, which were held at the same time, were as follows:
   Plebiscite: 1,214,238
   General Election: 1,324,994
2. The figures should be identical inasmuch as each voter was entitled to get a ballot paper and a plebiscite paper and as every copy of both papers, whether used properly, not used at all, or misused, should have been taken into account. The figures quoted above, however, indicate a discrepancy of 110,756, the

[15] Private Secretary to P.J. Ruttledge, Minister for Justice.

figure in respect of the Plebiscite being less than that of the General Election voting to that extent.

3. It is possible that the figures are wrong, but the discrepancy is sufficiently large to justify an investigation of the facts.
4. I have drawn the attention of the Returning Officer, Mr Wilfred Browne, of the Department of Local Government, to the matter and he will examine it fully as soon as the exact figures are available.[16]

No. 225: NAI, DT S9711

Memorandum by Michael McDunphy

Department of the President
10 July 1937

Constitution: Holding of Plebiscite, 1937

1. On 14 June, 1937, the Draft Constitution of Ireland was approved by Dáil Éireann. Article 62 of the Constitution provides as follows:

   Article 62:
   This Constitution shall come into operation
   i. on the day following the expiration of a period of one hundred and eighty days after its approval by the people signified by a majority of the votes cast at a plebiscite thereon held in accordance with law, or,
   ii. on such earlier day after such approval as may be fixed by a resolution of Dáil Éireann elected at the general election the polling for which shall have taken place on the same day as the said plebiscite.
2. The law referred to in the article in question had already been enacted on the 2 June 1937 under the title of Plebiscite (Draft Constitution) Act, 1937.[17]
3. The plebiscite was duly held on the same day as the General Election, viz. 1 July, 1937, the result being that the Draft Constitution was approved by a majority of the votes of the people.

[16] See document no. 228.
[17] The Plebiscite (Draft Constitution) Act, 1937 became law on 2 June. The drafting of the bill was begun in March 1937, and received final Cabinet approval on 21 May. The bill was introduced to Dáil Éireann on 25 May. All other stages were disposed of on 1 June, when the Bill received a minor amendment to correct a mistake made by the printers on the ballot paper, NAI, DT S9710.

No. 226: NAI, DT S9734

Memorandum from Arthur Matheson to Maurice Moynihan 'Legislation consequential on the passing of the Constitution'

Parliamentary Draftsman's Office
15 July 1937

Legislation consequential on the passing of the Constitution
In pursuance of our recent telephone conversations, I send you herewith a schedule containing the long and short titles of the Bills (five in number) which will be available for introduction on or immediately after the 21st instant. The drafts of these Bills, in so far as this Office is concerned, will be ready in time to enable the Bills to be circulated to Deputies at the beginning of next September.

There is a point arising on the long titles of these Bills and other similar Bills to which the President's special attention should be called. Each of these Bills will contain a provision to the effect that it will come into law immediately after the coming into operation of the new Constitution; further, provision will be made either in the Bills themselves or in the new Interpretation Act, that each of these Bills is to be construed with reference to the new Constitution, that is to say, references to the Oireachtas will be construed as referring to the Oireachtas established by the new Constitution, references to Dáil Éireann will be construed as referring to the Dáil Éireann similarly established, and so on. It appears to me to be very desirable that the long titles of all these Bills should contain some indication of the fact that they have reference to the new Constitution; the exact words by which that indication is given are more a matter of policy than of drafting. It is for the President to decide whether he will accept the form of the words which I have inserted for that purpose in the accompanying long titles; as alternative suggestions, would the President prefer that the new Constitution should be referred to simply as 'the Constitution of Ireland'? Would he prefer the words 'for the purpose of' instead of the words 'as from the coming into operation of'?

The Bill usually referred to as the Adaptation of Enactments Bill is being considered in this Office, but I would like to postpone the final drafting and publication of it to as late a date as possible so as to give time to discover all the points which will have to be covered in it; it will however have to be passed before the new Constitution comes into operation.

Schedule
Long and short titles of Bills which will be available for introduction on 21 July, 1937.

1. Interpretation Bill, 1937
   A Bill entitled an Act to make, for the purpose of the Constitution of Ireland lately enacted by the people, divers provisions in relation to the form, operation and interpretation of Acts of the Oireachtas and of instruments made under such Acts.[18]
2. Presidential Elections Bill, 1937
   A Bill entitled an Act to regulate, for the purpose of the Constitution of Ireland lately enacted by the people, elections for the office of President of Ireland, and to provide for matters incidental to or connected with such elections.[19]
3. Seanad Electoral (Panel Members) Bill, 1937
   A Bill entitled an Act to regulate, for the purpose of the Constitution of Ireland lately enacted by the people, elections of those elected members of Seanad Éireann who are required by that Constitution to be elected from panels of candidates, to define the electorate for such elections, and to provide for matters incidental to or connected with such elections.[20]
4. Seanad Electoral (University Members) Bill, 1937
   A Bill entitled an Act to regulate, for the purpose of the Constitution of Ireland lately enacted by the people, elections (including bye-elections as well as general elections) of those elected members of Seanad Éireann who are required by that Constitution to be elected by universities, to define the franchise on which such members are to be elected, and to provide for matters incidental to or connected with such elections.[21]
5. Electoral (Chairman of Dáil Éireann) Bill, 1937
   A Bill entitled an Act to make provision, for the purpose of the Constitution of Ireland lately enacted by the people, enabling the member of Dáil Éireann who is the Chairman immediately before a dissolution of Dáil Éireann to be deemed

[18] Enacted as 'Interpretations Act', No. 38 of 1937, on 8 December 1937. See NAI, DT S9834A, DT S9834B and DT S9834C.
[19] Enacted as 'Presidential Elections Act', No. 32 of 1937, on 19 November 1937. See NAI, DT S9785.
[20] Enacted as 'Seanad Electoral (Panel Members) Act', No. 43 of 1937, on 21 December 1937. See NAI, DT S10087A and DT S10087B.
[21] Enacted as 'Seanad Electoral (University Members) Act', No. 30 of 1937, on 19 November 1937. See NAI, DT S10088.

without any actual election to be elected as a member of Dáil Éireann at the ensuing general election.[22]

No. 227: NAI, DT S9734

Memorandum from Maurice Moynihan to Arthur Matheson

Department of the President
17 July 1937

Mr Matheson,
With reference to your letter of the 15th instant and enclosure in regard to the long and short titles of the Bills which will be available for introduction on or before the 21st idem, I send you herewith a schedule of the Bills with the alterations in the long titles as agreed with you today.[23]

The Executive Council has authorised the introduction of the five Bills concerned in Dáil Éireann on Wednesday the 21st instant, and the necessary steps are being taken to give effect to their decision.

No. 228: NAI, DT S9952

Wilfred Browne[24] to Michael McDunphy

Department of Local Government and Public Health
11 August 1937

Dear Michael,

[Matter omitted]

The number of ballot papers issued at the General Election was 1,352,544. The number of ballot papers issued at the Plebiscite was 1,346,207, that is 6,357 less or about forty-four per cent.

If each presiding officer made the usual error in making out his return, this would account for the discrepancy, or if only two people at each table told the officer they did not want a Plebiscite paper, the discrepancy would be even more. In any case it is too small to have any significance. The big discrepancy between the valid votes at the General

[22] Enacted as 'Electoral (Chairman of Dáil Éireann) Act', No. 25 of 1937, on 1 November 1937.
[23] See document no. 226.
[24] Head of Elections Section, Department of Local Government and Public Health.

Election and at the Plebiscite is altogether due to the 100,426 Plebiscite Ballot papers rejected as invalid being unmarked or void for uncertainty.[25]

No. 229: NAI, DT S9855A

Memorandum from Arthur Matheson to Maurice Moynihan 'The Council of State'

Parliamentary Draftsman's Office
28 August 1937

The Council of State
In reference to your minute of 21 June, I do not think any legislation is necessary in relation to the procedure of the Council of State, and in particular I do not see any necessity for this Council to have a seal.[26]

The Council of State has, without any legislation, full power to regulate its own procedure; whatever the actual details may be. I take it that the general lines of the procedure at meetings of the Council will follow the customary practice at meetings of councils and committees, that is to say, there will be a chairman who will preside, definite decisions will be made by resolutions passed by the members present, the proceedings will be recorded by the secretary in the form of minutes in a Minute Book, and those Minutes will be signed by the chairman of the meeting to which they relate or by the chairman of the next meeting.

The procedure where the President consults the Council of State is outlined in Article 32; that Article seems to contemplate a mere formless discussion, but there is nothing in it to prevent the Council passing a resolution expressing the opinion of the Council or giving specific advice. The proceedings on any such consultation are a matter between the President and the Council and have no legal significance; from the legal point of view all that is necessary is that the President shall have 'consulted' the Council in the manner stated in Article 32.

If the Council of State should ever be called upon to exercise the power conferred by Section 4 of Article 14, I would think that the Council would act by means of resolutions passed at meetings of the Council.

If it ever became necessary to prove in Court a resolution of the Council of State, such proof should strictly be given by the secretary producing the Minute Book in Court; normally, however, a Court would

[25] See document no. 224.
[26] See document no. 222.

accept a copy of the relevant Minute verified by the affidavit of the secretary.

The only other point in relation to the procedure of the Council of State which requires comment is as to the quorum necessary to constitute a meeting of the Council. Section 4 of Article 14 expressly requires the concurrence of 'a majority of its members', which I think clearly means a majority of the total membership of the Council, and therefore no question of quorum arises. The position in regard to Article 32 is not so clear as the last sentence would appear to be open to two conflicting constructions; no difficulty arises in regard to the phrase 'convened a meeting', as that phrase obviously means that all the members must be summoned; it is in regard to the phrase 'the members present at such meeting' that the difficulty arises. I would personally think that the phrase means 'the members who actually come to the meeting, however many or few that may be', and that therefore no question of quorum arises; it is however very arguable that in the said phrase the word 'meeting' means a properly constituted meeting, on the ground that members could not be present at a meeting unless there was a properly constituted meeting for them to be present at; if that argument is accepted the question of quorum does arise. As the Constitution does not fix the quorum for meetings of the Council, the ordinary law must apply, viz., that, in the absence of a provision to the contrary, the presence of a majority (i.e. more than half) of the total membership is necessary to constitute a meeting. The difficulty cannot be met with legislation, because an enactment fixing the quorum necessary to constitute a meeting of the Council would be inconsistent with the Constitution as it would give to the word 'meeting', where it occurs in the Constitution in relation to the Council, a meaning which is different from the meaning which it would otherwise have.

No. 230: NAI, DT S9976

Memorandum from Arthur Matheson to Maurice Moynihan
'Constitution (Consequential Provisions) Bill'

Parliamentary Draftsman's Office
28 August 1937

Constitution (Consequential Provisions) Bill
There is a matter in connection with this Bill to which I would suggest that you should call the attention of the President.

The Acts of the Oireachtas passed before last December conferred a large number of powers on 'the Governor General on the advice of the Executive Council'; all those powers were, by the Executive Powers (Consequential Provisions) Act, 1937, transferred to and are now vested in the Executive Council. The Constitution (Consequential Provisions) Bill, now in the course of preparation in this Office, will contain a provision adapting all references to the Executive Council in Saorstát Éireann legislation by substituting the expression 'the Government' for the expression 'the Executive Council'; that adaptation will have the effect of transferring all the above mentioned powers to the Government.

It has occurred to me that the President might possibly prefer that the said powers, or some particular classes of them, should be transferred to and vested in the President of Ireland acting on the advice of the Government; such transfer would appear to be authorised by Sections 10 and 11 of Article 13 of the Constitution. There are also some powers conferred directly on the Executive Council by legislation passed since last December to which similar considerations would apply.[27]

No. 231: NAI, DT S9976

Memorandum from Michael McDunphy to Maurice Moynihan

Department of the President
6 September 1937

Secretary,

1. I have discussed with Mr Matheson his letter of 28th ultimo.[28]
2. The object of paragraph 3 is not to make a specific recommendation, but rather to draw attention to the fact that the Bill can, if so desired, be utilised to confer certain powers on the President by law as authorised by Article 13.10 of the Constitution.
3. The transfer to the President of former functions of the Governor General could either be general or limited to specific classes, e.g., appointments to judicial or quasi-judicial posts apart from those governed by Article 35, the making of orders corresponding to former Orders in Council, etc., particularly those having an international bearing.

[27] See document no. 231.
[28] See document no. 230.

4. As far as powers conferred by Acts of the Oireachtas are concerned, the compilation of information regarding powers of the Governor General presents no difficulty, and has in fact been effected in connection with the drafting of the Executive Powers (Consequential Provisions) Act, 1937, which became law on 8 June last.
5. The preparation, however, of an exhaustive list of functions which descended, so to speak, from Pre-treaty law and practice would, I fear, be extremely difficult.
6. Apart from the mechanics of the matter, however, I think that, as a matter of policy, it would not be desirable to make use of a consequential statute of this nature—which is really a mere clearing up measure—to do anything so fundamental as to confer additional powers on the President, particularly in view of the controversy which this whole subject has aroused in the Dáil and outside.
7. I would suggest, therefore, that it would be better to wait until we have had some practical experience of the working of the new Constitution, and of the type of powers which it would be desirable to confer on the President, and then, having got a clear picture of the situation, to deal with the matter by ad hoc legislation.[29]

No. 232: NAI, DT S9855A

Memorandum from Michael McDunphy to Maurice Moynihan

Department of the President
15 September 1937

Secretary,

1. The essence of Mr Matheson's note of 28th ultimo, attached, is, as far as the immediate aspects of the matter are concerned, contained in Paragraph 1 thereof, namely, (a) that legislation is not necessary in relation to the procedure of the Council of State, and (b) that the Council does not need a Seal.[30]

[29] Annotated by Moynihan: 'President, I agree that the Consequential Provisions Bill should not include any provisions conferring additional powers or functions on the President of Ireland. 6/9/37'. On 8 September Moynihan informed Matheson that the Constitution (Consequential Provisions) Bill should not be used to confer any additional powers or functions on the President of Ireland, NAI, DT S9776.
[30] See document no. 229.

2. I think we may be safely guided by him in respect of both.
3. With regard to the reference to the Secretary of the Council, I do not think there would be any justification for the appointment of a whole-time official for this purpose. Apart from the question of the amount of work to be done, I think it is desirable that the Secretary of the President of Ireland should also be *ex officio* the Secretary of the Council of State, in respect of such matters as that body is likely to require the services of a Secretary.

[Matter omitted]

No. 233: NAI, DT S10150

Memorandum by Michael McDunphy
'Constitution (Consequential Provisions) Bill, 1937'

Department of the President
30 September 1937

The Parliamentary Draftsman, on 28 August 1937, raised the question as to whether the Constitution (Consequential Provisions) Bill should be availed of to vest in the President of Ireland certain powers formerly exercised by the Governor General.

The President ruled that the Bill should not be utilised to confer any additional powers and functions on the President.

[Matter omitted]

No. 234: NAI, DT S9881

Michael McDunphy to all Ministers

Department of the President
11 October 1937

[Matter omitted]

The Constitution was approved by the people on 1 July 1937, and consequently, in the absence of a resolution by Dáil Éireann under Clause ii of [Article 62], the Constitution will come into operation on Wednesday, 29 December next.

No. 235: NAI, DT S9957

Memorandum from Michael McDunphy to Maurice Moynihan

Department of the President
19 October 1937

Secretary,

1. I have been examining for some time past—in consultation with the Parliamentary Draftsman, Mr Matheson, as the occasion arose—the procedure with regard to the preparation, for enrolment in the Supreme Court, of the signed copy of the Constitution provided for in Article 63 of the Constitution, and the position is now clear, subject to the President's ruling on certain details.
2. The Article in question provides that the copy shall be signed by the Taoiseach, the Chief Justice and the Chairman of Dáil Éireann.
3. Mr Matheson agrees that the signatures might be preceded by the following words: 'Signed by us at Dublin this...day of...'
4. He expressed the opinion that while this inscription could be typed on the document, the titles of the respective offices should be written by the signatories after their signatures in their own handwriting as being essential parts of the process of signature.
5. No other entry whatever should be made on the document.
6. I think that this important document, which, as will be seen from the copy attached, has been printed specially for this purpose on very good quality paper, should be bound suitably in high grade leather. Samples of binding in any desired quality, colour, finish and format can be obtained from the Stationery Office.
7. Furthermore, both the cover and the fly leaf, which will not, of course, be part of the essential document and are therefore not affected by paragraph 5, should, in my opinion, contain an inscription somewhat as follows:

Constitution of Ireland, 1937
Signed copy provided for in Article 63

8. To this major heading might be added the following informative material in smaller print:
   Approved by Dáil Éireann on 14 June 1937
   Enacted by the people 1 July 1937
   In operation as from 29 December 1937
9. The whole inscription would be in both Irish and English, in conformity with the text of the Constitution itself.
10. Actual signature cannot, of course, take place until there is a Taoiseach, but as this will automatically happen on the coming into operation of the Constitution, the preparation should be put in hand without delay.
11. Before the document is prepared in final form I think it would be as well if the Chief Justice and the Ceann Comhairle, as potential signatories, were consulted as to the suggested arrangement.
12. The text will, of course, be checked word for word with the text as approved by Dáil Éireann which is also the text approved by the people at the plebiscite on 1 July 1937. In this connection see my note of 25 August last.[31]
13. A ruling from the President would seem to be desirable in regard to the points covered by paragraphs 6, 7, 8, 9 and 11.

No. 236: NAI, DT S10332A

Memorandum by Michael McDunphy
'Michael McDunphy—Appointment as Secretary to President of Ireland'

Department of the President
5 November 1937

It was agreed that an announcement should be made through the Press that Mr Michael McDunphy, Assistant Secretary of the Department of the President of the Executive Council, had been designated for appointment as Secretary to the President of Ireland.[32]

[31] McDunphy's memo of 25 August 1937 mentioned that arrangements were being made to have the wording of the Constitution to be enrolled checked. This was accordingly done by S.B. Ó Faoilleacháin of the Stationery Office in June 1937, NAI, DT S9957.
[32] Notices of the appointment were carried in the *Irish Press*, *Irish Times* and *Irish Independent* on 6 November 1937.

No. 237: NAI, DT S9734

Memorandum by Michael McDunphy

Department of the President
14 December 1937

1. Replies have now been received from all Departments.
2. With the exception of the President's salary and Establishment Bill, the draft of which we have not yet received from Finance, it would appear that all Bills which ought to be law before the Constitution comes into operation on the 29 December have already been enacted or are in course of enactment.
3. The other measures referred to in the various Departmental communications can be passed into law in the early Spring, viz:

   (a) Remuneration of the Attorney General
   (Dept. of Finance)
   (b) Remuneration of the Chairmen of both Houses
   (Dept. of Finance)
   (c) Payment of members of the Oireachtas
   (Dept. of Finance)
   (d) Referendum
   (Dept. of Local Government)
   (e) Seanad Bye-elections
   (Dept. of Local Government)
   (f) Measure to Replace Article 2A
   (Dept. of Justice)

Constitution: Consequential Legislation

Department	Measure	Observations
Defence	Defence Forces Bill	Already introduced
Finance	Remuneration of Attorney General	Not urgent, can wait
	Remuneration of House Chairmen	Ditto
	Payment of members of Oireachtas	Ditto

Department	Measure	Observations
Lands		None
Ind. and Comm.	None	
Posts and Telegraphs		None
Local Govt.	Referendum	Can wait
	Seanad Bye Elections	Ditto
Education		None
Agriculture		None
External Affairs		None
Justice	Measure to replace Article 2A	Can wait

No. 238: NAI, DT S10428

Michael McDunphy to all Ministers and Patrick Lynch

Department of the President
16 December 1937

I am desired by the President to enquire whether, as a result of the coming into operation of the Constitution on the 29th instant, it will be necessary for (a) the Government, or (b) the Taoiseach to take any specific action on that date on any matter affecting your Department.

If so, I shall be glad if I may be favoured with immediate particulars.[33]

No. 239: NAI, DT S10428

J.J. Irwin[34] to Maurice Moynihan

Department of Defence
[?] December 1937

I am desired by the Minister for Defence to refer to Mr McDunphy's minute of the 16th instant enquiring as to whether it will be necessary for the Government or the Taoiseach to take any specific action on the

[33] Replies were received from the Departments of Lands, External Affairs, Finance, Posts and Telegraphs, Industry and Commerce, Education, Local Government and Public Health, Agriculture, and Patrick Lynch to state that no specific action would be required. See also document no. 239.

[34] Private Secretary to Frank Aiken, Minister for Defence.

29th instant in matters affecting this Department and to state that having regard to the provisions of the Defence Forces Act, 1937, the following matters will require suitable action on the 29th instant:

1. Appointments to the following offices in accordance with Section 4 of the Defence Forces Act, 1937, viz.:
   (a) the office of the Chief of Staff of the Defence Forces;
   (b) the office of the Adjutant General of the Defence Forces;
   (c) the office of the Quarter Master General of the Defence Forces;
   (d) the office of the Judge Advocate General.

   The Office of Inspector General of the Defence Forces is not filled at present.
2. The transmission from the Government by way of minute to the Minister of authority under Section 3 of the Defence Forces Act, 1937, to deal without necessary reference to the Government with certain matters relating to the command and administration of the Defence Forces which hitherto have been provided for by practice or by specific legislation.

   A separate submission in regard to these matters is being made to the Executive Council forthwith.

No. 240: NAI, DT S10428

Memorandum by Michael McDunphy 'Constitution Day, 29 December 1937'

Department of the President
20 December 1937

The following things will require to be done on Constitution Day:

1. Divine Service will be held in both Catholic and Protestant Cathedrals.
2. Ministers will return immediately thereafter to Government Buildings for the purpose of holding a meeting of the Government.
3. Before the meeting, however, the Chief Justice will take and subscribe his Declaration of Office before the Taoiseach, as required by Article 58.3 of the Constitution.

[Matter omitted]

No. 241: NAI, DT S10437

Padraig Ó Cinnéide to D.F.R. Wilson[35]

Department of the President
21 December 1937

Dear Mr Dean,
I am desired by the President to inform you that he is anxious that special Religious Services should be held on the occasion of the inauguration of the Constitution of Ireland on the 29th instant, and I am to enquire whether you could see your way to arrange for the holding of such a Service in St Patrick's Cathedral on that date. It is suggested, if convenient, that the Service should be timed to commence at 10 a.m.

As the matter is extremely urgent I am to request that you will intimate by telephone today, if possible, whether you will be in a position to co-operate in the matter.[36]

No. 242: NAI, DT S10437

Memorandum by Padraig Ó Cinnéide 'Constitution day—Religious Services'

Department of the President
22 December 1937

The following matters require attention with regard to the religious Services to be held on Constitution Day:

1. The Administrator, Pro-cathedral to be notified regarding the celebration of Mass.
2. Arrangements to be made for the hiring of a car from the Shelbourne Garage to call at St Stephen's Green Club a quarter hour before the commencement of the Protestant ceremony, for the purpose of bringing Mr D.L. Robinson, who will represent the President, to St Patrick's Cathedral.
3. The Police authorities to be notified of the number of the car in which Mr Robinson will be travelling, so that it may be given precedence over other traffic.

[35] Dean, St Patrick's Cathedral Dublin.
[36] Wilson telephoned the Department of the President on 22 December to state that 'he would be glad to arrange to have Divine Services in the Cathedral', NAI, DT S10437.

4. Stewarding arrangements at the Pro-Cathedral. Mr Christie of the Oireachtas staff is to call here this afternoon to settle the matter.
5. The Department of External Affairs are to let us know what arrangements are usually made for the hiring of cars for the use of the President and Ministers in connection with the St Patrick's Day Divine Service.
6. The Secretary, Department of External Affairs, to whom I spoke this morning on the suggestion of our own Secretary, is to consult with the President on the question of inviting representatives of foreign countries to the ceremony. He himself was inclined to take the view that they should not be asked.
7. The Department of Justice to be notified of the route of the procession in order that the necessary police arrangements may be made; the route to be settled with the Department of Defence.
8. The Department of Education to be asked to make the space in front of the Department's buildings in Marlboro Street available for the parking of cars.
9. Information bureau to be notified for the purpose of issuing a press statement.[37]

No. 243: NAI, DT S10437

Maurice Moynihan to Joshua Baker

Department of the President
23 December 1937

Dear Dr Baker,
I am desired by the President of the Executive Council to refer to the attached Notice relative to Religious Services which it is proposed to hold on Wednesday next, the 29th instant, in connection with the inauguration of the Constitution of Ireland.[38]

It occurs to the President that possibly the Jewish Congregation might also wish to solemnise the occasion in a special manner. If so, he

[37] On 22 December a letter was issued to all Ministers, the Parliamentary Secretaries, Frank Fahy, Patrick Lynch and Joseph P. Walshe, requesting them to assemble at Government Buildings at 9.20 a.m. on 29 December, in order to proceed in procession to the Votive Mass due to be celebrated at the Pro-Cathedral, NAI, DT S10437.

[38] Notice not printed.

presumes that you will take steps with a view to the making of such arrangements as may seem fit, having regard to the time available and the circumstances of the occasion.[39]

No. 244: NAI, DT S10428

Memorandum from Padraig Ó Cinnéide to Michael McDunphy

Department of the President
28 December 1937

Dear McDunphy,

[Matter omitted]

4. There are three matters with which the [Presidential] Commission will be concerned tomorrow: 1) to receive intimation of your appointment as Secretary to the President; 2) to appoint Judge [Daniel] O'Brien as Chairman of the Railway Tribunal for a period of one year as from the 29th instant; 3) to make certain Army appointments as provided in Section 4 of the Defence Forces Act, 1937.

[Matter omitted]

No. 245: NAI, DT S10437

Richard L. Cole[40] to Maurice Moynihan

Methodist Centenary Church, Dublin
30 December 1937

Dear Sir,
Your letter to the Rev. W.H. Massey of the 23rd instant reached me this afternoon. Mr Massey died last June, and the letter was delayed in his office during the Christmas season.

You may see, from this morning's *Irish Times* that on behalf of the Methodist Church in Ireland I made appropriate references last evening

[39] Identical letters, referring to the Presbyterian Church, the Methodist Church and the Society of Friends, were sent to Robert Crossett of St Andrew's Presbytery, W.H. Massey of Wesley College and Leonard Webb, respectively, on the same date. Services were arranged for the Religious Society of Friends at the Friends' Meeting House, Eustace St, Dublin, and for the Jewish Congregation at Adelaide Road Synagogue, Dublin, NAI, DT S10437. For the response of the Methodist Church, see document no. 245.
[40] Richard Lee Cole (1878–1963).

in the Centenary Methodist Church. I did so, not knowing that you had already addressed a communication to us.

Perhaps you would be so good as to note that I am the representative of our Church in this District, being Chairman of the Dublin Synod and Executive President of the Conference.

No. 246: NAI, DT S9957

Memorandum from Padraig Ó Cinnéide to Maurice Moynihan

Department of the Taoiseach
31 December 1937

Secretary,

1. As I did not feel quite satisfied with the proposed arrangements in connection with the enrolment of the signed copy of the Constitution provided for in Article 63, and as the matter is urgent in view of the possibility of the institution of Court proceedings involving the validity of the Constitution itself or portions thereof, I discussed the matter yesterday with Mr Philip O'Donoghue. He agrees with me that the signed copy should be deposited with the registrar of the Supreme Court as soon as possible.
2. As a result of our discussion I submit the following suggestions for approval.
3. The first consideration is to ensure that the signed copy enrolled in the Supreme Court is identical in every respect with the draft Constitution approved by Dáil Éireann and at the subsequent plebiscite. From the purely mechanical point of view this has already been secured by the printing by the Stationery Office, on special paper, of five copies which are certified to have been printed from the same type without alteration as the copies approved by Dáil Éireann on the 14 June, 1937, and the copies published for the purposes of the Plebiscite held on 1 July, 1937.

[Matter omitted]

10. This return [of the plebiscite results, published in *Iris Oifigiúil* on 16 July 1937] is conclusive evidence that the draft Constitution approved by Dáil Éireann was subsequently approved by the people at a plebiscite, and all that is necessary

for us now is to ensure that the signed copy of the Constitution provided for in Article 63 shall be connected directly with the draft Constitution approved by Dáil Éireann on the 14 June last

11. To secure this, it will be necessary to have a certificate from the Clerk of the Dáil on the copy in question to the effect that it is identical with the draft approved by the Dáil. Each page of the certified copy will, I think, require to be initialled by the Clerk of the Dáil. Unfortunately, a copy which has already been certified and initialled by the Clerk is described as a draft Constitution and could not, therefore, be utilised for the purpose of Article 63.

[Matter omitted]

13. It may, I daresay, also be considered necessary for each of the signatories to initial each page of the signed copy, but this is a matter which they themselves may wish to determine.
14. As the completion of all these steps may take some time, and as the matter is urgent, I suggest that, if the Taoiseach approves, a memorandum embodying the above proposals should be transmitted to the Chief Justice and to the Chairman of Dáil Éireann and that they should be asked to state whether they are satisfied with them. If they are, the necessary steps to finish off the matter then will be taken at once.

[Matter omitted].[41]

No. 247: NAI, DT S9957

Frank Fahy to Maurice Moynihan

Leinster House, Dublin
5 January 1938

A chara,
Outside the items relating to signatures and identification your memo on the Bunreacht does not call for comment from me.

[41] De Valera indicated his consent to these proposals, including that suggesting that each of the signatories initial the individual pages of the Constitution (Memo by Maurice Moynihan, 1 January 1938). Letters setting out the above procedure to be followed (though there is no mention of signatories being required to initial each page, later correspondence suggests that this was still envisaged) for enrolling the Constitution in the Supreme Court were sent to Chief Justice Timothy Sullivan and Frank Fahy. On 3 January. Sullivan indicated his consent to the procedure on 5 January, NAI, DT S9957. For Fahy's response see document no. 247.

It is true that the practice has been for the Seanascal—or recently, the Ceann Comhairle—and Cléireach na Dála to initial every page of a Bill. It seems to me that it would be sufficient to initial every leaf of the Bunreacht, but that is only a minor matter.

As to identification Cléireach na Dála would like to see the wording of whatever certificate he is to give. It is not clear to him that he has any authority to certify, as he had discharged his statutory duty when he delivered the certified *dreacht*-bhunreacht to the Ard-Comhairle. However he will certify if desired. It would not be amiss if you had a word with him. Indeed it appears to me that excessive precautions are being taken in this matter of identification—perhaps it is as well to make assurance doubly sure.

No. 248: NAI, DT S10449

Memorandum from P.S. Ó Muireadhaigh to John Leydon

Department of the Taoiseach
5 January 1938

I have to inform you that at the meeting of the Executive Council on the 21st ultimo an informal discussion took place on the question of an Annual Public holiday to commemorate the coming into operation of the Constitution. The 29 June was suggested as a suitable date subject, inter alia, to its being acceptable to your Department. I shall be glad to have the favour of your observations in the matter.[42]

No. 249: NAI, DT S9957

Memorandum from Padraig Ó Cinnéide to Maurice Moynihan

Department of the Taoiseach
6 January 1938

Secretary,
The Chief Justice approves of the procedure proposed in connection with the enrolment of the signed copy in the Office of the Registrar of the Supreme Court.

[42] Leydon replied on 2 February, stating that 29 June presented no problems to the Department of Industry and Commerce, NAI, DT S10449. See document nos 251–3.

As regards the Ceann Comhairle, he seems to be satisfied himself with what we propose, but Cléireach na Dála appears to have some scruples about the matter. The certificate which we are asking Cléireach na Dála to give does not rest on any statutory authority, but he is a necessary link in the chain of identification and is undoubtedly the proper, if not the only, person who could certify that the signed copy is identical with the draft Constitution approved by Dáil Éireann.

I would suggest that the certificate might be worded as follows:

> 'I hereby certify that this copy of the Constitution is a true and correct copy of the draft Constitution which was approved by Dáil Éireann on the 14th day of June, 1937.'

It may be a fact that we are being excessively careful in this matter but as it is most probable that sooner or later an effort will be made to upset the Constitution or at any rate portions thereof, it is better to be sure than sorry.

No. 250: NAI, DT S10437

Padraig Ó Cinneide to Michael Murphy[43]

Department of the Taoiseach
21 January 1938

A Athair, A Chara,
With reference to the Solemn Votive Mass which was celebrated in the Pro-Cathedral on 29 December last, in connection with the inauguration of the Constitution of Ireland that day, I am desired by the Taoiseach to express the hope that you will accept the accompanying offering of £25.[44]

No. 251: NAI, DT S10449

Memorandum from Maurice Moynihan to Seán Moynihan

Department of the Taoiseach
28 March 1938

I have to inform you that at a recent meeting of the Government a discussion took place on the question of fixing an annual public holiday

[43] Administrator, Pro-Cathedral, Marlborough St, Dublin.
[44] Murphy replied on 24 January, expressing his appreciation for the offering, NAI, DT S10437.

to commemorate the Constitution. The 29 June was suggested as a suitable date, subject to there being no serious objection from the point of view of the Ecclesiastical authorities, Government Departments or other important interests involved.

I am to request that you will be good enough to ascertain from Government Departments and other Institutions, such as Banks, whether there is any objection to the date indicated and that you will inform this Department of the result of your inquiries at as early a date as possible.

I am to add that the Department of Industry and Commerce have already intimated that there is no objection to the date suggested from their point of view.[45]

No. 252: NAI, DT S10449

Memorandum from Seán Moynihan to Maurice Moynihan

Department of Finance
20 April 1938

I am directed by the Minister for Finance to refer to your minute of 28th ultimo relative to the question of fixing 29 June as an annual public holiday to commemorate the Constitution, and to state that this Department has now received the replies of other Departments as to whether there are any objections to the proposed date. In general, the replies are in the negative. A few points have, however, been raised to which it is thought desirable to direct your attention.

The first of these points concerns the Registry of Deeds where it is pointed out that this Office should be kept open for business, in accordance with the Registry of Deeds Office (Ireland) Holidays Act, 1883, 'from the hour of ten in the forenoon until the hour of four in the afternoon on every day in the year, excepting Saturdays, on which days the office shall be closed at the hour of two in the afternoon; provided that the office shall be kept closed on Sundays, Good Friday, Easter Monday, Whitsun Monday, Christmas Day, and the two week days next after Christmas Day, and on days of Public Fast or Thanksgiving'. When the Bank Holiday (Ireland) Act, 1903, was enacted making St Patrick's Day a general holiday in Ireland, no special mention was made of the position of the Registry of Deeds. Accordingly, it is suggested that in any arrangements that may be made for proclaiming 29 June, or any other

[45] See document nos 248, 252–3.

date, a public holiday to commemorate the Constitution, no special provision need be made for the Office of the Registry of Deeds as that Office will conform to the usual arrangements made for Government Offices.

The second point has been made by the Department of Education which states that there is no objection from a departmental point of view to 29 June but as this is a Church Holiday it would be a holiday for the children in any event. Having regard to this fact, it is suggested that more interest would be taken by children in the commemoration of the Constitution if the proposed holiday took place on a day which is not already a school holiday.

The Office of Public Works draws attention to the following points:

(a) Under Section 7 of the Conditions of Employment Act, 1936, and under Section 30 of the Shops (Conditions of Employment) Act, 1938, 29 June can be substituted by the employer in the first case and by the Minister in the second case for certain statutory public holidays.

(b) It is presumed that the intention is that if 29 June or any other day is proclaimed a public holiday the employers would grant pay to persons who did no work on that day, as otherwise the workers generally would not appreciate any advantage in the public holiday.

The legal officers, who have been consulted in regard to the question raised at (a) expressed the view that no legal point is concerned. If 29 June, or any other day, is proclaimed a public holiday, it will be a matter for employers themselves to decide whether they will grant pay for that day or not. If, however, any Government Department has already indicated that 29 June would be substituted for any one of the public holidays mentioned in the Conditions of Employment Act, 1936, or in the Shops (Conditions of Employment) Act, 1938, the State would, it is believed, have to grant another day in lieu of 29 June with pay. As industrial employees will be concerned, the State would otherwise normally follow the practice in outside employment.

As regards to the point referred to at (b), it would be necessary, if it were the intention of the Government that employers should give workers pay for the day appointed as a public holiday to commemorate the Constitution, to pass special legislation to that effect, otherwise it would be open to employers to pay the workers or not for the day that is proclaimed a public holiday. Subject to what is stated in the preceding paragraph, the State would normally follow the practice adopted by outside employers.

It should be stated that in some observations that have been received from officials of this Department it has been pointed out that in the first six months of the year State employees enjoy a total of five public and privilege holidays in all, viz., St Patrick's Day, Good Friday, Easter Monday (plus a privilege holiday) and Whit Monday, whilst there is nothing between Whit Monday and Christmas, save the August Bank Holiday. There is thus a long stretch for the staffs that are obliged to take their leave comparatively early in the year before a rest day is secured. Another break in this long period at the end of the year might have a good effect on the health of staffs. The first Monday in July or last Monday in September have been suggested as alternatives. The Monday is suggested for the reason that it would guarantee a fairly substantial weekend rest and holiday for the entire population and would have advantages over a single day probably in the middle of a week. It must be borne in mind, however, that there is considerable advantage in having the public holiday to commemorate the Constitution coincide with a Church Holiday.

In accordance with the arrangements semi-officially agreed, institutions such as Banks have not been consulted pending a further communication from you.

No. 253: NAI, DT S10449

Memorandum from Padraig Ó Cinnéide to Maurice Moynihan

Department of the Taoiseach
22 April 1938

Secretary,

1. There are only one or two points mentioned in Finance minute of the 28th [sic 20th] instant which merit serious consideration.[46]
2. The first concerns the question of payment of workers for the proposed holiday. I do not know whether this aspect of the matter was adverted to by the Government when it was decided to proclaim 29 June as a public holiday. If the view was taken that the matter should be left to individual

[46] See document no. 252.

employers, we need not take any further action. On the other hand, if the question was not considered at all, it might be advisable to hear what the Department of Industry and Commerce have to say about the matter.[47]

3. The only other point of substance raised is that relating to the uneven spread of the existing public holidays under which there is only one bank holiday between Whit Monday and Christmas. I do not think that there is very much in this point having regard to the fact that fully 80 per cent of Civil Servants and probably as many persons in outside employment take their holidays in the period June to September every year. There is not, consequently, the same necessity for a break in the later part of the year as there is in the first half which comes immediately after the winter months when the beneficial effect of the previous year's holidays has worn off.[48]
4. As regards the suggestion to hold the holiday on a fixed day such as a Monday, I think that the proposal to have it on a day which is already observed as a holiday in rural Ireland is a greater advantage in so far as it would result in the least possible inconvenience or dislocation of business or employment.[49]
5. I have not yet approached the Church Authorities in the matter which I was leaving over until after Easter when they would probably have more time to consider it. I propose to make a move next week.[50]

[47] Annotated by Moynihan: 'We should have obs[ervations] from D. of I[ndustry] and C[ommerce]'.

[48] Annotated by Moynihan: 'I agree. Finance are not disposed to press the point'.

[49] Annotated by Moynihan: 'I agree'.

[50] Annotated by Moynihan: 'This may now be done'. A later memorandum of Ó Cinnéide's, dated 3 May 1938, noted that the Archbishop of Dublin welcomed the proposal to commemorate the Constitution with a public holiday, and was enthusiastic about the idea of it coinciding with an existing Church holiday, NAI, DT S10449. The Department of Finance were duly informed, and instructed to approach other institutions, including banks, to ascertain their viewpoints.
On 19 May, the Department of Industry and Commerce submitted a lengthy memorandum to the Department of the Taoiseach on the subject. Referring to three separate pieces of legislation (Conditions of Employment Act, 1936 (Industrial Workers), Shops (Conditions of Employment) Act, 1938 and Shops (Hours of Trading) Act, 1938), the memo outlined the difficulty raised by appointing 29 June as a public holiday, in addition to the six already allowed. At a Cabinet meeting on 24 May, it was decided that no further action should be taken with a view to fixing 29 June as an annual Public Holiday. Subsequent correspondence from institutions such as the Association of Chambers of Commerce of the Irish Free State, the Currency Commission and the Irish Banks Standing Committee intimated that a bank holiday on 29 June would be opposed by members of the commercial sector, NAI, DT S10449.

No. 254: NAI, DT S9783A

P.J. Ruttledge, Gerald Boland, James Dillon and Thomas O'Higgins to Douglas Hyde

Leinster House, Dublin
22 April 1938

A Dhuine Uasail,
On behalf of the Fianna Fáil and Fine Gael parties we cordially invite you to accept nomination to the office of President of Ireland. We should be glad if you would favourably consider this invitation and inform us of your decision as soon as you may find it convenient to do so.[51]

No. 255: NAI, PRES P159

Memorandum by Michael McDunphy 'President: Election 1938'

Office of the Secretary to the President
23 April 1938

Date of Election of Dr Douglas Hyde

1. It is now clear that there will be only one nomination for the Presidency of Ireland, namely that of Dr Douglas Hyde.
2. Section 12.1 (c) of the Presidential Elections Act, 1937 (No. 32) provides that

   'At twelve o'clock on the last day of receiving nominations...the presidential returning officer shall attend at the place appointed...and if only one person is declared to stand nominated (a) declare such person to have been elected, and (b) send to the Taoiseach and publish in *Iris Oifigúil* a certificate in the form set out in the Second Schedule to the Act.

3. The position is therefore that in the event of no other candidate being nominated, Dr Hyde will at 12 noon Wednesday 4 May be declared to be President of Ireland.

[51] The letter was sent to the Chief Clerk of the Translation Staff in Leinster House, with the request that it be translated into Connacht Irish for transmission to Hyde.

No. 256: NAI, DT S9783A

Certificate of the Result of the Presidential Election

Wilfred Browne, Presidential Returning Officer
4 May 1938

I hereby certify that Dubhghlas de hÍde of Rath Réidh, Dún Gar, Co. Ros Comáin, was the only candidate duly nominated at the abovementioned election and that I therefore declare him to have been elected President of Ireland.

Chapter XIII

First Amendment of the Constitution Act, 1939

The Munich crisis of September 1938 brought the prospect of a European war into sharp focus. While Article 28.3.3° of the Constitution provides complete constitutional immunity for legislation 'which is expressed to be for the purpose of securing the public safety and the preservation of the State in time of war or armed rebellion', the critical question was whether the phrase 'time of war' extended 'to a war in which this country is not a participant'.[1] This question was central to the whole policy of neutrality. A European war involving Britain would require the Government to have emergency powers, yet the constitutionality of such powers would depend on whether they enjoyed the cover of Article 28.3.3° and this in turn brought one back to the question of whether 'time of war' had a narrow (i.e., in the sense of a war in which Ireland was a belligerent) or a more extended meaning (i.e., a war in which Ireland was a neutral, but which clearly affected our vital interests).

On 25 October 1938, Arthur Matheson provided a detailed memorandum to the Attorney General on this topic.[2] While accepting that this issue was not clear-cut, Matheson argued convincingly that 'the great weakness' in Article 28.3.3° was the presence of the words:

> 'armed rebellion' immediately after the words 'time of war'; the phrase 'armed rebellion' seems to me necessarily to connote something happening within the State…[and these words] carry a strong suggestion that the preceding

[1] Fanning, *Department of Finance*, 309.
[2] See document no. 259.

> words 'time of war' refer only to a war in which our State is engaged as a belligerent, whether the actual fighting does or does not occur within our State.

From that point on, it appears to have been agreed that an amendment would be necessary, the only issue then being on the form such an extended definition of time of war might take. Various suggestions were contemplated. Matheson had himself tentatively suggested that it be extended to include 'neighbouring states', but acknowledged that this raised its own problems. (Was France, for example, a neighbouring state?) Nor was it clear that an extended definition of time of war would solve all problems. If, for example, the Spanish Civil War[3] was an 'armed rebellion', then the question arose as to whether it was within the scope of the amendment:

> It may be argued that nothing that could happen in Spain could lead to a national emergency here, but we must not forget that the Spanish affair did have repercussions in this country (e.g., the O'Duffy Brigade) which might have become very serious.[4]

But, by as early as November 1938, Hearne and O'Donoghue had argued in a joint memorandum that what was necessary was an amendment to Article 28.3.3° which gave the Dáil (or both Houses of the Oireachtas) the right to determine that there was a national emergency arising out of a European war in which Ireland was not engaged as a belligerent, but which was so determined by one or more of the Houses of the Oireachtas 'to threaten the vital interests of the community'.[5] The arguments for and against the various forms of amendments were considered in a conference on 11 January 1939 involving Moynihan,[6] O'Donoghue and Hearne,[7] Matheson's first draft having been submitted to the Attorney General on 22 December 1938.

Further re-working of the draft amendment took place in the opening months of 1939, but the First Amendment of the Constitution Bill 1939 (which extended the 'time of war' definition) was not published until 2 September 1939, the day before Britain and France declared war on Germany.[8] The Emergency Powers Bill 1939 was

[3] Which ended in March 1939.
[4] Padraig Ó Cinnéide to Maurice Moynihan, 7 January 1939. See document no. 294.
[5] See document no. 287.
[6] With Padraig Ó Cinnéide and Sarsfield Hogan also representing the Department of the Taoiseach.
[7] See document no. 269.
[8] The German invasion of Poland had begun on the previous day, Friday, 1 September 1939.

published at the same time. As the Taoiseach made clear, it was envisaged that the Oireachtas would pass all stages of the First Amendment Bill and that this would be signed immediately by the President. Following that, both Houses would pass resolutions in the terms of (by then amended) Article 28.3.3°, declaring a state of emergency. The passage of the Emergency Powers Bill would then complete this sequence of events. The actual method whereby the First Amendment Bill passed both Houses is, however, of some interest.

On 2 September 1939 the Dáil sat at 3 pm and the First Amendment Bill had passed all stages at 4.05 pm.[9] The Taoiseach explained the rationale for the constitutional amendment:

> When we were considering the powers that it would be necessary to secure for the Government in an emergency such as has arisen, some doubt was expressed by legal officers as to whether 'time of war' might not be narrowly interpreted by courts to mean a time in which the State was actually a participant, a belligerent. That narrow interpretation I do not think had occurred to any body when the Constitution was being considered in the Dáil. I do not know what view a court might take on the matter, but I think you will all agree that in circumstances like the present, in which you would have several nations all around you engaged in war, creating conditions of a type here which are altogether abnormal and which could not exist except in a time of such a general war, an amendment of the Constitution, so that that particular meaning will be applicable to it, is in accord with the general idea of the Article of the Constitution.
>
> We are, therefore, extending 'time of war' or, if not extending it, we are making it clear that 'time of war' should mean a crisis such as the present, provided, when there are hostilities and conflict about us, there is a resolution both by the Dáil and the Seanad indicating that such an emergency exists, that such a condition exists. You will, therefore, observe that in that particular measure we are simply resolving a doubt, or, if it is not resolving a doubt—if somebody were to hold that legally there is no doubt; that a time of war can only mean a time at which the State is an active participant—we are, under that

[9] 77 *Dáil Debates*, Cols 1–19 (2 September 1939).

> assumption, extending the meaning to be that which, I think, everybody would reasonably expect it to cover when we were passing the Constitution.[10]

At the close of the debate, the following exchange took place:

> **Patrick McGilligan (Fine Gael):** This Bill, presumably, now goes to the Seanad and is then going to be presented to the President for signature. Is there not an Article of the Constitution which deals with a time limit?
> **Eamon de Valera (Fianna Fáil):** A resolution will have to be passed in the Seanad to meet that.
> **Patrick McGilligan (Fine Gael):** That a shorter time is necessary?
> **Eamon de Valera (Fianna Fáil):** Yes.[11]

The First Amendment Bill then went immediately to the Seanad where it passed all stages by 5.55pm. The Bill appears to have been signed immediately by the President within a matter of minutes. The Dáil then resumed, declared a state of emergency and then went on to pass the Emergency Powers Bill 1939. The Seanad equally declared a state of emergency and passed the Emergency Powers Bill. At the close of that debate early on Sunday morning, 3 September, the Seanad passed an early signature motion pursuant to Article 25.2.2°.[12] That Bill was duly signed by the President later that day.

As the First Amendment Bill debate concluded in the Seanad, the following exchange took place:

> **D. FitzGerald (Fine Gael):** Surely we must pass a resolution that the President is to sign this Bill in less than five days.
> **Eamon de Valera (Fianna Fáil):** I think I did not reply correctly in the Dáil to a question of that sort. We will have to do that with regard to the other Bill, but not in regard to this one which will be signed forthwith.[13]

The question of the actual method of amendment during the transitional period had, indeed, been a matter on which the Taoiseach had sought the advice of the Attorney General.[14] During the transitional period, there

[10] 77 *Dáil Debates*, Col. 5 (2 September 1939).
[11] 77 *Dáil Debates*, Col. 19 (2 September 1939).
[12] 23 *Seanad Debates*, Col. 1092 (2 September 1939).
[13] 23 *Seanad Debates*, Col. 1043 (2 September 1939).
[14] See memorandum from Maurice Moynihan to the Attorney General of 25 March 1939 (document no. 273). The Attorney General subsequently advised de Valera that he could see no objection to immediate signature: see Moynihan memorandum to Patrick Lynch, 25 August 1939 (document no. 277).

were, in fact, two methods of amending the Constitution. One involved Article 46, i.e., passage of the Bill through both Houses followed by a referendum. The other involved Article 51 (one of the transitional articles) which provided:

> 1. Notwithstanding anything contained in Article 46 hereof, any of the provisions of this Constitution, except the provisions of the said Article 46 and this Article[15] may, subject as hereinafter provided, be amended by the Oireachtas, whether by way of variation, addition or repeal, within a period of three years after the date on which the first President shall have entered upon his office.[16]
> 2. A proposal for the amendment of this Constitution under this Article shall not be enacted into law, if, prior to such enactment, the President, after consultation with the Council of State, shall have signified in a message under his hand and seal addressed to the Chairman of each of the Houses of the Oireachtas that the proposal is in his opinion a proposal to effect an amendment of such a character and importance that the will of the people ought to be ascertained by Referendum before its enactment into law.

O'Donoghue and Hearne replied to Moynihan's queries on 31 March 1939.[17] While recognising the difficulties of interpretation presented by the fact that two separate methods of amendment were open, they concluded that, during the transitional period, 'Article 46 must be read as subject to the qualifications of Article 51 and, as a consequence, that every amendment should and, indeed, would in practice be proceeded with under the latter Article'.

This issue was also relevant to the question of whether the President was entitled to sign the Bill immediately, even in the absence of the early signature motion from the Seanad.[18] Article 25.1 provides that every Bill 'other than a Bill expressed to be a Bill containing a proposal for the

[15] This thus avoided the drafting omission that had allowed the eight year transitional period of Article 50 of the Irish Free State Constitution to be extended itself by ordinary legislation: see Chapter I.

[16] The first President (Dr Douglas Hyde) entered office on 25 June 1938, so that the transitory period ended on 25 June 1941.

[17] See document no. 274.

[18] Article 25.2.2° provides:

> At the request of the Government, with the prior concurrence of Seanad Éireann, the President may sign any Bill the subject of such request on a date which is earlier than the fifth day after such date as aforesaid.

amendment of this Constitution' shall be presented by the Taoiseach to the President for the latter's signature. Article 25.2.1° then provides that:

> Save as otherwise provided by this Constitution, every Bill so presented to the President for his signature and for promulgation by him as a law shall be signed by the President not earlier than the fifth and not later than the seventh day after the date on which the Bill shall have been presented to him.

But if O'Donoghue and Hearne were correct, then it equally followed that an amendment Bill which followed the Article 51 route was subject to the requirements of Article 25:

> Plainly, therefore, the provisions of Article 25, so far as they make any special provisions for Bills to amend the Constitution, apply to Bills passing *both* Houses after 25 June 1941; this, indeed, is plain from the wording of Article 25.1 which speaks of 'a Bill containing a proposal for the amendment of this Constitution', a form of words appropriate to a Bill which is to be submitted to referendum, but not appropriate to a Bill passed by two Houses during the transitional period when no referendum was necessary. The ratio of Article 25.1, in excluding from the fifth to seventh days signature rule to a Bill to amend the Constitution, is patently related to the post-1941 necessity to submit such Bills to referendum.[19]

If this analysis is correct, then Senator FitzGerald was right—and the Taoiseach wrong—to say that an early signature motion was required from the Seanad before the President could sign the First Amendment Bill in advance of the fifth day.

These very issues—pertaining to the validity of the First Amendment of the Constitution Act, 1939—came before the High Court and the Supreme Court in the summer of 1940 in *Re McGrath and Harte.*[20] Here the two prisoners had been convicted of the murder of two detectives and sentenced to death by a military tribunal constituted by orders made under the Emergency Powers Act, 1939. Of course, the validity of that Act rested on the assumption that the First Amendment Act had been

[19] Kelly, *Irish Constitution*, 443–5; Davis, *History and Development of the Special Criminal Court*, 86–7.

[20] [1941] IR 38. A further objection to the validity of the First Amendment of the Constitution Act, 1939 would have been that the amendment was enacted in English only, but this point was not raised in *McGrath and Harte*. That omission was not rectified until the Irish text to Article 28.3.3° was supplied by the Second Amendment of the Constitution Act, 1941: see Kelly, *Irish Constitution*, 396–7.

validly enacted. Both Gavan Duffy (in the High Court) and the Supreme Court tersely dismissed these arguments, saying (without elaborate explanation) that Article 25.2.1° did not apply to this constitutional amendment. The Supreme Court gave its decision on 4 September 1940[21] and it is hard to avoid the conclusion that, after the events of *The State* (*Burke*) *v. Lennon* the previous December,[22] a degree of legal realism had set in and that the courts were no longer in the mood (if, indeed, the special case of Gavan Duffy apart, they ever had been) for judicial activism in cases of this kind so long as the very survival of the country was at stake.

No. 257: NAI, DT S10834B

Memorandum from Philip O'Donoghue to Maurice Moynihan

Office of the Attorney General
30 September 1938

Mr Moynihan,
The following observations have occurred to me after a perusal of the further draft of the Defence of the State (Emergency Powers) Bill, 1938, which was sent to you yesterday direct from the Draftsman.[23]

[Matter omitted].

It is considered a safer course to have Part II of the Bill drafted on the lines that the arrangements for setting up the special courts can be operated by the Government whenever they are not satisfied that the ordinary courts are adequate to secure the effective administration of justice and the preservation of the public peace and order, and that it

[21] McGrath and Harte had been arrested on 16 August 1940 following a shoot-out in which two detectives had been murdered. They were brought before the Military Court the following day. They were found guilty on 20 August 1940 and sentenced to death. They applied to Justice Gavan Duffy at his residence on 23 August for a *habeas corpus* inquiry under Article 40 of the Constitution. Gavan Duffy granted leave for the holding of such an inquiry , but indicated that the prospects at full hearing were remote, [1941] IR 68, 70–71. At the full hearing on 26 August, Gavan Duffy refused the application and the applicants' appeal was dismissed by the Supreme Court on 4 September 1940 without counsel for the State having even been called upon to address the Court. The applicants were subsequently executed by firing squad on 6 September 1940: see Coogan, *The IRA* (London, 1995), 148.
[22] For which see Chapter XIV of this volume.
[23] Authority was given by the Government on 20 September 1938 for the drafting of this Bill. Originally entitled 'Defence of the State (Emergency Powers) Bill, 1938', the first draft was submitted by Arthur Matheson on 24 September 1938, NAI, DT S10834A. According to Sarsfield Hogan: 'The Bill was drafted on the assumption that Article 28.3.3° will be amended. If the Bill had to be introduced while that Article remains in its present form the Law Department have stated that it would be advisable to delete [certain] subsections', NAI, DT S10834C.

would be open to the Government at any time to terminate by a simple order the continued functioning of such special courts. The draft sent you, however, proceeds on the basis that the operation of the Special Criminal Court is to be an integral part of the Emergency Legislation and would really derive its validity from Article 28.3 of the Constitution. While this would have the advantage of relying solely on one Article in the Constitution it would also have the obvious drawbacks of such a course. Article 38.3 recognises as normal constitutional organisation the establishment of Special Criminal Courts in certain contingencies and, in my opinion, it would be most advisable to utilise the formula contained in Article 38.3 as a preface for the establishment of the Special Courts without any express mention of that Article.

[Matter omitted].

No. 258: NAI, DT S11039

Memorandum from Maurice Moynihan to Patrick Lynch

Department of the Taoiseach
20 October 1938

Attorney General,
In connection with the drafting of the Defence of the State (Emergency Powers) Bill, a doubt arose as to how far the drastic powers proposed to be taken by that measure should be regarded as covered by the terms of the Constitution. Reliance was placed on Article 28.3.3° and the Preamble of the Bill was drafted so as to indicate that any abrogation of the constitutional rights of citizens were justified by the necessity of securing the public safety and the preservation of the State in time of war. For that purpose it was necessary to assume that the phrase 'in time of war' included not only a war in which this State was a participant but also circumstances in which the vital interests and security of this country were threatened by an outbreak of war between other European Powers, including Great Britain. An Taoiseach desires that the question should now be examined further and that a suggestion should be made as to the most appropriate manner in which Article 28.3.3° of the Constitution could be amended for the purpose of removing any doubt that, notwithstanding the Constitution, the widest possible powers could be taken in the public interest during a war in which this country was not

a belligerent but in which the nearness and character of the conflict necessitated emergency measures. I am to request you to be good enough to give the matter your early consideration and to furnish your views to An Taoiseach.

No. 259: NAI, DT S11039

Memorandum from Arthur Matheson to Patrick Lynch 'Defence of the State (Emergency Powers) Bill'

Parliamentary Draftsman's Office
25 October 1938

Defence of the State (Emergency Powers) Bill
Mr O'Donoghue has discussed with me the Minute of 20th instant from Mr Moynihan to you in relation to the meaning of the phrase 'time of war' in Article 28.3.3° of the Constitution; I have also seen your opinion thereon dated 21st instant. Having considered the matter to the best of my ability, I am moved to submit to you the following comments as representing my personal views on the subject.

The Constitution is intentionally drafted in general terms and in language readily comprehensible by persons who are not lawyers, and there is throughout a definite avoidance of the precision of parliamentary drafting. That course has the advantage of importing into the working of the Constitution a certain flexibility and a freedom from the hampering rigidity of parliamentary drafting; at the same time, that course carries with it some uncertainty as to the precise meaning and effect of particular clauses or phrases and a consequent uncertainty as to what can or cannot be done under particular provisions. In regard to all questions of the meaning or construction of passages in a document, a legal adviser is always hampered by the fact that any written clause does not necessarily always convey the same meaning to every person who reads it; therefore a legal adviser is very frequently in the position of being quite clear as to the meaning a clause conveys to him but quite uncertain as to whether it would convey that particular meaning to a particular other person. For that reason it often happens that the only opinion a legal adviser can give is—'In my opinion the clause means ABC, but any judge might quite reasonably take the view that it means XYZ'.

The foregoing observations apply with special force to the phrase 'in time of war' in Article 28.3.3° of the Constitution; different persons could quite reasonably take different views as to its meaning, and the opinion of any particular person would probably be considerably influenced by the state of affairs and the general circumstances in relation to which he is asked to apply and interpret the phrase. That uncertainty has its advantages, and reasons could be advanced for its retention; if however it is decided that the disadvantages of such uncertainty are so great that the Constitution must be so amended as to secure certainty and precision in that particular clause, then it is necessary to consider by what amendment that object is to be attained. On that aspect of the matter I submit the following observations:

1. To my mind, the great weakness in clause 3.3° of Article 28 is the presence of the words 'armed rebellion' immediately after the words 'time of war'; the phrase 'armed rebellion' seems to me necessarily to connote something happening within the State; to my mind the clause cannot reasonably apply to an armed rebellion in another State unless that armed rebellion amounts to civil war; to my mind therefore the words 'armed rebellion' carry a strong suggestion that the preceding words 'time of war' refer only to a war in which our State is engaged as a belligerent, whether the actual fighting does or does not occur within our State.
2. I would respectfully submit that the insertion of a reference to a war in a neighbouring State only partially removes the uncertainty attaching to the phrase 'time of war'; the insertion of the said reference would make it clear that the phrase is not limited to a war in which we are participants, but it brings in a new uncertainty as to what is a neighbouring State (I should mention that I have been unable to find any better word than 'neighbouring'). On a strict construction, Northern Ireland is only a neighbouring territory to ours; if a wider construction is adopted, difficulties arise at once—for instance, is France a neighbouring State, and would a Franco-Italian war be a war in a neighbouring State? It might even be argued that the events at present taking place in Spain constitute an armed rebellion in a neighbouring State.
3. I would myself prefer an approach on the lines of a war which, in Mr Moynihan's words, threatens the vital interests and security of this country; the objection to such an approach is the difficulty of deciding whether a particular war does or does not threaten our vital interests and security. The present

Minute is based on the assumption that it is, from the practical point of view, impossible to leave the determination of that question to the Courts; from the constitutional point of view, it is objectionable to leave the decision to the Government, as that would in effect be giving the Executive power to suspend the Constitution. It occurs to me that the solution is to vest the power in the Legislature, and to say that 'time of war' means when there is a war which is declared by the Oireachtas to threaten our vital interests.

4. I would strongly recommend that the proposed amendment of Article 28.3.3° should take the form of deleting the words 'or armed rebellion' in paragraph 3°, and adding a paragraph defining in detail what is meant by war; I would suggest that the added paragraph should read somewhat as follows:

    '4° For the purposes of this section of this Article, a time of war shall be deemed to exist during the occurrence of any of the following events: (1) an armed rebellion against the organs of government established by this Constitution; (ii) a war in which Ireland is involved as a belligerent (whether alone or with an ally or allies) against another State or other States; (iii) a war between other States in which Ireland is not involved as a belligerent but which is declared by the Oireachtas so to affect the normal administration of government and the normal life of the community within the State that it is expedient that extra-constitutional measures should be adopted for the preservation of law and order and the continuance of essential supplies and services; (iv) a civil war or armed rebellion in another State in respect of which such declaration as aforesaid is made by the Oireachtas.'

5. I would further suggest that the words 'for the purpose of securing the public safety and the preservation of the State' in the said Section 3.3° require reconsideration; those words seem to me to be applicable only to a war in which the State is a belligerent; I have difficulty in seeing how a war in which we are not involved as a belligerent would require special measures for the *preservation of the State*. I would suggest that the words quoted above should be deleted and that some such words as 'rendered expedient because of the existence of a state of war'

should be substituted; the exact words would depend largely on the precise wording of the definition of a time of war, but the underlying principle should be that:

(a) an armed rebellion in the State or a war in which we are belligerents are themselves sufficient reason for extra-constitutional legislation, and
(b) in the case of any other rebellion or war, the clause would only apply if the rebellion or war had been declared by the Oireachtas to be such as to justify extra-constitutional legislation.

No. 260: NAI, DT S11039

Memorandum by John Hearne and Philip O'Donoghue 'Article 28.3.3° of the Constitution'

16 November 1938

War in which Ireland is involved as a belligerent:

1. Article 28.3.3° of the Constitution permits the most comprehensive and drastic legislation being passed at any time provided it can be related to a time of war that is a conflict in which this country is involved as a belligerent. The Article would also, it is thought, be sufficient to cover action taken during a reasonable period before actual hostilities commence.

National emergency arising out of a war in which Ireland is not involved as a belligerent:

2. (1) Article 28.3.3° cannot be relied upon, however, with any degree of confidence to support extra-constitutional legislation, or action based on such legislation, during a national emergency arising out of a war in which Ireland is not in fact involved as a belligerent, in other words, a war in which Ireland is neutral. In this memorandum such an emergency is referred to as 'a neutrality emergency'.
(2) The draft Emergency Powers Bill has been examined with a view to ascertaining how far in its present terms it would contravene the Constitution if not protected by Article 28.3.3°, in other words, if Article 28.3.3° does not apply to legislation expressed to be passed for the purpose of a

neutrality emergency. It could, of course, be expressed to have for its object the preservation of public order and thus be brought within the scope of Article 40.6 in so far as the matters referred to in Article 40.6 are dealt with in the legislation. But that would not, we consider, cover the whole field.

(3) In particular we think that the general powers proposed to be taken by Subsection 1 of Section 2 of the draft Bill could not be conferred and acted upon unless Article 28.3.3° applies. It is impossible to say, before a neutrality emergency actually arises, that a general powers section in the terms of Subsection 1 of Section 2 of the draft Bill would not be necessary. We are satisfied that the safe course to take would be to amend the Constitution so as to confer on legislation expressed to be for the purpose of the protection of the State in a neutrality emergency—the same protection as Article 28.3.3° now confers on the legislation therein referred to.

(4) The specific powers proposed to be taken in the various paragraphs of the draft Bill (with the exception of paragraphs (f) and (n)) can in our view be taken without raising any constitutional issue. With regard to [these] paragraphs the observations contained at (3) above apply.

(5) The form of Section 12 of the draft Bill might perhaps be reconsidered.

Form of Amendment of the Constitution

3. The Constitution could be amended in any of the following ways:
   (a) by the insertion of a new Article in the same general terms as Article 28.3.3° supporting legislation expressed to be for the purpose of the preservation of the State in a neutrality emergency, or
   (b) by the insertion of a new subsection to that effect in Article 28 itself, or
   (c) by the insertion of appropriate additional words in Article 28.3.3°, or
   (d) by a definition in a new subsection 4° of the expression 'time of war' now contained in Article 28.3.3°.

We consider that whichever method is adopted by the Draftsman the words to describe a neutrality emergency should be some such words as the following:

> 'A national emergency arising out of a war in Europe in which Ireland is not engaged as a belligerent but which emergency is declared by Dáil Éireann (*or, alternately*, both Houses of the Oireachtas) to threaten the vital interests of the community.'

No. 261: NAI, DT S11039

Memorandum from G.P. Sarsfield Hogan to Maurice Moynihan

Department of the Taoiseach
22 November 1938

Secretary,
The Defence of the State (Emergency Powers) Bill has been redrafted in accordance with the instructions given by the Government at their meeting on 18th ultimo. While the Bill is still substantially the same as Parts I and IV of the original draft, there have been considerable verbal and drafting changes. It is possible that further amendments of detail may, on examination, be found to be necessary, but it is suggested that consideration of these should be postponed until the more important questions discussed below have been decided.

Covering the draft Bill is a memorandum by Messrs. O'Donoghue and Hearne, in which they discuss, *inter alia*, the question of the extent to which the present draft Bill is repugnant to the Constitution.[24]

Messrs. O'Donoghue and Hearne express their conviction that (1) Article 28.3.3° completely covers the draft Bill and any action taken thereunder, if it is passed during or immediately prior to a war in which this country is involved as a belligerent, and (2) that it would be unsafe to rely on Article 28.3.3° as validating the same legislation, if passed for the purpose of what they describe as a neutrality emergency.

If Article 28.3.3° cannot be relied upon, the present draft Bill is repugnant to the Constitution in the following respects:

> Section 2 (1), which confers on the Government a general power to deal with the emergency situation, as they think fit, by its nature involves the possibility of unconstitutional action by the Government.
>
> Section 2 (2) (f) in its present form is regarded as in conflict with Articles 43 and 44.

[24] See document no. 260.

> Section 2 (2) (n) is in conflict with Article 15.2.1° of the Constitution.
>
> Section 12 of the Bill, as at present drafted, is considered to involve conflict with Article 25.4.2°, and, moreover, the provisions of that section, in so far as it might be desired to apply them to offences committed against the Emergency Powers Order prior to the passage of legislation, would be repugnant to Article 15.5.

In view of the foregoing, the question arises whether it would be possible to meet a neutrality emergency by giving the Government only such powers as fall within the four walls of the existing Constitution. Undoubtedly, the Government would be considerably embarrassed if they could not take the widest powers to meet such emergency which, so far as can be foreseen, would involve dangers and difficulties just as great as those likely to be experienced 'in time of war'. The necessity for retaining Section 2 (1) in the Bill, even when related to a situation in which this country was endeavouring to maintain neutrality, can be justified by the considerations:

1. It is impossible to foresee all the detailed powers which the government might need to exercise in such an emergency, and
2. Even if it were possible to recite all such necessary powers there would be the danger that the statutory clauses might not give full effect to the Government's intentions or protect them sufficiently against attack in the Courts, and, consequently, a general overriding provision is a necessary safeguard.

From the purely administrative angle, therefore, it seems desirable that the full powers in the present draft Bill should be taken in a neutrality emergency, and that, to enable that to be done, the existing Constitution should be amended accordingly. There may be political considerations which would be directed against a proposal to amend the Constitution for such a purpose. These considerations must, however, be weighed against the dangers to which the Government might expose itself by attempting to deal with a neutrality emergency by a Bill which kept strictly within the terms of the existing Constitution.

If it is decided that the Constitution should be amended, the question that arises is when would be the most appropriate time to introduce such an amendment. Under Article 51 the Constitution can be amended by simple legislation at any time prior to 25 June 1941. Subsequent to that date any such proposal would have to be submitted to a referendum under Article 46. An amending Bill could be drafted now and held in readiness for introduction immediately on the outbreak of an emergency. If the emergency did not take place within the three-year period consideration should be given to the desirability of passing a Bill before 25 June 1941. Considerations of domestic and international policy will, no doubt, determine the view of the Government as to whether a Bill amending the Constitution for the purposes of meeting a neutrality emergency would be desirable in time of peace. It would obviously be easier to get such a Bill through the Oireachtas when the emergency had actually arisen. Another point which should be mentioned in considering this matter is the power of the President under Article 51.2 to refer an amending Bill for a referendum. The likelihood of that power being exercised would be considerably lessened if the Bill was introduced only when the emergency arose.

If it is decided that the Constitution (Amendment) Bill should be held in readiness for introduction on the outbreak of an emergency, it is most desirable that in that event there should be no delay in passing the measure into law, because Mr O'Donoghue's advice is that the Emergency Powers Bill could not be introduced until after the Constitution had been amended. Clearly, a referendum would involve delay, and this is an added factor in considering whether the Constitution should, in any event, be amended before 25 June 1941, if the emergency does not, in fact, arise before that date.

On the question of delay, another point that arises is that a Constitution (Amendment) Bill cannot be rushed through the Seanad under Article 24. Assuming a hostile or obstructive Seanad, 90 days, at least, would be required to pass such a Bill into law. In time of emergency it is, no doubt, unlikely that either the Dáil or the Seanad would endeavour to hamper the Government in the passage of the Constitution (Amendment) Bill, or the Emergency Powers Bill.

The rapid passage of both of these Bills would be of vital importance so as to legalise the Defence of the State (Emergency Powers) Order which would be promulgated immediately on the outbreak of an emergency. Any material time lag would cause embarrassment to the Government. There is particularly the danger of Court action during the period between the issue of the order and the passage of the covering legislation. To make the obvious case of the detention of aliens or suspected malcontents, against whom no statutory charge could be brought, I am advised that there would be no answer to *habeas corpus* proceedings if the detention had no other authority than the Order. A series of successful *habeas corpus* proceedings would be a blow to

Government prestige, and failure to apprehend dangerous persons on the outbreak of the emergency might have even more serious consequences. These dangers would, no doubt, be appreciated by the Dáil and Seanad and would fully justify the Government in pressing for rapid enactment of the necessary legislation.

If it is decided that the Constitution should be amended so as to provide for the passage of extraordinary legislation during a neutrality emergency, the question arises as to the form of such amendment. Messrs. O'Donoghue and Hearne have suggested four different methods of amendment. It is suggested that the methods (a) and (b), which contemplate an entirely new and independent provision in the Constitution, would be undesirable as creating the impression that the Government was attempting to undermine Constitutional safeguards. It would appear easier to justify such an amendment if it is directly related to the existing provisions in Article 28.3.3° covering Government powers in times of war or armed rebellion. The suggestions by Messrs. O'Donoghue and Hearne at (c) and (d) appear the most desirable methods of achieving the objective. The precise verbal form of the amendment is a matter for the Draftsman, but it is suggested that a new Subsection 28.3.4° might be inserted, as follows:

> 'For the purpose of the foregoing subsection of this Article and for that purpose only, the expression "time of war" shall be deemed to include a national emergency which (a) arises out of a war waged by or between European powers in which the State is not a belligerent, and (b) is declared by Dáil Éireann to threaten the vital interests of the State.'

Mr O'Donoghue strongly favours an amendment on these lines notwithstanding the objection offered to an attempt to define 'time of war' as something which is fundamentally opposed to a state of war, i.e., a state of neutrality. Such an objection is, in my view, more apparent than real, and the form of amendment indicated above would be simpler from the drafting point of view, than an attempt to graft additional words on the existing Article 28.3.3°.

I submit, accordingly, the following recommendations for approval:

1. That the full powers contemplated in the existing draft Emergency Powers Bill be taken in a neutrality emergency.
2. That for that purpose the Constitution be amended.
3. That the amendment of Article 28 of the existing Constitution should be on the lines suggested above.

4. That the Constitution (Amendment) Bill should be introduced immediately on the outbreak of the emergency or, alternatively, before the expiration of the three years' period under Article 51.
5. That the Emergency Powers (Defence of the State) Order on the lines of the present draft should be promulgated immediately the emergency occurs, and that the validating Bill should be passed into law with the greatest possible speed immediately after the enactment of the Constitution (Amendment) Act.[25]

No. 262: NAI, DT S11039

Memorandum from Maurice Moynihan to G.P. Sarsfield Hogan

Department of the Taoiseach
3 December 1938

Mr Hogan,
I have discussed with the Taoiseach. He approves of the recommendations at 1, 2 and 3 in the concluding paragraph of your minute of 22nd ultimo.[26] As to 4, he is of opinion that the necessary amendment to the Constitution should be introduced in advance of any emergency—say within the first six months of 1939. Subsequent to modifications consequent on his decision in regard to 4, he approves provisionally of the recommendations at 5.

The drafting of the amendment to Article 28 of the Constitution should proceed accordingly. The examination of the draft Bill by the Departments concerned should also proceed, with a view to the submission of the draft to the Government in due course.[27]

[25] Recommendations 1, 2, 3 and 5 are annotated with a 'yes' mark. Recommendation 4 is annotated by Moynihan: 'Introduce in the near future, in anticipation of any emergency?'.
[26] See document no. 261.
[27] The first draft of a bill to amend Article 28 of the Constitution, known as 'Amendment of the Constitution (Article 28) Act, 1939', was submitted by Arthur Matheson on 22 December 1938. See document no. 264.

No. 263: NAI, DT S11039

Memorandum from Maurice Moynihan to Patrick Lynch

Department of the Taoiseach
7 December 1938

Attorney General,
With reference to my minute of 20 October last on the subject of Article 28.3.3° of the Constitution and of the interpretation to be placed on the expression 'in time of war' in that Article,[28] I am to state that the Taoiseach is of opinion that the Constitution should be amended for the purpose of making it clear that nothing in the Constitution should be invoked to invalidate any law enacted by the Oireachtas for the purpose of securing the public safety and preservation of the State in time of national emergency arising from a war in which the State is not a belligerent.

The Taoiseach considers that the most appropriate method of amending the Constitution for the purpose indicated would be by the insertion in Article 28 of a new Subsection (28.3.4°) on the lines of the following tentative draft:

> 'For the purpose of the foregoing Subsection of this Article and for that purpose only, the expression "in time of war" shall be deemed to include a national emergency which (a) arises out of a war waged by or between European powers in which the State is not a belligerent, and (b) is declared by Dáil Éireann to threaten the vital interests of the State.'

In order that the Taoiseach may be in a position to submit this question to the Government at a very early date, I am to request you to be good enough to instruct the Parliamentary Draftsman to prepare a Bill amending the Constitution in the manner suggested above.

No. 264: NAI, DT S11039

Draft of 'Amendment of the Constitution (Article 28) Bill, 1939'

Arthur Matheson, Parliamentary Draftsman's Office
22 December 1938

Draft of bill entitled 'An Act to amend the Constitution in relation to the expression "time of war" in Section 3 of Article 28'.

[28] See document no. 258.

Be it enacted by the Oireachtas as follows:

1. Article 28 of the Constitution shall be and is hereby amended by inserting at the end of Section 3 of that Article the following additional Subsection, that is to say:

   '4° For the purpose of the next preceding subsection of this section and for no other purpose, the expression "time of war" shall be deemed to include a national emergency which (a) arises out of a war waged by or between European powers in which the State is not a belligerent, and (b) is declared by Dáil Éireann to threaten the vital interests of the State.'

2. This Act may be cited as the Amendment of the Constitution (Article 28) Act, 1939.[29]

No. 265: NAI, DT S11039

Memorandum from G.P. Sarsfield Hogan to Maurice Moynihan

Department of the Taoiseach
29 December 1938

Secretary,
We have now received from the Attorney General the draft Bill prepared by Mr Matheson to amend Article 28 of the Constitution in accordance with the instructions conveyed in your official minute of the 7th instant.[30]

Mr Matheson's covering memorandum is devoted to points arising on the Long and Short Titles of the Bill and I think that his views on these topics may be accepted. He has nothing to say in his memorandum as to the precise form of the proposed amendment of Article 28. In a recent conversation he explained to me that he regarded the instruction in your minute of the 7th instant as representing the settled views of the Taoiseach as to the form which the amendment should take and he had followed that form closely except for some necessary verbal changes. I said that, of course, we would be glad of any opinion he might like to

[29] Matheson's explanatory memorandum for this draft bill, dated 22 December, dealt exclusively with the issue of numbering acts to amend the Constitution. Matheson noted that the practice used under the 1922 Constitution of referring to amendments in numerical sequence could not be continued due to the confusion it would provoke. His suggestion was to use the short title of each amending act to express that it was a constitutional amendment, with the particular article(s) also referred to.
[30] See document nos. 263, 264.

give in regard to the amendment and he replied that he saw no objection to it and that it appeared adequately to fulfil the purpose in view. He added that he would have preferred personally a somewhat different form and no doubt he had in mind the suggestion in his own memorandum of 25 October last.[31] As you know we regarded Mr Matheson's suggestions as somewhat too verbose and complicated and the Taoiseach agreed to accept in principle the alternative form in my minute of the 2nd ultimo which was based on the suggestion made by Messrs. O'Donoghue and Hearne.[32]

What we are aiming at is some form of words which will expand 'time of war' to include what we envisage as a neutrality emergency. The form of words now set out in Section 1 of the draft Bill, i.e., the addition of a subsection to Article 28.3 gives effect to that intention, but on looking at it again I am not satisfied that it could not be improved upon. The objections that I see to the present draft are not perhaps of considerable importance but it is clear that the greatest possible care must be taken in drafting any amendment to the Constitution. For one thing I would prefer to avoid the use of lettered sub-paragraphs. I used this expedient in order to make the instruction to the Parliamentary Draftsman perfectly clear but this rather legal method of drafting may be out of harmony with the phraseology generally used throughout the Constitution.

Secondly, I feel that viewing the Constitution as a permanent document designed to meet all sorts of events and contingencies in the future, it would be wiser to avoid the reference to European powers. At the present time, no doubt, a neutrality emergency would not arise except as a result of a war in Europe in which Britain was engaged. Circumstances may change, however, and in any event it must be assumed that Dáil Éireann will not declare a national emergency to have arisen except as a result of a war which clearly involves a threat to the vital interests of this country, and it seems unnecessary to impose any geographical limitation on the exercise of this discretion.

Thirdly, I see a flaw in the present draft in as much as it does not define what is a national emergency. The intention is, no doubt, that Dáil Éireann would at one and the same time declare that a national emergency existed and that that emergency threatened the vital interests of the State. This intention could easily be achieved by a redrafting of the amendment.

I am somewhat surprised that Mr Matheson left in the somewhat redundant words 'and for no other purpose'. I had put these words in to

[31] See document no. 259.
[32] See document nos 260–1.

meet Mr Hearne's doubts as to the propriety of defining 'time of war' to mean a state of affairs in which Ireland was maintaining her neutrality but I thought that a drafting purist would have omitted them.

The following alternative draft amendment is suggested for consideration as meeting the objections mentioned above. If you think fit it might be well to discuss the matter with Mr O'Donoghue who, judging by his minute of the 22nd instant, may have something to say on the whole question:

> '4° For the purpose of the next preceding subsection in this section (and for no other purpose) the expression "time of war" shall be deemed to include a national emergency which arises out of a war in which the State is not a belligerent and threatens the vital interests of the State, provided that Dáil Éireann shall have first declared that such a national emergency exists.'

No. 266: NAI, DT S10299

Seán Moynihan to all Government Departments

Department of Finance
30 December 1938

Circular No. 34/38

Amendment of the Constitution in accordance with Article 51

I am directed by the Minister for Finance to refer to the provision in paragraph 1 of Article 51 of the Constitution which relates to amendments of the Constitution by the Oireachtas within a period of three years after the date on which the first President shall have entered upon his Office. Experience to date has shown that it will be necessary to enact a number of amendments, largely of a verbal nature, within the specified period. It will be appreciated that any measure for amending the Constitution which may be introduced should be as comprehensive as possible in order to avoid subsequent legislation of the same type. It has been decided accordingly that all Departments should keep a record of amendments which they may find from time to time, as a result of examination or experience of the Constitution, to be necessary or desirable. The record should be kept as up to date as possible and in such a form as to be available for use at short notice. It should indicate not only the nature of the suggested amendment but also the reasons therefore.[33]

No. 267: NAI, DT S11039

Memorandum from Padraig Ó Cinnéide to Maurice Moynihan

Department of the Taoiseach
7 January 1939

Secretary,
I agree generally with Mr Hogan's minute of the 29th ultimo on the draft Bill for the amendment of Article 28 of the Constitution.[34] I would, however, go even further than Mr Hogan suggests and insert an amendment of the widest possible scope to the Article.

My view as regards national emergencies, whether arising as a result of war, armed rebellion or any other cause, is that a Government must have unlimited and unrestricted powers to take whatever steps it may consider necessary to safeguard the State. No Government could function effectively during a time of emergency if it is hampered in any way either in the scope of its actions or as to the time, place or manner of carrying them out. It is virtually impossible to visualise and tabulate in advance either all the circumstances in which an emergency may arise or the steps which may have to be taken during the period of such emergency. For these reasons, authority for extra constitutional action must, if it is to be of any use at all, be as wide as possible and, accordingly, as I indicated above, I would favour an amendment of even a less restricted character than that suggested by Mr Hogan.

I am not certain that the form of amendment which he suggests would cover every type of situation which might lead to a national emergency. For example, could the state of affairs at present existing in Spain be described as a war (Italian troops are fighting Spanish and other forces there) or is it a Civil War, and, if so, is 'Civil War' covered by the amendment? The Parliamentary Draftsman (and many others) suggest that the Spanish affair might be described as an armed rebellion, in which case it is, I think, clearly outside the scope of the suggested amendment. It may be argued that nothing that could happen in Spain could lead to a national emergency here, but we must not forget that the Spanish affair did have repercussions in this country (e.g. the

[33] See Chapter XIV in this volume.
[34] See document no. 265.

O'Duffy Brigade) which might have become very serious and it is not outside the bounds of possibility that a similar and even graver state of affairs may arise again and in a country very much nearer to us geographically and economically than Spain. In 1926, during the general strike, England was on the verge of Civil War or armed rebellion. Another general strike there is not an impossibility and if it were to occur we would not be far removed from a state of national emergency in this country but we could not take any emergency measures under the proposed amendment. Again, would the word 'war' used in the proposed amendment include a conflict of the type which is now taking place between Japan and China? War has not been declared officially between these two countries and the Japanese insist on treating the matter as an 'incident'. I do not suggest that the Sino-Japanese conflict is likely to lead to an emergency here but a conflict of a similar type nearer home might do so.

I have given above a few examples which have occurred to me of circumstances in which a national emergency might arise which might not be covered by the proposed amendment. There are probably many other types of emergency which are equally outside its scope. I suggest, therefore, that serious consideration be given to the adoption of an amendment which would include every type of emergency. Such an amendment might be along the following lines:

> '4° For the purpose of the next preceding Subsection in this Section the expression "time of war" shall be deemed to include a national emergency which threatens the vital interests of the State provided that Dáil Éireann shall have first declared that such an emergency exists.'

Such an amendment would cover every class of war or rebellion. It may be that I am taking too extreme a view of the position but as an amendment of the Constitution is to be made I think that it would be most unwise for the Government to tie its hands in any way and that advantage should be taken of the opportunity now offered to provide against every possible contingency. Nowadays, international affairs are not governed by precedent and it is impossible to forecast from day to day not alone what emergency, but even what type of emergency or crisis, is likely to arise.

Another matter to which I think that attention might be given at this stage is the meaning of the phrase 'armed rebellion' in Article 28.3.3°. It seems to me that there might be considerable doubt as to what constitutes 'armed rebellion', and that a situation could arise in which a Government would legislate on the basis of the protection afforded by Article 28.3.3° to deal with what it might consider to be a state of armed rebellion within the country, whereas the Courts might hold that no such state existed. The amendment which I have suggested above would avoid any such difficulty by treating armed rebellion as a national emergency and thereby including it automatically in the scope of the expression 'time of war'.

There may be some objection from the legal point of view to giving the expression 'time of war' such a wide meaning as that which I have suggested. If this be so, perhaps a better solution would be to amend Article 28.3.3° itself by omitting the words 'of war or armed rebellion' in lines 4 and 5 and by substituting the words 'of national emergency' and providing either in the same or in a subsequent section that a time of national emergency shall not exist until Dáil Éireann has so declared. Personally I would prefer this course which appears to me to be simple and straightforward and to cover any conceivable type of emergency. Objection on the ground that it vests too much power in the Government may be answered by pointing out that nothing can be done without the prior knowledge and consent of Dáil Éireann and, secondly, that in a time of national emergency the ordinary safeguards of democratic government must be abrogated to a considerable extent if the system is to survive. It is one of the weaknesses of the democratic system that very often it cannot, by methods consistent with its own principles, protect itself in times of grave emergency.

No. 268: NAI, PRES P2

Memorandum by Michael McDunphy 'Council of State—Procedure'

Office of the Secretary to the President
10 January 1939

1. Article 32 of the Constitution provides

> 'The President shall not exercise or perform any of the powers or functions which are by this Constitution expressed to be exercisable or performable by him after consultation with the Council of State unless, and on every occasion before doing so, he shall have convened a meeting

of the Council of State and the members present at such meeting shall have been heard by him.'

2. It is clearly essential therefore that every member of the Council of State should be summoned to each meeting.
3. It is important to bear in mind that the right to be convened to a meeting of the Council of State of a person whose membership under Article 31.2.ii, is contingent on his being willing and able to act, and is not affected by his having at any time declined to act. Willingness or otherwise is a state of mind at any given moment, which has no permanent effect as regards this Constitutional provision.
4. Any such person is entitled to alter his attitude in regard to the Council of State at any time and without notice to anybody, and thereby requalify himself as a member of the Council of State.
5. It is essential therefore that the letter of summons to any meeting of the Council should be sent to every member and every potential member without exception.

No. 269: NAI, DT S11039

Minutes of interdepartmental conference held to discuss an amendment to Article 28 of the Constitution

Government Buildings, Dublin
11 January 1939

Present:	Maurice Moynihan	Dept. of the Taoiseach
	Padraig Ó Cinnéide	Dept. of the Taoiseach
	Sarsfield Hogan	Dept. of the Taoiseach
	Philip O'Donoghue	Office of the Attorney General
	John Hearne	Dept. of External Affairs

1. The Conference was convened for the purpose of considering whether and if so how far the Amendment to Article 28.3.3° of the Constitution embodied in the draft Bill prepared by the Draftsman should be widened to cover contingencies, other than those emerging from armed conflict, which might be so serious as to create what is termed a national emergency.

2. The draft amendment prepared by Mr Matheson defines 'time of war' to include a national emergency arising out of a war waged by or between European Powers in which the State is not a belligerent and is declared by Dáil Éireann to threaten the vital interests of the State. The suggestion has been made that the geographical limitation in this draft amendment should be removed so that the Dáil might be in a position to pass extra-constitutional legislation to deal with an emergency situation arising from a war anywhere, provided that the Dáil had declared that the war involved a threat to the vital interests of the State. The further suggestion was then made that if the Constitution was to be amended the opportunity should be taken to make provision for the legislature to pass extra-constitutional legislation for dealing with any form of national emergency whether that emergency arises from armed conflict within or without the State or whether it arose from some form of social or economic crisis unrelated to actual warfare
3. The views expressed at the conference indicated that if importance was to be attached to purely administrative and executive considerations and to the expediency of giving the Government the widest possible powers to deal with an emergency situation from whatever cause arising, the insertion of a provision in the Constitution on the lines of the annexed draft Article (A) should receive favourable consideration. On the other hand, if preference was to be given to the general principles on which a democratic Constitution is framed or to political expediency, the Conference felt that the Government might find difficulty in introducing an amendment of the kind suggested.
4. The arguments for and against the suggested wide form of amendment as stated at the Conference may briefly be summarised as follows:

For the Amendment:

1. *Salus populi suprema lex.* If this maxim is accepted, the Government should be in a position to ask the legislature for the widest possible powers to protect the community in time of national emergency.
2. The recent international crisis showed that by reason of the limiting expressions 'time of war' and 'armed rebellion', Article

28.3.3° could not be relied upon for the purposes of a neutrality emergency. Even if additional words or definitions are now inserted it may subsequently be found that in some future crisis the Government and the legislature are hampered in taking the necessary measures for the protection of the State, because the particular emergency does not fall strictly within the phraseology used in the Article.

3. A national emergency may arise from a cause not connected with a war or with armed rebellion inside the State. A Civil War or even a wide social upheaval in Great Britain might cause conditions of great insecurity in this country. Internal disorder not amounting to armed rebellion or some great economic disaster might create a state of affairs amounting to a national emergency which the Government of the day might find it necessary to deal with by extra-constitutional action.
4. The declaration of a state of national emergency could, under the suggested amendment, be effected only by a resolution of Dáil Éireann and it must be assumed that the majority in the Dáil would not take that drastic step without due reason such as would be manifest to the community as a whole.
5. The restricted form of amendment which deals with a situation in which Ireland is neutral while other Powers are at war cannot be introduced without provoking declarations and discussions as to our relations to Great Britain and the Commonwealth in present-day international affairs. The wider amendment, therefore, holds an advantage in that it need not be related to the requirements of an existing situation but to general considerations and to the long view as to the special powers which the Government should ask from the legislature in any time of national emergency.

Against the Amendment:

1. Power should not be given to Dáil Éireann or in effect to the majority party in Dáil Éireann to suspend the Constitution for an undefined national emergency.
2. It is difficult to give convincing illustrations of the type of national emergency for which such drastic powers would be necessary, other than those which arise from a state of war (whether Ireland is or is not a participant) or from armed rebellion.

3. Even if hypothetical examples could be cited, it is difficult to state with certainty that these hypothetical dangers could not be met by the exercise of executive powers within the framework of the present Constitution.
4. A Government introducing an amendment of the kind suggested will certainly be faced with the criticism that it is seeking to obtain these extraordinary powers, not for the reasons indicated but for the purpose of weakening the democratic basis of the Constitution and for removing the protection which the Constitution gives to all citizens to organise peaceful resistance to an unpopular or tyrannical Government.
5. It will also be urged by opponents of the amendment that if there is such a radical defect in the existing Constitution as is represented by the proposers of the amendment it should have been foreseen and provided for when the original Constitution was being drafted.
5. The Conference also considered whether, in the event of its being decided to adhere to the limited form of amendment, a change in wording in the draft prepared by Mr Matheson would be desirable. With the exception of Mr Hearne, those present agreed that it would be desirable to remove the geographical limitation as to European Powers and to leave it to Dáil Éireann to decide whether any war threatened the vital interests of the State. It was also suggested that the expression;'armed conflict' should be substituted for the word 'war' and the word 'participant' for 'belligerent' where they occur in sub-paragraph (a) of Mr Matheson's draft. War and belligerent have technical meanings in international law and the term 'armed conflict' would cover any form of war or, for instance, a Civil War or revolution by force in Great Britain. For the purpose of giving greater solemnity to the occasion and also to indicate clearly that the right of initiation rests with the Government and that no such declaration can be introduced without due cause, it is suggested that the declaration by Dáil Éireann should be preceded by a message from the President. Effect to these suggestions is given in the annexed rough draft of an alternative form of amendment—B.
6. It was suggested at the Conference that Bills amending the Constitution should be given a distinctive label or Short Title,

which would differentiate them from ordinary legislation, and that the present Bill might be described simply as 'The First Amendment of the Constitution'—later Bills being called Second Amendment, Third Amendment, and so on.

A: Suggested Amendment of the Constitution to provide for the enactment of extraordinary legislation in time of national emergency:

1. Delete existing Article 28.3.3°.
2. Insert a new subsection as follows:

> '3° Nothing in this Constitution shall be invoked to invalidate, or to nullify any act done or purporting to be done in pursuance of, any law enacted by the Oireachtas which is expressed to be for the purpose of securing the public safety and the preservation of the state in time of national emergency, provided that the President shall have signified by a Message addressed to Dáil Éireann and Dáil Éireann shall thereupon have declared by resolution, that a national emergency exists which threatens the vital interests of the State.'

B: Suggested revision of the amendment in the Draft Bill:

> '4° For the purpose of the next preceding subsection of this section the expression "time of war" shall be deemed to be a national emergency arising from an armed conflict in which the State is not a participant provided that the President shall have signified by a Message addressed to Dáil Éireann and Dáil Éireann shall thereupon have declared by resolution, that such armed conflict threatens the vital interests of the State.'

No. 270: NAI, DT S10484A

Memorandum by Padraig Ó Cinnéide 'Bills. Reference to Supreme Court'

Department of the Taoiseach
17 January 1939

1. Consideration will have to be given to the question of amending clause 2° of Section 1 of Article 26 of the Constitution, which

prescribes that reference of any Bill, to which the Article applies, to the Supreme Court shall be made not later than four days after the date on which such Bill shall have been passed or deemed to have been passed by both Houses of the Oireachtas.

2. The four day interval is much too short, having regard to the fact that one day will probably elapse in every case before the printing of a Bill can be completed, and another day to allow for transmission to the President.
3. It was obviously intended that the four days should run from the date of the presentation of the Bill by the Taoiseach to the President for signature.[35]

No. 271: NAI, DT S11039

Memorandum from Maurice Moynihan to G.P. Sarsfield Hogan and Padraig Ó Cinnéide

Department of the Taoiseach
25 January 1939

1. The discussion at yesterday's meeting of the Government in regard to the Amendment of Article 28.3.3° of the Constitution was centred mainly on the question of whether the amendment should take the wide or narrow form which has been under consideration on this file. It was agreed provisionally that the amendment should be prepared on the basis of declaring that the expression 'time of war' includes a time of armed conflict in which the State is not a participant but which threatens the vital interests of the State. It was further agreed provisionally that the resolution following the President's message should be taken in both Houses and not merely in Dáil Éireann.
2. A suggestion was made, however, that it might be possible to find a form of words which would cover emergencies additional to that referred to in the narrow amendment without going so far as was proposed in Drafts A and B attached. It was agreed that the Taoiseach would give further consideration to this point.

[35] See Chapter XIV of this volume.

3. I have had a discussion with the Taoiseach today in the course of which he decided that at this stage it is not necessary to pursue further the suggestion referred to in the preceding paragraph. Steps may therefore be taken for the preparation for the submission to the Government of a revised Bill embodying an amendment on the lines of Draft C attached subject to the change necessary to provide for the taking of the resolution in both Houses. Further special consideration should be given to the form of the Bill with a view to differentiating it as an amendment to the Constitution from an ordinary piece of legislation. The question of altering the Short Title to some such as 'The First Amendment to the Constitution' should also be considered. Mr John Hearne, Legal Adviser to the Department of External Affairs, should be consulted in regard to the terms of amendment and the form of the Bill.

Draft A:

'3° Nothing in this Constitution shall be invoked to invalidate, or to nullify any act done or purporting to be done in pursuance of any law enacted by the Oireachtas which is expressed to be for the purpose of protecting and preserving the vital interests of the State and the public welfare in time of war or armed rebellion, or during a national emergency arising from an armed conflict in which the State is not a participant, or from any other cause whatsoever; provided that this subsection of this Article shall not apply to laws enacted for the purpose of such national emergency unless the President shall have signified by a Message addressed to Dáil Éireann, and Dáil Éireann shall thereupon have declared by resolution, that a national emergency exists which involves a threat to the vital interests of the State.'

Draft B:

'4° Nothing in this Constitution shall be invoked to invalidate, or to nullify any act done or purporting to be done in pursuance of any law enacted by the Oireachtas which is expressed to be for the purpose of protecting and preserving the vital interests of the State and the public welfare during a national emergency arising from an armed conflict in which the State is not a participant or from any other cause whatsoever, provided that the President shall have signified by a Message addressed to Dáil Éireann, and Dáil

Éireann shall thereupon have declared by resolution, that a national emergency exists which involves a threat to the vital interests of the State.'

Draft C:

'4° For the purpose of the next preceding subsection of this section the expression "time of war" shall be deemed to include a national emergency arising from an armed conflict in which the State is not a participant, provided that the President shall have signified by a Message addressed to Dáil Éireann, and Dáil Éireann shall thereupon have declared by resolution, that a national emergency exists which involves a threat to the vital interests of the State.'[36]

No. 272: NAI, DT S11039

Memorandum from G.P. Sarsfield Hogan to Maurice Moynihan

Department of the Taoiseach
7 February 1939

Secretary,

1. Mr Matheson's revised draft Bill was discussed at a conference on the 3rd instant between Messrs. Matheson, Hearne, O'Donoghue and myself.
2. It was agreed that the Parliamentary Draftsman should prepare a memorandum of his views as to possible methods of procedure and form that might be adopted with regards to Bills amending the Constitution so as to take them outside the category of ordinary legislation. It would appear that without some change in Standing Orders and an amendment of the Interpretation Act, the Bill now in contemplation would have to fall into line with ordinary legislation.

[36] On 26 January, Moynihan wrote to Patrick Lynch to inform him that the decision had been made to amend the Constitution along the lines of the draft Bill submitted by Matheson on 22 December 1938, taking into account the following instructions: 'It is proposed that the expression "time of war"...should be deemed to include a national emergency arising from an *armed conflict* in which the State is not a *participant* subject to the condition that the President shall have signified by a message addressed to both Houses of the Oireachtas, and that both Houses of the Oireachtas shall thereupon have declared by resolutions that such a national emergency exists and involves a threat to the vital interests of the State'. Matheson submitted a revised draft of the amendment, titled 'First Amendment of the Constitution Bill, 1939', on 30 January 1939. The formula of words used was that of Draft C found in document no. 271, with minor verbal changes. Sarsfield Hogan remained unconvinced that the draft Bill was sufficient, proposing on 31 January to further refine the amendment by specifying that the meaning of 'time of war' was not to be *restricted* to armed conflicts in which the State was not a participant, NAI, DT S11039.

3. While the present draft Bill implements, subject to minor drafting amendments, the provisional agreement of the Government of the 24th ultimo, the Conference agreed to recommend the following points for the Government's consideration and Mr Matheson will embody these in a revised draft Bill:

   a. That the bill should bear on its face an indication that it is introduced under Article 51, i.e. within the 3 years' limit.
   b. That instead of defining the expression 'in time of war' in a new subsection, words should be added to the existing Article 28.3.3° stating that war shall be deemed to include an armed conflict in which the State is not a participant, subject to specified conditions. This amendment will, it is believed, not only achieve greater simplicity in drafting but will reinforce the point of view that the amendment is not of a drastic nature but rather for the purpose of clarifying the original provision. It will also have the advantage of leaving only one question open for discussion as a point of fact, i.e. whether there is or is not an armed conflict; the questions whether the armed conflict give rise to a national emergency of a character which involves a threat to the vital interests of the State would be determined by the Oireachtas.
   c. That the Message from the President should be deleted on the grounds that such a Message issued on the advice of the Government would, in fact, be an act of the Executive and would cut across the principle that the question of the existence of a national emergency should be determined by the legislature and not by either the Executive or the Judicial Power and also that the introduction of the President into the amendment might be a factor in influencing the President that the Bill should be the subject of a referendum. It should be added that Mr Hearne is still of opinion that the amendment should be restricted to 'an armed conflict in Europe'.
4. Mr Matheson will prepare two revised drafts one including the Message from the President and the other excluding that provision.[37]

[37] Annotated by Moynihan: 'No doubt work on the Offences Against the State Bill has prevented Mr Matheson from making further progress with the Constitution Amendment Bill. The matter might be brought forward again when the former Bill has been disposed of by Mr Matheson. 16 February 1939'. Matheson submitted the two alternative drafts on 21 March 1939, NAI, DT S11039.

No. 273: NAI, DT S11039

Memorandum from Maurice Moynihan to Patrick Lynch

Department of the Taoiseach
25 March 1939

Attorney General,
With reference to my minute of 26 January last and to previous correspondence relative to proposals for the amendment of Article 28.3.3° of the Constitution, I am directed by the Taoiseach to state that in connection with the drafting of the Bill certain questions have arisen in regard to which it is desired to have the benefit of your advice.

The annexed memorandum sets out the points on which your opinion is sought and the Taoiseach would be very grateful if you could give your early attention to this matter.

Questions for thc Attorney General

1. (a) Is the Constitution open to the construction that during the 'three year period' two separate methods of amendment exist, i.e. under Article 46 and under Article 51; or
(b) Can the Government, during that period, introduce a bill under Article 46 alone, without reference to Article 51, with the object of making it clear *ab initio* that the proposal is to be the subject of a referendum; or
(c) Must every Bill to amend the Constitution during that period be introduced under Articles 46 and 51 jointly, be in the same form, and follow the same procedure, up to the point at which the President takes action under Article 51.2, or does not take such action as the case may be;
(d) Does an affirmative answer to (c) involve the conclusion that during the three years period there can be no prior determination that an amending Bill will be submitted to the people and that this question can be decided only when the President has made up his mind under Section 51.2, i.e., after the Bill has passed both Houses of the Oireachtas?
2. Do the terms of Article 51.2 mean that a Bill 'under this Article' is dead if the President sends Messages to the Houses of the Oireachtas, having regard to the prohibitory words 'shall not be enacted; or

Is the subsection to be construed to mean that when these Messages have been sent by the President the Bill, as passed by both Houses, *must* be submitted to the people in the manner prescribed by Articles 46 and 47, thus leaving the Government no option but to withdraw the Bill and reintroduce it if they see fit under Article 46, possibly in a form more suitable for submission to referendum?

3. What provisions of the Constitution are held to govern the signing and promulgation of Bills passed by both Houses of the Oireachtas under Article 51.1 and in respect of which the President has not taken action under Article 51.2, having regard to the terms of Articles 25.1 and 46.5?
4. Having regard to Articles 46.2 and 47.4, is it the case that any proposal for the amendment of the Constitution which is to be submitted to the people is dependent on the prior enactment of a law regulating the Referendum?[38]

No. 274: NAI, DT S11039

Memorandum from Philip O'Donoghue to Patrick Lynch

Office of the Attorney General
31 March 1939

With reference to Mr Moynihan's minute of the 25th instant,[39] I have had a discussion with Mr Hearne who was present at some of the meetings which have taken place concerning amendments to the Constitution. The answers to the queries submitted should be as follows:

1. (a) The Constitution is, of course, open to the construction that two separate methods of amendment exist. At least it can be said that there is nothing in the Constitution which forbids this construction. It is, however, suggested that in practice the method prescribed by Article 51 will be adopted in every case during the first three years. Having regard to the fact that Article 51 contemplates important as well as trifling amendments it is a little difficult to see why it should be necessary to disregard Article 51 during the period of its application.

[38] A copy of this memorandum was also sent to Arthur Matheson. The memorandum had its genesis in a disagreement between Matheson and Hogan as to whether Article 46 or Article 51 had precedence during the three years' period, NAI, DT S11039.
[39] See document no. 273.

(b) See answer to (a).
(c) The form of every Bill to amend the Constitution should be the same. The procedure, it is suggested, during the first three years would be that laid down in Article 51.
(d) An affirmative answer to (c) does not necessarily involve the conclusion that during the three-year period there cannot be prior determination that an amendment will be submitted to a referendum. Again it is submitted that amendments within this period would be made in accordance with Article 51.

2. No: The Bill is not dead but would proceed in the usual course to a referendum. There appears to be nothing in the Constitution preventing a withdrawal by the Government if the President requires the amendment to be submitted to the people but the embarrassing consequences to any Government taking such a line will not fail to be appreciated. Article 51.2 speaks of a proposal for the amendment of the Constitution which must, I suggest, be taken to be equivalent to the Bill containing such a proposal. As any amendment during the first three years may be and every amendment thereafter must be submitted to a referendum, I consider that any Bill containing such a proposal should be drafted as far as possible in a form suitable for submission to a referendum.
3. Every Bill which is passed or is deemed to have been passed by both Houses of the Oireachtas requires the signature of the President for its enactment into law (Article 13.3). It must be inferred from Article 51.2 that if the President does not send his message the proposal for amendment should be enacted into law.
4. Yes, but this does not necessarily mean that any amendment cannot be enacted during the first three years in a case where the President does not require a referendum.

On the general question raised by the foregoing queries, I find myself in agreement with the views of the Parliamentary Draftsman contained in his minute to Mr Hogan of 22nd and 23rd instant.[40] While it is possible to read Articles 46 and 51 as prescribing two separate and independent methods capable of being employed at the same time, I prefer the view that during the preliminary period Article 46 must be read as subject to the qualifications of Article 51 and as a consequence that every

[40] Documents not printed.

amendment should and indeed would in practice be proceeded with under the latter Article.

In my opinion a Court would be very slow to lay undue emphasis on one particular provision on these questions arising under Articles 46 and 51 so as to frustrate the function of the clauses which confer power to amend the Constitution. The form of a petty amendment of the Constitution is in no way different from one involving a vital change and the legal effect is the same in the one case as in the other. The normal process for carrying out an amendment is to introduce the proposal in the form of a Bill, pass it through both Houses and then submit it to a referendum. This course has been modified during the first three years in that the referendum may be dispensed with if the President so signifies.

No. 275: NAI, DT S11039

Extract from Cabinet Minutes

Government Buildings, Dublin
14 April 1939

Article 28.3.3° of the Constitution Amendment
It was decided that a Draft Bill should be circulated to the Government with a view to further consideration of the question of principle as to whether the amendment of Article 28.3.3° of the Constitution should be proceeded with and consideration of the form which the Bill should take.

No. 276: NAI, DT S10108

Department of Education Circular to all Managers and Teachers of National Schools

Department of Education
[?] June 1939

An Bunreacht
It is of the greatest importance that all citizens should know, clearly understand and fulfil in practice the principles of the Constitution of their country, and it is essential, for the achievement of this aim, that the pupils of our schools should receive proper instruction in the Bunreacht and be led, through a sound knowledge of its matter and a

realisation of its spirit, to cherish the ideals of loyalty and service to the nation and to pay due honour to these ideals and to the unity of the nation, in the symbols of the National Flag and the National Anthem.

The Minister for Education has, accordingly, decided that, from 1 January 1940: 1) the study of the Bunreacht be introduced in Fifth and higher standards; 2) the National Anthem (Amhrán na bhFiann) be included as part of the programme of instruction in Music (Singing) for pupils in Third and higher standards.

The period allotted on the Time Table for Reading in the standards specified under (1) will be devoted on one day in each week to the study of the Bunreacht. Where pupils in the standards affected are doing all their work in the secular subjects through the medium of Irish, this special instruction should be in Irish: in other cases it may be in Irish and English or in Irish or English (according to the pupils' capacity to read and speak Irish) at the discretion of the Manager.

For the pupils in all the standards concerned, viz., fifth and higher standards, during the first school year which commenced on 1 July last, and for the pupils in fifth standard during the second and subsequent school years, this study will consist entirely of oral instruction by the teacher.

For the pupils of the sixth and higher standards in the second school year, and, for the pupils of the sixth standard, in the third and subsequent school years, the study will consist in the reading and discussion of the Bunreacht.

For the pupils in higher standards than sixth in the third and subsequent school years discussions and essay writing on subjects drawn from the Bunreacht will form the basis of this special instruction.

As an aid to the teacher an Explanatory Note which follows has been prepared suggesting matter for the oral instruction of the pupils and including an outline of the Bunreacht and an arrangement of its Articles for reading by the pupils. The teacher is at liberty, however, to make his own outline of the Bunreacht and the arrangement of the Articles for reading by the pupils if he so desires.

A supply of copies of the Bunreacht and of the Explanatory Note is being sent to each school for the use of the teachers in giving this instruction.

Copies of the Bunreacht will be on sale at the Government's Publications Sale Office, College Street, Dublin, at the reduced price of 1d. per copy for pupils of national schools and supplies for the pupils can be obtained from that Office by teachers.

The Minister is confident that Managers and Teachers will appreciate the necessity for giving the senior pupils of the National Schools—the citizens of tomorrow—a good grasp of the fundamental laws of their country in order that they may be prepared for the fulfilment of their national duty, and that the teachers will earnestly endeavour to give these pupils not merely a sound knowledge of the principles and provisions of the Bunreacht but to inspire them with the spirit in which it is written, the spirit of the tradition of the nation in its Christianity, its humanity, its devotion to principles, its tireless effort to live and develop, its unconquerable will.[41]

No. 277: NAI, DT S11039

Memorandum from Maurice Moynihan to Patrick Lynch

Department of the Taoiseach
25 August 1939

Attorney General,
With reference to previous correspondence relative to the proposed Bill to amend Article 28.3.3° of the Constitution, a question has arisen as to the time at which the Bill should be signed by the President, after it has been passed by both Houses of the Oireachtas. Bills amending the Constitution appear to be expressly exempted from the provisions of Article 25 of the Constitution. The present Bill to amend the Constitution will be introduced under Article 51 which contains no provision as to signing or promulgation. A Bill under Article 46 must be signed by the President forthwith (sub-paragraph 5). The Taoiseach would be glad to have your advice as to whether it would be in accordance with the Constitutional position if the Bill now proposed was immediately presented to the President after its passage by both Houses and was signed by him forthwith.[42]

[41] The Explanatory Note enclosed with this Circular ran to sixteen pages. Similar circulars were also drawn up for distribution to secondary and vocational schools. A scheme for introducing study of the Constitution into the school curriculum at all levels was first raised at an Executive Council meeting on 27 July 1937. There followed a lengthy series of correspondence between the Department of the President (later the Department of the Taoiseach), the Department of Education and the Department of Finance. Several drafts of explanatory memoranda were drawn up, with the assistance of John Hearne acquired in November 1938. Much of the delay in finalising the format of the proposed constitutional classes arose from a dispute between Education and Finance regarding the cost of the proposed classes.
Despite the finalisation of the scheme in the summer and autumn of 1939, it appears that the circulars and explanatory memoranda were never issued.

[42] Philip O'Donoghue's response noted that no objection could be seen to the Bill being immediately presented to the President for his signature: 'In my opinion...it would be in accordance with the Constitutional position if the Bill under consideration was presented to the President immediately after its passage by both Houses and thereupon signed by him', NAI, DT S11039.

Chapter XIV

Constitutional Challenges and the Second Amendment, 1939–41

Background to the Offences against the State Act, 1939

Although the Constitution had come into force on 29 December 1937, almost two years were to elapse before the first major item of litigation came before the courts. Of course, almost no sooner had the work on the Constitution been concluded than the Government's attention had turned to a resolution of the Anglo-Irish Economic War and, immediately thereafter, preparation in anticipation of the pending Second World War. The Attorney General's office had advised on the drafting of emergency legislation at the height of the Munich crisis in September 1938 and the Offences against the State Act, 1939 had become law by the end of June 1939.[1] While, of course, the 1939 Act partook of the character of emergency legislation, it was, in fact, a permanent statute which, in respect of many of its essential features, has remained virtually unchanged since its enactment.[2] While the 1939 Act has been—often justly—criticised, it was in its own way a more liberal and enlightened enactment than the earlier Article 2A of the Irish Free State Constitution and the Public Safety Acts which preceded it.[3]

[1] See Chapter XIII of this volume and Fanning, *Irish Department of Finance*, 308–9.

[2] The major changes were the Offences against the State (Amendment) Act, 1940 (which was necessitated by the High Court's decision in *The State (Burke) v. Lennon*, [1940] IR 136); Offences against the State (Amendment) Act, 1972 (which, *inter alia*, enabled the courts to treat the opinion of a Garda Superintendent that an accused was a member of an illegal organisation as evidence of that fact) and the Offences against the State (Amendment) Act, 1998 (which was enacted largely as a response to the Omagh bomb in August 1998 and which, *inter alia*, extended the powers of detention following an arrest under s.30 of the 1939 Act).

[3] Thus, for example, s.30 of the 1939 Act originally provided for a maximum of 48 hours' detention following an arrest for a scheduled offence and s.44 provided for a right of appeal to the Court of Criminal

On 2 March 1939 the Minister for Justice, Patrick Ruttledge, moved the Second Reading of the Offences against the State Bill in Dáil Éireann. His speech was restrained—almost low key[4]—but he drew attention to the fact that some months previously, in December 1938, the remaining Anti-Treaty members of the Second Dáil had purported to transfer the 'Government of the Irish Republic' to the 'Council of the Irish Republican Army'.[5] This was a threat which the legitimate Government of the State could not lightly ignore.[6] The Minister also emphasised the reluctance with which the Government had asked the Oireachtas for these powers:

> In 1932, when this Government was first elected, an amnesty was declared. In 1937, when the Constitution was passed, there was a similar position, a similar jail clearance...We have done everything possible to carry on as a Government with the least possible force and the least possible infliction of penalties on any citizen of our country. I am afraid, however, that we have reached a position that, I suggest, if allowed to develop, is bound to deteriorate until in a very short time this country would find itself in a catastrophe.[7]

On the powers of internment itself which were contained in Part VI of the Bill, the Minister did not elaborate at length:

> Part VI of this Bill provides for internment. It is intended to deal with offences against the State in connection with cases in which there is a moral certainty, although legal proof is lacking. There, again, that provision comes into operation on a proclamation by the Government when the Government are satisfied that such an emergency exists, and there, again, it goes out by proclamation and...the Dáil, by resolution, can annul this provision.[8]

[3] *contd.* Appeal against conviction in the Special Criminal Court (following the enactment of the Offences against the State (Amendment) Act, 1998, the maximum period of detention has been extended to 72 hours, but the further period of detention can only be ordered by the District Court following an application in that behalf by the Garda Síochána and having heard the legal representatives of the detainee). By contrast, s.14 of Article 2A provided for a maximum of 72 hours detention and s.6(5) of Article 2A not only provided that no appeal would lie against the decision of the Special Powers Tribunal, but also sought to exclude the jurisdiction of the High Court in respect of *certiorari* applications.

[4] Joe Lee describes Ruttledge as 'known for his IRA sympathies', Joe Lee, *Ireland 1913–1985: Politics and Society* (Cambridge, 1989), 219.

[5] See John Bowyer Bell, *The Secret Army—The IRA* (Dublin, 1998), 154.

[6] 74 *Dáil Debates*, Cols 1285–90 (2 March 1939).

[7] 74 *Dáil Debates*, Cols 1291–2 (2 March 1939).

[8] 74 *Dáil Debates*, Col. 1291 (2 March 1939). For the background to the drafting of the 1939 Act, see Lee, *Ireland, 1913–1985*, 219–24.

The Offences against the State Act was duly signed into law on 14 June 1939. Pursuant to s.19 of the 1939 Act, the IRA was immediately proclaimed to be an illegal organisation,[9] but no move was taken either to establish the Special Criminal Court or to activate the power of internment.

The challenge to the internment powers

Following the resumption of the IRA bombing campaign in Britain in January 1939, which in turn had followed its 'declaration of war' on the United Kingdom and the imminent outbreak of hostilities between Germany and the United Kingdom, the Government could no longer afford to remain inactive.[10] On 22 August 1939 the Special Criminal Court was established following a Government proclamation[11] and Part VI of the 1939 Act—which provided for the power of internment—was duly activated. It was the exercise of these powers which led directly to *The State (Burke) v. Lennon* and, subsequently, *In re Article 26 and the Offences against the State (Amendment) Bill*, the first major items of litigation involving the new Constitution. Not surprisingly, Justice Gavan Duffy's judgment in the High Court in *Burke*, whereby he held the internment provisions of Part VI of the 1939 Act to be unconstitutional, provoked a major constitutional crisis which was only remedied when the Supreme Court subsequently upheld the constitutionality of the Offences against the State (Amendment) Bill, 1940.

The State (Burke) v. Lennon

On 16 September 1939 the Minister for Justice issued a warrant pursuant to section 55(1) of the 1939 Act[12] directing the arrest and internment of James Burke. On 22 November 1939, James Burke's brother, Redmond, swore an affidavit which grounded an application for *habeas corpus*. The substantive application for *habeas corpus* was first due to be heard by a Divisional High Court[13] (Conor Maguire (President) and Justices O'Byrne

[9] Unlawful Organisation (Suppression) Order, 1939 (S.R. & O. No. 162 of 1939).

[10] Lee, *Ireland, 1913–1985*, 219–22; Coogan, *The IRA*, 124–5.

[11] *Iris Oifigiúil*, 22 August 1939. Section 54(2) of the 1939 Act provided that:

> If and whenever and so often as the Government makes and publishes a proclamation declaring that the powers conferred by this part of the Act are necessary to secure the preservation of public peace and order and that it is expedient that this Part of this Act shall come into force immediately, this Part of the Act shall come into force forthwith.

[12] This provided that:

> Whenever a Minister of State is satisfied that any particular person is engaged in activities calculated to prejudice the preservation of the peace, order or security of the State, such Minister may by warrant under his hand order the arrest and detention of such person under this section.

See Gerard Hogan, 'The Supreme Court and the Offences against the State (Amendment) Bill', in *Irish Jurist*, 35 (2000), 238; Davis, *History and Development of the Special Criminal Court*, 74–84.

[13] That is, where the High Court sits as a panel of three judges. The practice is nowadays quite rare and is reserved (in practice) for constitutional cases of great importance.

and Gavan Duffy) on Friday, 24 November 1939 when matters took a surprising turn of events. When the case was called on, Albert Wood[14] (for the applicant) said that he had to make his position clear:

> It was, he submitted, a fundamental right of the citizen bringing a *habeas corpus* application to select the judge before whom he would move his application. Having selected his judge, he wished to have that judge dispose of the application. Mr Wood cited a number of judgments of the King's Bench Division and of the High Court which, he said, laid it down that a person was entitled to proceed from judge to judge and that it was the duty of each judge to form his own independent opinion on the application. He submitted that he had never abrogated their right to have the application heard by one judge. The application for a conditional order had been made before one judge, Mr Justice Gavan Duffy, who had directed them to serve a notice of motion. They had served the notice of motion in a form which preserved that right and with the intent to protect that right he was forced with respect, to decline to make his application before the court as now constituted and he would, when Mr Justice Gavan Duffy found it convenient to hear him, make the application before him.
> Mr Justice O'Byrne—'You served a notice of motion. Is not that notice of motion returnable to the High Court?'
> Mr Wood—'In its express terms, no.'
> The President: 'I wonder if I might ask you if your attitude would be affected by my informing you that this court was constituted at the request of Mr Justice Gavan Duffy?'
> Mr Wood—'Not in the slightest. If I agreed it would be an abrogation of the constitutional right which my client has. The moment that I conceded that the Court as now constituted has jurisdiction to try my case would be to abrogate my right to the extent of at least two judges.'
> Mr Justice Gavan Duffy—'Having regard to the important issues raised, I should have thought that the larger the court the better…If an application is being made to me to hear the case sitting alone, I should feel bound to accede, but that application has not been made to me.'

[14] Wood, Robert Albert Ernest (1874–1941) KC: Known by colleagues as 'The Thunderer': see Ferguson and Osborough (eds), *King's Inns Barristers 1868–2004* (Dublin, 2005), 320.

> Mr Wood—'My position is this. The citizen for whom I appear has the right to go to each judge in turn and I am here in assertion of that right.'
> Mr Justice O'Byrne—'May I take it that you are declining to make your application before this Court?'
> Mr Wood—'May it please your lordships, that is so.'[15]

At a later stage in the afternoon it was reported that Wood appeared before Gavan Duffy in another Court. The exchange then continued:

> Mr Justice Gavan Duffy—'I take it that this is the case which was listed before the High Court this morning. What are you asking me to do now?'
> Mr Wood—'I am asking for an order of *habeas corpus* directed to the Attorney General and the Governor of Arbour Hill prison.'
> Mr Justice Gavan Duffy—'Is this an *ex parte* application?'
> Mr Wood—'Yes.'
> Mr Justice Gavan Duffy—'The effect of the order of the High Court this morning is that the notice of motion was returnable to the High Court and not specifically to me. I cannot hear a substantive application for *habeas corpus* without notice to the other side.'
> Mr Wood—'They are here pursuant to your order.'
> Mr Justice Gavan Duffy—'If they are willing to go on and if the notice of motion is before me, but otherwise I would have to give them notice, however short, before hearing it.'

After further exchanges, Gavan Duffy is reported as having turned to Kevin Dixon SC (who appeared for the Attorney General and Commandant Lennon) and asked him for his view:

> Mr Dixon (who with Mr Haugh KC had appeared for the Attorney that morning) stated that he was here as a mere spectator.
> Mr Justice Gavan Duffy—'Then Mr Wood, I would rule against you on that application. You can always make a fresh application. If you make a fresh application, I am willing to hear the case and to give you an early return date.'
> Mr Wood—'At the moment, I will not make that application. I will consider my position.'

[15] *Irish Times*, 25 November 1939.

> Subsequently Mr Seán MacBride applied to Mr Justice Gavan Duffy at his residence for liberty to issue a notice of motion to be heard on Tuesday next and for an order that the order of *habeas corpus* be directed to the AG and Commandant Lennon to produce Seamus Burke before the Court. Mr Justice Gavan Duffy granted the application.

It is worth pausing to inquire why Burke's legal team took the stance which they did: it can only be because they believed that Gavan Duffy was likely to be outvoted by both Maguire and O'Byrne, and that the best prospect of securing the release of their client was to make the application before Gavan Duffy sitting alone.[16]

The substantive *habeas corpus* application was duly heard by Gavan Duffy sitting alone as a High Court judge on 28 and 29 November. Gavan Duffy reserved judgment at the conclusion of the second day of argument and delivered his ruling two days later on Friday, 1 December 1939. Bearing in mind that this was the first major constitutional case since the new Constitution had come into force two years earlier[17] and given the time pressures against which it was delivered, the judgment must be regarded as a remarkable *tour de force*. Having set out the background to the application and to the 1939 Act itself, Gavan Duffy then proceeded to give an admirable summary of the relevant provisions of the Constitution:

> As to personal liberty, it is one of the cardinal principles of the Constitution, proclaimed in the Preamble itself, that the dignity and freedom of the individual may be assured; Articles 40–44 of the Constitution set out the 'Fundamental Rights' comprising personal rights, the imprescriptible rights of the family, the inalienable right and duty of parents to

[16] The very fact that an applicant could select a judge in this way was regarded in Government circles as an abuse. Cf. the comments of Stephen Roche to Maurice Moynihan in a memorandum dated 13 September 1940:

> It was possible in this case for an applicant to select the most suitable Judge of the High Court, from his point of view, to prevent other Judges from sitting with him, and to obtain from that Judge, sitting alone, a decision which proved to be erroneous, that an Act of the Oireachtas is void as being contrary to the Constitution, with very serious practical consequences. This should not be possible. See document no. 300.

The *habeas corpus* procedure contained in Article 40.4.2° was later amended by the Second Amendment of the Constitution Act, 1941. See generally, Kevin Costello, *The Law of Habeas Corpus in Ireland* (Dublin, 2006), 134–5.

[17] Gavan Duffy himself recognised this fact, saying:

> I must look into the material provisions of the Constitution in order to see what place personal liberty finds there, and to see exactly what place personal liberty finds there, and to see whether the impugned enactment fits into the constitutional framework, and I must do so with special care, since this is the first case in which a claim of this kind has arisen for adjudication under the Constitution, [1940] IR 136, 143.

> educate their children, the natural right to private property and freedom of conscience and religion. The fundamental personal rights, which are the personal rights of free men, include (Article 40) the right to equal protection of the law, the inviolability of the home, the rights of free speech, peaceable association and, in particular, the liberty of the person…These rights are, of course, qualified, because under modern conditions the rights of the citizen must be subject to legal limitations and absolute rights are unknown, or virtually unknown, in a democratic State. But in a significant clause of Article 40 the State guarantees in its laws to respect the personal rights of the citizen and, as far as practicable, to defend and vindicate them…The right to personal liberty means much more than mere freedom from incarceration and carries with it necessarily the right of the citizen to enjoy the other fundamental rights, the right to live his life, subject, of course, to the law; and if a man is confined against his will, he has lost his personal liberty, whether the name given to the restraint be penal servitude, imprisonment, detention or internment…*habeas corpus* is the direct security for the right to personal liberty, but a constitutional separation of powers and constitutional directions for the administration of justice as an independent function of the State were necessary to make the remedy secure.[18]

This statement clearly placed the right to personal liberty in its proper context and clearly understood the role of the courts vis-à-vis the other branches of government in such matters. The judge continued by referring in some detail to the provisions dealing with state of war and emergency (Article 28.3.3°) and the provisions dealing with trial of offences (Article 38). He then added:

> Manifestly these penal jurisdictions are all contemplated as importing lawful restrictions under the Constitution upon personal liberty, and Article 40 must be read in the light of Article 38…There is no provision enabling the Oireachtas or the Government to disregard the Constitution in any emergency short of war or armed rebellion. And the Constitution contains no express provision for any law endowing the Executive with powers of internment without trial.

[18] [1940] IR 136, 144. See document no. 279.

Gavan Duffy then proceeded to examine the central question raised by the application, namely, whether the internment powers contained in section 55(1) of the 1939 Act unconstitutionally vested the Minister with judicial powers. Section 55(1) was in the following terms:

> Whenever a Minister of State is satisfied that any particular person is engaged in activities calculated to prejudice the preservation of the peace, order or security of the State, such Minister may by warrant under his hand order the arrest and detention of such person under this section.

Gavan Duffy admitted that there could be no *a priori* answer to the question of whether the Minister was exercising judicial powers, since the word 'satisfied' might or might not 'imply something in the nature of a judicial inquiry: its implication depends on the context'. And the quasi-criminal context of the present case was regarded by Gavan Duffy as crucial:

> The Minister has to be satisfied. There must be countless occasions in the official life of a Minister of State on which he has to be satisfied as to particular facts before taking a particular course, occasions on which nobody would for a moment expect him to act judicially in order to be satisfied: otherwise the daily routine of administration would become impossible. But under s.55 the Minister...is not exercising any normal functions of his office; he is exercising a most exceptional statutory power, and a man's liberty depends on his exercise of it. The nature of the duty imposed on a 'Minister of State' by s.55 is the best guide to the meaning of the word 'satisfied' in the section. Part VI of the Act is its own best dictionary, and the grave duty which the section imposes does not suggest any loose use of the word 'satisfied', but, in my opinion, clearly suggests a serious inquiry resulting in a serious finding of 'satisfied' or 'not satisfied' as the case may be.

The judge then proceeded to list five considerations which, in his view, were decisive on this question:

> First, the Constitution (Article 9) declares fidelity to the nation and loyalty to the State to be fundamental political duties of all citizens; there is, I think, much to be said for the proposition that the citizen engaged in activities

> conflicting with that fidelity and loyalty commits a misdemeanour for which he is liable to prosecution under the criminal law. Secondly, and quite apart from that consideration, it would be difficult, and I think, impossible, for a man to engage in activities calculated to prejudice the preservation of the peace, order or security of the State without offending the ordinary criminal law. Thirdly, I am further of opinion that the activities contemplated by s.55, if not otherwise unlawful, are made unlawful by this very enactment: if such activities are not in terms forbidden by our laws, they are at least prohibited by necessary implication in s.55 under pain of internment...Fourthly, the activities described by the section make the subject-matter of Part VI of the Act one 'which, by its very nature, belongs to the domain of criminal jurisprudence: cp. *In re Board of Commerce Act, 1919* [1922] 1 AC 191, 198. Fifthly, I am of opinion that indefinite internment under Part VI is indistinguishable from punishment for engaging in the activities in question and I consider that the decision of a Minister of State to order the arrest and internment of a man under s.55 is equivalent to a judgment pronounced against the internee for his dangerous activities. These considerations are—indeed, any one of them probably is—sufficient to show that the authority, not merely to act judicially, but to administer justice and an authority to administer criminal justice and condemn the alleged offender without charge or hearing and without the aid of a jury.[19]

Gavan Duffy then went on to hold that section 55 violated an internee's right to personal liberty. On this point he commenced first by observing that:

> ...a law for the internment of a citizen, without charge or hearing, outside the great protection of our criminal jurisprudence and outside even the special Courts, for activities calculated to prejudice the State, does not respect his right to personal liberty and does unjustly attack his person; in my view, such a law does not defend his right to personal liberty as far as practicable, first, because it does not bring him before a real Court and again because there

[19] [1940] IR 136, 144, 151–2.

> is no impracticability in telling a suspect, before ordering his internment, what is alleged against him and hearing his answer, a course dictated by elementary justice.[20]

The judge then proceeded to reject the positivism of the majority of the Supreme Court in *The State (Ryan) v. Lennon*[21] as applicable to the present Constitution:

> In my opinion, the saving words of the declaration that 'No citizen shall be deprived of his liberty save in accordance with law' cannot be used to validate an enactment conflicting with the constitutional guarantees. The opinion of Mr Justice Fitzgibbon in *Ryan's Case*...does not apply, in my judgment, to a Constitution in which fundamental rights and constitutional guarantees effectively fill the *lacunae* disclosed in the polity of 1922. The Constitution, with its most impressive Preamble, is the Charter of the Irish People and I will not whittle it away...The right to personal liberty and the other principles which we are accustomed to summarise as the rule of law were most deliberately enshrined in a national Constitution, drawn up with the utmost care for a free people, and the power to intern on suspicion or without trial is fundamentally inconsistent with the rule of law as expressed in the terms of the Constitution. The legal position would be different, were I concerned with a war measure, a law 'expressed to be for securing the public safety and the preservation of the State in time of war' under Article 28; but I am not, for the Offences against the State Act, 1939, is not such a law.[22]

The Government was later to express considerable surprise at this decision. In some ways, this surprise might have been justified, given Gavan Duffy's comments on the draft Constitution prior to its enactment. In his first submission in late March 1937, the judge had first suggested an amendment to Article 38.1 which would have prevented internment without trial.[23] This suggestion was not acted upon and in his subsequent 'Notes on Final Draft Constitution' Gavan Duffy remarked in respect of Article 38.1 that 'A law for internment without trial is not forbidden.'[24] These comments might suggest that in 1937 Gavan Duffy

[20] [1940] IR 136, 144, 154.
[21] See Chapter III of this volume.
[22] See document no. 279.
[23] See document no. 114.
[24] See document no. 134.

did not consider that the proposed new Constitution prevented the enactment of a law providing for internment, yet two years later he—convincingly, it is submitted—arrived at the opposite conclusion.[25]

The unsuccessful appeal to the Supreme Court

At all events, following the decision of Gavan Duffy releasing the applicant, the State sought to appeal this *habeas corpus* order to the Supreme Court. However, when the appeal opened on 11 December 1939, Mr MacBride (who appeared for the applicant) raised the question as to whether the Court had jurisdiction to hear the appeal and the Court accordingly proceeded to determine this jurisdictional issue as a preliminary issue. Mr MacBride relied on the standard pre-Constitution authorities which established that the

> mere use in a statute of general words, which, taken literally, might comprehend an appeal against an order of discharge, cannot be held to involve such a grave departure from the constitutional right to personal freedom...There is no real distinction between an order of discharge and an acquittal on a criminal prosecution, and if the appellants' contention be correct, an appeal will lie against an acquittal by the Central Criminal Court.[26]

In response, Maguire relied on the express language of Article 34.4.4° of the Constitution which provides that:

> No law shall be enacted excepting from the appellate jurisdiction of the Supreme Court cases which involve questions as to the validity of any law having regard to the provisions of the Constitution.

A majority of the Supreme Court, however, found for Mr MacBride on the jurisdictional question. The Court accepted that there had been no legislation enacted subsequent to the enactment of the Constitution which had regulated or excepted that appellate jurisdiction, so that, to all intents and purposes, Article 34.4.3° might be read for the purposes of the appeal as saying: 'The Supreme Court shall have appellate jurisdiction from all decisions of the High Court.'[27]

[25] For a discussion of Gavan Duffy's judgment in this and other similar emergency cases, see G.M. Golding, *George Gavan Duffy, 1882–1951* (Dublin, 1982), 98–115.
[26] [1940] IR 136, 158–9.
[27] Chief Justice Sullivan noted (166) that the corresponding provisions contained in Article 66 of the Irish Free State Constitution had been interpreted as referring to 'exceptions and regulations prescribed by Act of the Oireachtas after the Constitution came into force and did not carry on the limitations upon appeals

This did not conclude the matter, since Chief Justice Sullivan led the majority of the Court to hold that Article 34.4.3° could not be read in isolation from the rest of the Constitution and that the special nature of the *habeas corpus* procedure served to create an exception from the general language of Article 34.4.3°:

> In the present case in determining the meaning of Article 34.4.3° of the Constitution I am entitled to have regard to the provisions of Article 40.4 and in considering that Article I am entitled to consider the principles formerly applicable in *habeas corpus* cases. I have already stated my opinion that the latter Article contemplates summary application, upon the hearing of which the right to release will be summarily determined. I think that in accordance with settled principles and established practice that determination is, and was intended to be, final. It follows that in my opinion an appeal does not lie to this Court from an order of the High Court made under Article 40.4 discharging a person from illegal custody....[In] this Court counsel for the Attorney General relied upon certain articles of the Constitution as indicating that an appeal should lie to this Court in any case in which the validity of any law is involved, having regard to the provisions of the Constitution. But that consideration cannot affect the jurisdiction of this Court to entertain an appeal from an order under Article 40.4 discharging a person from custody.[28]

It is clear that Chief Justice Sullivan's argument did, perhaps, less than justice to the language of Article 34.4.4° in particular. The language of Article 34.4.4° clearly preserves the right of appeal where the validity of a 'law'[29] was at issue and it is hard to see how the plain import of this special provision could be diluted by reference to factors such as pre-1922 *habeas corpus* practice. At the same time, while this aspect of *Burke* was subsequently overruled by the Supreme Court in *The State (Browne)*

[27] *contd.* imposed by statutes of the Parliament of the United Kingdom': see *Warner v. Minister for Industry and Commerce*, [1929] IR 582, and *In re MM*, [1933] IR 299. The Chief Justice continued by observing that:

> We should give a similar interpretation to these words in Article 34.4.3° of the present Constitution and if we do so we cannot hold that the exception from the jurisdiction of the Court of Appeal established [by the House of Lords] in *Cox v. Hakes* 15 App. Cas. 506 is an 'exception prescribed by law' within the meaning of that Article.

[28] [1940] IR 136, 186.

[29] That is, as here, a law enacted by the Oireachtas created by the Constitution: see *The State (Sheerin) v. Kennedy*, [1966] IR 379.

v. Feran,[30] this literal approach to the interpretation of Article 34.4.3° has itself given rise to manifold difficulties, not least with regard to the issue of whether an appeal lies against an acquittal in the Central Criminal Court.[31]

The Magazine Fort raid and its aftermath

Following the failure of the Supreme Court to entertain the State's appeal against Gavan Duffy's decision, the Government concluded that it had no option but to release all the other prisoners who had been detained under Part VI of the 1939 Act, even though no formal application for *habeas corpus* appears to have been made by or on behalf of any other prisoner. This decision to release the other prisoners appears to have led to consequences which were potentially catastrophic. On 23 December 1939, the Magazine Fort at Phoenix Park—the Defence Forces main ammunition depot—was raided by the IRA in a military style operation and over one million rounds of ammunition were stolen by over 50 men using four lorries.[32] In the immediate post-Christmas period, an Army cordon was placed around Dublin and in surrounding areas and significant quantities of the stolen ordnance were recovered.[33] This raid had not only depleted the necessary reserves of the Defence Forces in a time of war—and munitions were already in short supply—but it gave a major propaganda boost to the IRA. The *Irish Times* was certainly not impressed with the resulting state of affairs:

> It is obvious that the Government must have new powers to replace those of which it has just been deprived by the courts. It is still possible by ordinary legislation to amend the Constitution and we shall not be surprised if a Bill for that purpose is introduced in Dáil Éireann on Wednesday. The same result, we understand, can be obtained by an amendment to the Emergency Powers Act. Whatever method may be used, one thing is essential: there must be no legal loopholes. The position is far too grave for constitutional or juridical niceties. We yield to nobody in our belief in democratic institutions, but, if those very

[30] [1967] IR 147.

[31] See generally the debate in cases such as *The People v. O'Shea*, [1982] IR 384, and *The People v. Quilligan (No. 2)*, [1989] IR 46. Cf. the arguments of Seán MacBride in the Supreme Court in *Burke*, [1940] IR 136, 159: 'There is no real distinction between an order of discharge and an acquittal on a criminal prosecution, and if the appellant's contention be correct, an appeal will lie against an acquittal by the Central Criminal Court.'

[32] See Coogan, *The IRA*, 135–6.

[33] *Irish Times*, 26 December 1939; 28 December 1939.

> institutions are to be preserved for us and our children and this country, there must be an end to all forms of play-acting. There must be only one Government in the State and that Government's writ must be allowed to run without let or hindrance. It is all very well to regard the raid on the Magazine Fort as a rather clever jape—an encounter of wits in which the Government came off as second best: but, when all is said and done, it was an act of treason against the State. To mince words on such an occasion would be cowardice.[34]

The situation disclosed by *Burke's* case was clearly equally unacceptable to the Government and a new strategy was thereafter decided on. At a special meeting of the Government on New Year's Day 1940, the Government decided to approve the circulation of the Offences against the State (Amendment) Bill 1940. This again provided for internment, save that the Minister for Justice was now required to 'be of opinion' (rather than 'satisfied') that the individual in question was engaged in subversive activities.[35] On the same day, the *Irish Press* reported that the President 'may shortly refer a Bill to the Supreme Court, in accordance with Article 26 of the Constitution, for a decision as to whether any law is "repugnant to this Constitution".' It further indicated that this 'probability arises out of the Government's plans for dealing with the present emergency', as these plans involved asking the Oireachtas to re-enact with 'certain amendments' Part VI of the 1939 Act.[36] As the *Irish Press*—with its very close links to Fianna Fáil—was apparently so certain of its facts, this might suggest that the Article 26 reference was part of a

[34] *Irish Times*, 30 December 1939. As Eunan O'Halpin has observed:

> The Magazine Fort raid soon gave de Valera cause to regret his own leniency towards IRA hunger strikers. A humiliation for the army, and a tremendous shock to the Government and public, it underlined the real dangers posed by domestic subversives and it demonstrated that the IRA's ambitions had grown despite…the delicacy of the national position. As well as displacing any residual national complacency, the raid prompted a flood of information from the public to both the Garda and the Army, O'Halpin, *Defending Ireland: The Irish State and its Enemies* (Oxford, 1999), 247–8.

[35] In fact, the distinction between the phraseology of the Bill ('of opinion') and that of the 1939 Act ('satisfied') was to all intents and purposes immaterial. The rationale for Gavan Duffy's conclusion was based on the effect of the ministerial warrant (which was held by him to be an 'authority to administer criminal justice') as opposed to any mental element leading to the making of the warrant. Indeed, as Justice Henchy later observed in *The State (Lynch) v. Cooney*, [1982] IR 337, 378:

> Indeed, it might well be contended that if s.55(1) of the Act of 1939 had used the words 'is of opinion' —thus connoting a laxer and more arbitrary level of ministerial assessment—Justice Gavan Duffy might well have treated those words as an *a fortiori* reason for his finding of unconstitutionality.

Of course, had the modern orthodoxy—whereby all discretionary powers are presumed to be exercised fairly and in a constitutional fashion (*East Donegal Co-Operative Ltd. v. Attorney General*, [1970] IR 317)—then prevailed this would have been a ground for upholding the constitutionality of the Bill.

[36] *Irish Press*, 1 January 1940.

pre-arranged plan on the part of the Government whereby the Article 26 procedure would operate as a substitute form of an appeal from Gavan Duffy's decision.[37]

The 1940 Amendment Bill in the Houses of the Oireachtas

As it happens, two Bills were debated in the Oireachtas in the first week of January 1940. In the first of these, the Emergency Powers (Amendment) Bill, 1940, it was proposed to allow for the internment of Irish citizens. This had not been provided for in the original measure, the Emergency Powers Act, 1939, but the amending Bill sought to rectify this. The point here, of course, was that the Emergency Powers Acts were enacted under cover of Article 28.3.3° of the Constitution and were, accordingly, immune from judicial review. This meant that even if the companion measure, the Offences against the State (Amendment) Bill 1940, was adjudged to be unconstitutional, the Minister for Justice would still have had the legal power to intern Irish citizens for so long as the Article 28.3.3° emergency remained operative.

During the sombre debate which took place that week, the Government made no secret of the fact that it viewed the situation as one of the utmost gravity.[38] Nor did de Valera conceal his surprise and disappointment at the recent turn of events:

> The Government, and all those interested in the passing of the Constitution were taken by surprise when they found that an Act which was passed by the Oireachtas last year was held to be unconstitutional. We were still more surprised when we found that the Supreme Court held that there was not a right of appeal even in a case in which the validity of an Act—in view of the Constitution—was in

[37] This was clearly hinted at by de Valera when speaking in the Dáil on 3 January 1940 on the Emergency Powers (Amendment) Bill 1940 (this Bill also allowed for the internment of Irish nationals), but with reference to the Offences against the State (Amendment) Bill, 1940, which was going through the Dáil at the same time:

> The view of the legal advisers of the Government is that in view of all the circumstances and the situation as a whole the proper line to take is, if possible, to re-enact Part VI of the Offences against the State Act, giving an opportunity of having it referred to the Supreme Court for a decision as to whether internment is within the Constitution. In this matter I cannot presume to know what attitude the President will take, but again...we would say to ourselves that the President is likely, having seen a judge of the High Court rule to the effect that this Act as it stood originally was unconstitutional, and being possessed of a power before signature, to refer a Bill to the Supreme Court, we would say that he is likely to refer it, 78 *Dáil Debates*, Cols 1351–2.

[38] Thus, speaking on the Emergency Powers Bill, the Minister for Justice (Gerard Boland) commented that:

> I am satisfied that if it had not been for the decision of the courts—I do not want to comment on the decision of the judge—that raid would not have occurred, 78 *Dáil Debates*, Col. 1323 (3 January 1940).

> question...Last June we passed a certain Act intended to meet, not merely times of crisis, but the peculiar circumstances of our conditions here in ordinary peace time. That instrument for preserving the safety of the public was broken in our hands by the Court's decision. We have got to remedy that situation.[39]

Indeed, speaking in the Dáil, de Valera seemed to hint that the whole system of judicial review might have to be re-considered if the judiciary were to continue to surprise the Government in this fashion:

> I say if the Constitution which was brought in here, which used common-sense language and which had to be submitted to the people for enactment is not to have the meaning which the Legislature and which the people think it has and if we cannot get some common ground on which there is an understanding of words, then we certainly cannot get on. If the Legislature and the judiciary are going to be at loggerheads in that way we shall have to change the situation.[40]

It is possible to interpret these words as containing something of a veiled threat to the Supreme Court and, indeed, J.M. Kelly described these comments as having been uttered in a manner as 'a vein less plaintive and a good deal more disquieting' than the comments which were made in the Seanad by de Valera on the following day.[41] However, in fairness to de Valera, it is important to note that the particular words in question were uttered in response to an opposition charge that the Emergency Powers (Amendment) Act, 1940 might not enjoy constitutional protection on the ground that the 'emergency' did not constitute a 'state of war' for the purposes of Article 28.3.3°. That contingency had already been dealt with in the First Amendment of the Constitution Act, 1939 and de Valera's response was to the hypothetical possibility that the extended meaning now given to 'time of war' in Article 28.3.3° might be judicially interpreted as not including our state of neutrality while our European neighbours were at war.[42] All the same, de Valera did not

[39] 24 *Seanad Debates*, Col. 511 (4 January 1940).

[40] 78 *Dáil Debates*, Col. 1353 (3 January 1940).

[41] Kelly, *Fundamental Rights*, 25.

[42] This is made clear by a passage in the Taoiseach's speech immediately before the words just quoted:

> We think that in this present emergency, which creates a particularly difficult situation, unless the language of the ordinary man is to have no meaning, the [Emergency Powers (Amendment) Bill] is covered by Article 28.3.3°...I think that Deputy Costello suggested that as this had only a reference to a time of war, it might be held that that the present was not a time of war. But

mince his words and the Supreme Court cannot have been under any illusions as to where he and the Government stood on the matter.[43]

The Council of State meeting

Following the passage of the Bill by both Houses of the Oireachtas on 5 January 1940 it was then submitted to the President for signature. As anticipated, the President duly convened a Council of State meeting on 8 January 1940.[44] This was the first meeting of the Council of State and the members who attended were first required by Michael McDunphy, the Secretary to President Hyde, to make the declaration required by Article 31.4 of the Constitution.[45] The President also exercised his constitutional prerogative under Article 31.3 and appointed six members to the Council of State.[46] Although the minutes of that meeting are concise to the point of brevity,[47] an aide memoire prepared for de Valera clearly demonstrates that he was in favour of the reference:

> Is é mo thuairm-se gur ceart an Bille seo do chur fé bhreith na Cúirte Uachtaraighe. Bheinn ar a mhalairt de thuairim

[42] *contd.*

> there was an amendment passed a short time ago which assimilated a situation such as this to a time of war and which defined the expression 'time of war' as meaning a time such as the present. It seems to me, therefore, that unless words in the ordinary common way in which a man expresses himself are to have no meaning—in which case, of course, there is an end to everything—unless words in their plain meaning are to have no sense, it should mean that legislation under the present circumstances and under the present conditions cannot be nullified by an appeal to the Constitution, 78 *Dáil Debates*, Cols 1352–3.

[43] Thus, speaking in the Seanad on 4 January on the Emergency Powers Bill, 1940, the Taoiseach said:

> If a case was made…and I have heard no case that this Bill is unconstitutional—perhaps I will wake up and find I have been dreaming all the time and that the Supreme Court will show me otherwise. But I hope that I am not dreaming. It will be a serious matter, if when people are interned under the Bill, when it is enacted, we should have a habeas corpus application action again and the people who are interned in the interests of the State have to be released again. It will be serious. It will be bad for the prestige of the Government.
>
> Senators: Hear, hear! 24 *Seanad Debates*, Cols 518–19.

[44] *Irish Press*, 6 January 1940 forecast that the President would convene a meeting of the Council of State to consult them on the question of whether he should refer the Bill to the Supreme Court.

[45] *Irish Press*, 9 January 1940. It was further reported by the *Irish Press* that the meeting had lasted approximately one hour and that all members of the Council of State, with the exception of William Cosgrave, had duly attended. Cosgrave's absence may be explained by the fact that such was the level of his distrust of de Valera that he tried to avoid all social contact with him: see M.G. Valiulis, '"The Man They Could Never Forgive"–the View of the Opposition', in J.P. O'Carroll and J.A. Murphy (eds), *De Valera and his Times* (Cork University Press, 1983), 92. Cosgrave's rather curmudgeonly attitude to the entire procedure is, perhaps, best summed up by his comments at the Inaugural Meeting of the UCD Law Society (as reported in the *Irish Times*, 29 February 1940) a few weeks after the Supreme Court decision:

> We have reached a stage in the making of laws when on one occasion recently the proceedings were suspended and the question 'how's that, Umpire' was fired by the President from the Council of State gun at the Supreme Court. The consideration of that question was costly in terms of time and money. By a majority the Supreme Court gave its decision–a rare tribute to the ambiguity of the Constitution or the Bill or both.

[46] The President appointed three Dáil Deputies and three Senators as his nominees. All six were members of the opposition: Deputy James M. Dillon; Senator Robert Farnan; Senator Sir John Keane; Deputy Richard Mulcahy; Deputy William Norton and Senator Michael Tierney: *Irish Press*, 8 January 1940.

[47] See document no. 282.

> muna mbéadh an bhreith a thug duine de bhreithiúnaibh na hArd-Chúirte uaidh le déanaí. Is tuigthe ó bhreithiúntas an Bhreithimh sin go bhfuil sé i n-aghaidh an Bhunreachta comhacht do bhronnadh chun daoine do ghabháil agus do choinneáil gan a dtriail agus a gciontú os comhair Cúirte. B'é tuairim an Riaghaltais ná raibh comhachta den tsaghas san i n-aghaidh an Bhunreachta agus is dóigh liom go bhfuil an oiread san tábhachta ag baint leis an gceist nach mór í a shocrú go húdarásach.[48]

Against this background of legal uncertainty and (we may fairly assume) widespread political consensus in favour of a reference, it is scarcely surprising that the President decided it was appropriate to refer the Bill to the Supreme Court.

The fact that the 1940 Bill had been referred at the time that it was gave rise to an interesting situation regarding the composition of the Court. As of the date of the reference the Court consisted of the following judges: Chief Justice Sullivan and Justices Murnaghan, Meredith, Geoghegan and Johnston. The President of the High Court, Conor Maguire, was also an *ex-officio* member of the Court. As it happened, Johnston was due to retire on 18 January 1940 and the timetable for the reference made it impossible that the matter could have been disposed of in advance of that day.[49] This accordingly gave the Government an opportunity to make an appointment to the Court at a very sensitive time.

At all events, on 18 January 1940 the Government nominated O'Byrne to fill the vacancy caused by the retirement of Justice Johnston.[50] Although O'Byrne was then a senior judge of the High Court with fourteen years' experience and was a judge of some considerable distinction,[51] from the standpoint of the then Government there were several reasons why he might not have been promoted. First, O'Byrne had served from 1924 to 1926 as Attorney General in the Cosgrave administration as successor to Hugh Kennedy before he was himself appointed to the High Court. Secondly, O'Byrne had proved to be something of a thorn in the side of the Government during the turbulent years of 1933 and 1934. He had, for example, ordered the release of General O'Duffy

[48] See document no. 281 for translation.

[49] Thus, the *Irish Press*, 10 January 1940, observed that it had been reported in legal circles that:

> In view of the fact that counsel will have to be nominated, and that they will have to be given an opportunity of studying the case, apart altogether from the difficulty of estimating how long the case will take, it is very likely that the appeal will not be heard until after 18 January.

[50] *Iris Oifigiúil*, 23 January 1940.

[51] The *Irish Law Times and Solicitor's Journal* noted that the promotion of O'Byrne had 'given much satisfaction following a distinguished academic and legal career'; *ILTSJ* 74 (1940), 28.

following his arrest in December 1933 during the height of the Blueshirt controversy,[52] a decision which had been greeted 'with jubilation by Fine Gael leaders, who interpreted it as a major setback and embarrassment for the government'.[53] The third reason is far more speculative: as a Supreme Court Judge O'Byrne turned out to be something of a judicial activist[54] and perhaps he could not safely be regarded as a certain vote in favour of upholding the constitutionality of the Bill.

There is, however, some evidence pointing in the opposite direction and, on this view, O'Byrne was nominated in the belief that he would be, so to speak, a 'safe pair of hands' on issues of this kind. First, O'Byrne was chosen in preference to Justice Hanna who was then the senior ordinary judge of the High Court. It is true that Hanna was due in any event to retire in two years' time, but similar considerations had not prevented the Government nominating Johnston to the Supreme Court in March 1939, even though he had less than one year to serve on that Court before his retirement.[55] Secondly, O'Byrne had been a member of the Divisional High Court before whom Mr Wood had declined to press the constitutional argument. Might this not have suggested to well-informed observers that O'Byrne would uphold the constitutionality of any internment provisions or, at least, that the Burke legal team had no confidence that he would not do so? Finally, it has been suggested that any liberal sympathies which O'Byrne may have harboured did not extend to cases involving political subversion or State security. After all, O'Byrne had been a pro-Treaty supporter whose views on security matters and the threat posed by IRA violence had been hardened by the bitter experience of the Civil War and its aftermath. Of course, this speculation may be entirely misplaced and the Government may well have sought to make the best possible appointment without any regard whatsoever to the potential composition of the Court on the Article 26 reference. In this regard, it is only fair to add that de Valera appears to have been largely fair minded regarding judicial appointments and that his Government had previously promoted several judges to the Supreme Court who had either no Fianna Fáil links or who had been closely associated with Fine Gael.[56]

[52] [1934] IR 550.
[53] Manning, *The Blueshirts*, 116.
[54] He was, after all, the judge who subsequently delivered the judgment of the Supreme Court in *Buckley v. Attorney General*, [1950] IR 67, invalidating a key section of the Sinn Féin Funds Act, 1947.
[55] One possibility is that Justice Hanna had been the High Court judge who had been highly critical of the special Garda forces in the politically sensitive case of *Lynch v. FitzGerald*, [1938] IR 382.
[56] These promotions included those of Timothy Sullivan, then President of the High Court to Chief Justice (December 1936), Justice Meredith (from High Court to Supreme Court) (December 1936) and Justice Johnston (from High Court to Supreme Court)(March 1939).

However, the actual composition of the Supreme Court when it sat on Wednesday, 24 January 1940 to commence hearing arguments regarding the constitutionality of the Bill is of interest. On that day the Court consisted of Chief Justice Sullivan, High Court President Conor Maguire and Justices Murnaghan, Geoghegan and O'Byrne. The Political Correspondent of the *Irish Press* had previously reported that:

> An interesting situation arises owing to the fact that one member of the Supreme Court, Mr Justice Johnston, retires on 18 January. Under the Constitution, a Bill referred to the Supreme Court by An t-Uachtarain, must be heard by five judges.
>
> The President of the High Court may sit on the Supreme Court, but, I am informed, that it is unlikely that he will be asked to do so, while there are five Supreme Court judges able to act. If the Supreme Court does not hear and decide the case before 18 January, then either the President of the High Court would sit on the Supreme Court or the vacancy on the Supreme Court would be filled before the hearing.[57]

But while the vacancy had subsequently been filled by O'Byrne, the President of the High Court, contrary to predictions in earlier press reports, nonetheless sat on the Court. It was reported on the morning of the hearing that Justice Meredith 'may be unable to attend owing to indisposition'[58] and it appears that Maguire replaced him as a result.

The 1940 Bill before the Supreme Court

The oral argument commenced on Wednesday, 24 January 1940 and continued until the following Tuesday, 31 January. Leading counsel for the Attorney General, Martin Maguire SC,[59] opened the case in support

[57] *Irish Press*, 9 January 1940.

[58] *Irish Press*, 24 January 1940. On the following day, the *Irish Press* reported that Meredith 'had been unable to attend owing to indisposition'. Meredith appears to have been judicially active during the previous week, since he is reported as having delivered a judgment on 16 January 1940: see *Great Northern Railway Co. v. Commissioner of Valuation*, [1940] IR 247, 273. Meredith also appears to have sat on the Supreme Court in *Irish Industrial Benefit Building Society v. O'Brien*, [1940] 74 ILTR 52, where the case was at hearing on 15, 17 and 18 January 1940. Meredith also spoke at the inaugural meeting of the Literary and Historical Society on the previous Friday, 19 January 1940: see James Meenan (ed.), *Centenary History of the Literary and Historical Society of University College Dublin* (Tralee, 1956), 273. It may be noted, however, that the date of this meeting was given by the *Irish Law Times and Solicitor's Journal* as 12 January 1940: see *ILTSJ* 74 (1940), 21.

[59] Kevin Haugh, SC and Kevin Dixon, Barrister-at-Law appeared with Conor Maguire for the Attorney. This was an exceptionally distinguished team. Immediately after the arguments on the Bill concluded, Maguire was appointed a judge of the High Court to replace O'Byrne: *Iris Oifigiúil*, 6 February 1940. Martin Maguire was a member of the Supreme Court from 30 January 1954 until his retirement on

of the Bill and A.K. Overend SC[60] and Cecil Lavery SC[61] argued against the validity of the Bill.[62] If one can judge by newspaper accounts, Maguire seems to have made a better impression on the Court. Whereas counsel opposing the Bill never seem to have quite struck the right note,[63] Maguire's submissions read as having been fluently presented and well-argued.

Towards the close of Maguire's argument, Justice Murnaghan intervened to say that the question arose:

> whether in our Constitution there was room for what they called 'preventive justice.' Could it be shown that, under the Constitution, the State could arrest anyone on the prospect that he might commit a crime?
> Mr Maguire –It depends on the Constitution and what is meant by the rule of law within the Constitution.
> Mr Justice Murnaghan said he understood that the British Parliament could do anything—that they could pass a law that anybody who was likely to commit a crime could be interned.
> Mr Justice Geoghegan—If the two Houses of Parliament here passed a Bill which purported to authorise the arrest and internment of a person merely because some person

[59] *contd.* 8 February 1961. The *Irish Law Times and Solicitors' Journal* described his appointment to the High Court as being one that would 'give general satisfaction', adding that Maguire had been a 'popular figure' at the Bar: [1940] 74 ILTSJ 41, 42. Kevin Haugh SC was shortly thereafter appointed Attorney General (*Iris Oifigiúil*, 5 March 1940) and was later a judge of the High Court and Supreme Court. Kevin Dixon took silk later that year and was Attorney General from 1942–6. He was a judge of the High Court from 1946 until his death at the age of 57 in 1959 and it has been justly said that his 'early death deprived the Irish judiciary of one of its more promising members who would probably have been promoted to the Supreme Court' (Redmond, *Modern Irish Lives*, 83).

[60] Later judge of the High Court, 11 January 1943 until his death on 16 April 1947. Appointed to the High Court at the relatively late age of sixty-six, Overend did not appear to have had any party affiliation, but he did appear for the applicants in most of the major Article 2A cases during the mid-1930s. On his appointment he was described by the *Irish Law Times and Solicitor's Journal* as 'an able lawyer, particularly in the field of constitutional law', and it was said that 'the new judge was a popular and busy member of the Senior Bar': *ILTSJ* 77, (1943), 12. On his death, the Irish judiciary was said to have 'suffered its greatest loss since the death of Chief Justice Kennedy' and that 'after the death of W.M. Jellet in 1936', Overend had generally been regarded 'as leader on the Chancery side': *Irish Jurist*, 13 (1947), 11.

[61] Later Attorney General (1948–50) and judge of the Supreme Court (1950–66). It has been said that by 1940 'he was regarded by his colleagues as the ablest advocate in practice', Redmond, *Modern Irish Lives*, 166.

[62] Art O'Connor, Barrister-at-Law was the junior counsel appointed by the Court to argue against the validity of the Bill. It is interesting to note that Seán MacBride, Barrister-at-Law was not so appointed by the Court, presumably because of the fact that memories of his IRA connections were still fresh in official minds. Perhaps even more pertinently MacBride had been suspected of involvement in the murder of Kevin O'Higgins, then Minister for Justice, in July 1927. O'Higgins was related to Chief Justice Sullivan by marriage.

[63] Thus, at a key point, Overend could merely observe:

> Although it would be exceedingly difficult to put one's finger upon any precise provision of the Constitution to which it was directly contrary, nevertheless, it might be plainly contrary to the spirit of the Constitution, *Irish Press*, 26 January 1940.

> contemplated that he would commit an offence, which is the Article that would enable that?
> Mr Maguire—There is no specific Article directing the likelihood of that. If there was, surely we would not be here arguing it at all.
> In reply to further questions by Mr Justice Geoghegan, Mr Maguire said that the Constitution proceeded upon the basis that it prohibited certain things and enabled everything else. It enabled laws to be passed for the peace, good order and good government of the country.
> Mr Justice Murnaghan—If this Constitution does preserve *habeas corpus*, it seems to me that if it enables people to be put into imprisonment because it is contemplated that they might commit a crime, you might as well take out *habeas corpus*.[64]

On 14 February 1940, much to the relief, no doubt, of the Government, the Supreme Court upheld the constitutionality of the Bill. Having set out the background to the reference and having observed that Article 26 'admittedly refers to a Bill such as this which had been duly passed by both Houses of the Oireachtas', Chief Justice Sullivan first drew attention to the fact that several internment statutes had been enacted by the Oireachtas of the Irish Free State prior to the enactment of the Constitution:

> The existence and effect of these Acts must have been within the knowledge of the framers of the Constitution and, nevertheless, there is no express prohibition against such legislation. This is a matter to which we are bound to attach considerable weight in view of the fact that many Articles of the Constitution prohibit the Oireachtas, in plain and unambiguous language from passing certain laws therein specified.

[64] *Irish Press*, 26 January 1940. These remarks of Murnaghan were not accepted by the Court, thus providing further evidence for the contention that he dissented. On this issue, Chief Justice Sullivan said:

> It was contended that the effect of the Bill is to take away the right to *habeas corpus*. There is no foundation for this contention. Notwithstanding the provisions of the Bill, a person who is detained is entitled under Article 40.4.2° to have the legality of his detention enquired into and to obtain an order for his release, unless the Court or Judge, enquiring into the matter, is satisfied that all the provisions of the Bill have been complied with and that the detention is legal. No doubt the Bill, when enacted, will have the effect of altering the law and, to that extent, will justify a detention which might otherwise be unlawful. This, however, cannot rightly be described as taking away the right to *habeas corpus*. (582)

Sullivan was, of course, formally correct in that the 1940 Bill did not formally abridge the right to apply to the High Court for an order enquiring into the legality of a detention. Murnaghan's comments were directed to the fact that the substance of the Constitution's guarantees of personal liberty were substantially eroded by the Bill.

> Where any particular law is not expressly prohibited and it is sought to establish that it is repugnant to the Constitution by reason of some implied prohibition or repugnancy, we are of opinion, as a matter of construction, that such repugnancy must be clearly established.[65]

The Chief Justice then quickly proceeded to dismiss arguments based on the Preamble[66] and on the alleged administration of justice by the Minister for Justice in making the detention orders.[67]

Sullivan next rejected the contention—upon which Gavan Duffy had laid so much emphasis in *Burke*—that the 1940 Bill enabled the Minister to try the accused in respect of criminal offences in a manner contrary to Article 38.1 and that the detention thereby contemplated constituted a form of punishment in respect of a criminal offence:

> In the opinion of this Court neither s.4 nor s.5 of the Bill creates or purports to create a criminal offence. The only essential preliminary to the exercise by a Minister of the powers contained in s.4 is that he should have formed opinions on the matters specifically mentioned in the section. The validity of such opinions is not a matter that could be questioned in any Court. Having formed such opinions, the Minister is entitled to make an order for detention: but this Court is of opinion that the detention is not in the nature of punishment, but is a precautionary measure taken for the purpose of preserving the public peace and order and the security of the State.[68]

In this context, Sullivan quoted extensively with approval from the judgments of the House of Lords in *R. (Zadig) v. Halliday*[69] where the validity of detention regulations made under the Defence of the Realm

[65] [1940] IR 470, 478.

[66] The Chief Justice commented:

> Apart from the grammatical construction of the words of the Preamble, it seems to us difficult to understand how the dignity and freedom of the individual member of the State can be attained unless social order is maintained in that State. There is nothing in this clause of the Preamble which could be invoked to necessitate the sacrifice of the common good in the interests of the freedom of the individual, [1940] IR 478–9.

[67] The Chief Justice said:

> In order to rely upon [Article 34] it would be necessary to establish that the Minister, in exercising the powers conferred upon him by the Bill, is administering justice within the meaning of the Article. This proposition seems to us to be wholly unsustainable, [1940] IR 479.

But whereas in *Burke's* case, Gavan Duffy went to great lengths to develop his argument that the exercise of internment powers by the Minister amounted to the administration of justice, Sullivan simply stated—without further explanation—that this argument was unsustainable.

[68] [1940] IR 470, 479.

[69] [1917] AC 260.

Consolidation Act, 1914 was upheld. As Lord Finlay L.C. said in that case:

> On the face of it the statute authorises in this sub-section provisions of two kinds—for prevention and for punishment. Any preventative measures, even if they involve some restraint or hardship upon individuals, do not partake in any way of the nature of punishment, but are taken by way of precaution to prevent mischief to the State.[70]

The Chief Justice then continued by saying:

> The principle underlying the decision in [*Zadig*] was acted upon and applied in this country in the case of *R. (O'Connell) v. Military Governor of Hare Park Camp*.[71] In that case the applicant was detained in custody under an order of an Executive Minister made under section 4 of the Public Safety (Powers of Arrest and Detention) (Temporary Provisions) Act, 1924 which authorised such Minister to make such an order where he was of opinion that the public safety would be endangered by such person being set at liberty. It was contended that the section was repugnant to the Constitution of the Irish Free State, which, in our opinion, was, in this respect, substantially to the same effect as the Constitution of Ireland. That contention was rejected and an application for *habeas corpus* was refused.[72]

This analysis of *O'Connell* is correct so far as it goes, but, of course, this case had been decided in the context of a purely temporary item of legislation which had been enacted just as the Civil War was coming to a close. Moreover, so far as the Divisional High Court was concerned, two of the three judges[73] clearly doubted the constitutionality of permanent internment legislation.[74] In addition, the Court of Appeal

[70] [1917] AC 260, 265.

[71] [1924] 2 IR 104.

[72] [1940] IR 470, 481.

[73] Chief Justice Molony, Justices Pim and Dodd.

[74] Justice Dodd was quite emphatic on this point. He said:

> It would be possible, I think, to argue successfully that a permanent law giving the Executive power to deprive any citizen of his liberty without trial was contrary to the spirit of Article 6, and therefore, a violation of the Constitution; but that is a very different thing from a temporary law made in abnormal times and for a temporary purpose, [1924] 2 IR 118.

Dodd went on to refer with approval to the judgment of Lord Haldane in *Re Board of Commerce Act*, 1922] 1 AC 191, where the Privy Council expressly recognised the right of a Dominion Parliament 'where the interest of the State is of permanent and overriding importance' to do 'by temporary Act what would be unconstitutional if the Legislature attempted to make it permanent'. It was on this narrow basis alone—a temporary Act enacted at a time of emergency—that Dodd was prepared to uphold the constitutionality of the Public Safety Act, 1923.

simply held that it had no jurisdiction to consider the validity of a post-1922 law while the transitory eight-year period was still running and never even considered the merits of the constitutional point.[75] On any view, therefore, *O'Connell* could not be regarded as a particularly strong authority for the wider proposition advanced by Sullivan. In addition, however, Sullivan's statement regarding the non-reviewability of a Minister's opinion is no longer regarded as good law. Although this view was subsequently endorsed by Chief Justice Maguire for the Supreme Court in *Re Ó Láighleis*,[76] by 1982 different views had prevailed. In *The State (Lynch) v. Cooney* [77] the Supreme Court expressly departed from these decisions, with Chief Justice O'Higgins stating:

> While the opinion of the former Supreme Court, expressed in 1940 and in 1957, reflected what was then current judicial orthodoxy, judicial thinking has since then undergone a change. Decisions given in recent years show that the power of the courts to subject an administrative decision to judicial review is seen as having a wider reach than that delimited by those decisions of 1940 and 1957... The Court is satisfied that [s.31 of the Broadcasting Authority Act, 1960 authorising the prohibition of certain broadcasts] does not exclude review by the courts and that any opinion formed by the Minister thereunder must be one which is bona fide held and factually sustainable and not unreasonable.[78]

Returning to the Offences against the State Bill reference, Sullivan then proceeded to reject the arguments based on the personal rights provisions of Article 40.3.1°:

> The guarantee in this clause is not in respect of any particular citizen, or class of citizens, but extends to all of the citizens of the State and the duty of determining the extent to which the rights of any particular citizen, or class

[75] In the High Court in *Burke*, Gavan Duffy was decidedly unimpressed by arguments based on the authority of *O'Connell*. He said:

> [Counsel for the State] vigorously pressed upon me...the decision in O'Connell's Case whereby a transient Court upheld internment without trial under the Constitution of 1922; in my opinion, that case, if its authority survived the appeal, bears only a superficial resemblance to this, because it was decided under a Constitution differing radically from the Constitution in its provisions to secure personal liberty, [1940] IR 146–7.

[76] [1960] IR 93.

[77] [1982] IR 337. This case concerned, *inter alia*, the reviewability of a ministerial decision, pursuant to s.31 of the Broadcasting Authority Act, 1960, to ban television broadcasts by representatives of political parties closely associated with illegal organisations.

[78] [1982] IR 337.

> of citizens, can properly be harmonised with the rights of the citizens as a whole seems to us to be a matter which is peculiarly within the province of the Oireachtas, and any attempt by the Oireachtas to control the exercise of this function, would, in our opinion, be a usurpation of its authority.[79]

These comments regarding Article 40.3.1° are not only at odds with the entire tenor of the text of this provision, but, even by the end of the decade, it was clear that the Supreme Court would no longer endorse this analysis. Thus, some seven years later in *Buckley v. Attorney General*[80] Justice O'Byrne took a radically different approach, rejecting the argument of the Attorney that the task of harmonising personal rights lay exclusively with the Oireachtas:

> It is claimed that the question of the exigencies of the common good is peculiarly a matter for the Legislature and that the decision of the Legislature on such a question is absolute and not subject to, or capable of, being reviewed by the Courts. We are unable to give our assent to this far-reaching proposition. If it were intended to remove this matter entirely from the cognisance of the Courts, we are of the opinion that it would have been done in express terms as it was done in Article 45 with reference to the directive principles of social policy, which are inserted for the guidance of the Oireachtas and are expressly removed from the cognisance of the Courts.[81]

Finally, Sullivan disposed of the argument based on the personal liberty provisions of Article 40.4.1° by saying:

> The phrase 'in accordance with law' is used in several Articles of the Constitution and we are of opinion that it means in accordance with the law as it exists at the time when the particular Article is invoked and sought to be applied. In this Article, it means the law as it exists at the time when the legality of the detention arises for determination. A person in custody is detained in accordance with the provisions of a statute duly passed by the Oireachtas; subject always to the qualification that such

[79] [1940] IR 470, 481.
[80] [1950] IR 67.
[81] [1950] IR 83.

> provisions are not repugnant to the Constitution or to any provision thereof. Accordingly, in our opinion, this Article cannot be relied on for the purposes of establishing the proposition that the Bill is repugnant to the Constitution—such repugnancy must be established by reference to some other provision of the Constitution.[82]

Of course, Sullivan's decision must be viewed in its proper historical context. Gavan Duffy's audacious—if legally correct—decision nearly caused a national catastrophe and the Supreme Court must have been conscious of such considerations.

Disclosure that the opinion was a majority opinion

There was, in any event, a slight sting in the tail of Sullivan's judgment. At the date of the reference of this Bill, Article 26.2.2° read as follows:

> The decision of the majority of the judges of the Supreme Court shall, for the purposes of this Article, be the decision of the Court and shall be pronounced by such one of those judges as the Court shall direct.

Accordingly, as the Constitution then stood, Article 26 required the Court to give one judgment following a reference of the Bill, but it did not preclude the Court revealing that this judgment was not (apparently) a unanimous one. Sullivan commenced his judgment by indicating that the Court had been divided on the constitutionality of the Bill: 'The decision now announced is the decision of the majority of the Judges and is, within the meaning of Article 26.2.2° of the said Article, the decision of the Court.'[83]

President Hyde duly signed the Bill following the Supreme Court's decision. When the Ceann Comhairle announced to the Dáil on 21 February that he had received a message to this effect, an exchange then took place between James Dillon and de Valera. The former drew the latter's attention to the fact that of the six judges who had considered the constitutionality of the internment provisions (i.e., Gavan Duffy in respect of Part VI of the 1939 Act and the five members of the Supreme

[82] [1940] IR 475, 482.

[83] [1940] IR 470, 475. These comments prompted a re-consideration of the necessity for a 'one judgment' rule in constitutional cases and led directly to such changes being effected by the Second Amendment of the Constitution Act, 1941. Cf. the comments of Chief Justice Finlay in *Attorney General v. Hamilton*, [1993] 2 IR 252, 269:

> This was apparently seen to indicate a dissenting opinion which it was felt could greatly reduce the authority of the decision of the Court and, we are informed, and it is commonly believed, led directly to the insertion of the additional [one judgment provisions of Article 26.2.2° and Article 34.4.5°] by the Act of 1941 in both Article 26 and Article 34.

Court who had considered the 1940 Bill), three had adjudged the measure in question to be constitutional and three had formed the opposite view, with Deputy Dillon expressly naming Murnaghan and Geoghegan as the dissenting judges.[84]

Perhaps the real surprise, however, was that (again, apparently) at least one and, quite possibly, two, members of the Supreme Court were prepared to find the Bill unconstitutional and that the Bill only narrowly survived challenge. Given that the Supreme Court had never previously held any legislative measure to be unconstitutional, the Government must surely have expected that the Bill would have had a relatively easy passage. This belief was probably re-inforced by the fact that this was a war time measure and where the security implications of a finding against the Bill were plain to behold, as witnessed by the calamitous aftermath of Gavan Duffy's original ruling in the High Court. The fact that the judiciary had been so evenly divided over the constitutionality of sensitive security legislation at a time when a question mark hung over even the very survival of the State ought to have sent its own signal that the Constitution had indeed endowed the judiciary with potent powers which might well be used to rebuff the other organs of government in more settled times.

The transitional amendment provisions

Obviously conscious of the disastrous experience which had befallen the Constitution of the Irish Free State, the drafters of the Constitution had provided for an elaborate mechanism whereby that Constitution could only be amended by way of referendum, subject only to strictly limited transitional arrangements which were made unalterable by ordinary legislation. The special transitional arrangements were contained in

[84] It is not absolutely clear that there was, in fact, ever any dissent. It is possible that Chief Justice Sullivan in speaking of the decision being that of the majority of the judges was simply meticulously following the language of the then Article 26. It may be pedantic to say so, but a unanimous decision is also a decision of the majority and there was, in any event, no constitutional prohibition *at that time* on the delivery of a dissent: see Ronan Keane, 'The "One Judgment" Rule in the Supreme Court', in N.M. Dawson (ed.), *Reflections on Law and History* (Dublin, 2006), 312–13. Dillon's actions were heavily criticised by the *Irish Law Times and Solicitors' Journal.* In an anonymous piece entitled 'An Insult to the Judiciary', the writer first complained that Dillon's comments 'clearly overstep the bounds of propriety' and then continued:

> The Chief Justice, in delivering judgment, referred to it as a dissenting judgment, but the names of the dissenting Judge or Judges were never mentioned. Nor did any of the Judges at any time during the hearing express an opinion that the Bill was unconstitutional. In face of that, it is manifestly untrue to say that any members of the Court 'held' the Bill to be unconstitutional. What makes the matter particularly serious is that it is obviously impossible, and, in any event, incompatible with the dignity of the judicial office for the learned Judges whose names have been made use of in an undignified controversy to step down from the Bench to correct the false implications which have been spread abroad. Our public representatives are charged with the duty of upholding and maintaining our national institutions. To make use of the names of the Judges as weapons in a political controversy is scarcely in accord with that duty, *ILTSJ* 74 (1940), 83.

Article 51 which provided in relevant part that:

> 1. Notwithstanding anything contained in Article 46 hereof, any of the provisions of this Constitution, except the provisions of the said Article 46 and this Article may, subject as hereinafter provided, be amended by the Oireachtas, whether by way of variation, addition or repeal, within a period of three years after the date on which the first President shall have entered upon his office.
> 2. A proposal for the amendment of this Constitution under this Article shall not be enacted into law, if, prior to such enactment, the President, after consultation with the Council of State, shall have signified in a message under his hand and Seal addressed to the Chairman of each of the Houses of the Oireachtas that the proposal is in his opinion a proposal to effect an amendment of such a character and importance that the will of the people thereon ought to be ascertained by Referendum before its enactment into law.
> 3. The foregoing provisions of this Article shall cease to have the force of law immediately upon the expiration of the period of three years referred to in section 1 hereof.

These elaborate precautions were designed to ensure that what de Valera described as 'the foundations of the Constitution' were not upset through the use of the special amendment procedure in this three-year interval.[85] During the course of the Dáil debate on the Constitution, de Valera had, in fact, rejected an amendment put down by Deputy Frank McDermott at re-committal stage to extend the three-year period to eight years. He explained his thinking thus:

> If some minor, some verbal amendment reveal themselves as necessary during the period laid down, I think it is only right that it should be possible to pass them easily...Otherwise you are going to have what I would regard as a very unfortunate position created and that is that an amendment to the Constitution, as such, will become a feature, so to speak, of our political life. I think that would be undesirable.[86]

[85] 68 *Dáil Debates*, Col. 289 (10 June 1937).
[86] 68 *Dáil Debates*, Col. 285 (10 June 1937).

A little later in the debate de Valera added that 'any matters of principle certainly should go to the people and that any other changes should only be changes of a minor character which were necessary to deal with some oversight'.[87]

The first President, Dr Douglas Hyde, entered upon his office on 25 June 1938 so that, by virtue of Article 51.1, the period for the transitional amendment of the Constitution by ordinary legislation expired on 25 June 1941. The First Amendment of the Constitution Act, 1939 was enacted on 3 September 1939—following the outbreak of the Second World War—in order to amend Article 28.3.3° by extending the definition of 'time of war' and, hence, to allow for the enactment of emergency legislation even though the State was neutral during that conflict. In contrast to that specific measure, the Second Amendment of the Constitution Act, 1941 consisted of a series of heterogeneous changes which were the result of a systematic study of the entire Constitution. Neither of these measures was judged by the President to be of such a momentous character as to require a referendum and both measures duly passed into law in accordance with Article 51.1.

The 1940 Constitution Review Committee

As early as January 1938 the Department of the Taoiseach had established a working file dealing with possible amendments to the Constitution which might be included in an omnibus amendment during the transitional period. This was further formalised by a Department of Finance circular in December 1938[88] and a subsequent letter of 1 December 1939 to all Departments setting out 'the procedure to be adopted in connection with amendments to the Constitution which may come up for consideration during the three-year period'.[89] The replies were duly received in the first half of 1940 and in April 1940 a Committee was established by de Valera to review proposed amendments to the Constitution. The new Committee consisted of Maurice Moynihan (the Secretary to the Government, Chairman of the Committee); Dr Michael Rynne (legal adviser to the Department of External Affairs); Philip O'Donoghue (Legal Assistant to the Attorney General) and William Fay (Parliamentary Draftsman's Office).[90] The

[87] 68 *Dáil Debates* Cols 288–9 (10 June 1937).
[88] See document no. 266.
[89] See document no. 278.
[90] See document no. 299. As it happens, Arthur Matheson was indisposed with a minor illness at the date of the formation of the new Committee. De Valera wrote on 27 April 1940 to Matheson at home wishing him a speedy recovery and explaining why he had appointed Fay to the Committee:

composition of the Committee had altered somewhat from its predecessor in 1934 and, of course, the key figure of the 1936–7 drafting committee—John Hearne—was no longer available, having been made High Commissioner to Canada in 1939, largely in recognition of his work on the new Constitution. Michael McDunphy had been appointed Secretary to President Hyde. However, the presence of Moynihan and O'Donoghue provided continuity from the 1936–7 drafting committee and, of course, O'Donoghue had been a member of the 1934 Constitution Review Committee.

The Committee held its first meeting on 1 May 1940 and had 16 meetings in all before concluding its business on 30 June 1940. Just as with the 1934 Committee, the 1940 Committee discharged its business with great speed and efficiency, especially given the circumstances in which it operated and the other very considerable burdens which must have rested on the shoulders of these men during this anxious time.[91]

In addition to matters raised by members of the Committee itself, it also had to consider a large variety of possible amendments from the different Departments and certain individuals.[92] Among the various proposals were some which potentially impacted on the structure of judicial review. These were: aspects of Article 26 practice; the finality of a finding under Article 26; the 'one judgment' rule; the right of applicants for *habeas corpus* to move from judge to judge and the right of appeal from decisions of the High Court in *habeas corpus* cases involving the constitutionality of a law. All of these proposals can trace their origin to either *The State (Burke) v. Lennon* or the Offences against the State Bill reference and the debate concerning each of them will be presently considered in turn.

In its main Report the Committee set out its manner of operation:

[90] *contd.*

> I regard Fay's membership as desirable...because I understand that he takes a special interest in constitutional questions and he may be able to make valuable suggestions. I take it that the committee will have the benefit of consulting with you personally as occasion may arise.

Matheson promptly responded to thank the Taoiseach for his warm wishes and indicated that he agreed with the suggested course of action, NAI, DT S10299.

[91] The US Minister to Dublin, David Gray, wrote to Roosevelt on 19 June 1940 that there was a 'before the battle atmosphere' prevailing in Dublin and that a German invasion was thought to be 'probable and imminent': John Bowman, *De Valera and the Ulster Question* (Oxford, 1982), 225. See also Catriona Crowe *et al* (eds), *Documents on Irish Foreign Policy* vol. 6 1939–41 (Dublin, 2008), 170–367, *passim*.

[92] Including Seán Malone (Clerk of the Seanad); Stephen Roche and John Hearne (the High Commissioner to Canada). Rynne cabled Hearne in Ottawa on 4 September 1940 asking for comments and suggestions, adding that:

> In view of your very special knowledge of the Constitution the Taoiseach feels that final preparation of amending measures should not be undertaken before you have time to re-examine the substance of the Constitution in light of present world trends, recent political developments at home and your personal experience of Canadian constitutional matters. (See document no. 297.)

> All suggestions were considered by the Committee in the order in which they affected the various Articles of the Constitution. Where necessary, suggestions were re-drafted for the purpose of stating in a net form the proposals for amendment contained in them. In regard to each proposal, the Committee made a recommendation. All these proposals and the recommendations thereto are set out in the First Annex to this report. This Annex is in three parts: viz., I, the proposals recommended for acceptance; II, the proposals regarded as matters of policy; III, proposals not accepted.[93]

In their Report, the Committee commented that:

> Such amendments as appeared to be either of a purely drafting character, or such as, though containing points of substance, were thought to be unlikely to be submitted to a referendum, should be included in one Bill and placed before the Oireachtas for enactment without reference to a referendum. If it was found on the passage of this Bill through the Oireachtas, that substantial opposition was offered to any proposal in the Bill, such proposal could be dropped and later submitted in a separate Bill for ultimate reference to the people…Where any proposed amendment to be made within the said period is likely to be submitted to the people by referendum, the amendment should be incorporated in a separate Bill. It was recognised that, despite the suggestion in Article 46.4, that more than one proposal might be contained in the same Bill, there would obviously be difficulties in submitting more than one proposal in a Bill which was to be referred to the people.

In the end, the Second Amendment of the Constitution Act, 1941 took the form of thirty separate heterogeneous amendments which had no particular relationship with each other. It may be convenient to mention the amendments which were inserted as a result—either directly or indirectly—of the decision in *Burke* and the Offences against the State (Amendment) Bill reference.

[93] For the report, see document no. 299. There was a second annex to the Report which contained a memorandum from Stephen Roche that, in essence, argued against key features of the Constitution and that contended (a) that the powers of judicial review given to the judiciary were too extensive and (b) that the constitutional safeguards with regard to the administration of justice were too extensive. Parts II and III of the first annex are not reproduced in this volume.

The time limits for Article 26 references

Article 26.1.2° originally provided that any reference of a Bill by the President to the Supreme Court would have to take place within four days after the date on which the Bill was passed or was deemed to have been passed by the Houses of the Oireachtas. The Department of Finance was noting as early as January 1939 that the time-period in question was much too short and recommending that consideration be given to an amendment of this provision.[94] Following the reference of the 1940 Bill by the President, the matter again became topical and, accordingly, Michael McDunphy wrote on 19 January 1940 to Maurice Moynihan about this issue.[95] McDunphy raised two issues: first, the time ran from the date of the passage of the Bill by the Houses of the Oireachtas as opposed to the date of its presentation to the President and, secondly, the four-day period was too short. The Secretary concluded by requesting that Article 26 be amended accordingly within the three-year transitional period. The proposal was then formally transmitted to the Department of Finance in accordance with its 1938 circular.

The 1940 Committee agreed with the first proposal and agreed that time should run from the date of the presentation of the Bill. They disagreed, however, with the second proposal:

> In their opinion, to allow a longer period than four days for a decision to refer a Bill to the Supreme Court would unduly encroach on the period allowed to the President for the signature of the Bill.

De Valera, however, agreed with McDunphy and Article 26.1.2° was amended accordingly to provide for a seven-day period in which the decision to refer might be made, such period to run from the date of presentation of the Bill.

The finality of a finding under Article 26

Article 34.3.3° now provides that:

> No Court whatever shall have jurisdiction to question the validity of a law, or any provision of a law, the Bill for which shall have been referred to the Supreme Court by the President under Article 26 of this Constitution, or to

[94] Article 26.1.2° now provides that the President must make his/her decision 'not later than the seventh day after the date on which the Bill shall have been presented by the Taoiseach to the President for his signature'.
[95] See document no. 291.

> question the validity of a provision of a law where the corresponding provision in the Bill for such law shall have been referred to the Supreme Court by the President under Article 26.

This provision had not been included in the Constitution as originally enacted and it was John Hearne who put forward the idea for such an absolute rule of finality to the 1940 Committee. Hearne's proposal was that Article 34.3.2° should be amended to provide:

> that a Bill or provision which has been the subject of decision of the Supreme Court under Article 26 pronouncing it valid shall when enacted into law be beyond reach of original jurisdiction conferred on the High Court by [this Article].[96]

Although Hearne's formal proposal was not made until September 1940, he did set forth his thinking regarding the purpose of the Article 26 procedure in a letter to Rynne on 4 May 1940. The letter first made reference to a speech of Professor Michael J. Ryan KC where the latter had been reported as saying that the Constitution contained 'elements of a conflict between the legal mind and laymen' and gave as an example the aftermath of the Supreme Court's decision in respect of the reference:

> The reference of a Bill to the Supreme Court before it became law was not worth the paper on which it was written. The courts were there to interpret the law and a Bill was not law until it had been passed by the Oireachtas and had received the consent of the Uachtaráin. It was an interesting question to consider whether the advice given by the Supreme Court in that case was not in the same position as advice given by the Judicial Committee of the British Privy Council to the King and was not binding therefore on the courts of this country.[97]

Ryan's views evidently caused some concern to Rynne and the fellow members of the drafting team since the appropriate newspaper cutting appears to have been sent to Hearne asking for his comments. Given the novelty of the entire procedure and having regard to the fact that it was not a decision of the Court based on facts assumed or proved (the traditional starting point at common law for the doctrine of precedent)

[96] Hearne's telegram also recommended that: '2. An amendment removing jurisdiction conferred by [Article 40.4.2°] from single judge' (see document no. 298).
[97] *Irish Times*, 29 February 1940.

there is, perhaps, something to be said for Ryan's view that the Supreme Court decision was not binding.[98] Nevertheless, as we have already seen, Matheson had already advised de Valera in early March 1937 to change the wording of Article 26 from 'advice' to 'decision' in order to ensure that any such decision of the Court would be regarded as binding and not simply an advisory opinion.[99] To that extent Ryan was incorrect to describe the Supreme Court as having given advice to the President in much the same way as the Privy Council gives advice to the British Monarch: Article 26 referred to a decision which was intended to be binding.

At all events, Hearne referred to Professor Ryan's argument and continued:

> The effect of the reference procedure under Article 26 of the Constitution, as I understand it, is as follows:
>
> > It protects the President from having to sign a Bill automatically on the advice of a Government who have used their parliamentary majority to drive an invalid measure through both Houses. If the Supreme Court holds that the Bill is contrary to the Constitution, the President must refuse to sign it and it cannot become law. The 'reference' procedure, including the decision of the Supreme Court, should, therefore, be considered in the context only of the machinery of law making.
> >
> > At the time of the framing of the Constitution, we had many discussions as to whether a provision should not be inserted prohibiting a challenge in the Courts to the validity of any statute the Bill for which had been signed by the President after a reference thereof to the Supreme Court and a decision by that Court under Article 26 of the Constitution pronouncing the Bill valid. It was decided not to insert such a provision. The reason for that decision was as follows: There is little likelihood, it was said, of a Supreme Court which had decided, on a reference to them under Article 26, that a Bill is valid, holding that the same Bill when enacted into law is invalid. In order to insure that that would be

[98] No less an authority than Justice Kenny expressed the very same view in *Ryan v. Attorney General*, [1965] IR 297, regarding the precedential status of any 'advice' given by the Supreme Court to the President following an Article 26 reference. In practice, however, the judgments given by the Privy Council are regarded as binding in the same way as decisions of other courts.

[99] See document no. 82.

so, it was agreed to put in a provision contained in Article 26.2.1° that the Supreme Court should consist of not less than five judges for the purposes of the Article.[100]

There is nothing in the Constitution which prevents any litigant from raising in a proper court the question of the validity or otherwise of a statute the Bill for which has been decided by the Supreme Court on a reference under Article 26 to be valid in very respect. The High Court and Supreme Court have the same power over such a statute as they have over a statute which has never been referred to the Supreme Court by the President under Article 26. The provision (Article 34.3.2°) which confers original jurisdiction on the High Court alone in all cases in which the validity of any law is in issue makes no exception of a law the Bill for which has been declared valid under Article 26.

In my view, the High Court is not bound by the decision of the Supreme Court sitting under Article 26 and pronouncing that a Bill referred to them thereunder is valid. But, should the High Court hold that the statute is invalid, the Supreme Court on appeal would in 99 cases out of a 100 decide as they had done when the Bill was before them under Article 26. You might conceivably have a case where a sound argument against the validity of a law is adduced in the High Court which had completely escaped the attention of the Supreme Court when considering the Bill. But that is extremely unlikely. You might have again a complete change of personnel of the Supreme Court Bench who would take different views of the law and the Constitution from that held by their predecessors when the Bill was before them. And in that case it is still possible under the Constitution as it stands to have the situation in which a law would be declared invalid perhaps some years after the Bill for the

[100] It is interesting that this conclusion was quite independently arrived at by the Constitution Review Group in its *Report* almost 60 years later:

> The Review Group is of the view that there should be at least five judges. This ensures a large judicial input into these important decisions. Five represents more than half the total proposed Supreme Court membership and allows the Court to deliver a judgment even if a number of judges cannot sit for such reasons as illness or absence abroad. If immunity from challenge is removed [Article 34.3.3°], the case for retaining the five judge minimum would be all the stronger, *Report of the Constitution Review* Group, 85–6.

> law had been declared valid by the Supreme Court under Article 26.[101]

Hearne's proposal evoked a broadly sympathetic response from the Committee:

> The Committee are inclined to sympathise with this suggestion and if it is desired to give effect to it, this could be done by a comparatively simple amendment to Article 34.3, preferably by the addition of a new Subsection 3° to that section, excluding from the jurisdiction conferred on the High Court by Subsection 2°, any law or any provision of a law the Bill for which had been referred to and pronounced valid by the Supreme Court under Article 26.
>
> The Committee however are of opinion that it is extremely unlikely that the High Court would ever enquire into, let alone question, the validity of a law where the Bill for such law had been pronounced valid by the Supreme Court, and it is accordingly for consideration whether any amendment of the Constitution is really necessary for this purpose.

In passing it may be noted that in 1964 in *Attorney General v. Ryan's Car Hire Ltd.*[102] the Supreme Court indicated that it was no longer so strictly bound by its previous decisions. But this relaxation of the doctrine of precedent does not, of course, mean that the High Court can question a Supreme Court decision[103] even if that decision has been given in the course of an Article 26 reference.[104]

Moynihan noted in his hand-writing on the margin on 31 October 1940:

> The Taoiseach feels that there is much force in the arguments both for and against this proposal. He desires

[101] NAI, DT S10299. See www.irishconstitution.ie.

[102] [1965] IR 642.

[103] In *Moynihan v. Greensmyth*, [1977] IR 55, the Supreme Court raised the issue of whether *O'Brien v. Keogh*, [1972] IR 144, had been correctly decided. In *Campbell v. Ward*, [1981] ILRM 60, Justice Carroll was asked to treat as valid the section of the Statute of Limitations 1957 which the Supreme Court had held to be unconstitutional in *O'Brien v. Keogh*. This she refused to do, saying that she considered herself 'bound by the existing decision of the Supreme Court in that case until such time as the Supreme Court reviews its decision'.

[104] In *Ryan v. Attorney General*, [1965] IR 294, Justice Kenny concluded that the High Court was not bound by the 'advice' given by the Supreme Court to the President in an Article 26 reference 'in the same way as does a decision of the Supreme Court in a case between parties'. It may be noted, however, that the balance of authority lies clearly the other way. In *Director of Public Prosecutions v. Best*, [2000] 2 ILRM 1, Justice Keane observed that:

> Dicta in other cases would appear to support the view the High Court and Supreme Court are bound by the *ratio decidendi* of judgments arising from a reference under Article 26: see, in particular, the observations of Justice Henchy in *The State (Lynch) v. Cooney*, [1982] IR 337, 33.

> that a draft amendment based thereon should be included provisionally in the list of amendments to be submitted to the Government.

The Committee then produced a draft—which corresponded exactly to the present wording of Article 34.3.3°—for their meeting on 25 November 1940. Moynihan noted on the same day that the Committee recommended 'the acceptance of the proposal' and 'the Taoiseach agrees'.

The 'one judgment' rule

The idea of a one judgment rule in certain constitutional cases seems to have originated during the course of the original drafting, possibly as an aspect of earlier ideas for a Constitutional Court. In the draft of 13 February 1937, Article 28.4 proposed to vest the Supreme Court with exclusive jurisdiction to determine all questions as to the validity of a law having regard to the provisions of the Constitution, but there was no provision for one judgment in ordinary constitutional cases. However, a different rule had been envisaged for Article 26 references, as that draft of Article 26.2.2° then provided that:

> The decision of the majority of the judges of the Supreme Court shall, for the purposes of this Article, be the decision of the Court and dissenting opinions shall not be disclosed.

As we have already seen, shortly afterwards these drafts were forwarded to both the President of the High Court, Conor Maguire, and Justice Gavan Duffy who were asked for their observations on these drafts. Gavan Duffy expressed himself trenchantly in relation to the one-judgment rule which the drafters had proposed for Article 26:

> The silencing of dissenting opinions comes from the British Privy Council, where its purpose is to conceal dissent from India and African nations, and from the Court of Criminal Appeal, where the purpose is to conceal dissent from the criminal. Surely it would be most undemocratic to apply the same policy to judicial opinions on the Constitution, and the people are entitled to know what their judges think. This would give an artificial sanction to the opinion of 3 Judges against 2, and those 2 are fully entitled to be heard, especially as they may be right.[105]

In the light of these comments, the words 'and dissenting opinions shall not be disclosed' were omitted when Article 26.2.2° was originally

[105] See document no. 114. These notes are undated, but certainly do date from the second half of March 1937.

enacted.[106] The effect of this was to require the Supreme Court to deliver a collective judgment in respect of the Article 26 reference, but it did not prevent the Court revealing that this judgment was that of the majority. But this change proved to be simply a temporary reprieve given the aftermath of the Offences against the State (Amendment) Bill, 1940 reference.

The one judgment issue was subsequently then considered by the 1940 Constitution Revision Committee. As far as Article 26 was concerned, the Committee observed that:

> Where a Bill, or a provision of a Bill, is referred to the Supreme Court under Article 26 of the Constitution, it is desirable that the certainty attaching to the Court's decision should not be impaired by the pronouncement of a dissenting judgment. The amendment accordingly provides that the decision shall be pronounced by one Judge of the Supreme Court and that 'no other opinion, whether assenting or dissenting, shall be pronounced nor shall the existence of any such other be disclosed'.

The Committee took a similar view with regard to ordinary constitutional challenges:

> Having regard to the statement contained in their [recommendations regarding Article 26], the Committee gave consideration to the question of providing that the Supreme Court should pronounce only one judgment in constitutional cases. The Committee understand, after consultation with the Attorney General, that the Chief Justice [Sullivan] considers that the Supreme Court should pronounce only one judgment in all constitutional matters, whether they arise on a reference under Article 26 or otherwise. Accordingly they recommend an amendment be made for this purpose in Article 34.4.[107]

Moynihan noted in handwriting on 4 November 1940 that the Attorney General (Kevin Haugh SC) was of opinion that it was 'undesirable' that the one judgment rule should be extended to ordinary constitutional cases. Haugh was also noted as having drawn attention to practical difficulties that might be encountered:

[106] However, speaking in the Dáil during the course of the Second Amendment of the Constitution Bill, 1941, de Valera commented: 'In an early draft of the Constitution there was a provision such as this [providing for the one judgment rule] but it finally disappeared. I have not been able to find how it got out', 82 *Dáil Debates*, Col. 1857, 24 April 1941.
[107] See document no. 299.

> [Suppose that] three judges A, B and C say [the law is] valid [and] two [judges] D and E [say the law is] invalid. [Judge] B holds the other ground in favour of party pleading unconstitutionality. Then, in AG's views, case should be decided in favour of that party.

This was prescient advice, as the practical difficulties which Haugh identified have subsequently come to pass. De Valera, however, agreed with the views of the Committee and recommended that its proposals for change should be incorporated into the Second Amendment of the Constitution Bill, 1941.

The one judgment proposals excited some controversy during the course of the Dáil debate. As far as the Article 26 amendment was concerned, it was proposed to add the following to Article 26.2.2°:

> ...and shall be pronounced by such one of those judges as the Court shall direct, and no other opinion, whether assenting or dissenting, shall be pronounced nor shall the existence of any such other opinion be disclosed.

A similar amendment was proposed for Article 34:

> The decision of the Supreme Court on a question as to the validity of a law having regard to the provisions of this Constitution shall be pronounced by such one of the judges of that Court shall direct and no other opinion on such question, whether assenting or dissenting, shall be pronounced, nor shall the existence of any such other opinion be disclosed.

During the course of the Dáil Debates, de Valera admitted that while from an educational point of view a multiplicity of judgments might be desirable, yet the desirability of a definite opinion was for him the decisive consideration:

> The one thing I am looking for, and which I think we all ought to look for here, is that there should be a definite decision; that it should not be bandied about from month to month that, in fact, that decision was only come to by a mere majority of the Supreme Court. Then you would have added in, perhaps, the number of judges who dealt with the matter in the High Court before it came to the Supreme Court, as might happen in some cases. You would then have an adding up of judges and people saying: 'There

> were five on this side and three on the other, and therefore the law is the other way. That would be altogether undesirable. While there might be advantages on the other side, I think, on the whole, we ought to keep it here in a single judgment.[108]

The allusion to the adding up of judges etc. is clearly a reference to what had occurred in the aftermath of the Offences against the State Bill reference.

Habeas corpus procedure

There were several suggestions for change of the Article 40.4.2° procedure. All of these suggestions were prompted by aspects of what had occurred during the course of *The State (Burke) v. Lennon* where, as we have seen, to the consternation of the authorities, the applicant declined to move his application before a Divisional High Court, but instead selected his own judge—Gavan Duffy—to hear both the leave and substantive applications. Upon hearing the substantive application, Gavan Duffy promptly found Part VI of the 1939 Act to be unconstitutional and the Supreme Court refused to hear an appeal from that decision, the wording of Article 34.4.4° notwithstanding. The Government was then forced to release all internees, with potentially disastrous consequences.

It was, however, far from clear that Gavan Duffy had been correct in allowing the applicant, in effect, to select his own judge, as the Supreme Court had recently seemed to dispel that notion in *The State (Dowling) v. Kingston*.[109] Indeed, one of the judges on that Court, Fitzgibbon,[110] wrote to de Valera on 4 April 1941 concerning the decision in *Dowling* as the Second Amendment of the Constitution Bill 1941 made its way through the Oireachtas.[111] Fitzgibbon had noticed that in the course of the debate in the Dáil, John A. Costello ('for whose ability as a lawyer I have a very sincere respect') had stated that the proposed amendment would deprive a citizen of his 'immemorial right to go from one judge of the High Court to another' in search of a writ of *habeas corpus*. Fitzgibbon wrote to express his disagreement with this point of view:

> In one of the last judgments delivered by me in the Supreme Court [*The State (Dowling) v. Kingston*] I believed

[108] 82 *Dáil Debates*, Col. 1859 (24 April 1941). See also Keane, 'The One Judgment Rule'.
[109] [1937] IR 699. See also the discussion of this issue in the letter sent by the President of the High Court (Conor Maguire) to the Taoiseach on 5 March 1941 (see document no. 320) and the memorandum of Philip O'Donoghue of the Attorney General's Office on 22 April 1941 (see document no. 321).
[110] Fitzgibbon had, however, retired from the Supreme Court in October 1938.
[111] NAI, DT S11663.

> that I had disposed of this error once [and] for all, so far as Éire is concerned; and I thought that I had demonstrated, with the concurrence of the Chief Justice at any rate, that the view now expressed by Mr Costello was founded upon a mistaken reading by Lord Hailsham of an old case in the House of Lords [*Cox v. Hakes*] and that the right of the citizen was *not* to go from one *Judge* of a Court to another, but from one *Court* to another, at a time when there were four independent and co-ordinate *Courts*—our own old *Four Courts*—Chancery, King's Bench, Common Pleas and Exchequer and seek the opinion of each of these independent Courts, through one of *its* Judges, as to his right to a *habeas corpus*. But it has never been conceded, or even, so far as I know, contended in these days that a man could go from one Judge to another of the same Court. The Courts were all fused into one High Court in 1875 and so the right to go from Court to Court disappeared.

Apart from the intrinsic interest of yet further correspondence between de Valera and Fitzgibbon on constitutional matters,[112] it seems clear from the latter's letter that he understood that the right to go from court to court had disappeared with the union of the four courts into one single court by the Supreme Court of Judicature (Ireland) Act, 1875. In any event, such common law rights as existed in 1922 had been at least supplanted by the enactment of Article 6 of the 1922 Constitution which referred to applications 'to the High Court and any and every judge thereof'. In the only case in which these words had been judicially examined—*The State (Dowling) v. Kingston*—Chief Justice Sullivan and Justice Murnaghan had reached opposite conclusions as to what they meant. Although precisely similar language had been used in the version of Article 40.4.2° as originally enacted in 1937, the meaning of those words 'had not yet been judicially determined and about which there [was] still a great deal of confusion'.[113] Against that background one could not confidently assert that the right to go from judge to judge (insofar as it existed) included the right to have a particular judge of the

[112] They had previously corresponded in 1937 on the issue of the Article 26 procedure: See document nos 168–9. In fact, de Valera responded warmly in a letter of 18 April 1941, assuring Fitzgibbon that following the latter's suggestion:

> ...he has been in consultation with the Attorney General and has seen your judgment in the case of *The State (Dowling) v. Kingston (No. 2)* (1937), all of which is receiving full consideration.

Philip O'Donoghue of the Attorney General's Office prepared a memorandum on this very point on 22 April 1941, see document no. 321, and he appears to have independently arrived at the same conclusion.

[113] Anon., '*Habeas Corpus* Procedure under the Constitution of Éire', in *ILTSJ* 74 (1940), 1, 3.

High Court hear the application, as happened in *The State (Burke) v. Lennon.*

It is not altogether surprising, therefore, that in the light of what had actually occurred in *Burke's* case that various Government Departments sought amendments to Article 40.4.2°. Stephen Roche submitted a lengthy memorandum to the Committee on 13 September 1940 in which he was frankly sceptical of the value of constitutional guarantees and in which he maintained the courts had been given excessively wide powers of judicial review. The following extracts give a flavour of his forthright views:

> The general line adopted in the Constitution in relation to the Courts of Justice and the punishment of offences in normal times is to provide, as the ordinary or permanent code, a system characterised mainly by precautions designed to prevent any possibility of injustice or undue severity. With this object, very explicit and far-reaching guarantees are given; justice is to be administered by Judges and by nobody else; in addition to the Judge there must be, except in the case of minor offences, a jury: the *habeas corpus* procedure is explicitly made a portion of the Constitution; a High Court Judge is given the right to declare an Act of the Oireachtas to be invalid. (This last provision was inserted, it will be remembered, after considerable hesitation, and on the assumption that it would always be open to the State to appeal to the Supreme Court, an assumption which seemed perfectly safe having regard to the words of Article 34.4.4° but which was defeated, in a very unexpected and unfortunate way, in connection with *habeas corpus* procedure.)[114]

Roche's reference here to the hesitations concerning the vesting of the power of judicial review in the High Court reflect the fact that—as we have already seen—the draft Constitution as introduced in Dáil Éireann had originally proposed that the Supreme Court would enjoy exclusive original jurisdiction in constitutional matters. At Committee Stage de Valera yielded to opposition concerns[115] and restored the High Court's jurisdiction in constitutional matters, but Article 34.4.4° sought to safeguard the right of appeal against a finding of constitutionality. Roche's memorandum continued:

[114] See document no. 300.
[115] 68 *Dáil Debates*, Cols 1492–4 (2 June 1937).

> We have not only adopted the old safeguards but we have also bound ourselves to them in a way which the English, who invented them, have never adopted. *Habeas corpus* or no *habeas corpus*, Bill of Rights or no Bill of Rights, the Westminster Parliament acknowledge no restraint over what it may do for the better government of Great Britain. No Court can take a new statute of that Parliament for examination and pronounce it invalid, because it is, in its view, 'contrary to the Constitution'. When *habeas corpus* threatens to become troublesome in England it is simply suspended.
>
> In my view (I admit being prejudiced against a written Constitution at all) it is unwise to put much detail about the Court system and the criminal law into a statement of fundamental law.

Roche then proceeded to give four examples of where express constitutional protections gave the courts too great a role vis-à-vis the Oireachtas and the Executive. The first three were Article 34.1 (what constituted the administration of justice and must it always be held in public); Article 34.3.1° (one High Court with a full original jurisdiction); Article 38.5 (trial by jury). The fourth concerned the procedure under Article 40.4.2°:

> [Article 40.4.2°] is a good illustration of the danger inherent in any attempt to translate what is quite a good general principle into a flat and final statement of constitutional law. Even those who do not like 'safeguards' must admire the vigour and simplicity of the *habeas corpus* procedure but it is, I think, safe to say that when this provision was inserted in the Constitution nobody anticipated the mischievous use which would actually be made of it.

Quite independently of the Roche memorandum, proposals for change came from both Hearne and the Department of the Taoiseach. As we have already noted, Hearne had cabled from Ottawa with the suggestion that Article 40.4.2° should be amended 'by removing the jurisdiction thereby conferred from single judge of the High Court'. The Department of the Taoiseach made a similar suggestion:

> It is suggested that this provision under which an applicant in a *habeas corpus* case can have the matter dealt with by

> any and every judge of the High Court should be amended. It may be necessary or desirable to take steps to ensure that persons are not released from custody on purely technical grounds or because of some trifling flaw in procedure. There is also the issue that *habeas corpus* proceedings are of such importance as to justify their being heard by more than one judge.
>
> It is suggested further that where a *habeas corpus* application is granted on the ground that a particular statute is unconstitutional there should be an appeal to the Supreme Court. It is undesirable that constitutional issues should in a *habeas corpus* case be decided by the judgment of a single member of the High Court without any appeal to the Supreme Court.

These proposals met with a mixed response from the Committee:

> The Committee are of opinion that no change should be made in the present position in regard to *habeas corpus* save in the direction of an appeal to the Supreme Court in cases where the applicant obtains his release on the ground that the law under which he is detained is unconstitutional. In this respect, they agree with the proposal and recommend that provision should be made by the amendment of Article 40.4 for enabling a Court or Judge which or who is of opinion, on application under that section, that the applicant is detained in accordance with a law which is unconstitutional, to refer the question of its constitutionality to the Supreme Court for its determination, and not to release the applicant until that question is determined.

The Committee then furnished an early draft of what was ultimately to become Article 40.4.3°:

> 3. Where, on an inquiry by the High Court or a judge thereof into a complaint made under this section, the Court or judge is satisfied that the person detained is being detained in accordance with a law, but that such a law is invalid having regard to the provisions of this Constitution, the Court or judge may refer the question of the validity of such law by way of case stated to the Supreme Court for its determination thereon, and in

> that case, shall not order the release of the person detained pending the determination of the Supreme Court.

Moynihan noted in the margins on 16 October 1940 that it had been approved 'provisionally' by de Valera, but that it be 'very carefully considered from the judge's point of view'. The words 'that such a law is invalid' were underlined and it seems clear from the crossed out words in the margins that alternative drafts were being considered. About a week later Moynihan noted he had discussed the matter further with de Valera on 23 October 1940:

> With regard to [the] suggested draft, he now agrees that we should let the words 'that such law is invalid' stand.
>
> He desires that we should add words to the draft indicating that where the person concerned in a [H]abeas [C]orpus application is under sentence of death, such sentence shall not be executed pending the final determination of the question whether he is lawfully detained. This, he directs, might be effected by deleting the words 'shall not order the release of the person detained' and substituting the words 'shall order that the person detained shall be held in custody' or words to the like effect.
>
> He desires further, that any other suggestions affecting *habeas corpus* including Mr Hearne's suggestion should be fully examined and submitted to him.[116]

By mid-November 1940 several drafts corresponding in broad measure to the present Article 40.4.2-5° were produced and these were approved by de Valera. At this stage, however, the draft Article 40.4.2° provided that every substantive *habeas corpus* application (i.e., apart from the initial application for an inquiry) would have to be heard and determined by a Divisional High Court consisting of not less then three judges.

Replying at the close of the Second Stage debate, de Valera indicated that, if necessary, he would be prepared to re-insert the words 'any and every judge thereof' in Article 40.4.2° to make it plain that the applicant had the right to go from judge to judge at the application for leave stage. De Valera, however, stoutly defended the three-judge rule:

> If there is an important matter to be decided as to whether a certain law is constitutional or not, it is not proper that

[116] See document no. 299.

> that should be dealt with in a haphazard way of finding some judge with a particular view, and allowing him to decide. You try, in other words, to choose the person whose opinion happens to be in a certain direction and then get your verdict. We would not stand for that and I think, therefore, that for the final determination, if it is regarded by the President of the High Court, who is removed from politics, as of sufficient importance to have three judges, there is no harm done to anybody.[117]

At the Committee Stage de Valera moved an amendment to clarify the position regarding the right of the applicant to go from judge to judge at leave stage. The version of Article 40.4.2° contained in the 1941 Bill as originally published provided that:

> Upon complaint being made by or on behalf of any person to the High Court or such [any][118] judge thereof alleging that such person is being unlawfully detained, the High Court or such judge thereof shall forthwith inquire into the said complaint and may order the person in whose custody such person is detained to produce the body before the High Court on a named day and to certify in writing the grounds of his detention and the High Court [consisting of not less than three judges][119] shall, upon the body of such person being produced before the Court and after giving the person in whose custody he is detained an opportunity of justifying the detention, order the release of such person from such detention unless satisfied that he is being detained in accordance with the law.

De Valera moved two amendments at Committee Stage to replace the words 'or such judge thereof' (which appeared twice) with in each case the words 'and any and every judge thereof to whom such complaint is made'.[120] He explained that:

> The amendment is intended to make quite clear that the complaint of a person that he is being unlawfully detained may be made in the first instance to any and every judge of

[117] 82 *Dáil Debates*, Cols 1265–6 (2 April 1941).
[118] The version as originally drafted by the 1940 Committee read 'or any judge thereof'. This made it clear—which the words 'or such judge thereof' did not—that the applicant had the right to apply to any judge of the High Court asking for an inquiry into the legality of an applicant's detention.
[119] The words in brackets were contained in the version drafted by the 1940 Committee.
[120] 82 *Dáil Debates*, Cols 1906–7 (24 April 1941).

> the High Court and that upon refusal by one or more judges the application may be renewed before the other judges or any of them. In other words, that you may make your application for a conditional order of which is usually the first step in a *habeas corpus* application to the various judges of the High Court in succession. That is to meet a point that was made by some speakers on the other side on the Second Reading.[121]

The new wording did represent an improvement, since, whatever the intention may have been, the original wording ('the High Court or such judge thereof…') of the revised Article 40.4.2° as presented to the Oireachtas did not readily lend itself to the argument that there was a right to go from judge to judge once the initial application for an inquiry has been refused.

De Valera did not, however, give way on the other points raised. The opposition expressed concern that the President of the High Court would be given the power to determine whether Court hearing the substantive application for release would consist of one or three judges and would also be in a position to determine whether the judge who granted leave should sit on that Court, but de Valera, dismissed those concerns.

On the whole, however, the changes to *habeas corpus* procedure effected by the 1941 Act were probably warranted. The common law rules had evolved in the pre-Judicature Act era in which there had been no right of appeal and these had given rise to endless confusion about the extent of the right to go from judge to judge. Nor did this confusion end following the enactment of Article 6 of the 1922 Constitution and the very similar language of Article 40.4.2° as originally enacted, since—as *Dowling's* case revealed—no one could be sure what the words 'and any and every Judge thereof' actually meant as they appeared in these provisions.[122] The new version of Article 40.4.2°, while preserving the right to go from judge to judge in respect of the initial *ex parte* application for leave, made it clear that there was no right to go to another judge of the High Court once that Court had pronounced following a full hearing that detention was valid. Moreover, unlike the position at common law, the disappointed applicant could always exercise his constitutional right to appeal that decision to the Supreme Court. And while the case-stated provisions of Article 40.4.3° were

[121] 82 *Dáil Debates* Cols 1906–7.

[122] It is, of course, true that similar language is used in Article 40.4.2°, but the crucial difference is that the words 'to whom such complaint is made' follow the words 'and any and every judge thereof'.

something of a novelty in 1941, they were justifiable on the ground that—unlike the position of the common law courts—the High Court had been given the enormous power of judicial review of legislation. If a prisoner was to be released from custody on the sole ground that an Act of the Oireachtas was unconstitutional—with, as in *Burke's* case, possibly enormous implications for many other detained persons[123]—it does not seem unfair that the Supreme Court should be given the final say on an issue of such potentially far-reaching importance.

President Hyde signed the Second Amendment of the Constitution Act, 1941 on 30 May 1941, just before the transitory period expired. After all the turmoil of the preceding twenty years, the constitutional system attained some stability, since another thirty-one years would elapse—with the passage of the Third Amendment of the Constitution Act, 1972 allowing Ireland to join the (then) European Economic Community—before the next amendment to the Constitution. But in 1941 all of that lay in the future. Yet, it is evident once again from the care and attention which was given to the (admittedly technical) issues that dominated the debate on the Second Amendment that the drafters had some sense of the potential impact which judicial review might have in the future.

No. 278: NAI, DT S10299

Seán Moynihan to all Government Departments

Department of Finance
1 December 1939

We have been requested by the Department of the Taoiseach to direct the special attention of Departments to the instructions contained in Finance Circular No. 34/38[124] regarding amendments to the Constitution, and to remind them of the necessity of keeping up-to-date the record referred to in the Circular. It will be appreciated that although the period within which the Constitution may be amended, in accordance with the provisions of Article 51, does not expire until 25 June 1941, it will, of course, be necessary to give full consideration to any suggested amendments, and to prepare any amending legislation required, well in advance of that date. It is important, therefore, that Departments should

[123] This issue was very much in view in *A v. Governor of Arbour Hill Prison*, [2006] 4 IR 84, where the Supreme Court was obliged to consider the retroactive effects of a declaration of unconstitutionality following the invalidation of section 1 of the Criminal Law (Amendment) Act, 1935.
[124] See document no. 266.

be in a position to furnish at short notice particulars of amendments which they may have found as a result of examination or experience of the Constitution to be necessary or desirable.

No. 279: [1940] IR, pp 141–57

Justice Gavan Duffy's Judgment in *The State (Redmond Burke) v. The Governor of Arbour Hill Military Barracks*

Four Courts, Dublin
1 December 1939

Seamus Burke, a spirit grocer and provision merchant, of Ballinrobe, Co. Mayo, who is an Irish citizen, applies for an order of *habeas corpus*, on the ground that he is being unlawfully detained by the Governor of Arbour Hill Military Detention Barracks, Dublin, being interned in the Barracks without trial.

The Governor justifies on a warrant emanating from the Minister for Justice under s. 55 (authorising internment under certain circumstances) of the Offences Against the State Act, 1939 (No. 13 of 1939), and the Regulations made under that Act.

I shall speak throughout of Seamus Burke as the applicant; he has made an affidavit and is the applicant in effect, but in form the applicant is his brother; no objection has been made on this score, but I am not to be taken as construing Art. 40 of the Constitution to sanction an application by a third party where the person detained can make the application himself.

Sects. 55 and 54 of the Act, and s.59, to which I shall refer, appear in Part VI of the Act, headed 'Powers of Internment', and subsection. 2 of s.54 enacts that that Part of the Act shall come into force forthwith, 'if and whenever and so often as the Government makes and publishes a proclamation declaring that the powers conferred by this Part of this Act are necessary to secure the preservation of public peace and order and that it is expedient that this Part of this Act should come into force immediately.'

The proclamation is thus a condition precedent. The Act was passed on the 14th of June, 1939 and a proclamation in the terms of sub-s.2 of s.54 was made and gazetted by the Government on the 22nd of August, 1939. On the same day the Government, under s.35 of the same Act, made and gazetted a proclamation declaring that they were 'satisfied that the ordinary Courts are inadequate to secure the effective administration of justice and the preservation of public peace and order and that it is therefore necessary that Part V' of the Act should come into force; Part V is headed 'Special Criminal Courts' and such Courts are the subject of a special provision in Article 38 of the Constitution. It is noteworthy that a determination that the ordinary Courts are inadequate to their functions is necessary to bring Part V into force, whereas that condition does not apply to bringing into force Part VI. Any Judge of the High Court must regret interfering with executive action at this time, when in fact the Government, with its special means of knowledge, has officially declared that the ordinary Courts are inadequate to secure the effective administration of justice, but any such consideration is subsidiary to the right of the citizen under the Constitution to an order of *habeas corpus*, if that right be established.

The applicant has been interned without trial since the 16th of September, 1939, in pursuance of s.55 of the Act, under a warrant by the Minister of that date, on the ground that the Minister is satisfied that he is engaged in activities calculated to prejudice the preservation of the security of the State. He now challenges the right of the Oireachtas to make a law conferring the power of internment on a Minister. I have thus to determine a matter of high constitutional importance. I am not concerned with policy, for problems of statesmanship belong essentially to the legislative and executive domains, and not to the judicial; I have to decide a question of law.

The Attorney General is represented on this application in pursuance of the Rules of Court, and he sustains the validity under the Constitution of Part VI of the Offences Against the State Act, 1939. I must look into the material provisions of the Constitution in order to see exactly what place personal liberty finds there, and to see whether the impugned enactment fits into the constitutional framework, and I must do so with special care, since this is the first case in which a claim of this kind has arisen for adjudication under the Constitution.

I wish to place on record the fact that there has been no suggestion on behalf of the State that the Offences Against the State Act, 1939, may be treated as having amended the Constitution by implication. If I may say so, I think counsel for the State were quite right in making no case of that kind under the present Constitution.

The Constitution was enacted by the People of Ireland on the 1st of July, 1937, and came into force on the 29th of December, 1937.

With the greatest solemnity, the People, invoking the Most Holy Trinity, gave to themselves 'Dochum Glóire Dé agus onóra na hÉireann':

a noble Christian polity; they enshrined the guiding principles in language simple and direct; and they entrusted to the Judiciary the tremendous responsibility of maintaining their constitutional monument against legislative attack.

Article 9 deals with citizenship and declares fidelity to the nation and loyalty to the State to be fundamental political duties of all citizens. For the rest, the salient features of the Constitution, for the purposes of the present case, are (1) its declaration of the fundamental right of the citizen to personal liberty; (2) its measures for the protection of constitutional rights; (3) its outlook on the criminal law; and (4) its provisions for times of emergency. There is no express authority for internment without trial.

As to personal liberty, it is one of the cardinal principles of the Constitution, proclaimed in the Preamble itself, that the dignity and freedom of the individual may be assured; Articles 40 to 44 of the Constitution set out the 'Fundamental Rights', comprising personal rights, the imprescriptible rights of the family, the inalienable right and duty of parents to educate their children, the natural right to private property, and freedom of conscience and religion. The fundamental personal rights, which are the personal rights of free men, include (Article 40) the right to the equal protection of the law, the inviolability of the home, the rights of free speech, peaceable assembly and association, and, in particular, the liberty of the person, expressed in the words: 'No citizen shall be deprived of his personal liberty save in accordance with law'; this right is secured by a strongly worded *habeas corpus* clause, to protect the citizen against unlawful imprisonment, except as against the Defence Forces during the existence of a state of war or armed rebellion.

These rights are, of course, qualified, because under modern conditions the rights of the citizen must be subjected to legal limitations, and absolute rights are unknown, or virtually unknown, in a democratic State. But in a significant clause of Article 40, the State guarantees in its laws to respect the personal rights of the citizen and, as far as practicable, to defend and vindicate them; in particular, the State is charged by its laws to protect, as best it may, from unjust attack the person of the citizen as well as his life, good name and rights of property.

The right to personal liberty means much more than mere freedom from incarceration and carries with it necessarily the right of the citizen to enjoy the other fundamental rights, the right to live his life, subject, of course, to the law; and, if a man is confined against his will, he has lost his personal liberty, whether the name given to the restraint be penal servitude, imprisonment, detention or internment; see *Dunne v.*

Clinton.[125] *Habeas corpus* is the direct security for the right to personal liberty, but a constitutional separation of powers and constitutional directions for the administration of justice as an independent function of the State were necessary to make the remedy secure.

The architects of the Constitution were alive to the need for protecting the rights declared in the Constitution; accordingly, in Article 5, they characterised the State as a democratic State, in which (Article 6) all powers derive under God from the People and are to be exercised only by or on the authority of the legislative, executive and judicial organs established by the Constitution; effect is given to the division of powers by Articles 15, 28 and 34 and 35. Laws in any respect repugnant to the Constitution are expressly forbidden and invalidated by Article 15 and, as a special safeguard, exclusive original jurisdiction in cases raising the constitutionality of any law is assigned to the High Court, together with a veto, a matter of first importance, upon any statutory encroachment on the appellate jurisdiction of the Supreme Court in any such case (Article 34); the Supreme Court is thus made the ultimate constitutional guardian of constitutional right.

Under Articles 34 and 35 an independent judiciary is constituted, charged with the administration of justice in public Courts established by law. The High Court is invested with full original jurisdiction to determine all matters and questions, whether of law or fact, civil or criminal; the inference is that there are two categories, and two categories only, of matters and questions of law or fact: (a) the civil and (b) the criminal. The Constitution recognises in Articles 29 and 13, as exceptions from the general jurisdiction of the High Court, international agreements (unless the Oireachtas otherwise determines) and the exercise of his powers and functions by the President.

Articles 30 and 38 enjoin that all crimes and offences are to be prosecuted in the name of the People, that no person shall be tried on any criminal charge save in due course of law, minor offences only being tried in Courts of summary jurisdiction, and that no person shall be tried on any criminal charge without a jury, except under the summary jurisdiction for minor offences, or military law for military offenders, or where military tribunals are dealing with a state of war or armed rebellion, or under the jurisdiction of special Courts, established by law when the ordinary Courts are inadequate to secure the effective administration of justice and the preservation of public peace and order. Manifestly these penal jurisdictions are all contemplated as importing

[125] [1930] IR 366.

lawful restrictions under the Constitution upon personal liberty, and Art. 40 must be read in the light of Art. 38.

The need to provide for times of emergency was clearly foreseen and the emergencies in contemplation were defined. Besides making the declaration of war subject to the assent of Dáil Éireann, the Constitution, where express amendment of the Constitution is not involved, facilitates the enactment of a Bill declared by the Government to be urgent and immediately necessary to preserve public peace and security or by reason of a public emergency (Article 24), sanctions the establishment of special Courts, as I have said, where the ordinary Courts are inadequate (Article 38), and declares that a law made expressly to secure the public safety and the preservation of the State in time of war or armed rebellion is not to be invalidated by any provision of the Constitution (Article 28); see now as to 'time of war' the First Amendment (1939).

There is no provision enabling the Oireachtas or the Government to disregard the Constitution in any emergency short of war or armed rebellion. And the Constitution contains no express provision for any law endowing the Executive with powers of internment without trial.

I am now in a position to ask myself whether s.55 of the Offences Against the State Act, 1939, is a valid law under the Constitution. The section purports to authorise a Minister of State (after the necessary proclamation has been made and published under s.54), to order the arrest and indefinite detention of any person engaged in activities calculated to prejudice the preservation of the peace, order or security of the State, whenever the Minister is satisfied, a condition precedent, that the person is so engaged; the Minister makes his order by a 'warrant' under his hand, which entitles any Gárda, without other warrant, to arrest that person; and the section requires the person arrested to be detained in a prescribed place. The detained man may apply in writing to the Government, under s.59, to have his detention considered by a non-judicial Commission, whereupon the Government must refer the matter to the Commission; its duty is to inquire into *the grounds* of the detention and with all convenient speed report to the Government; the Minister for Justice must furnish to the Commission all relevant information and documents for which it may call; if it reports that no reasonable grounds exist for the detention, the internee must within one week either be released or charged according to law with an offence. He may be held for a week despite the Commission's report that no reasonable grounds exist for detaining him–a provision hard to defend. Mr Maguire for the Attorney-General says that it is the plain duty of the Commission to inquire what the internee has to say for himself, either orally or in writing; any such inquiry must, I think, involve divulging the grounds of internment to the internee. Mr Maguire's candour, a conspicuous feature of his argument, invites the inquiry why, if he is right as to the duty of the Commission, fair play does not impose a similar duty on the Minister; I do not know the answer. But, as neither the prosecutor nor the State has argued that the Minister's duty under the section involves any hearing of, or statement from, the suspect, I pass on to the specific complaints of the applicant.

Let me say here, in order to avoid recurring to the case that Mr Haugh vigorously pressed upon me, in answer to most of those complaints, the decision in *O'Connell's Case*[126] whereby a transient Court upheld internment without trial under the Constitution of 1922; in my opinion, that case, if its authority survived the appeal,[127] bears only a superficial resemblance to this, because it was decided under a Constitution differing radically from the present Constitution in its provisions to secure personal liberty; and because in that case, unlike this, there was 'nothing except the inner consciousness of the Minister expressed in the written order' for interment (*per* Molony C.J. at 112), for the authority to intern was the arbitrary opinion of the Minister that the enlargement of the internee would imperil the public safety: that position is not reproduced in the Act of 1939.

The applicant complains that s.55 violates the equality of citizens before the law (Article 40); I cannot so hold without much closer examination of the authorities. It is recognised in America that a similar provision for equal protection of the laws in the 14th Amendment to the Constitution of the United States does not prevent all limited legislation and is not infringed by a law imposing on all citizens the like penalties for the like offences. But I need not decide this point.

I shall now examine the contention that s.55 of the Act of 1939 is repugnant to the Constitution because it authorises an invasion by the Executive of the judicial domain by requiring a Minister of State to administer justice. In order to determine this question, I shall investigate the duty of a Minister under the section, in order to see its essential character and so to ascertain whether a Minister acting under s.55 is acting judicially. That is the first of two associated, but distinct, questions. Upon an affirmative answer to the first question, the second inquiry is whether, besides acting judicially, he is administering justice.

The Minister has authority to order arrest and internment only upon condition that he shall first have been 'satisfied' that the person concerned

[126] [1924] IR 104.
[127] [1935] IR 247.

is engaged in prejudicial activities of the sort described in the section. The word 'satisfied' may or may not imply something in the nature of a judicial inquiry; its implication depends on the context. And, if the section erects the Minister into a tribunal, is he a judicial or a so-called administrative tribunal? A judicial tribunal, besides acting judicially, administers justice, determining rights and liabilities according to law, upon the ascertainment of the relevant facts. An administrative tribunal is sometimes required to act judicially; more often it is not, but, whether or not it acts judicially, it does not administer, and does not claim to administer, justice. Such is not its function; normally its characteristic function is to administer policy as it sees best in the public interest. Its decisions may, therefore, properly be influenced by subjective standards; it generally has the widest discretion, a very much wider power of acting on personal opinion than is involved in the limited judicial discretion familiar to a court of law, administering justice. That is why an appeal to the Courts from an administrative tribunal so frequently fails.

The Minister has to be satisfied. There must be countless occasions in the official life of a Minister of State on which he has to be satisfied as to particular facts before taking a particular course, occasions on which nobody would for a moment expect him to act judicially in order to be satisfied; otherwise the daily routine of administration would become impossible. But under s.55 the Minister, who may be any Minister of State, is not exercising any normal function of his office; he is exercising a most exceptional statutory power, and a man's liberty depends on his exercise of it. The nature of the duty imposed on 'a Minister of State' by s.55 is the best guide to the meaning of the word 'satisfied' in the section. Part VI of the Act is its own best dictionary, and the grave duty which the section imposes does not suggest any loose use of the word 'satisfied', but, in my opinion, clearly suggests a serious inquiry resulting in a serious finding of 'satisfied' or 'not satisfied', as the case may be. Mr Haugh points out that in the Public Safety Act of 1924 (No. 1 of 1924), there were sections empowering a Minister to act, if 'satisfied' that there were grounds of suspicion, but those sections were not considered by the Court in *O'Connell's Case.*[128]

In examining the duty imposed on the Minister, I have in mind two well-known authorities in particular, *The Dublin Corporation Case,*[129] and *Webster's Case.*[130] In the earlier case C.J. May says (at 376):

128 [1924] IR 104; [1935] IR 247.
129 2 LR IR 371.
130 [1902] 2 IR 349.

> 'It is established that the writ of *certiorari* does not lie to remove an order merely ministerial, such as a warrant'—he is, of course, speaking of the purely ministerial warrant—'but it lies to remove and adjudicate upon the validity of acts judicial. In this connection the term 'judicial' does not necessarily mean acts of a Judge or legal tribunal sitting for the determination of matters of law, but for the purpose of this question a judicial act seems to be an act done by competent authority, upon consideration of facts and circumstances, and imposing liability or affecting the rights of others';

and he instances the making of a rate. In the later case L.J. Fitzgibbon accepts this statement, as applied to the cases under consideration, with the proviso that the acts must involve the exercise, or assumed exercise, of some jurisdiction (383), while C.B. Palles (373) enunciates this much quoted proposition:

> 'I have always considered, and still consider, the principle of law to be as stated by the Chief Justice, assuming that there is nothing in the statute constituting the particular tribunal or investing it with the particular power which indicates a contrary intention.' He is speaking of an intention to exclude *certiorari*. 'I have always thought that to erect a tribunal into a "Court" or "jurisdiction", so as to make its determinations judicial, the essential element is that it should have power, by its *determination* within jurisdiction, to impose liability or affect rights. By this I mean that the liability is imposed, or the right affected by the determination only, and not by the fact determined, and so that the liability will exist, or the right will be affected, although the determination be wrong in law or in fact.'

This passage represents accepted law, save that the words 'determine liability' would, it has been suggested, be more accurate than 'impose liability', but for my present purpose the difference is not material. These statements, though directed to *certiorari,* help to clarify the aims of my present inquiry.

Let me examine the duty of the Minister under the section a little more closely. Before issuing his warrant for arrest with a view to internment, the Minister must make up his mind upon certain matters of fact; the evidence placed before him will generally, I suppose, be contained in the Gárda records; I assume that it is not required by the section to be legal evidence. Often the Minister may be in a better position to reach a correct conclusion than the man in the street, and he is not bound by the view which he thinks a jury would probably take, if on the evidence that view appears to him to be wrong. I recognise all that in favour of the State, but I come back to the need for the Minister to be satisfied, to be satisfied as to facts, and to be satisfied as to facts which will form 'the grounds' of detention for the Commission of inquiry, if there be one. First, the Minister, to have the right to intern, must be satisfied that the person concerned is in fact engaged in specific activities; that is the kind of question that one may fairly classify as a 'jury question'; if he finds against the man on that issue of fact, the Minister, before he can intern, must consider whether those activities by that person are calculated to prejudice the peace, order or security of the State and be satisfied that they are; the phraseology here is indefinite, but I need not pause to consider whether, on the analogy of American decisions, it is too vague under our Constitution for a penal enactment; this second determination may be said to depend on opinion, because different minds may so easily on the same facts reach different conclusions; but it is emphatically not a matter of discretion, which the Minister is free to determine as he feels inclined in accordance with his view of the public interest; it is essentially a matter of fact to be determined with due regard to the evidence; the Minister has to be satisfied, as a matter of fact, that the activities in question are calculated to prejudice the State, as being hurtful to the public peace, public order or public security. Sometimes a strong opinion may inevitably affect his judgment upon this kind of fact, but it remains a matter of fact. Having reached a conclusion adverse to the man concerned on both issues of fact, having been 'satisfied' within the meaning of the section, the Minister by his dual determination of fact, be it right or wrong, at once puts the man into the category of persons liable to be arrested and interned. In my opinion, it is clear that, so far as his investigation has now gone, the Minister in this weighing of the evidence has been acting judicially; to give an example illustrating the limits of his power, the Minister could not be satisfied within the terms of the section, merely because he ascertained that the Gárda Síochána had the worst opinion of the man by reason of his past activities, and that he was a person whom it would be prudent to lock up; but the Minister must be satisfied on the evidence that his present activities are calculated to prejudice the State. If I am right in holding that the Minister is acting judicially in his essential inquiry, in finding 'the grounds' for internment, I cannot hold that the essential character of his duty under the section is altered by his discretion (if any, for it is not clear that he has a discretion) as to proceeding to apply the statutory sanction, if he does not prosecute. Now many civil servants are called upon in divers directions to act judicially, without thereby administering justice; hence this test does not by itself determine whether under the section the Minister is administering justice or acting merely in an administrative capacity, but the test is useful because it goes a long way towards ascertaining the essential character of this particular statutory function.

The border line between the powers that may, and the powers that may not, be exercised by a Minister of State or a Department of Government is not easy to define with accuracy. The solution of the problem is expressed by Professor Willoughby in his Constitution of the United States, 2nd edn., (1,619 and 1,620) in the following statement, which, as a general enunciation of principle, I adopt, as applicable under our Constitution, for the purpose of my present inquiry:

'It is not a correct statement of the principle of the separation of powers to say that it prohibits absolutely the performance by one department of acts which, by their essential nature, belong to another. Rather, the correct statement is that a department may constitutionally exercise any power, whatever its essential nature, which has, by the Constitution, been delegated to it, but that it may not exercise powers not so constitutionally granted, which, from their essential nature, do not fall within its division of governmental functions, unless such powers are properly incidental to the performance of its own appropriate functions....Generally speaking, it may be said that, when a power is not peculiarly and distinctly legislative, executive or judicial, it lies within the authority of the Legislature to determine where its exercise shall be vested.'

Before applying the principle, let me record certain relevant conclusions to which I have come on s.55, remembering that I am dealing with a man whom a Minister has found to be engaged in activities calculated to prejudice the State. First, the Constitution (Art. 9) declares fidelity to the nation and loyalty to the State to be fundamental political duties of all citizens; there is, I think, much to be said for the view that the citizen engaged in activities conflicting with that fidelity and loyalty commits a misdemeanour, for which he is liable to prosecution under the criminal law. Secondly, and quite apart from that consideration, it would be difficult, and I think impossible, for a man to engage in activities calculated to prejudice the preservation of the peace, order or security of the State without offending the ordinary criminal law. Thirdly, I am further of opinion that the activities contemplated by s.55, if not otherwise unlawful, are made unlawful by this very enactment, authorising internment as their reward; if such activities are not in terms forbidden by our laws, they are at least prohibited by necessary implication in s.55, under pain of internment; Mr Maguire agrees with me here. Fourthly, the activities described by the section make the subject-matter of Part VI of the Act one 'which, by its very nature, belongs to the domain of criminal jurisprudence'; *cp. In re Board of Commerce* Act, 1919.[131] Fifthly, I am of opinion that indefinite internment under Part VI of the Act is indistinguishable from punishment for engaging in the activities in question, and I consider that the decision of a Minister of State to order the arrest and internment of a man under s.55 is equivalent to a judgment pronounced against the internee for his dangerous activities.

These considerations are, indeed any one of them probably is, sufficient to show that the authority conferred on a Minister by s.55 is an authority, not merely to act judicially, but to administer justice and an authority to administer criminal justice and condemn an alleged offender without charge or hearing and without the aid of a jury. But, to apply Professor Willoughby's principle, the administration of justice is a peculiarly and distinctly judicial function, which, from its essential nature, does not fall within the executive power and is not properly incidental to the performance of the appropriate functions of the executive; consequently a law endowing a Minister of State, any Minister, with these powers is an invasion of the judicial domain and as such is repugnant to the Constitution.

My conclusion in favour of the applicant is fortified by Article 37 of the Constitution, expressly authorising a law to empower an officer who is not a Judge to exercise limited functions and powers of a judicial nature in non-criminal matters; the Article must imply that no such jurisdiction can be conferred by law in a criminal matter, so that criminal justice is exercisable only by a person who is a Judge under the Constitution. The Constitution, no doubt, makes exceptions for military law and for special Courts in specified circumstances of danger, but those exceptions do not apply here and I observe that the Constitution does not contemplate internment without trial even by the special Courts set up in time of emergency.

If my analysis of the Minister's statutory duty is accurate, the document which the Act calls a warrant is really a combination of a conviction, an order to arrest and a warrant of committal. Its character

[131] [1922] 1 AC 191, 198.

as a conviction in the case of the present applicant seems to me particularly clear on the evidence. Sergeant Conway deposes that on the 15th of September, 1939, he arrested the applicant at Ballinrobe, because, having searched his house and found 'a number of what appeared to me to be seditious and incriminating documents' unspecified, he suspected 'that he was concerned in the commission of an offence' under the Offences Against the State Act, 1939, 'namely, possession of seditious or incriminating documents'; that is an offence under s.12 of the Act and 'incriminating document' is defined in s.2; the penalty is a fine or imprisonment (up to three months) or both. As I understand the evidence, a report (I rather think verbal) was then sent to Chief Superintendent Carroll in Dublin, whereupon the Chief Superintendent deposes that on the morning of the 16th he 'got into touch with the Department of Justice and a warrant for the arrest and detention' of the applicant under s.55 of the Act was signed by the Minister. This was done at 11.30 a.m. This rather elusive evidence of the ministerial activity must mean that the warrant was signed by the Minister because the seditious or incriminating documents were found in Mr Burke's house. The inescapable conclusion, in my opinion, is that the Executive Authority of the State, having under the Act the right to prosecute for the alleged offence, elected to take the alternative course of directing indefinite imprisonment without trial for the 'activity' of possessing seditious or incriminating documents. And I am quite seriously asked to hold that this internment was not punishment at all, but merely 'a deterrent'. I shall refrain from painting this lily of speech.

But, if the Minister does act only to deter, I reach the same result. If the Minister's action was not an act of punitive justice, I should have to classify it, despite the resultant internment, as an act of deterrent or preventive justice. Now, the jurisdiction to bind a man over to be of good behaviour, when his conduct has given ground for anticipating misbehaviour by him, has been a regular feature of the ordinary administration of justice for centuries; it is a venerable part of the most ancient jurisdiction of justices and is perhaps as old as the jurisdiction to try and punish crime; see Bacon's Abridgement, 7th edn., vol. VII, titles 'Surety of the Peace' and 'Surety of the Good Behaviour' and the corresponding titles in Burn's Justice of the Peace, vol. V, and O'Connor's Justice of the Peace, vol. I, chapter III (2nd edn.); see also the judgments of Lord Fitzgerald in *Father Feehan's Case*,[132] and of C.B. Palles in *Dr*

[132] 10 LR IR, 294, 301.
[133] Judgments of the Superior courts in Ireland in cases under the Criminal Law (Ir.) Act, 1887, 340, 353 *et seq.*

Tanner's Case.[133] If the Minister's action was preventive justice, it cannot be defended under Art. 37 of the Constitution, because preventive justice, though no offence be charged, is in its nature a criminal matter or proceeding; this characteristic of preventive justice emerges from the terms of the traditional commission of the peace, coupled with the fact that the suspect may be imprisoned in default of finding sureties; from the inclusion of the subject-matter in the Criminal Justice Administration Act, 1914—see s.43, sub-s.13; and from the decisions in *Hilton v. Byron*,[134] in *Father Feehan's Case*,[135] *per* C.J.May; and in *Halpin v. Rice*,[136] *per* Justice Gibson. Hence, if the Minister was exercising preventive justice by interning the applicant, he was administering criminal justice. This point is material also on the applicant's contention that the warrant must show jurisdiction on its face, a matter to which I shall refer at the conclusion of this judgment.

In my opinion, the long title of the 'Offences Against the State Act' and indeed its short title, would show that the intention of the Legislature was to punish wrongdoers, if the Act left any doubt on the question; as Mr Maguire says, the Act was passed to deal with offenders against Article 9 of the Constitution, which lays down the citizen's fundamental duty of fidelity and loyalty; that is the setting in which I find s.55.

The Minister's action was attacked as unconstitutional by Mr MacBride, in his very careful and elaborate argument, upon a number of other grounds, with which it is now unnecessary for me to deal. But one contention is too important to pass over in silence, especially as I think it well founded. Mr MacBride relies very strongly on the constitutional guarantees for the personal rights of the citizen. Sect.55, he says, infringes those rights and cannot stand. He says that the right to be free is denied. Article 40, if I understand it, guarantees that no citizen shall be deprived of liberty, save in accordance with a law which respects his fundamental right to personal liberty, and defends and vindicates it, as far as practicable, and protects his person from unjust attack; the Constitution clearly intends that he shall be liable to forfeit that right under the criminal law on being duly tried and found guilty of an offence. In my opinion, a law for the internment of a citizen, without charge or hearing, outside the great protection of our criminal jurisprudence and outside even the special Courts, for activities calculated to prejudice the State, does not respect his *right* to personal

[134] 12 Mod. 243.
[135] 10 LR IR 294, 300.
[136] [1901] 2 IR 593, 605.

liberty and does unjustly attack his person; in my view, such a law does not defend his right to personal liberty as far as practicable, first, because it does not bring him before a real Court and again because there is no impracticability in telling a suspect, before ordering his internment, what is alleged against him and hearing his answer, a course dictated by elementary justice. I am inclined to think that, if a Minister be properly satisfied under s.55, he could have the suspect bound over to be of good behaviour under the ordinary law, so that, if the case be not one for prosecution, a law defending his liberty as far as practicable would take his recognisance, with or without sureties, in order to allow him to enjoy all his fundamental rights, to carry on his business and live his life; certainly the Act could have so provided, with the ordinary imprisonment in default.

In my opinion, the saving words in the declaration that 'No citizen shall be deprived of his liberty save in accordance with law' cannot be used to validate an enactment conflicting with the constitutional guarantees. The opinion of Mr Justice Fitzgibbon in *Ryan's Case*[137] is relied upon by Mr Maguire, but it does not apply, in my judgment, to a Constitution in which fundamental rights and constitutional guarantees effectively fill the *lacunae* disclosed in the polity of 1922. The Constitution, with its most impressive Preamble, is the Charter of the Irish People and I will not whittle it away. There is nothing novel in the solemn recognition of the right to personal freedom as an essential basis of the social structure of a society of free men. In my opinion, the Constitution intended, while making all proper provisions for times of emergency, to secure his personal freedom to the citizen as truly as did Magna Carta in England. Whatever abuses were perpetrated in this country, despite the Magna Carta Proclamation for Ireland of 1216, in England Magna Carta was taken to mean what it said. Lord Shaw's citation in *O'Brien's Case*,[138] from Hallam's 'penetrating judgment' affirms that from the era of King John's Charter it must have been a clear principle of the Constitution in England that no man can be detained in prison without trial. The same principle is established in the Constitution of the United States, where a law which may prejudice person or property must be a law which hears before it condemns, which proceeds upon inquiry, and renders judgment only after trial, so that every citizen shall hold his life, liberty and property, and immunities, under the protection of the general rules which govern society; see the citation from Webster, adopted by the Supreme Court, in Willoughby,

137 [1935] IR 170, 229, 231.
138 [1923] AC 603, 646.

2nd edn., at 1691. It would be idle to multiply quotations. In my opinion, the right to personal liberty and the other principles which we are accustomed to summarise as the rule of law were most deliberately enshrined in a national Constitution, drawn up with the utmost care for a free people, and the power to intern on suspicion or without trial is fundamentally inconsistent with the rule of law and with the rule of law as expressed in the terms of our Constitution.

The legal position would be different, were I concerned with a war measure, a law 'expressed to be for securing the public safety and the preservation of the State in time of war' under Article 28, but I am not, for the Offences Against the State Act, 1939, is not such a law.

The Minister's procedure and his warrant under s.55 of the Act of 1939 are also attacked. I shall confine myself to the single objection that the warrant is bad on its face because it fails to show jurisdiction, so that it is no authority to the Governor of the Barracks to hold the applicant.

If the warrant were an ordinary act of a civil department administering its functions, it would have to be liberally construed, without regard to technicalities derived from the necessity of surrounding personal liberty with safeguards against errors of inferior Courts administering laws of a penal character. But it is nothing of that kind. I have held that this 'warrant' amounts to a conviction, an order to arrest and a warrant of committal; if I am right in that view, the warrant must show jurisdiction. Baron Parke in *Gossett v. Howard* says:

'In the case of special authorities given by statute to justices or others acting out of the ordinary course of the common law, the instruments by which they act, whether warrants to arrest, commitments, or orders, or convictions, or inquisitions, ought, according to the course of decisions, to show their authority on the face of them by direct averment or reasonable intendment.'[139]

This passage is endorsed by C.B. Palles in *R. (Boylan) v. Londonderry JJ*;[140] and the Chief Baron's enunciation of the principle is taken to be the true rule by Mr Justice O'Byrne in *Hughes's Case*.[141] The warrant here purports to be made by the Minister for Justice 'in exercise of the powers conferred on me by s.55 of the Offences Against the State Act, 1939', but it contains no statement that the Government has made and published the proclamation necessary to give the Minister any jurisdiction at all in the matter and no reference to s.54 (authorising such a proclamation), which might justify this Court in reading a reference to an existing

[139] 10 QB 411, 452.
[140] [1912] 2 IR 374, 382.
[141] [1935] IR 128, 150.

proclamation into the warrant. In *Hughes's Case* an order, containing better recitals but omitting an averment essential to jurisdiction, was held void, despite very strong validating provisions in the governing enactment, provisions which have no counterpart here. The applicant is, therefore, held under an invalid warrant and I shall, under Art. 40 of the Constitution, order his release accordingly.

I had at one time expected to confine my judgment to the single point on the warrant, but I was able to ascertain the true character of that document only after a laborious investigation of the duty imposed on the Minister, and this involved an examination of the separation of powers in the Constitution to ascertain his lawful powers. Since that examination showed the applicant to be right on both the constitutional and the technical issues, I have felt obliged to deal with both matters.

I have only to add that there is no application before me to quash the Minister's warrant and I am not doing so; it is well settled in this country that the absence of any such application does not affect the duty of the Court with regard to *habeas corpus*, when satisfied that the detention is not authorised by law; see *Reg. v. Riall*,[142] and *In re Sullivan*,[143] a case which on this point is good law.

No. 280: NAI, PRES P2

Memorandum by Michael McDunphy
'Council of State—procedure re consultation'

Office of the Secretary to the President
11 December 1939

Time Limits for Consultation

[Matter omitted]

2. A convening of a meeting of the Council of State connotes the summoning of every individual member thereof, and for this purpose each member is entitled to reasonable notice.
3. The need for a meeting of the Council will almost always arise at very short notice, and the question of what period of time it is necessary to envisage for the summoning and holding of such a meeting, in any circumstances which are likely to arise, is of considerable importance, in view of the fact that in most

[142] 11 IR CLR, 279.
[143] 22 LR IR 98.

cases a time limit is fixed by the Constitution for the completion of Presidential acts involving consultation with the Council.

4. In the event of a member being in some out of the way place in the extreme south or west of Ireland, the time taken for a communication to reach him may be as much as two days, and may be longer if he is out of Ireland, particularly if he is on tour in a motor car.
5. Having regard to such a possibility it seems to me that a minimum period of four days between the date of issue of the convening notices and the date on which the meeting to which they relate is to be held, should be available.
6. I am informed that a period of four days is regarded as normal notice to members of the Dáil summoning a meeting of that body, though in exceptional cases it may be summoned by wire at shorter notice.
7. Any hasty summoning of the Council of State should be exceptional. In normal circumstances ample time should be available.
8. There is one type of case in which as the Constitution stands at present the period of four days suggested in paragraph 5 is not likely to be available.
9. Article 27, which provides in certain terms for the reference of a Bill by the President to the Supreme Court on the question of its Constitutionality, requires that this reference which involves consultation with the Council of State, must be made not later than the fourth day after the Bill has been passed or deemed to have been passed by both Houses of the Oireachtas.
10. It is rare indeed that a Bill reaches the President on the day on which it is so passed; seldom in fact does it reach him before the second day after that event. In certain cases it is possible that it might not reach him until after the lapse of the period of four days within which reference to the Supreme Court must be made.
11. Even without taking into consideration the time necessary for the prior examination by the President of a Bill from the point of view of the application of this Article, the time available is not sufficient even for the summoning of the Council of State.

12. I am of opinion that the first definite change to be made is to make the period run from the date of presentation of the Bill by the Taoiseach to the President, that is to say, from the date on which the President becomes officially cognisant of the Bill, instead of from the date of its passage, actual or deemed, by both Houses of the Oireachtas, as at present.[144]
13. This would prevent the operation of the Article being rendered impossible by reason of lapse of time not cognisable by the President.
14. The second desirable change is to extend the period of four days which might in certain circumstances be found to be too restrictive.
15. In view of the fact that the latest date for the signature of a Bill which is capable of being, but is not in fact, referred to the Supreme Court, is the seventh day after the date of its presentation by the Taoiseach to the President; there seems to be no reason why this date should not also be the latest date on which the President can refer such a Bill to the Supreme Court.
16. This period would be ample for the completion of all steps leading to a decision by the President to refer or not to refer the Bill to the Supreme Court, including the convening and holding of a meeting of the Council of State.
17. The two changes which I would recommend in this connection are therefore
    (a) That the date from which the period within which the President may refer a Bill to the Supreme Court should run, should be the date on which the Bill is presented to him by the Taoiseach for signature.
    (b) The period within which such reference may be made should be seven days from that date instead of the present four.[145]

[Matter omitted]

[144] Annotated by McDunphy: 'This change has now in fact been made'.
[145] Annotated by McDunphy: 'Both changes have now in fact been made'.

No. 281: NAI, DT S10484A

Eamon de Valera's statement at the first meeting of the Council of State

[Department of the Taoiseach]
[8] January 1940

Is é mo thuairim-se gur ceart an Bille seo do chur fé bhreith na Cúirte Uachtaraighe. Bheinn ar a mhalairt de thuairim muna mbéadh an bhreith a thug ~~Seoirse Gabhánach Ó Dubhthaigh, Breitheamh den Ard-Chúirt~~ (duine de bhreithiúnaibh na hArd-Chúirte uaidh le déanaí).[146] Is tuigthe ó bhreithiúntas an Bhreithimh sin go bhfuil sé i n-aghaidh an Bhunreachta comhacht do bhronnadh chun daoine do ghabháil agus do choinneáil gan a dtriail agus a gciontú os comhair Cúirte. B'é tuairim an Riaghaltais ná raibh comhachta den tsaghas san i n-aghaidh an Bhunreachta agus is dóigh liom go bhfuil an oiread san tábhachta ag baint leis an gceist nach mór í a shocrú go húdarásach.[147]

No. 282: NAI, PRES P2

Minutes of the first meeting of the Council of State

Áras an Uachtaráin
8 January 1940

The President presided.

a. Members Present:
   Ex - Officio Members (Article 31.2.i)

The Taoiseach	Eamon de Valera
The Tánaiste	Seán T. O'Kelly

[146] This document is in typescript, with the words indicated crossed out manually, and the section in parentheses added manually above the deleted words.

[147] 'I am of the opinion that it is proper that this Bill should be referred to the Supreme Court. I would have been of the opposite opinion but for the judgment given recently by ~~George Gavan Duffy, Judge of the High Court~~ (one of the judges of the High Court). It is understood from the judgment of that judge that it is contrary to the Constitution to confer power to arrest individuals and to keep them without having a trial and a conviction before the Courts. The Government were of the opinion that powers of this kind were not contrary to the Constitution, and I am of the view that there are so many important matters relating to this question that it is necessary that it should be determined authoritatively.'

The statement has been annotated by Maurice Moynihan on 8 January as follows: 'Cóip is eadh seo thuas den mhéid a bhí beartaithe ag an dTaoiseach a rá ag an gcruinniú den Chomhairle Stáit inniú'. (Herewith a copy of what the Taoiseach had decided to say at the meeting of the Council of State today).

The Chief Justice	Hon. Timothy O'Sullivan
The President of the High Court	Hon. Conor A. Maguire
The Chairman of Dáil Éireann	Frank Fahy, T.D.
The Chairman of Seanad Éireann	Seán Gibbons, T.D.
The Attorney General	Patrick Lynch, K.C.

Members under Article 31.2.ii:
[Nil]
Members appointed by the President:
Deputy James M. Dillon
Senator Robert P. Farnan
Senator Sir John Keane
Deputy General Richard Mulcahy
Deputy William Norton
Senator Michael Tierney

b. Members Absent:
Deputy William T. Cosgrave

c. Others Present:
Secretary to the President Michael McDunphy, B.L.

1. The President stated that he had convened the meeting of the Council for the purpose of consulting them on the following matter, that is to say, whether the Offences Against the State (Amendment) Bill, 1940, should be referred by him to the Supreme Court under Article 26 of the Constitution for a decision on the question of whether the Bill is repugnant to the Constitution or to any provision thereof.
2. Each of the members present took and subscribed the Declaration prescribed by Article 31.4 of the Constitution.
3. The members present having been heard by the President, the meeting terminated at 4.40p.m.[148]

[148] The scant nature of the information presented in the minutes of the Council of State meeting is covered by an explanatory memorandum by Michael McDunphy, dated 10 January 1940. He noted that due to the sensitive nature of matters discussed at such meetings, 'it is clear that the minutes should not contain anything which would indicate any views expressed by individual members at the meeting', and should be confined to particulars of attendance, the relevant issue to be discussed and the fact that the members had been heard by the President', NAI, PRES P2.

No. 283: NAI, PRES P1488

Reference of Offences Against the State (Amendment) Bill 1940 to the Supreme Court by Douglas Hyde

Áras an Uachtaráin
8 January 1940

To: The Honourable Timothy Sullivan, Chief Justice.
In pursuance of the provisions of Article 26 of the Constitution, I, Douglas Hyde, President of Ireland, after consultation with the Council of State, do hereby refer the annexed Bill entitled Offences Against the State (Amendment) Bill, 1940, to the Supreme Court for a decision on the question as to whether the said Bill is repugnant to the Constitution or to any provision thereof.

Given under my hand and Seal this 8th day of January, 1940.

No. 284: NAI, PRES P2

Memorandum by Michael McDunphy 'Council of State—Procedure'

Office of the Secretary to the President
10 January 1940

Absence of A Member

1. Prior to the first meeting of the Council of State held on 8 January 1940, one of the members, Deputy William T. Cosgrave, had already intimated verbally to the Secretary to the President, that he did not intend to attend any meeting.
2. The Secretary explained that it was his duty to convene every member on every occasion.
3. This was done in the case of the first meeting.
4. Mr Cosgrave duly acknowledged the Convening Notice and expressed his inability to attend.[149]

[Matter omitted]

[149] Cosgrave's response to the Council of State Convening Notice may be found at NAI, PRES P1210.

No. 285: NAI, PRES P1488

Memorandum by Michael McDunphy
'Council of State—Procedure'

Office of the Secretary to the President
10 January 1940

Attendance of Persons Other Than Members

1. The only person, other than the President and members of the Council, who will normally be present at a meeting of the Council of State will be the Secretary to the President, who, as provided by Section 6.5 of the Presidential Establishment Act, 1938, will act as Clerk to the Council.
2. On the occasion of the first meeting of the Council on 8 January 1940, the Taoiseach discussed with me whether his Private Secretary, who is also Secretary to the Government, might be present or not. I expressed the opinion that it would be quite wrong for other than the President, members and the Secretary to the President to be present, who is ex-officio Clerk of the Council.
3. Apart from the question of principle, it would create a precedent which, if followed by other members, would entirely destroy the confidential nature of the Council of State.
4. The Taoiseach agreed with this view.

No. 286: NAI, PRES P2

Memorandum by Michael McDunphy
'Council of State—Procedure'

Office of the Secretary to the President
10 January 1940

Basic Rules of Discussion

i. Statement by President at opening of meeting

1. At the first meeting of the Council of State on 8 January 1940, the President in the course of his opening statement laid down

three rules or principles to be observed in the conducting of the meeting, viz:

(a) The proceedings should be strictly private.
(b) Political references should be avoided.
(c) Legal arguments should be equally avoided.[150]

ii. Privacy

2. The following is a relevant extract from the President's statement at the first meeting:

 'Before commencing the formal portion of the meeting I think it no harm that I am sure it is the wish of every member that the proceedings here should be regarded as strictly private, so that each of you may feel free to speak his mind on the question on which I seek your advice.

 'For the same reason it is not intended that any record should be made of the discussion here. The Secretary, who is Clerk to the Council, will take such brief notes as may be necessary to assist me in taking the requisite decision, but these notes will be destroyed immediately my decision has been made.'

3. The undertaking given by the President was duly honoured.

iii. Reference to Politics

2. The following is an extract from the President's statement in this regard:

 'I think you will agree with me also that reference to political considerations should be carefully avoided. We are not concerned here with whether the Bill is a desirable one or not, or with what consequences may or may not result, in the event of its becoming law.

 'The only matter which is before the meeting is whether or not I should refer the Bill to the Supreme Court.'

D. Legal Arguments to be Avoided

5. The following is an extract from the President's statement on the matter:

 'I think you will agree with me also that anything in the nature of legal arguments would be equally out of place. It is not the purpose of the meeting to express any opinion on the Constitutionality of the Bill. This is a matter entirely

[150] Annotated by McDunphy: 'Re. (b) and (c), see however my later note of 1 March 1943'.

for the Supreme Court, in the event of my deciding to refer the Bill to that Court.'

6. Strict adherence to this principle was particularly essential at the meeting in question for the reason stated in the President's statement.

E. Scope of Discussion may vary according to subject

7. At the first meeting of the Council of State the nature of the subject, viz., the question of whether or not a certain Bill should be referred to the Supreme Court under Article 26, naturally limited the scope of discussions within very narrow limits.
8. A much broader basis of discussion would of course be available in the case of a matter of public interest not involving purely legal considerations, such as the question of whether a Bill should or should not be referred to the people.
9. At the same time, the three basic principles referred to in the preceding paragraphs must always remain inviolable.[151]

No. 287: NAI, DT S10484A

Memorandum by Maurice Moynihan

Department of the Taoiseach
10 January 1940

The Taoiseach informed me today that Mr McDunphy, Secretary to the President, rang him last evening on the telephone and drew his attention to a point in regard to the procedure under Article 26 of the Constitution. Mr McDunphy pointed out that no provision is made in that Article for notification by the President to the Taoiseach and the Chairmen of the Houses of the Oireachtas of a decision to refer a Bill to the Supreme Court. He referred to the provisions in Article 27.4 and Article 51.2 where notification is required in the case of the reference of

[151] Annotated by McDunphy: 'See, however, my later note of 1 March 1943'. A portion of the text of this March 1943 note, arising out of the proceedings of the second meeting of the Council of State on 25 February 1943, is worth reproducing for the light it sheds on the meeting of 8 January 1940:

> On the occasion of the first meeting of the Council of State...the President expressed a wish that (a) reference to political situations and (b) legal arguments, should be avoided. The result was that members of the Council confined themselves merely to simple expressions of opinion for or against reference of the Bill to the Supreme Court, and that there was practically no discussion. On the occasion of the second meeting...the President decided to relax both these restrictions. The result was that the discussion was much freer, fuller and more informative, NAI, PRES P2.

Bills to the people and raised the question whether the Constitution should not be amended so as to provide for notification in the case of a reference of a Bill to the Supreme Court. The Taoiseach informed Mr McDunphy that he would mention the point to me and that I would reply to it.

I had previously spoken on the 8th instant to the Taoiseach about the claim of direct access to him which Mr McDunphy recently appears to be inclined to assert. The Taoiseach fully agrees that in cases where Mr McDunphy has a communication to make which affects him the communication should be made through this Department and not directly by Mr McDunphy to the Taoiseach himself. In any future case in which Mr McDunphy may communicate with him personally the Taoiseach proposes to refer him to me. He does not wish however to lay down a rigid rule since he feels that circumstances may arise in which direct communication by the Secretary to the President to himself may be unavoidable.

I undertook to have the point raised in regard to Article 26 examined.[152]

No. 288: NAI, DT S10484A

Memorandum from Maurice Moynihan to Michael McDunphy

Department of the Taoiseach
11 January 1940

I am directed by the Taoiseach to state that consideration has been given to the fact that no provision is made in Article 26 of the Constitution for notification by the President to the Taoiseach and the Chairman of each House of the Oireachtas of a decision under Article 26 of the Constitution to refer a Bill to the Supreme Court. It is understood that you drew attention to this point in a recent conversation with the Taoiseach.

As to the question whether Article 26 should be amended so as to provide for such notification, I am to state that if you are of opinion that the matter is of sufficient importance to justify consideration being given

[152] Annotated by Moynihan: 'Does the Office of the President come within the scope of the arrangements under which Departments generally have been requested to draw attention to points involving questions of amending the Constitution? 10/1/40'. Padraig Ó Cinnéide wrote to Moynihan the next day, informing him that the guidelines regarding suggested amendments to the Constitution had indeed been sent to McDunphy, and that McDunphy's telephone conversation with de Valera was 'quite unnecessary as well as being incorrect', NAI, DT S10484A.

to it in connection with possible amendments to the Constitution it should be dealt with on the lines laid down in Finance circular No. 34/38 of 30 December 1938, and Finance semi-official circular letter of 1 December 1939, and noted for consideration when the appropriate time comes.[153]

With regard to the practice which should be established, the Taoiseach considers it desirable that the President should inform him and the Chairman of each House of the Oireachtas in writing under his hand and seal of a decision under Article 26 of the Constitution to refer a Bill to the Supreme Court. He would suggest that this procedure should be followed in the case of the Offences Against the State (Amendment) Bill.

No. 289: NAI, DT S11484A

Memorandum from Maurice Moynihan to Padraig Ó Cinnéide

Department of the Taoiseach
11 January 1940

[Matter omitted]

I think it is now time to give preliminary consideration to the arrangements for the examination of any points that Departments may have noted in connection with the amendment of the Constitution. The three years' period will expire on 25 June 1941. I should be glad to have your views as to the steps that might be taken. The setting up of a small committee representing this Department, the Attorney General and one or two other Departments may be necessary.[154]

No. 290: NAI, DT S10484A

Memorandum from Michael McDunphy to Maurice Moynihan

Office of the Secretary to the President
18 January 1940

1. I am in receipt of your letter of 11th instant, on the question of keeping the Taoiseach and the Chairman of each House of

[153] See document nos 266, 278.
[154] See document no. 299.

the Oireachtas duly informed of any action which may be taken by the President from time to time under Article 26 of the Constitution.

2. The President agrees that, although not obligatory as in the case of Articles 27 and 51, such notification is desirable. He concurs further in the suggestion that the requisite communications should, following the headline set by those Articles, take the form of messages under his hand and Seal.
3. This procedure has been adopted in connection with the recent reference of the Offences Against the State (Amendment) Bill, 1940, to the Supreme Court under Article 26, and will be followed in future cases.
4. With reference to the question raised in paragraph 2 of your letter, I do not think that any amendment of the Constitution is either necessary or desirable in this regard.
5. Amendments of the Constitution should, in my opinion, be limited to matters of major principle, leaving procedure as far as possible to be established by practice.
6. In these early stages a very important code of Presidential procedure is being developed in the light of experience, and in harmony with the general scheme of the Constitution. The precedents created in this manner, while free from the rigidity of Constitutional requirement, will not be departed from except for very good reasons.

No. 291: NAI, DT S10484A

Memorandum from Michael McDunphy to Maurice Moynihan

Office of the Secretary to the President
19 January 1940

1. I find from my notes that about 20 January 1938, I mentioned to you in the course of a telephone conversation that I was not satisfied with the provisions of Subsection 2 of Section 1 of Article 26 of the Constitution as to the time within which a Bill could be referred by the President to the Supreme Court under that Article.
2. The matter was not the subject of any written correspondence, and I propose to remedy that omission now.

3. The Subsection referred to provides that where it is decided by the President to refer a Bill to the Supreme Court that reference must take place not later than four days after the date on which the Bill has been passed or is deemed to have been passed by both Houses of the Oireachtas.
4. The fact that the period runs from the date of passage of the Bill, rather than from the date of its presentation to the President for signature creates a difficulty at the very outset.
5. It rarely occurs that a Bill is received by the President from the Taoiseach before the first day after passage by the Oireachtas. In the majority of cases it is not received before the second day. In the case of a lengthy Bill in which there have been numerous amendments in the final stages, it is possible that it may not be received by the President until the four-day period prescribed by Subsection 2 above has expired, due to the fact that the Bill has to be printed after it has been passed by both Houses.
6. Even in the most favourable circumstances the time limit of four days is far too short, as a Bill cannot be referred to the Supreme Court by the President except after consultation with the Council of State, for which purpose a meeting of that Council must be convened and held.
7. It will be borne in mind that the five-day period which must elapse before a Bill can be signed under Article 25 runs from the date of its *presentation* by the Taoiseach to the President. It seems to me to be only reasonable that the period allowed for reference to the Supreme Court under Article 26 should run also from the same basic date.
8. This at least would prevent the operation of Article 26 being rendered impossible in the case of any particular Bill by reason of lapse of time not cognisable by the President.
9. The second point which I wish to make is that the period of four days available for such reference is too restricted.
10. It must be borne in mind that the Bill if not referred to the Supreme Court must be signed not later than seven days after the date of its presentation by the Taoiseach to the President. There seems to be no reason why this period of seven days should not also be available to the President for the reference of the Bill to the Supreme Court.
11. This period would be ample for the completion of all steps necessary arising out of his decision to refer the Bill to the

Supreme Court, including the convening and holding of a meeting of the Council of State.

12. The two changes which I would recommend in this connection are therefore:
    (a) The basic date of the period within which the President may refer a Bill to the Supreme Court should be the date of its presentation to him for signature and not the date of its passage, deemed or actual, by both Houses.
    (b) The period available for such reference should be seven days instead of the four days as at present.
13. In my considered opinion an amendment of the Constitution to effect these changes should be made before the lapse of the three-year period within which the Constitution may be amended by ordinary legislation, and I recommend accordingly.
14. I shall be glad, therefore, if my recommendation may be submitted to the Taoiseach for a ruling, and if I may be informed in due course of the result.[155]

No. 292: NAI, DT S10299

Memorandum from Padraig Ó Cinnéide to Maurice Moynihan

Department of the Taoiseach
22 January 1940

Secretary,

I agree that the time has arrived to take up and examine the various matters in connection with the amendments of the Constitution which it is proposed to make within the three-year period.

We might, accordingly, ask Finance to call on Departments to furnish information as to the points noted by them following the Finance instructions which were issued in the matter. These, when received, could be referred to the Committee mentioned in your minute. In

[155] Moynihan replied on 25 January, again pointing out the procedure with regard to amendments of the Constitution laid out in Finance Circular 34/38 of 30 December 1938 (see document no. 266). McDunphy's reply to this letter, dated 29 January, stated that he was aware of this procedure. However, he believed that any proposal affecting the office of the President should first receive the imprimatur of de Valera, but conceded that if de Valera did not wish to deviate from the general procedure he would comply with his wishes. Moynihan wrote to McDunphy on 31 January informing him that all important suggested amendments of the Constitution would be laid before de Valera before any final decision was made, and that the general procedure should therefore be followed, NAI, DT S10484A.

addition to representatives from this Department and the Department of the Attorney General who would be permanent members of the Committee, I suggest that other members representing different Departments which might be concerned with suggested amendments should be appointed *ad hoc* when these amendments are under consideration by the Committee. I do not think that it will be necessary to have a permanent representative of the Department of Finance on the Committee though I see no objection to one being appointed.

No. 293: NAI, DT S10299

Memorandum from Arthur Codling to all Government Departments

Department of Finance
29 January 1940

I am directed by the Minister for Finance to refer to this Department's Circular No. 34/38 of 30 December 1938, relative to suggestions from Departments as to necessary or desirable amendments of the Constitution in accordance with Article 51 thereof.[156] I am to state that the Department of the Taoiseach proposes to give preliminary consideration to any such amendments, and the Minister for Finance will be glad accordingly if your Department will furnish not later than 20th proximo particulars of such suggested amendments as have been recorded up to date in accordance with the request in this Department's Circular No. 34/38.

Each amendment suggested by your Department should be dealt with comprehensively in a separate statement, which should be furnished to this Department in quintuplicate.

No. 294: NAI, DT S9797

Seán Moynihan to [?]

[Department of Finance?]
7 February 1940

Leas Rúnaí,

1. Article 63 of the Constitution provides as follows: 'A copy of this Constitution signed by the Taoiseach, the Chief Justice,

[156] See document no. 266.

and the Chairman of Dáil Éireann, shall be enrolled for record in the office of the Registrar of the Supreme Court, and such signed copy shall be conclusive evidence of the provisions of this Constitution. *In case of conflict between the Irish and English texts, the Irish text shall prevail.*'

2. We have already noted on file S.10299[157] the question of the need for amending the Constitution to provide for the enrolment of the text of Constitution Amendments and apropos of this the following matter may cause difficulties later.
3. The first and only amendment to the Constitution, unlike the Constitution itself, was passed by the Oireachtas in English only, an Irish translation being issued afterwards in accordance with Article 25.4.5°. The view might perhaps be taken that there is no *Irish text* of the Amendment but merely a translation and that consequently the Irish text of the Constitution which is predominant, was not amended at all or was amended by the insertion of English words. If this view be correct, it would be necessary when republishing the amended constitution to insert the English text of the amendments in the present Irish version.[158]

No. 295: [1940] IR, pp 470

Judgement of the Supreme Court on the Constitutionality of the Offences Against the State (Amendment) Bill, 1940

Four Courts, Dublin
8 February 1940

In pursuance of the provisions of Article 26 of the Constitution, the President of Ireland, on 8 January 1940, after consultation with the Council of State, referred to this Court a Bill, entitled 'Offences Against the State (Amendment) Bill, 1940', for a decision on the question whether the said Bill is repugnant to the Constitution or to any provision thereof.

The said Article admittedly refers to a Bill such as this which has duly passed by both Houses of the Oireachtas. Under the Article it is provided

[157] NAI, DT S10299.
[158] Annotated by Seán Moynihan: 'This matter was cleared up in the Second Amendment to the Constitution Bill, 1941. The Irish version of the first amendment was passed as part of the second amendment. 5/7/'41'.

that the Court, consisting of not less than five Judges, shall consider every question referred to it by the President and, having heard arguments by or on behalf of the Attorney General and by Counsel assigned by the Court, shall pronounce its decision in open Court as soon as may be, and in any case not later than sixty days after the date of reference.

The Article further provides that the decision of the majority of the Judges of this Court shall, for the purposes of this Article, be the decision of the Court (Clause 2.2°).

It is further provided that, in every case in which this Court decides that the provision of a Bill so referred to the Court, is repugnant to the Constitution or to any provision thereof, the President shall decline to sign such Bill, and that, in every other case, the President shall sign the Bill as soon as may be after the date on which the decision of this Court shall have been pronounced.

In accordance with the provisions of the Article the Court assigned Counsel and, subsequently the Court heard arguments by Counsel on behalf of the Attorney General and by Counsel so assigned by the Court, and at the conclusion of the arguments reserved its decision; and the decision now announced is that of the majority of the Judges and is, within the meaning of Clause 2.2° of the said Article, the decision of the Court.

The Long title of the Bill, so referred to this Court is 'An Act to repeal Part VI of the Offences Against the State Act, 1939, and to make other provisions in relation to the detention of certain persons'.

Section 2 which is contained in Part I of the act repeals Part VI of the Offences Against the State Act, 1939. The part of the Act of 1939 so repealed is substantially to the same effect as Part II of the Bill now before this Court. Part II of the Bill consists of seven Sections.

Section 3 provides that Part II of the Act is to come into force when and so often as the Government makes and publishes a Proclamation declaring that the powers conferred by the said Part of the Act are necessary to secure the preservation of public peace and order, and that, if the Government makes and publishes a Proclamation declaring that the said Part of the Act shall cease to be in force, same shall forthwith cease to be in force. It further provides that it shall be lawful for Dáil Éireann, at any time while said Part of the Act is in force, to pass a resolution annulling such first-mentioned Proclamation and thereupon such Proclamation shall be annulled and said Part of the Act shall cease to be in force, but without prejudice to the validity of anything done after the making of the Proclamation and before the passing of the resolution.

Section 4 provides as follows:

'4.1 Whenever a Minister of State is of opinion that any particular person is engaged in activities which, in his opinion, are prejudicial to the preservation of public peace and order or to the security of the State, such Minister may by warrant under his hand and sealed with his official seal order the arrest and detention of such person under this Section.'

'4.2 Any member of the Garda Síochána may arrest without warrant any person in respect of whom a warrant has been issued by a Minster of State under the foregoing subsection of this section.'

'4.3 Every person arrested under the next preceding subsection of this section shall be detained in a prison or other place prescribed in that behalf by regulations made under this part of this Act until this Part of this Act ceases to be in force or until he is released under the subsequent provisions of this Part of this Act, whichever first happens.'

'4.4 Whenever a person is detained under this section, there shall be furnished to such person, as soon as may be after he arrives at a prison or other place of detention prescribed in that behalf by regulations made under this Part of this Act, a copy of the warrant issued under this section in relation to such person and of the provisions of section 8 of this Act.'

'4.5 Every warrant issued by a Minister of State under this section shall be in the form set out in the Schedule to this Act or in a form to the like effect.'

Section 5 confers on any member of the Garda Síochána power, in respect of any person arrested and detained under this Part of the Act, (a) to demand his name and address, (b) to search him or cause him to be searched, (c) to photograph him or cause him to be photographed and (d) to take or cause to be taken his finger-prints. It also provides that any person who obstructs or impedes a member of the Garda Síochána in the exercise of the said powers or who refuses to give a member of the Garda Síochána his correct name and address shall be guilty of a contravention of the regulations to be made under this Part of the Act and shall be dealt with accordingly.

Section 6 provides that a Minister of State may, by writing under his hand, order the release of any person who is being detained, and such person shall forthwith be released.

Section 7 empowers a Minister of State to make regulations for all or any of the following purposes, that is to say: (a) prescribing the prisons, internment camps, and other places in which persons may be detained under this Part of this Act; (b) providing for the efficient management, sanitation, control, and guarding of such prisons, internment camps, and other places; (c) providing for the enforcement and preservation of discipline amongst the persons detained in any such prison, internment camp, or other place as aforesaid; (d) providing for the punishment of persons so detained who contravene the regulations; (e) prescribing or providing for any other matter or thing incidental or ancillary to the efficient detention of persons detained under this Part of this Act.

Subsection 2 of the said Section provides that: Every regulation made under this Section shall be laid before each House of the Oireachtas as soon as may be after it is made, and if a resolution annulling such regulation is passed by either House of the Oireachtas within the next subsequent twenty-one days on which such House has sat after such regulation is laid before it, such regulation shall be annulled accordingly, but without prejudice to the validity of anything previously done under such regulation.

Section 8 provides for the setting up of a Commission to which any person detained under this Part of the Act may apply in writing to consider the continuation of his detention, and requires the Minister for Justice to furnish to the Commission such relevant information and documents, in the possession or procurement of the Government, or of any Minister of State as shall be called for by the Commission, and further provides that if the Commission reports that no reasonable grounds exist for the continued detention of such person, he shall, with all convenient speed, be released.

Section 9 provides that the Government shall, once at least in every six months, furnish to each House of the Oireachtas certain particulars therein specified with reference to persons detained.

Counsel so assigned by the Court, contended that the Bill was repugnant to the Constitution and, in particular, they relied upon the Preamble and on Articles 34.1, 38 and 40.

We propose to deal specifically with the aforesaid Articles, but in arriving at our conclusion we have had regard not only to those Articles but also to all such other Articles as seemed to us material to the question which we have to determine.

Before dealing, however, with the said Articles, we desire to point out that several Acts authorising the detention or persons had been passed by the Oireachtas of the Irish Free State prior to the enactment of the Constitution which we are now considering. The existence and effect of these Acts must have been within the knowledge of the framers of the Constitution and nevertheless, there is no express prohibition in the Constitution against such legislation. This is a matter to which we are bound to attach considerable weight in view of the fact that many of the Articles of the Constitution prohibit the Oireachtas, in plain and unambiguous language, from passing certain laws therein specified.

Where a particular law is not expressly prohibited and it is sought to establish that it is repugnant to the Constitution by reason of some implied prohibition or repugnancy, we are of opinion, as a matter of construction, that such repugnancy must be clearly established.

The material portion of the Preamble is that which declares that, in enacting the Constitution, the People of Ireland are:

> 'Seeking to promote the common good, with due observance of Prudence, Justice and Charity, so that the dignity and freedom of the individual may be assured, true social order attained, the unity of our country restored, and concord established with other nations.'

In dealing with the Preamble, Counsel laid great stress on the words 'dignity and freedom of the individual' and focused their attention upon those words exclusively. This does not seem to us to be the correct method of arriving at the true meaning and effect of the Preamble. The main object aimed at is the promotion of the Common Good, which, it is contemplated, will assure the dignity and freedom of the individual, the attainment of Social Order, the restoration of the unity of our country and the establishment of concord with other nations. Apart from the grammatical construction of the words of the Preamble, it seems to us difficult to understand how the dignity and freedom of the individual member of a State can be attained unless social order is maintained in that State. There is nothing in this clause of the Preamble which could be invoked to necessitate the sacrifice of the Common Good in the interests of the freedom of the individual.

Article 34 deals with the establishment of Courts and the administration of Justice therein, and the particular clause on which reliance was placed, is clause 1, which provides that justice shall be administered in public Courts established by law by Judges appointed in the manner provided by the Constitution. In order to rely upon this Article it would be necessary to establish that the Minister, in exercising the powers conferred upon him by the Bill, is administering justice without the meaning of the Article. This proposition seems to us to be wholly unsustainable.

Article 38 deals with the trial of offences and provides, in clause 1, that no person shall be tried on any criminal charge save in the course of law. The remaining clauses of the Article prescribe the methods in which criminal charges may be tried and specify various Courts for this purpose. The argument necessarily proceeds upon the basis that the Minister, in performing his function under the Bill, is engaged in the trial of a criminal charge and that the detention contemplated by the Bill is punishment in respect of a criminal offence.

In the opinion of this Court neither Section 4 nor Section 5 of the Bill creates or purports to create a criminal offence. The only essential preliminary to the exercise by a Minister of the powers contained in Section 4 is that he should have formed opinions on the matters specifically mentioned in the Section. The validity of such opinions is not a matter that could be questioned in any Court. Having formed such opinions the Minister is entitled to make an order for detention; but this Court is of opinion that the detention is not in the nature of punishment but is a precautionary measure taken for the purpose of preserving the public peace and order and the security of the State. This distinction has been recognised in several cases.

In the case of *The King (Zadig) v. Halliday* (1917), A.C. 260, a question arose as to the power of the Home Secretary in England to make an order for detention under the Defence of the Realm (Consolidation) Regulations 1914, made under s.1(1) of the Defence of the Realm Consolidation Act, 1914. In the course of his speech in that case Lord Finlay L.C. says at 265:

> 'On the face of it the Statute authorises in this subsection provisions of two kinds—for prevention and for punishment. Any preventive measures, even if they involve some restraint or hardship upon individuals, do not partake in any way of the nature of punishment, but are taken by way of precaution to prevent mischief to the State.'

In a later passage he says at 269:

> 'One of the most obvious ways of taking precautions against dangers such as are enumerated is to impose some restriction on the freedom of movement of persons whom there may be any

> reason to suspect of being disposed to help the enemy. It is to this that re.14B is directed. The measure is not punitive but precautionary. It was strongly urged that no such restraint should be imposed except as the result of a judicial inquiry, and indeed counsel for the appellant went so far as to contend that no regulation could be made forbidding access to the seashore by suspected persons. It seems obvious that no tribunal for investigating the question whether circumstances of suspicion exist warranting some restraint can be imagined less appropriate than a Court of law. No crime is charged. The question is whether there is ground for suspicion that a particular person may be disposed to help the enemy. The duty of deciding this question is by the order thrown upon the Secretary of State, and an advisory Committee, presided over by a Judge of the High Court is provided to bring before him any grounds for thinking that the order may properly be revoked or varied.'

Lord Atkinson, in the course of his speech in the same case, says at 273:

> 'Preventive Justice, as it is styled, which consists in restraining a man from committing a crime he may commit but has not yet committed, or doing some act injurious to members of the community which he may do but has not yet done, is no new thing in the laws of England.'

Again:

> 'One of the most effective ways of preventing a man from communicating with the enemy or doing things such as are mentioned in s.1, subsection 1 (a) and (c) of the statute is to imprison or intern him. In that as in almost every case where preventive justice is put in force some suffering and inconvenience may be caused to the suspected person. That is inevitable. But the suffering is, under this statute, inflicted for something much more important than his liberty or convenience, namely, for securing the public safety and defence of the realm.'

The principle underlying the decision in that case was acted upon and applied in this country in the case of *The King (O'Connell) v. The Military Governor of Hare Park Camp* [1924] 2 IR 104. In that case the applicant was detained in custody under an Order of an Executive Minister made under Section 4 of the Public Safety (Powers of Arrest and Detention) Temporary Act, 1924, which authorised such Minister to make such an

Order where he was of opinion that the public safety would be endangered by such person being set at liberty. It was contended that the Section was repugnant to the Constitution of the Irish Free State, which in our opinion, was, in this respect substantially to the same effect as the Constitution of Ireland. That contention was rejected and an application for *habeas corpus* was refused.

Article 40 deals with personal rights. Clause 3 thereof provides that the State guarantees by its laws to respect, and, as far as practicable, by its laws to defend and vindicate the personal rights of the citizen, and to protect from unjust attack and in case of injustice done, to vindicate the life and person of every citizen. It is alleged that the provisions of the bill are repugnant to the guarantee contained in this clause. It seems to us impossible to accede to this argument. The guarantee in the clause is not in respect of any particular citizen or class of citizens but extends to all the citizens of the State and the duty of determining the extent to which the rights of any particular citizen or class of citizens can be properly harmonised with the rights of the citizens as a whole seems to us to be a matter which is peculiarly within the province of the Oireachtas and any attempt by this Court to control the Oireachtas in the exercise of this function would, in our opinion, be a usurpation of its authority.

The people, by the Constitution, have provided for the setting up of three great Departments of State—the Oireachtas, the Executive and the Judiciary—and it is essential for the harmonious working of the machinery of State that each Department should confine itself to its own constitutional functions. If the Oireachtas enacts a law within the scope of its legal and constitutional powers, it is for the Courts to construe and apply such law. Any criticism by the Courts of the manner in which the Oireachtas exercises the discretion and powers vested in it would be as much open to objection as would any suggestion, in either House of the Oireachtas, that a decision of a court, within the scope of its authority, was not in accordance with law.

Clause 4 of the said Article provides that no citizen shall be deprived of his liberty save in accordance with law, and makes provision for the release of any person who is being detained otherwise than in accordance with law.

The phrase 'in accordance with law' is used in several Articles of the Constitution and we are of opinion that it means in accordance with the law as it exists at the time when the particular Article is invoked and sought to be applied. In this Article, it means the law as it exists at a time when the legality of the detention arises for determination. A person in custody is detained in accordance with law if he is detained in accordance with the provisions of a Statute duly passed by the Oireachtas; subject always to the qualification that such provisions are not repugnant to the Constitution or to any provision thereof.

Accordingly, in our opinion, this Article cannot be relied upon for the purpose of establishing the proposition that the Bill is repugnant to the Constitution—such repugnancy must be established by reference to some other provision of the Constitution.

It was contended that the effect of the Bill is to take away the right to *habeas corpus*. There is no foundation for this contention. Notwithstanding the provisions of the Bill, a person who is detained is entitled under Article 40.4.2° to have the legality of his detention enquired into, and to obtain an Order for his release, unless the Court or Judge, enquiring into the matter, is satisfied that all the provisions of the Bill have been complied with and that the detention is legal. No doubt the Bill, when enacted, will have the effect of altering the law, and to that extent, will justify a detention which might otherwise be unlawful. This, however, cannot rightly be described as taking away the right to *habeas corpus*.

The arguments based upon Sections 5 and 7 of the Bill can be disposed of very shortly. If, as this Court holds, the arrest and detention contemplated by Section 4 are lawful, it is obviously necessary that provision should be made as to the place and mode of detention and other matters incidental thereto. Sections 5 and 7 seem to us framed with this object in view. The purposes for which regulations may be made are set out in Section 7 and, in framing the regulations, the Minister is bound by the terms of the Section. There is nothing in the Section to suggest that any regulation made thereunder could contravene any Article of the Constitution. It is not for us to assume that the Minister will exceed the powers conferred upon him by the Section and, should he do so, it seems to us that the Regulations would, to that extent, be *ultra vires* and invalid.

It was contended before us that the Bill is unnecessary and oppressive. This is not a matter for our consideration and we express no opinion on it. The only question before us is whether it is in the power of the Oireachtas, consistently with the Constitution, to enact such legislation.

In the opinion of the Court it is, and we shall advise the President accordingly.

No. 296: NAI, DT S11577A

Douglas Hyde to Eamon de Valera

Áras an Uachtaráin
9 February 1940

I, Douglas Hyde, President of Ireland, do hereby inform you that the Supreme Court has decided that the Bill entitled Offences Against the State (Amendment) Bill, 1940, is not repugnant to the Constitution or to any provision thereof. I have accordingly this day signed the said Bill.

No. 297: NAI, DFA 247/21

Telegram from the Department of External Affairs to John Hearne

Department of External Affairs
4 September 1940

Owing to short time still available for amendment of Constitution by way of ordinary legislation, the Taoiseach hopes at forthcoming session to introduce one or more amending bills to cover a number of minor changes in the Constitution, which practice has shown to be desirable.

Some five months ago all State Departments were asked to submit suggestions for amendments, and, although response was not considerable, the material received sufficient to occupy a special Constitution Amendment Committee until present date. It is understood that most of the proposals submitted to the Committee are likely to be rejected when report is issued shortly. Only about twenty suggestions relating almost exclusively to purely verbal or translation points are likely to be recommended for adoption or for fuller consideration by the Government.

In view of your very special knowledge of the Constitution the Taoiseach feels that final preparation of amending measures should not be undertaken before you have had time to re-examine substance of Constitution in light of present world-trends, recent political developments at home, and your personal experience of Canadian constitutional matters.

Kindly consider this matter urgently and cable suggestions for any amendments which in your view should now be introduced.

No. 298: NAI, DFA 247/21

Telegram from John Hearne to the Department of External Affairs

Irish Legation, Ottawa, Canada
16 September 1940

Have carefully re-examined Constitution in light of facts and trends referred to in your telegram no. 53 of September the 4th.[159] Would suggest for consideration of committee two amendments as follows (1) An amendment providing that a bill or provision which has been the subject of decision of the Supreme Court under Article 26 pronouncing it valid shall when enacted into law be beyond reach of original jurisdiction conferred on High Court by Subsection 2° of Section 3 of Article 34. (2) An amendment removing jurisdiction conferred by Subsection 2° of Section 4 of Article 40 from single judge. Submit no amendment necessary to authorise membership of or association with any European organisation or world system hereafter established and composed of independent political communities. Statute similar to League of Nations (Guarantee) Act, 1923 may be called for if such organisation or system is established and Ireland enters into relations therewith. Article 29 needs no alteration. Procedure etc based on Subsection 2° of Section 4 and the relevant existing Act is optional and in contemplation of the act temporary. Suggest final re-examination of Article 49. My view is that this Article is water tight but owing to its importance submit should receive special final approval of committee. Would suggest establishment of a statute revision or codification of law committee to put an end to temporary situation created by Article 50.

No. 299: NAI, DT S12506

Report of the Committee to consider Amendments to the Constitution

[September] 1940

In April, 1940, a Committee was appointed by An Taoiseach, to consider and report as to what (if any) amendments to the Constitution should be enacted before the expiration of the period of three years ending on

[159] See document no. 297.

the 26th June, 1941, (the triennial anniversary of the entry upon office of the first President) during which amendments might be made, under Article 51, by the Oireachtas.

The following persons were appointed to be members of the Committee:

> Mr Muiris O'Muimhneachain, Secretary to the Government and to the Department of an Taoiseach, who acted as Chairman; Dr Michael Rynne, Legal Adviser to the Department of External Affairs; Mr Philip O'Donoghue, Legal Assistant to the Attorney-General and Mr William P. Fay, of the Parliamentary Draftsman's Office, who acted as Secretary to the Committee.

The Committee held its first meeting on the 1st May, 1940, and between that date and the 30th June, 1940, held two meetings a week, in all about sixteen meetings. In addition various informal meetings were held between various members of the Committee to consider a draft memorandum and to settle points of detail.

The principal work of the Committee consisted in considering and making recommendations in regard to various proposals for amendment of the Constitution put forward by a number of public officers and Departments.

Proposals of this kind were received from the following:

> The Secretary to the President;[160] the Clerk of the Dáil;[161] the Clerk of the Seanad;[162] the Department of An Taoiseach; the Department of Finance; the Department of Justice; the Department of the Attorney-General; the Department of Local Government and Public Health; the Department of Lands (Gaeltacht Services) and the Quit Rent Office.

In addition to these proposals, the Committee had the advantage of hearing the views of the Clerk of the Seanad and of the Secretary of the Department of Justice, expressed by those officers in person, in relation to proposals put forward by them.

In response to enquiries addressed to them, the Department of Finance furnished the Committee with a detailed and valuable exposition of their views in relation to certain important proposals touching on the functions of that Department.

In response also to a cable sent from the Department of External

[160] Michael McDunphy.
[161] Gearóid Mag Canainn.
[162] Seán Malone.

Affairs, the Committee had the advantage of having an expression of his views from the High Commissioner to Canada, Mr J. J. Hearne.

The Committee also considered various proposals put forward by members of the Committee themselves.

All these suggestions were considered by the Committee in the order in which they affected the various Articles of the Constitution. Where necessary, suggestions were re-drafted for the purpose of stating in a net form the proposals for amendment contained in them. In regard to each proposal, the Committee made a recommendation. All these proposals and the recommendations thereto are set out in the First Annex to this report. This Annex is in three parts: viz. 1) the proposals recommended for acceptance; 2) the proposals regarded as matters of policy; 3) the proposals not recommended. Certain of the proposals have annexed to them memoranda prepared either by the Department of Finance or by members of the Committee on various points touched on in the proposals.

In the Second Annex is contained a memorandum setting forth the views of the Secretary of the Department of Justice in regard to a suggested comprehensive change in the administration of Criminal Justice.[163]

Lastly, the question arises as to what would be the most suitable method for dealing with amendments to the Constitution to be enacted within the three-year period specified in Article 51 thereof. This question was considered by the Committee at the outset of their deliberations, and they decided to make the following recommendations in regard to the machinery for enacting any proposed amendments which the Government thought fit to adopt:

1. Such amendments as appeared to be either of a purely drafting character, or such as, though containing points of substance, were thought to be unlikely to be submitted to a Referendum should be included in one Bill and placed before the Oireachtas for enactment without reference to a Referendum. If it was found on the passage of this Bill through the Oireachtas, that substantial opposition was offered to any proposal in the Bill, such proposal could be dropped and later submitted in a separate Bill for ultimate reference to the people.
2. Provision should be made, either in the Bill already referred to, or in a separate Bill for the re-enrolment of a revised text of the Constitution as a whole after the expiration of the three-year period mentioned in Article 51, the new text to contain the amendments made within that period.

[163] See document no. 300.

3. Where any proposed amendment to be made within the said period was submitted to the people by referendum, the amendment should be incorporated in a separate Bill. It was recognised that, despite the suggestion in Article 46.4, that more than one proposal might be contained in the same Bill, there would obviously be difficulties in submitting more than one proposal in a Bill which was to be referred to the people.

Annex 1, Part 1: Proposals Recommended[164]

Article 12.3.3°
Proposal 13: Department of the Taoiseach
No election may be held after the date of termination of office of an outgoing President. It is not inconceivable that a person elected as President would either die or become permanently incapacitated before entering upon his office, but so close to the date of expiration of office of the outgoing President that there would be no time to hold a second election before that date. In such circumstances it would be necessary to invoke the emergency powers of the Council of State (Article 14.4.) and to operate under that section without a President until the situation could be relieved by an amendment of the Constitution.

Recommendation: The proposal should be accepted. The Committee consider that the point might be met by an amendment of Article 12.3.3° to the effect that in the event of the death, resignation or permanent incapacity of a President elect a new election will be held within 60 days.[165]

Article 12.10.5°
Proposal 2A: Clerk of the Dáil
It would seem that the words 'under this section' should be inserted in line 2 after the word 'Oireachtas' in the English version.

Recommendation: The Committee is in agreement with this proposal.[166]

Articles 13.1.1° & 28.5.1°
Proposal 92: Department of the Taoiseach
It is suggested that the term 'Prime Minister' should be deleted from these Articles. It was not intended as a title but as a description and is sufficiently covered by the term 'Head of the Government'.

[164] Annotated by Moynihan: 'Proposals recommended discussed with Taoiseach on 4 September 1940. His views are noted in pencil'. All annotations are made by Moynihan. De Valera's views are included here as footnotes to the document.
[165] Annotated with a 'yes' mark.
[166] Annotated: 'Taoiseach doubtful on its necessity'. A later annotation, dated 16 October 1940, states: 'Not necessary'.

Recommendation: The Committee is in agreement with this proposal.[167]

Article 13.2.1°
Proposal 17: Department of Finance
It is not clear that Dáil Éireann could be summoned if the Taoiseach failed to advise the President to summon it. An amendment to provide for this contingency would be desirable.

Recommendation: The Committee considers that the point should be met, but more properly form the subject of an amendment to Article 16.4.2° than to Article 13.2.1°. See recommendation in regard to Article 16.4.2°.[168]

Article 13.6
Proposal [Blank]: Department of Justice.
'Pardon', etc.
Query, provide for *postponement* of execution of death sentence.

The present position is very unsatisfactory in that respect. Is postponement 'commutation or remission'? Hardly, but arguable. If the President postpones, it may be argued that he has no power. If somebody else postpones, it may be argued, contrary-wise, that that is reserved to the President as a 'commutation or remission' in a 'capital case'.

In England, I understand, it is regarded as part of the prerogative but is exercised in fact by the Home Secretary. There is no Irish example in our time.

Recommendation: The Committee is of opinion that the point should be met by a simple amendment to Article 13.6: namely to substitute the words 'to commute, remit or defer' for the words 'to commute or remit' and to insert the words 'remission or deferment' in lieu of the words 'or remission'.[169]

Article 13.7
Proposal 20A: Attorney-General's Department.

A. Paragraph 1° provides that the President may communicate with the Houses of the Oireachtas 'by message or address' but paragraph 2° provides that he may 'address a message' to the Nation. The use of 'address' as a verb in the latter paragraph seems undesirable in this context on account of its use as a noun contrasted with 'message' in the preceding paragraph.

[167] Annotated with a 'yes' mark.
[168] Annotated: 'Taoiseach says this change is hardly necessary and would not appreciably strengthen the existing [position?]'. A later annotation, dated 16 October 1940, states: 'Not necessary'.
[169] Annotated: 'On further consideration on 23/10/40, Committee thinks this can be done by ordinary legislation'.

'Give', 'send', 'communicate' or 'convey' might be considered more appropriate in paragraph 2.

B. The Gaelic version of paragraph 1° seems to contemplate the President *sending* either a message (teachtaireacht) or an address (aitheasc) to 'An Oireachtas' (which includes himself). The English version seems to indicate that the President may communicate with the *Houses* of the Oireachtas by message (i.e. a communication, written or oral, conveyed by some other person) or by *address* (i.e. by himself addressing or speaking to the Houses). The Gaelic version of this paragraph should refer to Tighthibh an Oireachtas as does paragraph 2° of section 8. The English or Irish version would seem to require amendment according as it is desired that the President should have power to address the Houses in person or not.

Recommendation: As regards suggestion 'A', the Committee do not consider it necessary to amend the Constitution for the purpose of a purely verbal change.

As regards suggestion 'B', the Committee are in agreement that the Irish text needs amendment for the reasons suggested.[170]

Article 14
Proposal 23: Secretary to the President[171]

1. An examination of Article 14 of the Constitution reveals a discrepancy between the wording of Section 1 and the corresponding portion of Article 57, as regards the scope of the power and functions of the respective Presidential Commission set up by those Articles.
2. While Article 57 refers to 'the powers and functions of the President *under this Constitution*', the phrase used in Article 14 is 'the powers and functions *conferred on the President by this Constitution*'.
3. On a strict reading, the use of the word 'by' in Article 14 might be held to suggest that the Commission provided for in that Article is entitled to exercise only the powers and functions conferred on the President by the Constitution itself, and is precluded from exercising those conferred on the President by ordinary statute. No such limitation is implied by the wording of Article 57.

170 Annotated with a 'yes' mark.
171 Michael McDunphy.

4. I have had some informal discussions on the matter with the Attorney General's Office and the view is held that the Constitution should be interpreted liberally, and that it would be better to assume that the intention of Article 14 is to provide for the exercise of all Presidential functions by the Commission, rather than to contemplate any restriction which might lead to difficulties in practice.
5. Whether the Courts would also take this view is a matter for conjecture. In any case, there is sufficient lack of certainty to justify a careful examination of the whole question, with a view to seeing whether it might not be desirable to rectify any defect by a Constitutional amendment under Article 51, before the expiration of the initial three-year period.

Recommendation: The proposal should be accepted. The point raised might be met by substituting the words 'by or under' for the word 'by' in Article 14, Section 1, and Section 5.1° and 5.2°.[172]

Article 15.7
Proposal 27: Clerk of the Seanad
The precise meaning to be attached to this provision has never been clear, nor has the object it is expected to achieve. In essence the provision derives from British constitutional practice—with an origin in the middle ages. The difficulty felt in regard to the section, however, is as to what the description 'session' covers. In view of the fact that in the succeeding Section (Section 8) the description 'sitting' is used in reference to a single meeting of a House of the Oireachtas, it can be inferred that the description 'session' in Section 7 is intended to apply to a number of sittings of the Houses to which there is a definite beginning and termination each year. From the dictionary point of view the words 'session' and 'sitting' are synonymous, but a distinction has been made in parliamentary practice. For instance, in Britain, the practice is to open the 'session' with a King's speech and to close the sitting of the year by a Proclamation proroguing Parliament. Only twice since 1922 was there an opening of the Parliamentary year here with a formal statement of Government business, and the Houses of the Oireachtas were never prorogued. Instead the Houses have been adjourned over Recesses by formal Resolutions, and the duration of the parliamentary session has come to be regarded as coterminous with the life of the Dáil. That practice is of great inconvenience and enables Bills to be introduced and given a first reading before a Recess, and to have them taken up on

[172] Annotated with a 'yes' mark.

second reading or in committee, as the case may be, when the House resumes.

Apart from these considerations, doubt is felt as to whether the description 'The Oireachtas' is strictly applicable. If the section is retained, it is suggested that the more correct wording would be: 'Each House of the Oireachtas shall hold at least one sitting each year'.

Proposal 27A: Department of the Attorney General

The reference to 'session' in the English version seems inappropriate. The Gaelic version can be translated 'the Oireachtas must *sit* at least once every year'. This conveys the meaning which Cléireach an tSeanaid suggests is desirable and agrees with section B.

Recommendation: The Committee is in agreement with the sense of the proposal, but suggests that the word 'meeting' is more suitable than 'sitting'. The Committee accordingly suggests that the following Section should be substituted in lieu of Section 7 of Article 15: 'Each House of the Oireachtas shall meet at last once a year'.

If this suggestion is accepted, corresponding amendments would be desirable in Article 15.8.[173]

Article 16.4.2°

Proposal 35: The Committee.

The Committee consider that the suggestion contained in proposal 17 (Department of Finance) should be met by adding to or inserting in this Subsection (as appears to the Draftsman to be suitable) some such words as 'whether duly summoned or not'.[174]

Article 22.1.1°

Proposal 50: Clerk of the Dáil

In Subsection 1° the expression 'public moneys', 'public money' occur. In Subsection 2° there is a definition of 'public money' only.

Note in Article 17, Section 2 the reference is to 'appropriation of revenue or other public moneys'. In the definition in Article 22 above the expression is 'appropriation…of public money'.

Proposal 51: Clerk of the Seanad

The definition of a Money Bill, now included in this Subsection, was taken from the Constitution of Saorstát Éireann, and originally from the Parliament Act of 1911.

The definition provides that a Bill to be a Money Bill, within the meaning of the Article, does not have actually to impose a charge on public

[173] Annotated with a 'yes' mark.

[174] Annotated: 'Not necessary in T[aoiseach]'s view. 16/10/40'.

money. It may deal only with the subject-matter on the imposition. It provides, further, that the subject of imposition must be for the payment of debt, *or other financial purposes*. There is no explicit definition in the Constitution of the expression 'or the financial purposes', nor is there one in the British Parliament Act of 1911. The expression is certainly vague.

Dealing with this point in the House of Lords during a debate on the second reading of the Parliament (Reform) Bill, 1933 (H.L. No. 7 of 1933), the Marquess of Salisbury is reported as saying (Column 80 of Volume 92 of the House of Lords Debates):

> 'In the Parliament Act there are the general words 'or other financial purposes' as well as those I have described, and the words 'other financial purposes' are so wide that they cover almost everything.'

Previously in the same debate, the Marquess had said that 'according to the best opinion as the Parliament Act stands now, almost anything could be passed under the section which provides that a Money Bill is to be passed straight through Parliament'.

There is also in the definition the expression 'charges on public moneys'. The expression used in the Parliament Act is 'charges on the Consolidated Fund or on moneys provided by Parliament'—a much more precise expression. A discussion on the point arose at the Committee of Privileges on the Land Purchase (Guarantee Fund) Bill, 1935. During that discussion the Attorney General appeared to contend that the expression covered all moneys raised by the Exchequer for national purposes and by local authorities and bodies for purposes other than local purposes. That contention would seem to be a very wide extension in scope of the 'moneys' which it was considered the expression was intended to cover.

The Parliament (Reform) Bill, to which reference has been made, proposed an amendment of the definition of a Money Bill contained in the Parliament Act of 1911. It may be desired to have the terms of the amended definition, and they are as follows:

> '12. For sub-sections (2) and (3) of section one of the Parliament Act, 1911, there shall as from the date of the dissolution of the present Parliament be substituted the following sub-sections:
>
> A Money Bill means a Public Bill which according to the certificate of the Speaker of the House of Commons contains only provisions dealing with all or any of the following subjects, namely:
>
> (a) which, whatever their form, have in substance no other intention than the raising variation or reduction of revenue

through the imposition, repeal, remission, alteration or regulation of taxation;

(b) the imposition for the payment of debt of charges on the Consolidated Fund, or on moneys provided by Parliament or the variation or repeal of any such charges;

(c) supply;

(d) the appropriation, receipt, custody, issue or audit of accounts of public money;

(e) the raising or guarantee of any loans or the repayment thereof. In this subsection the expressions 'taxation', 'public money' and 'loan' respectively do not include any taxation, money or loan raised by local authorities or bodies for local purposes.'

Recommendation: In view of the annexed note containing the views of the Department of Finance on these proposals, the Committee recommends that the word 'money' be amended to read 'moneys' but that no other change be made in this section.[175]

'Note by Department of Finance on Article 21.1':
While there seems no clear difference between the meaning of the word 'money' and the word 'moneys', especially having regard to the rule of interpretation laid down in Section 11 (a) of the Interpretation Act, 1937, it seems desirable to have consistency throughout this sub-article and to use the phrase 'public moneys' in preference to 'public money'.

It is true that the phrase 'financial purposes' is somewhat vague, but it is difficult to see what definition could be given or even if that definition is desirable. Many terms used in the Constitution are not defined and in this instance the purposes are probably quite sufficiently indicated by the context stating that 'payment of debt' is a financial purpose and that charges on public moneys are concerned, the clear implication being that the purposes relate to State finance. The line of argument adopted in the Debate in the House of Lords which is referred to has more than a suggestion of being *ex parte* and it is to be noted that Section 12(b) of the Parliament Reform Bill, which is quoted in the Memo, goes to the other extreme when it allows charges to be imposed only in respect of the payment of debt. The suggested Clause would, for instance, rank Bills as Money Bills if they contained only matters dealt with in Accounts Nos XIV and XXI of the Finance Accounts but would exclude from the category Bills dealing solely with such items as those set out in Accounts Nos XVII to XX.

[175] Annotated with a 'yes' mark.

Public Money

Without investigating the reasons for adopting the phrase 'charges on public moneys' instead of the phrase 'charges on the Central Fund or on moneys provided by the Oireachtas' (which would correspond with the phrase used in the Parliament Act of 1911, viz., 'charges on the Consolidated Fund or on money provided by Parliament') it may be said that the need for absolute precision is not apparent. If words corresponding to the British phrase were employed, it might be open to doubt whether such items as Appropriations-in-Air and the revenue which is intercepted by the Revenue Commissioners and by the Department of Posts and Telegraphs and used for current expenses instead of being put into the Exchequer, would come within the meaning of the phrase. Sufficient definition for practical purposes seems to be attained by Article 22.1.2°. In this connection it cannot be admitted that there is any real force in the objection which the Memo apparently raises to the effect that 'public moneys' should not include moneys raised by local authorities or bodies for '*other* than local purposes'. In the view of this Department moneys paid into the Exchequer under such enactments as Section 14(1) of the Damage to Property (Compensation) Act, 1923 (No. 15 of 1923) or moneys raised by a local authority and paid to a Minister and appropriated-in-aid, as is the case under section 26 of the Unemployment Assistance Act, 1933 (No. 46 of 1933), as amended, must be held to become public moneys when paid over.

Articles 23.1, 25 and 27

Proposal 51A: Attorney General's Department

The opening provision of Section 23.1 dealing with the application of the Article, is not numbered either as a Section or a Subsection. A similar remark applics to the opening provisions of Articles 26 and 27. Numbering of these provisions seems to be desirable for ease of reference and for consistency with the method of numbering of sections and subsections throughout the Constitution.

Recommendation: The Committee does not consider it necessary to support this recommendation in full, but would draw attention to the fact that the opening paragraph in Article 23 is included in Section 1 while in Articles 26 and 27 similar introductory paragraphs are not numbered. Perhaps Article 23 might be brought into conformity with Articles 26 and 27.[176]

Article 24.2

[176] Annotated: 'Committee, on recommendations, feels this need not be proceeded with as an amendment. 23/10/40'.

Proposal 52: Clerk of the Seanad
There is an implication in this Subsection that the Seanad may *pass* a Money Bill with recommendations. The Seanad, however, has no such power, and it is suggested that the section might be amended to read:

> 'Where a Bill...is within the period specified in the resolution, either rejected by Seanad Éireann or is passed by Seanad Éireann with amendments to which Dáil Éireann does not agree, or is returned by Seanad Éireann with recommendations which Dáil Éireann does not accept, or is neither passed with or without amendments or returned with or without recommendations nor rejected by Seanad Éireann within the period so specified' etc.

Recommendations: The Committee considers that the proposal should be accepted in principle.[177]

Article 25.1
Proposal 55: Clerk of the Seanad
The matter of excluding Money Bills from the operation of this section might be considered—particularly so, as Money Bills are excluded from Section 1 of Article 26 and Section 1 of Article 27. The greater number of such Bills are purely formal Bills, e.g. Central Fund Bills, Appropriation Bills—in the full enactment of which there is frequently a time factor.

Recommendation: The Committee understands that the object of this proposal is to avoid unnecessary delay in the signature of Money Bills. It also understands that the Department of Finance would welcome an amendment for this purpose as difficulty is often experienced in ensuring that the annual Central Fund Bill becomes law before the 31st March in each year. Accordingly, the Committee recommends that the Article should be amended, not as suggested, but by a simple amendment of Article 25.3 to the following effect:

Before the word 'Every' in line 1 of the section to insert 'Every Money Bill and'.

'Amendment of Article 25'[178]
To delete section 4 and substitute the following:

> 4.1° This section applies to every Bill signed by the President under this Constitution, including a Bill expressed to be a Bill containing a proposal for the amendment of this Constitution.[179]

[177] Annotated: 'Agreed on P[arliamentary] D[raftsman]'s suggestion that this should be done by having a separate section or subsection for Money Bills. 23/10/40'.
[178] This portion of the document is a draft amendment of Article 25, drawn up by the Committee. It is annotated: 'Preliminary discussions by Committee on 30/10/40'.
[179] The annotation 'Necessary' appears in the margin opposite this subsection.

2° Every Bill to which this section applies shall become and be law as on and from the day on which it is signed by the President under this Constitution, and shall, unless the contrary intention appears, come into operation on that day.
3° Every such Bill shall be promulgated by the President as a law by the publication, by his direction, of a notice in *Iris Oifigiúil* stating that the Bill has become law.
4° Every such Bill shall be signed by the President in the text in which it was enacted, and if a Bill is enacted in both the official languages, the President shall sign the text of that Bill in both languages.[180]
5° Where any such Bill is enacted in one only of the official languages, an official translation shall be issued in the other official language.
6° As soon as may be after the signature and promulgation of any such Bill as a law, the signed text of such law, or where the President has signed the text in both the official languages, both those signed texts, shall be enrolled for record in the office of the Registrar of the Supreme Court, and the text or both texts so enrolled shall be conclusive evidence of the provisions of such law.
7° Where the text of a law is enrolled under this section in both the official languages, the text in the national language shall prevail in case of conflict between those texts.
5.1° It shall be lawful for the Taoiseach, from time to time as occasion appears to him to require, to cause to be prepared under his supervision a text, in both the official languages, of this Constitution as then in force having regard to all amendments theretofore made therein.
2° A copy of every text so prepared shall be signed by the President and countersigned by the Taoiseach and the Chief Justice, and when so signed shall be enrolled for record in the office of the Registrar of the Supreme Court.
3° The copy so signed and enrolled of the text which is for the time being the latest text so prepared shall upon such enrolment be conclusive evidence of the provisions of this Constitution and shall for that purpose supersede all copies of this Constitution previously so signed and enrolled.
4° In case of conflict between the texts of any copy so enrolled, the text in the national language shall prevail.

180 The word 'enacted' in this subsection has been crossed out, with 'passed by both Houses of the Oireachtas' written in the margin.

5° The provisions of this section shall be without prejudice to the omission of the Transitory Provisions, in accordance with Articles 51 and 52 of this Constitution, from every official text of this Constitution published after the dates specified in those Articles respectively.[181]

Article 63[182]

1. A copy of this Constitution signed by the Taoiseach, the Chief Justice, and the Chairman of the Registrar of the Supreme Court, and such signed copy shall be conclusive evidence of the provisions of this Constitution. In case of conflict between the Irish and the English texts, the Irish text shall prevail.
2. Where a Bill containing a proposal for the amendment of this Constitution has been signed and promulgated by the President in both the Irish language and the English language, both the Irish text and the English text of such Bill shall be enrolled in accordance with Article 25 of this Constitution, and in case of conflict between those texts, the Irish text shall prevail.
3. 1° It shall be lawful for the Taoiseach, from time to time as occasion appears to him to require, to cause to be prepared under his supervision a text, in both the Irish language and the English language, of this Constitution as then in force having regard to all amendments theretofore made therein.

2° A copy of every text so prepared shall be signed by the Taoiseach, the Chief Justice, and the Chairman of Dáil Éireann and when so signed shall be enrolled for record in the office of the Registrar of the Supreme Court.[183]

3° The copy so signed and enrolled of the text which is for the time being the latest text so prepared shall upon such enrolment be conclusive evidence of the provisions of this Constitution and shall for that purpose supersede all copies of this Constitution previously so signed and enrolled.

4° In case of conflict between the Irish and the English texts of any copy so enrolled, the Irish text shall prevail.

[181] Annotated: 'Submission to Taoiseach deferred pending further consideration and preparation of amended draft. 31/10/40'.

[182] Annotated: 'Sections 2 and 3 to be dealt with in Article 25. 22/10/40'.

[183] Annotated: 'Or President and countersigned by T[aoiseach] and C[hief] J[ustice]. 23/10/40'.

Articles 25.4 & 63
Proposal 88
Article 63 is not a transitory provision and should not be included in the provisions which, under Article 52, are omitted from future official texts.

Proposal 90: Department of Finance
It is considered that the provision that 'in case of conflict between the Irish and the English texts, the Irish text shall prevail' should appear as a permanent part of the Constitution rather than as a 'transitory provision'.

It is presumed that amendments of the Constitution will be enrolled for record in the Office of the Registrar of the Supreme Court and that the original text will be duly amended accordingly.

Proposal 91: Department of the Taoiseach
The Constitution contains no special provision at present for the enrolment of Constitutional Amendments.

Recommendation: The Committee is in agreement with the substance of the various proposals relating to Article 63 which are set out above, but, after full consideration, they are of opinion that Article 63 itself should be left as it is even though this means that it will not be printed in the future official texts. In substance, the provisions of that Article are transitory and its operation is now spent, once the original text of the Constitution has been enrolled. Even the provision for the priority of the Irish text will not survive if, as the Committee recommends, periodical revised versions of the Constitution as amended up to date are issued from time to time, because it is the Irish version of the latest such revised text which will prevail in the future, as it will supersede all former versions.

The Committee is of opinion, however, that provision should be made in the Constitution for the following matters:

1. Enrolment in the office of the Registrar of the Supreme Court of all amendments to the Constitution;
2. Provision for the priority of the Irish texts of such amendments;
3. The enrolment and publication from time to time of a revised text of the Constitution, with all amendments incorporated therein, prepared under the supervision of the Taoiseach.

Such revised text, when enrolled, to contain all the provisions (including the Transitory provisions) of the Constitution, though the Transitory provisions would of course be omitted from every official text published after the expiration of the respective dates mentioned in Article 51 and 52.

After full consideration the Committee decided to recommend that provisions for the purpose mentioned would most suitably be inserted in Article 25. It is to be observed that Article 25.4 already appears to provide for the enrolment of Constitutional amendments as well as ordinary bills, as in terms it applies to all Bills signed by the President under the Constitution. But the Committee is of opinion that, in view of the exclusion of Constitutional amendments from Section 1 of Article 25 and the possibility that this might be held to govern the whole Article, constitutional amendments should be expressly included in the application of Section 4. Moreover, the provisions of that Section are defective in relation to priority of the Irish text of Bills passed in both official languages and in fact the present form of the Section does not seem to contemplate that a Bill might be passed in more than one language. Accordingly the Committee recommend a comprehensive amendment of Article 25.4 to meet the points mentioned.

Such amendment might be to the following effect: To delete section 4 and substitute the following:

> 4.1° This section applies to every Bill signed by the President under this Constitution, including a Bill expressed to be a Bill containing a proposal for the amendment of this Constitution.
> 2° Every Bill to which this section applies shall become and be law as on and from the day on which it is signed by the President under this Constitution, and shall, unless the contrary intention appears, come into operation on that day.
> 3° Every such Bill shall be promulgated by the President as a law by the publication, by his direction, of a notice in *Iris Oifigiúil* stating that the Bill has become law.
> 4° Every such Bill shall be signed by the President in the text in which it was passed by the Oireachtas, and if a Bill is passed in both the official languages, the President shall sign the text of that Bill in both those languages.
> 5° Where any such Bill is passed in one only of the official languages, an official translation shall be issued in the other official language.
> 6° As soon as may be after the signature and promulgation of any such Bill as a law, the signed text of such law, or where the President has signed the text in both the official languages both

those signed texts, shall be enrolled for record in the office of the Registrar to the Supreme Court, and the text or both the texts so enrolled shall be conclusive evidence of the provisions of such law.
7° In case of conflict between the texts of a law enrolled under this section in both the official languages, the text in the national language shall prevail.
5.1° It shall be lawful for the Taoiseach, from time to time as occasion appears to him to require, to cause to be prepared under his supervision a text, in both the official languages of this Constitution as then in force having regard to all amendments theretofore made therein.
2° A copy of every text so prepared shall be signed by the President and countersigned by the Taoiseach and the Chief Justice, and when so signed shall be enrolled for record in the office of the Registrar of the Supreme Court.
3° The copy so signed and enrolled of the text which is for the time being the latest text so prepared shall upon such enrolment be conclusive evidence of the provisions of this Constitution and shall for that purpose supersede all copies of this Constitution previously so signed and enrolled.[184]
4° The copy so signed and enrolled of the text which is for the time being the latest text so prepared shall upon such enrolment be conclusive evidence of the provisions of this Constitution and shall for that purpose supersede all copies of this Constitution previously so signed and enrolled.[185]

Article 26.1.2°
Proposal 61: Secretary to the President.

1. Subsection 2 of Section 1 of Article 26 provides that where it is decided by the President to refer a Bill to the Supreme Court that reference must take place not later than four days after the date on which the Bill has been passed or is deemed to have been passed by both Houses of the Oireachtas.
2. The fact that the period runs from the date of passage of the Bill, rather than from the date of its presentation to the President for signature, creates a difficulty at the very outset.

[184] Annotated: 'Does this [?] immediate re-enrolment following every amendment? 14/11/40'.
[185] Annotated: 'Discussed with Taoiseach 16/11/40. He agrees in principle but wider consideration to be given to possibility of bringing style of drafting more into harmony with that adopted in the Constitution generally. Spoke to Mr Fay accordingly'. A further annotation at the foot of the page reads: 'Try to break up into short paragraphs and make phraseology less legal. 16/11[/40]'.

3. It rarely occurs that a Bill is received by the President from the Taoiseach before the first day after its passage by the Oireachtas. In the majority of cases it is not received before the second day. In the case of a lengthy Bill in which there have been numerous amendments in the final stages, it is possible that it may not be received by the President until the four-day period referred to in paragraph 1 above has expired, due to the fact that the Bill has to be printed after it has been passed by both Houses.
4. Even in the most favourable circumstances the time limit of four days is far too short, as a Bill cannot be referred to the Supreme Court by the President except after consultation with the Council of State, for which purpose a meeting of that Council must be convened and held.
5. It will be borne in mind that the five-day period which must elapse before a Bill can be signed under Article 25 runs from the date of its *presentation* by the Taoiseach to the President. It seems to me to be only reasonable that the period allowed for reference of the Bill to the Supreme Court under Article 26 should run also from the same basic date.
6. This at least would prevent the operation of Article 26 being rendered impossible in the case of any particular Bill by reason of lapse of time not cognisable by the President.
7. The second point is that the period of four days available for such reference is too restricted.
8. Under Article 25.2.1° a Bill, if not referred to the Supreme Court, must be signed not later than seven days after the date of its presentation by the Taoiseach to the President. There seems to be no reason why this period of seven days should not also be available to the President for the reference of the Bill to the Supreme Court.
9. This period would be ample for the completion of all steps necessary antecedent to and arising out of his decision to refer the Bill to the Supreme Court, including the convening and holding of a meeting of the Council of State.
10. The two changes which I would recommend in this connection are therefore –
    (a) the basic date of the period within which the President may refer a Bill to the Supreme Court should be the date of its presentation to him for signature and not the date of its passage, deemed or actual, by both Houses.

(b) The period available for such reference should be seven days instead of four days as at present.

11. In my considered opinion an amendment of the Constitution to effect these changes should be made before the lapse of the three-year period within which the Constitution may be amended by ordinary legislation and I recommend accordingly.

Recommendation: The Committee agree with the suggestion contained in paragraph 10 (a) of this proposal. They recommend a simple amendment to meet the point in Article 26.1.2°.

The Committee do not agree with the suggestion contained in paragraph 10 (b) of the proposal. In their opinion, to allow a longer period than four days for a decision to refer a Bill to the Supreme Court would unduly encroach on the period allowed to the President for the signature of the Bill.[186]

Article 26.2.2°
Proposal 62: Dept. of the Taoiseach
It is suggested that provision should be made for one judgment only to be provided, i.e. the judgment of the majority.

It is clearly undesirable that in the important type of constitutional case which the Supreme Court will be called upon to decide under this Article divergent views should be expressed from the Bench.

Recommendation: The Committee are in agreement with this proposal which, they understand, originated from a suggestion made by the Chief Justice to the Attorney General.

The Committee also decided to give consideration, under Article 34, to making a similar provision to that suggested in the present proposal in relation to cases coming before the Supreme Court which raise questions as to the validity of a law having regard to the Constitution. They are of opinion that the same consideration applies to judgments of the Supreme Court in all constitutional cases, namely, that it is desirable in the public interest to have only one judgment.[187]

Articles 26 & 27
Proposal 63: A member of the Committee
It is suggested that a Bill might be referred to the Supreme Court under Art. 26, and also submitted for the approval of the People under Art. 27. It is intended that there should be the possibility of such a double

[186] Recommendations are annotated with a 'yes' mark.
[187] Annotated with a 'yes' mark.

reference? If so, provision should be made to prevent a conflict in regard to the time available to the President under each Article to enable him to make a reference thereunder. The present position in this respect is not satisfactory. Compare Art. 26.1.2° with Art. 27.3. The unqualified statement in Art. 26.3.2° also needs harmonising with Art. 27.

Recommendation: The Committee consider that it was intended by the framers of the Constitution that a Bill referred to the Supreme Court under Article 26 might also be submitted to the People under Art. 27 provided, of course, that the Supreme Court found in favour of the constitutionality of the Bill. In their opinion it was also intended that a Bill approved by the People under Art. 27 might have its constitutionality tested under Art. 26. See proposal 64 and recommendation thereto.

Although the Committee consider it unlikely that any Bill would at the same time be referred to the People and the Supreme Court, they nevertheless consider that the possibility should be provided for.

If this recommendation be accepted, a number of interlocking amendments will be required in Articles 26 and 27, notably, a qualification in regard to Article 27 in Article 26.3.2° and qualifications in regard to Article 26 in Article 27.3.

The qualification referred to in Article 27.3 might be to the following effect—to add at the end and as part of the section the following words:

> 'or in the case of a Bill which is referred to the Supreme Court under Article 26, not later than ten days after the decision of the Supreme Court on such reference is pronounced.'[188]

Article 27

Proposal 65: Clerk of the Seanad

In informal conference with the Secretary to the President on the 9th February, 1939, the question of the procedure to be followed in verifying names signed to a petition was raised for discussion. It was agreed that verification of the names appeared not to be a matter for an officer of the Oireachtas, and it was felt that a Bill implementing Article 27 in this regard should be introduced. Doubt, however, it was understood, was expressed by the Parliamentary Draftsman as to whether this course was possible and the recollection of the conversation is that the opinion was that an amendment of the Constitution was required. That opinion was understood to be based on the fact that there was no authority in the Constitution to prescribe the procedure by law.

[188] Annotated with a 'yes' mark and the following: 'Note: Alternative provisions should so far as conveniently possible be in *separate* subsections'.

Proposal 66: Secretary to the President

1. The operation of Article 27 of the Constitution under which the President may in certain circumstances decline to sign a Bill until the will of the people thereon has been ascertained, depends in the first instance upon the receipt by him of a joint petition in writing signed by:
   (a) a majority of the members of Seanad Éireann,
   and
   (b) not less than one-third of the members of Dáil Éireann.
2. In an important matter of this nature bearing directly on the enactment of legislation, it is essential that the validity of any action taken by the President as a result of such petition may not be open to challenge on any ground e.g.,
   (a) that some of the signatories do not possess the necessary qualification as members of the appropriate house of the Oireachtas, or
   (b) that any signature on the petition is not in fact that of the person by whom it purports to have been written.
3. The question arises as to how certainty in this regard may be achieved.
4. The Constitution makes no provision for proof, and as the time available to the President for the completion of all action arising out of such petition is in practice only six or seven days, it is clearly desirable that some procedure should be arranged which will secure that the bona fides of any such petition shall have been established beyond question, in all respects, before it reaches the President.
5. It was thought that arrangements could be made whereby such a petition would be transmitted to the President by the Chairman or Clerk of either house of the Oireachtas, his covering signature being accepted without question as a certification of the genuineness of the petition.
6. This proposal was fully discussed with, and examined by officers of the Oireachtas, but the view was held by them that neither the Chairman nor the Clerk of either House had any function in the matter. For that reason none of them was prepared to accept responsibility for the transmission of petitions of this nature, or to do anything which would imply certification of the bona fides of the signatures thereto.

7. In the present circumstances, the presentation of such a petition to the President would create a very difficult situation for which the Constitution as it stands provides no solution.
8. It has been suggested that the defect might be remedied by ordinary law, without having recourse to a constitutional amendment. On that matter legal advice will, no doubt, be sought.
9. In any case, the question should be resolved without delay, so that if necessary, the Constitution may be appropriately amended under Article 51.

Recommendation: The Committee is in agreement with the suggestion contained in the proposals. They consider that the point could be met by a simple amendment to Article 27.2, to the following effect—to insert after the word 'petitioners' the words 'and verified in the manner prescribed by law'.[189]

Article 27.4.2°
Proposal 67: A member of the Committee
The words 'Every such Bill' appear to have been inserted in error. It is not the *Bill* but the *proposal* which is submitted to the people under Article 27. Accordingly, it is suggested that the words 'Every such Bill' should be deleted, and in their stead the following inserted 'Every Bill containing a proposal, etc.'

Recommendation: The Committee is in agreement with this proposal which involves a merely verbal change.[190]

Article 34.4.4°
Proposal 76: The Committee
Having regard to the statement contained in their recommendation to proposal 62, the Committee gave consideration to the question of providing that the Supreme Court should pronounce only one judgment

[189] Annotated: 'P[arliamentary] D[raftsman] suggests split 27.2 into 2 subsections. Committee agree. 23/10/40'.

[190] Annotated: 'Approved by Taoiseach in principle but he is not satisfied that the words suggested are sufficient to identify the Bill. A different Bill might contain the same proposal'.

Moynihan later made a second annotation, as follows: 'I again discussed this proposal with the Taoiseach on 23 October 1940. He still feels that our suggested amendment would not sufficiently identify the Bill in question. The Government, having got approval for a proposal, might include it in a new Bill containing other obnoxious proposals and having got the new Bill passed by both Houses submit it to the President. I expressed the view that this was most unlikely. It seems questionable [that] it would be permissible under the Section or could have any value since the new Bill would also be made the subject of a petition. I suggested however that the P.D might be asked to consider an amended draft on the following lines: "Whenever a proposal contained in a Bill the subject of a petition under this Article shall have been approved either...section, such Bill should..." The Taoiseach agreed. The Taoiseach directed that a further amendment should be prepared whereby the President would not be obliged to sign a Bill containing a proposal approved under the Article if it also contained a proposal vetoed'.

in Constitutional cases. The Committee understands, after consultation with the Attorney General, that the Chief Justice considers that the Supreme Court should pronounce only one judgment in all Constitutional matters, whether they arise on a reference under Article 26 or otherwise. Accordingly they recommend that an amendment be made for this purpose in Article 34.4.[191]

Article 40.4.2°
Proposal 81: Department of the Taoiseach
It is suggested that the provision under which an applicant in a *habeas corpus* case can have the matter dealt with by any and every judge of the High Court should be amended.

It may be necessary or desirable to take steps to ensure that persons are not released from custody on purely technical grounds or because of some trifling flaw in procedure. There is also the issue that *habeas corpus* proceedings are of such importance as to justify their being heard by more than one judge.

It is suggested further that where a *habeas corpus* application is granted on the ground that a particular statute is unconstitutional there should be an appeal to the Supreme Court.

It is undesirable that constitutional issues should in a *habeas corpus* case be decided by the judgment of a single member of the High Court without any appeal to the Supreme Court.

Proposal 81A: The High Commissioner to Canada[192]
It is suggested that this subsection should be amended by removing the jurisdiction thereby conferred from a single judge of the High Court.
Recommendation: The Committee are of opinion that no change should be made in the present position in regard to *habeas corpus* save in the direction of an appeal to the Supreme Court in cases where the applicant obtains his release on the ground that the law under which he is detained is unconstitutional. In this respect, they agree with the proposal and recommend that provision should be made by amendment of Art. 40.4 for enabling a Court or judge which or who is of opinion, on an application under that section, that the applicant in detained in accordance with a law which is unconstitutional, to refer the question of constitutionality to the Supreme Court for its determination, and not to release the applicant until that question is determined.

[191] Annotated: 'A.G. thinks undesirable to further have [?] cases where the *sole* issue is that of validity of a law. Two drafts to be prepared, one on this basis and the other on basis indicated above, A.G. to consult [?]. 4 November 1940'.
[192] John Hearne, appointed High Commissioner to Canada in 1939.

The suggested amendment to Article 40. 4 might take the form of a new Subsection 3° inserted in the section, the Subsection being to the following effect:

> '3° Where, on an inquiry by the High Court or a judge thereof into a complaint made under this section, the Court or judge is satisfied that the person detained, is being detained in accordance with a law, but that such law is invalid having regard to the provisions of this Constitution, the Court or judge may refer the question of the validity of such law by way of case stated to the Supreme Court for its determination thereon, and in that case, shall not order the release of the person detained pending the determination of the Supreme Court.'[193]

Alternative drafts of Amendments to Article 40.4.2° of the Constitution.[194]

[Draft A]
To insert, immediately after Subsection 2°, a new Subsection as follows:

> '3° Where, on an inquiry by the High Court or a judge thereof into a complaint made under this section, the Court or judge is satisfied that the person detained is being detained in accordance with a law, but that such law is invalid having regard to the provisions of this Constitution, the Court or judge may refer the question of the validity of such law by way of case stated to the Supreme Court for its determination thereon, and in that case, shall not order the release of the person detained pending the determination of the Supreme Court, but may, pending such determination, allow him to be at liberty on bail subject to such conditions as may be fixed by the Court or judge, and, if the person detained is under sentence of death, the Court or judge shall direct that the execution of the sentence shall be deferred pending such determination as aforesaid.'

[193] Annotated: 'Provisionally approved by Taoiseach subject to amendment shown [The above Subsection has been edited to read as manually amended by Moynihan]. Requires to be very carefully considered from judge's point of view'.

Moynihan later made a second annotation, as follows: 'I discussed this matter further with the Taoiseach on 23 November 1940. With regard to suggested draft, he now agrees that we should let the words "that such law is invalid" stand. He desires that we should add words to the draft indicating that where the person concerned in a *H[abeas] C[orpus]* application is under sentence of death, such sentence shall not be executed pending the final determination of the question whether he is lawfully detained. This, he directs, might be effected by deleting the words "shall not order the release of the person detained" and substituting the words "shall order that the person detained shall be held in custody" or other words to the like effect. He desires further, that any other suggestions affecting *Habeas Corpus* including Mr Hearne's suggestion should be fully examined and submitted to him'.

[194] Annotated: 'Discussed with Taoiseach 16 November 1940. Combine drafts A and C'.

[Draft B]
In lieu of Article 40.4.2°, to substitute a new Subsection as follows:

> '2° Upon complaint being made by or on behalf of any person that he is being unlawfully detained, the High Court consisting of at least three judges shall forthwith enquire into the same and may make an order requiring the person in whose custody such person is detained to produce the body of the person so detained before the Court without delay and to certify in writing as to the cause of the detention, and the High Court shall thereupon order the release of such person unless satisfied that he is being detained in accordance with the law.'

[Draft C]
In Section 4, the deletion of Subsection 2° and the insertion in its place of two new Subsections as follows, that is to say:

> '2° Upon complaint being made by or on behalf of any person to the High Court or any judge thereof alleging that such person is being unlawfully detained, the High Court or such judge thereof shall forthwith enquire into the said complaint and may order the person in whose custody such person is detained to produce the body of such person before the High Court on a named day and to certify in writing the grounds of his detention, and the High Court, consisting of not less than three judges, shall, upon the body of such person being produced before that Court and after giving the person in whose custody he is detained an opportunity of justifying the detention, order the release of such person from such detention unless satisfied that he is being detained in accordance with the law.
>
> '3° Where an order is made under this section by the High Court or a judge thereof for the production of the body of a person who is under sentence of death, the High Court or such judge thereof shall further order that the execution of the said sentence of death shall be deferred until after the body of such person has been produced before the High Court and the lawfulness of his detention has been determined by that Court in accordance with this section.'

Article 56.5

Proposal 89: Department of Finance
The wording of this section in the English version is faulty and has already been the subject of controversy before the Civil Service

(Compensation) Board. The Irish version correctly speaks of 'terms of office, conditions of office, salary or tenure of office', whereas the English version speaks of 'the terms, conditions, remuneration or tenure of any person'. The English version should be amended to bring the text into conformity with the current Irish version.

Recommendation: The Committee agrees that the English text should be brought into conformity with the Irish text.[195]

Annex 1, Part 2: Proposals Regarded as Matters of Policy

Article 12.2
Proposal 10: Department of Finance
Article 16.1.4° provides that 'no voter may exercise more than one vote at an election for Dáil Éireann…' It seems desirable that a similar provision should be embodied in this Article in connection with the election of a President (See also Article 18).

Recommendation: The provision suggested in this proposal is already covered by legislation which, in the opinion of the Committee, is perfectly valid, namely, Section 26.3 of the Presidential Elections Act, 1937 (No. 32 of 1937).

If, however, it is desired to amend the Constitution in the manner indicated, a simple amendment on the lines of Article 16.1.4° would be sufficient.[196]

Article 13.7
Proposal 20: Secretary to the President

1. The question has arisen as to whether a President, on the occasion of his formal entry on office, under Section 8 of Article 12 of the Constitution might not wish to make a brief statement or speech.
2. It has been suggested that any such statement, unless confined to a mere formality such as an expression of thanks etc., would be an address to the Nation within the meaning of Section 7 of Article 13 of the Constitution, and as such would require
   (a) prior consultation with the Council of State, and
   (b) prior approval by the Government.
3. It is obvious that compliance with these conditions would not be possible in the circumstances, and the question arises as to whether the Constitution should not be amended so as to cover the contingency.

[195] Annotated: 'Further amendment to be suggested by Mr Philip O'Donoghue. 16 November 1940'.
[196] Annotated: 'Put in provisionally for submission to the Government'.

4. The matter, however, is one of policy, and should be the subject of a positive direction by the Taoiseach before any action is taken in regard to it.

Recommendation: The Committee is in agreement with the suggestion contained in the last paragraph of the proposal.[197]

Article 16.1.2°
Proposal 33: Quit Rent Office
I would suggest the desirability of limiting the implied powers of the Oireachtas to create disqualifications under Article 16.1.2°. At present the only limits imposed are that any citizen who has reached the age of twenty-one years cannot be disqualified on the grounds of (1) age or (2) sex. The most important statutory incapacity existent is that created by section 5 of the Electoral Act, 1923 in relation to members of Police Forces.

It is only a step from the Garda Síochána to the Army and the Civil Service and other public officials but what is more important is that so long as questions of age or sex are left untouched there seems to be nothing to prevent the Oireachtas from confining the franchise to £10 rated occupiers or from going back to a register of freeholders.

It may of course be argued that the force of public opinion is a strong enough brake on the Oireachtas in this matter. That may seem so at the present time to some people but only to some people. We live in a changing world, and in my opinion this power is too vital and basic to be left to the discretion of the Legislature.

There may be difficulty in devising a suitable form or amendment to meet all the circumstances, but I would suggest that most of the difficulty is caused by the existence of Section 5 of the Electoral Act, 1923. To my mind there is no need for that section now though in the clash of principle and practice it could have been justified by expediency at the time of its enactment.

A similar amendment in Article 16.1.1° would seem desirable but amendment in that subsection is not so vital and necessary as in Article 16.1.2°.

Recommendation: The Committee considers that the proposal is one of policy. They observe that the suggestion contained in it would impose a further restriction on the legislative freedom of the Oireachtas.

The disqualifications at present imposed by law on the exercise of the Dáil Franchise are:

[197] Annotated: 'No amendment necessary'.

1. Legal incapacity to be registered or to vote e.g. insanity (Electoral Act, 1923 (No.12 of 1923), sections 1(1), 4(2))
2. Membership of a police force on full pay (Electoral Act, 1923 section 5).
3. During seven years after conviction of a corrupt practice (Prevention of Electoral Abuses Act, 1923 (No.38 of 1923), s.6. (3))
4. During five years after conviction of an illegal practice (Electoral Act, 1923 s.15).[198]

Article 18, Sections 1, 3 and 10
Proposal 38: Clerk of the Seanad
Copies of Minutes exchanged with the Department of the Taoiseach in reference to the procedure regarding the appointment of members of the Seanad nominated by the Taoiseach are attached hereto. It will be seen from the Minute of the 26 October that it was considered that if the procedure was to be regulated by law, authority to do so should be taken under the Constitution.

Copy of minute dated 13.3.40 received from Mr P. P. O'Donoghue also attached.[199]

Proposal 39: Dept. of Local Government and Public Health
This Article might be amended so that the nominations may only be made by the Taoiseach who, after a General Election, secures the support of a majority in Dáil Éireann.

Recommendation: The minutes referred to in the proposal of the Clerk of the Seanad (and annexed hereto) deal with two matters: (1) the question of providing by law for the procedure for nominating the members of Seanad Éireann who are to be nominated by the Taoiseach: (2) the question of securing that the said members shall be nominated by the incoming and not by the outgoing Taoiseach; this latter question also forms the kernel of the proposal of the Department of Local Government and Public Health.

As regards (1), the Committee consider that it should be dealt with by practice rather than by legislation, and are in agreement with the view that legislation purporting to control the discretion of the Taoiseach might be held unconstitutional.

As regards (2), the Committee consider it unlikely that an outgoing

[198] Annotated: 'No amendment necessary'.

[199] Correspondence not printed. In brief: On 23 November 1939, Padraig Ó Cinnéide wrote to Seán Malone, noting that legislation for regulating the appointment of members of the Seanad Éireann was under consideration, principally to ensure that members were nominated by the incoming, not the outgoing, Taoiseach.

Taoiseach would ever attempt to nominate members for a new Seanad. Nevertheless, if it is desired to provide against the possibility of such an occurrence, adequate provision could be made by a simple amendment to Article 18.3. It is suggested that the section, as amended, might read as follows:

> '3 The nominated members of Seanad Éireann shall be nominated, with their prior consent, by the Taoiseach appointed, after the reassembly of Dáil Éireann following a general election.'[200]

Article 18.4
Proposal 40: Department of Local Government and Public Health
It is suggested that university representation in Seanad Éireann should be provided by statute law rather than by the Constitution.

On the re-integration of the national territory, it may be an article of the Agreement that representation be given to the University in Belfast, and it would be easier to meet the position by amendment of the law than by amendment of the Constitution.

Recommendation: The Committee consider that the suggestion contained in this proposal is a matter of policy. If it is desired to give effect to the proposal, the Committee are of opinion that this could be done by a comparatively simple amendment to Article 18.4 on the following lines:

To delete paragraphs i and ii now contained in that section and substitute the following:

> 'i. Such number, not less than six nor more than nine, as may be provided by law shall be elected by the Universities in the State in such manner that each university shall be entitled to equal representation'.

If this amendment were accepted, a consequential amendment would be required in Article 18.1, to the following effect: In Article 18.1, before the word 'sixty' to insert the word 'not less than'.[201]

First Amendment of the Constitution—Article 28.3.3°
Proposal [Blank]: Department of the Taoiseach
In view of the constitutional function vested in the President of safeguarding the Constitution, it is thought that when as at present the Constitution is suspended under the First Amendment during a time

[200] Annotated: 'Taoiseach agrees in principle that amendment should be made. He would like the suggested wording to be reconsidered, with a view to simplifying'. The annexed minutes refer to correspondence between the Department of the Taoiseach and Seán Malone.
[201] Annotated: 'No amendment necessary'.

while the State is at peace, the President should concur in the suspension. It is accordingly suggested that the First Amendment of the Constitution should be amended by inserting after the words 'shall have resolved', some such words as 'and the President, after consultation with the Council of State shall have concurred'.

Recommendation: The Committee is of opinion that the suggestion contained in this proposal is largely a question of policy. They observe, however, that if it were adopted and ultimately enacted the effect would be that the Emergency Powers Act, [1939] and other emergency legislation would require re-enactment.[202]

Draft Amendment of Article 28.3.3°
In Subsection 3° of section 3 of Article 28, to insert the words 'or for the purpose of dealing with a conspiracy against the State' immediately after the words 'armed rebellion'.[203]

Article 28.3.3°
Proposal 69: Department of Lands (Gaeltacht Services)
The question arises whether the reference to laws 'for the purpose of securing the public safety, etc.,' is sufficient to cover disturbance, civil commotion and national or international emergency and whether additional words should be inserted.

Proposal 69A: Department of Finance
The advisability of further amending this subsection to provide for an emergency unconnected with a war situation might be considered.

Recommendation: The Committee recognise that, in the circumstances of this country, it is necessary to have a strong machinery for dealing effectively with the activities of treasonable conspiracies.

Such machinery should not be hampered by being questioned on constitutional grounds, for the principle involved is nothing less than that the Constitution and the organs of government established there-

[202] Annotated: 'The Taoiseach is now of opinion that no amendment need be introduced on the basis of this proposal. 31 October 1940'. A further annotation, also dated 31 October, notes: 'Tentatively suggested at Committee meeting (30 October) that Art. 28.3.3° might be further amended so as to cover laws expressed to be for the purpose of [?] against any conspiracy or activities designed to upset by force the State or the Constitution. The Taoiseach is of opinion that this suggestion should be carefully considered and made the basis of a draft amendment to be submitted for his consideration'.

[203] Annotated: 'Discussed with Taoiseach, 16 November 1940. Include provisionally in draft Bill'. Later annotation reads: 'Since the discussion with the Taoiseach on 16 November, the Taoiseach has directed that the wording of this amendment should be further considered and an alternative draft prepared. He also wished to have a brief on the amendment for the purposes of explaining its effect to the Government. At a meeting of the Committee today [25 November] it was agreed to submit the following form of words: "or for the purpose of dealing, at any time, with an attempt by force to undermine the organs of state established by this Constitution".' An annotation of 26 November reads: 'The Taoiseach fears that the form recommended above might be interpreted as safeguarding only legislation dealing with actual violence. He thinks that the following alternative, which I submitted to him, should be considered: "or for the purpose of dealing, at any time, with a conspiracy to undermine by force the organs etc., etc".'

under shall be clothed with the power of self protection and preservation and that the Constitution shall not be invoked to cause its own destruction. Moreover, those who by their acts and attitude proclaim themselves outlaws should not, on any ground of justice or equity or even commonsense, be accorded the benefit of the Constitutional guarantees framed to protect the citizen who fulfils his fundamental political duty of fidelity to the Nation and loyalty to the State (Article 9).

Accordingly the Committee recommend that Article 28.3.3° should be strengthened to protect from constitutional attack legislation designed to deal with conspiracies of violence against the State, and they recommend the addition of words to that Subsection for the purpose.

Article 28.9.2°
Proposal 70: Department of Finance
As it is clear from subsection 3° of this section that the President may in certain circumstances refuse to accept the resignation of a member of the Government, it is suggested that 'resign' in subsection 2° should be altered to 'tender his resignation'.

Recommendation: The Committee consider that the present form of Article 28.9 is sufficiently clear, but if, in view of the fact that the word 'resign' has a different meaning in Subsection 1° to that which it has in Subsections 2° and 3°, it is thought desirable to put the matter beyond doubt, this can be done by a simple amendment to Subsection 2°—namely, in Article 28.9.2° to delete the words 'resign from office by placing' and to substitute the word 'place'.[204]

Article 34.3.2°
Proposal [Blank]: The High Commissioner to Canada
It is suggested that this Article should be amended to provide that a Bill or provision which has been referred to the Supreme Court under Article 26, and has been pronounced valid by that Court, shall, when enacted into law, be beyond the reach of the original jurisdiction conferred on the High Court by this Article.

Recommendation: The Committee are inclined to sympathise with this suggestion and if it is desired to give effect to it, this could be done by a comparatively simple amendment to Article 34.3, preferably by the addition of a new Subsection 3° to that Section, excluding from the jurisdiction conferred on the High Court by Subsection 2°, any law or any provision of a law the Bill for which had been referred to and pronounced valid by the Supreme Court under Article 26.

[204] Annotated: 'Make it "place his resignation from office"'.

The Committee however are of opinion that it is extremely unlikely that the High Court would ever enquire into, let alone question, the validity of a law where the Bill for such law had been pronounced valid by the Supreme Court, and it is accordingly for consideration whether any amendment of the Constitution is really necessary for this purpose.[205]

[Proposed amendment to] Article 34
The deletion of Subsection 2° of Section 3 and the insertion in its place of two new Subsections as follows:

> 2° Save as otherwise provided by this Article, the jurisdiction of the High Court shall extend to the question of the validity of any law having regard to the provisions of this Constitution, and no Court, save only the High Court and the Supreme Court on appeal from the High Court, shall have jurisdiction to determine any such question.
> 3° No Court whatever shall have jurisdiction to question the validity of a law, or any provision of a law, the Bill for which shall have been referred to the Supreme Court by the President under Article 26 of this Constitution, or to question the validity of a provision of a law where the corresponding provision in the Bill for such law shall have been referred to the Supreme Court by the President under the said Article 26.

And the alteration of the number of Subsection 3° of the said Section 3 from '3°' to '4°'.[206]

No. 300: NAI DT S12506

Memorandum from Stephen Roche to Maurice Moynihan

Department of Justice
13 September 1940

Dear O'Muimhneacháin,
In the opening paragraph of the attached memorandum you will find the reasons why it was written and why it is addressed to you.

I had originally intended to have a dozen or so copies made so that a separate copy could be given to each of the persons interested but before

[205] Annotated: 'The Taoiseach feels that there is much force in the arguments both for and against this proposal. He desires that a draft amendment based thereon should be included provisionally in the list of amendments to be submitted to the Government. 31 October 1940'.
[206] Annotated: 'Discussed by Committee on 25 November. Agreed to recommend the acceptance of the proposal. The Taoiseach agrees'.

I had finished the memorandum I made up my mind that a single copy would be sufficient at this stage and that it would be a waste of paper to make any more. The attached copy is, therefore, the only one in existence: I have not kept even the usual carbon. It might perhaps be given, in turn, to each of the persons interested to read: at a later stage copies can be made, if necessary, of any portions which are considered to be useful.

'Some aspects of the Constitution, and judicial System, considered from the point of view of the effective administration of criminal justice', September 1940

Enforcement of Criminal Law—Restraints and delays arising out of Constitution and otherwise—Disadvantages of relying too much on 'Emergency' provisions—possibility of improving ordinary law and procedure.

Mr O'Muimhneachain,
These notes are written as a result of a discussion (in connection with possible amendments of the Constitution) which took place in your room some months ago. You will remember that Mr O'Donoghue and Mr Fay, both of the Attorney General's Office, and Dr Rynne, of the Department of External Affairs, were present. I expressed certain views on them and it was suggested that it might be useful if I put these views in writing and submitted them for more leisurely consideration. I have tried to do this and I may say frankly that I doubt if I have made a very impressive case: I still feel that there is room for reform, but since the above-mentioned discussion took place the position has improved to the extent at least that the validity of both the Special Criminal Court and the Military Court has been finally established and we have probably seen the end, for the present at least, of the legal difficulties, delays, and uncertainties which have made the last nine months so unpleasantly memorable. Also, under the pressure of other work, I have not been able to deal with the very wide and important subject in anything like a satisfactory manner and these notes are put together in a loose and rather incoherent manner. As I have written the paper, however, I may as well submit it such as it is: some of it, here or there, may be of some use, now or afterwards. Any further delay in attempting to improve it would probably result in its not being submitted at all.

There will be found in the Appendix summaries of five cases which came before the High Court in one form or another. These cases seem to me to illustrate the following points:

Case No. 1: The Superior Courts are inclined to take too critical and destructive a line with Orders of the District Court which come before them for revision. The District Court is the Court upon which the greatest burden of ordinary criminal work falls; the work is done, very often, under difficulties and an Order which is in essence perfectly just should not be set aside on a technicality. Is there any *real* reason why the Superior Courts should not *amend* instead of setting aside in such cases and do so on such terms as would not encourage such appeals?

Case No. 2: The same observations apply to the High Court in its dealings with the Constitution (Special Powers) Tribunal.

Case No. 3: It was possible in this case for an applicant to select the most suitable Judge of the High Court, from his point of view, to prevent other Judges from sitting with him, and to obtain from that Judge, sitting alone, a decision which proved to be erroneous, that an Act of the Oireachtas is void as being contrary to the Constitution, with very serious practical consequences. This should not be possible.[207]

Case No. 4: *Habeas corpus* procedure should not be used, at the last moment, to delay the execution of a man who was convicted of murder and who refused either to defend himself or to appeal, as he was entitled to do, to the Court of Criminal Appeal.

Case No. 5: This case illustrates two points, viz:

(a) the misuse of *habeas corpus* as at (4) above, and
(b) the extraordinary nature of the circumstances which made it possible to bring about a result which, under an effective Criminal Code, would be quite ordinary and natural, viz., the convictions and execution, within a reasonable time, of men apprehended in the act of murder.

The view which I expressed at the meeting was, in general, that the recurring necessity for 'emergency' laws was due, at least partly, to certain weaknesses of the ordinary system in criminal administration and that one way of approaching the problem was, not to open the door wider for 'emergency' laws, but to revise the Constitution, and the Court system in criminal matters with a greater regard to the actual needs and the actual dangers of our time and our country—the chief danger being that our democracy may collapse by reason of its failure to defend itself against its enemies.

[207] This was a reference to the events surrounding *The State (Burke) v. Lennon*. See Chapter XIII.

The general line adopted in the Constitution in relation to the Courts of Justice and the punishment of offences in normal times is to provide, as the ordinary or permanent code, a system characterised mainly by precautions designed to prevent any possibility of injustice or undue severity. With this object, very explicit and far-reaching guarantees are given; justice is to be administered by Judges and by nobody else: in addition to the Judge there must be, except in the case of minor offences, a jury: the *habeas corpus* procedure is explicitly made a portion of the Constitution: a High Court Judge is given the right to declare an Act of the Oireachtas to be invalid. (This last provision was inserted, it will be remembered, after considerable hesitation, and on the assumption that it would always be open to the State to appeal to the Supreme Court, an assumption which seemed perfectly safe having regard to the works of Article 34.4.4° but which was defeated, in a very unexpected and unfortunate way, in connection with *habeas corpus* procedure).

In my view, the importance of the safeguards contained in the Constitution and in the law and in inherited court practice, supposedly for the prevention of tyrannical action by the Executive against the ordinary citizen, is much exaggerated. Many of these safeguards have been taken from the English law, having originated in England in circumstances which no longer exist either there or here. They originated at different times but, in general, they arose in circumstances almost inconceivable nowadays and probably now known, even as historical facts, to ten per cent of our people. They were rightly regarded as valuable, to the comparatively few who really could avail of them, in times when the dependence of the Executive on a Parliament elected by adult suffrage and the modern power of public opinion expressed through daily papers, read by practically everybody, were unknown. The English safeguards existed side by side with transportation, the slave trade, examination by torture, public hangings by the thousand (the victims being frequently so young that we would not send them to a Reformatory), general illiteracy, the burning of 'witches' and 'heretics', branding, disembowelling, quartering, and flogging. Magna Carta did not prevent an accused person from being starved and pressed to death if he refused to plead when put on trial—a procedure which would no doubt disagreeably surprise the modern offender who refuses to plead but at the same time expects the full benefit of all Constitutional rights. If formal safeguards of a legal character can really protect us against a repetition of such things, and are really necessary for that purpose, let us by all means have them, but let us not, by way of superstition, retain unnecessary safeguards which only harm us. No Government in this country dares to exercise, or to tolerate in its servants, injustice or cruelty to the individual citizen, and this is not because of Magna Carta or *habeas corpus* but because no Government in this modern and very democratic State could survive if it alienated public opinion, and if there is anything against which there is a strong public opinion in this country it is cruelty or injustice by the Government. The real difficulty, in fact, is not to restrain the Government from committing excesses but to get public opinion to support the Government in any action, however just and necessary, which inflicts pain or hardship on anybody. Just as the Department of Finance has constantly to struggle against the popular idea that there is plenty of public money for everybody, so the Department of Justice has constantly to struggle against the popular idea that all punishment is cruel and unnecessary.

We have not only adopted the old safeguards but we have also bound ourselves to them in a way which the English, who invented them, have never adopted *habeas corpus* or no *habeas corpus*, Bill of Rights or no Bill of Rights, the Westminster Parliament acknowledges no restraint over what it may do for the better government of Great Britain. No Court can take a new statute of that Parliament for examination and pronounce it invalid, because it is, in its view, 'contrary to the Constitution'. When *habeas corpus* threatens to become troublesome in England it is simply suspended.

In my view (I admit being prejudiced against a written Constitution at all) it is unwise to put much detail about the Court system and the criminal law into a statement of fundamental law. For example, our Constitution lays down the following four principles, viz:

(1) Justice is to be administered *by Judges*.
(2) Trial by jury is to be the normal method of trying offences, except minor offences.
(3) There is to be one High Court 'with full original jurisdiction in…all matters and questions whether of law or fact, civil or actual'.
(4) Any High Court Judge may, on application, order the release of any person, if such Judge is of opinion that he is not being detained in accordance with the law.

Taking these principles in turn, as numbered above:-

(1) This involves the consequence that District Justices, just as much as the Chief Justice, must be classed as 'Judges' and

appointed in the same way. It seems to make any system of administration of summary justice by local Committees (Parish Councils) impossible, whereas this is just the sort of thing we would all like to see. It raises the almost unanswerable question of what is 'justice'—e.g. are the granting of dance-hall licences, and the supervision of the Probation Officer system for youthful offenders functions of 'justice', to be performed only by 'Judges' and 'in public Courts'?

(2) On the broad issue, is trial by jury really so bound up with our traditions, so suitable to us, or so sacred in itself as to be a basic principle of our law? On details, what *is* trial by jury?—Is it the English system as it at present exists?

(3) The provision excludes the possibility (which is well worth being considered) of having two sets of High Courts or Judges—one at the head of the civil courts, the other at the head of the criminal courts. The provision assumes that the qualities which go to make a first class civil lawyer are the same qualities which go to make a first class judge in criminal matters. That may well be questioned and it may well be suggested that the present system had led to the introduction into criminal law of refinements and niceties which are not only unnecessary but positively harmful.

(4) This provision is a good illustration of the danger inherent in any attempt to translate what is quite a good general principle into a flat and final statement of constitutional law. Even those who do not like 'safeguards' must admire the vigour and simplicity of the *habeas corpus* procedure but it is, I think, safe to say that when this provision was inserted in the Constitution nobody anticipated the mischievous use which would actually be made of it: see, for instance, cases Nos 3, 4, and 5 in the Appendix.

It was foreseen to some extent when the Constitution was in preparation that it was not strong enough to protect the State against certain kinds of crime, or during certain critical periods. Special provision was made accordingly, which may be classed under two heads, viz., (a) in peace, (b) in war. The provision made for exceptional cases IN PEACE TIME took the following form:

'Special Courts may be established by law for the trial of offences in cases where it may be determined in accordance with such law

> that the ordinary Courts are inadequate to secure the effective administration of justice and the preservation of public peace and order.
>
> The constitution, powers, jurisdiction and procedure of such Special Courts shall be prescribed by law.
>
> The provisions of Article 34 and 35 shall not apply to any such Special Court.'

By way of provision FOR TIMES OF WAR it was laid down that 'Military Tribunals may be established...to deal with a state of war or armed rebellion' and any doubts as to the adequacy of this second provision (the war time provision) were removed by the provisions in another part of the Constitution (Article 28.3.3°) whereby laws passed by the Oireachtas to deal with war conditions are freed entirely from the restrictions of the Constitution.

We may take it, therefore, that while there is a state of war or armed rebellion, either actual or constructive, (meaning by 'constructive' a situation like the present as contemplated in the First Amendment to the Constitution) there should be no real difficulty in the matters in which we are concerned: the Oireachtas can do anything it liked, though even in these circumstances there is, as we have recently seen, a possibility of undesirable delay by reason of an appeal to the High Court or the Supreme Court, an appeal which has to be dealt with, however hopeless its prospects of success may be. However, broadly speaking, it remains true that there are no legal or constitutional problems once a state of war or armed rebellion has been declared to exist.

We may, therefore, concentrate on examining the provision made for special cases in peace time. That provision, which is quoted above, was, on the whole, ingenious and has been of great utility, but the following points may be mentioned by way of criticism, viz:

(1) It obviously suggests that a Special Court will not be a Military Court. (Military Courts being specially mentioned elsewhere) whereas in practice the Special Court is a Military Court in the sense that it is composed entirely of military officers. It was feared at one time that this point might be successfully made in the Courts so as to invalidate the proceedings of the Special Criminal Court: the point was in fact raised, but without success, and that particular danger is over:

(2) The Special Criminal Court is a temporary Court coming into existence only after proclamation by the Government

to the effect that the ordinary Courts are inadequate and, in theory, at least, ceasing to exist as soon as that unsatisfactory state of affairs has passed away:

(3) Its operations are subject, expressly, to an appeal to the Court of Criminal Appeal and it ranks generally, in law, as an inferior Court:

(4) Its powers are restricted, by the words of the relevant Article of the Constitution, to the *trial* of offences: if it were desired to confer upon it powers other than powers of trial, e.g., powers of interrogation or of internment, awkward questions of law would arise.

It appears to be worthy of consideration whether a Court, upon which such heavy responsibilities are placed and which is in fact, from the point of public safety, the most important Court in the State, enjoys under these conditions the confidence, continuity, authority and prestige which it might reasonably expect to have, or which it should have, for the proper performance of its duties. Is it better, on the whole, for the State to treat the form of crime which cannot safely be dealt with by juries as something transient which can adequately be dealt with by a subordinate and temporary Court composed solely of military officers, or would it be better to create a permanent Tribunal, of the highest authority, for this work and, perhaps, having got such a Tribunal together for this purpose, to extend its functions so far as they can usefully be extended to criminal matters other than merely those which are too dangerous to leave to juries?

We have had within nine years the Constitution (Special Powers) Tribunal (1931), the Special Criminal Court (1939), and now the Military Court (1940). Every new experiment in emergency legislation creates new technical difficulties, distracts the attention of the Government and its servants from other business, raises new questions on which appeals can be made to the Courts, and disturbs public confidence. In the latest development, also, the Government itself has had to take an active part in the prosecution of individual offenders: the Government itself formally sends the offenders for trial and even fixes the date of execution. This should not be so: the Government's concern with individual offenders should be limited as far as possible to the exercise of the prerogative of mercy in proper cases. That the Government as such should have to take an active part in the prosecution seems to indicate that there is something wrong with the system. It is true that in dealing, in critical times, with offences arising from political motives it seems almost inevitable that the Government itself should decide whether the offender should be prosecuted at all and, if prosecuted, before what Tribunal and under what penalties, (where there are alternative Tribunals and alternative penalties) but it will probably be agreed that it is the kind of development which should not be allowed to grow beyond the inevitable minimum. It seems to be indicated that some better machinery is required to deal with this important aspect of criminal administration—the things *before* trial—in order to relieve the Government as much as possible of this new burden.

I have now stated, at, I fear, undue length some of the points in the Constitution, &c., which I think might be improved from the point of view of the better administration of criminal justice. As to just how they should be improved I do not propose to make any suggestions here. I believe, after fairly lengthy experience, that to suggest any specific remedy in advance in a case of this kind would probably be harmful to the prospect of reform. If it appears to your Committee, in the first instance, and then to the Government, *some* reform is desirable, the next step might well be to have the matter considered by some such body as the present Defence Conference, at which it has proved possible for all political parties represented in the Dáil to discuss subjects of national importance on their merits. An agreement arrived at in that way seems to me the only avenue to reform: it would be very unwise (in my opinion) for the Government first to make up its own mind and then to put its decision before the Oireachtas as is done in the case of ordinary Bills. If that were the only possible course by which reform could be effected I think that the whole idea should be dropped: no reform that could be hoped for would be worth the waste of time and the re-opening of old controversies which would be involved in a public debate on such a matter conducted on Party lines.

Very much subject to the above observations on the danger of producing specific remedies prematurely, I may perhaps give the following rude outlines of various possibilities. I have set them down without any attempt either to arrange them in order or to indicate how far they overlap one another or which of them would involve amendment of the Constitution and not merely an amendment of ordinary law:

(1) Cut down to a minimum the period of uncertainty as to whether a law is or is not unconstitutional so that a law cannot be set aside on this ground except during the period of three months following its enactment and then only by

the Supreme Court on the petition of not less than one third of the members of the Dáil.

(2) Establish a High Commission of the Peace or a separate (criminal) division of the High Court and confer upon it the most extensive powers possible for the preservation of peace and order, so as to relieve the Oireachtas and the Government of the necessity for tightening up the law, appointing Special Courts, etc., etc. The idea is to create something which will concentrate upon this task a great variety of powers at present dispersed between the Oireachtas, the Government, the Courts and the Police.

(3) Make appeals on purely technical grounds against Orders of the Inferior Criminal Courts impossible or unprofitable.

(4) So far as the criminal jury system must be retained, consider the desirability of a highly localised jury, selected by the District Justice and working locally under a District Justice, instead of the unwieldy county juries, selected mechanically and dealing with cases not affecting the peace of the jurymen's own districts. (Incidentally the Circuit Court should probably be abolished. It is not, in its present form, the Circuit Court as originally intended. It does not seem to serve any purpose which could not be better served by the High Court and the District Court. The clashes between the Circuit Judge and the District Justice in certain districts bring the Courts generally into discredit. Some of the individual Judges are excellent and might be transferred either to the High Court or to the High Commission of the Peace which is suggested above).

(5) Amend *habeas corpus* procedure so as to avoid repetition of the recent abuses.

(6) Reduce to the unavoidable minimum the references in the Constitution to Courts of Justice and the trial of offences. Aim at something very short and very general such as:

> 'No person shall be imprisoned, tried, fined, or otherwise punished save under the authority of law.'

No. 301: NAI, DT S12172A

Memorandum from Maurice Moynihan to Kevin Haugh

Department of the Taoiseach
19 November 1940

Attorney General,
I am directed by the Taoiseach to request that you will be good enough to instruct the Parliamentary Draftsman to proceed with the drafting of a Bill providing for the amendment of the Constitution on the lines which have been agreed upon by the Committee which has been considering the question of amendments to be effected within the limit prescribed by Article 51 of the Constitution.[208]

No. 302: NAI, DT S12172A

Memorandum from Phillip O'Donoghue to Maurice Moynihan

Office of the Attorney General
19 November 1940

Mr Moynihan,
I enclose draft of the Constitution Bill, 1940, which has been received from the Parliamentary Draftsman.[209] The Attorney General has not considered the draft and I am sending it on to you so that the Taoiseach would be able to take an early opportunity of discussing the matter with the Attorney General.[210]

[208] A preliminary draft, incorporating sample amendments to articles, had been drawn up by William Fay on 22 October 1940, NAI, DT S12172A.
[209] Not printed.
[210] On 21 November Fay submitted to Moynihan draft amendments to the Irish text of the Constitution to keep it in harmony with the English text, NAI, DT S12172A. On 27 November, the Second Amendment of the Constitution Bill, 1940, was introduced in the Dáil. De Valera informed the Dáil that he was uncertain as to the exact amendments that the Bill would include, but that they would receive the draft Bill by the end of December, 81 *Dáil Debates*, Cols 698–9. The second stage of the Bill was not taken until 2 April 1941. The draft Bill of 19 November was revised on several occasions before the end of December: 28 November, 3 December, 6 December, 10 December and 11 December.

No. 303: NAI, DT S12172A

Memorandum by Maurice Moynihan

Department of the Taoiseach
4 December 1940

In connection with the Second Amendment of the Constitution Bill, I am engaged in reading to the Taoiseach the entire English text of the Constitution. On the 2nd and 3rd instant I read Articles 1 to 31, inclusive. The following points have arisen:

1 In dealing with the second stage of the Bill in the Dáil, the Taoiseach would like to indicate that in some cases it would have been possible to improve the phraseology of provisions of the Constitution or perhaps even to make their intention clearer but that in the case of a number of suggestions with these objects it was decided not to introduce amendments, the Government's desire being to restrict the amendments to those shown to be really necessary.

2 In connection with Article 15.10 of the Constitution it is understood that the preparation of a Powers and Privilege Bill has been under consideration for a considerable time. The Taoiseach desires to know the position in this regard.

3 The position of the Emergency Powers Acts and Orders at the end of the war should be carefully examined and the need for a further amendment to Article 28.3.3° in this regard considered.[211] For example, it might be provided that nothing in the Constitution shall be invoked to invalidate the Emergency Code for a period ending not later than twelve months after the termination of the 'time of war' or earlier on the passing of resolutions to that effect by both Houses of the Oireachtas.

4 The question of extending the period of 90 days referred to in Article 24.3 of the Constitution should be considered. In this connection, the feasibility of enacting identical permanent legislation before the expiration of the period during which an Act passed in accordance with Article 24 remains in operation should be examined in particular reference to the

[211] Article 28.3.3° was originally amended by the First Amendment of the Constitution Act, 1939. See Chapter XIII.

question whether the introduction of such identical legislation would be in accordance with the rules of order in the two Houses of the Oireachtas. The Taoiseach is inclined to think that 120 days might be substituted for 90 days.

5 Special copies should be made for the Taoiseach of Articles or Sections to be amended embodying the proposed amendments and the provisions affected should be marked in the Taoiseach's copy of the Constitution.

6 Consideration should be given to the question of amending Article 27 so as to provide that no Bill shall be referred to the people under that Article until it has first been referred to the Supreme Court under Article 26 and the Supreme Court has announced a decision to the effect that the Bill or the provision referred to them is not repugnant to the Constitution.[212]

No. 304: NAI, DT S12172A

Maurice Moynihan to Gearóid Mag Canainn

Department of the Taoiseach
4 December 1940

Cléireach na Dála,
I am directed by the Taoiseach to refer to the Second Amendment of the Constitution Bill, 1940, and to state that he has under consideration the question of including in the Bill an amendment extending to 120 days the period of ninety days referred to in Article 24.3 of the Constitution.

In this connection the Taoiseach has in mind the possibility that a Bill, the time for the consideration of which by Seanad Éireann has been abridged under Article 24, may contain proposals required in the public interest to be enacted as permanent legislation, and consideration is being given to the feasibility of enacting such permanent legislation within the limited period referred to in Article 24.3.

It is recognised that, under the terms of Article 24.3, a law the Bill for which was dealt with under Article 24 may be continued in force for longer than ninety days, by agreement between the two Houses of the Oireachtas. In certain circumstances, however, the agreement of Seanad Éireann to such a course might not be forthcoming. It might be possible to gain time by the passage of a further Bill under the procedure of

[212] Annotated by Moynihan: 'Spoke [to] Mr O'Donoghue and Dr Rynne regarding 3, 4 and 6. They will consider'. See document nos 305–6.

Article 24 within the period of ninety days, but this is a course to which objection would possibly be seen.

The Taoiseach would be glad to have your observations generally on the foregoing points. In particular I am to request your views as to whether, in the event of the passing of a Bill under Article 24, it would be in conformity with the rules of order to introduce within the period of ninety days (or longer period if agreed upon under Article 24.3) (a) a second Bill the time for consideration of which by the Seanad would be abridged under Article 24 and (b) a further Bill, the time for consideration of which would not be abridged, both such Bills being identical in terms with the original Bill dealt with under Article 24.[213]

No. 305: NAI, DT S12172A

Memorandum by Maurice Moynihan

Department of the Taoiseach
6 December 1940

On the 4th instant Mr O'Donoghue and Dr Rynne considered the points referred to in paragraphs 3, 4 and 6 of that date. I discussed the points with Mr O'Donoghue on the 5th instant. The following is the result of the consideration given to the points:

Point 3: It is agreed that a further amendment to Article 28.3.3° is necessary. Mr O'Donoghue is of opinion that this amendment should be by way of an addition to the first amendment of the Constitution. He is apprehensive as to the possible effect on the existing emergency code if the wording of the first amendment were altered otherwise than by way of addition. We agreed that the additional words should be something to the following effect:

> 'and a time after the termination of such armed conflict up to such date as may be determined by resolutions of both Houses of the Oireachtas.'

The Parliamentary Draftsman will be requested to draft an amendment accordingly.[214]

[213] An identical letter was sent to Seán Malone, Clerk of the Seanad, on the same date. Malone responded on 7 December stating that, in his view, extending the period in question to 120 days would have little practical effect and that Article 24 'should not be thrown open for amendment'. In Malone's opinion, it was highly unlikely that the Seanad would 'display the irresponsibility of refusing a more extended period of operation of a law recommended to it by the Government on the grounds that it was urgent and necessary for the preservation of the public peace and security', NAI, DT S12172A.

[214] Annotated by Moynihan: 'Draft received. 6 December 1940'.

Point 4: If under the procedure indicated in Article 24 of the Constitution a Bill had been passed through both Houses of the Oireachtas and signed by the President on 5th December 1940, it would remain in force for a period of ninety days from 5th December unless a longer period were agreed upon by both Houses. If a similar resolution were passed by the Dáil and sent to the Senate on 6th December 1940 then, assuming that the Senate did not agree to the measure, it could be deemed to have been passed by both Houses of the Oireachtas on the ninety-first day from 6th December but it could not be signed by the President until five days later. There would thus be a gap of some days between the expiration of the temporary measure and the coming into force of the permanent measure.

Mr O'Donoghue points out, however, that Article 24, in view of the terms of Section 1 thereof, must be regarded as contemplating temporary rather than permanent legislation. If the emergency giving rise to the legislation still exists, further legislation under Article 24 can be passed before the expiration of the ninety days. In these circumstances, Mr O'Donoghue does not think that an extension of the period of ninety days by amendment of the Constitution is necessary.

Point 6: It is agreed that the suggested amendment to Article 27, with possible consequential amendments to Article 26, is undesirable. There is a presumption in favour of the constitutionality of every Bill introduced by way of ordinary legislation since the legal advisers to the Government would undoubtedly draw attention to any provision the validity of which was, in their view, open to question. In ordinary circumstances therefore, no occasion for a reference to the Supreme Court should arise unless some question as to the constitutionality of a Bill is raised after its introduction. Further, a provision for automatic reference to the Supreme Court in advance of any Bill the subject of a petition under Article 27 might result in a delay of sixty days before action for reference to the people could be taken (see Article 26.2.1°). This would be an undesirable encroachment on the period of eighteen months given to the Government under Article 27.4 in which to decide whether they should drop the Bill or take a referendum or dissolve the Dáil. A Bill, the subject of a petition under Article 27, is likely to be one of such importance that an early decision would be desirable as to whether it should or should not be passed into law.

If the Taoiseach wishes, however, to proceed with an amendment to Article 27 on the lines suggested, Mr O'Donoghue thinks that the Chief Justice should be consulted.

On the 4th instant I completed the reading of the English text of the Constitution to the Taoiseach. In connection with proposed amendments 20 and 30 affecting Articles 26 and 34 respectively, the Taoiseach directed that consideration should be given to the question of having the amendments redrafted so as to provide that no contrary opinion should be pronounced or indicated. He pointed out that the Judge pronouncing the decision of the Court might, as the amendments have been drafted, indicate that some of his colleagues dissented from the judgment. Mr O'Donoghue strongly advised against any such change in the form of the amendments. He is satisfied that, as the amendments stand, no reference would be made to any dissenting judgment or indication given that there had been any dissent. He appears to think that a provision in the form suggested by the Taoiseach would, to some extent, imply a reflection on the discretion of members of the Supreme Court.

The Taoiseach also inquired whether the word 'lawful' in Article 42.3.1° would be construed as meaning rightful, as was intended. He apprehends that the expression 'lawful preference' might be construed as 'preference in accordance with law'. Mr O'Donoghue is satisfied that in the context the word 'lawful' would be construed as 'rightful'

[Matter omitted]

No. 306: NAI, DT S12172A

Memorandum from Michael Rynne to Maurice Moynihan

Department of External Affairs
6 December 1940

Dear Mr Moynihan,
I don't know that I have anything very useful to remark in regard to the three points on the amendment of the Constitution raised by the Taoiseach.[215] However, here are some observations:

1. Article 28.3.3°: As the present emergency code depends for its validity on the periodical extension by special statutes of the Emergency Powers Act, 1939, and as that Act is securely tied up in its long title to 'time of war', it would seem, at first glance, that all we have to do is to extend the sense of the expression 'time of war' in the Constitution so that a period of

[215] See document no. 305.

one year or less after any war will henceforth be comprised in the expression. On second thoughts, however, the difficulties of such an approach become apparent. First of all, there is going to be some difficulty in deciding from what date the extra year of emergency government is to run. That is a problem which we will have to overcome one day, whatever line we adopt about the Taoiseach's suggestion on Article 28.3.3°. Will an Anglo-German armistice terminate the present war? Or must it be an Anglo-German peace treaty? Or one of a number of other possible alternatives? The next and most real difficulty about extending the meaning of 'time of war' to cover a year of peace lies in the amended Constitution Article itself. Whatever 'time of war' may have meant when first used in the Constitution, it clearly, since the first amendment became law, connotes 'an armed conflict' 'taking place' somewhere. An endeavour now to extend the sense of 'time of war' to a time when no armed conflict would be taking place anywhere, would not only entail radical changes in the amended part of Article 28, but would, I think, look absurd on the face of it. I suggest therefore, that we should after all, adopt the less obvious method of letting 'time of war' stand as it is in Article 28, while supplementing it with a new set of contingencies one of which would cover a period of post war abnormality, and then, on the basis of such supplementary definition or expression, set about enacting a statute which would be in effect the Emergency Powers Act, 1939, with a differently worded long title to relate to the appropriate period or state of affairs for which the Act was being made. Alternatively, the only plan I can suggest is that of letting the Oireachtas keep on enacting Emergency Powers (Continuance) Acts on the ground that although the war is over, 'a national emergency exists affecting the vital interests of the State', '*arising out of* the armed conflict. Personally, I do not feel that these words of the Constitution would carry the Acts, because I do not imagine they were ever meant to do so except during actual wartime. It might, however, be worth putting the idea to Philip O'Donoghue for his view.

2. Article 24.3: I can see the 'policy' arguments for extending the ninety-day period to a period of, say, 120 days. I presume that Seán Malone will enlighten us on the technical or practical

arguments (pro and contra), if any. Therefore, there is nothing to be said except that, if it is decided to amend the Article the Parliamentary Draftsman's task will be extremely easy.

3. Article 27 (and, perhaps Article 26): The Taoiseach's idea of ascertaining the constitutionality of every proposal which is about to be submitted to the people's referendum, seems to me an excellent one. At present there is no guarantee that a law which has been deliberately and individually approved by the people—from whom all powers of Government legislative, etc., under God, derive—is not going to be thrown out of Court by a mere creature of the people's judicial power of government. Maybe, put like that, it sounds more serious than it really is. But, the change should and could, I suggest, be made so that the President, having taken all the preliminary steps necessary at present for a referendum would immediately refer the subject matter of the proposed referendum to the Supreme Court on the question of repugnancy to the Constitution. Philip O'Donoghue, with whom I spoke regarding this matter, seemed inclined to think (1) that the necessary amendment and consequential changes would not be easy to draft and (2) that, owing to the provision at Article 27.4.1°.ii, which makes a parliamentary dissolution a possible alternative to a referendum, the Supreme Court might sometimes be compelled to decide on the constitutionality of a proposal which in fact would never go to the people at all. My only reply to these objections, which Philip put up in an informal way on the phone and which he may since have dropped, is, (1) that even if the drafting of the amendment is going to be tricky, it is not impossible. There must be a point of time before every referendum when it is virtually certain that the referendum is so-to-speak physically possible and probable. At that point the Supreme Court should be consulted and it is up to the Parliamentary Draftsman to locate the point and insert the new proviso thereat. (2) As regards the extra trouble which might be occasioned to the Supreme Court, I must say I have not much sympathy for them. It will rarely happen that notice of a dissolution is so long delayed that all arrangements for the referendum, including the reference to the Supreme Court, have been put under way.

As a matter of policy, it might be a very good thing for the Supreme Court to give their decision even when a dissolution was practically arranged for by the Government. If the Supreme Court's decision was to the effect that the Bill at issue was repugnant to the Constitution, both the referendum and the dissolution might be avoided, thus saving the country expense and upset.

No. 307: NAI DT S12172A

Preliminary Draft of Second Amendment of the Constitution Bill, 1940

Parliamentary Draftsman's Office
10 December 1940

See www.irishconstitution.ie.
This draft was distributed to all Government departments for observations on 10 December 1940.

No. 308: NAI, DT S12172A

Memorandum: Observations by Departments on Preliminary Draft of the Second Amendment of the Constitution Bill, 1940[216]

Department of the Taoiseach
[20?] December 1940

Department of Justice:[217]
Ref. No. 25, Article 28.3.3°
Thinks the placing of the words 'at any time' in the phrase to be inserted is perhaps a little awkward.[218]

Ref. No. 33, Article 40
Habeas corpus procedure. Question of fixing date of execution after final rejection of application by person under sentence of death.[219]
Secretary to the President:[220]

[216] At the head of the document is the following annotation by Moynihan: 'The manuscript notes are the result of the consideration given to the various points by Mr P. O'Donoghue, Dr M. Rynne and Mr W. Fay during week ended 4 January 1941'.
[217] Submitted by Stephen Roche on 11 December, NAI, DT S12172A.
[218] Annotated: 'These words are needed to bring out the contrast with the legislation contemplated by the Article for time of war or armed rebellion. Their position will not affect the long title of any Act to be enacted'.
[219] Annotated: 'Has already been dealt with'.
[220] Submitted by Michael McDunphy on 12 December, NAI, DT S12172A.

Preamble, etc.
Use of words 'Amendment in Title of Bill, 'Several Amendments' in Preamble, 'Particulars of Amendments' in Schedule and 'Ref. No.' instead of Amendment No.' or 'Number' in Schedule.[221]

Ref. No. 2, Article 12
Suggests that the wording of Article 12.4.5° is inconsistent with Article 12.2.1° and that an amendment is necessary.[222]

Ref. No. 3, Article 12
No observations on amendment proposed. Suggests that wording of Article 12.3.1° and 3° indicates that the basic event from which action commences runs from actual occurrence of incapacity not from date of judicial determination of the fact. Amendment should be inserted to provide that the period for holding an election for President as a result of incapacity of a President should run from date of establishment of that fact by the Supreme Court, and not from date of the occurrence of the incapacity itself.[223]

Ref. No. 13, Article 22
Article 22.2.2° empowers the Seanad at a meeting with attendance of thirty to resolve by simple majority that a Money Bill should be presented to a Committee of Privileges to decide whether it is in fact a Money Bill. Article 15.10 would permit the Seanad subsequently to accept the Bill by a simple majority as a Money Bill and return it to the Dáil. On being presented with the Bill by the Taoiseach, the President could (under Article 25.3 as amended by Ref. No. 16) sign the Bill on the same day or await the completion of operations under Article 22, set in train by first resolution of [the] Seanad.

To obviate this dilemma he suggests a provision that a resolution by the Seanad (Article 22.2.2°) should automatically suspend operation of the Article by the Ceann Comhairle under Article 22.2.1° and preclude any further action towards enactment of the Bill pending receipt of message from the President as to the result.[224]

[221] Annotated: 'Appears to be wholly a matter of drafting which might be left to P.D. No change is recommended'.
[222] Annotated: 'No inconsistency in reality'.
[223] Annotated: 'Interpretation suggested would not be correct. Incapacity can only date from its establishment. No amendment is necessary: "such event" refers to the establishment of the incapacity, and to no earlier date'.
[224] Annotated: 'Seanad may rescind resolution under 22.2.2° up to date on which President refers question under 22.2.3° to Committee of Privileges. Once this is done the matter is out of the hands of the Seanad and the matter becomes a question of law as to whether Bill is or is not a Money Bill. Dilemma therefore does not arise as President must wait for decision of Committee'.

Ref. No. 16, Article 25
Observations on Ref. No. 13 (Article 22) have some bearing on this amendment.[225]

Ref. No. 17, Article 25.4.5°
Objection on grounds of euphony to use of simple past followed by perfect present.[226]

Ref. No. 19, Article 26
Amendment should go further. Period of four days for the President to decide whether he should send the Bill to Supreme Court in certain circumstances is too short (intervention of weekend, Bank Holidays, difficulty of contact with Council of State, etc.) Since a maximum of seven days is allowed to President to sign any Bill to which the Article applies, the same period instead of four days should be allowed to him for completion of action referred to. A maximum period of six days is allowed to the President for similar action under Article 27.

Refers also to ambiguity of words in Article 26.1.2° 'not later than…days after' and to amend under Ref. No. 15 in respect of Article 25.2.1°.[227]

Ref. No. 21, Article 26
Suggests that in Section 3.2° the words 'that Article shall be complied with' should read 'the provisions of that Article shall', etc.[228]

Ref. No. 22, Article 27
Questions whether amendment is wide enough. Ceann Comhairle should certify (a) that every signatory has qualification as a member of either House, (b) genuineness of each signature and (c) adequacy of number of signatures from each House, so that petition may be accepted without question as being fully valid.[229]

Ref. No. 23, Article 27
Suggests division into two Subsections:

1. Bill declared by Supreme Court not to be repugnant to the Constitution.
2. Bill in respect of which contrary decision is given.[230]

[225] Annotated: 'See previous note'.
[226] Annotated: 'No observations subject to views of P.D.'.
[227] Annotated: 'On reconsideration we feel inclined to suggest that period for reference under Article 26 should be the same as the maximum period allowed to President for signing a Bill under Article 25, viz., seven days. If adopted we also suggest that it should be 'the seventh' day to conform with Article 25 as amended'.
[228] Annotated: 'We do not consider any change necessary'.
[229] Annotated: 'Present amendment fully covers these points'.
[230] Annotated: 'No change thought necessary: a drafting point purely'.

Ref. No. 30, Article 34
Wording of amendment should be brought into line with Article 26.2.2° supplemented, if necessary, by Ref. No. 20 amendment.[231]

Article 14
Suggests amendment to cover defects in personnel provisions of Article 14 unless it can be dealt with under powers given by Article 14.4 to Council of State.[232]

Department of Local Government and Public Health:[233]
Article 27
No provision made for re-numbering Section 4 (Also Section 5?).[234]

Department of Defence:[235]
Articles 28.3.3° and 40.4.3° should be combined. A question of the amendment of Article 40.4.3° arises on consideration of the question of the powers of the military in time of war.[236]

Gaeltacht Services:[237]
Ref. No. 1, Article 11
Suggests 'stát-cíos' instead of 'cíos' in view of use of latter word in Article 17.2.

Article 20
Use of the word 'breathnú' (consider) in Article 20.2. This word is not used in this sense in Article 20.1. If it is to be used it is suggested that 'by Seanad Éireann' should be inserted after 'considered'; and 'would' after 'as'.

In the English text the words 'shall be considered as' appears to mean 'shall thereupon be deemed to be' and accordingly in the Irish text the words should be 'ní folair a mheas uiome sin gur Bille é a tionnscnadh I nDáil Éireann'.

In this connection Article 23.2.1° should be examined also.[238]

Ref. No. 17, Article 25
Suggests insertion of the following saving clause in the new 4.3° as follows: 'provided that in the case of Bills expressed to be Bills to amend the

[231] Annotated: 'The context is different in each case and the wording is accordingly different. In cases coming within ordinary jurisdiction of Supreme Court under Article 34 the judgment is always the judgment of the majority; express provision only appropriate for special kind of jurisdiction conferred by Article 26'.
[232] Annotated: 'Suggested amendment not necessary. General question of providing for emergencies is fully covered by Article 14.4'.
[233] Submitted on 14 December, NAI, DT S12172A.
[234] Annotated: 'Needs attention. Being met'.
[235] Submitted in December, date unspecified, NAI, DT S12172A.
[236] Annotated: 'Not practicable at this stage. Powers are adequate'. Also annotated by Moynihan: 'Memorandum [from Department of Defence] promised'.
[237] Submitted on 13 December, NAI, DT S12172A.
[238] Annotated: 'Requires consideration'.

Constitution such bills must in all cases be passed or deemed to have been passed in both official languages' in view of provision of the last sentence in Article 63. An error which the above amendment is intended to obviate has already occurred in connection with the First Amendment Act.[239]

Article 28
'Éigeandáil' instead of 'práinn' for 'emergency'.[240]

Clerk of the Dáil:[241]
Preamble

1. Reference to Article 46 is unnecessary, as Article 51 is sufficiently inclusive.
2. Insert 'except the provisions of Article 46 and that Article' between 'Constitution' and 'may' in second paragraph of preamble.[242]

Ref. No. 14, Article 24.2
Insert at end of new Section 2 the words 'or on the date (if it is later) on which Dáil Éireann shall, in the case of a Bill which is not a Money Bill, disagree to the amendments (if any) made by Seanad Éireann or, in the case of a Money Bill, reject the recommendations (if any) made by Seanad Éireann'. Insert at end of Article 21.2.2° words of similar import. These are to cover the event of the Seanad submitting amendments, etc., too late to allow the Dáil to consider them before the provisions of the Article, whereby the Bill deemed to be passed by both Houses, can operate.[243]

Ref. No. 17, Article 25
'The President shall sign…each of the official languages' is ambiguous. It may mean the President shall sign his name in both languages.[244]

Ref. Nos 17 and 18
'National language' should be in conformity with Articles 8 and 61 read 'Irish language'.[245]

Ref. No. 22
Alterations in numbering should read '2, 3, 4 & 5' to '3, 4, 5 & 6'.[246]

239 Annotated: 'Not recommended: we consider the suggestion to be a matter of policy'.
240 Annotated with a 'yes' mark.
241 Submitted by Gearóid Mag Canainn on 17 December, NAI, DT S12172A.
242 Annotated: '1. Omission not recommended. 2. "Subject as therein after provided" is enough'.
243 Annotated: 'Drafting point which it is considered is sufficiently met'.
244 Annotated: 'Not considered necessary. The P. is required to sign the *text* as distinct from his *name*'.
245 Annotated: 'The National language is already defined in Article 8 to mean Irish language'.
246 Annotated: 'Accepted'.

Ref. No. 31, Article 34.4
New Section implies that the Supreme Court decision on appeal from High Court shall be a majority one. This is explicitly stated in Article 26.2.2°. Is it necessary to re-state it here?[247]

Department of Finance:[248]
Preamble
Second paragraph does not mention the two Articles which are exempted from amendment by Article 51.[249]

Ref. No. 1, Article 11 (Irish text)
'Cíos' as meaning 'revenue'. 'Cios' has come to mean rent derived from property. 'Saor-cíos' [means] Quit rents paid by State. 'Stát-cíos' would indicate rents out of State property. Amendment requires further consideration. Irish word should not exclude non-tax revenue whereas it is doubtful if 'cíos' covers anything obtained otherwise than by levy or impost. See also Article 17.2.

Ref. No. 5, Article 13.6
Insert 'an' before 'comhacht' and carry out consequential amendments.

Ref. No. 10, Article 15.15 (Irish text)
Alter 'go ndeonfaidhe' to 'go ndeanfar' which after present tense in principal clause 'Tig leis an Oireachtas, etc.' seems more appropriate.

Ref. No. 3, Article 12
Intention of Article 12.3.3° is presumably to ensure that another election may be held in the event of the President Elect ceasing for one reason or another to be capable of holding office. The Constitution does not refer to the President Elect and if he dies a further election should take place. But election for President can only take place (1) on sixtieth day before date of expiration of term of office of a President or (2) within sixty days of a President ceasing to hold office by reason of removal, death, resignation, or permanent incapacity. In case mentioned neither of these conditions would be satisfied.

Amendment would therefore require further clarification. This could be done if, instead of the scheduled amendment, an additional Subsection to Article 12.3 were inserted, e.g. '3.4°: In the event of the death, resignation or permanent incapacity established as aforesaid, of a President Elect before he enters upon his office, an election for the office

[247] Annotated: 'See observation on Ref. No. 30 (Secretary of the President)'.
[248] Submitted on 18 December, NAI, DT S12172A.
[249] Annotated: 'See observation to preamble by Clerk of Dáil'.

of President may be held within sixty days of the death…of such President elect'.[250]

Ref. No. 14, Article 24.2

Words in brackets in new Subsection 2 (b) are superfluous. The omission of the words might allow of a simplification of paragraph (b).[251] Neither existing Article 24.2 nor proposed amendment make it clear whether, in the event of the Dáil disagreeing with or not accepting some only of the amendments made by the Seanad, the Bill as originally sent to Seanad Éireann will be deemed to have been passed, or whether any amendments or recommendations made by the Seanad and accepted by Dáil Éireann can be embodied in the Bill.

The point may be covered by Article 21.2.1° in the case of Money Bills but difficulty seems to arise under Article 23 in respect of other Bills.[252]

Ref. No. 17, Article 25.4

1. New Section presupposes that 'every Bill' will be signed by the President and promulgated. But under Article 23.3.1° he may decline to sign a Bill.[253]
2. New Subsection 4.3°. What is the position of a Bill in which both English and Irish are used, e.g. the present Bill.[254]
3. Insert 'so' before 'passed' where it last occurs in Subsection 3° in order to convey the meaning apparently intended in latter part of Subsection.
4. Reconsider wording of Subsections 3° and 4° to avoid likelihood of 'deeming' being taken as relating to the language and not merely to the passing.
5. In Subsection 4° (?3°) insert 'by both Houses of the Oireachtas' after 'passed' where latter occurs secondly.[255]

Ref. No. 18, Article 25

1. Can proposed new Section be added in this Article which deals exclusively with the 'signing and promulgation of *laws*' and is so headed.[256]

[250] Annotated: 'Interpretation at (1) is incorrect. Although the amendment does not mention the President elect, we think it is sufficiently clear to cover the contingency envisaged'.
[251] Annotated: 'Agreed'.
[252] Annotated: 'It is reasonably clear in existing Article as amended'.
[253] Annotated: 'This has been changed'.
[254] Annotated: 'There is an English and an Irish text. The fact that Irish appears in one and English in the other is quite immaterial'.
[255] Annotated: 'This is changed and doesn't arise'.
[256] Annotated: 'Promulgation includes publication and constitutional amendments are laws. Title is therefore sufficient'.

2. Subsection 5.1°. The use of 'under his supervision' may cause administrative difficulty and does not appear to be necessary.[257]
3. Conflict between this Article and Article 52. Article 52 and subsequent ones must be included in text to be prepared at the instance of the Taoiseach under the new Section while under Article 52 such text must not be included.[258]

Ref. No. 19, Article 26
Omit 'by the Taoiseach' since in his absence the Tánaiste might do the presentation.[259]

Ref. No. 36, Article 56.5.1°
Amendment will not remove existing objections. Suggested that the Subsection should be amended by insertion between 'terms' and 'of any person' the words 'and conditions of service, or the tenure of office or the remuneration' in lieu of the words in the original.[260]

Ref. No. 37, Article 56.5.2°
Draft amendment seems open to the construction of confirming the unchangeable position of the rights which it is proposed to take power to modify at any time. Following alternative is suggested:

> Nothing in this Article shall operate to invalidate or restrict any legislation ~~enacted or to be enacted hereafter~~ notwithstanding that ~~any~~ such legislation may be in conflict with the provisions of any former Constitution or statute applying to all or any of the matters contained in the next preceding Subsection.[261]

No. 309: NAI, DT S12172A

Seán MacBride to Eamon de Valera

Clonskeagh, Dublin
8 January 1941

Dear Chief,
I know that a time such as this is not a good one to choose to raise abstract questions of Constitutional Law. However, the recent

[257] Annotated: 'No observations. Administrative difficulty is not appreciated'.
[258] Annotated: 'All articles will be enrolled but those directed to be omitted will be omitted from future published texts'.
[259] Annotated: 'See Article 28.6.2° and 3°'.
[260] Annotated: 'Suggest that amendment should follow the Irish text literally'.
[261] Annotated: 'Accept with the change in ink' [illustrated by line through relevant words].

announcement that it was proposed to amend the Constitution has prompted me to draw your attention to some matters arising out of Article 28, which, if not corrected, might at some future date give rise to grave difficulties. I enclose herewith a Memorandum giving an outline of my submissions in this connection.

I raised most of these matters in the Supreme Court in the McGrath and Harte case. But the Supreme Court refrained, and I think rightly so, from expressing any views about most of the points raised in the memorandum, as they had not actually arisen in that case.

Another matter I had intended to draw your attention to at the time of the McGrath and Harte case in the Supreme Court was the position in regard to Statutory Rules and Orders. In this case the Supreme Court in its Judgment expressed the view that the Oireachtas might well consider the advisability of enacting legislation to deal with the publication and promulgation of Statutory Rules and Orders to replace the Rules Publication Act of 1893. This portion of the Judgment was, I think, not published in the newspapers and may have, accordingly, escaped your notice.

I hope that your recent operation has proved quite successful and that you have quite recovered from its effects.[262]

Memorandum concerning Article 28 of the Constitution and the First Amendment of the Constitution in relation to the other provisions of the Constitution:

This memorandum is intended to deal with a certain ambiguity which is contained in [Article 28.3.3°] of the Constitution as amended, and with certain conflicts between this Article as amended and other Articles of the Constitution. It is respectfully submitted that this Article in its present form might, in certain contingencies, give rise to very grave difficulties of legal interpretation. Inasmuch as a Constitution is a fundamental law intended to provide for all emergencies any ambiguity should, as far as possible, be removed and the possible remoteness of some of the contingencies envisaged in this memorandum should not be allowed to reduce the necessity of making the Constitution a fundamental law applicable to all emergencies.

For the purposes of this memorandum it is convenient to consider Article 28.3.3° in the first instance in its original form before it was amended, and in the second instance to consider it in relation to the first amendment to the Constitution.

[262] Annotated by Moynihan: 'This letter was received under cover of a personal note to Miss O'Connell, who is acknowledging'.

Article 28.3.3° in its original form reads as follows:

> Nothing in this Constitution shall be invoked to invalidate any law enacted by the Oireachtas which is expressed to be for the purpose of securing the public safety and the preservation of the State in time of war or armed rebellion, or to nullify any act done or purporting to be done in pursuance of any such law.

The first and gravest difficulty of interpretation arises on the interpretation of the first four words in this Section: 'Nothing in this Constitution'. What exactly is excluded by these four words? Do the four words apply to some or all of the Constitutional guarantees given to citizens by the Constitution only, or do they include as well the institutions set up by the Constitution? If they include the institutions set up by the Constitution, do they include them all or only some of them?

A strict interpretation of the words 'Nothing in this Constitution…' would bring within the ambit of this Section not only abstract declarations of rights contained in the Constitution, but also the institutions set up by the Constitution. From such a strict construction stupendous results would follow, for the institutions set up by the Constitution include not only the Courts of Justice, but the Council of State, the President, the Senate, the Dáil, the Government, the Attorney General and the Auditor General. In addition, of course, on such a strict interpretation, the right of suffrage provided for by Article 16 and the Referendum would be included.

While the question of the interpretation of these words has not been decided upon by our Courts, I believe that judicial support would be found for the view that these words include the very institutions set up by the Constitution. Certainly the word 'nothing' when parsed into 'no thing' supports such a construction.

Assuming such a construction to be a correct one it becomes necessary to consider the results which flow from it. In so doing it should be remembered that the Section is not limited to laws passed by the Oireachtas, for it also includes acts done or purporting to be done in pursuance of any such law. In this connection, therefore, this Section reads as follows:

> Nothing in this Constitution shall be invoked…to nullify any act done or purporting to be done in pursuance of any such law.

Assuming a strict construction to be the correct one it then becomes impossible for the Government (I take the Government merely as an instance as it is one of the institutions set up by the Constitution) to nullify any act done by one of its servants, or indeed, by anyone, provided that the person doing the act says he purports to have done it in pursuance of an Emergency Law coming within the definition of the Section. For instance, if a police officer or a military officer chose to arrest a member of the Government under the powers invested in him by virtue of the Emergency Powers Act, the Government, the Courts, and all the other institutions set up by the Constitution would be powerless to nullify his act. This may be a very far-fetched example, but it is only one of countless others which, in other times and circumstances might not be so far-fetched.

Apart from the absurd consequences referred to, graver and more probable difficulties arise if the strict construction of that Section be the correct one. The following are but a few instances of such difficulties:

(a) The jurisdiction of the Courts is ousted in any matter arising out of legislation coming within the scope of Article 28.3.3°. It should be borne in mind that nowadays emergency legislation and Orders are not confined to matters affecting the liberty of the citizens and that the Courts have to deal with numerous cases arising from Emergency Orders.
(b) The Council of State could be abolished.
(c) The powers of the President could be usurped.
(d) The Senate could be abolished.
(e) The Constitution could be amended, or even abrogated, by ordinary legislation.
(f) There would be no machinery to remedy any unconstitutional act.

If, on the other hand, the strict interpretation of the words 'nothing in this Constitution…' is not the correct one and if these words do not bring within their scope the institutions set up by the Constitution, but are intended to apply only to the constitutional guarantees contained in the Constitution an anomalous position still results, for there is nothing to indicate whether they apply to all the constitutional rights and guarantees contained in the Constitution or only to some of them.

A cursory consideration of the constitutional guarantees and declarations contained in the Constitution will show clearly that an impossible position would result if these were to cease to exist whenever the situation provided for by Article 28 was in existence.

Every Article of the Constitution contains a constitutional declaration and an equivalent right to have that declaration observed.

For instance Article 16 provides that every citizen without distinction of sex who has reached the age of 21 shall be eligible for membership of Dáil Éireann and shall have the right to vote at election, and that the system of proportional representation shall be the method used at election. These provisions create constitutional rights, to which, I am sure, the provisions of Article 28 were never intended to apply. Yet if by means of a snap division, or otherwise, a Bill was passed through the Oireachtas limiting suffrage to men of over seventy years of age and doing away with proportional representation, there would be no way of having that Bill declared unconstitutional provided it came within the ambit of Article 28.

It is apprehended that the provisions of Article 28 were intended to apply principally to the constitutional guarantees contained in Article 40. However, as there is nothing in Article 28 to limit the application of this Article it applies to the whole Constitution. Reading through the Constitution it will be found that practically every Article of it grants a constitutional right to the citizen or to the State or to some of the institutions created by the Constitution.

If all the constitutional rights contained in the Constitution come within the ambit of the words 'nothing in this Constitution…' then it is open to any person '*purporting*' to act in pursuance of a law coming within the provisions of Article 28 to do violence to any of the Articles in the Constitution with absolute impunity. Likewise, it would be open to the Oireachtas to legislate with complete disregard for any Article in the Constitution provided the legislation came within the wide scope of Article 28.

It is now necessary to consider the First Amendment to the Constitution. It has two characteristics: firstly, it extends the meaning of the words 'time of war' to include a time when there is no actual conflict in Ireland; secondly, it limits the application of this extended definition of 'time of war' to Article 28.3.3°.

Apart from the difficulties hereinbefore referred to, Article 28.3.3° before it was amended did not directly conflict with any of the other provisions of the Constitution. The Amendment, however, does set up a direct conflict between Article 28.3.3° as amended and the other provisions of the Constitution which deal with a state of war or armed rebellion to which the extended definition of time of war does not apply.

For instance, Clauses 4 and 5 of Article 38 specifically preclude military tribunals from trying civilians except to deal with a state of war of armed rebellion. The provisions of Clause 5 of Article 38 amount to a constitutional prohibition. Before the enactment of the First Amendment to the Constitution there would probably have been no conflict between Article 28 and Article 38 as the 'time of war' provided for by Article 28 would have coincided with the 'state of war' provided for by Article 38. Since the passing of the Amendment, however, the position is that a time of war within the meaning of Article 28 exists while a state of war within the meaning of Article 38 does not exist.

Accordingly, the resultant position is that despite the fact that Article 38 prohibits the trial of civilians by military tribunals except to deal with a state of war or armed rebellion (i.e. martial law) Article 28 as amended enables civilians to be tried by military tribunals. The provisions of Article 38 therefore become meaningless.

This memorandum is merely intended to draw attention to the ambiguities and conflicts referred to and I have not attempted to suggest the remedies therefore. The question of remedying the difficulties referred to would depend largely on the interpretation it is wished to give to the words 'nothing in this Constitution…'

In a recent case in the Supreme Court I attempted three alternative constructions of these words. The Supreme Court, probably quite wisely, did not accept any of these alternative constructions. I give them hereunder, however, as they may be of assistance in analysing the difficulties which arise on the construction of Article 28 as amended. But it should be remembered that they were only put forward in an attempt to reconcile, by means of judicial interpretation, conflicting Articles of the Constitution.

Suggested alternative constructions of the words 'Nothing in this Constitution…'

1. The words 'nothing in this Constitution…' refer to those declaratory statements of right, (a) of a non-specific nature, (b) which are contained in the Constitution and (c) which had no independent existence prior to the enactment of, or apart from the Constitution, or (d) which are not expressly, or impliedly, maintained under all emergencies short of actual war or armed rebellion.
2. The words 'nothing in this Constitution…' refer to those declaratory statements of right, (a) which are contained in the Constitution, and (b) which are not expressly, or impliedly, maintained under all emergencies, short of actual war or armed rebellion.
3. The words 'nothing in this Constitution…' refer to all the rights and institutions created by the Constitution (a) whether

> or not they had an independent existence prior to or apart from the Constitution and (b) whether or not they are maintained expressly, or impliedly, by other provisions of the Constitution at all times short of actual war or armed rebellion.

Constructions No. 1 and No. 3 represent the opposite extremes. A large number of intermediate constructions could be found.

No. 310: NAI, DT S12172A

Memorandum from Maurice Moynihan to Kevin Haugh

Department of the Taoiseach
9 January 1941

I am directed by the Taoiseach to refer to the draft Second Amendment of the Constitution Bill, 1940, and to state that, following examination of the draft by Departments generally and by the Committee set up to examine proposals for the amendment of the Constitution, it is proposed that the draft should be amended in the following respects:

Ref. No. 5, Article 13:
The proposed amendment is not now regarded as essential and should be deleted.

Ref. No. 11, Article 18:
Section 3 of Article 18, if amended as proposed, would appear to imply that the power of the Taoiseach to nominate members of the Seanad is confined to the making of the nominations immediately occasioned by a dissolution of Dáil Éireann. If this interpretation is correct, a further amendment is necessary in order to preserve the Taoiseach's right to nominate persons to fill casual vacancies among the nominated members.[263]

Article 20.2.2°:
The following additional amendment to the Irish text should be inserted:

> The deletion of the words 'é bhreathnú mar bhreathnóchaí Bille a tionnscnóchaí I nDáil Éireann' and the insertion, in their place, of the words 'a mheas é bheith 'na Bhille a tionnscnadh I nDáil Éireann'.[264]

[263] Annotated by Moynihan: 'In raising this point I overlooked Art. 18.10.2°. 20 January 1941'.
[264] Annotated: 'Amendment to be inserted at Ref. No. 12'.

Ref. No. 14, Article 24:
It is considered that the words and brackets '(with or without amendments)' in paragraph (a) and the words and brackets '(with or without recommendations)' in paragraph (b) of the proposed new Section 2 are superfluous and should be deleted.

Ref. No. 18, Article 25:
In Subsection 2° of the proposed new Section 5, it is for consideration whether the words 'and countersigned' should be inserted immediately after the word 'signed' where that word secondly occurs. This point also affects Subsection 3°.

Ref. No. 19, Article 26:
A further amendment should be made in Article 26.1.2° deleting the words 'four days' and inserting in their place the words 'the seventh day'.

Ref. No. 20, Article 26:
The amendment should be strengthened so as to make it clear that if there is a dissenting opinion among the judges of the Supreme Court as to whether a Bill is repugnant to the Constitution, the existence of such a dissenting opinion shall not be disclosed. It is understood that a revised draft has been prepared by the Parliamentary Draftsman in the following terms:

> The decision of the majority of the Judges of the Supreme Court shall, for the purposes of this Article, be the decision of the Court and shall be pronounced by such one of those Judges as the Court shall direct, and no other opinion (whether assenting or dissenting) shall be pronounced nor shall the existence of any such other opinion be disclosed.

Ref. No. 22, Article 27:
The comma immediately following the word 'petitioners' in the existing Article 27.2 should be deleted, as well as the words 'shall be in writing signed by the petitioners'. The numbers of Sections 4 and 5 of the Article should be altered to 5 and 6 respectively.

Ref. No. 23, Article 27:
It appears necessary to insert in the amendment, immediately after the words 'repugnant to the Constitution', the words 'or to any provision thereof'. (Cf. Article 26.1.1°).

The words 'six days' should be substituted for 'ten days'.

Ref. No. 27, Article 28:
The Taoiseach is inclined to the opinion that a limit of, say, two years should be set to the time, after the termination of the armed conflict, during which the national emergency occasioned thereby may be deemed to be still in existence. He has not, however, come to a definite decision on this point and he would be glad to have your observations. It is appreciated that the date of termination of the armed conflict may be difficult to determine precisely and, further, that the national emergency caused by the conflict may continue for several years and, conceivably, be as grave after the lapse of two or three years from the end of the war as at any previous time. On the other hand, the Taoiseach sees strong objections to the possibility of the continuance for an indefinite period, after the war, of the extraordinary powers given by Article 28.3.3°.[265]

Ref. No. 30, Article 34:
It is understood that a revised draft of the new Section 3.2° has been prepared as follows:

> Save as otherwise provided by this Article, the jurisdiction of the High Court shall extend to the question of the validity of any law having regard to the provisions of this Constitution, and no such question shall be raised (whether by pleading, argument or otherwise) in any Court established under this or any other Article of this Constitution other than the High Court and the Supreme Court.

The Taoiseach desires that the draft Bill should be amended accordingly.

Ref. No. 31, Article 34:
It is understood that the proposed new Subsection 5° of Article 34.4 has been revised so as to read as follows:

> The decision of the Supreme Court on a question as to the validity of a law having regard to the provisions of this Constitution shall be pronounced by such one of the judges of that Court as that Court shall direct, and no other opinion on such question (whether assenting or dissenting) shall be pronounced nor shall the existence of any such other opinion be disclosed.

I am to request that the draft Bill be amended accordingly.

[265] Annotated: 'No amendment made as a result of clarification. No observations submitted'.

Ref. No. 33, Article 40:
The Taoiseach desires that, in the proposed new Subsection 3° of Article 40.4, the word 'may' where it occurs immediately before the words 'refer the question' should be deleted and the word 'shall' inserted in its place. As the Subsection stands, it would apparently be open to the High Court, in a *habeas corpus* case, to pronounce a law invalid and at the same time to refrain from referring the question of the validity of the law to the Supreme Court. The position thus created would be most unsatisfactory from the point of view of the State, which would have no right of appeal to the Supreme Court.

Ref. No. 36, Article 56:
The Department of Finance have suggested, in effect, that, in lieu of the proposed amendment, Article 56.5 should be amended by the deletion of the words 'terms, conditions, remuneration or tenure' and the insertion in their place of the words 'terms and conditions of service, or the tenure of office or the remuneration'. The Taoiseach agrees with this suggestion.

Ref. No. 37:
Having regard to the observations of the Department of Finance, I am to request that the following draft should be inserted in lieu of this amendment:

> Nothing in this Article shall operate to invalidate or restrict any legislation notwithstanding that such legislation may be in conflict with the provisions of any former Constitution or statute applying to all or any of the matters contained in the next preceding Subsection.

The draft Bill is returned herewith for amendment by the Parliamentary Draftsman.[266]

No. 311: NAI, DT S12172A

Memorandum from General Peadar MacMahon to Maurice Moynihan

Department of Defence
10 January 1941

I am directed by the Minister for Defence to refer to this Department's minute of 14th ultimo relative to the preliminary draft of the Second

[266] A further draft of the Bill was submitted by the Parliamentary Draftsman on 16 January. It carried the following annotation by Moynihan: 'Prepared following examination of first draft by Departments and this Department's letter of 9 January to Attorney General'.

Amendment of the Constitution Bill, 1940, and to state that, as indicated therein, the question of the Amendment of Article 40.4.3° of the Constitution arises in connection with the introduction, in time of war, of what is known in other countries as martial law.[267] It was proposed to deal with the amendment of the Constitution in a general memorandum which it is intended to submit to the Government on the subject of martial law, but as it is understood from Mr Kennedy of your Department that the proposed amendment is required for urgent consideration by the Committee dealing with the Bill, particulars are now forwarded herewith.

At a conference held in the Attorney General's Office on the 6th ultimo, representatives of this Department pointed out that apart from the proposed Military Courts (No. 2) Order and the instructions issued to Regional and County Commissioners to subordinate themselves to the military authorities in certain circumstances, the military would not appear to have any of the powers conferred on the armed forces of other countries by martial law, e.g. the imposition of curfew, prohibition on civilian transport, etc.

The Attorney General pointed out that the Constitution does not permit the introduction of martial law but expressed the opinion that, in the event of hostilities, the military should assume whatever powers the situation rendered necessary, relying for protection on an Indemnity Act at the close of hostilities.

The Minister considers, however, that it would be much more desirable that the constitutional position should be adjusted beforehand in order that the powers of the Defence Forces may be quite clear and that military officers should not, during hostilities, be influenced by the fear of possible consequences in taking any action necessary to meet situations which might then arise.

Article 40.4.3° of the Constitution suspends personal liberty in so far as acts of the Defence Forces are concerned during the existence of a state of war or armed rebellion. The Minister considers that, in regard to property, and other rights as well as to personal liberty, the Constitution should uphold the principle that in war *salus populi suprema lex*.

He suggests, therefore, that Article 40.3.3° should be amended by substituting the word 'Constitution' for 'section' and deleting the word 'however'; that Articles 28.3.3° (as amended by the First Amendment of the Constitution Act, 1939, and proposed to be amended by the Second Amendment of the Constitution Bill), 37 and 40.4.3° should be

[267] For details of the Department of Defence's proposals, see reference to the Department of Defence in document no. 308.

combined in the one Article, and that such Article, embodying all the exceptions or suspensions, should appear either at the beginning or at the end of the Constitution.[268]

No. 312: NAI, DT S12172A

Memorandum by Maurice Moynihan 'Second Amendment to the Constitution Bill'

Department of the Taoiseach
15 January 1941

Mr Seán Malone, Clerk of the Seanad, suggests the deletion of Amendments 4, 8, 9, 11, 13 and 16 on the ground that they are not necessary and that it is difficult to justify them by reference to the words in the preamble to the Bill, '*experience* has shown that certain amendments of the Constitution are desirable'.

Mr Codling, Department of Finance, does not wish to press Amendments 13 and 16, if the Government are inclined to delete them with a view to reducing the number of amendments to a minimum.

No. 313: NAI, DT S12172A

Memorandum from Maurice Moynihan to General Peadar MacMahon

Department of the Taoiseach
15 January 1941

I am directed by the Taoiseach to refer to your minute of the 10th instant relative to the Second Amendment of the Constitution Bill and to state that the suggestions contained therein have been examined by the Committee set up for the purpose of considering proposals for the amendment of the Constitution. Following consideration by him of the Committee's views, the Taoiseach has instructed me to convey the following reply.

I am to point out that under Article 28.3.3° of the Constitution, the Government, in case of actual invasion, are empowered to take whatever

[268] Annotated by Moynihan: 'Discussed by Committee on Amendment of the Constitution on 11 January 1941. Decided that draft reply, on lines agreed upon by Committee, should be prepared for submission to the Taoiseach. 13 January 1941'. A draft reply was prepared and submitted to de Valera, who suggested amendments. See document no. 313 for reply as sent to MacMahon.

steps they may consider necessary for the protection of the State. The Taoiseach is advised that this provision would enable the Government, in the event of invasion, not only to confer on the Defence Forces whatever additional specific powers may be necessary to deal with the situation, including such powers as the imposition of curfew and prohibition on civilian transport, which are expressly referred to in your minute, but to give general authority to the Defence Forces to take such steps and exercise such powers as might be necessary for the protection of the State.

Further, Article 28.3.3° of the Constitution and the legislation enacted thereunder enable the Government by Order to make provision for securing the public safety or the preservation of the State in time of war or armed rebellion, and both the legislation and action taken in accordance therewith are protected against the possibility of being invalidated or nullified by reference to the Constitution. Extensive powers have already been conferred on the Defence Forces by means of Emergency Power Orders, and any additional powers that might be required in the event of hostilities can also be conferred by Orders in accordance with the Emergency Powers Acts. It is open to your Department to consider what additional powers are required, with due regard being had to the existing relevant provisions contained in the Emergency Powers Order, 1939, and subsequent Orders, and to seek the authority of the Government for the drafting of further Orders, if necessary. Such further Orders could either be drafted and held in readiness to be made should the necessity arise or, alternatively, made in advance with a provision whereby they would come into operation on a date to be determined by means of some subsequent specific action, e.g. the issue of directions by the Taoiseach.

Having regard to the foregoing considerations, the Taoiseach is of opinion that no amendment of the Constitution is necessary in order to enable such additional powers as may be required to be conferred on the Defence Forces. He would be glad to be informed, at an early date, whether the Minister for Defence now agrees with this view.[269]

[269] See document no. 311. A reply was received from the Department of Defence on 20 January stating that the Minister for Defence agreed with the Taoiseach's view, and that the Department would submit to the Government suggested powers for the Department of Defence in the event of invasion, NAI, DT S12172A.

No. 314: NAI, DT S12172A

Memorandum from Maurice Moynihan to Kevin Haugh

Department of the Taoiseach
15 January 1941

Attorney General,
I am directed by the Taoiseach to refer to Article 28.3.3° of the Constitution and to state that a question has been raised as to the construction of the opening words of that provision, viz., 'Nothing in this Constitution'. Possible alternative constructions of these words have been suggested as follows:

1. The words 'nothing in this Constitution…' refer to those declaratory statements of right, (a) of a non-specific nature, (b) which are contained in the Constitution, and (c) which had no independent existence prior to the enactment of, or apart from the Constitution, or (d) which are not expressly, or impliedly, maintained under all emergencies short of actual war or armed rebellion.
2. The words 'nothing in this Constitution…' refer to those declaratory statements of right, (a) which are contained in the Constitution, and (b) which are not expressly, or impliedly, maintained under all emergencies, short of actual war or armed rebellion.
3. The words 'nothing in this Constitution…' refer to all the rights and institutions created by the Constitution (a) whether or not they had an independent existence prior to or apart from the Constitution and (b) whether or not they are maintained expressly, or impliedly, by other provisions of the Constitution at all times short of actual war or armed rebellion.[270]

It has been suggested that constructions No. 1 and No. 3 represent the opposite extremes and that a large number of intermediate constructions could be found.

The Taoiseach would be glad if you would be so good as to furnish your opinion on this matter having regard to any views that may have been expressed by the Courts in cases in which the construction of article

[270] Taken from the memorandum submitted by Seán MacBride on 8 January 1941. See document no. 309.

28.3.3° arose for consideration. He regards the point as being one of the greatest importance on which the Government should be in a position to feel reasonably secure as to the view which would be taken by the Supreme Court.

As a particular case to which the construction of Article 28.3.3° might be relevant the Taoiseach has in mind the possibility that if the emergency were to continue for a long period it might be considered necessary to extend the life of the Dáil beyond the period of seven years referred to in Article 16.5 of the Constitution. He assumes that by means of ordinary legislation the life of the Dáil could at any time be extended to a maximum period of seven years. He would be glad, however, to have your advice as to whether by legislation under Article 28.3.3° of the Constitution or by Order under the existing Emergency Powers Acts it would be possible to extend the period of seven years.[271]

No. 315: NAI, DT S12172A

Memorandum from Philip O'Donoghue to Kevin Haugh

Office of the Attorney General
16 January 1941

Attorney General,

1. The only case in which Article 28.3.3° has come before the Supreme Court is that of the *habeas corpus* application of McGrath and Harte, the report of which has not yet appeared in the Irish Reports but in which the certified judgment is available. In the judgment of the court, delivered by the Chief Justice, the following extract is the only relevant observation on the point raised by Mr Moynihan in his inquiry of the 15th instant:[272]

    We are, therefore, of the opinion that the Acts come within the protection of the Article as amended, and on the construction of the Article itself none of the suggested alternative constructions proposed by Counsel can have any foundation in view of the clear language of the Article, which, in the times and circumstances contemplated, makes it impossible to invoke other Articles of the

[271] See document no. 315.
[272] See document no. 314.

Constitution to invalidate Acts passed by the Oireachtas and expressed to be for the purpose of securing the public safety and the preservation of the State within the terms of the Article.

2. In my opinion, the true construction of the 28th Article is to be found in the literal and plain meaning of the words contained in it. No argument or submission based on any other Article in the Constitution can prevail against legislation enacted within the protection of Article 28.3.3°. I would, therefore, prefer to take the widest possible interpretation suggested at No. 3 of Mr Moynihan's minute as being nearest to the correct meaning of the reach and extent of Article 28.3.3°.
3. It cannot be overlooked that the twin objects of the Article are the preservation of the State and the safety of the public. It is always open to object to the creation of wide and unfettered powers that in the exercise of such powers grave and horrible abuses may happen. It is submitted, however, that this is not a sufficient reason for withholding powers where the object is fundamental and the need is imperative. It is impossible, to my mind, to insert any safeguards or limitations on the exercise of such wide powers without endangering the achievement of the purposes laid down in Article 28.3.3°. In a time of war the Executive Authority has to carry out work in the nature of a gigantic salvage operation and the imposition of limitations upon the Executive in attempting to do this is likely to lead to frustration. The test should be that the Government is to have all the power necessary to deal as they consider best with any aspect of the emergency situation. The Courts may be unable to function or the legislature to meet but the Executive, at least, should not be embarrassed by any such breakdown. The wide interpretation of Article 28.3.3° may beget disturbing reflections, but any narrow construction might result in an Executive being hampered by constitutional niceties at a time when most issues would be determined by the forces at the disposal of the Government.
4. In the light of the foregoing I do not see that any objection could be taken to the extension of the life of the Dáil to a period exceeding seven years by ordinary legislation during the present crisis, notwithstanding the existence in the Constitution of the

maximum limitation of seven years. In view of the subject matter of such legislation it might be more appropriate to carry it into effect by a Bill rather than by an Emergency Order, although there is no sufficient reason, of which I am aware, why this step could not be taken by an Emergency Order.[273]

No. 316: NAI, DT S12172B

Extract from Cabinet Minutes relating to the Second Amendment of the Constitution Bill

Government Buildings, Dublin
21 January 1941

Second Amendment of the Constitution Bill, 1940

Consideration was given to the draft of the Second Amendment of the Constitution Bill, 1940, submitted by the Department of the Taoiseach. The draft Bill was approved subject to:

(a) Such drafting changes as may be decided upon by the Taoiseach;
(b) The deletion of the proposed amendments indicated at the following Reference Numbers in the Schedule to the Bill, viz., 2, 4, 5, 8, 9, 13, 16, 25, 28, 29 and 34.
(c) The amendment of the proposed amendment at Reference Number 33 to provide that the body of the person in custody should be produced before the High Court consisting of one or three judges, as may be determined by the President of the High Court, instead of before the High Court consisting of not less than three judges;
(d) The further consideration of the amendment at Reference Number 37, by the Parliamentary Draftsman in consultation with the Department of Finance, with a view to the omission of any reference to the former Constitution.

It was also decided that Reference Number 27 should stand as drafted.

It was further decided that a white print of the Bill should be submitted to the Government in due course.[274]

[273] Annotated: by Kevin Haugh, 14 March 1941 'I agree'.

[274] A memorandum was sent to the Department of Finance on 22 January setting out the above details, along with the proposed wording for Reference Number 37: '2° Nothing in this Article shall operate to invalidate or restrict any legislation whatsoever affecting all or any of the matters contained in the next preceding Subsection'. For the reply of the Department of Finance, see document no. 317.

No. 317: NAI, DT S12172B

Memorandum from Seán Moynihan to Maurice Moynihan

Department of Finance
31 January 1941

With reference to Mr Ó Cinnéide's minute of the 22nd instant relative, inter alia, to the amendment indicated at Ref. No. 37 in the Schedule to the draft Second Amendment of the Constitution Bill, 1940, I am directed by the Minister for Finance to state that, as you are aware from the discussions that took place at the Conference held on the 27th instant, some doubt is felt as to the absence of a specific removal of rights based on the former Constitution or on existing Statutes, to validate legislation passed in the interim between the coming into operation of the Constitution and the passing of the amendment, or to empower the removal of such rights by simple legislation after its passing. It is feared that the judicial view would be strongly against the retrospective validation of penal legislation such as the Emergency Powers (No. 30) Order, 1940, suspending the operation of the Civil Service (Transferred Officers) Compensation Act, 1929, unless such a construction were clearly inescapable. It is accordingly suggested that the amendment might be expressed in the following form:

> 2° Nothing in this Article shall operate to invalidate or restrict any legislation whatsoever which has been enacted or may be enacted hereafter applying to or prejudicing or affecting all or any of the matters contained in the next preceding Subsection.

No. 318: NAI DT S12172B

Draft Second Amendment of the Constitution Bill, 1941

Parliamentary Draftsman's Office
31 January 1941

See www.irishconstitution.ie

No. 319: NAI, DT S12172B

Memorandum from Maurice Moynihan to all Cabinet members

Department of the Taoiseach
24 February 1941

1. The Government at a meeting held on 21 January 1941 approved of the draft of the Second Amendment of the Constitution Bill, 1940, subject to certain deletions and amendments.
2. These deletions and amendments have now been carried out and a proof of the White Print of the resultant text is attached.[275]
3. At its meeting on 21 January the Government decided that further consideration should be given to the amendment at Ref. No. 37 (now Ref. No. 28) of the Schedule which deals with the amendment of Article 56 with a view to the omission of any reference to the former Constitution. The amendment then proposed reads as follows: 'Nothing in this Article shall be held to invalidate or restrict any legislation by reason of any provision in any former Constitution or Statute.' The substitute amendment which will be found at Ref. No. 28 of the Schedule omits any reference to the former Constitution.
4. Apart from the amendment at Ref. No. 28 and a few unimportant drafting changes the Bill is now in the form approved by the Government at its meeting of 21 January. In order to save time the proof copies are being circulated exactly as they have been received from the printers. They contain a number of small printers' errors but these will be corrected before the final print is prepared.
5. The approval of the Government is sought for the circulation of the text now submitted subject to the correction of the printers' errors contained therein.[276]

[275] Not printed.
[276] At a Cabinet meeting on 25 February, the text of the Bill was approved for circulation to Dáil members. Corrected proofs were sent to Conor Maguire and Timothy Sullivan on 3 March, and to Gearóid Mag Canainn on 5 March.

No. 320: NAI, DT S12172B

Conor Maguire to Eamon de Valera

Four Courts, Dublin
5 March 1941

Dear Taoiseach,
I have looked through the white paper of the Second Amendment to the Constitution Bill, 1940. The only particular amendment which seems to call for comment is that of [Reference no.] 25 dealing with *habeas corpus*. Personally I see no objection to the proposal that the Court, before which it is ordered, that the body of a prisoner be produced should the President of the High Court so direct before a Court of three Judges. I imagine that this provision will be attacked from two angles. It will be said that to deprive an applicant for *habeas corpus* of the right to choose his Judge is to deprive him of a valuable privilege which was allowed him even under British Law. It is I think correct to say that the very precise terms of Article 6 of the 1922 Free State Constitution were inspired by a desire to make clear that the citizen should be entitled to insist upon any Judge he chose hearing and determining his application and also to ensure that he should be entitled to go from Judge to Judge in his search for a favourable decision. In practice applications for an order of *habeas corpus* go through two stages.

The first step is to apply ex-parte for a conditional order of *habeas corpus* directed to the jailor. This is almost always made to a single Judge. If any sort of reasonable case is made out he grants the conditional order, gives direction as to service and fixes a day for the return. In practice the Court to which the return is made consists of three Judges. Only during the vacation or in cases where no important point of law appears to be involved has it been the practice to have the argument on the sufficiency of the return take place before less than three Judges. The Supreme Court however has held that the Article of the Constitution (40.4) obliges the Judge to whom application is made for *habeas corpus* to hear and determine it. It was following this decision that Judge Gavan Duffy was compelled to hear and determine the Burke case. It is unlikely that many similar cases will arise in future and it may be argued that to amend the Constitution in the manner proposed is carrying caution too far.

Another objection which may be urged is that if the amendment remains in its present form a refusal of the Court of three Judges to grant an order of *habeas corpus* will not prevent a further application to a single

Judge who may give a conditional order and necessitate the constitution of another High Court of three Judges. *This objection should be met if the amendment is being made by making the decision of the Court of three Judges final, subject of course to a right of appeal to the Supreme Court.*

There seems no reason why this should not be done. In any other type of case a decision of the High Court is binding on all Judges of that Court and can only be reviewed by the Supreme Court.

Undoubtedly however it will be argued that such a provision further limits the existing freedom allowed to applicants for *habeas corpus* applications.

An objection which will meet with more support amongst lawyers is that the amendment deals with the working of the machinery of the Courts and would for that reason be more appropriately made in an Act amending the law embodied in the various Courts of Justice Acts.

I should perhaps have made more clear in what I have said about the present practice that the amendment proposed can be defended on the basis that for many years all applications on what is called the State side of the Court have been argued before three or more Judges.

Nothing else occurs to me as calling for any comment nor have I been able to discover any point upon which to make suggestions for other changes or additions to the amendment proposed.[277]

No. 321: NAI, DT S12172B

Memorandum by Philip O'Donoghue 'Amendment to Article 40.4.2°'

Office of the Attorney General
22 April 1941

Memorandum on Amendment to Reference No. 25 and Article 40.4.2° of the Schedule to the Second Amendment of the Constitution Bill, 1940.

The amendment is intended to make quite clear that the complaint of a person that he is being unlawfully detained may be made in the first instance to any and every Judge of the High Court and that upon refusal by one or more Judges the application may be renewed before the other Judges or any of them. In other words that you may make your application to the various Judges of the High Court in succession.

The second step when a conditional order has been granted, is to have

[277] Annotated by Moynihan: 'Pending observations by Justice and A.G.'s Departments, the Taoiseach is inclined to take the point suggested at "X". 6 March 1941'. The suggestion Moynihan was referring to has been italicised above, beginning with 'This objection'. See document no. 321.

a careful judicial inquiry carried out into the legality of the detention. It has been suggested by Deputy Costello that before 1922 there was a right to go from Judge to Judge after the legality of the detention was enquired into, and established. I think he will find on consulting the Law Reports that this right was to go from Court to Court and not from Judge to Judge. There must be some finality even in a *habeas corpus* proceeding and it is expected that under the Article as amended a decision by the High Court that a detention is legal will determine the matter so far as that Court is concerned, but will leave it open to the applicant to appeal to the Supreme Court. That was the old position which prevailed and it has not been disturbed by this amendment.

No. 322: NAI, DT S12172B

Memorandum from Maurice Moynihan to Gearóid Mag Canainn

Department of the Taoiseach
24 April 1941

A Chara,
I am to transmit herewith three certified copies of an amendment which the Taoiseach desires to move on the Committee Stage of the Second Amendment of the Constitution Bill, 1940.

Proposed amendment to the Second Amendment of the Constitution Bill, 1940:

> At Reference Number 25, in the new Subsection [40.4.]2° to delete the words 'to the High Court or any judge thereof' and to delete the words 'or such judge thereof' and substitute for those words the words 'and any and every judge thereof'.[278]

No. 323: NAI DT S12279

Memorandum from Philip O'Donoghue to Padraig Ó Cinnéide

Office of the Attorney General
19 August 1941

Mr Kennedy,
Under Article 26, the President cannot refer a Bill to the Supreme Court

[278] The text of the amendment had been delivered by the Parliamentary Draftsman's Office to the Department of the Taoiseach on 18 April. Following a protracted debate in Dáil Éireann, the Second Amendment of the Constitution Act, 1941 was passed by the Oireachtas on 30 May. See www.irishconstitution.ie.

without consulting the Council of State. He may, of course, decline to so refer it, acting in his own discretion and without any consultation. In view of the terms of Article 13.9, the Government does not enjoy any function as such, and is not competent to tender any advice, in relation to a reference or a proposal for a reference. The practice on the initiation of a proposal for the reference of a Bill under Article 26 is for the President alone and, no doubt, will develop as a matter of constitutional usage.

No. 324: NAI DT S12279

Memorandum by Padraig Ó Cinnéide

Department of the Taoiseach
19 August 1941

By direction of the Taoiseach I spoke to Mr [Philip] O'Donoghue regarding the circumstances in which the President might consider it appropriate to consult the Council of State with a view to referring Bills to the Supreme Court under the provisions of Article 26 of the Constitution.

Mr O'Donoghue agreed with me that it was difficult to lay down any general principles in the matter and after reading the papers on this file[279] he sent me the attached note dated 19th instant.

I subsequently spoke to the Taoiseach again about the matter and the latter, after consideration, suggested that I might seek an opportunity of telling Mr McDunphy that in his, the Taoiseach's, opinion, the President should only consult the Council of State under the provisions of Article 26.1.1° of the Constitution if, in his opinion, there was a *prima facie* case for referring the Bill to the Supreme Court. He added that if Mr McDunphy had any doubt about the matter an informal discussion with the Chief Justice might prove helpful.[280]

[279] The papers referred to related to the Trade Union Act, 1941, NAI, DT S12279.
[280] Annotated by Ó Cinnéide: 'I conveyed this information to Mr McDunphy today. 22/8/41'.

Appendix 1: Select Bibliography

Anonymous, 'The Amendment of the Saorstát Constitution', in *Irish Law Times and Solicitors' Journal*, 55 (1935).

Akenson, D.H. and Fallin J.F., 'The Irish Civil War and the Drafting of the Irish Free State Constitution,' *Éire-Ireland*, 1 (1970), 10–26; 2, 42–93; 4, 28–70.

Aughey, Arthur, 'Obstacles to reconciliation in the South,' *Building Trust in Ireland: Studies Commissioned by the Forum for Peace and Reconciliation* (Belfast, 1996).

Casey, James, *Constitutional Law of Ireland* (3rd edn., Dublin, 2000).

Cooney, John, *John Charles McQuaid: Ruler of Catholic Ireland* (Dublin, 1999).

Costello, Declan, 'The Natural Law and the Irish Constitution' in *Studies* (Dublin, 1956).

Costello, Kevin, *The Law of Habeas Corpus in Ireland* (Dublin, 2006).

Curran, J.M., *The Birth of the Irish Free State 1921–1923* (Alabama, 1980).

Davis, Fergal Francis, *The History and Development of the Special Criminal Court, 1922–2005* (Dublin, 2006).

Fanning, Ronan, 'Mr de Valera Drafts a Constitution', Brian Farrell (ed.), *De Valera's Constitution and Ours* (Dublin, 1988).

Fanning, Ronan, *The Irish Department of Finance, 1922–1958* (Dublin, 1978).

Farragher, Sean, *De Valera and his Alma Mater* (Dublin, 1984).

Farrell, Brian, 'The Drafting of the Irish Free State Constitution', *Irish Jurist*, 5 (1970), 115–40; 343–56; 6 (1971), 111–35, 345–59.

Faughnan, Sean, 'The Jesuits and the Drafting of the Irish Constitution of 1937', in *Irish Historical Studies*, xxvi (1988).

Foster, R.F., *Modern Ireland 1600–1972* (London, 1988).

Gallagher, Michael, 'The Constitution and the Judiciary', in John Coakley and Michael Gallagher (eds), *Politics in the Republic of Ireland* (4th edn., London, 2005).

Gaughan, A.N. (ed.), *Memoirs of Senator James G. Douglas, Concerned Citizen* (Dublin, 1998).

Gwynn Morgan, David, *Separation of Powers in Irish Constitutional Law* (Dublin, 1997).

Hand, Geoffrey, 'A Reconsideration of a German Study (1927–1932) of the Irish Constitution', in Bieber and Nickel eds, *Das Europa der zweiten Generation: Gedächnisschrift für Christophe Sasse* (Baden Baden, 1981).

Heuston, Robert Francis Vere, *Lives of the Lord Chancellors, 1885–1940* (Oxford, 1964).

Hogan, Gerard, 'Constitutional Interpretation', in Frank Litton (ed.), *The Constitution of Ireland, 1937–1987* (Dublin, 1988).

Hogan, Gerard, 'Unenumerated Personal Rights, Ryan's Case Re-evaluated' in *Irish Jurist*, 25–7 (1990–1992).

Hogan, Gerard, 'Hugh Kennedy, The Childers *Habeas Corpus* Application and the Return to the Four Courts' in Caroline Costello (ed.), *The Four Courts: 200 Years* (Dublin, 1996).

Hogan, Gerard, 'The Constitution Committee of 1934' in Fionan Ó Muircheartaigh (ed.), *Ireland in the Coming Times: Essays to Celebrate TK Whitaker's 80th Year* (Dublin, 1997).

Hogan, Gerard, 'The Constitution, Property Rights and Proportionality in *Irish Jurist*, 32 (1997).

Hogan, Gerard, 'A Fresh Look at Tilson's Case' in *Irish Jurist*, 33 (1998).

Hogan, Gerard, 'The Supreme Court and the Reference of the Offences Against the State (Amendment) Bill 1940' in *Irish Jurist*, 35 (Dublin, 2000).

Hogan, Gerard, 'A Desert Island Case Set in the Silver Sea: *The State (Ryan) v. Lennon* (1934)' in E. O'Dell (ed.), *Leading Cases of the 20th Century* (Dublin, 2000).

Hogan, Gerard, 'Directive of Principles, Socio-Economic Rights and the Constitution' in *Irish Jurist*, 36 (2001).

Hood Philips, O., 'Ryan's Case' in *Law Quarterly Review*, 52 (1936).

Humphreys, Richard 'Interpreting Natural Rights' in *Irish Jurist*, 28–30 (1993–1995).

Humphreys, Richard, 'Constitutional Interpretation' in *Dublin University Law Journal*, 15 (1993).

Jennings, Ivor, 'The Statute of Westminster and Privy Council Appeals' in *Law Quarterly Review*, 52 (1936).

Kavanagh, Aileen 'The Quest for Legitimacy in Constitutional Interpretation' in *Irish Jurist*, 32 (1997).

Kelly J.M., *Fundamental Rights in Irish Law and the Constitution* (Dublin, 1967).

Kelly, J.M., *The Irish Constitution* (Dublin), 2003.

Kennedy, Finola, 'Two Priests, The Family and Irish Constitution' in *Studies*, 87 (Dublin, 1998).
Keogh, Dermot, 'The Irish Constitutional Revolution: The Making of the Constitution: An Historical Analysis' in Litton (ed.), *The Constitution of Ireland 1937–1987* (Dublin, 1988).
Keogh, Dermot, 'Church State and Society', in Farrell (ed.), *De Valera's Constitution and Ours.*
Keogh, Dermot and McCarthy, Andrew, *The Making of the Irish Constitution, 1937* (Dublin, 2007).
Kohn, Leo, *The Constitution of the Irish Free State*, (London, 1932).
Litton, Frank (ed.), *The Constitution of Ireland, 1937–1987* (Dublin, 1988).
Lyons, F.S.L., *Ireland since the Famine* (London, 1972).
Manning, Maurice, *The Blueshirts* (Dublin, 1970).
Mansergh, Nicholas, *The Unresolved Question: The Anglo-Irish Settlement and its Undoing, 1912–1972* (Yale, 1991).
McGarry, Ferghal, *Eoin O'Duffy, A Self Made Hero* (Oxford, 2005).
McGuire, James and Quinn, James (eds), *Dictionary of Irish Biography* (9 vols, Cambridge, 2009) and *Dictionary of Irish Biography Online* (dib.cambridge.org) (2011, ongoing)
McMahon, Deirdre, *Republicans and Imperialists: Anglo-Irish Relations in the 1930s* (Yale, 1982).
Mohr, Thomas, 'Law without Loyalty' in *Irish Jurist*, 37 (2002).
Mohr, Thomas, 'The Rights of Women under the Constitution of the Irish Free State' in *Irish Jurist*, 41 (2006).
Møse, Erik M., 'Norway' in Blackburn and Polakiewicz, *Fundamental Rights in Europe, the ECHR and its Member States 1950 to 2000* (Oxford, 2001).
Ó Cearúil, Micheál, *Bunreacht na hÉireann: A Study of the Irish Text* (Dublin, 1999). (www.constitution.ie/publications/irish-text.pdf)
Ó Cearúil, Micheál, *Bunreacht na hÉireann: Two Texts or Two Constitutions?* (Dublin, 2002).
Ó Cearúil, Micheál, *Bunreacht na hÉireann: Divergences and Inconsistencies? Neamhréireachtaí agus Easpa Leanúnachais?* (BÁC, 2003).
O'Halpin, Eunan, *Defending Ireland: The Irish State and its Enemies Since 1922* (Oxford, 2000).
O'Rahilly, Alfred, *Thoughts on the Constitution* (Dublin, 1937).
O'Sullivan, Donal, *The Irish Free State and its Senate* (London, 1940).

Quinn, Gerard, 'Reflections on the Legitimacy of Judicial Activism in the Field of Constitutional Law' in *Dlí*, 29 (1989).

Regan, John M. *The Irish Counter-Revolution, 1931–1936* (Dublin, 1999).

Report of the Constitution Review Group Pn. 2632 (1996). (http://www.constitution.ie/reports/crg.pdf)

Sexton, Brendan, *Ireland and the Crown 1922–1936: The Governor Generalship of the Irish Free State* (Dublin, 1989).

Walsh, Rachel, 'The Constitution, Property Rights and Proportionality' in *Dublin University Law Journal*, 31 (2009).

Walsh, Rachel, 'Private Property Rights in the Drafting of the Irish Constitution: A Communitarian Approach' in *Dublin University Law Journal*, 33 (2011).

Ward, A.J., *The Irish Constitutional Tradition: Responsible Government and Modern Ireland 1782–1922* (Dublin, 1994).

Wheare, K.C., *The Statute of Westminster and Dominion Status* (Oxford, 1938).

Whyte, John, *Church and State and Modern Ireland, 1923–1979* (Dublin, 1980).

Index